ANDERSON'S MANUAL
FOR
NOTARIES PUBLIC

A COMPLETE GUIDE FOR NOTARIES PUBLIC AND
COMMISSIONERS OF DEEDS, WITH FORMS,
CHARTS AND INSTRUCTIONS

FOR USE IN ALL STATES

QUALIFICATIONS, APPOINTMENT, JURISDICTION,
TERM, POWERS, DUTIES, FEES, RECORDS, SEAL,
LIABILITIES, PENALTIES, REMOVAL

Fifth Edition

BY

WESLEY GILMER, JR., B.A., M.S.L.S., J.D.

Assistant Law Librarian, and
Lecturer on Law and Legal Bibliography
University of Cincinnati, College of Law
Member of the Ohio and Kentucky Bars

D1462819

anderson publishing co./cincinnati

Twelfth Printing—October, 1988

Library of Congress Catalog Card Number: 76-5600

ISBN: 0-87084-039-8

PREFACE

A very large number of persons hold commissions as notaries public under the laws of the 50 states of the United States, the District of Columbia, Puerto Rico, and the Virgin Islands. While the laws of each of the jurisdictions under which the notaries are appointed are different, there are also large areas of common ideas and rules which appear in the law of each of those jurisdictions. In the main, notaries have the same duties and authority, and labor under the same constraints, regardless of the state or other jurisdiction by which they are appointed.

Most notaries are not full-time "professional" notaries. Instead, they hold their commissions as incidents to other occupations, such as accountant, attorney, automobile dealer, banker, bookkeeper, court reporter, insurance agent, legal assistant, loan officer, real estate broker, secretary, and the like. Despite the fact that they are not full-time "professional" notaries, their every act as a notary must be accomplished in a professional manner, however, because they are held to high accountability and are relied upon by the public because of the high degree of responsibility which they exercise. For this reason, among others, each notary public needs a reliable manual at hand to which he or she may turn for prompt answers to the questions, problems, and dilemmas which from time to time present themselves. With such a need in mind, it was this reviser's goal to prepare, as best the various statutes permitted, a manual of concrete statutes and text which would be responsive to a large number of such needs.

The chapters are classified according to various topics with which a notary public is likely to be concerned, such as appointment, authority and duties, fees chargeable, oaths, affidavits, acknowledgments, depositions, seals, commercial paper, and the like. Within each such topic, there is some general text material and the statutes of each state, the District of Columbia, Puerto Rico, and the Virgin Islands relative to the topic, edited if appropriate, and cross references.

The best way to consult this book is through the index in the back. It provides an alphabetical analysis of the book's contents. The table of contents in the front is useful, however, for the purpose of scanning the sequence of the contents of the book and generally locating topics and specific state or other jurisdictions' statutes concerning the topics therein. The reader is encouraged to utilize both avenues of access.

Attention is called to the charts which are provided in the book; they have been prepared for the purpose of providing graphic comparisons of the variations among the jurisdictions. The glossary of definitions should also be remembered; its purpose is to aid the reader to grasp the meanings of the legal terms which a notary public is obligated to understand.

Although periodic supplementation is a common characteristic of law books, it is unusual for other books to be supplemented. Because the legislatures of the various states and other jurisdictions tend to make periodic changes in the law of notaries public, and other legal innovations occur which bear on the appointment, authority, and duties of notaries, however, it is the intention of the publisher and this reviser to supplement this work from time to time with a cumulative pamphlet-like volume, so that readers will be periodically apprised of the changes in the law, if any, which would make this book out-of-date and inaccurate if it were not for the supplementation. This book, when kept current with its cumulative supplement, should, therefore, be more useful to the reader as a dependable source of up-to-date information. After all, it is a "law book" and deserves the same kind of supplementation as other law books.

This reviser would be grateful if readers who have suggestions to offer concerning the future improvement of *Anderson's Manual for Notaries Public* would communicate those suggestions to him or to the publisher.

June 1, 1976   W. G.

SUMMARY OF CONTENTS

DIVISION ONE: INTRODUCTION

DIVISION TWO: STATE AND OTHER STATUTES

DIVISION THREE: OATHS; ACKNOWLEDGMENT; DEPOSITION; COMMERCIAL PAPER (U.C.C.)

CONTENTS

DIVISION ONE: INTRODUCTION

CHAPTER 1: AUTHORITY

CHAPTER 2: THE OFFICE OF NOTARY PUBLIC

APPOINTMENT

DIVISION TWO: STATE AND OTHER STATUTES

CHAPTER 3: APPOINTMENT

STATE AND OTHER STATUTES

CHAPTER 4: QUALIFICATIONS

STATE AND OTHER STATUTES

CHAPTER 5: AUTHORITY AND DUTIES

STATE AND OTHER STATUTES

CHAPTER 6: SEAL

STATE AND OTHER STATUTES

CHAPTER 7: RECORDS

STATE AND OTHER STATUTES

CHAPTER 8: FEES

STATE AND OTHER STATUTES

CHAPTER 9: OFFENSES

STATE AND OTHER STATUTES

DIVISION THREE: OATHS; ACKNOWLEDGMENT; DEPOSITION; COMMERCIAL PAPER (U.C.C.)

CHAPTER 11: OATHS AND AFFIDAVITS

OATHS

AFFIDAVITS

CHAPTER 12: ACKNOWLEDGMENTS

ESSENTIAL REQUISITES

STATE AND OTHER AUTHORITIES

CHAPTER 13: DEPOSITIONS

STATUTORY PROVISIONS AND FORMS

STATE AND OTHER STATUTES

CHAPTER 14: COMMERCIAL PAPER UNDER THE UNIFORM COMMERCIAL CODE

CHAPTER 15: COMMISSIONERS OF DEEDS

APPOINTMENT AND POWERS

STATE AND OTHER STATUTES

DIVISION ONE: INTRODUCTION

CHAPTER 1:   AUTHORITY

§ 1.1   Generally.

A notary public (sometimes called a notary) is a public official appointed under authority of law with power, among other things, to administer oaths, certify affidavits, take acknowledgments, take depositions, perpetuate testimony, and protest negotiable instruments. Notaries are not appointed under federal law; they are appointed under the authority of the various states, districts, territories as in the case of the Virgin Islands, and the commonwealth in the case of Puerto Rico. The statutes which define the powers and duties of a notary public frequently grant the notary authority to do all acts justified by commercial usage and the law merchant.

The law merchant, or custom of merchants as it is occasionally called, is the general body of commercial usages which have become an established part of the law of the United States and England and which relate chiefly to the transactions of merchants, mariners, and those engaged in trade. Unless displaced by particular provisions of the Uniform Commercial Code, the law merchant supplements its provisions.

For other definitions see *Glossary*, page 853. Concerning the Uniform Commercial Code see *Commercial Paper under the Uniform Commercial Code*, page 690.

1

§ 1.2   Origin and early history of office.

In the early days of the Roman Republic there were persons who made it a business to draw important documents, and do other writing for whoever might employ them. Their number and importance increased with the growth of the wealth and power of the Roman Empire, under various titles such as *scriba, cursor, tabularius, tabellio, exceptor, actuarius,* and *notarius,* according to the time in which they lived and the duties which they performed. In the latter days of the Empire, they had become more or less subject to regulation by law. Some of their acts had been accorded such a degree of authenticity as to be specially designated as public instruments themselves, and were required to be deposited in public archives.

These quasi officials, and the regulations by law concerning them, spread to a greater or lesser degree into the various provinces of Rome, including, among others, the present nations of France, Spain, and England.

They were well known functionaries in the territories of Charlemagne, who invested their acts with public authority and provided for their appointment by his deputies in every locality. He provided that each bishop, abbot, and count should have a notary. That they acted as conveyancers, in some instances at least, in England, even before the Norman conquest, is shown by the fact that a grant of lands and manors was made by King Edward the Confessor, to the Abbot of Westminster by a charter written and attested by a notary.

In England, notaries have always considered themselves authorized to administer oaths, and this power is now expressly conferred on them by statute. They protest foreign bills of exchange, and their certificate of the presentment, demand, and dishonor of such bills, and of their protest thereof on account of such dishonor, is itself proof of these matters. The law in the United States is similar, and is often so declared by the statutes of the various states and other jurisdictions.

§ 1.3   What a notary should know.

Before entering upon his duties, a notary public should know and understand:

The qualifications necessary for his appointment;

How to prepare an application for a commission;

Who appoints notaries public in his state, district, or other jurisdiction;

The amount of the bond which he must furnish, if one is required;

The fee which he must pay for his commission;

Where his commission must be recorded;

The number of years he holds office;

The extent of his territorial jurisdiction;

The scope of his powers and duties;

Circumstances which will disqualify him from acting;

The manner of signing his official certificate;

The requisites of his official seal, or stamp, if one is required;

What records he must keep;

The fees which he may charge for performing particular services;

His, and his surety's liability for negligent and fraudulent acts;

The fines and penalties to which he may be subject;

The grounds for his removal from office;

The manner of administering oaths;

The form and purpose of affidavits;

His duties in connection with taking acknowledgments, depositions, the perpetuation of testimony, and safe deposit boxes;

His duties in presenting and protesting commercial paper, sometimes called negotiable instruments; and

What constitutes the unauthorized practice of law.

§ 1.4   What a notary may not do.

A notary public, who is not also a licensed attorney at law in the particular state, district or other jurisdiction, has no authority to perform any act or service which constitutes practicing law, as that term has been defined by the courts of the various states, districts and other jurisdictions. Like any other individual, he is free to prepare legal documents under directions from a competent person, but it is contrary to law for him to draft legal papers, such as deeds, mortgages, wills, trust agreements, and the like, at his own discretion and charge a fee for the service rendered. Such constitutes the practice of law, even though the individual so engaged makes no attempt to appear in court or to give the impression that he is entitled to do so.

A notary public may be enjoined from preparing instruments for compensation, and from giving legal advice to those for whom he prepares them. A person who gives legal advice to those for whom he draws instruments, or holds himself out as competent to do so, does work of a legal nature, when the instruments he prepares either define, set forth, limit, terminate, specify, claim, grant, or otherwise affect legal rights. Instruments coming within the scope of this limitation are deeds, mortgages, leases, agreements, contracts, bills of sale, security agreements, wills, promissory notes, options, powers of attorney, liens, bonds, mortgage assignments, releases, or satisfactions, and any other documents requiring the use of knowledge of law in their preparation.

CHAPTER 2:   THE OFFICE OF NOTARY PUBLIC

APPOINTMENT

§ 2.1   Qualifications of applicant.

Ordinarily, an applicant must be of legal age, which for many purposes today is 18 years old, a citizen of the state, district, or other jurisdiction, and a person of good moral character.   In many instances he must be a resident of the county or judicial district within which he is to act. Several of the states require filing some evidence of qual- to file a certificate from a judge or other local official that ifications.   As an example, an applicant might be required he is of good moral character, of legal age, a citizen of the county in which he resides, and is possessed of suffi- cient qualifications and ability to discharge the duties of the office.   In some states a similar certificate must be signed by a certain number of ordinary citizens.   The specific qualifications for applicants in the various states, the Dis- trict of Columbia, Puerto Rico, and Virgin Islands are described below.   See Qualifications: State and Other Statutes.

§ 2.2   Eligibility of women.

The statutes in some of the states expressly provide that women may be appointed as notaries.[1]   Such statutes are

---

[1] See summary of statutory provisions, § 2.10, p. 9.

probably unnecessary, because dissimilar treatment for men and women who are similarly situated is arbitrary when mandated solely on the basis of sex, and violates the United States Constitution, Amendment XIV.[2]

§ 2.3   Application.

An applicant usually obtains the necessary forms from the governor, secretary of state, or other appointing authority. As a matter of convenience, surety companies occasionally furnish forms.

In recent years there has developed a practice of submitting questionnaires to each applicant, preliminary to the approval of the application. Questions such as the following must be answered: how long the applicant has lived in the county; place and date of his birth; his business or employment; education; whether his commission has ever been revoked; whether he has ever been convicted of any offense; and the name and address of surety company or individual who will execute indemnity bond.

§ 2.4   Appointment.[3]

In most of the states, notaries public are appointed by the governor of the state. In some states the appointments are made by the governor by and with the advice and consent of the senate, or with the advice of his council. In other states the secretary of state has authority to make the appointment. Notaries are appointed by courts in a few of the states.

§ 2.5   Bond.

In most states, and other jurisdictions, a notary is required to file a bond with approved sureties. The public

---

[2] Reed v. Reed, 404 U.S. 71, 92 S.Ct. 251 (1971); Brenden v. Independent School District 742, 477 F.2d 1292, 1297 (8th Cir. 1973); Gilpin v. Kansas State High School Activities Ass'n., 377 F.Supp. 1233 (D. Kan. 1973).

[3] See summary of statutory provisions, § 2.10, p. 9.

officer with whom the bond must be filed is designated by the statutes of the various states and other jurisdictions. For a summary of the amount of bond required in various states and other jurisdictions, see the summary of statutory provisions, § 2.10, page 9. The specific statutes relating to bonds are quoted verbatim in Appointment: State and Other Statutes, page 15.

The amount of bond required varies among the several states and other jurisdictions, from none up to $10,000.[4] The purpose of the bond is often stated in the specific statute applicable,[5] but may be generally described as being to assure the faithful performance of duties, and to compensate any person who may suffer a loss as a result of the notary's misconduct.

§ 2.6   Oath.

An oath of office is required in every state. Occasionally the oath is endorsed on the notary's commission or on his bond. Both the oath and bond are ordinarily filed with the secretary of state or other designated public officer.

§ 2.7   Commission.

Upon the payment of a fee, usually to the secretary of state, a commission will be issued to a qualified applicant. The amount of this fee varies among the states and other jurisdictions from $1.00 up to $100.00. In a few jurisdictions, there is apparently no fee. For concrete information in this regard, see the summary of statutory provisions, § 2.10, page 9, and the specific statutes applicable in Appointment: State and Other Statutes, page 15.

The commission, signed by the appointing power, is evidence of the notary's official authority. In many states the notary, before entering upon his duties, must leave the commission with some officer designated by law, generally

---

[4] See summary of statutory provisions, § 2.10, p. 9.

[5] See Appointment: State and Other Statutes, page 15.

the clerk of court, to be recorded. A small additional fee is charged by the clerk, to cover the cost of recording the commission.

§ 2.8   Term of office.

The statutes of most states and other jurisdictions prescribe a certain number of years as the term of office of a notary public. These terms range from two to ten years, and in some jurisdictions the term of office is indefinite.[6] In some instances a particular statute provides that a notary holds office during good behavior, during the pleasure of the governor, or. during the term of the appointing judge.

The death of a notary will terminate his office, although he was appointed for a definite term. It will not create a vacancy for the unexpired part of his term.

§ 2.9   Territorial jurisdiction.[7]

In some jurisdictions a notary public can act only within the county or judicial district for which he has been appointed, or within the locality named in his commission. The statutes of many states, however, permit a notary to act anywhere throughout the state. He has no jurisdiction outside the state of his appointment.

Some states allow the notary to act in any other county, or in a county adjoining the county of his residence, if he files a certified copy of his appointment with the clerk of such other county. Where the city in which a notary resides is located in two or more counties, he may often perform his duties in either county.

These matters are strictly controlled by the concrete provisions of the specific state, district or other jurisdiction statutes, however. For the various applicable statutes, see Authority and Duties: State and Other Statutes, page 127.

---

6 See summary of statutory provisions, § 2.10, page 9.

7 See summary of statutory provisions, § 2.10, page 9.

§ 2.10 Summary of statutory provisions.

The following chart is arranged alphabetically according to the various states, the District of Columbia, Puerto Rico, and the Virgin Islands. It sets out: source of appointment, jurisdictions in which the statutes specify that women are eligible, the fees payable relating to the commission, the amount of bond required, the term of office in years, and territorial jurisdiction. It also provides references to applicable statutes, and various remarks. For the concrete provisions of the specific statutes relative to appointment, see Appointment: State and Other Statutes, page 15.

	(A) APPOINTMENT					(B) WOMEN ELIGIBLE	(C) COMMIS- SION FEE [10]
	Governor	Governor, with consent of Senate	Governor, with advice of council	Secretary of State	Court		
Alabama					X	X	$1.00
Alaska				X		X	20.00
Arizona				X		X	
Arkansas	X					X	
California				X		X	2.00
Colorado				X		X	
Connecticut				X		X	20.00
Delaware	X					X	20.00
District of Columbia	[9]					X	10.00
Florida	X					X	10.00
Georgia					X	X	5.00
Hawaii	[10a]					X	25.00[10b]
Idaho	X					X	10.00
Illinois				X		X	2.00[11b]
Indiana	X					X	5.00
Iowa				X		X	7.50
Kansas	X					X	3.00[11]
Kentucky				X		X	5.00
Louisiana		X				X	5.00
Maine			X			X	5.00
Maryland		X[11a]				X	11.00
Massachusetts			X			X	7.00
Michigan	X					X	3.00
Minnesota		X				X	5.00
Mississippi	X					X	

[9]   Appointed by the Council of District of Columbia.
[10] The absence of a figure in column C indicates that no fee is required.
[10a] Appointed by the attorney general.
[10b] $10.00 for renewal.
[11] $1.00 to clerk; $2.00 to secretary of state.
[11a] With consent of senator for particular district involved.
[11b] $1.25 fee if county population is less than 100,000.
[12] The absence of a figure in column D indicates that no bond is required.
[13] The Judges of Probate may appoint competent number for state at large who will give $2,000 bond.
[13a] Postmasters are automatically notaries public. State employees may be commissioned notaries public by secretary of state. Neither state employees nor postmasters need post bond.

(D) BOND [12]	(E) TERM (years)	(F) JURISDICTION State	County	(G) STATUTORY REFERENCES
$1,000	4	x[13]	x	Code, 1958, Tit. 40, §§ 1-23
1,000	4	x[13a]		Statutes, §§ 44.50.010-44.50.190
1,000	4	x[14]	x	Revised Statutes, 1956, §§ 41-311 to 41-316
1,000	4	x[14a]	x	Statutes Ann., 1947, §§ 12-1401 to 12-1410 (1968 Replacement)
5,000	4	x		Government Code, §§ 8200-8218 (1976 Supp.)
1,000	4	x		Revised Statutes, 1973, §§ 12-55-101 to 12-55-104
	5	x		General Statutes, Ann., 1958, §§ 3-91 to 3-99
	2	x		Code, Tit. 29, §§ 4301 to 4309
2,000	5			Code, 1973, §§ 1-501 to 1-518
500	4	x[15]		Statutes, 1973, §§ 117.01-117.08
	4		x	Code, Ann., §§ 71-101 to 71-113
1,000[16]	4		x[16a]	Revised Statutes, §§ 456-1 to 456-18
1,000	4	x		Code, §§ 51-101 to 51-112
1,000	4	x		Revised Statutes, 1963, c. 99, §§ 1 to 14
1,000	4	x		Statutes (Burns), 1964 Repl., §§ 49-3501 to 49-3517
500	3	x		Code, 1950, §§ 77.1 to 77.19
1,000	4		x[17a]	Statutes Ann., §§ 53-101 to 53-113
Required[18]	4	x[17]		Revised Statutes, §§ 423.010 to 423.990
1,000[19]	Indefinite[20]		x	Revised Statutes, 1950, §§ 35.1 to 35.555
	7	x		Revised Statutes, 1964, Tit. 4, §§ 951 to 958
	4	x		Ann. Code of Maryland, 1957, Art. 68, §§ 1-10
	7	x		Annotated Laws, 1974, c. 222, §§ 1, 8 to 10
1,000	4	x		Mich. Statutes Ann., 1973, §§ 5.1041-5.1071 Mich. Compiled Laws, 1967, §§ 55.107-55.251
2,000	7	x		Minn. Statutes Ann., 1966, §§ 359.01 to 359.12
2,000	4		x	Code, Ann., 1972

[14]   As to acknowledgments.
[14a] As to swearing witnesses, taking affidavits, depositions and acknowledgments.
[15]   As directed by governor.
[16]   In first judicial circuit; $500 in other judicial circuits.
[16a] In judicial circuit for which appointed.
[17]   Has power to act in any county of state in which certificate is filed.
[17a] And in any adjoining county.
[18]   Amount not stated.
[19]   Outside Orleans Parish; $10,000 in Parish of Orleans
[20]   During good behavior.

	(A) APPOINTMENT					(B) WOMEN ELIGIBLE	(C) COMMIS- SION FEE [21]
	Governor	Governor, with consent of Senate	Governor, with advice of council	Secretary of State	Court		
Missouri	x					x	$5.00
Montana	x					x	2.50[22]
Nebraska	x					x	
Nevada	x					x	25.00
New Hampshire			x			x	
New Jersey				x		x	15.00
New Mexico	x					x	10.00
New York				x		x	10.00
North Carolina				x		x	10.00
North Dakota				x		x	10.00
Ohio	x					x	2.00[23]
Oklahoma				x		x	5.00[24]
Oregon	x					x	5.00
Pennsylvania				x		x	25.00
Rhode Island	x					x	25.00
South Carolina	x					x	10.00
South Dakota	x					x	
Tennessee					x[25]	x	3.00
Texas				x		x	1.00
Utah	x					x	
Vermont					x	x	
Virginia	x					x	3.00
Washington	x					x	10.00
West Virginia	x					x	1.00
Wisconsin	x					x	10.00
Wyoming	x					x	

[21] The absence of a figure in column C indicates that no fee is required.
[21 a] Appointed by secretary of state, commissioned by the governor.
[22] $200 to the state, 50 cents to the county clerk.
[23] Attorneys pay $5.00
[24] $2.00 to secretary of state; $3.00 to county clerk.
[25] Appointed by the court, commissioned by the governor.

(D) BOND [26]	(E) TERM (years)	(F) JURISDICTION		(G) STATUTORY REFERENCES
		State	County	
$2,000[27]	4		x	Statutes, Ann., § 486.010-486.100 (Supp. 1975)
1,000	3	x		Revised Code, 1947, §§ 56-101 to 56-117
4,000[28]	4		x[29]	Revised Statutes, 1943, §§ 64-101 to 64-115 (1971)
2,000	4	x		Revised Statutes, §§ 240.010 to 240.330
	5	x		Revised Statutes Ann., 1968, ch. 455
	5	x		Revised Statutes, 1937, §§ 52:7-1 to 52:7-8
500	4	x		Statutes, 1953, ch. 35 §§ 1-1 to 1-24
	2	x		Executive Law, §§ 130 to 138
	5	x		General Stats., §§ 10-1 to 10-10 (1975 Supp.)
500	6	x		Century Code Annotated, §§ 44-06-01 to 44-06-14
	5[29a]		x[30]	Revised Code (Page), §§ 147.01 to 147.14
1,000	4	x		Statutes Ann., Tit. 49, §§ 1-10 (Supp. 1975)
500	4	x		Revised Statutes, §§ 194.010 to 194.990
[31]	4	x		Statutes (Purdon), Title 57, §§ 147 to 168
	5	x		General Laws, 1956, § 42-30 (Supp. 1975)
	10	x		Code of Laws, §§ 49-1 to 49-12 (1975 Supp.)
500	8	x		Compiled Laws Ann., 1967, § 18-1-1 et seq.
5,000	4		x[32]	Code Ann., 1973, §§ 8-1601 to 8-1627
1,000	2		x	Statutes (Vernon), Arts. 5949 to 5960 (1975 Supp.)
500	4	x		Code, 1953, § 46-1-1 et seq.
	2		x	Statutes, Ann., Tit. 24, §§ 441-444
500	4	x[33]	x	Code, 1950, § 47-1 et seq.
1,000	4	x		Revised Code Ann., §§ 42.28.010-42.28.110
	10		x[34]	Code, §§ 29-4-1 to 29-4-16 (1971)
500	4[35]	x		Statutes, Ann., ch. 137.01 (1974)
500	4	x		Statutes, 1957, §§ 32-1 to 32-15 (1975 Supp.)

[26] The absence of a figure in column D indicates that no bond is required.
[27] In counties having over 100,000 in population, $5,000.
[28] $6,000 bond for statewide notary.
[29] May be commissioned to act throughout state.
[29a] Attorneys may be commissioned for life without renewal.
[30] Attorneys have statewide jurisdiction. Adjacent county for lay notary if judge of common pleas so certifies.
[31] Fixed by secretary of commonwealth.
[32] Notary may apply to secretary of state for certificate authorizing him to act in all counties. Fee, $2; bond $5,000.
[33] Governor may also appoint notaries for state at large; fee $25.
[34] Governor may appoint notaries for state at large with additional fee of $40.00 and with a $500 bond.
[35] Attorneys may receive permanent commission.

DIVISION TWO: STATE AND OTHER STATUTES

CHAPTER 3: APPOINTMENT

ALABAMA

[ALA. CODE]

Commercial Notaries

Tit. 40, § 1. Appointment; term of office. A competent number of notaries public for each county shall be appointed and commissioned by the judges of probate of the several counties of the state and shall hold office for four years from the date of their commissions. The judges of probate shall collect a fee of $1.00 for each such notary commission issued.

§ 2. Women eligible. Women may be appointed notaries public, who shall have the power and authority of commercial notaries only.

§ 3. Removal vacates office. Notaries public shall vacate their office by removal from the county; and may be removed by the governor, in his own discretion.

§ 4. Bond. Notaries public must give bond with sureties, to be approved by the judge of probate of the county for which they are appointed, in the sum of one thousand dollars, payable to the state of Alabama, and conditioned to faithfully discharge the duties of such office, so long as they may continue therein, or discharge any of the duties thereof; which bond must be executed, approved, filed, and recorded in the office of judge of probate before they enter on the duties of such office.

15

Notaries Ex Officio Justices of the Peace

§ 15. Appointment and term of office. The governor may appoint one notary public for each election precinct in counties, and one for each ward in cities of over five thousand inhabitants, who, in addition to the powers of notary, as defined by law, shall have and exercise the same jurisdiction, and the same powers, as justices of the peace, within the precinct or ward for which he is appointed; and shall hold office for the term of four years from the first Monday after the second Tuesday in January, 1911, and every four years thereafter.

§ 16. Governor may remove. The governor may, in his discretion, remove, at any time, the notary appointed as provided in the preceding section.

§ 17. Vacation of office. A notary public having the jurisdiction of a justice of the peace, vacates his office by removal from the precinct or ward for which he is appointed.

§ 18. Official bond. A notary public having the jurisdiction of a justice of the peace, before entering on the duties of his office, must give bond with sufficient sureties, in the penalty of one thousand dollars, payable to the state of Alabama, with condition that he will faithfully discharge all the duties of his office during the time he continues therein, or discharges any of the duties thereof; which bond must be approved by the judge of probate of the county, and filed and recorded in his office.

Notaries for State at Large

§ 21. Appointment, term of office. A competent number of notaries public for the state at large shall be appointed and commissioned by the judges of probate of the several counties of the state, and shall hold office for four years from the date of their commission. Such notaries public for the state at large shall perform all the acts and exercise all authority now performed and exercised by notaries public under the general laws of the state of Alabama; the jurisdiction of such notaries public shall not be limited to the counties of their residence but shall extend to any county of the state. The judges of probate shall collect a fee of one dollar ($1.00) for each such notary commission issued.

§ 22. Bond. Notaries public appointed under this chapter must give bond with sureties to be approved by the judge of probate of the county of their residence in the sum of two thousand dollars ($2,000.00), payable to the state of Alabama, and conditioned to faithfully discharge the duties of such office, so long as they may continue therein, or discharge any of the duties thereof; which bond must be executed, approved, filed and recorded in the office of the judge of probate of the county of their residence before they enter on the duties of such office. Such notaries public for the state at large, in the event of any breach of the conditions of their official bonds, may be sued in the county of their residence, or in the county in which the breach was committed, or in the county where the party, or parties, who suffered damages from the breach reside.

Notaries Generally

Tit. 41, § 178. Who may be impeached; grounds of impeachment. The following officers may be impeached and removed from office, to-wit: ° ° ° notaries public, ° ° ° for the following causes, to-wit: Wilful neglect of duty, corruption in office, incompetency or intemperance in the use of intoxicating liquors or narcotics to such an extent in view of the dignity of the office and importance of its duties as unfits the officer for the discharge of such duties, or any offense involving moral turpitude while in office, or committed under color thereof, or connected therewith.

ALASKA

[ALASKA STAT.]

§ 44.50.010. Appointment and commission. The lieutenant governor may appoint and commission notaries public for the state.

§ 44.50.030. Term of office. The term of office of a notary public is four years from the date of commission.

§ 44.50.040. Fees. A fee of $20 shall be paid to the lieutenant governor for each commission issued other than to a state employee.

§ 44.50.050. Chapter not a limitation on postmasters. Nothing in this chapter requires a postmaster to post a bond or to have a commission.

§ 44.50.110. Application of Administrative Procedure Act to revocation of notary commission. The procedures set out in the Administrative Procedure Act (AS 44.62) shall be followed in the revocation of the commission of a notary public.

§ 44.50.120. Bond. Every person appointed a notary public after July 1, 1961, shall execute an official bond of $1,000, approved by the clerk of the superior court.

§ 44.50.130. Filing oath and bond. (a) An application for a notary public commission shall include a statement under oath that the applicant is a citizen of the United States and a resident of Alaska, as defined in § 20 of this chapter.

(b) A person appointed a notary public shall file his bond and the oath set out in AS 39.05.130 with the lieutenant governor. The oath must be notarized and signed by the appointee.

§ 44.50.160. . Misconduct or neglect.   A notary and the sureties on his official bond are liable to persons injured for the damages sustained on account of misconduct or neglect of the notary.

§ 44.50.180. Postmasters as notaries.   (a) Each postmaster in the state may perform the functions of a notary public in the state.

(b) Each official act of a postmaster as a notary public shall be signed by the postmaster, with a designation of his title as post-master, shall have the cancellation stamp of the post office affixed, and shall state the name of the post office and the date on which the act was done.

(c) The postmaster may charge and receive the same fees as a notary for similar services.

ARIZONA

[ARIZ. REV. STAT. ANN.]

§ 41-126.   Fees.   The secretary of state shall receive the following fees:

°   °   °

4.   Filing and recording each official bond for a notary public, ten dollars.

°   °   °

§ 41-311.   Appointment; term; oath and bond.   A.   The secretary of state may appoint notaries public in each county to hold office for four years who shall have jurisdiction in the county in which they reside and in which they are appointed.   Acknowledgments of instruments may be taken and executed by a notary public in any county of the state although the commission is issued to the notary public in and for another county.

B.   The secretary of state shall transmit the commission of the person appointed as notary public to the clerk of the superior court of the county for which the notary was appointed.   The clerk shall give notice thereof to the person appointed, who shall, within twenty days after receiving such notice, take the oath prescribed by law, and give a bond to the state, with sureties approved by the chairman of the board of supervisors, in the amount of one thousand dollars, and file it with the clerk.   Upon filing the official oath and bond the clerk shall deliver the commission to such person, and give notice to the secretary of state of the time and filing of the oath and bond.

ARKANSAS

[ARK. REV. STAT. ANN.]

§ 12-201.   Officers commissioned by governor.   Each ° ° ° [among others] ° ° ° notary public, ° ° ° shall be commissioned by the Governor.

§ 12-202. Fee for commission forwarded to secretary of state—Forwarding duplicate oath—Time limits. All state and county officers, both civil and military, who are required by law to be commissioned by the Governor of this State, are required to forward the legal fee for their said commissions to the Secretary of State within sixty [60] days after their election, and they shall, after said commissions have been received, forward within fifteen [15] days their duplicate oath to the Secretary of State, to be by him recorded and filed in his office.

§ 12-1401. Appointment—Bond—Term of office. The Governor may appoint a convenient number of notaries public for each county, who shall be citizens of the county for which they are appointed, and who shall file in the office of the Recorder of Deeds for the county a bond to the State, for the faithful discharge of their duties, in the sum of one thousand [dollars] [$1,000], with security to be approved by the Clerk of the Circuit Court of the county, and who shall hold office for the term of four [4] years.

§ 12-1701. Secretary of state. The following fees shall be allowed for services performed by the Secretary of State, and paid into the treasury in the same manner that all other fees are or shall be directed to be paid, viz.:

*   *   *

For every commission to notary public 5.00

*   *   *

CALIFORNIA

[CAL. GOV'T CODE]

§ 8200. Appointment and commission; number; jurisdiction; fees. The Secretary of State may appoint and commission notaries public in such number as he deems necessary for the public convenience. Notaries public may act as such notaries in any part of this state, and they shall receive for their services such fees as are provided by law.

§ 8201.5. Application form; confidential nature; use of information. The Secretary of State shall require an applicant for appointment and commission as a notary public to complete an application form prescribed by the Secretary of State. Information on this form filed by an applicant with the Secretary of State, except for his name and address, is confidential and no individual record shall be divulged by an official or employee having access to it to any person other than the applicant, his authorized representative, or an employee or officer of the federal government, the state government, or a local agency, as defined in subdivision (b) of Section 6252 of the Government Code, acting in his official capacity. Such information shall be used by the Secretary of State for the sole purpose of carrying out the duties of this chapter.

§ 8202.5. County employees. The Secretary of State may appoint and commission such number of county employees as notaries public in the several counties of the state to act for and on behalf of the county by whom they are employed as he deems proper. Whenever such a notary is appointed and commissioned, the county, through its duly authorized representatives, shall execute a certificate that the appointment is made for the purposes of the county, and whenever such certificate is filed with any state or county officer, no fees shall be charged by the officer for the filing or issuance of any document in connection with such appointment.

Any county for which a notary public is appointed and commissioned pursuant to this section may pay from any funds available for its support the premiums on any bond and the cost of any stamps, seals or other supplies required in connection with the appointment, commission or performance of the duties of such notary public.

Any fees collected or obtained by any notary public whose documents have been filed without charge and for whom bond premiums have been paid by a county shall be remitted by him to the county by whom he is employed and paid into the county treasury to the credit of the fund from which his salary is paid.

§ 8202.6. School district employees. The Secretary of State may appoint and commission such number of school district employees as notaries public in the several school districts of the state to act for and on behalf of the school districts by whom they are employed as he deems proper. Whenever such a notary is appointed and commissioned, the school district, through its duly authorized representatives, shall execute a certificate that the appointment is made for the purposes of the school districts, and whenever such certificate is filed with any state or county officer, no fees shall be charged by the officer for the filing or issuance of any document in connection with such appointment.

Any school district for which a notary public is appointed and commissioned pursuant to this section may pay from any funds available for its support the premiums on any bond and the cost of any stamps, seals or other supplies required in connection with the appointment, commission or performance of the duties of such notary public.

Any fees collected or obtained by any notary public whose documents have been filed without charge and for whom bond premiums have been paid by a school district shall be remitted by him to the school district by whom he is employed and paid into the district treasury to the credit of the fund from which his salary is paid.

§ 8204. Term of office. The term of office of a notary public is four years from and after the date of his commission.

§ 8212. Bond, amount, approval. Every person appointed a notary public shall execute an official bond in the sum of five thousand dollars ($5,000). Unless the bond is executed by an admitted surety insurer, it shall be approved by a judge of the superior court of the county in which the person maintains his principal place of business.

§ 8213. Bond, filing, recording fees; oath, filing; disposition of bond; record as evidence. No later than 20 days after the beginning of the term prescribed in his commission, every person appointed a notary public shall file his official bond, and take, subscribe, and file his oath of office in the office of the county clerk of the county within which he maintains his principal place of business as shown in the application submitted to the Secretary of State, and the commission shall not take effect unless this is done within the 20-day period. Upon filing the oath and bond, the county clerk shall forthwith transmit to the Secretary of State his certificate setting forth the fact of such filing and containing a copy of the official oath, signed by the notary with his own proper signature, and shall forthwith deliver the bond to the county recorder for recording.

If he transfers his principal place of business from one county to another, he may file a new oath of office and bond, or a duplicate of the original bond with the county clerk to which he transfers. In such a case, the same filing and recording fees are applicable as in the case of the original filing and recording of the bond. Promptly after the filing with the county clerk of the county to which he transfers, the notary public shall cause his old seal to be altered, or shall obtain a new seal, and such altered or new seal shall include the name of the county to which he transfers.

A recording fee of three dollars ($3) shall be paid by the person appointed a notary public. Said fee may be paid to the county clerk who shall transmit it to the county recorder.

The county recorder shall record the bond and return it to the county clerk who shall keep the bond for one year following the expiration of the term of the commission for which the bond was issued after which said bond may be disposed of. Such disposition shall not affect the time for commencement of actions on the bond. A certified copy of the record of the official bond with all affidavits, acknowledgments, endorsements and attachments, may be read in evidence with like effect as the original thereof, without further proof.

§ 8214. Misconduct or neglect. For the official misconduct or neglect of a notary public, he and the sureties on his official bond are liable to the persons injured thereby for all the damages sustained.

§ 8214.2. **Revocation of commission by proceedings under sections 3060-3072.** Notwithstanding the provisions of Section 8214.1, the commission of any notary public may also be revoked by the same proceedings as those provided by Sections 3060 through 3072 of this code for the removal of certain public officers, such proceedings to be brought in the county in which the notary public maintains his principal place of business.

Note: For § 8214.1, see Chapter 4, *Qualifications.*

§ 8215. **State employees as notaries.** The Secretary of State may appoint and commission such number of state employees as notaries public in the several counties of the state to act for and in behalf of a state agency as he deems proper. Whenever such a notary is appointed and commissioned, the head of the agency shall execute a certificate that the appointment is made for the purposes of the agency, and whenever such certificate is filed with any state or county officer, no fees shall be charged by the officer for the filing or issuance of any document in connection with such appointment.

Any agency for which a notary public is appointed and commissioned pursuant to this section may pay from any funds available for its support the premiums on any bond and the cost of any stamps, seals, or other supplies required in connection with the appointment, commission, or performance of the duties of such notary public.

Any fees collected or obtained by any notary public whose documents have been filed without charge and for whom bond premiums have been paid by a state agency shall be remitted by him to the state agency by which he is employed and paid into the State Treasury to the credit of the fund from which his salary is paid.

Any expenditures made or costs incurred by a state agency prior to the effective date of this section for the appointment, commission, or qualification of a notary public to act as such for the agency may be paid from funds available for the support of the agency.

§ 12197.1. **Issuing notary public commission.** The fee for issuing a commission as notary public is six dollars ($6).

COLORADO

[COLO. REV. STAT. ANN.]

§ 12-55-101. **Appointment—term.** The secretary of state shall appoint and commission and issue certificate of appointment to such number of notaries public as occasion may require, each of whom shall hold his office for four years unless sooner removed.

§ 12-55-106. **Oath and bond.** Every notary public before entering upon the duties of his office shall take the oath of office prescribed by law, and shall give bond to the state of Colorado in the sum of one thousand dollars, with, as surety thereon, a company qualified to write surety bonds in this state, conditioned that he will faithfully perform the duties of his office.

§ 12-55-107. Certificate of appointment—recording. (1) The secretary of state is authorized to issue a certificate that a person is a notary public, the date of expiration of his commission, and any other fact concerning such notary public as is required by the laws of any state.

(2) A notary public may record in any county of the state his certificate of authority, and after such recording, the clerk and recorder of such county may issue a certificate that such person is a notary public, the date of expiration of his commission, and any other fact concerning such notary public as is required by the laws of any state.

(3) A notary public may exhibit to the judge or clerk of any court of record his certificate of authority, and the said judge or clerk may thereupon issue a certificate that such person is a notary public, the date of expiration of his commission, and any other fact concerning such notary as is required by the laws of any state.

§ 12-55-108. Bond—action on—limitation. Such bond and oath shall be delivered to the secretary of state and may be sued on by any person injured on account of the unfaithful performance of said notary's duties; provided, that no suit shall be instituted after three years have elapsed from the time the cause of action accrued.

§ 24-21-104. Fees of secretary of state. It shall be the duty of the secretary of state to charge as fees the following sums of money for papers officially executed, and other official work which may be done in his office: ° ° ° for each notary public's commission, five dollars; ° ° ° and he shall not deliver any such commission, or file for record any certificate, or do any such official work until the fee or sum so fixed to be collected therefor shall first be paid to him.

CONNECTICUT

[CONN. GEN. STAT. ANN.]

§ 1-25. Forms of oaths. The forms of oaths shall be as follows, to wit:

FOR MEMBERS OF THE GENERAL ASSEMBLY, EXECUTIVE AND JUDICIAL OFFICERS AND NOTARIES PUBLIC

You do solemnly swear (or affirm, as the case may be) that you will support the constitution of the United States, and the constitution of the state of Connecticut, so long as you continue a citizen thereof; and that you will faithfully discharge, according to law, the duties of the office of .... to the best of your abilities. So help you God.

❖   ❖   ❖

§ 3-91. **Appointment, term and qualifications of notaries public.** The secretary may, upon application as hereinafter provided, accompanied by a fee of twenty dollars, appoint a convenient number of notaries public, each for the term of five years from April first in the year of appointment and may revoke any such appointment for cause. Appointees shall be at least eighteen years of age and shall have resided in the state at least one year immediately preceding their appointment. The secretary shall cause a certificate, bearing a facsimile of his signature and countersigned by his executive assistant or an employee designated by the secretary, to be issued to each such appointee. A notary public may exercise the functions of his office at any place in the state. Each application for appointment to such office, except for the renewal of a certificate, shall be in the handwriting of the applicant and shall bear the recommendation of the clerk of the county where such applicant resides, made after investigation, and shall be upon a form furnished by the secretary of the state.

§ 3-92. **Record of certificate and oath of notary.** The certificate of each notary public, and his oath of office taken and subscribed to by him before proper authority, shall be recorded by the clerk of the superior court in the county in which such notary resides, in a book provided for that purpose; and in addition, the certificate and oath of any notary residing in New Haven county may be recorded in like manner in the office of the clerk of the superior court at Waterbury, and the certificate and oath of any notary residing in New London may be recorded by the clerk or assistant clerk of the court of common pleas in New London county, in books kept for that purpose; and any notary having his principal place of business in a county other than that in which he resides may also have his certificate and oath recorded in the county in which he has such place of business; and such clerks or assistants may certify to the authority and official acts of any notary whose certificate and oath have been recorded in the books in their charge. The clerk of the superior court for Litchfield county shall keep at the courthouse in Winchester a duplicate copy of the record of all notaries public in Litchfield county and also a duplicate of the seal of said court.

§ 3-93. **Notice of revocation of appointment.** Notice of the revocation of the appointment and certificate of any notary public shall be given in such manner as the secretary directs, and the executive assistant or the employee designated by the secretary shall, within five days after such revocation, give notice thereof to the clerk of the court or courts in the records of which such certificate is required to be recorded under the provisions of section 3-92. Such clerk shall note such revocation and its date upon the original record of such certificate.

§ 7-33a. **Issuance of certificates of authority of justices of peace, notaries and superior court commissioners.** The town clerk of a town wherein a justice of the peace, notary public or commissioner of the superior court resides or is employed shall be deputized by the clerk of the superior court of the county within which such town is located to issue certificates of the authority of such person.

§ 51-170. **Clerks of superior court to be county and judicial district clerk. Custody of records of former county courts.** The clerk of the superior court of each county and for the judicial district of Waterbury, for the purpose of certifying to the authority of justices of the peace, notaries public and commissioners of the superior court, shall be the clerk for such county or district. ° ° °.

§ 52-259. **Court fees.** ° ° ° [Clerks shall receive] for recording the commission and oath of a notary public or certifying under seal to the official character of any magistrate, two dollars; ° ° ˒.

DELAWARE

[DEL. CODE ANN.]

Tit. 29, § 4301. Appointment of notaries in general; number from each county; qualifications; revocation. (a) In addition to the notaries public authorized to be appointed under sections 4302-4304 of this title, the Governor may appoint as many notaries public as he may decide is necessary and proper in each county of the State.

(b) [Omitted. See *Qualifications.*]

(c) The Governor may revoke any notary commission for cause.

§ 4302. **Appointment of certain officers as notaries; term.** (a) The Governor shall appoint every person who is appointed by him to the office of justice of the peace and as collector of State revenue also as a notary public.

The collector of State revenue shall only act as a notary public in connection with work performed in carrying out the duties of his office.

The term of office of any person appointed a notary public under the provisions of this section—

(1) whose appointment as a justice of the peace or collector of State revenue is not confirmed by the Senate; or

(2) who fails to qualify, resigns or is removed from the office of the justice of the peace or collector of State revenue,

shall terminate at the same time his term of office as justice of the peace or collector of State revenue terminates.

(b)   The Governor shall appoint as a notary public the Register in Chancery in Kent County, and his successors, from time to time, in the office.

The term of office of the Register in Chancery in Kent County as a notary public shall expire at the same time as his term of office as such Register in Chancery.

§ 4303.   **Appointment of notary for each bank or branch.**   The Governor shall appoint one notary public for each trust company, bank, banking association, or branch or branches thereof in this State, whether state or national, chartered or organized under the laws of this State, or of the United States.

§ 4303A.   **Appointment of court reporters as notaries public.** The Governor may, upon the request of the Chief Justice of the Supreme Court, appoint any of the official Court reporters as a notary public.   Such Court reporter need not be a legal resident of this State for one year at the time of his appointment, if he is a resident of this State at the time of his appointment as a notary public.

§ 4304.   **Appointment of notaries for certain service organizations; limitations.**   (a)   The governor may, upon the request of the department commander of the Spanish-American War Veterans, of the Veterans of Foreign Wars of the United States, of the Disabled American Veterans, of the Jewish War Veterans, of the American Legion, and of the Paralyzed Veterans of America, appoint one notary public for each requesting organization for a term of 4 years, without charge to any appointee, commander or organization.

(b)   Any such notary, so appointed, shall have no authority to perform any duties with respect to such office or to take affidavits or acknowledgments, except on documents and papers in connection with and for the benefit of any veteran, their families or dependents. The notaries public, so appointed, shall make no charge for any service rendered.

§ 4305.   **Term of office.**   Notaries public shall be commissioned for the term of 2 years.

Any one who is a notary public by virtue of holding the office of justice of the peace or collector of State revenue shall hold the office of notary public in accordance with the provisions of section 4302 of this title.

§ 4306.   **Oath; State tax.**   The notaries shall severally take and subscribe the oath or affirmation prescribed by Article XIV of the Constitution.

Notaries shall each pay to the Secretary of State for the use of the State a fee of $20.

§ 4312. Commission; signature of Governor; seal. (a) The Commission appointing a notary public shall be in such form as the Secretary of State shall designate; shall be executed with the signature of the Governor or with a facsimile signature of the Governor, which may be engraved, printed, or stamped thereon and shall be signed by the Secretary of State.

(b) The Commission shall have placed thereon the impression of the Great Seal of the State, or a facsimile of the Great Seal shall be engraved or printed thereon.

§ 2316. Fees. The fees to be charged by the Secretary of State for the use of the State are as follows:

o   o   o

For commission to Attorney General, Registers in Chancery, Coroners, and Notaries Public, each, ... 10.00

o   o   o

DISTRICT OF COLUMBIA

[D.C. CODE ENCYCL. ANN.]

§ 1-501. Appointment—Representation of clients before government departments—Administration of certain acknowledgments—License fee—Rules and regulations. The Commissioners of the District of Columbia shall have power to appoint such number of notaries public, residents of said District, or whose sole place of business or employment is located within said District, as, in their discretion, the business of the District may require: *Provided,* That the appointment of any person as such notary public, or the acceptance of his commission as such, or the performance of the duties thereunder, shall not disqualify or prevent such person from representing clients before any of the departments of the United States Government in the District of Columbia or elsewhere: *Provided further,* That such person so appointed as a notary public who appears to practice or represent clients before any such department is not otherwise engaged in Government employ, and shall be admitted by the heads of such departments to practice therein in accordance with the rules and regulations prescribed for other persons or attorneys who are admitted to practice therein: *And provided further,* That no notary public shall be authorized to take acknowledgments, administer oaths, certify papers, or perform any official acts in connection with matters in which he is employed as counsel, attorney, or agent, or in which he may be in any way interested before any of the departments aforesaid.

Each notary public before obtaining his commission, and for each renewal thereof, shall pay to the Collector of Taxes of the District of Columbia a license fee of $10: *Provided,* That no license fee shall be collected from any notary public in the service of the United

States Government or the District of Columbia Government whose notarial duties are confined solely to Government official business: *And provided further,* That no notary fee shall be collected at any time by a notary public who is exempted from the payment of the license fee. The Commissioners are hereby authorized to refund, in the manner prescribed by law for the refunding of erroneously paid taxes, the amount of any fee erroneously paid or collected under this section.

The Commissioners are hereby authorized to prescribe such rules and regulations as they may deem necessary to carry out the purposes of this chapter.

§ 1-502. **Tenure of office.** Said notaries public shall hold their offices for the period of five years, removable at discretion.

§ 1-504. **Oath and bond.** Each notary public, before entering upon the duties of his office, shall take the oath prescribed for civil officers in the District of Columbia, and shall give bond to the District of Columbia in the sum of $2,000, with security, to be approved by the Commissioners of the District of Columbia or their designated agent, for the faithful discharge of the duties of his office. Where any such notary public is an officer or employee of the Government of the District of Columbia whose notarial duties are confined solely to government official business, any bond covering such officer or employee for the faithful performance of such notarial duties obtained by the Commissioners of the District of Columbia pursuant to the authority conferred on them by law shall be in lieu of the bond required by the first sentence of this section.

FLORIDA

[FLA. STAT. ANN.]

§ 113.01. **Fee for commissions issued by governor.** A fee of ten dollars is prescribed for the issuance of each commission of every kind issued by the governor of the state and attested by the secretary of state; except that no fee shall be required for issuance of commissions to officers of the Florida national guard; and, except that no fee shall be required for the issuance of a commission as a notary public to a veteran of the Spanish American war, world war I, world war II, the Korean war or one who serves from August 4, 1964, to the date of cessation of hostilities in the Vietnam conflict, as determined by the United States government, who has a disability rating by the United States of fifty per cent or more; such disability being subject to verification by the secretary of state who shall have authority to adopt reasonable procedures to implement this act.

§ 117.01. **Appointment, application, fee, term of office, powers, bond and oath.** (1) The governor may appoint as many notaries public as to him shall deem necessary, each of whom shall be at least twenty-one years of age, a citizen of the United States, and a permanent resident of the state for one year.

(2) Application for appointment shall be signed by the applicant, accompanied by a fee of ten dollars, and the oath and bond required by subsection (4), and be in the following form:

APPLICATION FOR APPOINTMENT AS NOTARY PUBLIC STATE OF FLORIDA

Miss
Mr.
Mrs.

NAME ....
(Type or print your legal name in which commission will issue)

HOME ADDRESS ....
                            Street   City   State

BUSINESS ADDRESS ....
                            Street   City   State

HOME PHONE .... BUSINESS PHONE ....

HOW LONG A RESIDENT OF FLORIDA? ....
    (1 year required)

ARE YOU A CITIZEN OF THE U.S.? YES .... NO........
    (Citizenship Required)

DATE OF BIRTH ....
    (Must be over 21)   Month   Day   Year

IS THIS A RENEWAL? YES .... NO ....

EXPIRATION DATE ....
    (If yes, give date present commission expires)

HAVE YOU EVER BEEN CONVICTED OF A FELONY?
YES .... NO ....

IF SO, HAVE YOUR CIVIL RIGHTS BEEN RESTORED?
YES .... NO ....

                     ....
                     Legal Signature of Applicant

SIGNATURES OF TWO CHARACTER WITNESSES WHO PERSONALLY KNOW APPLICANT AND WILL VOUCH FOR HIS GOOD MORAL CHARACTER, REQUIRED:

1. ....
       Name   Street   City   State

2. ....
       Name   Street   City   State

(3) Said notaries public shall hold their respective offices for four years, and shall use and exercise such office of notary public for such

places and within such limits and precincts as the governor shall direct, to whose protestations, attestations and other instruments of publication due credence shall be given. The governor may remove any notary public for cause.

(4) Every notary public shall, prior to his or her executing the duties of said office, give bond to the governor for the time being, in the penalty of $500.00 conditioned for the due discharge of his said office, and also take an oath that he will honestly, diligently and faithfully discharge the duties of a notary public. Said bond shall be approved and filed in like manner and placed as the bonds of county officers of the county in which the person so appointed notary public shall reside; provided, however, where such bond is executed by a surety company for hire, duly authorized to transact business in Florida, said bond may be approved by the department of banking and finance.

(5) No person shall obtain nor use a notary public commission in other than his legal name. Any person applying for a notary public commission may be required to submit proof of his identity to the department of state if so requested. Any person violating the provisions of this subsection shall be guilty of a felony of the third degree, punishable as provided in § 775.082, § 775.083, or § 775.084.

Note: Concerning the punishment, see *Offenses*, FLA. STAT. ANN. §§ 775.082 to 775.084.

§ 117.02. **Women eligible.** (1) Women over twenty-one years of age are eligible to appointment by the governor as notaries public, and to hold and exercise the office thereof upon the same terms and conditions, and with the same powers and emoluments, as notaries now appointed by the governor.

(2) Any woman who is commissioned as a notary public and subsequently changes her name by marriage or any other method, may continue to hold her commission under the name in which it was issued until said commission shall have expired. Upon expiration, she shall then apply for a new commission using her correct name, except those married women who use their maiden name, or the name in which said commission was issued, in their occupation or profession.

GEORGIA

[GA. CODE ANN.]

§ 71-101. **By whom and when appointed.** The power to appoint notaries public is vested in the clerks of the superior courts, and may be exercised by them at any time.

§ 71-103. **Oath of office.** Before entering on the duties of their office, they shall take and subscribe before the clerk of the superior court the following oath, which shall be entered on his minutes: "I, ..., do solemnly swear, or affirm, that I will well and truly perform the duties of a notary public to the best of my ability; and I further swear, or affirm, that I am not the holder of any public money belonging to the State, and unaccounted for. So help me God."

§ 71-104. **Term of office.** They shall hold their offices for four years, revocable at any time by the clerk of the superior court, at the end of which time on petition their commissions may be renewed by order of the clerk for a like term. The clerk of the superior court shall issue to them certificates of their appointment and qualifications, which certificates shall contain the name, the residence, the age and the sex of the appointee, the date the certificate is issued, and the term for which the appointment runs, and the clerk shall also keep a record of their names and addresses.

§ 71-105. **Fees to be paid.** Before a certificate shall be issued to the appointee, he shall pay to the clerk of the superior court the sum prescribed by section 24-2727, relating to fees of clerks of the superior courts, as amended, of which amount the clerk shall be entitled to cover his services in issuing certificate of appointment as notary public, administering the oath and recording the same, the amount by which the sum prescribed by said section 24-2727 exceeds the amount which the clerk is required by this section to forward to the Secretary of State. With a copy of the certificate of appointment, under his seal of office, the clerk shall immediately send $2 to the Secretary of State who shall keep a record in his office showing the names of the notaries public appointed with their address, age, sex, and the term for which their commission runs, and such amount shall cover the cost of the Secretary of State in keeping such records. On reappointment as notaries public, the sum prescribed by said section 24-2727 shall be paid to the clerk of the superior court and dispersed in the same manner as provided herein for the original appointment.

§ 24-2727. **Fees enumerated.** The clerks of the superior courts of this State shall be entitled to charge and collect the following fees for official duties performed by them; provided, that in all counties in this State where the clerk of the superior court is on a salary basis the fees herein provided shall be paid into the county treasury, to-wit:

Civil Cases

⁂   ⁂   ⁂

For issuing certificates of appointment to notaries public and for issuing certificates of reappointment as provided by section 71-105, relating to the issuance of such certificates and the fees therefor, as amended, 5.00

⁂   ⁂   ⁂

Notaries Public Ex-Officio Justices of the Peace

§ 24-403.   **Oath; form.**   Justices of the peace, including commissioned notaries public who are ex-officio justices of the peace, before entering on the duties of their office besides the oath required for all civil officers, must take the following oath: "I do swear that I will administer justice without respect to persons, and do equal rights to the poor and to the rich, and that I will faithfully discharge all the duties incumbent on me as a justice of the peace for the county of ——————, agreeably to the Constitution and laws of this State, and according to the best of my ability and understanding. So help me God."

§ 24-404.   **Before whom oaths taken.**   Such oaths shall be taken and subscribed before the ordinary of the county.

§ 24-501.   **Appointment, number, term of office, and removal.** Commissioned notaries public, not to exceed one for each militia district, may be appointed by the judges of the superior courts in their respective circuits, upon recommendation of the grand juries of the several counties. They shall be commissioned by the Governor for the term of four years, and shall be ex-officio justices of the peace, and shall be removable on conviction for malpractice in office.

Accord, GA. CONST. § 2-4301.

§ 24-502.   **Commissions, when to be issued.**   The Governor shall not issue a commission to any notary public and ex-officio justice of the peace, unless it shall appear from the order of appointment that such appointment was made at the term of the court next preceding the vacancy, or at some succeeding term after such vacancy has occurred.

§ 24-503.   **List of notaries public ex-officio justices of the peace.** The clerk of the superior court of each county shall prepare and keep in his office a correct list of all· the notaries public who are ex-officio justices of the peace of the county, showing the time of the expiration of the term of office of each one; and such list shall be accessible to the grand jury of the county at each term of the court.

HAWAII

[HAWAII REV. STAT.]

§ 456-1.   **Appointment; tenure.**   The attorney general may, in his discretion, appoint and commission such number of notaries public for each of the several judicial circuits of the State as he deems necessary for the public good and convenience.

The term of office of a notary public shall be four years from the date of his commission, unless sooner removed by the attorney general for cause after due hearing; provided, that after due hearing the commission of a notary public may be revoked by the attorney general in any case where any change occurs in the notary's office, occupation, or employment which in his judgment renders the holding of such commission by the notary no longer necessary for the public good and convenience. Each notary shall, upon any change in his office, occupation, or employment, forthwith report the same to the attorney general.

Editorial comment

The attorney general may, for public convenience and necessity, commission a notary for any number of judicial circuits, and the notary shall keep a separate record for each circuit. See *Qualifications*, HAWAII REV. STAT. § 456-2.

§ 456-4. Filing copy of commission; authentication of acts. Each person appointed and commissioned a notary public under this chapter shall forthwith file a literal or photostatic copy of his commission, an impression of his seal, and a specimen of his official signature with the clerk of the circuit court of the judicial circuit for and in which he is commissioned to act. Thereafter the clerk, when thereunto requested, shall certify to the official character and acts of any such notary public whose commission, impression of seal, and specimen of official signature is so filed in his office.

§ 456-5. Official bond. Each notary public forthwith and before entering upon the duties of his office shall execute, at his own expense, an official surety bond which, for the first judicial circuit, shall be in the sum of $1,000 and, for the other judicial circuits, shall be in the sum of $500. Each bond shall be approved by the judge of the circuit court of the judicial circuit for and in which any such notary public is commissioned to act.

The obligee of each bond shall be the State and the condition contained therein shall be that the notary public will well, truly, and faithfully perform all the duties of his office which are then or may thereafter be required, prescribed, or defined by law or by any rule or regulation made under the express or implied authority of any statute, and all duties and acts undertaken, assumed, or performed by the notary public by virtue or color of his office. The surety on any such bond shall be a surety company authorized to do business in the State. After approval the bond shall be deposited and kept on file in the office of the clerk of the circuit court of the judicial circuit for and in which the notary public is commissioned to act. The clerk of each circuit court shall keep a book to be called the "bond record", in which he shall record such data in respect to each of the bonds deposited and filed in his office as the attorney general may direct.

§ 456-6. **Liabilities on official bond.** For the official misconduct or neglect of a notary public or breach of any of the conditions of his official bond, he and the surety on his official bond shall be liable to the party injured thereby for all the damages sustained. The party shall have a right of action in his own name upon the bond and may prosecute the action to final judgment and execution.

§ 456-8. **Rules.** The attorney general, subject to chapter 91, may prescribe such rules and regulations as he deems advisable concerning the administration of this chapter, the appointment and duties of notaries public and the duties of other officers thereunder. The rules or regulations shall have the force and effect of law.

§ 456-9. **Fees.** The attorney general shall charge and collect the following fees:

For issuing the original commission, $25;

For renewal of commission, $10.

The clerk of each circuit court shall charge and receive the following fees:

For filing a copy of a commission, $1;

For each certificate of authentication, 25 cents.

The foregoing fees collected by the attorney general shall be deposited with the director of finance to the credit of the general fund.

IDAHO

[IDAHO CODE]

§ 51-101. **Appointment and commission—Term of office.** The governor may appoint and commission as many notaries public, having the qualification of electors, as he may deem necessary, who shall be appointed for the state and shall hold office for the term of four years.

§ 5-102. **Oath and bond.** Each notary public before entering upon the duties of his office must take the usual oath of office, which must be indorsed upon his bond, and must execute a bond to the state of Idaho in the sum of $1000, with two or more sufficient sureties, to be approved by the probate judge of the county in which said notary resides: provided, that any bond being furnished by any bonding or surety company authorized to do business in the state, shall not be required to be approved by the probate judge.

§ 51-103. **Filing of bond, oath and signature—Fee for commission.** The bond, with the oath of office endorsed thereon and duly subscribed and sworn to, together with a specimen of the signature, and impress of the official seal of the appointee, must be filed in the office of the secretary of state. At the issuance of any commission each appointee must pay the sum of ten dollars to said secretary, who must keep an account of and remit the same to the state treasurer for the general fund.

§ 51-109. Certificate to be transmitted to clerk. Each notary, as soon as he has taken his official oath and filed his official bond, must transmit a certificate of the facts, under the hand and seal of the secretary of state, to the clerk of the district court for his county.

§ 51-110. Liability for misconduct. For the official misconduct or neglect of a notary public, he and the sureties on his official bond are liable to the parties injured thereby for all the damages sustained.

ILLINOIS

[ILL. ANN. STAT.—(Smith-Hurd)]

Ch. 53, § 26. Notary public—Commission. All persons before they shall be commissioned a notary public shall pay to the Secretary of State a fee of $5.

Ch. 99, § 1. Appointment. The Secretary of State may appoint and commission as notaries public as many persons resident in a county in this State for which they are appointed as he may deem necessary, but no person shall be appointed a notary public who is under 18 years of age, is not a citizen of the United States, and has not resided in this State one year preceding the appointment.

§ 3. Term of office. Each notary public so appointed and commissioned shall hold his office for a term of 4 years, unless sooner removed by the Secretary of State.

§ 4. Bond—Oath of office. Before entering upon the duties of his office, he shall give a bond, payable to the People of the State of Illinois, in the sum of $1,000, with sureties to be approved by the Secretary of State, conditioned for the faithful discharge of the duties of his office, and shall take and subscribe the oath of office prescribed by the Constitution. The oath and bond shall be deposited in the office of the Secretary of State.

§ 5. Certificate of appointment— Notice of rejection—Memorandum of appointment and expiration—Entry—Fee—Delivery of commission. The Secretary of State shall forward the applicant's certificate of appointment or notice of rejection to the county clerk of the county of residence. Upon receipt thereof the county clerk shall notify the applicant of the action taken by the Secretary of State and, if a certificate of appointment is issued by the Secretary of State, the applicant shall appear at the county clerk's office to record the same and receive his certificate. The applicant shall have a memorandum of his appointment, and the time when his office will expire, entered in the office of the county clerk of his county in a book to be kept for that purpose by said clerk, for which entry he shall pay a fee of $1 to the county clerk. The county clerk shall then deliver the commission to the applicant.

§ 6. **Certificate of magistracy.** The county clerk of the county in which the memorandum is entered, or the Secretary of State, may grant certificates of magistracy of notaries public. The certificate of a clerk shall be under his hand and official seal, and that of the Secretary of State under the great seal of the state. The fee for the certificate is $1.

§ 15. **Forms.** The Secretary of State shall prescribe or provide suitable forms of applications for a commission as a notary public or for renewal thereof, and no other person is authorized to duplicate such forms without the express written consent of the Secretary of State.

§ 16. **Solicitation.** No person shall solicit any applicant for a commission or renewal thereof, and offer to provide a Surety Bond for the Notary Commission unless any such solicitation specifically sets forth in bold face type not less than ¼ inch in height the following:

> "THE LAW PRESCRIBES EITHER PERSONAL SURE-
> TIES OR A SURETY BOND. WHERE PERSONAL
> SURETIES ARE APPROVED BY THE SECRETARY OF
> STATE, NO SURETY BOND IS REQUIRED.
>
> WE ARE NOT ASSOCIATED WITH ANY STATE OR
> LOCAL GOVERNMENTAL AGENCY."

Nor shall any person solicit any applicant renewing a Notary's Commission and offer to provide a Surety Bond more than 30 days in advance of the expiration of such Commission.

Nothing contained in this Section shall apply to a letterhead proper, or general listings or advertising of a general nature, or general publications of any duly licensed insurance broker or agent or company which merely lists surety bonds along with other bonds or policies.

§ 17. **Enforcement and audits.** The Secretary of State is empowered to enforce the provisions of this Act, and to audit the books, records, letters, contracts or other pertinent documents of any person soliciting or offering to provide any applicant for a commission or renewal thereof a surety bond for a Notary Commission contrary to the provisions of Section 16. When a violation is found, the Secretary of State shall impose an audit fee of $25.00 per day per auditor, or $12.50 per half-day per auditor plus, in the case of out-of-state audits, air or rail expense incurred by such auditor or auditors.

§ 18. Injunction. Whenever it shall appear to the Secretary of State that any person is engaged or is about to engage in any acts or practices which constitute or will constitute a violation of the provisions of Section 16 of this Act, or of any rule or regulation prescribed under the authority thereof, the Secretary of State may in his discretion, through the Attorney General, apply for an injunction without notice, and upon a proper showing, any court of competent jurisdiction shall have power to issue a permanent or temporary injunction or restraining order without bond, to enforce the provisions of this Act, and either party to such suit shall have the right to prosecute an appeal from the order or judgment of the Court.

INDIANA

Notaries Public Generally

[INDIANA CODE]

§ 5-7-1-1. Fees charged by secretary of state. The secretary of state, Provided That no fees shall be charged against the United States, or this, or any other state, or any county of this state, nor against any officer of either of them, for any attestation, certificate or paper required by them for official use, shall be authorized to charge and collect on behalf of the state of Indiana, the following fees, to be paid by the parties requiring the service: For each commission to notaries public, one dollar [$1.00]; ° ° °.

§ 33-16-2-1. Appointment—Oath—Bond. (a) Any applicant for a commission as a notary public shall possess the following qualifications:

1. Be at least eighteen [18] years of age; and

2. Be a legal resident of the state of Indiana and of the county for which application is made.

(b) A notary public shall be appointed and commissioned by the governor upon a certificate of qualification and moral character from the judge of the circuit or superior or probate court of the applicant's county. The applicant, before entering upon the duties of a notary public shall take an oath of office before the clerk of the circuit or superior court of the applicant's county of residence, and file therewith an official bond, with freehold or corporate security, to be approved by the clerk, in the penalty of one thousand dollars [$1,000]. A notary public shall hold office for four [4] years. A notary public, when so qualified shall be authorized to act within the state of Indiana.

§ 33-16-2-2. Cause for revocation of appointment. No notary public shall do the following:

(1) Use any other name or initial in signing acknowledgments, other than that by which he has been commissioned;

(2) Acknowledge any instrument in which his name appears as a party to the transaction;

(3) Take the acknowledgment of or administer an oath to any person whom he actually knows to have been adjudged mentally ill by a court of competent jurisdiction and who has not been restored to mental health as a matter of record;

(4) Take the acknowledgment of any person who is blind, without first reading the instrument to him; and

(5) Take the acknowledgment of any person who does not speak or understand the English language, unless the nature and effect of the instrument to be notarized is translated into a language which such person does speak or understand.

In the event any notary public violates any of the provisions of this act his appointment may be revoked by the judge of the court in which the notary made his application.

§ 33-16-2-3. Appointment—Governor's discretion. Notaries now in office may serve out the terms for which they were respectively appointed; and the governor may appoint notaries public in the several counties whenever, in his judgment, the public interest would be thereby promoted.

Members of General Assembly

§ 2-3-4-1. General assembly—Members as notaries. Any member of the general assembly may take acknowledgment to deeds, or other instruments in writing, administer oaths, protest notes and checks, take the deposition of a witness, (to) take and certify affidavits and depositions, and perform any duty now conferred upon a notary public by the statutes of Indiana. And acknowledgments to deeds or other instruments to be recorded the same as though acknowledged before a notary public.

§ 2-3-4-2. General assembly—Members as notaries—Seal, impression, attestation. No member of the general assembly shall be authorized to perform any of the duties mentioned in section one [§ 49-3513] hereof until he shall have procured such seal as will stamp upon paper a distinct impression, in words or letters, sufficiently indicating his official character, to which may be added such other device as he may choose. All acts not attested by such seal shall be void.

§ 2-3-4-3. General assembly—Members as notaries—Date of election appended to jurat—Jurisdiction. It shall be the duty of every member of the general assembly performing any of the acts as set forth in this act [§§ 49-3513—49-3516], at the time of signing any certificate of acknowledgment of a deed, mortgage or other instrument, or any jurat or other official document, to append to such certificate the date of his election to the general assembly. The jurisdiction of any such member to perform the duties herein mentioned shall be coextensive with the state of Indiana.

§ 2-3-4-4. General assembly—Members as notaries—Fees—Violation of law—Repeal. Any such member performing any of the acts or duties hereunder shall be entitled to the same fees as those charged by notaries public, and where any act by a notary public would be a violation of the law, it shall likewise be a violation of the law if committed by a member of said general assembly in the performance of any of the duties or acts authorized hereunder. All laws and parts of laws in conflict herewith are hereby repealed.

Court Reporters

Concerning court reporters, see *Depositions,* IND. CODE 33-15-24-1.

IOWA

[IOWA CODE ANN.]

§ 77.1. Appointment. The secretary of state may at any time appoint one or more notaries public and may at any time revoke such appointment.

§ 77.2. Terms—expiration date. All terms shall be for a period of three years and shall expire on the thirtieth day of September.

§ 77.3. Notice of expiration of term. The secretary of state shall, on or before August 1 preceding the expiration of each commission, notify each notary public of such expiration and furnish him with a blank application for reappointment and a blank bond.

§ 77.4. Conditions. Before any such commission is delivered to the person appointed, he shall:

❉   ❉   ❉

2. Execute a bond to the state of Iowa in the sum of five hundred dollars conditioned for the true and faithful execution of the duties of his office, which bond, when secured by personal surety, shall be approved by the clerk of the district court of the county of his residence; all other bonds shall be approved by the secretary of state.

3. Write on said bond, or a paper attached thereto, his signature, and place thereon a distinct impression of his official seal.

4. File such bond with attached papers, if any, in the office of the secretary of state.

5. Remit the sum of seven dollars fifty cents for the three-year period provided by law to the secretary of state.

When the secretary of state is satisfied that the foregoing requirements have been fully complied with, he shall execute and deliver a commission to the person appointed.

A facsimile signature of the secretary of state and the seal of his office may be affixed to the certificate of commission in lieu of a personal signature.

Note: For the provisions of IOWA CODE ANN. § 77.4(1), see *Seal.*

§ 77.6. Revocation—notice. Should the commission of any person appointed notary public be revoked by the secretary of state, he shall immediately notify such person through the mail.

§ 77.17. Change of residence. If a notary remove his residence from the state of Iowa, such removal shall be taken as a resignation.

KANSAS

[KAN. STAT. ANN.]

§ 53-101. State and local notaries; appointment, terms, age; not considered state officers. The governor shall appoint and commission, as occasion may require, state and local notaries public, who shall hold their office for four (4) years. Any person who is at least eighteen (18) years of age shall be eligible to be appointed and commissioned as a state or local notary public as provided in this act. The provisions of this section shall not affect the unexpired commissions of notaries public issued prior to the effective date of this act; and notaries public holding such unexpired commissions on July 1, 1963, may exercise notarial acts within the county for which appointed and in any adjoining county of the state during the remainder of the unexpired terms of such commission. State or local notaries public shall not be considered as state officers within the meaning of K.S.A. 46-132.

§ 53-102. Oath and bond; filing official signature and seal impression. (a) Every local notary public before entering upon the duties of his office shall file with the clerk of the district court of the county for which he was commissioned his oath of office, and a good and sufficient bond to the state of Kansas in the sum of one thousand dollars ($1,000), with one or more sureties to be approved by said clerk conditioned for the faithful performance of the duties of his office; and he shall also file with said clerk and with the secretary of state his official signature and an impression of his official seal.

(b) Every state notary public before entering upon the duties of his office shall file with the secretary of state his oath of office, and a good and sufficient bond to the state of Kansas in the sum of two thousand five hundred dollars ($2,500), with one or more sureties to be approved by the said secretary of state, conditioned for the faithful performance of the duties of his office; and he shall also file with the secretary of state his official signature and an impression of his seal.

§ 53-103. Blanks for bond and oath. Blanks for bonds and oath of office shall be furnished with the commission by the secretary of state.

§ 53-104. Commission, bond and oath; recordation, filing and indexing; fees of clerk and secretary of state. Such commission, bond and oath shall be recorded in the office of the clerk of the district court of the county in which the notary public shall reside, and immediately thereafter said bond and oath shall be transmitted to the secretary of state, and by him filed and properly indexed in his office. The said clerk shall be entitled to a fee of one dollar ($1) for recording the papers and the said secretary of state shall be entitled to a fee of two dollars ($2) for his services.

§ 54-106. Form of oath to be taken by officer. All officers elected or appointed under any law of the state of Kansas shall, before entering upon the duties of their respective offices, take and subscribe an oath or affirmation, as follows:

"I do solemnly swear [or affirm, as the case may be] that I will support the constitution of the United States and the constitution of the state of Kansas, and faithfully discharge the duties of ———————. So help me God."

KENTUCKY

[KY. REV. STAT. ANN.]

§ 423.010. Appointment, term and qualifications of notaries; oath; bond; certificate. The Secretary of State may appoint as many notaries public as he deems necessary, who shall hold office for four years. Any person desiring to be appointed a notary public shall make written application to the Secretary of State. The application shall be approved by the circuit judge, circuit clerk, county judge, county clerk, justice of the peace or a member of the General Assembly of the county of the residence of the applicant. No officer shall charge or accept any fee for approving the application. A notary public must be eighteen years of age, a resident of the county from which he makes his application, of good moral character and capable of discharging the duties imposed upon him by this chapter, and the endorsement of the officer approving the application shall so state. The Secretary of State, in his certificate of appointment to the applicant, must designate the limits within which the notary is to act. Before a notary acts, he must take an oath in the county court of his county that he will honestly and diligently discharge the duties of his office. He must in the same court give an obligation with good security for the proper discharge of the duties of his office. Every certificate of a notary public shall state the date of the expiration of his commission. The Secretary of State shall give to each notary appointed a certificate of his appointment under the seal of the Commonwealth of Kentucky in lieu of a commission heretofore required to be issued to said notary by the Governor of Kentucky, and receive the same fee for the certificate that he now receives for attesting the commission issued by the Governor.

Editorial comment

The official oath of any officer may be administered by any judge, notary public, clerk of a court, or justice of the peace, within his district or county. See *Authority and Duties*, KY. REV. STAT. ANN. § 62.020.

§ 62.050. Bonds, when to be given. (1) No officer required by law to give bond shall enter upon the duties of his office until he gives the bond.

(2) Each person elected to an office who is required to give bond shall give the bond on or before the day the term of office to which he has been elected begins.

(3) Each person appointed to an office who is required to give bond shall give the bond within thirty days after he receives notice of his appointment.

Editorial comment

Concerning the penalties for violations of the foregoing section, see *Offenses*, KY. REV. STAT. ANN. § 62.990.

§ 14.090. Fees. (1) The Secretary of State shall charge and collect for the state the following fees:

       ✿   ✿   ✿

For issuing commission with Seal of Commonwealth
    to a notary public $2.00

       •   ✿   ✿

(2) No fee shall be collected for affixing the State Seal to a commission issued to any public officer other than commissioner of foreign deeds or notary public, or to a grant, or to a pardon of a felony.

LOUISIANA

General Provisions

[LA. REV. STAT.]

§ 35:1. Appointment of notaries public. The governor is authorized to appoint, by and with the advice and consent of the Senate, as many notaries public in the different parishes as may be deemed necessary.

Note: Cf. Qualifications, LA. REV. STAT. § 35:191.

§ 35:71. Renewal of bonds; suspension of notaries. All notaries shall renew their bonds every five years. They may be suspended by any court of competent jurisdiction for failure to pay over money instrusted to them in their professional character, for failure to satisfy any final judgment rendered against them in such capacity, or for other just cause.

§ 35:72. Continuing to act so long as bonds renewed. All notaries qualified under this Title are authorized, and shall continue, to act as such so long as they renew their bonds, unless suspended.

§ 35:191. Appointment, qualifications and bond; examination; examiners. [Omitted. See *Qualifications*, LA. REV. STAT. § 35:191].

§ 35:192. Execution and recordation of bond; filing of certificate of competency. The bond required of notaries by R.S. 35:191 shall be executed before the clerk of court and ex-officio recorder of mortgages for the parish where the notary will exercise the functions of his office, and together with the certificate of competency above provided for, shall be filed in the office of the state auditor. The bond shall be subscribed in favor of the governor, approved by the clerk, and if secured by personal surety, recorded in the mortgage office of the said parish in a special book kept for that purpose.

Bossier Parish and Webster Parish

§ 35:621. Appointments. The governor of this state shall, by and with the advice and consent of the Senate and upon a certificate of competency granted by the twenty-sixth judicial district court of Louisiana, as hereafter provided, make the necessary appointment of notaries public for the parishes of Bossier and Webster, respectively.

§ 35:623. Application; certificates. Every applicant for a commission as notary public for either the parish of Bossier or the parish of Webster shall apply to the twenty-sixth judicial district court for the parish in which he resides and shall furnish a certificate establishing his citizenship, residence and good reputation, sworn to and subscribed by at least two reputable citizens of said parish. Said court, pursuant to the rules thereof adopted for such purpose, shall cause said applicant to be examined by a committee of lawyers appointed by said court and, if found competent and possessed of the necessary qualifications, the court shall issue to the applicant appropriate certificate signed by a judge of said court.

§ 35:624. Commissions previously issued. Commissions as notaries public for Bossier Parish or Webster Parish issued prior to August 1, 1962, shall remain in effect.

§ 35:625. Limitation on actions. Actions against sureties on said bonds shall prescribe in ten years from date of act of commission or omission.

Caddo Parish

§ 35:391. Appointment by governor. The governor shall, by and with the advice and consent of the senate, and upon a certificate of competency granted by the First Judicial District Court of Louisiana, make the necessary appointment of notaries public in and for the Parish of Caddo.

§ 35:393. Application for appointment; examination and other prerequisites. Applications for a notarial commission shall be made to the first district court of the Parish of Caddo. Applicants shall furnish with their application a certificate establishing citizenship, residence, and good reputation, sworn to and subscribed by at least two reputable citizens of Louisiana. The court, pursuant to the rules adopted therefor, shall cause the applicant to be examined by a committee of lawyers appointed by it. If the applicant is found competent and possessed of the necessary qualifications, the court shall issue him the appropriate certificate signed by a judge thereof.

§ 35:394. Notarial commissions previously issued. Notarial commissions issued prior to July 28, 1948 for the Parish of Caddo shall remain in effect provided that, at the expiration of the bonds given therewith, they are renewed in the amount of five thousand dollars and in the manner provided in R.S. 35:392.

For LA. REV. STAT. § 35:392 mentioned in the foregoing section, see *Qualifications*. *Note:* Cf. *Qualifications*, LA. REV. STAT. § 35:392.

Jefferson Parish

§ 35:601. Appointments. The governor shall, by and with the advice and consent of the senate and upon a certificate of competency granted by the twenty-fourth judicial district court of Louisiana, make appointments of notaries public in and for the parish of Jefferson.

§ 35:603. Applications; certificates; examinations. Applications for a notarial commission shall be made to the twenty-fourth judicial district court in and for the Parish of Jefferson. Applicants shall furnish with their applications a certificate establishing citizenship, residence, and good reputation, sworn and subscribed to by at least two reputable citizens of Louisiana. Said court, pursuant to rules thereof adopted for such purpose, shall cause said applicant to be examined in writing by a committee of three notaries appointed by said court, two of whom shall be attorneys and one of whom shall not be an attorney and, if found competent and possessed of the necessary qualifications, the court shall issue to the applicant an appropriate certificate signed by a judge of said court. The examination may be dispensed with by the court if the applicant has been duly admitted to practice law in this state.

§ 35:604. **Commissions previously issued.** Notarial commissions issued prior to August 1, 1956, for the parish of Jefferson shall remain in effect.

Orleans Parish

§ 35:251. **Number of notaries.** No appointment of notaries public in and for the parish of Orleans shall be made by the governor unless the number of those holding commissions be less than nineteen hundred, which shall be the limit of the notaries hereinafter provided for.

§ 35:252. **Appointment to fill vacancies.** When the number of notaries public for the parish of Orleans is less than nineteen hundred, the governor shall, by and with the advice and consent of the Senate and upon a certificate of competency granted by the civil district court, as hereinafter provided, make the necessary appointment of notaries public to fill vacancies within the limit of nineteen hundred.

§ 35:254. **Publication of intention to apply for commission; examination of applicant; issue of certificate.** Every applicant for a commission as notary public for the Parish of Orleans, shall give, during ten consecutive days, public notice in one of the daily papers published in the City of New Orleans, of his intention to apply for a commission; and shall furnish with his application to the Civil District Court for the Parish of Orleans proof of the publication, together with a certificate establishing his citizenship, residence, and character, sworn to and subscribed by two reputable citizens of this state. Said court, pursuant to rules thereof adopted for such purpose, shall cause said applicant to be examined in writing by a committee of three notaries, two of whom shall be attorneys, and one of whom shall not be an attorney appointed by said court, and if found competent and possessed of the necessary qualifications, the court shall issue to the applicant an appropriate certificate, signed by at least three judges of the court. The examination may be dispensed with by the court if the applicant has been duly admitted to practice law in this state, and maintains an office for the practice of law in the Parish of Orleans.

§ 35:255. **Granting of commission, prerequisites.** Before the governor shall issue to the applicant a commission of notary public for the Parish of Orleans, he shall require of him the production of:

(1) The certificate provided by R.S. 35:254;

(2) His oath of office;

(3) His bond, properly executed, approved and registered as provided in R.S. 35:253;

(4) His official signature; and

(5) The impress of his official seal; all of which shall, upon the issuing of the commission, be deposited in the office of the Secretary

of State and annexed in the margin of a book to be kept for that purpose by the Secretary of State to be styled "The Notarial Book of Orleans Parish."

Note: For LA. REV. STAT. § 35:253, mentioned in the foregoing section, see *Qualifications.*

§ 35:256. **Renewal of bond; duration of authority to act.** All notaries public for the Parish of Orleans shall renew their bonds every five years or whenever one or both sureties on their bonds shall die or become insolvent, and they shall continue to act as notaries so long as they renew their bonds, unless suspended or removed for cause.

Webster Parish

See Bossier Parish and Webster Parish.

MAINE

[ME. CONST.]

Art. V, pt. 1, § 8. **To nominate officers.** He [the Governor] shall nominate, and, with the advice and consent of the Council, appoint all ° ° ° and notaries public; ° ° °; and every such nomination shall be made seven days, at least, prior to such appointment.

[ME. REV. STAT. ANN.]

Tit. 4, § 955-A. **Removal from office.** Whenever the Governor and Council, upon complaint, after due notice and hearing, shall find that a notary public or justice of the peace has performed any duty imposed upon him by law in an improper manner, or has performed acts not authorized by law, the Governor may remove such notary public or justice of the peace from office. Notice of a hearing shall be given to the accused by service in hand by a sheriff or his deputy or by registered mail at least 30 days prior to the hearing.

Tit. 5, § 87. **Fees payable by public officers.** A fee of $10 shall be paid to the Secretary of State by any person appointed to the office of justice of the peace, notary public, commissioner to take depositions and disclosures, disclosure commissioner and commissioner appointed under Title 33, section 251, before such person enters upon the discharge of his official duties.

MARYLAND

[MD. CONST.]

Art. 4, § 45. **[Coroners, elisors and] notaries public.** [Coroners, Elisors, and] Notaries Public may be appointed for each county, and the city of Baltimore, in the manner, for the purpose, and with the powers now fixed, or which may hereafter be prescribed by Law.

[MD. ANN. CODE]

Art. 68, § 1. Appointment, qualifications, application, term, commission and fees. (a) *Appointment.*—The Governor, on approval of the application by a senator representing the senatorial district and subdistrict in which the applicant resides, shall appoint and commission in his discretion and judgment any number of persons as notaries public, as provided herein.

(b) [Omitted. See *Qualifications.*]

(c) *Application; notice of appointment.*—Applications for original appointment as a notary public shall be made on forms prepared by the Secretary of State and shall be sworn to by the applicant, and must bear thereon or be accompanied by the written approval of a senator representing the senatorial district and subdistrict in which the applicant resides. Completed applications shall be filed with the Secretary of State. When the appointment is made by the Governor, the Secretary of State shall so notify the applicant.

(d) *Term.*—Appointments made and commissions issued following the effective date of the section shall be for a term ending July 1, 1974, and July 1 of each fourth year thereafter. Terms which commenced on or after July 1, 1967, are extended to July 1, 1970.

(e) *Renewal of commission; qualifying; revocation and reinstatement.*—Notary public commissions may be renewed from term to term, and the Secretary of State shall issue notice of renewal to the notary public at or prior to the expiration of the term of the existing commission. Within thirty (30) days after the issuance by the Secretary of State of notice of appointment or renewal the notary public shall qualify before the appropriate clerk of the court and pay the fees herein prescribed. The appointment and commission of any notary public who fails to qualify and pay the fees within said time shall stand revoked, and in such case the court clerk shall return the commission of the notary public to the Secretary of State with a certification that the notary public failed to qualify and pay the fees within the required time, but the Secretary of State for good cause shown may reinstate the appointment and commission.

(f) *Fees.*—At the time the notice of appointment by the Governor or the notice of renewal is issued, the Secretary of State shall forward to the clerk of the Superior Court of Baltimore City, if the notary resides therein, or the clerk of the circuit court of the county in which the notary public resides, a commission signed by the Governor and Secretary of State under the great seal of the State. The clerk of the court shall deliver the commission to the notary public upon qualification and payment of the prescribed fees by the notary public. Each notary public shall pay to the clerk a fee of one dollar ($1.00) for qualifying the notary public and registering the name and address of the notary public; and a fee of ten dollars ($10.00) or such lesser amount as may be prescribed by the Secretary of State for the commission issued, which shall be paid by the clerk to the treasury of the State of Maryland. The Secretary of State may fix such other reasonable fees as may be required for the processing of applications and the issuance and renewal of notarial commissions.

(g) *Forms.*—The Secretary of State may prepare and adopt forms as required under this section, including the form of original applications, the form of commissions, and forms for renewal of commissions.

§ 2. **Removal.** Any notary public may be removed from office by the Governor for good cause either in his own initiative or upon a request made to him in writing by the Senator who approved the appointment. After notice to the notary and the opportunity for a hearing before the Secretary of State, the Secretary of State shall submit his recommendation to the Governor for action as the Governor determines to be required in the case.

MASSACHUSETTS

[MASS. CONST.]

§ 106. **Art. IV. Appointment, Tenure, etc., of Notaries Public.** Notaries public shall be appointed by the governor in the same manner as judicial officers are appointed, and shall hold their offices during seven years, unless sooner removed by the governor with the consent of the council, [upon the address of both houses of the legislature]. Women shall be eligible to appointment as notaries public. Upon the change of name of any woman, she shall re-register under her new name and shall pay such fee therefor as shall be established by the general court.

§ 139. **Art. XXXVII. Removal of Certain Officers.** The governor, with the consent of the council, may remove justices of the peace and notaries public.

[MASS. ANN. LAWS]

Ch. 9, § 15. **Notice of Expiration of Commissions.** The secretary shall send by first class mail to every justice of the peace or notary public a notice of the time of expiration of his commission, not more than thirty nor less than fourteen days before such expiration.

§ 15A. **Validation of Acts Performed by Notary Public, etc., after Change of Name or Expiration of Commission.** If a notary public, whose name has been changed by marriage or decree of court and who has failed to re-register as required by law, or a notary public or justice of the peace whose commission has expired, continues to act as such after such change of name or expiration the state secretary, upon the application of such person and the payment of a fee of five dollars, may issue a certificate validating all such acts done after such change of name or expiration.

Ch. 30, § 12. Failure to Qualify. A person appointed to an office by the governor with or without the advice and consent of the council shall be notified of his appointment by the state secretary and his commission delivered to him, and if he does not, within three months after the date of such appointment, take and subscribe the oaths of office, his appointment shall be void, and the secretary shall forthwith notify him thereof and require him to return his commission, and shall also certify said facts to the governor. This section shall be printed on every such commission.

§ 13. Fees for Certain Commissions, etc. Before the delivery of a commission to a person appointed commissioner under section three or four of chapter two hundred and twenty-two, master in chancery or justice of the peace, he shall pay to the state secretary a fee of twenty-five dollars. Before the delivery of a commission to a person appointed a notary public he shall pay to the state secretary a fee of twelve dollars. A person whose acts as a notary public or justice of a peace have been validated by the general court or the state secretary shall pay a fee of one hundred dollars before the delivery of the first commission for either of said offices to be delivered after such validation. Upon the change of name of any woman who has been appointed and qualified as a notary public, she shall re-register under her new name and shall pay to the state secretary a fee of one dollar.

Ch. 222, § 1. Justices of the Peace and Notaries Public; Appointment and Jurisdiction. Justices of the peace and notaries public shall be appointed, and their commissions shall be issued, for the commonwealth, and they shall have jurisdiction throughout the commonwealth when acting under the sole authority of such a commission. Unless otherwise expressly provided they may administer oaths or affirmations in all cases in which an oath or affirmation is required and take acknowledgments of deeds and other instruments.

MICHIGAN

[MICH. COMP. LAWS ANN.]

§ 16.133. Certain powers, duties and functions of governor; transfer. All or any portion of the powers, duties and functions of governor under section 107 of chapter 14 of the Revised Statutes of 1846, as amended, being section 55.107 of the Compiled Laws of 1948, relating to notaries public, may be delegated by executive order to the department of state.

§ 55.101. Delegation of notaries public functions. [EXECUTIVE ORDER dated February 9, 1970.]

Whereas, the Governor may appoint one or more persons notaries public in each county of this state, and;

Whereas, persons desiring to be appointed as notaries public shall make written application to the Governor for his approval, and;

Whereas, all or any portion of the Governor's functions respecting notaries public may be delegated by Executive Order to the Department of State.

Therefore, I, William G. Milliken, Governor of the State of Michigan, pursuant to Act No. 380, paragraph 33 of the Public Acts of 1965, do hereby transfer and delegate to the Department of State all ministerial and clerical duties and functions relative to processing applications for notaries public.

§ 55.107. Appointment, term, eligibility; application; revocation; fees; indorsement of application in blank; deposit of fees. The governor may appoint 1 or more persons notaries public in each county of this state, who shall hold their offices respectively for 4 years from the date of their appointment, unless sooner removed by the governor. No person shall be eligible to receive such an appointment unless he or she shall be, at the time of making application for appointment, of the age of 18 years, a resident of the county of which he or she desires to be appointed notary public, and a citizen of this state. The person desiring to be appointed shall make a written application on an official form distributed by the county clerk of each county, stating the age of the applicant, which application shall be indorsed by a member of the legislature, or some circuit or probate judge of the county, district or circuit of which the applicant is a resident, and be presented to the governor, accompanied by a fee of ° ° °. Effective April 1, 1972 the fee shall be $3.00. Under no circumstances shall such application form be indorsed in blank, prior to completion and signature by the applicant. The governor may revoke a commission issued to a notary public upon presentation to him of satisfactory evidence of official misconduct or incapacity. The governor shall revoke the commission issued to a notary public upon presentation to him of satisfactory evidence of the notarization of a paper or document prior to completion by the person whose signature is notarized. On the last days of March, June, September and December of each year, the governor shall deposit all fees so received by him during the last preceding quarter with the state treasurer, which shall be placed in the general fund.

Any notary public whose name has been changed pursuant to law subsequent to the issuance of a commission shall continue to use the name set forth in the commission for all purposes authorized under such commission until the expiration thereof.

§ 55.108. Commission transmitted, notice. Whenever the governor shall appoint a notary public, the secretary of state shall transmit his commission to the clerk of the county for which such notary was appointed; and the county clerk, on receiving such commission, shall give notice thereof to the person so appointed.

§ 55.109. **Oath; quarterly lists to secretary of state; fee.** The person so appointed shall, before entering upon the duties of his office, and within 90 days after receiving notice from the county clerk of his appointment, take and file with the county clerk the oath prescribed by the constitution, and the said clerk shall file the oath thus taken in his office, and on the last day of December, March, June and September in each year, he shall transmit to the secretary of state a written list, containing the names of all persons to whom, during each preceding quarter he has delivered commissions, the date of filing their oaths and bonds, and their respective postoffice addresses with his certificate that such persons have fully complied with the provisions of law in regard to their qualification for the discharge of the duties of the office of notary public; and said clerk, for all his services required by this act, shall be entitled to receive the sum of $1.00 from each person so qualifying: Provided, Whenever the county clerk of any county shall be appointed to the office of notary public, the oath of office required of him by the constitution shall be filed with the judge of probate of such county.

§ 55.110. **Bond, approval.** Each notary public shall, also, before entering upon the duties of his office, and within the time limited for filing his official oath, give bond to the people of this state, with 1 or more sureties, to be approved by the county clerk, in the penal sum of 1,000 dollars, the condition of which bond shall be that such notary shall duly and faithfully discharge the duties of his office, and he shall file the same with said clerk: Provided, Whenever the county clerk of any county shall be appointed to the office of notary public, the bond required by this section shall be approved by, and filed with the judge of probate of such county.

§ 55.111. **Delivery of commission; notice to secretary of state.** Upon the filing of the official oath and bond, as required in the 2 next preceding sections, the clerk shall deliver to the person so appointed the commission received by him for such person: Provided, That where such oath and bond shall have been filed with the judge of probate, as provided in the 2 next preceding sections, he shall give the same notice thereof to the secretary of state as is required in this section to be given by the county clerk.

MINNESOTA

[MINN. CONST.]

Art. 5, § 4. Powers and duties of governor. The governor ° ° ° shall have power, by and with the advice and consent of the Senate, to appoint notaries public, and such other officers as may be provided by law. ° ° °.

Editorial comment

The governor may appoint and commission as many notaries public as he deems necessary. The fee for each commission shall not exceed $10.00 and shall be paid to the governor's private secretary. See *Qualifications*, MINN. STAT. ANN. § 359.01.

[MINN. STAT. ANN.]

§ 359.02.　**Term, bond, oath, reappointment.** Every notary so commissioned shall hold office for seven years, unless sooner removed by the governor or the district court; and, before entering upon the duties of his office, he shall give a bond to the state in the sum of $2,000, to be approved by the governor, conditioned for the faithful discharge of the duties of his office, which, with his oath of office, shall be filed with the secretary of state. Within ten days before the expiration of his commission he may be reappointed for a new term to commence and to be designated in his new commission as beginning upon the day immediately following such expiration. The reappointment so made shall go into effect and be valid although the appointing governor may not be in the office of governor on said day.

§ 359.06.　**Record of commission, certificates.** The commission of every notary shall be recorded in the office of the clerk of the district court of the county for which he is appointed, in a book kept for that purpose, on payment of a fee of $1; and thereafter such clerk, when requested, shall certify to his official acts in the same manner and for the same fees allowed by law for similar certificates to authenticate acts of justices of the peace.

§ 359.12.　**Removal from office.** Every notary who shall charge or receive a fee or reward for any act or service done or rendered by him under this chapter greater than the amount allowed by law, or who dishonestly or unfaithfully discharges his duties as notary, shall, on complaint filed and substantiated as in other civil cases in the district court of the county in which he resides, be removed from office by such court. The fact of such removal shall thereupon be certified by the clerk to the governor, and the person so removed shall thereafter be ineligible to such office.

MISSISSIPPI

[MISS. CODE ANN.]

§ 25-33-1.　**Governor may appoint for each county.** The governor may appoint one or more notaries public for each county, who shall hold his office for the term of four years. He shall give bond, with sufficient sureties in the penalty of two thousand dollars, conditioned and approved as bonds of county officers are required to be, and shall take the oath of office prescribed by § 268 of the constitution. The oath and bond shall be filed in the office of the clerk of the chancery court of the county, and the bond shall be recorded.

MISSOURI

[MO. ANN. STAT.]

§ 28.160. State entitled to certain fees. The state shall be entitled to fees for services to be rendered by the secretary of state as follows:

* * *

For issuing commission to notary public 5.00
For issuing commission to commissioners of deeds 7.50

* * *

§ 486.010. Notaries—how appointed—term of office—qualifications. The governor shall appoint and commission in each county and incorporated city in this state, as occasion may require, a notary public or notaries public, who may perform all the duties of such office in the county for which such notary is appointed and in adjoining counties, and in any or all other counties of the state in which he has previously filed a certified copy of his appointment with the county clerk of that county. Each such notary shall hold office for four years, but no person shall be appointed who has not attained the age of twenty-one years, and who is not a citizen of the United States and of this state. * * *.

§ 486.050. Oath of office and size of bond—exception in class one counties—liability on bond—sureties on bond may petition for discharge. Every notary, before entering upon the discharge of the duties of his office, shall take the oath of office, which shall be endorsed on his commission, shall give bond to the state in the sum of two thousand dollars, except in counties of the first class, in which they shall give bond in the sum of five thousand dollars, with at least two good and sufficient sureties, to be approved by the clerk of the county court (in the city of St. Louis such approval shall be by the clerk of the circuit court), which commission, oath and bond shall be filed and recorded in the office of said county clerk, and in the city of St. Louis in the office of the circuit clerk. Said bond, after having been so recorded, shall be filed in the office of the secretary of state, and may be sued on by any person injured; but no suit shall be instituted against any such notary or his sureties more than three years after such cause of action accrued. Sureties on the bond of any notary may be discharged from all future liability on such official bond, by petition in writing addressed to the county court (in the city of St. Louis to the circuit court), by conforming to the requirements, with the same rights and remedies as provided by sections 433.140 to 433.220, RSMo 1949, relating to sureties.

§ 486.060. **Insufficient bond, procedure.** On the written statement of any citizen, verified by oath, that the bond of any notary has become or is insufficient, said county clerk, and in the city of St. Louis the circuit clerk, shall cite such notary to appear before him, and to give a new and sufficient bond. If said clerk shall find his bond to be insufficient, he shall order a new bond to be given, and if such new and sufficient bond shall not be given within ten days after said order, such notary public shall forfeit his office, and thereafter cease to exercise the powers and duties thereof.

§ 486.070. **Commission, disposition of.** Whenever a commission is issued to any person as notary public, the secretary of state shall forward such commission to the county clerk, and the commissions for those in the city of St. Louis to the circuit clerk. Said clerk shall not deliver the same to the person commissioned until such person shall have given the bond required by section 486.050, and taken and subscribed the oath of office; and should the person so commissioned fail or neglect to so qualify within three months after the date of said commission, the clerk shall return the commission to the secretary of state with his endorsement thereof of such failure or neglect, and the governor shall cancel and annul said commission.

MONTANA

[MONT. REV. CODES ANN.]

§ 56-101. **Appointment and jurisdiction.** The governor may appoint and commission as many notaries public for the state of Montana as in his judgment may be deemed best, whose jurisdiction shall be co-extensive with the boundaries of the state, irrespective of their place of residence within the state.

§ 56-103. **Term of office.** The term of office of a notary public is three years from and after the date of his commission.

§ 56-110. **Bond and commission of notary public.** Each notary public must give an official bond in the sum of one thousand dollars, which bond must be approved by the secretary of state. Upon the approval of said bond and the filing in the office of the secretary of state of the official oath of such notary public, the governor shall issue a commission.

§ 56-111. **Liabilities on official bond.** For the official misconduct or neglect of a notary public, he and the sureties on his official bond are liable to the parties injured thereby for all damages sustained.

§ 56-112. **Certificates of official character.** The secretary of state may certify to the official character of such notary public, and any notary public may file a copy of his commission in the office of any county clerk of any county in the state, and thereafter said county clerk may certify to the official character of such notary public.

§ 56-113. Fees for filing commission and issuing certificates.
The secretary of state shall receive for each certificate of official
character issued, with seal attached, the sum of two dollars ($2.00).
The county clerk of any county in this state with whom a copy of
notarial commission has been filed, shall receive for filing same the
sum of fifty cents, and for each certificate of official character issued,
with seal attached, the further sum of fifty cents.

§ 56-114. Revocation of commission. Upon ten days notice, the
governor may revoke the commission of any notary public for any
cause he may deem sufficient.

NEBRASKA

[NEB. REV. STAT.]

§ 33-102. Notary public commission; fees. The Secretary of
State shall be entitled, for receiving, affixing the great seal to, and
forwarding the commission of a notary public, to the sum of two
dollars and the additional sum of three dollars for filing and approving the bond of a notary public.

§ 64-101. Notary public; appointment; qualifications; term. (1)
The Governor is hereby authorized to appoint and commission such
number of persons to the office of notary public as he shall deem
necessary. (2) There shall be one class of such appointments
which shall be valid in the entire state and referred to as general
notaries public. (3) The term effective date, as used with reference to a commission of a notary public, shall mean the date of the
commission unless the commission shall state when it goes into effect,
in which event that date shall be the effective date. (4) A general
commission may refer to the office as notary public and shall contain a provision showing that the person therein named is authorized
to act as a notary public anywhere within the State of Nebraska or,
in lieu thereof, may contain the word general or refer to the office as
general notary public.

[Subsections (5) and (6) omitted. See *Qualifications*, NEB. REV.
STAT. § 64-101.]

(7) Each person appointed a notary public shall hold office for
a term of four years from the effective date of his or her commission
unless sooner removed.

§ 64-102. Commission; how obtained; bond. Any person may
apply for a commission authorizing the applicant to act as a notary
public anywhere in the State of Nebraska, and thereupon the Governor may, at his discretion, issue a commission authorizing such
notary public to act as such anywhere in the State of Nebraska.
A general commission shall not authorize the holder thereof to act
as a notary public anywhere in the State of Nebraska until a bond
in the sum of four thousand dollars, with an incorporated surety

company as surety, has been executed and approved by and filed in the office of the Secretary of State. Upon the filing of such bond with the Secretary of State and the issuance of such commission, such notary public shall be authorized and empowered to perform any and all the duties of a notary public in any and all the counties in the State of Nebraska. Such bond shall be conditioned for the faithful performance of the duties of such office. Such person so appointed to the office of notary public shall make oath or affirmation, to be endorsed on such bond, and subscribed by him before some officer authorized by law to administer oaths, and by him certified thereon, that he will support the Constitution of the United States and the Constitution of the State of Nebraska, and will faithfully and impartially discharge and perform the duties of the office of notary public.

§ 64-103. **Commission; signature; sealing; filing and approval of bond; delivery of commission.** When any person shall be appointed to the office of notary public, the Governor shall cause his signature or a facsimile thereof to be affixed to the commission and deliver the same to the Secretary of State. Upon the receipt of the commission by the secretary, he shall affix thereto the great seal of state. Upon the filing and approval of the bond, as provided for in section 64-102, the Secretary of State shall mail or deliver the commission to the applicant.

§ 64-109. **Civil liability of notary public; actions.** If any person shall be damaged or injured by the unlawful act, negligence or misconduct of any notary public in his official capacity, the person damaged or injured may maintain a civil action on the official bond of such notary public against such notary public, and his sureties, and a recovery in such action shall not be a bar to any future action for other causes to the full amount of the bond.

§ 64-113. **Notary public; removal; grounds; procedure; penalty.** Whenever charges of malfeasance in office shall be preferred to the Governor against any notary public in this state, or whenever the Governor shall have reasonable cause to believe any notary public in this state is guilty of acts of malfeasance in office, he may appoint any disinterested person, not related by consanguinity to either the notary public or person preferring the charges, and authorized by law to take testimony of witnesses by deposition, to notify such notary public to appear before him on a day and at an hour certain, after at least ten days from the day of service of such notice. He may summon witnesses, in the manner provided by section 64-108,* to appear before him at the time specified in said notice, and he may take the testimony of such witnesses in writing, in the same manner as is by law provided for taking depositions, and certify the same to the Governor. The notary public may appear, at such time and place, and cross-examine witnesses, and produce witnesses in his behalf, which cross-examination and testimony shall be likewise certified to the Governor. Upon the receipt of such examination, duly certified in the manner prescribed for taking depositions to be used in suits in the district courts of this state, the Governor shall examine the same, and if therefrom he shall be satisfied that the charges are substantially proved, he may remove the person charged from the office of notary public. Within thirty days from such removal and notice thereof, such notary public shall deposit, with the Secretary of State, his commission as notary public. The commission shall be canceled by the Secretary of State. Thereafter such person so removed from office shall be forever disqualified from holding the office of notary public. The fees for taking such testimony shall be paid by the state at the same rate as fees for taking depositions by notaries public. The failure of the notary public to deposit his commission with the Secretary of State as required by this section shall subject him to a penalty of two hundred dollars, to be recovered in the name of the state.

* Concerning NEB. REV. STAT. § 64-108, see *Depositions.*

§ 64-114. **Notary public; change of name; continue to act.** Any person, whose name is legally changed after a commission as a notary public is issued to him or her, may continue to act as such notary public and use the original commission, seal, and name until the expiration or termination of such commission. The bond given by such notary public shall continue in effect, regardless of such legal change of name of such notary public, if the notary public uses the name under which the commission is issued.

§ 64-116. **Notary public; commission; renewal; procedure.** Commissions for general notaries public may be renewed within thirty days prior to the date of expiration by filing a renewal application along with the payment of a fee of five dollars and a new bond with the Secretary of State. The bond required for a renewal of such commission shall be in the same manner and form as provided in section 64-102.* The renewal application shall be in the manner and form as prescribed by the Secretary of State. Such renewal application made prior to the date of the expiration of any general notary public commission need not be accompanied by any petition. Any renewal application for such commission made after the date of expiration of the commission shall be made in the same manner as a new application for such commission as a general notary public.

* For § 64-102, see above.

NEVADA

[NEV. REV. STAT.]

§ 240.010. **Appointment by governor; number unlimited.** The governor is empowered to appoint and commission notaries public without limit in and for the several counties in this state, in any number in which applications may be made to him.

§ 240.020. **Term of office.** The term of office of a notary public shall be 4 years.

§ 240.030. **Fee for commission; oath and bond.** 1. Each notary public shall:

(a) Before entering upon the duties of his office and at the time he receives his commission, pay to the secretary of state the sum of $25 for the state general fund.

(b) Take the official oath as prescribed by law, which oath shall be endorsed on his commission.

(c) Enter into a bond to the State of Nevada in the sum of $2,000, to be approved by the clerk of the county for which the notary public may be appointed.

2. The bond, together with the oath of office, shall be filed and recorded in the office of the county clerk of the county.

NEW HAMPSHIRE

[N.H. REV. STAT. ANN.]

§ 5:10. **Office fees.** Except as otherwise provided, the following fees shall be paid to the secretary of state for the use of the state: For every commission issued to a justice of the peace or to a notary public, ten dollars; for every other commission to any person for an office of profit, five dollars, to be paid by such person; ° ° °.

§ 455:1. **Appointment.** Notaries public shall be appointed by the governor, with advice of the council, and shall be commissioned for five years.

NEW JERSEY

[N.J. STAT. ANN.]

§ 22A:2-29. **Fees for filing, indexing, entering or recording documents or papers in county clerk's office.** Upon the filing, indexing, entering or recording of the following documents or papers in the office of the county clerk or clerk of the law division of the County Court, such parties, filing or having the same recorded or indexed in the county clerk's office or with the clerk of the law division of the County Court of the various counties in this State shall pay the following fees in lieu of the fees heretofore provided for the filing, recording or entering of such documents or papers.

°   °   °

Commissions and oaths—

    Administering oaths to notaries public and commissioners of deeds 3.00

    For issuing certificate of authority of notary to take proof, acknowledgment of affidavit 1.00

For issuing each certificate of the commission and qualification of notary public for filing with other county
clerks 2.00

For filing each certificate of the commission and qualification of notary public, in office of county clerk of
county other than where such notary has qualified .. 2.00

* o o

§ 22A:4-1. Fees of Secretary of State and Governor. For services
herein enumerated the Secretary of State shall receive the following
fees:

o o o

For every commission granted to a notary public for a 5-year
term or a foreign commissioner of deeds for a 3-year term a fee
of $15.00.

For filing the seal of a foreign commissioner of deeds the Secretary of State shall receive a fee of $1.00.

* * o

§ 52:7-1. Appointment; term; removal. The governor may appoint and commission so many notaries public as he shall deem
necessary, who shall hold their respective offices for the term of
five years, but may be removed from office at the pleasure of the
governor.

§ 52:7-1.1. Appointment by Secretary of State; fees. All notaries
public shall hereafter be appointed by the Secretary of State but
shall be commissioned by the Governor as heretofore. No person
shall be appointed a notary public unless he shall be of the age
of twenty-one years or over.† The fees required to be paid for
the issuance of any commission shall be paid to the Secretary of
State, who shall account to the State Treasurer for the same.

The statement required to be made and signed pursuant to section
52:7-8 of the Revised Statutes° shall be addressed to the Secretary
of State and filed in his office and in such other offices as is now
required by law.

† It is likely that the age requirement has been reduced to 18
years. See *Qualifications*, N.J. STAT. ANN. § 9:17B-1.

° See *Authority and Duties*, N.J. STAT. ANN. § 52:7-8.

§ 52:7-2. Oath; filing; certificate of commission and qualification.
Within 3 months of the receipt of his commission, each notary
public shall take and subscribe an oath before the clerk of the county
in which he resides, faithfully and honestly to discharge all the
duties of his office, and that he will make and keep a true record
of all such matters as are required by law, which oath shall be filed
with said clerk. Upon the administration of said oath, the said

clerk shall cause the notary public to indorse a certificate of commission and qualification and shall deliver said certificate to the notary public, and the notary public shall transmit said certificate to the Secretary of State within 10 days of the administration of said oath.

The Secretary of State shall cancel and revoke the appointment of any notary public who fails to take and subscribe said oath within 3 months of the receipt of his commission, or who fails to transmit said certificate to the Secretary of State within 10 days of the administration of said oath, and any appointment so canceled and revoked shall be null, void and of no effect.

§ 52:7-3. Filing certificates of commission and qualification with county clerks. Any notary public, after having been duly commissioned and qualified, shall, upon request, receive from the clerk of the county where he has qualified, as many certificates of his commission and qualification as he shall require for filing with other county clerks of this state, and upon receipt of such certificates the notary public may present the same, together with his autograph signature, to such county clerks as he may desire, for filing.

§ 52:7-5. Fee to accompany application for commission. Each applicant for appointment as a notary public shall inclose with his application the fee prescribed by [§ 22A:4-1]* of the title Fees and Costs, which shall be returned if a commission is not issued to him.

* The statute says, "section 22:4-1". That former section has been transferred and renumbered as § 22A:4-1, however. See § 22A:4-1 above.

§ 52:7-6. Women as notaries. No person shall be denied appointment as notary public on account of sex.

NEW MEXICO

[N.M. STAT. ANN.]

§ 35-1-3. Application. Each applicant for appointment as a notary public shall submit to the secretary of state:

A. an application for appointment on a form prescribed by the secretary of state which includes a statement of the applicant's qualification and contains evidence of his good moral character as shown by signatures of two [2] citizens of this state;

B. the oath prescribed by the Constitution for state officers and an official bond to the state, with two [2] sureties, in the amount of five hundred dollars ($500) conditioned for the faithful discharge of duties as a notary public; and

C. an application fee in the amount of ten dollars ($10.00).

§ 35-1-4. Appointment—Term. Upon receipt of the completed application for appointment and the application fee, and upon approval of the applicant's bond, the secretary of state shall notify the governor who shall appoint the applicant as a notary public for a term of four [4] years from the date of appointment unless sooner removed by the governor. The secretary of state shall issue a commission to each notary public appointed by the governor.

§ 35-1-7. **Action on bond.** Any person damaged by an unlawful act, negligence or misconduct of a notary public in his official capacity may bring a civil action on the notary public's official bond.

§ 35-1-8. **Reappointment.** At least thirty [30] days before expiration of each notary public term, the secretary of state shall mail a notice of the expiration to the notary public's address of record. A notary public may be reappointed upon making application in the same manner as required for an original application.

§ 35-1-12. **Removal from office.** Any notary public may be removed from office by the governor for any malfeasance in office. Upon removal, the secretary of state shall give notice by certified mail to the person removed.

NEW YORK

[N.Y. EXEC. LAW]

§ 130. **Appointment of notaries public.** The secretary of state may appoint and commission as many notaries public for the state of New York as in his judgment may be deemed best, whose jurisdiction shall be co-extensive with the boundaries of the state. The appointment of a notary public whose appointment takes effect on the thirty-first day of March shall be for a term of two years, expiring on the thirtieth day of March. The appointment of a notary public whose appointment takes effect on a day other than the thirty-first day of March shall be for a term expiring on the thirtieth day of March occurring after the thirty-first day of March next following the day that the appointment takes effect. An application for an appointment as notary public shall be in form and set forth such matters as the secretary of state shall prescribe. ° ° ° The secretary of state may suspend or remove from office, for misconduct, any notary public appointed by him but no such removal shall be made unless the person who is sought to be removed shall have been served with a copy of the charges against him and have an opportunity of being heard.

§ 131. **Procedure of appointment; fees and commissions.** 1. Upon being satisfied of the competency and good character of the applicant for appointment as notary public, the secretary of state shall issue a commission to such person.

2. The secretary of state shall receive a non-refundable fee of ten dollars from applicants for appointment or reappointment, which fee shall be submitted together with the application.

3. The commission, duly dated, shall be transmitted by the secretary of state to the county clerk of the county in which the appointee resides. Upon receiving such commission, the county clerk shall forthwith notify each person so appointed to qualify by filing with him his oath of office, duly executed before any person authorized to administer an oath, together with his official signature, within thirty days from the date of such notice.

3-a. The county clerk may designate from among the members of his staff, by a certificate filed in his office, any assistant to administer oaths of office to persons appointed notaries public by the secretary of state who appear at the county clerk's office for the purpose of executing such oaths.

4. The county clerk shall make a proper index of commissions and official signatures filed with him. For filing and indexing the commission of appointment and official signature, the county clerk shall be paid a fee of one dollar by the appointee, which fee shall include the administration of the oath by the county clerk, should he administer the same.

5. If a person appointed notary public shall not file his oath of office as such notary public, in the office of the clerk of the county of his residence, within thirty days after the notice of his appointment as above provided, his appointment is deemed revoked and the fee filed with his application forfeited. However, after such revocation, any such notary public may reapply for a new appointment, but shall not be required to take and pass another examination during the term for which he was previously certified.

6. Each county clerk on or before the tenth day of each month shall, make a report to the secretary of state for the preceding month, indicating the name and date of the qualification of each notary public and also the name of each notary public whose appointment was revoked and fee forfeited by his failure to qualify.

§ 132. **Certificates of official character of notaries public.** The secretary of state or the county clerk of the county in which the commission of a notary public is filed may certify to the official character of such notary public and any notary public may file his autograph signature and a certificate of official character in the office of any county clerk of any county in the state and in any register's office in any county having a register and thereafter such county clerk may certify as to the official character of such notary public. The secretary of state shall collect for each certificate of official character issued by him the sum of one dollar. The county clerk and register of any county with whom a certificate of official character has been filed shall collect for filing the same the sum of one dollar. For each certificate of official character issued, with seal attached, by any county clerk, the sum of one dollar shall be collected by him.

§ 133. **Certification of notarial signatures.** The county clerk of a county in whose office any notary public has qualified or has filed his autograph signature and a certificate of his official character, shall, when so requested and upon payment of a fee of fifty cents affix to any certificate of proof or acknowledgment or oath signed by such notary anywhere in the state of New York, a certificate under his hand and seal, stating that a commission or a certificate of his official character with his autograph signature has been filed in his office, and that he was at the time of taking such proof or acknowledgment or oath duly authorized to take the same; that he is well acquainted with the handwriting of such notary public or has compared the signature on the certificate of proof or acknowledgment or oath with the autograph signature deposited in his office by such notary public and believes that the signature is genuine. An instrument with such certificate of authentication of the county clerk affixed thereto shall be entitled to be read in evidence or to be recorded in any of the counties of this state in respect to which a certificate of a county clerk may be necessary for either purpose.

§ 134. **Signature and seal of county clerk.** The signature and seal of a county clerk, upon a certificate of official character of a notary public or the signature of a county clerk upon a certificate of authentication of the signature and acts of a notary public or commissioner of deeds, may be a facsimile, printed, stamped, photographed or engraved thereon.

[N.Y. PUB. OFFICERS LAW]

§ 8. **Commissions of officers.** ° ° ° Commissions of notaries public shall be signed by the secretary of state, or by a person or persons in the department of state designated by the secretary of state, and shall be sent to the county clerk of the county in which such notaries public respectively reside. Commissions of commissioners of deeds in other states, territories and foreign countries, shall be signed by the secretary of state, or by a person or persons in the department of state designated by secretary of state.

°   °   °

Every such written appointment shall be deemed the commission of the officer appointed, and if of a state officer, a duplicate or a certified copy thereof shall be recorded in the office of the department of state; if of a local officer it shall be sent to the clerk of the county in which the officer appointed shall then reside, who shall file the same in his office, and notify the officer appointed of his appointment.

§ 10. **Official oaths.** Every officer shall take and file the oath of office required by law, and every judicial officer of the unified court system, in addition, shall file a copy of said oath in the office of the administrative board of the judicial conference of the state of New York, before he shall be entitled to enter upon the discharge of any of his official duties. An oath of office may be administered by a judge of the court of appeals or by any officer authorized to take, within the state, the acknowledgment of the execution of a deed of real property, or by an officer in whose office the oath is required to be filed or by his duly designated assistant, or may be administered to any member of a body of officers, by a presiding officer or clerk, thereof, who shall have taken an oath of office. An oath of office may be administered to any state or local officer who is a member of the armed forces of the United States by any commissioned officer, in active service, of the armed forces of the United States. In addition to the requirements of any other law, the certificate of the officer in the armed forces administering the oath of office under this section shall state (a) the rank of the officer administering the oath, and (b) that the person taking the oath was at the time, enlisted, inducted, ordered or commissioned in or serving with, attached to or accompanying the armed forces of the United States. The fact that the officer administering the oath was at the time duly commissioned and in active service with the armed forces, shall be certified by the secretary of the army, secretary of the air force or by the secretary of the navy, as the case may be, of the United States, or by a person designated by him to make such certifications, but the place where such oath was administered need not be disclosed. The oath of office of a notary public or commissioner of deeds shall be filed in the office of the clerk of the county in which he shall reside. The oath of office of every state officer shall be filed in the office of the secretary of state; of every officer of a municipal corporation, including a school district, with the clerk thereof; and of every other officer, including the trustees and officers of a public library and the officers of boards of cooperative educational services, in the office of the clerk of the county in which he shall reside, if no place be otherwise provided by law for the filing therof.

NORTH CAROLINA

[N.C. GEN. STAT.]

§ 10-1. **Appointment and commission; term of office; revocation of commission.** The Secretary of State may, from time to time, at his discretion, appoint one or more fit persons in every county to act as notaries public and shall issue to each a commission upon payment of a fee of ten dollars ($10.00). The commission shall show that it is for a term of five years and shall show the effective date and the date of expiration. The term of the commission shall be computed by including the effective date and shall end at midnight of the day preceding the anniversary of the effective date, five years thereafter. The commission shall be sent to the register of deeds of the county in which the appointee lives and a copy of the letter of transmittal to the register of deeds shall be sent to the appointee concerned.

The commission shall be retained by the register of deeds until the appointee has qualified in the manner provided in G.S. 10-2.

Any commission so issued by the Secretary of State or his predecessor, shall be revocable by him in his discretion upon complaint being made against such notary public and when he shall be satisfied that the interest of the public will be best served by the revocation of said commission. Whenever the Secretary of State shall have revoked the commission of any notary public appointed by him, or his predecessor in office, it shall be his duty to file with the register of deeds in the county of such notary public a copy of said order and mail a copy of same to said notary public.

✷   ✷   ✷

Note: Concerning the penalty for holding oneself out to the public as a notary public, or attempting to act in such capacity, after one's commission has been revoked by the Secretary of State, see *Offenses,* N.C. GEN. STAT. § 10-1.

§ 10.2. To qualify before register of deed; record of qualification. Upon appearing before the register of deed to which their commissions were delivered, the notaries shall be duly qualified by taking before the register an oath of office, and the oaths prescribed for officers. Following the administration of the oaths of office, the notary shall place his signature in a book designated as "The Record of Notaries Public." The record of Notaries Public shall contain the name of the notary, the signature of the notary, the effective date and expiration date of the commission, the date the oath was administered, and the date of revocation if the commission is revoked by the Secretary of State. The information contained in The Record of Notaries Public shall constitute the official record of the qualification of notaries public, and the register of deeds shall deliver the commission to the notary following his qualification and notify the Secretary of State of such qualification.

§ 147-15.1. Fees collected by private secretary. The secretary to the Governor shall charge and collect the following fees, to be paid by the person for whom the services are rendered: for the commission of a notary public, ten dollars ($10.00); for the commission of a special policeman, five dollars ($5.00). All fees collected by the secretary shall be paid into the State treasury.

NORTH DAKOTA

[N.D. CENT. CODE]

§ 44-06-01. Appointment and qualification of notaries public. The secretary of state shall appoint in each county in this state from among the citizens of either sex one or more notaries public, who shall hold office for six years unless sooner removed by the secretary of state.

✷   ✷   ✷

§ 44-06-02. Commission—Record—Fee—Notice. The secretary of state shall issue a commission and duplicate thereof to each notary public appointed by the secretary of state. One of such copies shall be posted by such notary in a conspicuous place in his office. The secretary of state shall collect ten dollars for the issuance of such commission and duplicate. Such sum shall be paid into the state treasury and credited to the general fund. The secretary of state shall keep in his office a record of such appointments and the date of the expiration of the same, and shall notify each notary public by mail at least thirty days before the expiration of his term of the date upon which his commission will expire. Such notice shall be addressed to such notary public at his last known place of residence.

§ 44-06-03. Oath and bond of notary public—Approval of bond. Each notary public, before entering upon the duties of his office, shall take the oath prescribed for civil officers and give to the state a bond in the penal sum of five hundred dollars conditioned for the faithful discharge of the duties of his office. Such bond may be furnished by a surety or bonding company authorized to do business in this state or by one or more sureties, and shall be subject to approval as follows:

1. If it is a surety bond, it shall be subject to approval by the secretary of state, and such approval shall be without charge; or

2. If it is a personal bond, it shall be subject to approval by the clerk of the district court of the county of which the notary public is a resident, or of the county to which such county is attached for judicial purposes.

Concerning the duties of a notary regarding filing of his oath, bond, and an impression of his notarial seal, see *Seal*, N.D. CENT. CODE § 44-06-04.

§ 44-06-11. Revocation of notary commission—Notice. In case the commission of any person appointed as a notary is revoked, the secretary of state shall give notice thereof by mail to such person immediately and to the clerk of the district court of the proper county.

OHIO

[OHIO REV. CODE ANN.]

§ 147.01. Appointment of notaries public; attorneys commissioned for entire state. The governor may appoint and commission as notaries public as many persons as he deems necessary, who are citizens of this state and are of the age of eighteen or over. A notary public, in addition to being appointed for the county in which he resides, may also be appointed as a notary public in any county adjacent to his county of residence in which a judge of the court of common pleas of such adjacent county has certified that he is possessed of sufficient qualifications and ability to discharge the duties of a notary public in such adjacent county. Citizens of this state of the age of eighteen or over, whose postoffice address is a municipal corporation, situated in two or more counties of the state, may be appointed and commissioned for all of the counties within which such municipal corporation is located. A citizen of this state who is admitted to the practice of law as an attorney in this state, or any person who has been certified by a judge of the court of common pleas of the county in which he resides as qualified for the duties of official stenographic reporter of such court, may be appointed and commissioned as a notary public for the state. The governor may revoke a commission issued to a notary public upon presentation of satisfactory evidence of official misconduct or incapacity.

§ 147.03. **Term of office; oath.** Each notary public, except a citizen of this state admitted to the practice of law by the Ohio supreme court, shall hold his office for the term of five years unless the commission is revoked. Before entering upon the duties of his office, he shall take and subscribe an oath to be indorsed on his commission.

A citizen of this state admitted to the practice of law by the Ohio supreme court shall hold his office as a notary public as long as such citizen is a resident of this state, is in good standing before the Ohio supreme court, and the commission is not revoked. Before entering upon the duties of his office he shall deposit with the secretary of state the certificate provided for in section 147.02 of the Revised Code and shall take and subscribe an oath to be indorsed on his commission.

A notary public who violates the oath required by this section shall be removed from office by the court of common pleas of the county in which he resides, upon complaint filed and substantiated in such court, and the court shall thereupon certify such removal to the governor. The person so removed shall be ineligible for re-appointment to the office of notary public.

Each citizen of this state holding office as a notary public on October 24, 1961, shall continue in such office until the expiration of his term and he shall thereafter hold office pursuant to this section.

§ 147.05. **Commission to be recorded; fee.** Before entering upon the duties of his office, a notary public shall leave his commission with the oath indorsed thereon with the clerk of the court of common pleas of the county in which he resides, and of each county for which he is appointed, but if an attorney at law and commissioned for the whole state, the record in the county of his residence is sufficient. Such commission shall be recorded by the clerk in a book kept for that purpose. The clerk shall indorse on the margin of the record and on the back of the commission the time he received it for record, and make a proper index to all commissions recorded by him. For recording and indexing such commission, the fee of the clerk shall be as provided for in division (S) of section 2303.20 of the Revised Code.

§ 147.06. **Certified copy of commission to be evidence; fees.** Upon application, the clerk of the court of common pleas shall make a certified copy of a commission and the indorsements thereon, under the seal of the court, which certified copy shall be prima-facie evidence of the matters and facts therein contained. For each certified copy of a commission the clerk shall be entitled to receive a fee of two dollars.

§ 147.32. **Commissioners of the state for veterans' affairs.** Representatives of the United Spanish War Veterans, The Disabled American Veterans, The American Legion, Veterans of Foreign Wars of the United States, and other congressionally chartered veterans' organizations, who are recognized as such representatives by the administrator of the veterans' administration, and who are engaged in the preparation and prosecution of claims of veterans and their dependents before the rating agencies of the veterans' administration within the state, may be appointed as commissioners of the state. Such commissioners shall continue in office for a term of three years. Each of such commissioners shall, before performing any of his duties, take and subscribe to an oath of office before a judge of a court of record within this state. Such oath, with his signature thereto and an impression of his seal of office and his residence address, shall forthwith be transmitted by him to the governor, and filed by the governor in the office of the secretary of state.

Each of such commissioners shall procure and employ a seal of the dimensions and inscription set forth and prescribed for notaries public, in section 147.04 of the Revised Code, except that the words shall be: "Commissioner of the State of Ohio for Veterans' Affairs."

Such commissioners may, without fee and within the state, administer oaths, take acknowledgments, and attest the execution of any instruments of writing only in connection with or used before the veterans' administration.

§ 147.37. **Fees for commissions.** Each person receiving a commission as notary public, except a citizen of this state admitted to the practice of law by the Ohio supreme court, shall pay a fee of two dollars. Each person receiving a commission as a notary public who is a citizen of this state admitted to the practice of law by the Ohio supreme court, shall pay a fee of five dollars.

§ 147.371. **Fees for duplicate commissions.** Upon receipt of a fee of two dollars and an affidavit that the original commission has been lost or destroyed a duplicate commission as notary public shall be issued by the governor.

§ 2303.20. Fees. The clerk of the court of common pleas shall charge the following fees and no more:

     o   o   o

(S) Seventy-five cents for recording commission of mayor or notary public;

     o   o   o

OKLAHOMA

[OKLA. STAT. ANN.]

Tit. 49, § 1. Appointment. The Secretary of State shall appoint and commission in this state as occasion may require, notaries public, who shall hold their office for four years. All of such commissions shall run in the name and by the authority of the State of Oklahoma, be signed by the Secretary of State and sealed with the Great Seal of the State of Oklahoma. Said commissions shall not be attested. Provided that the provisions of this Section shall not affect the unexpired commissions of notaries public issued prior to the effective date of this Act.

§ 2. Oath, signature, bond and seal—Fees. Before entering upon the duties of his office every notary public so appointed and commissioned shall file in the office of the court clerk, in his capacity as clerk of the district court, of the county in which such notary resides at the time he is commissioned, the commission issued to him, his oath of office, his official signature, an impression of his official seal, and a good and sufficient bond to the State of Oklahoma, in the sum of One Thousand Dollars ($1,000.00), with one or more sureties to be approved by the said court clerk, conditioned for the faithful performance of the duties of his office. Such commission, bond, and oath shall be recorded in the office of such court clerk, as clerk of the district court, and immediately thereafter said commission shall be returned to the notary, and said bond and oath shall be transmitted by said court clerk to the Secretary of State, and by him filed and recorded in his office. The filing of such commission, bond, official signature, and impression of official seal in the office of the court clerk shall be deemed sufficient evidence to enable such court clerk to certify that the person so commissioned is a notary public, duly commissioned and acting as such, during the time such commission is in force. Upon the filing of his commission with the court clerk, every notary public shall pay to the court clerk the sum of Three Dollars ($3.00), Two Dollars ($2.00) of which shall be remitted by the court clerk to the Secretary of State as filing and recording fees, the other One Dollar ($1.00) to be held and accounted for by the court clerk as fees of his office.

§ 2.1 Transmission of records by county clerk to court clerk. In order to enable the Court Clerk to certify that any person is commissioned as a Notary Public and duly authorized to act as such during the time such commission is in force, the County Clerk of each county in this State shall, within thirty (30) days after the effective date of this Act, transmit to the Court Clerk all oaths, bonds, official signatures, and impressions of official seals, and other records pertaining to the appointment and qualification of Notaries Public, in the office of such County Clerk before the effective date of this Act, and thereafter the same shall be deemed to be records and files of the office of the Court Clerk, and the Court Clerk shall be authorized to certify with reference thereto the same as though they had been filed originally in his office.

§ 3. **Blanks for bond and oath.** Blanks for bonds and oath of office shall be furnished with the commission by the Secretary of State.

Tit. 51, § 24.1. Suspension from office or employment upon conviction of felony. From and after the effective date of this act, any elected or appointed state officer or employee who, during the term for which he was elected or appointed, is, or has been, found guilty by a trial court of a felony in a court of competent jurisdiction shall be automatically suspended from said office or employment. Such suspension shall continue until such time as said conviction is reversed by the highest appellate court to which said officer or employee may appeal.

OREGON

[ORE. REV. STAT.]

§ 194.010. **Appointment of notary public; term; qualifications; office may be nonlucrative; functions not official duties.** (1) The Governor shall appoint notaries public for the term of four years unless the commission is revoked sooner by the Governor. A notary public may act throughout the state.

(2) Upon the appointment of a notary public, the Governor shall send the commission to the Secretary of State.

* * *

(5) The functions of a notary public are not considered official duties under Article III, section 1 of the Oregon Constitution.

§ 194.020. **Fee for application.** Each applicant for appointment as a notary public shall pay in advance to the Secretary of State a fee of $5, which shall be deposited in the State Treasury and credited to the General Fund, and is in lieu of any fee under ORS 177.130.

§ 194.040. **Record of commissions; Secretary of State's power to certify status and acts of notary.** The Secretary of State shall keep a record of each commission and promptly forward the commission to the appointee. The Secretary of State may certify as to the official character of such notary public and the genuineness of his signature and imprint upon all instruments requiring such certificates, and as to whether such instruments are executed according to the laws of Oregon.

§ 194.045. **Recording of commission in counties; county clerk's power to certify status and acts of notary.** (1) A duly commissioned notary public may record his commission with any county clerk of the state in the following manner:

(a) He shall, in person, present his commission to the county clerk for inspection.

(b) He shall file with the county clerk a specimen of his signature with an impression of his official seal or imprint of his official stamp.

(c) He shall pay to the county clerk a fee of $2.50 for this recording.°

(2) In recording a notary public commission as provided in subsection (1) of this section, the county clerk shall, in a special file, note the name and address of the notary, a specimen of the notary's signature, the impression of the notary's official seal or imprint of his official stamp and the effective and expiration dates of the commission.

(3) The county clerk may certify as to the official character of a notary public who has recorded his commission as provided in subsections (1) and (2) of this section°° and attest to the genuineness of the notary's signature and imprint upon all instruments requiring such certificates, and as to whether such instruments are executed according to the laws of Oregon.

° Compare the fee provided for by § 205.320(12), below.
°° See fee provided for by § 205.320(11), below.

§ 194.050. **Bond.** (1) Each notary public, before he enters upon his duties, shall take an oath to support the Constitution and laws of the United States and of the State of Oregon, and to faithfully discharge his duties, and shall give, subject to approval by the Secretary of State pursuant to standards prescribed by the Attorney General, a bond to the State of Oregon, with sufficient surety, in the penal sum of $500, conditioned for the faithful discharge of his duties.

(2) A notary public and the sureties on his bond, to the extent of their obligation on the bond, are liable to all persons for damages occasioned by the neglect or misconduct of the notary public in performing his official duties.

§ 194.063. **Application for new commission.** Upon the expiration of his commission a notary public may apply for a new commission in the manner provided by ORS 194.005 to 194.170, and subject to the qualifications prescribed therein. However, unless otherwise required by the Governor, such an application need not be accompanied by proof of good moral character, citizenship or continued residence in this state. Upon applying for a new commission, such notary public shall file a sample imprint of his official seal or official stamp in accordance with ORS 194.031.

§ 194.067. Grounds for revocation or denial of commission. The Governor may revoke the commission of a notary public, or deny an application for such a commission, if the applicant or notary public:

(1) Has failed to maintain the qualifications required under ORS 194.005 to 194.170 for his appointment.°

(2) Has been convicted of a felony or a misdemeanor involving moral turpitude.

(3) Has used officially a stamp or other device making an imprint or impression that does not conform to ORS 194.031°° or to the rules of the Secretary of State promulgated thereunder.

° See *Qualifications,* ORE. REV. STAT. § 194.010(3).

°° See *Seal,* ORE. REV. STAT. § 194.031.

Concerning removal from office for committing certain prohibited acts, see *Offenses,* ORE. REV. STAT. §§ 194.310, 194.320. ORE.

§ 205.320. Fees collected by county clerk. In every county there shall be charged and collected, in advance, by the county clerk for the benefit of the county, the following fees, and no more, for the following purposes and services:

°   °   °

(11) For certifying to the official character of a notary public, $1.

(12) For recording the commission of a notary public, $2.

PENNSYLVANIA

[PA. STAT. ANN.]

Tit. 16, § 11411. Counties of the second class; schedule. The fees to be charged and collected by the recorder of deeds, in counties of the second class, shall be as follows:

°   °   °

For recording or exemplifying of commission for notary public, with bond and oath, eight dollars ($8.00); ° ° °.

°   °   °

For affidavit and acknowledgment of bondsmen for notary public, justice of the peace, or alderman, one person, one dollar and twenty-five cents ($1.25); two persons, one dollar and seventy-five cents ($1.75).

°   °   °

Tit. 17, § 1593.1. Fees. The fees to be received by the pro-thonotary of the court of common pleas of this Commonwealth in

counties of the third, fourth, fifth, sixth, seventh and eighth class
shall be as follows:

           o   o   o

Notary Public

Registration of signature of notary public $1.00

Tit. 57, § 148. Appointment of notaries. The Secretary of the
Commonwealth is hereby authorized to appoint and commission, for
a term of four years from the date of appointment, as many notaries
public as, in his judgment, the interest of the public may require,
whose jurisdiction shall be co-extensive with the boundaries of the
Commonwealth, irrespective of their place of residence within the
Commonwealth.

§ 151. Application to become a notary public. Applications for
appointment to the office of notary public shall be made to the
Secretary of the Commonwealth, on forms prescribed and furnished
by him, and shall be accompanied by a fee of twenty-five dollars
($25), payable to the order of "State Treasurer," by money order,
certified check, or draft. Each application shall bear the endorsement of the Senator of the district in which the applicant resides,
or, in the case of a vacancy in that senatorial district, shall be
endorsed by the Senator of an adjacent district.

Before issuing to any applicant a commission as notary public, the
Secretary of the Commonwealth shall satisfy himself that the applicant is of good moral character, and is familiar with the duties and
responsibilities of a notary public. Such qualifying requirements may
be waived in the case of reappointment or appointments of persons
making application within six (6) months after the expiration of
a previous term as notary public, or appointments of persons who
were prevented from applying for reappointment or from applying
for appointment, within the six (6) month extension period mentioned above, by reason of their induction or enlistment in the armed
forces of the United States, if application is made within one (1)
year after military discharge of the applicant, under conditions other
than dishonorable.

§ 152. Application for reappointment. Applications for reappointment to the office of notary public shall be filed at least one
month prior to the expiration of the commission under which the
notary is acting.

§ 154. Oath of office; bond; recording. Every notary, on his appointment and before he enters upon the duties of the office of notary
public, shall take and subscribe the constitutional oath of office, and
shall give a surety bond, payable to the Commonwealth of Pennsylvania, in such amount as shall be fixed by the Secretary of the
Commonwealth, which bond shall, after being recorded, be approved
by and filed with the Secretary of the Commonwealth. Every such

bond shall have as surety a duly authorized surety company or two sufficient individual sureties to be approved by the Secretary of the Commonwealth, conditioned for the faithful performance of the duties of the office of notary public and for the delivery of his register and all other public papers into the office of the recorder of deeds of the proper county in case of his death, resignation, disqualification, or removal.   Such bond, as well as his commission and oath of office, shall be recorded in the office of the recorder of deeds of the county in which he maintains an office at the time of appointment or reappointment.   The commission of any notary hereafter appointed who shall, for the space of thirty (30) days after the beginning of his term, neglect to give bond and cause the same and his commission and oath to be recorded, as above directed, shall be null and void.

§ 155.   **Registration of notary's signature; fee.**   The official signature of each notary public shall be registered, in the "Notary Register" provided for such purpose in the prothonotary's office of the county wherein he maintains an office, within thirty (30) days after appointment or reappointment, and in any county to which he may subsequently move his office, within ten (10) days thereafter.   In counties of the second class, such signature shall also be registered in the clerk of courts' office within said period.   The fee to be charged by the prothonotary for recording a notary's signature shall be fifty ($.50) cents.

§ 157.   **Refund of fee.**   (a)   Whenever any person shall make application for a commission as notary public and shall pay into the State Treasury the fee for the same, and for any reason such commission shall not issue, or shall not be received, or the applicant fails or neglects to properly qualify for his commission, the State Treasurer, upon receipt of the proper warrant from the Board of Finance and Revenue, shall refund to such person or his personal representative the amount so paid into the State Treasury.

(b)   No such warrant shall be issued by the Board of Finance and Revenue until such person or his personal representatives shall have made application in writing to said board and, under oath or affirmation, on forms prescribed and furnished by said board therefor, setting forth such payment into the State Treasury, and averring that no commission has been received by such person, or that such person has failed or neglected to properly qualify for his commission; nor shall any such warrant issue until the Secretary of the Commonwealth shall have certified to the said board that a commission has not been issued to such applicant, or, if issued, has not been received by the applicant and has been cancelled, or that such person has failed or neglected to properly qualify for his commission.

§ 168.   **Rejection of application; removal.**   The Secretary of the Commonwealth may, for good cause, reject any application, or revoke the commission of any notary public, but such action shall be taken subject to the right of notice, hearing and adjudication, and the right of appeal therefrom, in accordance with the provisions of the Administrative Agency Law, approved the fourth day of June, one thousand nine hundred forty-five (Pamphlet Laws 1388), or any amendment or reenactment thereof, relating to adjudication procedure.

§ 169. **Revocation of commission of notaries issuing checks without funds on deposit.** The Secretary of the Commonwealth shall, upon written complaint of any aggrieved applicant, revoke the commission of any notary public who issues to the order of any State agency a personal check without funds on deposit in payment of money due the agency that were received by him from applicants. Any action taken by the Secretary of the Commonwealth shall be subject to the right of notice, hearing and adjudication and the right of appeal therefrom in accordance with the provisions of the Administrative Agency Law of June four, one thousand nine hundred forty-five (Pamphlet Laws 1388).

Tit. 72, § 3191. Tax on commissions. In lieu of the fees now receivable by the secretary of the commonwealth, for the use of the commonwealth, there shall be demanded by and paid to the recorder of deeds within the city of Philadelphia and of the respective counties, upon the several commissions hereafter named, at or before the delivery thereof, to the several officers commissioned, viz.: ° ° °; on the commission of a ° ° ° notary public, ° ° ° ten dollars.

PUERTO RICO

[P.R. LAWS ANN.]

Tit. 4, § 1002. Persons authorized to practice notarial profession; bond; oath of office; registry. On and after the date of approval of this chapter the notarial profession may be practiced in the Commonwealth only by those persons now authorized to practice it and by such attorneys as are hereafter admitted to the bar who are members of the Bar Association of Puerto Rico and are authorized by the Supreme Court of Puerto Rico to practice the notarial profession.

No person authorized to practice the notarial profession in Puerto Rico may practice same without first posting a bond in favor of the Commonwealth of Puerto Rico in the penal sum of two thousand five hundred (2,500) dollars conditioned upon the faithful performance of the duties of his office and to answer for any damages caused by any act or omission in the exercise of his functions. A notary's bond shall be a mortgage bond or an underwriting by a surety company authorized to do business in Puerto Rico, or by the Bar Association of Puerto Rico, which Association is hereby authorized to charge for such surety the fees it may deem reasonable. This bond requires approval by the Supreme Court of Puerto Rico, which shall also pass upon the sufficiency of mortgage bonds, which shall be recorded in the pertinent Registry of Property before final approval.

After the bond is approved the notary shall take the oath of office, if he has not already taken it, and shall register his signature, sign, mark and seal in the Department of State, as hereinafter provided, and also in a register which shall be kept for that purpose in the office of the Secretary of the Supreme Court of Puerto Rico and in which shall also appear his residence and the location of his notarial office, it being the duty of the notary to report any change of residence or notarial office to said official within the five days following such change. If in any judicial claim against a notary the claimant is awarded the whole or part of the bond, said notary shall discontinue practicing until he executes a new bond.

§ 1005. Oath of office; seal, signature, mark, and sign; registry in Department of State.

Before entering upon the duties of their office all notaries shall take an oath of allegiance to the Constitution and laws of the United States of America and to the Constitution and laws of the Commonwealth of Puerto Rico. They shall well and faithfully perform the duties of their office, and shall record in the register ad hoc kept in the Department of State the seal, signature, sign and mark to be used by them, which they shall not be permitted to alter unless as hereinafter provided. When a notary wishes to change the seal, it shall be his duty to impress same in the register kept in the Department of State and to surrender the useless seal to the Secretary of State for its destruction. In case a notary wishes to change his signature, mark and sign, or any of them, he shall address the Department of State for substitution of his signature, mark, or sign, and shall be under obligation to impress the new signature, mark, or sign in the register kept in the Department of State.

[P.R. R. SUP. CT.]

§ 9. Notaries.

(a) Any person entitled to practice law in the Commonwealth courts may be permitted to act as a notary. He shall file in the office of the secretary of his Court a petition together with a bond in duplicate for $2,500 in favor of the Commonwealth of Puerto Rico. Once the Court accepts said bond and the petitioner is permitted to act as notary, he shall take oath before the secretary of this Court. The notary shall then register in the Department of State of Puerto Rico and in the office of the secretary of this Court his signature, mark, seal, and paraph; and shall notify the Part of the Superior Court within his domicile, as well as the protocol inspectors, his residence address, the place of his notarial office, and the date on which he will open the latter. He shall forward to said Court on Monday of every week his indices of deeds and affidavits. The notaries shall likewise notify any change of residence or notarial office to the Secretary of the Supreme Court, the secretary of the corresponding Part of the Superior Court and to the protocol inspectors.

(b) When the bond is furnished by a surety company it shall be sent to the Insurance Commissioner of Puerto Rico, who shall certify as to its sufficiency. When a notary submits a mortgage security it must be accompanied by a certificate from the Secretary of the Treasury of Puerto Rico setting forth the assessed value of the mortgaged property, and a certificate from the corresponding register of property in connection with liens on said property.

*   o   o

RHODE ISLAND

[R.I. GEN. LAWS ANN.]

§ 36-1-3. **Issuance of commissions.** A commission shall issue to every person elected to office by the general assembly, to every justice of the peace elected by any town council, to the clerk and each deputy clerk of the Rhode Island district court, and to every person appointed to office by the governor.

§ 42-30-3. **Appointment of notaries and justices.** The governor shall, in the month of June, 1971, and in every fifth year thereafter, appoint as many notaries public for the state, and as many justices of the peace for the several towns and cities, as he may deem expedient; and every notary public and justice of the peace, so appointed, shall hold office until the first day of July, in the fifth year after his appointment. The governor may also appoint, from time to time, such other notaries public and justices of the peace as he may deem expedient, who shall hold office until the expiration of the tenure of office of those appointed under the preceding provisions of this section, or otherwise, until the first day of July, A.D. 1971.

§ 42-30-4. **Commission fee—Certificate of engagement.** Each notary public and justice of the peace shall, at the time of receiving his commission, pay to the secretary of state or the officer delivering the same, the sum of twenty-five dollars ($25.00) for the use of the state, and every such officer shall within thirty (30) days after the date of his commission, deliver to the secretary of state a certificate that he has been duly engaged° thereon, signed by the person before whom such engagement shall have been taken.

° The word "engaged" is construed to include either sworn or affirmed. See *Depositions,* R.I. GEN. LAWS § 43-3-11.

§ 42-30-9. **Lists of appointees—Certificates of appointment.** It shall be the duty of the secretary of state to make a list of all notaries public and justices of the peace appointed by the governor and duly qualified, and send a copy thereof to each of the clerks of the supreme and superior courts and to the clerks of the district courts for the second, third, fourth, ninth, tenth, eleventh and twelfth judicial districts, to be kept in the files of said courts, and said clerks shall, upon application, issue certificates of office to the person entitled thereto, and shall receive a fee of one dollar ($1.00) for every such certificate.

§ 42-30-10. **Removal of notaries, justices, and commissioners.** Any notary public, justice of the peace or commissioner of deeds, appointed by the governor, may be removed for cause by the governor, in his discretion, within the term for which such officer shall have been appointed, after giving to such officer a copy of the charges against him and an opportunity to be heard in his defense.

SOUTH CAROLINA

[S.C. CODE ANN.]

§ 49-1. **Appointment and term.** The Governor may appoint from the qualified electors as many notaries public throughout the State as the public good shall require, to hold their offices for a term of ten years. A commission shall be issued to each notary public so appointed and the record of such appointment shall be filed in the office of the Secretary of State. All commissions issued or renewed after July 1, 1967 shall be for the specified term. All commissions issued prior to July 1, 1967, unless renewed for the term herein provided, shall expire and terminate on January 1, 1970 for any person whose last name begins with A through K and on January 1, 1971 for any person whose last name begins with L through Z.

§ 49-3. **Fees.** The fee for the issuance or renewal of a commission shall be ten dollars, collected by the Secretary of State as other fees.

§ 49-4. **Oath.** Every notary public shall take the oath of office prescribed by the Constitution, certified copies of which shall be recorded in the office of the Secretary of State.

§ 49-5. **Enrollment of commission.** Every notary public shall, within fifteen days after he has been commissioned, exhibit his commission to the clerk of the court of the county in which he resides and be enrolled by the clerk.

§ 49-6.1. **Change of name.** Any notary public whose name is legally changed during his term of office may apply to the Secretary of State in such manner as may be prescribed by him, and the Secretary of State is hereby authorized to change the name of such notary upon proper application and upon payment of a fee of five dollars. The term shall expire at the same time as the original term expires.

SOUTH DAKOTA

[S.D. COMPILED LAWS ANN.]

§ 1-8-10. **Fees of secretary of state enumerated—Collection.**
Except as otherwise provided the secretary of state shall charge the
following fees for services performed in his office, and shall collect
the same in advance:

                    ○   ○   ○

(5) For filing application, bond, and issuing commission of notary
     public, five dollars;

                    ○   ○   ○

§ 16-2-29. **Fees and commissions charged by clerk of courts.**
The clerk of courts shall be required to charge and collect the
following fees, commissions, and per diem:

                    ○   ○   ○

(35) Approving bonds for notarial applications or other miscel-
      laneous bond, one dollar;

(36) Recording notary commissions, one dollar;

                    ○   ○   ○

§ 18-1-1. **Appointment by Governor—Terms of office—Authority.**
The Governor shall appoint in each of the organized counties in
this state from among the eligible citizens thereof, one or more
notaries public, who shall hold their office for eight years unless
sooner removed by the Governor, each of whom shall have authority
anywhere in this state to administer oaths and perform all other
duties required of him by law.

§ 18-1-2. **Oath and bond of notary.** Each notary public before
entering on the duties of his office, shall take an oath as required
by § 3-1-5, and shall give a bond to this state, to be approved by
the attorney general with one or more sureties, in the penal sum
of five hundred dollars, conditioned for the faithful discharge of
the duties of his office.

Editorial comment

Before entering on the duties of his office, every notary
must provide an official seal and file an impression of it,
together with his oath and bond, in the office of the
secretary of state. See *Seal*, S.D. COMPILED LAWS
ANN. § 18-1-3.

§ 18-1-4. **Issuance of commission—Posting—Records maintained
by secretary of state—Notice of expiration.** The secretary of state
shall issue a commission and duplicate thereof to each notary public
appointed by the Governor, one of which shall be by such notary

public posted in a conspicuous place in his office for public inspection. The secretary shall keep in his office a record of such appointments and the date of expiration, and shall notify each notary by mailing, postage prepaid, at least thirty days before the expiration of his term, a notice of the date upon which his commission expires, which notice shall be addressed to the notary at his last known place of residence.

§ 18-1-5.   **Recording of commission and seal by clerk of courts.** Every notary public before entering upon the duties of his office, shall file his commission for record with the clerk of courts of his county, and shall file with such clerk an impression of his seal, together with his official signature, and such clerk shall record the same in a book kept for that purpose, and it shall be deemed sufficient evidence to enable such clerk to certify that the person so commissioned is a notary public during the time such commission is in force.

§ 18-1-6.   **Recording of commission and seal in new county on change of residence.** Whenever any notary public shall change his place of residence from the county in which he was first appointed to another county, it shall be his duty to comply with the requirements of § 18-1-5 before he again enters upon the duties of his office.

§ 18-1-14.   **Notice to notary of revocation of commission.** Should the commission of any notary public be revoked, the secretary of state shall immediately notify such person by mail.

TENNESSEE

[TENN. CODE ANN.]

§ 5-512.   **Officers regularly elected by court.** The following officers are elected by the justices of the peace in county court assembled: Coroners, rangers, county surveyors, commissioners of the poor, workhouse commissioners, county standard keepers and sealers of weights and measures, notaries public, public administrators, public guardians, cotton and tobacco weighers, road commissioners, county revenue commissioners, and jail physicians or health officers.

Note: See also *Qualifications,* TENN. CODE ANN. § 8-1601, which is in accord with this section.

§ 8-1602.   **Commission.** All notaries shall be commissioned by the governor.

§ 8-1603.   **Term of office.** The term of office of notaries public shall be four (4) years, such term to begin on the date of the issuance of their commissions by the governor.

§ 8-1604.   **Surety bond.** Every notary public, before entering upon the duties of his office, shall give bond with good sureties, or one (1) corporate surety, in the penalty of five thousand dollars ($5,000), payable to the state of Tennessee, conditioned for the faithful discharge of said duties.

§ 8-1605. Oath of office. He shall also take and subscribe, before the county court clerk or his deputy, within his county, an oath to support the Constitutions of this state and of the United States, and an oath that he will, without favor or partiality, honestly, faithfully, and diligently discharge the duties of notary public.

§ 8-1606. Payment of fee—Issuance of commission. It shall be the duty of any person elected a notary public, who desires to qualify for such office, to pay to the county court clerk of the county in which he resides or has his principal place of business and was elected, the fee required to be paid into the office of the secretary of state for the issuance of a commission to a notary public, and thereupon it shall be the duty of the county court clerk to certify his election to the secretary of state and forward to the latter the fee, and it shall be the duty of the secretary of state, upon receipt of said certificate and fee, to forward such commission to the county court clerk, when the same shall have been issued by the governor, and the county court clerk shall promptly notify the person, to whom such commission is issued, that the same has been received in his office.

§ 8-1607. Delivery of commission—Clerk's record. The county court clerk shall not deliver the commission until the person elected shall have taken the oath and executed the bond, as required. The county court clerk shall make a record of the date of the issuance and the expiration of the commission, noting the same on the bond, executed by said notary public, and also in the minute entry showing his qualification as such notary public.

Editorial comment

Concerning the qualification of notaries in counties other than the county for which they are elected and commissioned, see *Authority and Duties,* TENN. CODE ANN. § 8-1609. Concerning the qualification of notaries for the state at large, see *Authority and Duties,* TENN. CODE ANN. § 8-1612.

§ 8-1614. Bond of notary at large. Before the secretary of state shall issue the certificate provided for in § 8-1612, the applicant therefor shall give a bond with two (2) good sureties or one (1) corporate surety in the penal sum of five thousand dollars ($5,000), payable to the state of Tennessee, conditioned for the faithful performance of the duties of a notary public, as provided for in § 8-1613, and the secretary of state, upon the issuance of the certificate provided for in § 8-1612 shall note the date of the issuance of the certificate, together with the expiration date of the commission of the said notary public on the face of the bond.

§ **8-1615. Oath of notary at large.** The secretary of state, upon the issuance of the certificate provided for in § 8-1612, shall be authorized and empowered to administer to notaries public granted the powers and privileges covered by §§ 8-1612—8-1618, the following oath: "I do solemnly swear that I will well and truly perform the duties of a notary public at large for the state of Tennessee, so help me God," which shall be taken and subscribed by such notaries public before entering upon the duties of their office before the secretary of state or any officer authorized to administer oaths.

§ **8-1618. Term of notary at large.** The term of any notary public thus authorized to act in any county in the state shall be coextensive with his term of service as regular notary public for the county of his residence and election, but the special authorization to act in any county of the state may be revoked, at any time, upon proper cause shown, by the secretary of state.

§ **8-2106. Secretary of state—Specific fees authorized.** The secretary of state is entitled to demand and receive, as above, and shall charge for the following services the fees annexed, among others, to be collected and paid into the state treasury:

*   °   *

(2)   For commission of each notary public 3.00

(3)   For commission of each commissioner of deeds 10.00

°   °   °

TEXAS

[TEX. CONST.]

Art. 4, § 26. Notaries public. (a) The Secretary of State shall appoint a convenient number of Notaries Public for each county who shall perform such duties as now are or may be prescribed by law. The qualifications of Notaries Public shall be prescribed by law.

(b) Nothing herein shall affect the terms of office of Notaries Public who have qualified for the present term prior to the taking effect of this amendment.

[TEX. REV. CIV. STAT. ANN.]

Art. 3914. Secretary of State. The Secretary of State is authorized and required to charge for the use of the State the following other fees:

For each commission to every officer elected or appointed in this State, Two Dollars ($2).

°   °   °

Art. 3930.   County Clerk and County Recorders.   County clerks
and county recorders are hereby authorized and required to collect
the following fees for services rendered by them to all persons,
firms, corporations, legal entities, governmental agencies and/or governmental representatives:

Fees for County Clerk and County Recorder Records and Mis-
cellaneous Services:

◦   ◦   ◦

(6)   For all clerical work in having appointment of notary public
made, administering oaths and qualifying the notary public, and
approving, filing and recording notarial bond, a fee (does not include
the fee for the Secretary of State), to be paid at the time the
executed oath and bond is filed, of $2.00

◦   ◦   ◦

Art. 5949.   Notary public: Appointment; number and terms.
1.   The Secretary of State of the State of Texas shall appoint a convenient number of Notaries Public to serve each county of the state.
Such appointments may be made at any time, and the terms of all
appointments shall end on the first day of June of each odd-numbered year, unless sooner revoked by the Secretary of State.

2.   [Omitted.]

**Procedure for appointment; application; contents;
duties of county clerks**

3.   Appointments to the office of Notary Public shall be made as
follows:

Any person desiring appointment as a Notary Public shall make
application in duplicate to the county clerk of his county of residence, or the county in which the applicant seeks to act as Notary
Public, on forms prescribed by the Secretary of State, which includes
his name as it will be used in acting as such Notary Public, his
post-office address, his social security number, if any, a statement
that he has never been convicted of a crime involving moral turpitude, and shall satisfy the clerk that he is at least twenty-one (21)
years of age and otherwise qualified by law for the appointment
which is sought.   One copy of each application, along with the
names of all persons making such application shall be sent in duplicate by the county clerk to the Secretary of State with the certificate of the county clerk that according to the information furnished
him, such person is eligible for appointment as Notary Public for
such county.   The Secretary of State shall act upon all such names
submitted at the earliest practicable time and notify the county
clerk whether such appointment or appointments have been made.
Upon receiving notice from the Secretary of State of such appointments, the county clerk shall forthwith notify all persons so appointed to appear before him within fifteen (15) days from the date of

such appointment and qualify as hereinafter provided. The appointment of any person failing to qualify within the time allowed shall be void, and if any such person desires thereafter to qualify, his name shall be resubmitted in the same manner as hereinabove provided.

Fees

4. At the time of such qualification the county clerk shall collect the fees allowed him by law for administering the oath and approving and filing the bond of such Notary Public, together with the fee allowed by law to the Secretary of State for issuing a commission to such Notary Public.

Notice to Secretary of State; issuance of commission; rejection of application; appeal

5. Immediately after the qualification of any Notary Public, the county clerk shall forthwith notify the Secretary of State that such person has qualified and the date of such qualification, and shall remit with such notice the fee due the Secretary of State, whereupon, the Secretary of State shall cause a commission to be issued for the county in which such Notary Public has qualified, which commission shall be effective as of the date of qualification in that county. All such commissions shall be forwarded to the proper county clerk for delivery to such persons entitled to receive them. Nothing herein shall prevent any qualified Notary Public from performing the duties of his office from and after his qualification and before the receipt of his commission.

*   *   *

Expiration of term; reappointment; changes of address; date of reappointment

6. Any qualified Notary Public whose term is expiring may be reappointed by the Secretary of State without the necessity of the county clerk resubmitting his name to the Secretary of State, provided such appointment is made in sufficient time for such Notary Public to be qualified on the expiration date of the term for which he is then serving; and provided that if any such Notary Public has removed his residence, or his principal place of business or employment, to a county or counties other than the one for which he has been appointed, his office in such county or counties shall be automatically vacated and if he desires to act as a Notary Public in such other county or counties, his commission in such county or counties shall be surrendered to the Secretary of State and his name shall be submitted by the clerk of such county or counties as hereinabove provided.

The Secretary of State shall reappoint Notaries Public on May 1 of each odd-numbered year, which reappointment shall be effective

June 1 of said year for the next term of office. The County Clerk of each county shall notify such persons, who are reappointed from his or her county, to qualify within the first fifteen (15) days of May of each odd-numbered year which qualifying shall become effective as of June 1 and shall not be effective prior thereto.

Bond

7. Any person appointed a Notary Public, before entering upon his official duties, shall execute a bond in the sum of One Thousand ($1,000.00) Dollars with two or more solvent individuals, or one solvent surety company authorized to do business in this State, as surety, such bond to be approved by the county clerk of his county, payable to the Governor, and conditioned for the faithful performance of the duties of his office; and shall also take and subscribe his name and social security number to the official oath of office which shall be endorsed on said bond with the certificate of the official administering the same. Said bond shall be deposited in the office of the county clerk and shall not be void on the first recovery, and may be sued on in the name of the party injured from time to time until the whole amount thereof has been recovered. Any such person shall be deemed to be qualified when he has taken the official oath of office, furnished the bond and paid the fees herein provided for, all within the time allowed therefor.

Failure or refusal of county clerk to perform duties

8. If any county clerk fails or refuses to forward the names of persons requesting appointments, notices of qualification, or to remit any fees due to the Secretary of State, or to notify any applicant of his appointment within sixty (60) days after receipt of same by the county clerk, the Secretary of State shall certify such failure or refusal to the State Comptroller, the County Auditor and Commissioners Court of such county, after which no claim or account in favor of such clerk shall be approved or paid until the Secretary of State shall certify to such officials that all requirements hereunder have been complied with.

Public records; inspection

9. All matters pertaining to the appointment and qualification of Notaries Public shall be public records in the offices of the county clerks and in the office of the Secretary of State after any such Notary Public has qualified, and shall be open to inspection of any interested person at such reasonable times and in such manner as will not interfere with the affairs of office of the custodian of such records; but neither a county clerk nor the Secretary of State shall be required to furnish lists of the names of persons appointed before their qualification nor lists of unreasonable numbers of qualified Notaries Public.

Administration and enforcement of act; regulations

10. The Secretary of State may make regulations necessary for the administration and enforcement of this Act consistent with all of its provisions.

Art. 5957. Removal. Any notary public who shall be guilty of any wilful neglect of duty or malfeasance in office may be removed from office in the manner provided by law.

Art. 5958. Office to become vacant. Whenever any notary public shall remove permanently from the county for which he was appointed, or an ex officio notary public from his precinct, his office shall thereupon be deemed vacant.

Art. 5988. Notary public. Any notary public indicted for and convicted of any wilful neglect of duty or official misconduct shall be removed from office. The order for his removal shall in each instance be embodied in the judgment of the court.

UTAH

[UTAH CODE ANN.]

§ 46-1-1. Qualifications — Appointment — Term — Removal. Notaries public shall have the qualifications of electors, and shall be appointed for the state at large. The governor may appoint and commission as many notaries public as he may deem necessary. They shall hold office for the term of four years from and after the date of their commissions, but the governor may remove from office any notary public during the term for which he was appointed. The commissions shall be filed with, and be recorded in the office of, the secretary of state.

§ 46-1-2. Master list of notaries public—Commissions certified to clerks of district courts—Names of governor and secretary of state printed on certificates. Hereafter, whenever a notarial commission is issued to any person, the governor and the secretary of state shall certify to a master list of notaries public. The issuance of all commissions shall be certified to each of the several clerks of the district courts giving the dates of issuance and expiration of same. All notary certificates shall have printed thereon the names of the governor and the secretary of state.

§ 46-1-3. Oath and bond. Each notary public before entering upon his official duties shall take the constitutional oath, and give bond to the state of Utah in the penal sum of $500, conditioned that he will faithfully perform the duties of his office. Such bonds shall be approved by the secretary of state and filed in his office.

§ 46-1-4. Action on bond—Parties—Limitation of action. The bond of a notary public may be sued on by any person injured through official delinquencies against which it is intended to provide; provided, that such action shall be instituted within three years from the time such cause of action shall have accrued.

VERMONT

[VT. STAT. ANN.]

Tit. 24, § 183. Certificate of appointment of notary public or master in chancery. Immediately after the appointment of a notary public or master in chancery, the county clerk shall send to the secretary of state a certificate of such appointment, on blanks furnished by such secretary, containing the name, signature, and legal residence of the appointee, and the term of office of each notary public. Such secretary shall cause such certificate to be bound in suitable volumes and to be indexed. Upon request, such secretary may certify the appointment, qualification and signature of such notary public or master in chancery on tender of his legal fees.

Tit. 24, § 441. Appointment; jurisdiction; ex officio notaries. The judges of the county court may appoint as many notaries public for the county as the public good requires, to hold office until ten days after the expiration of the term of office of such judges, whose jurisdiction shall extend throughout the state. The clerk of the supreme court, county clerks, district court clerks and town clerks and their depuities shall be ex officio notaries public.

Tit. 24, § 442. Oath; certificate of appointment recorded; form. A person appointed as notary public shall cause the certificate of his appointment to be filed and recorded in the office of the county clerk where issued. Before entering upon the duties of his office he, as well as an ex officio notary, shall take the oath prescribed by the constitution, and shall duly subscribe the same with his correct signature, which oath thus subscribed shall be kept on file by the county clerk as a part of the records of such county.

The certificate of appointment shall be substantially in the following form:

STATE OF VERMONT,

ss.

. . . . .County

This is to certify that A. B. of . . . . in such county, was, on the . . . . . . day of . . . ., 19..., appointed by the judges of the county court for such county a notary public for the term ending on February 10, 19...

Judges of the
county court.

. . . .

. . . .

. . . .

And at .... in such county, on this......
day of ...., 19... personally appeared A. B.
.... and took oath of office prescribed in the constitution.

Before me,

C. D. ....

(Designation of the officer administer-
ing the oath).

Tit. 24, § 443. Preservation of oaths. The county clerk at the
end of each biennial period shall cause the oaths aforesaid to be
bound into book form, which book shall then constitute the final
record thereof and shall be duly attested by the clerk as such.

VIRGIN ISLANDS

[V.I. CODE ANN.]

Tit. 3, § 771. Appointment of notaries public by Governor. The
Governor may appoint and commission not more than 200 notaries
public for the Virgin Islands, exclusive of notaries ex officio and
members of the Virgin Islands Bar, who shall hold office for a
period of 4 years.

•   °   °

§ 773. Commission fees; bonds; issuance of commission. (a)
Each notary public shall pay to the Treasury of the Virgin Islands
a fee of $20 for his commission and thereafter, on the first of January
of each year, an annual fee of $5. Upon failure to pay the annual
fee and representation thereof by the United States attorney, the
Governor shall cancel such appointment.

(b) Each notary public shall execute a bond in favor of the
government of the Virgin Islands, in the sum of $1,000 with two
resident sureties, who are owners, within the Virgin Islands, of real
property of the value of $2,000 over and above encumbrances
thereon, or with any bonding company doing business within the
Virgin Islands, which bond must be approved by the judge of the
District Court.

(c) Each notary public, upon the approval of his bond and after
having taken official oath, shall transmit such bond and oath, duly
signed by him, to the office of the Government Secretary, whereupon
the Governor may issue a commission.

§ 774. Liability of notaries and sureties. Each notary public
and the sureties on his bond shall be liable for all the damages
sustained by a party injured by the official misconduct or neglect
of that notary public.

Editorial comment

Concerning the appointment of government employees as notaries public, see *Qualifications*, "Special Notaries Public", V.I. CODE ANN. Tit. 3, §§ 801, 802, 803.

VIRGINIA

[VA. CODE ANN.]

§ 1-13.14. Notary or notaries. The word "notary" or "notaries" shall be construed as if followed by the word "public."

§ 14.1-103. Secretary of Commonwealth. The Secretary of the Commonwealth shall charge for services rendered in his office the following fees, to be paid by the person for whom the service is rendered at the time it is done:

*   *   *

For issuing a commission to a commissioner in another state .. 5.00
For issuing a commission to each notary and inspector
   appointed by the Governor 3.00

*   *   *

§ 14.1-112. Clerks of circuit courts; generally. A clerk of a circuit court shall, for services performed by virtue of his office, charge the following fees, to wit:

*   *   *

(19) For qualifying notaries public, including the making out of the bond and any copies thereof, administering the necessary oaths, and entering the order, five dollars.

*   *   *

§ 47-1. Notaries public for counties and cities. (1) *Appointment and term of office; powers; removal.* The Governor shall appoint in and for the several counties and cities of the State as many notaries as to him may seem proper, who shall hold office for the term of four years, and who shall exercise the powers and functions of conservators of the peace, and who shall be removable by the Governor at will for misconduct, incapacity or neglect of official duty; but in every case where the Governor shall remove a notary public from office, he shall report such action with his reasons therefor to the next session of the General Assembly.

(2) *Serving for two or more counties or cities; fees for commissions.* The Governor may appoint the same person to serve for two or more counties and cities, in which case only one commission shall be issued and the fee for issuing the same shall be three dollars for the first county or city and five dollars for each additional county or city, for which such notary is appointed to serve.

(3) *Acting in contiguous counties or cities.* A notary for a city shall also have authority to act as such in counties and cities con-

tiguous thereto, and a notary for a county shall also have authority to act as such in cities contiguous thereto.

(4) *Bond; time to qualify.* Each notary shall give bond with surety in the circuit court of the county, or corporation court of the city, for which the notary is appointed, or if the appointment be for more than one county or city, then in one of such courts, or before the judge of such court in vacation, or before the clerk thereof, within four months from the date of such notary's commission, in a penalty of not less than five hundred dollars, with condition for the faithful discharge of the duties of his office; and the clerk of the court shall immediately forward a certified copy of such bond to the Secretary of the Commonwealth. If any person appointed shall fail to qualify within four months from the date of his appointment the clerk of the court shall return his commission to the Secretary of the Commonwealth.

(5) [Omitted.]

(6) *Duties of Secretary of Commonwealth and clerks.* It shall be the duty of the Secretary of the Commonwealth when a commission is ordered by the Governor, to notify the party to whom the commission has been granted, that same has been granted and where and under what circumstances it may be secured, and to send the same to the clerk of the circuit court of the county or corporation court of the city in which, or in one of which, the notary public is required to qualify, to be delivered by him to the notary public after the notary public has given bond, and taken the oath of office; and the clerk of the court in which this is done shall forthwith report the fact to the Secretary of the Commonwealth, who shall keep a book stating the names and numbers of notaries public, when appointed and when qualified.

(7) [Omitted.]

§ 47-2. Notaries public for the State at large. The Governor may appoint in and for the State at large as many notaries public as to him may seem proper, who shall hold office for the term of four years. Any notary public so appointed may exercise the same powers and functions and shall be subject to the same restrictions and regulations as are prescribed by general law for notaries public for counties and cities, except that such notary public at large shall be empowered to act as notary public in any county or city in the Commonwealth. The fees for issuing a commission to such notary shall be twenty-five dollars, which shall include the tax on the seal of the State.

Every application for appointment as such notary shall state in what circuit or corporation court the applicant wishes to qualify, and any such notary so appointed shall qualify in the circuit or corporation court designated in the application, and the commission shall be sent by the Secretary of the Commonwealth to the clerk of such court to be delivered to the applicant upon compliance with the provisions of § 47-1.

§ 49-1. Form of general oath required of officers. Every person before entering upon the discharge of any function as an officer of this Commonwealth shall take and subscribe the following oath: "I do solemnly swear (or affirm) that I will support the Constitution of the United States, and the Constitution of the Commonwealth of Virginia, and that I will faithfully and impartially discharge and perform all the duties incumbent on me as .... according to the best of my ability, (so help me God)."

WASHINGTON

[WASH. REV. CODE ANN.]

§ 42.28.010. Appointment—Qualifications. The governor may appoint and commission, as notaries public, as many persons having the qualifications of electors as he shall deem necessary: *Provided,* That no person shall be appointed a notary public except upon the petition of at least ten freeholders of the county in which such person resides: *Provided, further,* That upon the expiration of his commission any notary public may obtain a new commission on application, without petition signed by freeholders, within one year from date of expiration of his preceding commission.

§ 42.28.020. Term of office. Every notary public shall be appointed for the state, and shall hold his office for four years, unless sooner removed by the governor.

§ 42.28.030. Bond, fee, seal, oath of office. Before a commission shall issue to the person appointed he shall—(1) execute a bond, payable to the state of Washington, in the sum of one thousand dollars, with sureties to be approved by the county clerk of the county in which the applicant resides, conditioned for the faithful discharge of the duties of his office; (2) pay into the state treasury the sum of ten dollars for special state library fund [state general fund], taking the treasurer's receipt therefor; (3) procure a seal, on which shall be engraved the words "Notary Public" and "State of Washington", and date of expiration of his commission, with surname in full, and at least the initials of his Christian name; (4) to take and subscribe the oath of office required of state officers; (5) file the said oath of office, bond and treasurer's receipt in the office of the secretary of state, and before performing any official acts, shall file in the office of the secretary of state a clear impression of his official seal, which seal shall be approved by the governor.

§ 42.28.100. Certification of appointment. After the delivery of a commission to a notary public, appointed and qualified as heretofore provided, the secretary of state shall make a certificate of such appointment, with the date of said commission, and file the same in the office of the county clerk of the county where such notary resides, who shall file and preserve the same, and it shall be deemed sufficient evidence to enable such clerk to certify that the person so commissioned is a notary public during the time such commission is in force.

§ 42.28.110. **Certificates of official character.** The county clerk of the county in which such notary resides, or the secretary of state, may grant certificates of official character of notaries public. The certificate of the clerk shall be under his hand and official seal, and that of the secretary of state, under the seal of the state.

§ 43.06.100. **May sign notarial papers by proxy.** The governor may designate an executive assistant on his staff who shall have authority to affix the governor's signature to the commission issued to any notary public or any other notarial paper requiring his signature. In affixing the governor's signature, the person designated may sign the governor's name either personally in writing or by facsimile reproduction, followed by the word "by" and the original signature of the person so designated. The governor's signature so affixed shall be valid for all purposes.

WEST VIRGINIA

[W. VA. CODE ANN.]

§ 6-2-10. **Bonds of county officers.** ° ° ° [E]very sheriff, surveyor of lands, clerk of a county court, assessor, county superintendent of schools, notary public, justice of the peace and constable shall give bond with good security, to be approved, unless otherwise provided by law, by the county court of the county in which such officer is to act. The penalty of the bond ° ° ° of a notary public [shall be] not less than two hundred and fifty nor more than one thousand dollars; ° ° °: Provided, however, that the bond herein required to be given by a notary public may be given before the clerk of the county court, in the vacation of said court, and approved by it at its next regular session.

§ 6-2-13. **Copies to be sent to the state tax commissioner; penalty for failure to send.** A copy of the official bond of every ° ° ° notary public, shall be sent to the state tax commissioner by the officer in whose office the original is filed, within two months after the same is filed in his office. If the officer whose duty it is to send any such copy fail to do so within the time specified, he shall forfeit fifty dollars.

§ 29-4-2. **New appointment; removal or vacation of office.** The governor shall appoint and commission so many notaries in this State, and for such counties, as he may deem proper, who shall hold their office respectively for a term of ten years from the date of their commission. Before such appointment is made, the applicant shall obtain from the county court of his county a certificate showing him to be a person competent to perform the duties of such office, of good moral character, and a resident of the county from which the appointment is made. Any notary may be removed or his office vacated in the manner prescribed by law.

§ 29-4-2a. Qualification by notary in another county; certificate by clerk of county court; fees. A notary public appointed for any of the counties of the State, upon filing in the office of the clerk of the county court in any other county in the State a certificate of the county clerk of the county for which he was appointed, setting forth the fact of his appointment, the date thereof, and qualifications as such notary public and paying to said clerk of the county court, where said certificate is filed, a fee of one dollar, without any further qualification, shall thereupon have the right to exercise all the functions of his office in the county in which such certificate is filed, with the same effect in all respects as if the same were exercised in the county in which he resides and for which he was appointed.

The clerk of the county court of the county in which a notary public resides and for which such notary public is appointed, upon request, shall issue to such notary public a certificate setting forth the fact of his appointment, the date thereof, and qualification as such notary public, and that such notary public is a resident of his county, and the clerk of the county court shall insert therein the name of the county in which such certificate is to be filed, for which certificate such notary public shall pay a fee of one dollar to the clerk of the county court for each such certificate so issued.

§ 29-4-2b. Appointments and commissions for entire state. The governor shall appoint and commission so many notaries for the State as he may deem proper, who shall hold their office respectively for a term of ten years from the date of their commission. Before such appointment is made, the applicant shall qualify as set forth in section two [§ 29-4-2, see above] and upon such appointment, without further qualification, shall thereupon have the right to exercise all the functions of his office in any county within the State. Any notary so appointed may be removed or his office vacated in the manner prescribed by law. The seal of any notary public so appointed shall contain the words "State of West Virginia" instead of any particular county designation. The fee for such appointment shall be forty dollars: Provided, however, that prior to such appointment, each applicant shall give a surety bond, to be approved by the secretary of state, in a penalty of five hundred dollars, which bond shall be filed and recorded in the office of the secretary of state.

§ 59-1-2. Fees to be charged by secretary of state. Except as may be otherwise provided in article one [§ 31-1-1 et seq.], chapter thirty-one of this Code, the secretary of state shall charge for services rendered in his office the following fees to be paid by the person to whom the service is rendered at the time it is done:

     °   °   °

For issuing commission to a notary public, or to a commissioner of deeds, which shall include the tax on the state seal thereon and other charges 5.00

     °   °   °

For issuing a commission to a commissioner in any other state   5.00

     °   °   °

WISCONSIN

[WIS. STAT. ANN.]

§ 19.01. **Oaths and bonds. (1) Form of oath.** Every official oath required by section 28 of Article IV of the constitution or by any statute shall be in writing, subscribed, sworn to, and except as provided otherwise by §§ 256.02 and 256.29, shall be in substantially the following form:

STATE OF WISCONSIN,

County of _____

I, the undersigned, who have been elected (Or appointed) to the office of _____, but have not yet entered upon the duties thereof, swear (or affirm) that I will support the constitution of the United States and the constitution of the state of Wisconsin, and will faithfully discharge the duties of said office to the best of my ability. So help me God.

Subscribed and sworn to before me this _____ day of _____, 19___.

_____ (Signature) ___.

(1m) Form of oral oath. If it is desired to administer the official oath orally in addition to the written oath prescribed above, it shall be in substantially the following form:

I, _____, swear (or affirm) that I will support the constitution of the United States and the constitution of the state of Wisconsin, and will faithfully and impartially discharge the duties of the office of _____ to the best of my ability. So help me God.

(2) Form of bond. (a) Every official bond required of any public officer shall be in substantially the following form:

We, the undersigned, jointly and severally, undertake and agree that _____, who has been elected (or appointed) to the office of _____, will faithfully discharge the duties of his said office according to law, and will pay to the parties entitled to receive the same, such damages, not exceeding in the aggregate _____ dollars, as may be suffered by them in consequence of his failure so to discharge such duties.

Dated _____, 19__

___ (Principal) ___,
___ (Surety) ___,

(b) Any further or additional official bond lawfully required of any public officer shall be in the same form and it shall not affect or impair any official bond previously given by him for the same or any other official term. Where such bond is in excess of the sum of $25,000, the officer may give 2 or more bonds.

(2m) **Effect of giving bond.** Any bond purportedly given as an official bond by a public officer, of whom an official bond is required, shall be deemed to be an official bond and shall be deemed as to both principal and surety to contain all the conditions and provisions required in sub. (2), regardless of its form or wording, and any provisions restricting liability to less than that provided in sub. (2) shall be void.

(3) **Official duties defined.** The official duties referred to in subs. (1) and (2) include performance to the best of his ability by the officer taking the oath or giving the bond of every official act required, and the nonperformance of every act forbidden, by law to be performed by him; also, similar performance and nonperformance of every act required of or forbidden to him in any other office which he may lawfully hold or exercise by virtue of his incumbency of the office named in his official oath or bond. Except as provided otherwise by § 59.22(3) and (4) the duties mentioned in any such oath or bond include the faithful performance by all persons appointed or employed by such officer either in his principal or his said subsidiary office, of their respective duties and trusts therein.

(4) **Where filed.** Official oaths and bonds shall be filed:

(a) In the office of the secretary of state: ° ° °; of all notaries public; ° ° °;

° ° °

(5) **Time of filing.** Every public officer required to file an official oath or an official bond shall file the same before entering upon the duties of his office; and when both are required, both shall be filed at the same time.

(6) **Continuance of obligation.** Every such bond continues in force and is applicable to official conduct during the incumbency of the officer filing the same and until his successor is duly qualified and installed.

(7) **Interpretation.** This section shall not be construed as requiring any particular officer to furnish or file either an official oath or an official bond. It is applicable to such officers only as are

elsewhere in these statutes or by the constitution or by special, private or local law required to furnish such an oath or bond. Provided, however, that whether otherwise required by law or not, an oath of office shall be filed by every member of any board or commission appointed by the governor, and by every administrative officer so appointed, also by every secretary and other executive officer appointed by such board or commission.

(8) Premium on bond allowed as expense. The state and any county, town, village, city or school district may pay the cost of any official bond furnished by an officer or employe thereof pursuant to law or any rules or regulations requiring the same if said officer or employe shall furnish a bond with a licensed surety company as surety, said cost not to exceed the current rate of premium per annum. The cost of any such bond to the state shall be charged to the proper expense appropriation.

§ 59.42. Clerk of court; fees. Except as otherwise provided in the statutes the clerk of circuit court and the clerk of any other court of record (in all actions and proceedings civil or criminal brought under jurisdiction concurrent with the circuit court, except those handled under essentially justice court or small claims procedure) shall collect the following fees:

✿   ✿   ✿

(12) Notary certificates. For filing certificates of notaries public, 50 cents.

✿   ✿   ✿

§ 137.01. Notaries. (1) Notaries public who are not attorneys.

(1)(a) The governor shall appoint notaries public who shall be Wisconsin residents and at least 18 years of age. Applicants who are not attorneys shall file an application with the secretary of state and pay a $10 fee.

(b) The secretary of state shall satisfy himself that the applicant is of good moral character, has the equivalent of an eighth grade education and is familiar with the duties and responsibilities of a notary public.

(c) If an application is rejected the fee shall be returned.

(d) Qualified applicants shall be notified by the secretary of state to take and file the official oath and execute and file an official bond in the sum of $500, with surety to be approved by the county judge or clerk of the circuit court of his county, or, when executed by a surety company, approved by the secretary of state.

(1)(e) The qualified applicant shall file his signature, post-office address and an impression of his official seal, or imprint of his official rubber stamp with the secretary of state.

(f) A certificate of appointment as a notary public for a term of

4 years stating the expiration date of the commission shall be issued to applicants who have fulfilled the requirements of this subsection.

(g) At least 30 days before the expiration of a commission the secretary of state shall mail notice of the expiration date to the holder of a commission.

(h) A notary shall be entitled to reappointment if of good moral character.

(2) Notaries public who are attorneys.

(2)(a) Any Wisconsin resident who is licensed to practice law in this state shall be entitled to a permanent commission as a notary public upon application to the secretary of state and payment of a $10 fee. Such application shall include a certificate of good standing from the supreme court, the signature and post-office address of the applicant and an impression of his official seal, or imprint of his official rubber stamp.

(b) The secretary of state shall issue a certificate of appointment as a notary public to persons who qualify under the requirements of this subsection. Such certificate shall state that the notary commission is permanent.

(c) The supreme court shall file with the secretary of state notice of the surrender, suspension or revocation of the license to practice law of any attorney who holds a permanent commission as a notary public. Such notice shall be deemed a revocation of said commission.

o　　o　　o

WYOMING

[WYO. STAT. ANN.]

§ 32-1. Appointment; commission; qualifications; exception as to federal clerks, etc.; new commission upon formation of new county. The governor shall appoint and commission in each county upon petition of not less than five reputable freeholders of the county wherein such applicant resides, as occasion may require, one or more notaries public, who shall hold their offices for four years, unless sooner removed according to law. No person shall be eligible for appointment to the office of notary public unless he is a person of good moral character, an adult citizen of the United States, who shall be able to read and write the English language and an actual resident of the State of Wyoming, and of the county for which he is appointed; provided, that any federal clerk, secretary, or stenographer who is otherwise qualified under the provisions of this section shall be eligible for appointment to the office of notary public. Any person holding a commission as a notary public for any county in this state, whose residence on account of the organization of a new county is no longer in the county for which the commission was originally issued, who shall file an affidavit with the governor, setting forth the fact at the time of the issuance of his commission he was a resident of the territory subsequently embraced in the newly organized county, and that he has resided there continuously, and is still residing there at the time of the filing of the affidavit, and shall in addition thereto return with such affidavit his original commission, shall receive from the governor a new commission as notary public for the new county, continuing during the time of the former commission, for the issuance of which no charge shall be made by the secretary of state, and the original commission shall thereupon be cancelled and placed on file in the office of the secretary of state.

§ 32-2. **Female notary marrying before expiration of commission; commission under name by which generally known.** (a) Whenever any woman in the State of Wyoming, who has been duly appointed or commissioned a notary public by the governor, shall marry before her commission expires, it shall not be necessary for her to apply for a new commission, but she may cause to be filed for record in the office of the county clerk in the county where her said notarial commission has been recorded, a certificate of her marriage, whether said marriage has been performed within or without this state. Upon filing with the secretary of state of the State of Wyoming a copy of such marriage certificate, duly certified by such county clerk, and paying to the secretary of state a fee of $1, she shall be entitled to continue as a notary public under the name in which the commission was granted to her, until the expiration thereof. Such notary public may continue to use her seal until the expiration of such commission, without changing the name thereon, and she shall sign her name as it appears upon her commission and seal except that her husband's surname shall be added thereto. If, however, the female notary public desires to continue to use on her commission the name by which she is generally known in her occupation or profession, she may do so by filing a written statement with the secretary of state of her intention to continue to use such other name instead of adopting her married name.

(b) A woman may be appointed or commissioned as a notary public under the name by which she is generally known in her occupation or profession instead of her married name.

§ 32-3. **Attesting and recording of commission; monthly list to be sent to county clerks.** When any person is appointed or commissioned a notary public by the governor, as provided in section 1 [§ 32-1], his commission shall be attested by the secretary of the state, under the seal thereof, which commission shall be transmitted by the secretary of the register of deeds [county clerk] of the county in which said appointee resides, who shall record the same in a book to be by him kept in his office, for the purpose of recording therein all commissions issued by the governor to officers in his county. On or before the tenth day of each month the secretary of state shall send to each county clerk a certified list of all notaries

public, notices of whose qualifications as notaries, have been filed
in the office of the secretary of state in accordance with the provisions of section 3 [§ 32-4], during the preceding month. Such list
shall contain the name of each such notary, the place of his residence,
the date of his commission, and the date of his qualification.

§ 32-4. Bond and oath. Each person so appointed to the office
of notary public shall, within sixty days from the date of his appointment, file with the register of deeds [county clerk] in whose office
his commission is filed for record a bond executed by himself and
two sureties, to be approved by said register of deeds [county clerk],
which bond shall run to the State of Wyoming, in the sum of five
hundred dollars, conditioned for the faithful performance of the
duties of his office, and shall take and subscribe an oath or affirmation before some officer in the county in which the said appointee
resides authorized to administer oaths or affirmation, that he will
support the constitution of the United States and the constitution of
this state, and that he will faithfully and impartially discharge and
perform all the duties of his office as notary public, and shall immediately transmit said oath to the said register of deeds [county clerk],
who shall preserve the bond in his office and record the commission
and oath in a book to be kept by him for that purpose, and shall
send to the secretary of state a written notice that the requirements
of the law are complied with, giving the date of qualification, which
notice shall be preserved by the secretary in his office.

§ 32-10. Action on notarial bond. If any person shall be damaged or injured by the unlawful act, negligence or misconduct of any
notary public, the person damaged or injured may maintain a civil
action on the bond of such notary public against such notary public,
and his sureties; and the recovery in such action shall not be a
bar to any future action for other cause, to the full amount of the
bond.

UNITED STATES

[11 U.S.C.]

§ 63. Qualifications of referees. Individuals shall not be eligible
to appointment as referees unless they are (1) competent to perform
the duties of a referee in bankruptcy; (2) not holding any office of
profit or emolument under the laws of the United States or of any
State or subdivision thereof other than conciliation commissioner or
special master under this Act [this title]: Provided, however, That
part-time referees may be commissioners of deeds, United States commissioners, justices of the peace, masters in chancery, notaries public,
retired officers and retired enlisted personnel of the Regular and
Reserve components of the Army, Navy, Marine Corps, and Coast
Guard, members of the Reserve components of the Army, Navy,
Marine Corps, and Coast Guard, members of the National Guard of

the United States and of the National Guard of a State, Territory, or the District of Columbia, except the National Guard disbursing officers who are on a full time salary basis, or either conciliation commissioners or supervising conciliation commissioners but not both; (3) at the time when originally appointed not relatives of any of the judges of the courts of bankruptcy or of the justices or judges of the appellate courts of the districts wherein they may be appointed; (4) resident and have their offices within the judicial district of the court or one of the courts of bankruptcy under which they are to hold appointment: Provided, however, That where a referee shall be temporarily transferred or permanently appointed to another judicial district, residence or office in such other district shall not be requisite for eligibility; and Provided further, That referees serving the District of Columbia shall reside in the District of Columbia, or within twenty miles thereof; and (5) members in good standing at the bar of the district court of the United States in which they are first appointed or, if appointed to serve in territory within more than one judicial district, at the bar of one of such district courts: Provided, however, That the requirement of membership at such bar shall not apply to referees holding office on the date when this amendatory Act takes effect.

CHAPTER 4: QUALIFICATIONS

STATE AND OTHER STATUTES

ALABAMA

The statutes are vague concerning the qualifications of notaries. Women are eligible for appointment as commercial notaries, and notaries must be able to give appropriate bond with sureties. See *Appointment*, ALA. CODE Tit. 40, §§ 2, 4, 18, 22.

ALASKA

[ALASKA STAT.]

§ 44.50.020. **Qualifications.** A person appointed a notary public shall be, at the time of submitting his application, a citizen of the United States and a resident at least 19 years of age. In this secton, "resident" means a person who maintains his permanent place of abode in Alaska, and is in fact living here.

ARIZONA

The statutes are vague concerning the qualifications of notaries. They must reside in a county of the state and must be able to give appropriate bond with sureties. See *Appointment*, ARIZ. REV. STAT. ANN. § 41-311.

ARKANSAS

The statutes are vague concerning the qualifications of notaries. They must be citizens of the county for which they are appointed and must be able to file appropriate bond with security. See *Appointment*, ARK. STAT. ANN. § 12-1401.

[ARK. STAT. ANN.]

§ 12-101. **Sex no bar to holding office.** Hereafter, sex shall not be a bar to the holding of any public or civil office in this State.

§ 12-102. **Women may hold office.** Women, where otherwise qualified, shall be entitled to hold public or civil office, whether elective or appointive, now created or authorized, or which shall be hereafter created or authorized under the Constitution and statutes of this State.

CALIFORNIA

[CAL. GOV'T CODE]

§ 8201. **Qualifications.** Every person appointed as notary public shall:

(a) Be at the time of appointment a citizen of the United States.

(b) Be at the time of appointment a legal resident of this state, except as otherwise provided in Section 8203.1.

(c) Be not less than 18 years of age.

(d) Satisfy the Secretary of State that he is of good moral character.

(e) Have satisfactorily answered a written questionnaire on a form prescribed by the Secretary of State to determine the fitness of the person to exercise the functions of the office of notary public. The questionnaire shall be answered before any notary public, and sworn to by such notary public who shall be entitled to a fee of two dollars ($2) for his services with respect thereto. All questions shall be elementary questions based on the statutory law of this state as set forth in the booklet of the laws of California relating to notaries public distributed without charge by the Secretary of State to all applicants for commission as notary public. Applicants shall be permitted to refer to such booklet while taking said examination.

§ 8202. **Ineligibility of county officers and deputies; exceptions.** No county officer, or his deputy, except as provided by Section 8202.5, is eligible to or may perform the duties of the office of notary public. This section does not apply to district attorneys, county counsels, treasurers, deputy county clerks who do not receive annual salaries, deputy county auditors, public administrators and public defenders.

Note: For § 8202.5, see *Appointment.*

§ 8203.1. **Military and naval reservations; appointment and commission of notaries; qualifications.** The Secretary of State may appoint and commission notaries public for the military and naval reservations of the Army, Navy, Coast Guard, Air Force, and Marine Corps of the United States, wherever located in the state; provided, however, that such appointee shall be a citizen of the United States, not less than 18 years of age, and must meet the requirements set forth in subdivisions (d) and (e) of Section 8201.

§ 8214.1 **Grounds for refusal, revocation or suspension of commission.** The Secretary of State may refuse to appoint any person as notary public upon any of the grounds set forth in subdivisions (a) through (d) hereof, and the Secretary of State may revoke or suspend the commission of any notary public upon any of the grounds set forth in subdivisions (b) through (i) hereof:

(a) Failure to meet the good moral character requirement set forth in subdivision (d) of Section 8201.

(b) Substantial and material misstatement or omission in the application submitted to the Secretary of State.

(c) Conviction of a felony or of a lesser offense involving moral turpitude or of a nature incompatible with the duties of a notary public.

(d) Revocation or suspension of a professional license, if such revocation or suspension was for misconduct or dishonesty.

(e) Failure to fully and faithfully discharge any of the duties required of him by this chapter.

(f) When adjudged liable for damages in any suit grounded in fraud, misrepresentation or violation of the state regulatory laws or in any suit based upon his failure to discharge fully and faithfully his duties as a notary public.

(g) The use of false or misleading advertising wherein he has represented that he has duties, rights or privileges that he does not possess by law.

(h) The practice of law in violation of Secton 6125 of the Business and Professions Code.

(i) Charging an individual more than the ten-dollar ($10) fee provided for assisting with each set of forms relating to change in that individual's immigration status.

If there is a revocation or suspension of a commission pursuant to this section, or a denial of a commission, the person affected shall have the right to a hearing on the matter and such proceeding shall be conducted in accordance with Chapter 5 (commencing with Section 11500) of Part 1 of Division 3 of Title 2 of the Government Code.

COLORADO

The statutes are vague concerning the qualifications of notaries. They must be able to give appropriate bond, with, as surety thereon, a company qualified to write surety bonds in the state. See *Appointment*, COLO. REV. STAT. ANN. § 12-55-106.

CONNECTICUT

Appointees shall be at least 18 years of age and shall have resided in the state at least one year immediately preceding their appointment. See *Appointment*, CONN. GEN. STAT. ANN. § 3-91.

DELAWARE

[DEL. CODE ANN.]

Tit. 29, § 4301. **Appointment of notaries in general; number from each county; qualifications; revocation.**

o   o   o

(b) Any citizen who desires to become a notary shall be at least 18 years of age and shall provide such evidence as the governor may require to show:

(1) Good character and reputation;

(2) A reasonable need for a notary commission; and

(3) Legal residence of at least 1 year within the State.

o   o   o

Official court reporters who are appointed as notaries public need not be a legal resident of the state for one year at the time of the appointment, if he or she is a resident of the state at the time of the appointment. See *Appointment*, DEL. CODE ANN. Tit. 29, § 4303A.

DISTRICT OF COLUMBIA

Notaries must be residents of the District of Columbia or have their sole place of business or employment located within the District. See *Appointment*, D.C. CODE ENCYCL. ANN. § 1-501. They must be able to give bond with appropriate security. See *Appointment*, D.C. ENCYCL. ANN. § 1-504.

FLORIDA

Applicants must be at least 21 years of age, a citizen of the United States, and a permanent resident of the state for one year. They must be able to give bond in the sum of $500.00. See *Appointment*, FLA. STAT. ANN. § 117.01.

GEORGIA

[GA. CODE ANN.]

§ 71-102. **Age and character of notary; attorneys at law.** A notary must be 18 years old, or an attorney at law; a citizen of the United States; a resident of Georgia, and a resident of the county from which he is appointed; and of good moral character.

§ 71-113. **Nonresidents commissioned as Georgia notaries public.** Any person who is a resident of a State bordering on the State of Georgia and who carries on a business or profession in the State of Georgia or who is regularly employed in the State of Georgia may be commissioned a notary public by the clerk of the superior court of the county in which they carry on said profession, business, or employment.

Such person wishing to be commissioned as a notary public shall be 18 years of age or more and of good character.

Such person shall make application to the clerk of the superior court in the county in which such profession, business or employment takes place and, upon the payment of the usual fees to the clerk, shall be issued a certificate as a notary public of this

State and shall be authorized to perform all of the duties and exercise all of the powers and authorities now in effect relating to notaries public who are residents of this State.

§ 79-207. Females, citizenship rights of. Females are entitled to the privilege of the elective franchise, to hold any civil office or perform any civil functions in as full and complete a manner as the same can be enjoyed by any male citizen: Provided, however, females shall not be liable to discharge any military, jury, police, patrol or road duty.

HAWAII

[HAWAII REV. STAT.]

§ 456-2. Qualifications; oath. Every person appointed a notary public shall, at the time of his appointment, be a resident of the State for one year, possess the other qualifications required of public officers and be at least eighteen years of age; provided, that the attorney general may, for public convenience and necessity, commission a notary for any number of judicial circuits, and the notary shall keep a separate record for each circuit. Every person appointed to that office shall, before entering thereon, take and subscribe an oath for the faithful discharge of his duties, which oath shall be filed in the department of the attorney general.

IDAHO

Notaries must have the qualifications of electors. See *Appointment,* IDAHO CODE § 51-101. Notaries must be able to execute bond in the sum of $1,000 with two or more sufficient sureties to be approved by the probate judge of the county in which the notary resides. See *Appointment,* IDAHO CODE § 51-102.

ILLINOIS

Appointees must be resident in a county in the state for which they are appointed; they must be 18 years of age or older, a citizen of the United States, and have resided in the state for one year preceding the appointment. See *Appointment,* ILL. ANN. STAT. ch. 99, § 1 (Smith-Hurd).

INDIANA

An applicant for a commission as a notary public must be at least 18 years of age and a legal resident of the state and of the county for which application is made. See *Appointment,* IND. CODE § 33-16-2-1. For provisions concerning certain disqualifications for serving as notaries public and certain disqualifications for appointment as notaries public, see *Authority and Duties,* IND. CODE § 33-16-2-7.

IOWA

The statutes are vague concerning the qualifications of notaries. They must be able to execute an appropriate bond and be a resident of the state. See *Appointment*, IOWA CODE ANN. §§ 77.4(2), 77.17.

KANSAS

Local notaries and state notaries must be eighteen years of age and must be able to file a good and sufficient bond in the sum of $1,000.00 for local notaries and $2,500.00 for state notaries, with one or more sureties. See *Appointment*, KAN. STAT. ANN. §§ 53-101, 53-102.

KENTUCKY

A written application to the Secretary of State must be approved by the circuit judge, circuit clerk, county judge, county clerk, justice of the peace or a member of the General Assembly of the county of the residence of the applicant. A notary must be eighteen years of age, a resident of the county from which he makes his application, of good moral character, and capable of discharging the duties imposed upon him by law, and the endorsement of the officer approving the application shall so state. The notary must be able to give an obligation with good security for the proper discharge of the duties of his office. See *Appointment*, KY. REV. STAT. ANN § 423.010.

[KY. CONST.]

§ 165. **Incompatible offices.** No person shall, at the same time, be a state officer or a deputy officer, or a member of the general assembly, and an officer of any county, city, town, or other municipality, or an employee thereof; and no person shall, at the same time, fill two municipal offices, either in the same or different municipalities, except as may be otherwise provided in this Constitution; but a notary public, or an officer of the militia, shall not be ineligible to hold any other office mentioned in this section.

LOUISIANA

[LA. REV. STAT.]

General Provisions

§ 35:191. **Appointment, qualifications and bond; examination; examiners.** Any citizen of the state may be appointed a notary public in and for the parish in which he resides, upon giving bond, with good and solvent security, in the sum of one thousand dollars conditioned for the faithful performance of all duties required by law toward all persons who may employ him in his profession of notary; and after being examined by written examination by an examining committee of three notaries, at least two of whom shall be attorneys appointed by the district court having jurisdiction of the parish in which the prospective notary resides and after having received a certificate from the court of having been found competent upon such examination, to exercise the profession of notary public. The examination may be dispensed with by the court if the applicant has been duly admitted to practice law in this state. ° ° ° Examinations shall be given on the second Monday in July and the second Monday in December of each calendar year beginning in December, 1966, and may be given at such other times as the examining committee shall determine. Application to take such examination must be filed with the examining committee no later than thirty days prior to the date as fixed herein for such examination. Results of the examination shall be announced to each applicant within forty-five days following the examination. If the examining committee fail to schedule and give the examinations as herein directed, then the said committee shall automatically be discharged and a new committee shall be appointed to fulfill the unexpired terms in accordance with the above provisions.

Note: Cf. *Appointment,* LA. REV. STAT. § 35:1.

§ 9:51. **Civil rights and duties.** Women have the same rights, authority, privileges, and immunities, and shall perform the same obligations and duties as men in the holding of office including the civil functions of tutor, under tutor, curator, under curator, administrator, executor, arbitrator, and notary public.

Assumption Parish and St. Mary Parish

§ 35:661. **Attorneys; appointment as notaries in parishes additional to or other than parish of residence.** In addition to the methods now provided by law for the appointment of notaries public in the parishes of Assumption and St. Mary, any attorney at law duly admitted to the practice of law before the courts of this state and any notary public who resides in either of such parishes may qualify and be appointed as a notary public in either parish; provided, however, that he meet the requirements established by law for the parish wherein he elects to act as notary public and after he has given bond, with good and solvent security, in the manner and in the amount provided by law for the parish in which he is appointed as notary public, conditioned for the faithful performance of all duties required by law toward all persons who may employ him in the profession of notary.

Notwithstanding any provision of this section to the contrary, this section shall not be construed to authorize notaries public to qualify and be appointed in more than one parish.

Bossier Parish and Webster Parish

§ 35:622. **Qualifications; bond; suspension.** Any citizen of the state over twenty-one years of age, a qualified elector in and a resident of the parish of Bossier, or the parish of Webster, for at least two years next preceding his appointment, being of good moral character, integrity, competency and sober habits, may be appointed under the provisions of this Chapter, a notary public in and for the parish in which he resides, upon giving bond with one or more good and solvent sureties, in the sum of one thousand dollars subscribed in favor of the governor of the state, and conditioned as the law directs for the faithful performance and discharge of his duties as a notary public, which bond shall be approved by the president of the police jury for the parish in which he resides and recorded in a special book kept for that purpose in the conveyance office for the parish in which he resides. Upon complying with the requirements of this Chapter, such appointment for life shall be during good behavior. Failure to keep the required bond in effect shall subject any such notary to suspension.

§ 35:622.1. **Qualifications; Webster Parish, exemptions.** Notwithstanding any provisions of R.S. 35:622 or any other provision of this Title to the contrary, any citizen residing in Webster Parish who changes his residence to another parish and who becomes an attorney at law duly admitted to the practice of law before the courts of this state and engages in the practice of law in said parish and who subsequently re-establishes his residence in Webster Parish, may qualify and be appointed as a notary public in and for Webster Parish without having been a resident and qualified elector therein for at least two years next preceding his appointment as a notary public; provided, however, that he shall be required to meet the other qualifications and requirements established by law for the appointment of notaries public in Webster Parish.

Caddo Parish

§ 35:392. **Qualifications; bond.** Any citizen of the state over twenty-one years of age, a resident of the parish of Caddo for at least two years next preceding his appointment, being of good moral character, integrity, competency and sober habits, may be appointed a notary public in and for the parish of Caddo, upon giving bond with one or more good and solvent sureties, in the sum of one thousand dollars subscribed in favor of the Governor of the state, and conditioned as the law directs for the faithful performance and discharge of his duties as a notary public, which bond shall be approved by the president of the police jury, for the parish of Caddo, and recorded in a special book kept for that purpose in the conveyance office for the parish of Caddo, and upon complying with the requirements of this section, for life during good behavior. Failure to keep bond in effect subjects notary to suspension.

Note: Cf. *Appointment,* LA. REV. STAT. § 35:394.

East Baton Rouge Parish

§ 35:651. Appointment as notary in East Baton Rouge Parish; qualification exceptions. Notwithstanding any provisions of this title to the contrary, any attorney at law duly admitted to the practice of law before the courts of this state who resides in the parish of Iberville or the parish of West Baton Rouge or the parish of West Feliciana and whose principal business office is in the parish of East Baton Rouge may qualify and be appointed as a notary public in the parish of East Baton Rouge; provided, however, that he meet the requirements established by law for the parish of East Baton Rouge and after he has given bond, with good and solvent security, in the manner and the amount provided by law for said parish, conditioned for the faithful performance of all duties required by law toward all persons who may employ him in the profession of notary. This section shall not be construed to authorize notaries public to qualify and be appointed in more than one parish.

Jefferson Parish

§ 35:602. Qualifications; bond. Any citizen of the state over twenty-one years of age, a resident of the parish of Jefferson for at least one year preceding his appointment, being of good moral character, integrity, competency and sober habits, may be appointed a notary public in and for the parish of Jefferson, upon giving bond with one or more good and solvent sureties, in the sum of one thousand dollars subscribed in favor of the governor of the state, and conditioned as the law directs for the faithful performance of his duties as a notary public, which bond shall be recorded in the office of the clerk of court, parish of Jefferson, and upon complying with the requirements of this Section shall retain the said office for life during good behavior.

See also Orleans Parish § 35:631.

Orleans Parish

§ 35:253. Eligibility for appointment; bond; corporate surety's right to cancel. A. Any citizen of the state over twenty-one years of age and a resident of the Parish of Orleans for at least two years next preceding his appointment, being of good moral character, integrity, competency and sober habits, may be appointed a notary public in and for the Parish of Orleans, upon giving bond with one or more good and solvent sureties, in the sum of

ten thousand dollars and upon complying with the other requirements of this Part. The bond shall be subscribed in favor of the
governor, and conditioned for the faithful performance and discharge of the duties of the notary as a notary public, and shall be
approved by the presiding judge of the civil district court for the
Parish of Orleans, and recorded in a special book kept for that
purpose in the conveyance office for the parish.

B. When the notary has given bond with corporate surety,
the surety has the right to cancel the bond for non-payment of the
premium by giving notice through registered mail to the custodian
of notarial records for the Parish of Orleans. This notice must be
given thirty days prior to any anniversary date of the bond, after
which anniversary date, the liability of the corporate surety on the
bond shall cease.

§ 35:631. **Attorneys; appointment as notaries in parishes additional to or other than parish of residence.** In addition to the
methods now provided by law for the appointment of notaries public in the parishes of Orleans, St. Tammany and Jefferson, any
attorney at law duly admitted to the practice of law before the
courts of this state and any notary public who resides in either
of such parishes may qualify and be appointed as a notary public
in either parish; provided, however, that he meet the requirements
established by law for the parish wherein he elects to act as notary
public and after he has given bond, with good and solvent security,
in the manner and in the amount provided by law for the parish
in which he is appointed as notary public, conditioned for the faithful performance of all duties required by law toward all persons who
may employ him in the profession of notary. Notwithstanding any
provision of this section to the contrary, this section shall not be
construed to affect the limitation on the number of notaries public
authorized by law for Orleans Parish, nor shall this section be construed to authorize notaries public to qualify and be appointed
in more than one parish.

St. Mary Parish

See Assumption Parish.

St. Tammany Parish

See Orleans Parish § 35:631.

Webster Parish

See Bossier Parish and Webster Parish.

MAINE

The statutes are vague concerning the qualifications of notaries.
Cf. *Appointment*, ME. CONST. art. V, pt. 1, § 8.

[ME. REV. STAT. ANN.]

Tit. 4, § 1056. Powers of attorneys. Attorneys at law duly admitted and eligible to practice in the courts of the State shall have all of the powers of justices of the peace and notaries public and be authorized to do all acts which may be done by justices of the peace and notaries public with the same effect thereof and have the same territorial jurisdiction.

MARYLAND

[MD. CONST.]

Art. 35. Holding more than one office prohibited; persons in public trust not to receive presents from other states, etc.; position of notary public not an office of profit. That no person shall hold, at the same time, more than one office of profit, created by the Constitution or Laws of this State; nor shall any person in public trust receive any present from any foreign Prince or State, or from the United States, or any of them, without the approbation of this State. The position of Notary Public shall not be considered an office of profit within the meaning of this Article.

[MD. ANN. CODE]

Art. 68, § 1. Appointment, qualifications, application, term, commission and fees.

°   °   °

(b) *Qualifications.*—Every person appointed shall be at least eighteen (18) years of age, of good moral character and integrity, a citizen of the United States, a resident in this State for a period of two (2) years prior to appointment, and a resident of the senatorial district and subdistrict from which he or she is appointed. The residence requirements shall not apply to persons having an appointment as an official court reporter by any court of any county or Baltimore City.

°   °   °

§ 9. Validation of acts by women notaries. All official acts heretofore done by women notaries public are hereby declared valid if any such act should have been done or performed by a man notary public appointed under the laws of this State.

MASSACHUSETTS

The statutes are vague concerning the qualifications of notaries. See generally, *Appointment.*

MICHIGAN

No person is eligible to receive an appointment as notary public unless he or she, at the time of making application for appointment, is 18 years old, a resident of the county of which he or she desires to be appointed notary public, and a citizen of the state. See *Appointment*, MICH. COMP. LAWS ANN. § 55.107. Notaries public must reside in the county for which they are appointed, but they may act as notaries in any part of the state. See *Authority and Duties*, MICH. COMP. LAWS ANN. § 55.117.

[MICH. COMP. LAWS ANN.]

§ 4.121. **Oaths, depositions, acknowledgments; power of legislators.** Sec. 1. During his term of office, every senator and representative in the state legislature is hereby authorized, by virtue of his office to administer oaths, take depositions and acknowledgments.

MINNESOTA

[MINN. STAT. ANN.]

§ 359.01. **Commission.** The governor may appoint and commission as notaries public, by and with the advice and consent of the senate, as many citizens of this state, over the age of 18 years, resident in the county for which appointed, as he deems necessary. The fee for each commission shall not exceed $10, and shall be paid to the governor's private secretary.

MISSISSIPPI

The statutes are vague concerning the qualifications of notaries. Notaries must be able to give bond with sufficient sureties in the penalty of $2,000.00. See *Appointment*, MISS. CODE ANN. § 25-33-1. Notaries, among others, are exempt from the provisions of MISS. CONST. art. 14, § 266 (See *Commissioners of Deeds*) which provides that no person holding or exercising an office of honor or profit under any foreign government or under the government of the United States may hold or exercise the rights and powers of any office of honor or profit under the laws or authority of the state.

[MISS. CONST.]

Art. 12, § 250. All qualified electors and no others shall be eligible to office, except as otherwise provided in this Constitution; provided, however, that as to an office where no other qualification than that of being a qualified elector is provided by this Constitution, the legislature may, by law, fix additional qualifications for such office.

[MISS. CODE ANN.]

§ 25-33-17. **Ex-officio notaries public.** All justices of the peace and clerks of the circuit and chancery courts are notaries public by virtue of their office, and shall possess all the powers and discharge all the duties belonging to the office of notary public, and may authenticate all their acts, instruments, and attestations by the common seal of office; and all acts done by them of a notarial character shall receive the same credit and legal effect as are attached to the acts of notaries public.

MISSOURI

No person shall be appointed a notary who has not attained the age of 21 years, and who is not a citizen of the United States and of the state. See *Appointment*, MO. ANN. STAT. § 486.010 (Vernon).

MONTANA

[MONT. REV. CODES ANN.]

§ 56-102. **Qualifications and residence.** Every person appointed as notary public must, at the time of his appointment, be a citizen of the United States and of the state of Montana for at least one year preceding his appointment, and must continue to reside within the state of Montana. Removal from the state vacates his office and is equivalent to resignation.

NEBRASKA

[NEB. REV. STAT.]

§ 64-101. **Notary public; appointment; qualifications; term.**

o   o   o

(5) No person shall be appointed a notary public unless his or her application is accompanied by the petition of at least twenty-five legal voters of the county in which he or she resides. (6) No appointment shall be made until such applicant shall have attained the age of twenty years nor unless such applicant shall certify to the Governor under oath that he or she has carefully read and understands the laws relating to the duties of notaries public and will, if commissioned, faithfully discharge the duties pertaining to said office and keep records according to law.

o   o   o

A removal from the state by a notary will terminate the term of his office. See *Authority and Duties,* NEB. REV. STAT. § 64-112.

NEVADA

The statutes are vague concerning the qualifications of notaries. Notaries must be able to enter into a bond to the state in the sum of $2,000, to be approved by the clerk of the county for which the notary public is appointed. See *Appointment*, NEV. REV. STAT. § 240.030(1)(c). The governor may appoint and commission notaries without limit in and for the several counties in the state. See *Appointment*, NEV. REV. STAT. § 240.010.

NEW HAMPSHIRE

[N.H. REV. STAT. ANN.]

§ 455:2. **Eligibility.** Any qualified voter may be appointed to the office of notary public.

NEW JERSEY

No person shall be appointed a notary public unless he shall be of the age of twenty-one years or over. See *Appointment*, N.J. STAT. ANN. § 52:7-1.1.

It is likely that the age provisions in § 52:7-1.1 have been modified, however, by the enactment of § 9:17B-1, which states as follows:

Rights of persons 18 years of age and older.

The Legislature finds and declares and by this act intends, pending the revision and amendment of the many statutory provisions involved, to:

a. Extend to persons 18 years of age and older the basic civil and contractual rights and obligations heretofore applicable only to persons 21 years of age or older, including the right to contract, sue, be sued and defend civil actions, apply for and be appointed to public employment, apply for and be granted a license or authority to engage in a business or profession subject to State regulation, serve on juries, marry, adopt children, attend and participate in horse race meetings and parimutuel betting and other legalized games and gaming, sell, purchase and consume alcoholic beverages, act as an incorporator, registered agent or director of a corporation, consent to medical and surgical treatment, execute a will, and to inherit, purchase, mortgage or otherwise encumber and convey real and personal property.

b. Abolish the right of a person between the ages of 18 and 21 years to disaffirm and be relieved of contractual obligations by reason of age.

[N.J. STAT. ANN.]

§ 52:7-1.3. **Nonresidents as notaries; oath.** No person shall be denied appointment as notary public on account of residence outside of this State; *provided*, such person resides in a State adjoining this State and maintains, or is regularly employed in, an office in this State. Before any such nonresident shall be appointed and commissioned as a notary public, he shall file with the Secretary of State an affidavit setting forth his residence and the address of his office or place of employment in this State. Any such nonresident who shall be appointed and commissioned as a notary public in this State shall file with the Secretary of State a certificate showing any change of residence or of his office or place of employment address in this State.

The oath of office required by the provisions of the chapter to which this act is a supplement shall be taken and subscribed before the clerk of the county in which he maintains his office or is employed in this State.

NEW MEXICO

[N.M. STAT. ANN.]

§ 35-1-2. **Qualifications.** Each notary public shall be a qualified elector of this state and a person of good moral character.

NEW YORK

[N.Y. EXEC. LAW]

§ 130. **Appointment of notaries public.**

o   o   o

Every person appointed as notary public must, at the time of his appointment, be a citizen of the United States and either a resident of the state of New York or have an office or place of business in New York state. A notary public who is a resident of the state and who moves out of the state but still maintains a place of business or an office in New York state does not vacate his office as a notary public. A notary public who is a nonresident and who ceases to have an office or place of business in this state, vacates his office as a notary public. A notary public who is a resident of New York state and moves out of the state and who does not retain an office or place of business in this state shall vacate his office as a notary public. A non-resident who accepts the office of notary public in this state thereby appoints the secretary of state as the person upon whom process can be served on his behalf. Before issuing to any applicant a commission as notary public, unless he be an attorney and counsellor at law duly admitted to practice in this state, the secretary of state shall satisfy himself that the applicant is of good moral character, has the equivalent of a common school education and is familiar with the duties and responsibilities of a notary public; provided, however, that where a notary public applies, before the expiration of his term, for a reappointment or where a person whose term as notary public shall have expired applies within six months thereafter for appointment as a notary public, such qualifying requirements may be waived by the secretary of state, and further, where an application for reappointment is filed after the expiration of the aforementioned renewal period by a person who failed or was unable to re-apply by reason of his induction or enlistment in the armed forces of the United States, such qualifying requirements may also be waived by the secretary of state, provided such application for reappointment is made within a period of one year after the military discharge of the applicant under conditions other than dishonorable. In any case, the appointment or reappointment of any applicant is in the discretion of the secretary of state.

○   •   ○

No person shall be appointed as a notary public under this article who has been convicted, in this state or any other state or territory, of a felony or any of the following offenses, to wit:

(a) Illegally using, carrying or possessing a pistol or other dangerous weapon; (b) making or possessing burglar's instruments; (c) buying or receiving or criminally possessing stolen property; (d) unlawful entry of a building; (e) aiding escape from prison; (f) unlawfully possessing or distributing habit forming narcotic drugs; (g) violating sections two hundred seventy, two hundred seventy-a, two hundred seventy-b, two hundred seventy-c, two hundred seventy-one, two hundred seventy-five, two hundred seventy-six, five hundred fifty, five hundred fifty-one, five hundred fifty-one-a and subdivisions six, eight, ten or eleven of section seven hundred twenty-two of the former penal law as in force and effect immediately prior to September first, nineteen hundred sixty-seven, or violating sections 165.25, 165.30, subdivision one of section 240.30, subdivision three of section 240.35 of the penal law, or violating sections four hundred seventy-eight, four hundred seventy-nine, four hundred eighty, four hundred eighty-one, four hundred eighty-four, four hundred eighty-nine and four hundred ninety-one of the judiciary law; or (h) vagrancy or prostitution, and who has not subsequent to such conviction received an executive pardon therefor or a certificate of good conduct from the parole board to remove the disability under this section because of such conviction.

A person regularly admitted to practice as an attorney and counsellor in the courts of record of this state, whose office for the practice of law is within the state, may be appointed a notary public and retain his office as such notary public although he resides in or removes to an adjoining state. For the purpose of this and the following sections of this article such person shall be deemed a resident of the county where he maintains such office.

[N.Y. PUB. OFFICERS LAW]

§ 3. Qualifications for holding office.

•   ○   ○

3. Nothing herein contained shall operate to prevent a person regularly admitted to practice as an attorney and counsellor in the

courts of record of this state, whose office for the practice of law is within the state, from accepting or retaining an appointment as a notary public, as provided in section one hundred thirty of the executive law, although he resides in or removes to an adjoining state. For the purposes of accepting and retaining an appointment as a notary public such person shall be deemed a resident of the county where he maintains such office for the practice of law.

○   ○   ○

NORTH CAROLINA

The statutes are vague concerning the qualifications of notaries. The Secretary of State may, from time to time, at his discretion, appoint one or more fit persons in every county to act as notaries public. The commission shall be sent to the register of deeds of the county in which the appointee lives. See *Appointment*, N.C. GEN. STAT. § 10-1.

NORTH DAKOTA

[N.D. CENT. CODE]

§ 44-06-01.   Appointment and qualification of notaries public.

○   ○   ○

A person, to be eligible to such appointment, at the time of appointment, must have the qualifications of an elector as to age, residence, and citizenship.

Note: The secretary of state shall appoint in each county in the state from among the citizens of either sex, one or more notaries public. See *Appointment*, N.D. CENT. CODE § 44-06-01.

OHIO

[OHIO REV. CODE ANN.—(Page)]

§ 147.02.   Certificate of qualifications.   Before the appointment of a notary public is made the applicant shall produce to the governor a certificate from a judge of the court of common pleas, court of appeals, or supreme court, that he is of good moral character, a citizen of the county in which he resides, and, if it is the fact, that the applicant is an attorney at law qualified and admitted to practice in this state, and possessed of sufficient qualifications and ability to discharge the duties of the office of notary public. No judge shall issue such certificate until he is satisfied from his personal knowledge that the applicant possesses the qualifications necessary to a proper discharge of the duties of the office, or until the applicant has passed an examination under such rules and regulations as the judge may prescribe. If the applicant is admitted to the practice of law in this state, this fact shall also be certified by the judge in his certification.

OKLAHOMA

The statutes are vague concerning the qualifications of notaries. Before entering upon the duties of his office a notary shall file in the office of the court clerk, in his capacity as clerk of the district court, of the county in which such notary resides at the time he is commissioned, among other things, a good and sufficient bond to the state in the sum of $1,000.00, with one or more sureties to be approved by the court clerk. See *Appointment*, OKLA. STAT. ANN. tit. 49, § 2.

OREGON

[ORE. REV. STAT.]

§ 194.010. **Appointment of notary public; term; qualifications; office may be nonlucrative; functions not official duties.**

°   °   °

(3) Every person appointed as a notary public at the time of appointment must be 21 years of age or older, of good moral character, a citizen of the United States and, for six months immediately prior to his appointment, a resident of Oregon.

°   °   °

Editorial comment

The Governor may revoke the commission of a notary public, or deny an application for such a commission, if particular grounds exist. See *Appointment*, ORE. REV. STAT. § 194.067.

PENNSYLVANIA

[PA. STAT. ANN.]

Tit. 57, § 149. **Eligibility.** Any citizen of Pennsylvania, being eighteen (18) years of age or over, of known character, integrity and ability, shall be eligible to the office of notary public, if he shall have resided within this Commonwealth for at least two (2) years immediately preceding the date of his appointment, and if he shall be a registered elector in the Commonwealth.

§ 150. **Disqualification; exception.** The following persons shall be ineligible to hold the office of notary public:

(1) Any person holding any judicial office in this Commonwealth, except the office of justice of the peace, magistrate, or alderman.

(2)   Every member of Congress, and any person, whether an officer, a subordinate officer, or agent, holding any office or appointment of profit or trust under the legislative, executive, or judiciary departments of the government of the United States, to which a salary, fees or perquisites are attached.

Editorial comment

Each application for appointment to the office of notary public must bear the endorsement of the Senator of the district in which the applicant resides, or, in the case of a vacancy in that senatorial district, must be endorsed by the Senator of an adjacent district.   Before issuing a commission as notary public, the Secretary of the Commonwealth shall satisfy himself that the applicant is of good moral character, and is familiar with the duties and responsibilities of a notary public.   Such qualifying requirements may be waived in certain cases.   See *Appointment,* PA. STAT. ANN. tit. 57, § 151.

Concerning the rejection of an application for appointment as a notary public, see *Appointment,* PA. STAT. ANN. tit. 57, § 168.

Incompatible Offices and Appointments

Tit. 65, § 1.   State and federal offices.   Every person who shall hold any office, or appointment of profit or trust, under the government of the United States, whether an officer, a subordinate officer or agent, who is or shall be employed under the legislative, executive or judiciary departments of the United States, and also every member of congress, is hereby declared to be incapable of holding or exercising, at the same time, the office or appointment of justice of the peace, notary public, mayor, recorder, burgess or alderman of any city, corporate town [or borough]°, resident physician of the lazaretto, constable, judge, inspector or clerk of election under this commonwealth: Provided, however, That the provisions hereof shall not apply to any person who shall enlist, enroll or be called or drafted into the active military or naval service of the United States or any branch or unit thereof during any war or emergency as hereinafter defined.

(°) The provision concerning boroughs has been repealed.

§ 1.1.   War defined.   As used in this act the term "war" shall mean the period between the opening and ending of hostilities and shall not include the period after the ending of hostilities, notwithstanding the fact that no treaty of peace has been negotiated or concluded, and the term "emergency" shall mean the period between a declaration that a state of emergency exists and a declaration that the state of emergency has been terminated.

§ 2.   **Offices so holden void.**   The holding of any of the aforesaid offices or appointments under this state, is hereby declared to be incompatible with any office or appointment under the United States, and every such commission, office or appointment, so holden under the government of this state, contrary to the true intent and meaning of this act, shall be and is hereby declared to be null and void.

§ 3.   **Penalty for exercising.**   If any person, after the expiration of six months from the passing of this act, shall exercise any offices or appointments, the exercise of which is by this act declared to be incompatible, every person so offending shall, for every such offense, being thereof legally convicted in any court of record, forfeit and pay any sum not less than fifty nor more than five hundred dollars, at the discretion of the court, one moiety of the said forfeiture to be paid to the overseers, guardians or directors of the poor of the township, district, county or place where such offense shall have been committed, to be applied to the support of the poor, and the other moiety thereof to the prosecutor who shall sue for the same.

PUERTO RICO

[P.R. LAWS ANN.]

Tit. 4, § 1002.°   **Persons authorized to practice notarial profession;**
° ° °

On and after the date of approval of this chapter the notarial profession may be practiced in the Commonwealth only by those persons now authorized to practice it and by such attorneys as are hereafter admitted to the bar who are members of the Bar Association of Puerto Rico and are authorized by the Supreme Court of Puerto Rico to practice the notarial profession.

° ° ° °

(°) For the complete text of P.R. LAWS ANN. tit. 4, § 1002, see *Appointment.*

RHODE ISLAND

[R.I. GEN. LAWS ANN.]

§ 42-30-5.   **Application for appointment.**   Any qualified elector or member of the bar of this state desiring to be appointed a notary public, or a justice of the peace, shall make written application to the governor over his own signature, and stating that he is a qualified elector or a member of said bar, who is an actual resident of the state of Rhode Island, as the case may be, such qualification as an elector of the state at the time of making application to be certified to by a member of the board of canvassers and registration, in cities having such boards, or by the city or town clerk of the city or town in which such applicant claims a right to vote, such qualification as a member of the bar shall be a certified copy of his certificate of admission to said bar.

§ 42-30-6. **Approval of application by court official.** Before said application for appointment to the office of notary public, or justice of the peace, shall be acted upon by the governor, and a commission issued thereon, the application shall be approved by a clerk, or assistant clerk, of the superior court of the county in which such applicant resides, or by a judge, or clerk of the district court.

Such clerk, assistant clerk of the superior court, or judge or clerk of the district court, shall satisfy himself that the applicant for appointment to the office of notary public, or justice of the peace, can speak[,] read and write the English language, and has sufficient knowledge of the powers and duties pertaining to such offices, and shall then approve such application in writing; provided, the provisions of this section shall not apply to any application made by a member of the Rhode Island bar; and provided, further, that all duly qualified notaries public and justices of the peace, whose commissions expire on the thirtieth day of June, 1971, or on the thirtieth day of June in every fifth year thereafter, shall be exempted from the provisions of this section and § 42-30-5.

§ 42-30-14. **Public officers having notarial powers.** Every state senator, state representative, clerk and assistant clerk of the superior court, during the period for which he has been elected or appointed, shall have the power to act as a notary public as in this chapter provided.

SOUTH CAROLINA

[S.C. CODE ANN.]

§ 49-1. **Appointment [and term.]** The Governor may appoint from the qualified electors as many notaries public throughout the State as the public good shall require, ° ° °.

°   °   °

§ 49-2. **Endorsement of application.** No notary public shall be appointed except upon the endorsement of at least one half of the members of the legislative delegation representing the county in which the applicant resides.

SOUTH DAKOTA

The Governor is directed to appoint in each of the organized counties in the state "from among the eligible citizens thereof", one or more notaries public. See *Appointment*, S.D. COMPILED LAWS ANN. § 18-1-1.

TENNESSEE

[TENN. CODE ANN.]

§ 8-1601. Election—Residence requirement. There shall be elected by the justices of the county court as many notaries public for their county as they may deem necessary. All notaries must be a resident of the county, or have their principal place of business in the county, from which they were elected. If an individual has his principal place of business in any county in the state of Tennessee he shall be eligible for election as a notary in said county, although he may reside in a state other than Tennessee.

TEXAS

[TEX. CONST.]

Art. 5, § 19.   Justices of the peace; ° ° ° ex officio notaries public; • ° ° And the justices of the peace shall be ex officio notaries public. ° ° •

[TEX. REV. CIV. STAT. ANN.]

Art. 2376.   [Justices of the peace.] Commissioned. Each justice of the peace shall be commissioned as justice of the peace of his precinct and ex officio notary public of his county.

Art. 5949.   Notary public.

•   °   °

Eligibility

2. To be eligible for appointment as Notary Public for any county, a person shall be a resident citizen of this state and at least twenty-one (21) years of age, and either a resident of the county for which he is appointed, or shall maintain his principal place of business or of employment in such county; provided that any person may be appointed, as hereinabove set out, in only one county in this state at the same time; provided further that where such person resides within the limits of a county with a population of more than fifty thousand (50,000), according to the last preceding federal census, containing an incorporated city, town or village partially located in another county, said person may be appointed a Notary Public for either of such counties; provided further that nothing herein shall invalidate any commission as Notary Public which has been issued and is outstanding at the time this Act becomes effective.

°   °   °

Editorial comment

An applicant for appointment as a notary must state on his application that "he has never been convicted of a crime involving moral turpitude." See *Appointment*, TEX. REV. CIV. STAT. ANN. art. 5949(3).

Art. 5949.   Notary   public.

°   °   °

° ° ° **Rejection of application; appeal.**

5.   ° ° °

The Secretary of State may, for good cause, reject any application, or revoke the commission of any Notary Public, but such action shall be taken subject to the right of notice, hearing and adjudication, and the right of appeal therefrom. Such appeal shall be made to the District Court of Travis County, Texas, but upon such appeal the Secretary of State shall have the burden of proof and such trial shall be conducted de novo.

"Good cause" shall include final conviction for a crime involving moral turpitude, any false statement knowingly made in an application, and final conviction for the violation of any law concerning the regulation of the conduct of Notaries Public in this state, or any other state.

°   °   °

UTAH

Notaries public shall have the qualifications of electors. See *Appointment*, UTAH CODE ANN. § 46-1-1.

VERMONT

The statutes are vague concerning the qualifications of notaries. The clerk of the supreme court, county clerks, district court clerks, and town clerks and their deputies are ex officio notaries. See *Appointment*, VT. STAT. ANN. tit. 24, § 441.

VIRGIN ISLANDS

[V.I. CODE ANN.]

Tit. 3, § 771.   Appointment of notaries public by Governor.

°   °   °

The Executive Secretary of the Legislature of the Virgin Islands shall be granted a commission by the Governor as a notary public ex officio. Each official court reporter of the Municipal Court of the Virgin Islands, the official court reporter of the District Court of the Virgin Islands, the official reporter of the Legislature of the Virgin Islands, and the Registrar and Deputy Registrars of Vital Statistics of the Department of Health shall be granted commissions by the Governor as notaries public ex officio. Any person admitted to practice law in the Virgin Islands as a member of the Virgin Islands Bar shall upon application and a showing of his membership be issued a commission for a period of four years.

§ 772. Qualifications. Every person appointed as a notary public shall—

(1) be a citizen of the United States at least 21 years of age and a resident of the Virgin Islands for at least 5 years preceding his appointment; Provided, however, That notaries ex officio and members of the Virgin Islands Bar commissioned in accordance with the provisions of section 771 of this title° shall not be required to comply with the five year residency requirement imposed by this section; and

(2) be a graduate of an accredited high school or have passed the high school equivalency test; and

(3) continue to reside within the Virgin Islands during the term of his office.

Removal from the Virgin Islands shall vacate his office and be the equivalent of a resignation.

(°) For § 771, see above.

Special Notaries Public

Tit. 3, § 801. Appointment of government employees as notaries public. In addition to the notaries public provided for in subchapter I of this chapter, the Governor may authorize and empower employees of the Government of the Virgin Islands or of the United States, not exceeding 30 in number, to take acknowledgments of deeds and administer oaths and affirmations, and such employees shall be appointed and commissioned as notaries public with terms of office at the pleasure of the Governor.

Tit. 3, § 802. Oath of office; ° ° ° Notaries public appointed and commissioned under section 801 of this title shall take an official oath ° ° °

Tit. 3, § 803. Commission fees; bonds. Notaries public appointed and commissioned under section 801 [above], of this title shall not be required to pay license fees, nor to give bond.

VIRGINIA

[VA. CODE ANN.]

§ 47-1. Notaries public for counties and cities.

o   o   o

(5) *Residence.*—A notary public may or may not be a resident of any county or city for which he is appointed. A nonresident of Virginia who is regularly employed in this State may be appointed a notary public in Virginia if, in the opinion of the Governor, such nonresident is otherwise qualified.

o   o   o

§ 47.3. Eligibility; liability for acts and omissions. Men and women eighteen years of age shall be eligible to the office of notary public and qualified to execute the bonds required of them in that capacity; and for acts and omissions in their official capacity, they shall be liable.

WASHINGTON

Persons appointed and commissioned as notaries public must have the qualifications of electors. No person may be appointed a notary public except upon the petition of at least ten freeholders of the county in which such person resides. Upon the expiration of his commission, a notary public may obtain a new commission on application, without the petition signed by freeholders, within one year from the date of the expiration of his preceding commission. See *Appointment,* WASH. REV. CODE ANN. § 42.28.010.

WEST VIRGINIA

Before the governor appoints a notary public, the applicant must obtain from the county court of his county a certificate showing him to be a person competent to perform the duties of the office, of good moral character, and a resident of the county from which the appointment is made. See *Appointment,* W. VA. CODE ANN. § 29-4-2.

If a person has reached the age of 18 years and is a citizen of West Virginia entitled to vote, he is eligible to be appointed a notary public, if he otherwise meets the qualifications for the office. OP. ATT'Y GEN. (W. VA.) July 31, 1973.

WISCONSIN

Persons appointed notaries public must be Wisconsin residents and at least 18 years of age. The secretary of state must satisfy himself that the applicant is of good moral character, has the equivalent of an eighth grade education and is familiar with the duties and responsibilities of a notary public. Any Wisconsin resident who is licensed to practice law in Wisconsin is entitled to a permanent commission as a notary public; his application to the secretary of state must include a certificate of good standing from the supreme court. See *Appointment*, WIS. STAT. ANN. § 137.01 (1), (2).

WYOMING

[WYO. STAT. ANN.]

§ 32-1. ° ° ° **qualifications;** ° ° °. The governor shall appoint and commission in each county upon petition of not less than five reputable freeholders of the county wherein such applicant resides, ° ° ° notaries public ° ° °. No person shall be eligible for appointment to the office of notary public unless he is a person of good moral character, an adult citizen of the United States, who shall be able to read and write the English language and an actual resident of the State of Wyoming, and of the county for which he is appointed; provided, that any federal clerk, secretary, or stenographer who is otherwise qualified under the provisions of this section shall be eligible for appointment to the office of notary public. ° ° °

Note: For the complete text of WYO. STAT. ANN. § 32-1, see *Appointment.*

CHAPTER 5: AUTHORITY AND DUTIES

Authority and duties

In the main, the authority and duties of notaries public are strictly controlled by the various state, district, territorial and other statutes. At common law, notaries had limited powers and functions, which were mainly commercial in nature. They related to dealings between mer--chants, were controlled by the law merchant, and were respected by the law of nations.

There are major differences between the notary public statutes of the various states, the District of Columbia, Puerto Rico, and the Virgin Islands. The statutes of each of these various jurisdictions concerning authority and duties of notaries are quoted below. In general, the statutes usually grant to a notary public power to administer oaths, certify affidavits, present and protest commercial paper (sometimes called negotiable instruments), take depositions, and take acknowledgments of instruments relating to the transfer or encumbrance of real property, and instruments relating to commerce and navigation. In addition, many jurisdictions by express statutory provision authorize a notary public to do all other acts justified by commercial usage and the law merchant.

The authority of a notary frequently corresponds with the authority of a justice of the peace. The right to issue subpoenas and compel the attendance of witnesses is occasionally granted.

Removal.

In a large number of states and other jurisdictions the statutes expressly specify grounds for the removal of a notary public, and designate the authority or officer who has the power to remove. Frequently those matters are stated in the same section that provides for the appointment of the notary. Concerning removal of notaries in specific states and other jurisdictions, see *Appointment: State and Other Statutes*, page 15.

STATE AND OTHER STATUTES

ALABAMA

[ALA. CODE]

Commercial Notaries

Tit. 40, § 5. Authority. Notaries public have authority:

(1) To administer oaths in all matters incident to the exercise of their office.

(2) To take the acknowledgment or proof of instruments of writing relating to commerce or navigation, and to certify the same, and all other of their official acts, under their seal of office.

(3) To demand acceptance and payment of bills of exchange, promissory notes, and all other writings which are governed by the commercial law as to days of grace, demand, and notice of non-payment; to protest the same for nonacceptance or nonpayment and to give notice thereof as required by law.

(4) To exercise such other powers as, according to commercial usage or the laws of this state, may belong to notaries public.

§ 11. Certificate of demand; notice and protest; evidence. The certificate of a notary public, under his hand and seal of office, or of any other authorized person, under his hand and seal, of the presentment for acceptance, or demand of payment, or protest for nonacceptance or nonpayment, of any instrument governed by the commercial law, or of service of notice of such presentment, demand, or protest, and the mode of giving the same, and the reputed place of residence of the party to whom the same was given, and the post office nearest thereto, is evidence of the facts contained in such certificate.

§ 12. Justices act as notaries. Where there is no notary public, or he is absent or incapable of acting, any justice of the peace may discharge the duties required of such notary by the laws of this state; for which he shall receive the fees allowed by law for such services; but when he acts as a notary public, he must set forth in his certificate, protest, or notice, that there is no notary public, or that the notary public is absent or incapable of acting, which certificate shall be evidence of such fact.

§ 13. Further authorities of notaries. Notaries public have the authority of justices of the peace to take and certify the acknowledgment and proof of conveyances, to administer oaths, and take and certify affidavits; and are either entitled therefor to the fee or fees allowed a justice of the peace, unless their seal of office is affixed, when they are entitled, in addition to a fee of twenty-five cents for affixing such seal, the seal to be affixed only at the request of the party for whom the service is rendered.

Notaries Ex Officio Justices of the Peace

§ 19. Jurisdiction; powers. A notary public having the jurisdiction of a justice of the peace, within the precinct or ward of his appointment, has all the jurisdiction, and must exercise all the powers of a justice of the peace, and is subject to all the liabilities to which a justice of the peace is subject; and all the remedies which may be pursued against a justice of the peace, and his sureties, or either of them, may be pursued against him, and his sureties, or either of them.

Notaries for State at Large

For authority and duties see *Appointment*, ALA. CODE tit. 40, § 21. Notaries for State at Large may perform all the acts and exercise all authority which is performed and exercised by notaries public under the general laws of the state.

ALASKA

[ALASKA STAT.]

§ 44.450.060. Duties. A notary public shall

(1) when requested, demand acceptance and payment of foreign and inland bills of exchange, or promissory notes, protest them for nonacceptance and nonpayment, and exercise the other powers and duties which by the law of nations and according to commercial usages, or by the laws of any other state, government, or country, may be performed by notaries;

(2) take the acknowledgment or proof of powers of attorney, mortgages, deeds, grants, transfers, and other instruments of writing, and give a certificate of the proof or acknowledgment endorsed on or attached to the instrument; the certificate shall be signed by the notary in his own handwriting;

(3) take depositions and affidavits, and administer oaths and affirmations, in all matters incident to the duties of the office, or to be used before a court, judge, officer, or board in the state; a deposition, affidavit, oath, or affirmation shall be signed by the notary in his own handwriting, and he shall endorse after his signature the date of expiration of his commission.

§ 44.50.070. Presence and identification required. A notary public shall require oaths and affirmations to be given in his presence and require persons appearing before him to produce identification.

§ 44.50.090. Protest of bill or note. The protest of a notary public, under his hand and official seal, of a bill of exchange or promissory note for nonacceptance or nonpayment is prima facie evidence of the facts recited in it, if the protest recites (1) the time and place of presentment; (2) the fact that presentment was made and the manner of presentment; (3) the cause or reason for protesting the bill; (4) the demand made and the answer given, or the fact that the drawee or acceptor could not be found.

§ 44.50.150. Copy of bond as evidence. A certified copy of the record of the official bond with all affidavits, acknowledgments, endorsements, and attachments may be read in evidence with the same effect as the original, without further proof.

§ 10.25.450. Directors, officers or members as notaries. No person authorized to take acknowledgments under the laws of this state is disqualified from taking acknowledgments of instruments to which a cooperative is a party because he is an officer, director or member of the cooperative.

ARIZONA

[ARIZ. REV. STAT. ANN.]

§ 33-1124. Mechanics' tools; professional tools and libraries. The following property of a debtor shall be exempt from execution, attachment or sale on ·any process issued from any court:

o   o   o

2. The notarial seal, records and office furniture of a notary public.

o   o   o

§ 41-312. Duties. Notaries public shall, when requested:

1. Demand acceptance and payment of foreign, domestic and inland bills of exchange or promissory notes, and protest them for nonacceptance and nonpayment, and exercise with respect thereto such other powers and duties as by the laws of other jurisdictions and according to commercial usages may be performed by notaries.

2. Take acknowledgments and give a certificate of them endorsed on or attached to the instrument.

3. Take depositions and administer oaths and affirmations.

4. Keep a record of all their official acts, and a record of the parties to, date and character of every instrument acknowledged or proved before them, date of acknowledgment and description of the property affected by the instrument, and furnish, when requested, a certified copy of any record in their office.

5. Provide and keep official seals upon which shall be engraved the words "Notary Public," the name of the county for which they are commissioned, and the name of the notary.

6. Authenticate with their official seals all official acts, and affix the date of the expiration of their commissions as such notaries on every certificate or acknowledgment signed and sealed by them.

§ 41-313. Protest or certificate of notary as evidence. A. The protest of the notary, under his hand and official seal, of a bill of exchange or promissory note for nonacceptance or nonpayment, stating the facts required by law to be stated in the protest, is prima facie evidence of the facts contained therein.

B. The certificate of a notary public under his hand and seal of office of official acts done by him as a notary shall be received in court as prima facie evidence of the facts therein contained.

§ 41-317. Competency of bank and corporation notaries. A. It is lawful for a notary public who is a stockholder, director, officer or employee of a corporation to take the acknowledgment or oath of any party to any written instrument executed to or by the corporation, or to administer an oath to any other stockholder, director, officer, employee or agent of the corporation, or to protest for non-acceptance or nonpayment of bills of exchange, drafts, checks, notes and other negotiable instruments which may be owned or held for collection by the corporation.

B. It is unlawful for any notary public to take the acknowledgment of an instrument executed by or to a corporation of which he is a stockholder, director, officer or employee, where the notary is a party to the instrument, either individually or as a representative of the corporation, or to protest any negotiable instrument owned or held for collection by the corporation where the notary is individually a party to the instrument.

ARKANSAS

[ARK. STAT. ANN.]

§ 12-1403. Power to administer oaths. Each notary public shall have power to administer oaths in all matters incident to or belonging to the exercise of his notarial office.

§ 12-1404. Acknowledgments and authentications. He may take the proof or the acknowledgment of all instruments of writing relating to commerce and navigation, receive and authenticate acknowledgments of deeds, letters of attorney, and other instruments of writing, make declarations and protests, and certify under his official seal the truth of all matters and things done by virtue of his office.

§ 12-1405. Power and authority coextensive with state. The powers and authority of notaries public shall be coextensive with the State for the purpose of swearing witnesses, taking affidavits and depositions, and taking acknowledgments of deeds and other instruments in writing and authorized by law to be acknowledged.

§ 12-1406. Statement of date of expiration of commission. All notaries public shall attach to any certificate of acknowledgment or jurat to an affidavit that he may make, a statement of the date on which his commission will expire. Provided, however, that no acknowledgment or other act of such notary shall be held invalid on account of the failure to comply with this act.

§ 12-1407. Penalty for failure to attach statement. If any notary public shall fail to attach such statement to any certificate of acknowledgment or other official act, he shall be guilty of a misdemeanor and be punished by a fine not to exceed five dollars [$5.00].

§ 12-1409. Instruments in writing so acknowledged admissible as evidence of facts stated. All declarations and protests made, and acknowledgments taken by notaries public, and certified copies of their records and official papers, shall be received as evidence of the facts therein stated in all the courts of this state.

§ 12-1411. Performance of duties for corporation. It shall be lawful for any notary public who is a stockholder, director, officer or employee of a bank or other corporation to take the acknowledgment of any party to any written instrument executed to or by such corporation, or to administer an oath to any other stockholder, director, officer, employee or agent of such corporation, or to protest for nonacceptance or nonpayment bills of exchange, drafts, checks, notes and other negotiable instruments which may be owned or held for collection by such corporation: Provided, it shall be unlawful for any notary public to take the acknowledgment of an instrument executed by or to a bank or other corporation of which he is a stockholder, director, officer, or employee, where such notary is a party to such instrument, either individually or as a representative of such corporation, or to protest any negotiable instrument owned or held for collection by such corporation, where such notary is individually a party to such instrument.

§ 28-205. Officials before whom made in state. An affidavit may be made in this State before a judge of the court, justice of the peace, notary public, clerk of a court, or mayor of a city or incorporated town.

CALIFORNIA

[CAL. GOV'T CODE]

§ 8205. Duties. It is the duty of a notary public:

(a) When requested, to demand acceptance and payment of foreign and inland bills of exchange, or promissory notes, to protest them for nonacceptance and nonpayment, and to exercise such other powers and duties as by the law of nations and according to commercial usages, or by the laws of any other state, government, or country, may be performed by notaries.

(b) To take the acknowledgment or proof of powers of attorney, mortgages, deeds, grants, transfers, and other instruments of writing executed by any person, and to give a certificate of such proof or acknowledgment, endorsed on or attached to the instrument. Such certificate shall be signed by him in his own handwriting.

(c) To take depositions and affidavits, and administer oaths and affirmations, in all matters incident to the duties of the office, or to be used before any court, judge, officer, or board in this state.

Any deposition, affidavit, oath or affirmation shall be signed by him in his own handwriting.

§ 8208. **Protest of bill or note for nonacceptance or nonpayment.** The protest of a notary public, under his hand and official seal, of a bill of exchange or promissory note for nonacceptance or nonpayment, specifying:

(a) The time and place of presentment.

(b) The fact that presentment was made and the manner thereof.

(c) The cause or reason for protesting the bill.

(d) The demand made and the answer given, if any, or the fact that the drawee or acceptor could not be found, is prima facie evidence of the facts recited therein.

§ 8213.5 **Change in location or address; notice.** A notary public shall notify the Secretary of State promptly in writing as to any change in the location or address of his principal place of business.

COLORADO

[COLO. REV. STAT. ANN.]

§ 12-55-102. **Powers—official acts—outside of county.** (1) A notary public, at any place within this state, has authority to take and authenticate any acknowledgment to any instrument, to administer any oath or affirmation, to take any deposition, to make any declaration or protest, and to do any other act usually done by a notary public, and to certify the truth of any of his official acts under his official seal.

(2) All acknowledgments heretofore taken and all official acts performed by a notary public within the state of Colorado but outside of the county within which his official bond is filed, are hereby confirmed and made valid, if otherwise correct.

CONNECTICUT

[CONN. GEN. STAT. ANN.]

§ 3-94. **Change of name of notary.** Whenever any notary public has his name changed by reason of marriage or by reason of a change of name legally adjudicated, the secretary shall change the name of such person on his records upon receipt of such proof of such change of name as said secretary deems sufficient and upon the payment of a fee of five dollars. Any clerk who is required to make record of the certificate and oath of a notary under section 3-92 shall record the change of name of such notary upon payment by such notary to such clerk of a fee of one dollar for such record.

§ 51-171a. **Certification to authority of justices of the peace, notaries public and commissioners of the superior court in Fairfield county.** The clerk of the superior court at Bridgeport shall, on the request of any justice of the peace, notary public or commissioner of the superior court in Fairfield county and on the receipt of a fee of one dollar, furnish to the clerk of the superior court at Stamford a duplicate of the certificate of qualification or appointment of such justice of the peace, notary public or commissioner of the superior court and said clerk at Stamford may thereafter certify to the authority of such justice of the peace, notary public or commissioner of the superior court.

Editorial comment

The Connecticut statutes are vague concerning the enumeration of a notary's authority and duties. In various statutes, notaries are given authority to, among other things, administer oaths, take acknowledgments of instruments, and take depositions. CONN. GEN. STAT. ANN. §§ 1-24, 1-29, 52-148.

DELAWARE

[DEL. CODE ANN.]

Tit. 29, § 4307. Seal and powers. The notary shall have a seal, and shall exercise the powers and perform the duties belonging to that office. He shall also have power to take the acknowledgment of deeds and other instruments.'

§ 4310. Duties and fees of notaries public with respect to conveyances of land in Sussex County. Notaries public in this State, before whom any deed conveying land situated in Sussex County is acknowledged, shall make a certificate on blanks to be furnished by the Board of Assessment of Sussex County, showing the transfer, and return the same to the Board of Assessment in the same month in which the transfer was made.

For every deed reported under the provisions of this section the notary public shall be entitled to a fee of 25 cents to be paid by the Levy Court of Sussex County.

Editorial comment

The authority and duties of certain state officers appointed as notaries public are limited to acts in connection with work performed in carrying out the duties of those offices. See *Appointment*, DEL. CODE ANN. tit. 29, § 4302. The authority and duties of notaries public appointed for certain service organizations are similarly limited to acts concerning certain documents and papers. See *Appointment*, DEL. CODE ANN. tit. 29, § 4304.

DISTRICT OF COLUMBIA

[D.C. CODE ENCYCL. ANN.]

§ 1-508. Foreign bills of exchange—Protest. Notaries public shall have authority to demand acceptance and payment of foreign bills of exchange and to protest the same for nonacceptance and nonpayment, and to exercise such other powers and duties as by the law of nations and according to commercial usages notaries public may do.

§ 1-509. **Inland bills and notes—Protest—Penalty.** Notaries public may also demand acceptance of inland bills of exchange and payment thereof, and of promissory notes and checks, and may protest the same for nonacceptance or nonpayment, as the case may require. And on the original protest thereof he shall state the presentment by him of the same for acceptance or payment, as the case may be, and the nonacceptance or nonpayment thereof, and the service of notice thereof on any of the parties to the same, and the mode of giving such notice, and the reputed place of business or residence of the party to whom the same was given; and such protest shall be prima facie evidence of the facts therein stated. And any notary public failing to comply herewith shall pay a fine of ten dollars to the District of Columbia, to be collected in the Superior Court of the District of Columbia as are other fines and penalties.

§ 1-510. **Other acts for use and effect beyond District.** Notaries public may also perform such other acts, for use and effect beyond the jurisdiction of the District, as according to the law of any state or territory of the United States or any foreign government in amity with the United States may be performed by notaries public.

§ 1-511. **Empowered to certify certain instruments, to administer oaths and affirmations—Affidavits.** Each notary public shall have power to take and to certify the acknowledgment or proof of powers of attorney, mortgages, deeds, and other instruments of writing, the acknowledgment of any conveyance or other instrument of writing executed by any married woman, to take depositions and to administer oaths and affirmations and also to take affidavits to be used before any court, judge, or officer within the District.

§ 1-513. **Copy of record as evidence.** The certificate of a notary public, under his hand and seal of office, drawn from his record, stating the protest and the facts therein recorded, shall be evidence of the facts in like manner as the original protest.

§ 20-110. **Authority of notaries public employed by banks or trust company.** It shall be lawful for any notary public who is a stockholder, director, officer, or employee of a bank, trust company, or other corporation to take the acknowledgment of any party to any written instrument executed to or by such corporation, or to administer an oath to any other stockholder, director, officer, employee, or agent of such corporation, or to protest for nonacceptance or nonpayment drafts, checks, notes, acceptances, or other negotiable instruments which may be owned or held for collection by such corporation: *Provided,* That it shall be unlawful for any notary public to take the acknowledgment of an instrument executed by or to a bank or corporation of which he is a stockholder, director, officer, or employee, where such notary is a party to such instrument, either individually or as a representative of such corporation, or to protest any negotiable instrument owned or held for collection by such corporation, where such notary is individually a party to such instrument: *Provided, further,* That it shall be unlawful for any notary public to take the oath of an officer or director of any bank or trust company of which he is an officer, or to take an oath of any person verifying a report of such bank or trust company to the Comptroller of the Currency.

Concerning the representation of clients before government departments and the administration of certain acknowledgments, see also *Appointment,* D.C. CODE ENCYCL. ANN. § 1-501.

FLORIDA

[FLA. STAT. ANN.]

§ 117.03. **May administer oaths.** In all cases in which it may be necessary to the due and legal execution of any writing or document whatever to be attested, protested, or published under the seal of his office, any notary public may administer an oath and make certificate thereof; and any person making a false oath before a notary public shall be guilty of perjury and be subject to the penalties, forfeitures, and disabilities that are prescribed by law in cases of willful and corrupt perjury.

§ 117.04. **May solemnize marriages and take acknowledgments.** Notaries public are authorized to solemnize the rites of matrimony and to take renunciation and relinquishment of dower and the acknowledgments of deeds and other instruments of writing for record, as fully as other officers of this state are; and for so doing they shall be allowed the same fees as allowed by law to other officers for like services.

Marriages

§ 741.07. **Persons authorized to solemnize matrimony.** All regularly ordained ministers of the gospel or elders in communion with some church, and all judicial officers and notaries public of this state may solemnize the rights of matrimonial contract, under the regulations prescribed by law. ° ° °

§ 741.08. **Marriage not to be solemnized without a license.** Before any of the persons named in § 741.07 shall solemnize any marriage, he shall require of the parties a marriage license issued according to the requirements of [law] and within ten days after solemnizing the marriage he shall make a certificate thereof on the license, and shall transmit the same to the office of the county court judge from which it issued.

GEORGIA

[GA. CODE ANN.]

§ 9-605. Authority to bind clients; administration of oaths. ° ° °
[A]ttorneys, who are otherwise authorized by law to take affidavits
and administer oaths, shall not be disqualified to take affidavits required of their clients in any matter or proceeding of any nature
whatsoever.

§ 16-429. Notaries not disqualified. No notary public or other
public officer shall be disqualified from taking the acknowledgment of
or witnessing any instrument, in writing, in which a State chartered
association or a Federal savings and loan association is interested,
by reason of his holding an office in or being a member of, or
being pecuniarily interested in or employed by such associations
so interested, and any such acknowledgments, or attestations heretofore taken are hereby validated.

§ 38-625. Notarial acts; proof by certificate. All notarial acts
of notaries public in relation to bills of exchange, drafts, and
promissory notes, required to be done by law, may be proved by
the certificate of such notary under his hand and seal: Provided,
such certificate is filed in the court at its first term, and permitted
there to remain until the trial.

**§ 71-106. Where notarial acts may be exercised. Office, how
vacated.** Notarial acts may be exercised in any county in the State
of Georgia. Removal from the State or conviction of any crime
involving moral turpitude shall vacate the office.

§ 71-108. Authority. Notaries public shall have authority:

1. To take the acknowledgments of all writings relating to commerce or navigation and to witness such deeds and papers as
they are permitted to by law.

2. To demand acceptance and payment of all commercial paper
and to note and protest the same for nonacceptance or nonpayment.

3. To certify to all official acts when required.

4. To administer oaths in all matters incidental to their duties
as commercial officers, and all other oaths which are not by law
required to be administered by a particular officer.

5. To exercise all other powers incumbent upon them by commercial usage or the laws of this State.

§ 71-109. Issuance of attachments and garnishments. It shall
not be lawful for notaries public to issue attachments or garnishments or to subscribe affidavits or approve bonds for the purpose
of issuing attachments or garnishments.

**§ 71-112. Authority of officers and employees of banks or other
corporations to act as notaries with respect to matters concerning**

their firms; protesting negotiable paper; exceptions. It shall be lawful for any notary public who is stockholder, director, officer or employee of a bank or other corporation to take the acknowledgment of any party to any written instrument executed to or by such corporation. Any such notary public may act and sign as official witness to the execution by any party of any written instrument executed to or by such bank or other corporation. Any such notary public may administer an oath to any other stockholder, director, officer, employee or agent of such bank or other corporation, or may protest for nonacceptance or nonpayment bills of exchange, drafts, checks, notes and other negotiable instruments which may be owned or held for collection by such bank or other corporation: Provided, that it shall be unlawful for any notary public to act and sign as official witness to, or take the acknowledgment of, an instrument executed by or to a bank or other corporation of which he is a stockholder, director, officer or employee where such notary would be witnessing or acknowledging his own signature as it appears on the instrument either in his capacity as an individual or in his representative capacity with the bank or other corporation, or to protest any negotiable instrument owned or held for collection by such bank or other corporation where such notary is individually a party to such instrument.

HAWAII

[HAWAII REV. STAT.]

§ 46-29. Certain notarial powers conferred upon county officers. Wherever by law any affidavit under oath or any statement or other document to be acknowledged is required to be filed with the chief of police, treasurer, director of finance, clerk, board of supervisors or city council of any county as a condition to the granting of any license or the performance of any act by any person, or by any county officer, the chief of police, treasurer, director of finance, or clerk, their deputy or deputies, or the county, shall take the oath or acknowledgment, free of charge, keeping records thereof as required by law of notaries public; provided, that nothing herein shall prevent any person desiring so to do from making the oath or acknowledgment before any duly authorized notary public, subject to his legal fees therefor.

§ 403-51. Notary connected with bank; authority to act. It shall be lawful for any notary public, although an officer, employee, shareholder, or director of a bank, to take the acknowledgment of any party to any written instrument executed to or by the bank, or to administer an oath to any shareholder, director, officer, employee, or agent of the bank, or to protest for nonacceptance or nonpayment of bills of exchange, drafts, checks, notes, and other negotiable instruments which may be owned or held for collection by the bank; provided, it shall be unlawful for any notary public to take the acknowledgment of any party to an instrument, or to protest any negotiable instrument, where the notary is individually a party to the instrument.

§ 407-36. **Notary public connected with association; authority to act.** It shall be lawful for any notary public, although an officer or employee of a building and loan association or a shareholder, member, or director thereof, to take the acknowledgment of any party to any written instrument executed to or by the association, or to administer an oath to any shareholder, member, director, officer, employee, or agent of the association, or to protest for nonacceptance or nonpayment of bills of exchange, drafts, checks, notes, and other negotiable instruments which may be owned or held for collection by the association; and in general, to do and perform any act pertaining to the powers and duties of a notary public; provided, that it shall be unlawful for the notary public to take the oath or acknowledgment of any party an instrument, or to protest any negotiable instrument, where the notary is individually a party to the instrument.

§ 456-10. **Duties, by mercantile usage.** It shall be a notary public's duty, when requested, to enter on record all losses or damages sustained or apprehended, by sea or land, and also all averages, and such other matters as, by mercantile usage, appertain to his office, and cause protest thereof to be made duly and formally.

§ 456-11. **Protests; negotiable paper.** All facts, extracts from documents, and circumstances, so noted, shall be signed and sworn to by all the persons appearing to protest. The notary public shall note, extend, and record the protest so made; and shall grant authenticated copies thereof, under his signature and notarial seal, to those who request and pay for the same. He shall also, in behalf of any person interested, present any bill of exchange, or other negotiable paper, for acceptance or payment to any party on whom the same is drawn or who may be liable therefor; and notify all indorsers or other parties to such bill or paper. He may, in general, do all the acts to be done by notaries public by the usages of merchants, or which are authorized by the laws of the State.

§ 456-12. **Protest, evidence of what.** The protest of any foreign or inland bill of exchange, or promissory note or order, duly certified by any notary public, under his hand or official seal, shall be legal evidence of the facts stated in the protest, as to the same, and also as to the notice given to the drawer or indorser in any court of law.

§ 456-13. **May administer oath.** Every notary public may administer oaths in all cases in which oaths are by law authorized or required to be taken or administered, or in which the administering of an oath may be proper. All oaths administered before June 23, 1888, by notaries public are declared valid and binding.

§ 456-14. **Notary connected with a corporation or trust company; authority to act.** It shall be lawful for any notary public, although an officer, employee, shareholder, or director of a corporation or trust company to take the acknowledgment of any party to any written instrument executed to or by the corporation or trust company, or to administer an oath to any shareholder, director, officer, employee, or agent of the corporation or trust company, or to protest for nonacceptance or nonpayment of bills of exchange, drafts, checks, notes, and other negotiable instruments which may be owned or held for collection by the corporation or trust company; provided, it shall be unlawful for any notary public to take the acknowledgment of any party to an instrument, or to protest any negotiable instrument, where the notary is individually a party to the instrument.

IDAHO

[IDAHO CODE]

§ 51-104. **General duties.** It is the duty of a notary public:

1. When requested, to demand acceptance and payment of foreign, domestic and inland bills of exchange, or promissory notes, and protest the same for nonacceptance and nonpayment, and to exercise such other powers and duties as by the law of nations and according to commercial usages, or by the laws of any other state, territory, government or country, may be performed by notaries.

2. To take the acknowledgment or proof of powers of attorney, mortgages, deeds, grants, transfers, and other instruments of writing executed by any person, and to give a certificate of such proof or acknowledgment indorsed on, or attached to, the instrument.

3. To take depositions and affidavits, and to administer oaths and affirmations, in all matters incident to the duties of the office, or to be used before any court, judge, officer, or board in this state.

4. To keep a record of all official acts done by him under the first subdivision of this section.

5. When requested, and upon payment of his fees therefor, to make and give a certified copy of any record in his office.

6. To provide and keep an official seal, upon which must be engraved his name, the words "Notary Public" and "State of Idaho."

7. To authenticate with his official seal all official acts.

8. To affix to his signature his official title and his place of residence.

§ 51-105. Protest as evidence of facts. The protest of a notary, under his hand and official seal, of a bill of exchange or promissory note, for nonacceptance or nonpayment, stating the presentment for acceptance or payment, and the nonacceptance or nonpayment thereof, the service of the notice on any or all of the parties to such bill of exchange or promissory note, and specifying the mode of giving such notice and the reputed place of residence of the party to such bill of exchange or promissory note, and of the party to whom the same was given, and the post-office nearest thereto, is prima facie evidence of the facts contained therein.

§ 51-112. Competency of real estate agent or broker, bank and corporation notaries. A person authorized by law to perform any duty, act or power, which notaries public may perform, is not disqualified therefrom by reason of being the real estate agent or broker of any person or corporation involved, or by reason of being a stockholder, director, officer, agent or employee of a bank or other corporation except only that such person shall not take the acknowledgment or proof of execution of an instrument where it appears therefrom that such person individually is a party to such instrument, or either signed the name, or attested the signature, of such bank or other corporation thereto, or acknowledging (acknowledged) the execution thereof by such bank or other corporation.

ILLINOIS

[ILL. ANN. STAT.—(Smith-Hurd)]

Ch. 99, § 4a. Failure to transmit money—Action for damages. If a Notary Public accepts or receives any money, from any one to whom he has administered an oath or taken an acknowledgment, for the purpose of transmitting or forwarding such money to another and wilfully fails to transmit or forward such money promptly, he is personally liable for any loss sustained because of such failure. The person or persons damaged by such failure may bring an action to recover damages, together with interest and reasonable attorney fees, against such Notary Public or his bondsmen.

§ 10. Notary's authority. A notary public duly qualified shall have authority, while he resides in the same county in which he was appointed, to execute the duties of his office throughout the state.

§ 14. Acknowledgment by officer or employee of corporation. It shall not be an objection to the validity of any act of a notary public done after the taking effect of this act, that such notary public is an officer, director, stockholder or employee of a corporation which is a party to the instrument acknowledged by such corporation or by any person on its behalf, or acknowledged by any other party to such instrument, or by any person signing, witnessing or acknowledging the execution of such instrument in any capacity, provided such notary public did not sign such instrument on behalf of the corporation.

INDIANA

[IND. CODE]

§ 33-16-1-1. Jurisdiction. The jurisdiction of any notary public duly qualified in this state shall be coextensive with the limits of the state; but no notary shall be compelled to act out of the limits of the county in which he resides.

§ 33-16-2-5. Powers. Every notary shall have power:

First. To do all such acts which, by common law and the custom of merchants, they are authorized to do.

Second. To take and certify all acknowledgments of deeds or other instruments of writing required or authorized by law to be acknowledged.

Third. To administer oaths generally, and to take and certify affidavits and depositions.

§ 33-16-2-7. Who can not be a notary public. No person, being an officer in any bank, corporation, or association possessed of any banking powers, shall act as a notary public in the business of such bank, corporation or association. The aforesaid prohibition shall not apply to employees of any such bank, corporation or association, and a person who is a shareholder or member of a building and loan association or savings and loan association may act as a notary public in the business of such association. No person holding any lucrative office or appointment under the United States or under this state, and prohibited by the Constitution of this state from holding more than one [1] such lucrative office, shall serve as a notary public, and his acceptance of any such office shall vacate his appointment as such notary; but this provision shall not apply to any person holding any lucrative office or appointment under any civil or school city or town of this state. No person, being a public official, or a deputy or appointee acting for or serving under the same, shall make any charge for services as a notary public in connection with any official business of such office, or of any other office in the governmental unit in which such persons are serving, unless such charges are specifically authorized by some statute other than the statute fixing generally the fees and charges of notaries public.

§ 33-16-3-1. Certificate—Date of commission. It shall be the duty of every notary public holding a commission as such from the state of Indiana, at the time of signing any certificate of acknowledgment of a deed, mortgage or other instrument, or any jurat or other official document, to append to such certificate a true statement of the date of the expiration of his commission as such notary public.

Note: For the penalty for failing or omitting to make the statement as required by this section, see *Offenses.* IND. CODE § 33-16-3-2.

§ 33-16-5-1.   Federal land bank association manager serving.   The manager of any federal land bank association located within the state of Indiana even though he be an officer of said association may, and is hereby authorized to become and act as a notary public in the business of such association to take acknowledgments of deeds and real estate mortgages and to take and certify affidavits.

§ 33-16-6-1.   Acknowledgments of sales by associations of cemetery lots.   Any notary public who may be a stockholder or officer of any cemetery association in which no officer or stockholder in such association can be a beneficiary from the sale of lots or otherwise, as provided by the constitution of such association, may and is hereby authorized to take acknowledgments of sales of such lots.

IOWA

[IOWA CODE ANN.]

§ 77.7.   Powers within state.   Each notary is invested, within the state of Iowa, with the powers and shall perform the duties which pertain to that office by the custom and law of merchants.

§ 77.9.   Oaths and protest by interested notary.   Any notary public, who is at the same time an officer, director, or stockholder of a corporation, is also hereby invested with the power to administer oaths to any officer, director, or stockholder of such corporation in any matter wherein said corporation is interested, and is hereby authorized to protest for nonacceptance or nonpayment, bills of exchange, drafts, checks, notes, and other negotiable or nonnegotiable instruments which may be owned or held for collection by such corporation, as fully and effectually as if he were not an officer, director, or stockholder of such corporation.

§ 77.10.   Corporation employee as notary.   Any employee of a corporation who is a notary public and who is not otherwise financially interested in the subject matter of said instrument, is hereby authorized to take acknowledgments of any person on an instrument running to such corporation, regardless of the title or position that said notary shall hold as an employee of such corporation.

§ 77.12.   Acting under maiden name.   When a female has, prior or subsequent to the adoption of this Code, been commissioned a notary public, and has, after the issuance of said commission and prior to the expiration thereof, contracted a marriage, the official acts of such notary public after said marriage and prior to the expiration of said commission shall not be deemed illegal or insufficient because, after said marriage, she performed said official acts under the name in which said commission was issued.

KANSAS

[KAN. STAT. ANN.]

§ 53-107. Powers and duties; exercise of notarial acts. State and local notaries public shall have authority to take the proof and acknowledgement of deeds and other instruments of writing required to be proved or acknowledged, and to administer oaths, including the acknowledgment of any such instrument when executed to or by any corporation, or the administering of oaths to officers, agents or employees of corporations in which any such notary public may be interested as a stockholder, officer, or employee: *Provided,* That no such notary public shall take an acknowledgment or administer an oath when acting himself in behalf of any such corporation; to demand acceptance or payment of foreign or inland bills of exchange and of promissory notes, and protest the same for nonacceptance or nonpayment, as the case may require; and to exercise such other powers and duties as by the law of nations and commercial usage may be performed by notaries public. Local notaries public appointed and commissioned on and after July 1, 1963, who have complied with other requirements of this act may exercise notarial acts within the county for which appointed and in any adjoining county of this state. State notaries public who have complied with other requirements of this act may exercise notarial acts anywhere within this state.

§ 53-109. Authcrity of notary connected with corporation. It shall be lawful for any notary public who is a stockholder, director, officer, or employee of a bank or other corporation to take the acknowledgment of any party to any written instrument executed to or by such corporation, or to administer an oath to any other stockholder, director, officer, employee, or agent of such corporation, or to protest for nonacceptance, or nonpayment bills of exchange, drafts, checks, notes, and other negotiable instruments which may be owned or held for collection by such corporation: *Provided,* It shall be unlawful for any notary public to take the acknowledgment of an instrument by or to a bank or other corporation of which he is a stockholder, director, officer or employee, where such notary is a party to such instrument either individually or as a representative of such corporation, or to protest any negotiable instrument owned or held for collection by such corporation, where such notary is individually a party to such instrument.

§ 53-113. Limitation of actions against notary and sureties. No suit shall be instituted against any such notary or his securities more than three years after the cause of action accrues.

KENTUCKY

[KY. REV. STAT. ANN.]

§ 62.020. Oath, who may administer official. The official oath of any officer may be administered by any judge, notary public, clerk of a court, or justice of the peace, within his district or county.

§ 289.241. [Savings and loan] [a]ssociation interest does not disqualify officer taking acknowledgment. No public officer qualified to take acknowledgments or proofs of written instruments shall be disqualified from taking the acknowledgment or proof of any instrument in writing in which an [savings and loan] association is interested by reason of his membership in or employment by an association so interested, and any such acknowledgment or proofs heretofore taken are valid.

§ 423.020. Notary may act in any county; validity of instruments notarized; certification of notary's authority. (1) A notary public may exercise all the functions of his office in any county of the state, by filing in the county clerk's office in such county his written signature and a certificate of the county clerk of the county for which he was appointed, setting forth the fact of his appointment and qualification as a notary public, and paying a fee of one dollar to the county clerk.

(2) When this has been done the instrument or instruments so proved or acknowledged and certified by the notary, whether prior or subsequent to this date, shall be entitled to be read as evidence or to be recorded in any county the same as if it were certified by a county clerk.

(3) The county clerk of a county in whose office any notary public has so filed his signature and certificate shall, when requested, subjoin to any certificate of proof or acknowledgment signed by the notary a certificate under his hand and seal, stating that such notary public has filed a certificate of his appointment and qualifications with his written signature in his office, and was at the time of taking such proof or acknowledgment duly authorized to take the same; that he is well acquainted with the hand-writing of the notary public and believes that the signature to such proof or acknowledgment is genuine.

Editorial comment

A copy of a protest made by a notary public, certified by the notary public under his notarial seal, is prima facie evidence in all the court of the state. See *Records,* KY. REV. STAT. ANN. § 423.030.

§ 423.040. Notice of dishonor; to whom sent. Notaries public shall upon protesting any instrument mentioned in KRS 423.030 give notice of the dishonor to such parties thereto as are required by law to be notified to fix their liability on such paper. When the residence of a party is unknown to the notary public, he shall send the notices to the holders of the paper, shall state in his protest the names of the parties to whom he gave notice, and the time and manner of giving the same and such statement in such protest shall be prima facie evidence that notices were given as therein stated.

LOUISIANA

General Provisions

[LA. REV. STAT.]

§ 35:2. **General powers.** Notaries public have power, within their several parishes, to make inventories, appraisements, and partitions; to receive wills, make protests, matrimonial contracts, conveyances, and generally, all contracts and instruments of writing; to hold family meetings and meetings of creditors; to receive acknowledgments of instruments under private signature; to affix the seals upon the effects of deceased persons, and to raise the same. All acts executed by them, in conformity with the provisions of article two thousand two hundred and thirty-four of the Civil Code,* shall be authentic acts.

    * For LA. CIV. CODE ANN. art. 2234, see below.

§ 35:3. **Oaths and acknowledgments.** Oaths and acknowledgments, in all cases, may be taken or made by or before any notary public duly appointed and qualified in this state.

§ 35:4. **Notaries connected with banks and other corporations; powers.** It is lawful for any notary public who is a stockholder, director, officer, or employe of a bank or other corporation to take the acknowledgment of any party to any written instrument executed to or by such corporation, or to administer an oath to any other stockholder, director, officer, employe, or agent of such corporation, or to protest for non-acceptance or nonpayment bills of exchange, drafts, checks, notes, and other negotiable instruments which may be owned or held for collection by such corporation. It is unlawful for any notary public to take the acknowledgment of an instrument by or to a bank or other corporation of which he is a stockholder, director, officer, or employe, where the notary is a party to such instrument, either individually or as a representative of such corporation, or to protest any negotiable instrument owned or held for collection by the corporation, where the notary is individually a party to the instrument.

§ 35:10. **Place of executing notarial acts.** All notarial acts shall be made and executed in the office of the notary, unless the illness of the party, or some other sufficient cause, shall prevent him from attending in such office.

§ 35:11. Marital status of parties to be given. Whenever notaries pass any acts they shall give the marital status of all parties to the act, viz:

If either or any party or parties are men, they shall be described as single, married, or widower. If married or widower the christian and family name of wife shall be given. If either or any party or parties are women, they shall be described as single, married or widow. If married or widow, their christian and family name shall be given, adding that she is the wife of or widow of . . . . the husband's name.

Concerning the fine for the violation of § 35:11, see *Offenses*, LA. REV. STAT. § 35:13.

§ 35.12. Christian names to be given in full, together with parties' permanent mailing addresses. Notaries shall insert in their acts the Christian names of the parties in full and not their initial letters alone, together with the permanent mailing addresses of the parties, and shall print or type the full names of the witnesses and of themselves under their respective signatures.

Concerning the fine, for the violation of § 35:12, see *Offenses*, LA. REV. STAT. § 35:13.

§ 35:131. Grant of leave of absence; designation of substitute notary. The governor may grant leave of absence to notaries public for a period not exceeding eight months, to date from the day of the permission granted by the governor.

Notaries public thus permitted to absent themselves shall be required to name and designate another notary public to represent them during their absence.

§ 35:132. Notaries in military service, leave of absence. A leave of absence may be granted by the governor to any notary public upon his application to the governor in writing certifying that he is a member of the Army, Navy, Marine Corps or any other branch of the military service of the United States, or of the State of Louisiana, and stating the expiration date of his bond; if the notary so desires, he may name and designate another notary to represent him during his absence, but the representation shall cease upon the expiration of the absent notary's bond.

§ 35:133. Notaries in military service, period of leave. The period of the leaves of absence granted in accordance with R.S. 35:132 shall date from the day of the permission granted by the governor and shall terminate sixty days after the date of discharge of the notary from the military service of the United States or the State of Louisiana.

§ 35:134. Expiration of bond during military service; renewal. When the notarial bond of a notary public expires during his term of military service, the notary shall have sixty days from the date of his discharge from military service in which to apply for a new bond.

§ 37:212. "Practice of law" defined. The practice of law is defined as follows:

* * *

Nothing in this Section prohibits any person from attending to and caring for his own business, claims, or demands; nor from preparing abstracts of title, or certifying, guaranteeing, or insuring titles to property, movable or immovable, or an interest therein, or a privilege and encumbrance thereon; or from performing, as a notary public, any act necessary or incidental to the exercise of the powers and functions of the office of notary public.

[LA. CIV. CODE ANN.—West]

Art. 2234. Authentic act, definition. The authentic act, as relates to contracts, is that which has been executed before a notary public or other officer authorized to execute such functions, in presence of two witnesses, aged at least fourteen years, or of three witnesses, if a party be blind. If a party does not know how to sign, the notary must cause him to affix his mark to the instrument.

All proces verbal of sales of succession property, signed by the sheriff or other person making the same, by the purchaser and two witnesses, are authentic acts.

Note: See LA. REV. STAT. § 35:2 above.

Orleans Parish

Every notary in and for the parish of Orleans must keep his office in a building covered with tile, slates or terrace, and keep his office open for the ready examination of his records every day from 10:00 a.m. to 3:00 p.m., Sundays and holidays excepted. See *Offenses*, LA. REV. STAT. § 35:257, wherein the penalty for the violation of this requirement is stated.

[LA. REV. STAT.]

§ 35:281. Act evidencing transfer of real property; filing with board of assessors. Whenever an act of sale or any other act evidencing a transfer of real property situated in the Parish of Orleans is passed before a notary public, it shall be the duty of the notary to file a copy of any such act with the board of assessors for the Parish of Orleans within fifteen days from the date of sale or transfer.

Concerning the penalty for the violation of §§ 35:281, 35:282, see *Offenses*, LA. REV. STAT. § 35:284.

§ 35:282. Duplicate copy of sketch, blueprint, or survey. Whenever there is annexed to any act of sale or other act of transfer of real estate any sketch, blue print, or survey which forms part of the act of sale or transfer, the notary public shall have attached to the copy of such act, a duplicate copy of the sketch, blue print, or survey.

Concerning the penalty for the violation of §§ 35:281, 35:282, see *Offenses*, LA. REV. STAT. § 35:284.

§ 35:283.   Obligations under existing laws not affected.   Nothing contained in R.S. 35:281 and R.S. 35:282 shall be construed as relieving notaries public from the obligations imposed upon them to file copies of their acts with other officials or in other offices.

§ 35:285.   Deposit of original acts when property affected situated outside New Orleans.   Notaries public within the Parish of Orleans shall deposit in the office of the clerk and recorder of the parish in which the property is situated, whenever the property affected is situated in this state outside of the Parish of Orleans, within fifteen days after the same shall have been passed, the original of all acts of sale, exchange, donation and mortgage of immovable property, passed before them, together with all resolutions, powers of attorney and other documents annexed to or made part of the acts, and in the order of their respective dates, first making a careful record of the acts in record books to be kept for that purpose.

Concerning the penalty for the violation of the foregoing section, see *Offenses*, LA. REV. STAT. § 35:286.

§ 35:287.   Deputies.   Every notary public in the Parish of Orleans may appoint one or more deputies to assist him in the making of protests and delivery of notices of protests of bills of exchange and promissory notes. Each notary shall be personally responsible for the acts of each deputy employed by him. Each deputy shall take an oath faithfully to perform his duties as such. The certificate of notice of protest shall state by whom made or served.

§ 35:323.   Central office, preservation of notarial records; permanent volumes.   A.   The [Custodian of Notarial Records in and for the Parish of Orleans (custodian)] shall maintain a central office in the city of New Orleans in the Civil District Court Building in quarters presently provided by the city of New Orleans or other quarters in said courthouse to be provided in the city of New Orleans. The custodian shall demand, take possession of, collect, keep and preserve in this office the notarial records of notaries in the parish of Orleans who have ceased to be such, either by death, removal or otherwise, and shall hereafter classify these records according to their date, serial number, and in such a manner as will most facilitate access to them.

B.   (1)   Every authentic act except chattel mortgages and acts relating to real property outside of Orleans Parish, passed before a notary public in Orleans Parish, and also every act, contract and instrument except money judgments and chattel mortgages filed for record in the office of either the recorder of mortgages or the register of conveyances for the parish of Orleans shall, as a condition precedent to such filing in the office of the recorder of mortgages or the register of conveyances for the parish of Orleans be first filed in the office of the custodian of notarial records for the parish of Orleans. The custodian shall endorse on each act, contract or instrument filed in his office, the date of such filing, a serial number, and shall attach to such act, contract or instrument a certificate of its filing, date and serial number. Such act, contract or instrument so endorsed, shall thereafter be filed for record, if otherwise required by law, with the recorder of mortgages or the register of conveyances for the parish of Orleans, or both, and shall be registered and/or recorded with the serial number furnished by the custodian, provided, however, that nothing herein be deemed to impose upon the custodian any obligation to file any act, contract or instrument with either the recorder of mortgages or the register of conveyances. The recorder of mortgages and register of conveyances for the parish of Orleans shall thereafter return said act, contract or instrument to the custodian, showing the date of filing and time, by the recorder of mortgages and the book and folio number, and the custodian shall thereupon have permanent custody of the said act, contract or instrument, which shall then be filed in his office according to the serial number endorsed thereon by the custodian. The recorder of mortgages and register of conveyances for the parish of Orleans shall endorse upon the certificate issued by the custodian for each act, contract or instrument the date and time, by the recorder of mortgages, book and folio number of its recordation or registry, and shall furnish such certificate to the notary public or other person who caused the same to be filed with the custodian.

(2) It shall be the duty of all notaries public filing acts for registration and/or recordation pursuant hereto to deposit with the custodian all certificates, tax researches, surveys and documents pertaining to any act passed before them and this deposit must be made within sixty days of the date of registration and/or recordation. It shall be the duty of the custodian to file in permanent form, according to serial number, all acts, contracts and instruments filed with him and all certificates, tax researches and documents furnished him pertaining to all such acts.

C. The custodian of notarial records shall charge the sum of three dollars for each act, contract or other instrument thus filed and deposited in his office. For the purpose of these charges, a sale and resale, and accompanying release and releases of mortgages, shall be considered as one act, and all certificates, surveys, tax researches and documents shall be considered as part of the original act pertaining thereto.

D. Every notary public for the parish of Orleans shall deliver for deposit to the office of the custodian, for permanent preservation, all acts executed before such notaries public prior to January 1, 1966, and the deposit of such acts shall not be optional, but shall be mandatory on the part of each notary public for the parish of Orleans. No charge shall be made by the custodian for the deposit of bound volumes of such acts. For the deposit of unbound acts, the custodian shall charge in accordance with the provisions of Subsection C of this section. The deposit of such acts shall be made not later than December 31, 1972. Whenever any notary public for the parish of Orleans shall fail to comply with the provisions aforestated then the custodian shall institute proceedings in accordance with the provisions of Subsection F of this section.

E. Every living, qualified notary public is authorized to certify true copies of any authentic act or any instrument under private signature hereafter or heretofore passed before him or acknowledged before him, and to make and certify copies, by any method, of any certificate, research, resolution, survey or other document annexed to the original of any authentic acts passed before him, and may certify such copies as true copies of the original document attached to the original passed before him.

F. Whenever any notary public for the parish of Orleans shall fail to comply with the provisions of this section then it shall be the duty of the custodian of notarial records to institute proceedings by rule in the Civil District Court for the parish of Orleans to require said notary public to show cause why his notarial commission should not be forfeited and why he should not be ordered to turn over all his notarial archives and records to the custodian of notarial records and pay all costs of said proceedings.

G. The indexing, binding and depositing of acts, contracts and instruments of writing executed before notaries public for the parish of Orleans, referred to in this section shall constitute an exception to the requirements of R.S. 35:329, and nothing contained in this section or in R.S. 35:329 shall be construed as requiring any notary public for the parish of Orleans to have an act executed before him in multiple originals.

§ 35:326. **Statement furnished custodian by notaries.** Each notary [in and for the Parish of Orleans] shall, annually, before September 1st, furnish to the [Custodian of Notarial Records in and for the Parish of Orleans] a statement showing his office and residence address, the date of his bond and the surety or sureties thereon, and their addresses. Failure to furnish this statement shall be cause for the revocation of the commission of the notary.

§ 35:327. **Fee payable to custodian by notaries.** Each notary [in and for the Parish of Orleans] shall pay an annual fee of fifteen dollars, on or before September 1st of each year, to the [custodian of Notarial Records in and for the Parish of Orleans], the said fees to be used by the custodian for additional compensation and expenses of his office.

MAINE

When authorized by the laws of the state, or of any other state or country, to do any official act, a notary may administer any oath necessary to the completion or validity thereof. See *Seal*, ME. REV. STAT. ANN. tit. 4, § 951. See also *Depositions*, ME. REV. STAT. ANN. tit. 4, § 202.

[ME. REV. STAT. ANN.]

Tit. 4, § 952. Protests of losses; record and copies. When requested, every notary public shall enter on record all losses or damages sustained or apprehended by sea or land, and all averages and such other matters as, by mercantile usage, appertain to his office, grant warrants of survey on vessels, and all facts, extracts from documents and circumstances so noted shall be signed and sworn to by all the persons appearing to protest. He shall note, extend and record the protest so made, and grant authenticated copies thereof, under his signature and notarial seal, to those who request and pay for them.

§ 953. Demand and notice on bills and notes. Any notary public may, in behalf of any person interested, present any bill of exchange or other negotiable paper for acceptance or payment to any party liable therefor, notify indorsers or other parties thereto, record and certify all contracts usually recorded or certified by notaries, and in general, do all acts which may be done by notaries public according to the usages of merchants and authorized by law. He may do all things that justices of the peace are or may be authorized to do and shall have the same territorial jurisdiction. He shall record all mercantile and marine protests by him noted and done in his official capacity.

§ 954. Acts of notary who is interested in corporation. Any notary public who is a stockholder, director, officer or employee of a bank or other corporation may take the acknowledgment of any party to any written instrument executed to or by such corporation, or may administer an oath to any other stockholder, director, officer, employee or agent of such corporation, or may protest for non-acceptance or nonpayment bills of exchange, drafts, checks, notes and other negotiable instruments which may be owned or held for collection by such bank or other corporation. It shall be unlawful for any notary public to take the acknowledgment of an instrument by or to a bank or other corporation of which he is a stockholder, director, officer or employee where such notary is a party to such instrument, either individually or as a representative of such bank or other corporation, or to protest any negotiable instrument owned or held for collection by such bank or other corporation, where such notary is individually a party to such instrument.

§ 955. Copies; evidence. The protest of any foreign or inland bill of exchange, promissory note or order, and all copies or certificates by him granted shall be under his hand and notarial seal and shall be received in all courts as legal evidence of such transactions and as to the notice given to the drawer or indorser and of all facts therein contained.

MARYLAND

[MD. ANN. CODE]

Art. 68, § 3. Administration of oaths; certificate under seal as evidence. Each notary public shall have the power of administering oaths according to law in all matters and cases of a civil nature in which a justice of the peace might have administered an oath prior to July 5, 1971, and with the same effect; and a certificate under the notarial seal of a notary public shall be sufficient evidence of his having administered such oath in his character as notary public.

§ 4. Acknowledgments; protests and declarations. A notary shall have power to receive the proof or acknowledgment of all instruments of writing relating to commerce or navigation and such other writings as have been usually proved and acknowledged before notaries public; and to make protests and declarations and testify the truth thereof under his seal of office concerning all matters done by him in virtue of his office.

§ 7. Acting outside of county or city for which appointed. A notary may exercise all functions of the office of notary in any other county or city than the county or city for which he may be appointed, with the same power and effect in all respects as if the same were exercised in the county or city for which he may be appointed.

§ 8. Form of protest. It shall not be lawful for any notary public to sign and issue any protest except in the form prescribed by the Comptroller.

§ 10. When notaries may not take acknowledgments and protests. It shall be lawful for any notary public who is a stockholder, director, officer or employee of a bank or other corporation to take the acknowledgment of any party to any written instrument executed to or by such corporation, or to administer an oath to any other stockholder, director, officer, employee or agent of such corporation, or to protest for nonacceptance or nonpayment bills of exchange, drafts, checks, notes and other negotiable instruments which may be owned or held for collection of such corporation; provided, it shall be unlawful for any notary public to take the acknowledgment of an instrument by or to a bank or other corporation of which he is a stockholder, director, officer or employee, where such notary is a party to such instrument, either individually or as a representative of such corporation, or to protest any negotiable instrument owned or held for collection by such corporation, where such notary is individually a party to such instrument.

MASSACHUSETTS

Notaries public have jurisdiction throughout the commonwealth when acting under the sole authority of their commission. Unless otherwise expressly provided, notaries may administer oaths or affirmations in all cases in which an oath or affirmation is required, and take acknowledgments of deeds and other instruments. See *Appointment*, MASS. ANN. LAWS ch. 222, § 1.

[MASS. ANN. LAWS]

Ch. 222, § 8.   Justices of the Peace, etc., to Print, etc., Name and Affix Date of Expiration of Commission. A justice of the peace or notary public, when taking acknowledgment of an instrument provided by law to be recorded, shall print or type his name directly below his signature and affix thereto the date of the expiration of his commission in the following language: "My commission expires ————." Failure to comply with this action shall not affect the validity of any instrument, or the record thereof.

§ 8A.   Same Subject. A justice of the peace, notary public or other person duly authorized, when taking an acknowledgment or administering an oath with relation to an instrument filed in a proceeding in the probate court shall print or type his name directly below his signature thereon. Failure to comply with this section shall not affect the validity of any instrument or the record thereof.

MICHIGAN

[MICH. COMP. LAWS ANN.]

§ 55.112.   Notary's powers. Notaries public shall have authority to take the proof and acknowledgments of deeds; to administer oaths, and take affidavits in any matter or cause pending, or to be commenced or moved in any court of this state; to demand acceptance of foreign and inland bills of exchange, and of promissory notes, and to protest the same for non-acceptance, or non-payment, as the case may require; and to exercise such other powers and duties, as by the law of nations, and according to commercial usage, or by the laws of any other state, government or country, may be performed by notaries public.

§ 55.113.   Certificate as presumptive evidence; exception. In all the courts of this state the certificate of a notary public, under his hand and seal of office, of official acts done by him as such notary, shall be received as presumptive evidence of the facts contained in such certificate; but such certificate shall not be evidence of notice of non-acceptance or non-payment in any case in which a defendant shall annex to his plea, an affidavit denying the fact of having received such notice.

§ 55.117. **Notary's residence; jurisdiction, fees.** Notaries public shall reside in the county for which they are appointed, but they may act as such notaries in any part of this state; and they shall receive for their services such fees as are provided by law.

§ 55.221. **Notaries public; typing, etc., name, etc., on affidavit, deposition, etc.; expiration date of commission; validity of instrument.** Notaries public shall legibly type, print or stamp on each affidavit, deposition, certificate and acknowledgment given or taken by them, and to all other instruments signed notarily, the date upon which their commissions shall expire, their commissioned names and the name of the county in which they are authorized to officiate: Provided, however, That where any such instrument has been heretofore or shall be hereafter recorded in the office of the register of deeds of any county without the date upon which said notary commission expires being affixed thereto, or shown on the record of such instrument, a certificate by a county clerk may be recorded in such register's office. Upon the recording of such certificate, showing that such person taking such acknowledgment was actually a notary public of such county on the date of such acknowledgment and giving the date on which his commission would expire, the record of such certificate and the record of such instrument shall be effectual for all purposes of a legal record, and the record of such instrument and such certificate or a transcript thereof may be given in evidence as in other cases, and such instrument shall be construed to be as valid and effectual as if such instrument had been in such respect duly executed.

§ 55.251. **Notary connected with bank or corporation, limited powers.** It shall be lawful for any notary public who is a stockholder, director, officer or employe of a bank or other corporation to take the acknowledgment of any party to any written instrument executed to or by such corporation, or to administer an oath to any other stockholder, director, officer, employe or agent of such corporation, or to protest for non-acceptance or non-payment bills of exchange, drafts, checks, notes and other negotiable instruments which may be owned or held for collection by such bank or other corporation: Provided, It shall not be lawful for any notary public to take the acknowledgment of an instrument by or to a bank or other corporation of which he is a stockholder, director, officer or employe, where such notary is named as a party to such instrument, either individually or as a representative of such bank or other corporation, or to protest any negotiable instrument owned or held for collection by such bank or other corporation, where such notary is individually a party to such instrument.

Note: Cf. § 489.862 below.

§ 489.862.   Acknowledgments not invalid by reason of member-ship [in savings and loan association].   No public officer qualified to take acknowledgments or proofs of written instruments shall be disqualified from taking acknowledgment or proof of any instrument in writing in which [a savings and loan] association is interested by reason of his membership in or employment by an association so interested, and any such acknowledgment or proofs heretofore taken are hereby validated.

Note: Cf. § 55.251 above.

MINNESOTA

[MINN. STAT. ANN.]

§ 51A.52.   Directors, employees, and members of [savings] associ-ation may acknowledge instruments to which it is a party.   No public officer qualified to take acknowledgments or proofs of written instru-ments shall be disqualified from taking the acknowledgment or proof of any instrument in writing in which [a savings association] is interested by reason of his membership in or employment by an association so interested, and any such acknowledgments or proofs heretofore taken are hereby validated.

§ 358.07.   Forms of oath in various cases.   An oath substantially in the following forms shall be administered to the respective officers and persons hereinafter named:

          ° ° °

(10)   To affiants:

"You do swear that the statements of this affidavit, by you sub-scribed, are true.   So help you God."

Note: For oaths to witnesses and interpreters, see *Depositions,* MINN. STAT. ANN. § 358.07.   For authority of notaries, and others, to take and certify acknowledgments within the state, see *Acknowl-edgments,* MINN. STAT. ANN. § 358.15.

§ 358.08.   Affirmation in lieu of oath.   If any person of whom an oath is required shall declare that he has religious scruples against taking the same, the word "swear" and the words "so help you God" may be omitted from the foregoing forms, and the word "affirm" and the words "and this you do under the penalties of perjury" shall be substituted therefor, respectively, and such person shall be con-sidered, for purposes, as having been duly sworn.

§ 358.09.   By whom and how administered.   Any officer autho-rized by this chapter to take and certify acknowledgments may ad-minister an oath, and, if the same be in writing, may certify the same under his official signature, and the seal of his office, if there be one, in the following form: "Subscribed and sworn to before me this .... day of ...., 19..." The mode of administering an oath commonly practiced in the place where it is taken shall be followed, including, in this state, the ceremony of uplifting the hand.

§ 358.25. **Power given for taking acknowledgments for protesting bills of exchange.** Any person authorized to take acknowledgments or administer oaths, who is at the same time an officer, director or stockholder of a corporation, is hereby authorized to take acknowledgments of instruments wherein such corporation is interested, and to administer oaths to any officer, director, or stockholder of such corporation as such, and to protest for non-acceptance or non-payment bills of exchange, drafts, checks, notes and other negotiable or non-negotiable instruments which may be owned or held for collection by such corporation, as fully and effectually as if he were not an officer, director, or stockholder of such corporation.

§ 359.04. **Powers.** Every such notary shall have power throughout the state, to administer all oaths required or authorized by law, to take and certify depositions, acknowledgments of deeds, and other instruments, and to receive, make out and record notarial protests.

§ 359.05. **Date of expiration of commission and name to be endorsed.** Each notary public so appointed, commissioned, and qualified, shall have power throughout this state to administer all oaths required or authorized to be administered in this state; to take and certify all depositions to be used in any of the courts of this state; to take and certify all acknowledgments of deeds, mortgages, liens, powers of attorney, and other instruments in writing, and to receive, make out, and record notarial protests.

Every notary public, except in cases provided in section 359.03,° subdivision 3, taking an acknowledgment of an instrument, taking a deposition, administering an oath, or making a notarial protest, shall, immediately following his signature to the jurat or certificate of acknowledgment, endorse the date of the expiration of his commission; such endorsement may be legibly written, stamped, or printed upon the instrument, but must be disconnected from the seal, and shall be substantially in the following form: "My commission expires ...., 19....". Except in cases provided in section 359.03,° subdivision 3, every notary public, in addition to signing his name to the jurat or certificate of acknowledgment, shall, immediately following his signature and immediately preceding his official description, endorse thereon his name with a typewriter or print the same legibly with a stamp or with pen and ink; provided that the failure so to endorse or print the name shall not invalidate any jurat or certificate of acknowledgment.

(°) For MINN. STAT. ANN. § 359.03, see *Seal.*

§ 359.07. **Notary in detached county. Subdivision 1. Powers.** In any county which has heretofore been detached from another county of this state, and which has been newly created and organized, any notary public residing in such newly created and organized county, who was a resident of the county from which the new county was detached and created, shall have the same powers during the unexpired term of his appointment as such notary public was authorized by law to exercise under the commission issued to him as a resident of the county from which the new county was detached and created and within which he was originally appointed such notary public; and all acts heretofore done by any such notary public, while residing in the newly created and organized county, otherwise in conformity of law, are hereby declared to be legal and valid and to the same effect as if the notary public had been originally commissioned as a resident of the newly created and organized county.

Subd. 2. Record of commission. Such notary public so residing in the newly created and organized county shall have his commission as such notary public recorded by the clerk of the district court of the newly created and organized county in which he resides, or of the county to which the newly created county is attached for judicial purposes, as provided in section 359.06,† and when so recorded shall be entitled to the same certificate of and from the clerk of the district court as provided in section 359.06.†

Subd. 3. Seal. Such notary shall, immediately upon the adoption of this section, provide himself with an official seal, as provided in and in conformity with section 359.03.°

(†) For MINN. STAT. ANN. § 359.06, see *Appointment.*
(°) For MINN. STAT. ANN. § 359.03, see *Seal.*

MISSISSIPPI

[MISS. CODE ANN.]

§ 25-33-9. Administer oaths. Every notary public shall have the power of administering oaths and affirmations in all matters incident to his notarial office.

§ 25-33-11. Powers and duties. Every notary public shall have power to receive the proof or acknowledgment of all instruments of writing relating to commerce or navigation, such as bills of sale, bottomries, mortgages, and hypothecations of ships, vessels, or boats, charter parties of affreightment, letters of attorney, and such other writings as are commonly proved or acknowledged before notaries; and to perform all other duties required of notaries by commercial usage, and also to make declarations and certify the truth thereof, under his seal of office, concerning all matters done by him in virtue of his office.

§ 25-33-13. Affixation of expiration date of commission. Every notary public, holding commission as such through appointment by the governor, shall be required to affix to any written or printed certificate of acknowledgment by him, in addition to his official seal and signature a written or printed recital of the date at which his commission expires. The failure of such notary public to affix such recital of date at which his commission expires shall not invalidate the acknowledgment of such instrument or such certificate of acknowledment, or otherwise affect the validity or recording of any instrument.

In case of the failure hereafter on the part of any notary public, so holding commission, to comply with the requirement of this section, his commission may be revoked by the governor.

§ 25-33-21. Acknowledgment by notary public as stockholder. It shall be lawful for any notary public who is a stockholder, director, officer, or employee of a bank or other corporation to take the acknowledgment of any party to any written instrument to or by such corporation, or to administer an oath to any other stockholder, director, officer, employee, or agent of such corporation, or to protest for nonacceptance or nonpayment bills of exchange, drafts, checks, notes, and other negotiable instruments which may be owned or held for collection by such corporation; provided, it shall be unlawful for any notary public to take the acknowledgment of an instrument by or to a bank or other corporation of which he is a stockholder, director, officer, or employee, where such notary is a party to such instrument, either individually or as a representative of such corporation, or to protest any negotiable instrument owned or held for collection by such corporation, where such notary is individually a party to such instrument.

MISSOURI

[MO. ANN. STAT.—Vernon]

§ 486.010. ° ° ° It shall be the duty of each such notary when he performs an official act outside his or her own county to state in his or her certificate that the county in which such act is performed adjoins the county within and for which he was appointed and commissioned or that he has filed a certified copy of his appointment with the county clerk of the county in which he performs his official act.

Editorial comment

Immediately below his signature in any certificate or acknowledgment which is to be recorded in the office of a recorder of deeds, a notary must print, stamp or type his name. He must designate in writing, in any certificate signed by him, the date of the expiration of his commission. See *Seal,* MO. ANN. STAT. § 486.040 (Vernon).

§ 486.020.   Powers and duties.   [Notaries public] may administer oaths and affirmations in all matters incident or belonging to the exercise of their notarial offices.   They may receive the proof or acknowledgment of all instruments of writing relating to commerce and navigation, take and certify relinquishments of dower and conveyances of real estate of married women; the proof or acknowledgment of deeds, conveyances, powers of attorney and other instruments of writing, in like cases and in the same manner and with like effect as clerks of courts of record or authorized by law; take and certify depositions and affidavits and administer oaths and affirmations, and take and perpetuate the testimony of witnesses, in like cases and in like manner as magistrates are authorized by law; make declarations and protests, and certify the truth thereof under their official seal, concerning all matters by them done by virtue of their offices, and shall have all the power and perform all the duties of register of boatmen.

§ 490.560.   Notary's certificate of protest.   The certificate of a notary public, protesting a bill of exchange or negotiable promissory note, without as well as within this state, setting forth the demand of payment, refusal, protest therefor, and notice of dishonor to parties thereto, and the manner of each of said acts, and verified by his affidavit, shall, in all courts in this state, be prima facie evidence of such acts; provided, such certificate be filed in the cause for at least fifteen days before the trial thereof.

§ 491.090.   Summons of witnesses.   In all cases where witnesses are required to attend the trial in any cause in any court of record, a summons shall be issued by the clerk of the court wherein the matter is pending, or by some notary public of the county wherein such trial shall be had, stating the day and place when and where the witnesses are to appear.

§ 491.100.   Subpoena, how issued—action of court when subpoena commands production of papers.   1.   Such summons shall be in the form of a subpoena, shall state the name of the court and the title of the action, and shall command each person to whom it is directed to attend and give testimony at a time and place therein specified. The clerk of the court wherein the matter is pending, or the notary public of the county wherein such trial shall be had, shall issue a subpoena, or a subpoena for the production of documentary evidence, signed and sealed but otherwise in blank, to a party requesting it, who shall fill it in before service.

2.   Where a subpoena commands the person to whom it is directed to produce the books, papers, or documents designated therein, the court upon motion may, promptly, and in any event at or before the time specified in the subpoena for compliance therewith, quash the subpoena if it is unreasonable and oppressive or condition denial of the motion upon the advancement by the person in whose

behalf the subpoena is issued of the reasonable cost of producing the books, papers, or documents.

MONTANA

[MONT. REV. CODES ANN.]

§ 56-104. Powers and duties. It is the duty of a notary public:

1. When requested, to demand acceptance and payment of foreign, domestic, and inland bills of exchange, or promissory notes, and protest the same for nonacceptance or nonpayment, and to exercise such other powers and duties as by the law of nations and according to commercial usages, or by the laws of any other state, government, or country, may be performed by notaries, and keep a record of such acts.

2. To take the acknowledgment or proof of powers of attorneys, mortgages, deeds, grants, transfers, and other instruments of writing executed by any person, and to give a certificate of such proof or acknowledgment, endorsed or attached to the instrument.

3. To take depositions and affidavits, and administer oaths and affirmations, in all matters incident to the duties of the office, or to be used before any court, judge, officer, or board in this state.

4. When requested, and upon payment of his fees therefor, to make and give a certified copy of any record in his office.

5. To provide and keep an official seal, upon which must be engraved the name of the state of Montana, and the words, "Notarial Seal," with the surname of the notary, and at least the initials of his Christian name.

6. To authenticate with his official seal all official acts. In all cases when the notary public signs his name officially as a notary public, he must add to his signature the words, "Notary Public for the State of Montana, residing at . . . ." (stating the name of his post office), and must endorse upon the instrument the date of the expiration of his commission.

§ 56-105. Jurisdiction of notaries. Every person receiving a commission as notary public shall have jurisdiction to perform his official duties and acts in every county of the state of Montana, and every notary now holding a commission from the governor of the state of Montana shall have like jurisdiction.

Note: See also *Appointment,* MONT. REV. CODES ANN. § 56-101, wherein it is provided that the jurisdiction of notaries is coextensive with the boundaries of the state, irrespective of their place of residence within the state.

§ 56-106. Authority of notaries who are stockholders or officers of corporations. It shall be lawful for any notary public who is a stockholder, director, officer, or employee of a bank or other corporation, to take the acknowledgment of any party to any written instrument executed to or by such corporation, or to administer an oath to any other stockholder, director, officer, employee, or agent of such corporation, or to protest for nonacceptance or nonpayment bills of exchange, drafts, checks, notes, and other negotiable instruments which may be owned or held for collection by such bank or other corporation; provided, it shall be unlawful for any notary public to take the acknowledgment of an instrument by or to a bank or other corporation of which he is a stockholder, director, officer, or employee, where such notary is a party to such instrument, either individually or as a representative of such bank or other corporation, or to protest any negotiable instrument owned or held for collection by such bank or other corporation, where such notary is individually a party to such instrument.

NEBRASKA

[NEB. REV. STAT.]

§ 25-1213. **Notarial protest as evidence of dishonor.** The usual protest by a notary public, without proof of his signature or notarial seal, is evidence of the dishonor and notice of a bill of exchange or promissory note.

§ 64-107. **Notary public; powers and duties; certificate or records; receipt in evidence.** A notary public is authorized and empowered, within the state: (1) To administer oaths and affirmations in all cases; (2) to take depositions, acknowledgments, and proofs of the execution of deeds, mortgages, powers of attorney, and other instruments in writing, to be used or recorded in this or another state; (3) to demand acceptance or payment of any foreign, inland, domestic bill of exchange, promissory note or other obligation in writing, and to protest the same for nonacceptance or nonpayment, as the case may be, and give notice to endorsers, makers, drawers or acceptors of such demand or nonacceptance or nonpayment; and (4) to exercise and perform such other powers and duties as by the law of nations, and according to commercial usage, or by the laws of the United States, or of any other state or territory of the United States, or of any other government or country, may be exercised and performed by notaries public. Over his signature and official seal, he shall certify the performance of such duties so exercised and performed under the provisions of this section, which certificate shall be received in all courts of this state as presumptive evidence of the facts therein certified to.

§ 64-112. **Removal from state; termination; notice to Secretary of State.** Every notary public removing from the State of Nebraska shall notify the Secretary of State of such removal. Such a removal shall terminate the term of his office.

Editorial comment

Concerning the authority of a notary public to issue a summons and to punish for contempt, see *Depositions,* NEB. REV. STAT. § 64-108 (Note following § 25-1229).

NEVADA

Concerning the duties of a notary in the authentication of official acts, and the use of a rubber or other mechanical stamp, see *Seal,* NEV. REV. STAT. § 240.040.

[NEV. REV. STAT.]

§ 240.050. Functions may be performed anywhere in state.

1. All notaries public may take acknowledgments of deeds, administer oaths and perform all other notarial acts and functions at any place within this state.

2. All acts of any notary public performed anywhere within this state shall be of the same force and validity as if performed within the county for which he was appointed and in which he resides.

§ 240.060. Powers of notaries public. Each notary public shall have power:

1. To administer oaths or affirmations.

2. To demand acceptance and payment of foreign and domestic bills of exchange, and to protest the same for nonacceptance and nonpayment, and to exercise such other powers and duties as by the laws of nations, and according to commercial usages, or by the law of any state, territory or country, may be performed by notaries public.

3. To demand acceptance of inland bills of exchange, and payment thereof, and of promissory notes, and may protest the same for nonpayment, or nonacceptance, as the case may require.

4. To take and to certify to the acknowledgment or proof of powers of attorney, mortgages, deeds and other instruments of writing, the acknowledgment of any conveyance, or the instrument of writing executed by any married woman, or to give a certificate of such proof or acknowledgment, which certificate shall be endorsed on the deed or other instrument, or attached thereto.

5. To take depositions and to administer oaths and affirmations in all matters incident or belonging to the duties of his office, and to take affidavits to be used before any court, judge or officer in this state.

§ 240.070. Acts of notaries public who are stockholders, directors, officers or employees of banks or other corporations. 1. It shall be lawful for any notary public who is a stockholder, director, officer or employee of a bank or other corporation:

(a) To take the acknowledgment of any party to any written instrument executed to or by the corporation.

(b) To administer an oath to any other stockholder, director, officer, employee or agent of the corporation.

(c) To protest for nonacceptance or nonpayment of bills of exchange, drafts, checks, notes and other negotiable instruments which may be owned or held for collection by the corporation.

2. It shall be unlawful for any notary public:

(a) To take the acknowledgment of an instrument by or to a bank or other corporation of which he is a stockholder, director, officer or employee, where the notary public is a party to the instrument, either individually or as a representative of the corporation.

(b) To protest any negotiable instrument owned or held for collection by the corporation, where the notary public is individually a party to the instrument.

NEW HAMPSHIRE

[N.H. REV. STAT. ANN.]

§ 455:2-a. **Competency.** It shall be lawful for any notary public or any other officer authorized to administer an oath or take an acknowledgment or proof of an instrument or make protest, who is a stockholder, director, officer or employee of a bank or other corporation, to take the acknowledgment of any party to any written instrument executed to or by such corporation, or to administer an oath to any other stockholder, director, officer, employee or agent of such corporation, or to protest for non-acceptance or non-payment bills of exchange, drafts, checks, notes and other negotiable instruments which may be owned or held for collection by such corporation; provided it shall be unlawful for any notary public or other officer authorized to administer an oath or take an acknowledgment or proof of an instrument or make protest, to take the acknowledgment of an instrument executed by or to a bank or other corporation of which he is a stockholder, director, officer or employee, where such notary or other officer is a party to such instrument, either individually or as a representative of such corporation, or to protest any negotiable instrument owned or held for collection by such corporation, where such notary or other officer is individually a party to such instrument. This section shall not be construed to imply that the acts herein made lawful may heretofore have been unlawful, and no instrument heretofore acknowledged or notarized before a notary public or other officer who would have been competent to act under the terms hereof shall hereafter be impugned or invalidated on the grounds that such notary public or other officer was incompetent to act.

§ 455:3. Powers. Every notary public, in addition to the usual powers of the office, shall have the same powers as a justice of the peace in relation to depositions and the acknowledgment of deeds and other instruments and the administering of oaths.

§ 455:4. Protest as evidence. The protest of a bill of exchange, note or order, duly certified by a notary public under his hand and official seal, shall be evidence of the facts stated in the protest and of the notice given to the drawer or indorsers.

Editorial comment

A notary may issue writs for witnesses to appear before himself or any other justice or notary, to give depositions in any matter or cause in which the same may be lawfully taken. A person neglecting or refusing to appear or testify or to give his deposition is subject to a penalty. See *Depositions,* N.H. REV. STAT. ANN. §§ 516:4, 516:7.

NEW JERSEY

[N.J. STAT. ANN.]

§ 2A:82-7. Certificate of protest as evidence. The certificate of a notary public of this state or of any other state of the United States, under his hand and official seal accompanying any bill of exchange or promissory note which has been protested by such notary for nonacceptance or nonpayment, shall be received in all the courts of this state as competent evidence of the official character of such notary, and also of the facts therein certified as to the presentment and dishonor of such bill or note and of the time and manner of giving or sending notice of dishonor to the parties to such bill or note.

§ 41:2-1. Before whom [oaths, affirmations, and affidavits] taken. All oaths, affirmations and affidavits required to be made or taken by law of this State, or necessary or proper to be made, taken or used in any court of this State, or for any lawful purpose whatever, may be made and taken before any one of the following officers:

°   °   °

Notaries public;
Commissioners of deeds,

°   °   °

This section shall not apply to official oaths required to be made or taken by any of the officers of this State, nor to oaths or affidavits required to be made and taken in open court.

§ 41:2-3. Oaths administered by notaries public in bank matters. A notary public who is a stockholder, director, officer, employee or agent of a bank or other corporation may administer an oath to any other stockholder, director, officer, employee or agent of the corporation.

§ 52:7-4. **County clerk to attach certificate of authority to notaries' certificates of proof or acknowledgment.** The county clerk of the county in which a notary public resides or the county clerk of any county where such notary public shall have filed his autograph signature and certificate, as provided in section 52:7-3° of this title, shall, upon request, subjoin to any certificate of proof, acknowledgment or affidavit signed by the notary public, a certificate under the clerk's hand and seal stating that the notary public was at the time of taking such proof, acknowledgment or affidavit duly commissioned and sworn and residing in this state, and was as such an officer of this state duly authorized to take and certify said proof, acknowledgment or affidavit as well as to take and certify the proof or acknowledgment of deeds for the conveyance of lands, tenements or hereditaments and other instruments in writing to be recorded in this state; that said proof, acknowledgment or affidavit is duly executed and taken according to the laws of this state; that full faith and credit are and ought to be given to the official acts of the notary public, and that the county clerk is well acquainted with the handwriting of the notary public and believes the signature to the instrument to which the certificate is attached is his genuine signature.

(°) See *Appointment*, N.J. STAT. ANN. § 52:7-3.

§ 52:7-7. **Signature of woman notary after marriage.** Whenever a woman notary public shall marry or remarry, she shall thereafter continue to sign her name the same as it was at the time of her appointment and commission, with a hyphen after the surname followed by the surname of her then husband.

§ 52:7-8. **Statement by woman notary after marriage; filing with governor; as evidence.** After the marriage of a woman notary public, and before she signs her name to any document which she is authorized or required to sign as notary public, she shall make and sign a statement in writing and under oath, on a form prescribed and furnished by the Secretary of State, setting out the date and place of her marriage, the name of her husband, and such other information as the Secretary of State shall require.

The statement shall be filed in the office of the Secretary of State and in the office of the clerk of the county where she qualified as a notary public and in the office of the clerk of any county in which she may have filed a certificate of her commission and qualification.

Such statement, or a certified copy thereof, shall be evidence of the right of said notary public to continue to exercise the powers and privileges and perform the duties of a notary public in her changed and new name.

NEW MEXICO

[N.M. STAT. ANN.]

§ 35-1-1. **Powers and duties.** The office of "notary public" is established. At any place within the state, a notary public may:

A. administer oaths;

B. take and certify acknowledgments of instruments in writing;

C. take and certify depositions;

D. make declarations and protests; and

E. perform other duties as provided by law.

§ 35-1-6. **Certification.** Upon request, the secretary of state shall certify to official acts of a notary public.

§ 35-1-9. **Protesting bills and notes—Notice.** Each notary public when any bill of exchange, promissory note, or other written instrument shall be by such notary protested for nonacceptance or nonpayment shall give notice in writing thereof to the maker and to each and every endorser of such bill of exchange, and to the maker of each security, or the endorsers of any promissory note or other written instrument, immediately after such protest shall have been made.

§ 35-1-10. **Service of notice of protest.** Each notary public may serve notice personally upon each person protested against by delivering to such person a notice in writing, or he may make such service by placing such notice in a sealed envelope with sufficient postage thereon addressed to the person to be charged, at his last place of residence, according to the best information that the person giving the notice may obtain, and by depositing such envelope containing such notice in the United States mail or post office.

§ 35-1-13. **Change of address.** Each notary public shall promptly notify the secretary of state of any change of his mailing address.

§ 35-1-14. **Change of name.** Upon any change of his name, a notary public shall promptly make application to the secretary of state for issuance of a corrected commission. The application shall be on a form prescribed by the secretary of state. Upon receipt of the completed application, the secretary of state shall issue a corrected commission showing the notary public's new name. The corrected commission expires on the same date as the original certificate it replaces.

§ 35-1-19. **Endorsing expiration date of commission.** Every notary public certifying to any acknowledgment, oath or other matter shall, immediately opposite or following his signature to the jurat or certificate of acknowledgment, endorse the date of the expiration of such commission; such endorsement may be legibly written, stamped or printed upon the instrument, but must be disconnected from the seal and shall be substantially in the following form:

"My commission expires (stating date of expiration of commission)."

§ 35-1-24. **Notary affiliated with bank or corporation—Power restricted.** It shall be lawful for any notary public who is a stockholder, director, officer or employee of a bank or other corporation to take the acknowledgment of any party to any written instrument executed to or by such corporation, or to administer an oath to any other stockholder, director, officer, employee or agent of such corporation, or to protest for nonacceptance or nonpayment bills of exchange, drafts, checks, notes and other negotiable instruments which may be owned or held for collection by such corporation; Provided, it shall be unlawful for any notary public to take the acknowledgment of an instrument by or to a bank or other corporation of which he is a stockholder, director, officer, or employee, where such notary is a party to such instrument, either individually or as a representative of such corporation, or to protest any negotiable instrument owned or held for collection by such corporation, where such notary is individually a party to such instrument.

NEW YORK

An instrument with a certificate of notarial signature by the county clerk affixed thereto shall be entitled to be read in evidence or to be recorded in any of the counties of the state in respect to which a certificate of a county clerk may be necessary for either purpose. See *Appointment*, N.Y. EXEC. LAW § 133.

[N.Y. EXEC. LAW]

§ 135. **Powers and duties; in general; of notaries public who are attorneys at law.** Every notary public duly qualified is hereby authorized and empowered within and throughout the state to administer oaths and affirmations, to take affidavits and depositions, to receive and certify acknowledgments or proof of deeds, mortgages and powers of attorney and other instruments in writing; to demand acceptance or payment of foreign and inland bills of exchange, promissory notes and obligations in writing, and to protest the same for non-acceptance or non-payment, as the case may require, and, for use in another jurisdiction, to exercise such other powers and duties as by the laws of nations and according to commercial usage, or by the laws of any other government or country may be exercised and performed by notaries public, provided that when exercising such powers he shall set forth the name of such other jurisdiction.

A notary public who is an attorney at law regularly admitted to practice in this state may, in his discretion, administer an oath or affirmation to or take the affidavit or acknowledgment of his client in respect of any matter, claim, action or proceeding.

For any misconduct by a notary public in the performance of any of his powers such notary public shall be liable to the parties injured for all damages sustained by them.

o   o   o

§ 137. **Statement as to authority of notaries public.** In exercising his powers pursuant to this article, a notary public, in addition to the venue of his act and his signature, shall print, typewrite, or stamp beneath his signature in black ink, his name, the words "Notary Public State of New York," the name of the county in which he originally qualified, and the date upon which his commission expires and, in addition, wherever required, a notary public shall also include the name of any county in which his certificate of official character is filed, using the words "Certificate filed . . . . County." A notary public who is duly licensed as an attorney and counsellor at law in this state may in his discretion, substitute the words "Attorney and Counsellor at Law" for the words "Notary Public." A notary public who has qualified or who has filed a certificate of official character in the office of the clerk in a county or counties within the city of New York must also affix to each instrument his official number or numbers in black ink, as given to him by the clerk or clerks of such county or counties at the time such notary qualified in such county or counties and, if the instrument is to be recorded in an office of the register of the city of New York in any county within such city and the notary has been given a number or numbers by such register or his predecessors in any county or counties, when his autographed signature and certificate are filed in such office or offices pursuant to this chapter, he shall also affix such number or numbers. No official act of such notary public shall be held invalid on account of the failure to comply with these provisions. If any notary public shall wilfully fail to comply with any of the provisions of this section, he shall be subject to disciplinary action by the secretary of state. In all the courts within this state the certificate of a notary public, over his signature, shall be received as presumptive evidence of the facts contained in such certificate; provided, that any person interested as a party to a suit may contradict, by other evidence, the certificate of a notary public.

§ 138. **Powers of notaries public or other officers who are stockholders, directors, officers or employees of a corporation.** A notary public, justice of the supreme court, a judge, clerk, deputy clerk, or special deputy clerk of a court, an official examiner of title, or the mayor or recorder of a city, a justice of the peace, surrogate, special surrogate, special county judge, or commissioner of deeds, who is a stockholder, director, officer or employee of a corporation may take the acknowledgment or proof of any party to a written instrument executed to or by such corporation, or administer an oath to any other stockholder, director, officer, employee or agent of such corporation, and such notary public may protest for non-acceptance or non-payment, bills of exchange, drafts, checks, notes and other negotiable instruments owned or held for collection by such corporation; but none of the officers above named shall take the acknowledgment or proof of a written instrument by or to a corporation of which he is a stockholder, director, officer or employee, if such officer taking such acknowledgment or proof be a party executing such instrument, either individually or as a representative of such corporation, nor shall a notary public protest any negotiable instruments owned or held for collection by such corporation, if such notary public be individually a party to such instrument, or have a financial interest in the subject of same. All such acknowledgments or proofs of deeds, mortgages or other written instruments, relating to real property heretofore taken before any of the officers aforesaid are confirmed. This act shall not affect any action or legal proceeding now pending.

NORTH CAROLINA

[N.C. GEN. STAT.]

§ 10-5. **Powers of notaries public.** (a) Subject to the exception stated in subsection (c), a notary public commissioned under the laws of this State acting anywhere in this State may:

(1) Take and certify the acknowledgment or proof of the execution or signing of any instrument or writing except a contract between a husband and wife governed by the provisions of G.S. 52-6;

(2) Take affidavits and depositions;

(3) Administer oaths and affirmations, including oaths of office, except when such power is expressly limited to some other public officer;

(4) Protest for nonacceptance or nonpayment, notes, bills of exchange and other negotiable instruments; and

(5) Perform such acts as the law of any other jurisdiction may require of a notary public for the purposes of that jurisdiction.

(b) Any act within the scope of subsection (a) performed in another jurisdiction by a notary public of that jurisdiction has the same force and effect in this State as full, as if such act were performed in this State by a notary public commissioned under the laws of this State.

(c) A notary public who, individually or in any fiduciary capacity, is a party to any instrument, cannot take the proof or acknowledgment of himself in such fiduciary capacity or of any other person thereto.

(d) A notary public who is a stockholder, director, officer, or employee of a corporation is not disqualified to exercise any power, which he is authorized by this section to exercise, with respect to any instrument or other matter to which such corporation is a party or in which it is interested unless he is individually a party thereto.

§ 10-6. **May exercise powers in any county.** Notaries public have full power and authority to perform the functions of their office in any and all counties of the State, and full faith and credit shall be given to any of their official acts wheresoever the same shall be made and done.

§ 10-7. **Certificates of official character.** The Secretary of State and the register of deeds in the county in which the notary public qualified may certify to the official character and authority of such notary public.

§ 10-9. **Official acts of notaries public; signatures; appearance of names; notarial stamps or seals; expiration of commissions.** Official acts of notaries public in the State of North Carolina shall be attested:

(1) By their proper signatures;

(2) By the readable appearance of their names, either from their signatures or otherwise;

(3) By the clear and legible appearance of their notarial stamps or seals;

(4) By a statement of the date of expiration of their commissions; provided, that the failure to comply with the provisions of subdivisions (2) and (4) shall not invalidate their official acts.

§ 10-14. **Validation of acknowledgment wherein expiration of notary's commission erroneously stated.** All deeds, deeds of trust, mortgages, conveyances, affidavits, and all other paper writings similar or dissimilar to those enumerated herein, whether or not permitted or required to be recorded or filed under the laws of this State heretofore or hereafter executed, bearing an official act of a notary public in which the date of the notary's commission is erroneously stated, are, together with all subsequent acts or actions taken thereon, including but not limited to probate and registration, hereby declared in all respects to be valid to the extent as if the correct expiration date had been stated and shall be binding on the parties of such paper writings and their privies; and such paper writings, together with their certificates may, if otherwise competent, be read in evidence as a muniment of title for all intents and purposes in any of the courts of this State: Provided, that at the date of such official act the notary's commission was actually in force.

§ 47-8. **Attorney in action not to probate papers therein.** No practicing attorney at law has power to administer any oaths to a person to any paperwriting to be used in any legal proceedings in which he appears as attorney.

NORTH DAKOTA

[N.D. CENT. CODE]

§ 44-06-01. **Appointment and qualification of notaries public.**

o   o   o

Each notary shall have power and authority anywhere in the state to administer oaths and perform all other duties required of him by law.

§ 44-06-06. **Duty of notary as to instrument protested by him.** Each notary public, when any bill of exchange, promissory note, or other written instrument, shall be by him protested for nonacceptance or nonpayment, shall give notice thereof in writing to the maker, to each and every endorser of such bill of exchange, and to the maker of each security or the endorsers of any promissory note or other written instrument, immediately after such protest shall have been made.

§ 44-06-07. **Service of notice by notary public.** Each notary public shall serve notice personally upon each person protested against, or by properly folding the notice, directing it to the person to be charged at his place of residence according to the best information that the person giving the notice can obtain, depositing it in the United States mail or post office most conveniently accessible, and prepaying the postage thereon.

§ 44-06-12. **Notary public commission — Date of expiration.** Every notary public taking an acknowledgment to any instrument, immediately following his signature to the jurat or certificates of acknowledgment, shall legibly print, stamp, or type his name and shall endorse the date of the expiration of such commission. Such endorsement may be written legibly, stamped, or printed upon the instrument but must be disconnected from the seal, and shall be substantially in the following form:

My commission expires . . . ., 19 . . . .

OHIO

[OHIO REV. CODE ANN.]

§ 147.07. **Powers; jurisdiction.** A notary public may, within the county for which he is appointed, or if commissioned for the whole state, throughout the state, administer oaths required or authorized by law, take and certify depositions, take and certify acknowledgments of deeds, mortgages, liens, powers of attorney, and other instruments of writing, and receive, make, and record notarial protests. In taking depositions, he shall have the power which is by law vested in judges of county courts to compel the attendance of witnesses and punish them for refusing to testify. Sheriffs and constables are required to serve and return all process issued by notaries public in the taking of depositions. If the post office address of a notary public which is recorded in the governor's office is in a municipal corporation situated in two or more counties or if such notary public is an attorney at law commissioned throughout the state such notary public may receive, make, and record notarial protests within the established limits of such municipal corporation.

§ 147.09. Protests are evidence. The instrument of protest of a notary public appointed and qualified under the laws of this state or of any other state or territory of the United States, accompanying a bill of exchange or promissory note, which has been protested by such notary public for nonacceptance or for nonpayment constitutes prima-facie evidence of the facts therein certified. Such instrument may be contradicted by other evidence.

§ 147.12. Acts done by notary public after term valid. An official act done by a notary public after the expiration of his term of office is as valid as if done during his term of office.

Note: A notary is prohibited from doing or performing any act as a notary, knowing that his term of office has expired. See *Offenses,* OHIO REV. CODE ANN. § 147.10 (Page). The penalty for violation of § 147.10 is specified in § 147.11. See *Offenses,* OHIO REV. CODE ANN. § 147.11 (Page).

OKLAHOMA

[OKLA. STAT. ANN.]

Tit. 6, § 904. Stockholder, director, officer or employee of bank as notary public—Administration of oaths—Protests. It shall be lawful for any notary public who is a stockholder, director, officer or employee of a bank to take the acknowledgment of any party to any written instrument executed to or by such bank, or to administer an oath to any other stockholder, director, officer, employee or agent of such bank, or to protest for nonacceptance or nonpayment bills of exchange, drafts, checks, notes and other negotiable instruments which may be owned or held for collection by such bank; provided, it shall be unlawful for any notary public to take the acknowledgment of an instrument executed by or to a bank of which he is a stockholder, director, officer or employee, where such notary is a party to such instrument, either individually or as a representative of such bank, or to protest any negotiable instrument owned or held for collection by such bank where such notary is individually a party to such instrument.

Tit. 49, § 6. Authority of notary. Notaries public shall have authority within any county in this state to make the proof and acknowledgment of deeds and other instruments of writing required to be proved or acknowledged; to administer oaths; to demand acceptance or payment of foreign or inland bills of exchange and promissory notes, and protest the same for nonacceptance or non-payment, as the same may require, and to exercise such other powers and duties as by law of nations and commercial usage may be performed by notaries public.

Tit. 51, § 21. Oaths, officers authorized to administer. The following officers are authorized to administer oaths:

      *   *   *

5. Justices of the peace and notaries public within their respective counties.

      *   *   *

OREGON

[ORE. REV. STAT.]

§ 194.010. Appointment of notary public; ° ° ° functions not official duties. (1) ° ° ° A notary public may act throughout the state.

      *   *   *

(5) The functions of a notary public are not considered official duties under Article III, section 1 of the Oregon Constitution.

§ 194.070. Protesting commercial paper. Each notary public who protests any commercial paper° shall take such actions as are required by ORS 73.5090 [Uniform Commercial Code].

(°) Definition of commercial paper. As used in ORS 194.005 to 194.170, "commercial paper" means such instruments as are within the scope of ORS chapter 73 [Uniform Commercial Code], including drafts, checks, certificates of deposit and notes. § 194.005.

Note: Concerning Uniform Commercial Code, see Chapter 14, page 690.

§ 194.100. Powers of notary connected with corporation; limitations. (1) A notary public who is a stockholder, director, officer or employe of a bank or trust company or other corporation may:

(a) Take the acknowledgment of any party to any written instrument executed to or by such corporation;

(b) Administer an oath to any other stockholder, director, officer, employe or agent of such corporation; and

(c) Protest commercial paper owned or held for collection by such corporation.

(2)   A notary public shall not:

(a)   Take the acknowledgment of an instrument executed by or to a bank or trust company or other corporation of which he is a stockholder, director, officer or employe, if the notary is a party to such instrument, either individually or as a representative of such corporation; or

(b)   Protest any commercial paper owned or held for collection by such corporation, if the notary is individually a party to the instrument.

See also, to similar effect, *Acknowledgments*, ORE. REV. STAT. § 722.250.

§ 194.110.   **Power to take acknowledgment.**   Notaries public may take acknowledgments of deeds.

§ 194.120.   **Faith and credit given acts of notary.**   Full faith and credit shall be given to all the protestations, attestations and other instruments of publication of all notaries public appointed under ORS 194.010.

PENNSYLVANIA

[PA. STAT. ANN.]

Tit. 28, § 223.   **Official acts of foreign notaries to be prima facie evidence.**   The official acts and exemplifications of foreign notaries in accordance with the laws of their respective countries shall be prima facie evidence of the matters therein set forth: Provided, That the consul or vice consul of the United States, at or near the place where such notaries public may reside, shall certify on his consular seal that such notaries are the proper officers, and that such official acts and exemplifications are in accordance with the laws of their respective countries, which seal, affixed to the said consular certificate, shall be presumed prima facie to be the genuine consular seal, and shall be evidence that the person so certifying was, at the date of the certificate, an acting consul or vice consul as represented, and that the signature is his genuine handwriting, and that the seal was affixed thereto by him: Provided however, That any party may be permitted to contradict, by other evidence, any such acts, exemplifications or certificates.

Tit. 57, § 148.   **Appointment of notaries.**   ° ° °   [Notaries' public] jurisdiction shall be co-extensive with the boundaries of the Commonwealth irrespective of their place of residence within the Commonwealth.

§ 153.   **Vacation of office; change of residence.**   In event of any change of address within the Commonwealth, notice in writing shall be given the Secretary of the Commonwealth and the recorder of deeds of the county of original appointment by a notary public within five (5) days of such change. For the purpose of this section, "address" means office address. A notary public vacates his office by removing from the Commonwealth, and such removal shall constitute a resignation from the office of notary public as of the date of removal.

§ 156. **Change of name.** Whenever the name of any notary is changed by decree of court, or whenever any female notary shall marry, or is divorced and assumes her maiden name thereafter, such notary may continue to perform official acts, in the name in which he or she was commissioned, until the expiration of his or her term, but he or she shall, within thirty (30) days after entry of such decree, or after marriage or divorce, notify the Secretary of the Commonwealth and the recorder of deeds of the county in which he or she maintains an office of such change of name. Application for reappointment of such notary shall be made in the new name.

§ 159. **Date of expiration of commission.** Every notary public in this Commonwealth shall note upon each certificate, attestation, or official notarial act, either written, typed, or stamped, a statement, in plain, legible characters, in the English language, of the date upon which his commission expires, and the name of the political subdivision and the county in which he maintains his office.

§ 160. **[Position of seal and] date of expiration of commission.**

○   ○   ○

(b) The date of expiration of a notary's commission and the location of his office shall be written, typed or stamped immediately below the signature of the notary.

§ 162. **Power to administer oaths and affirmations.** Notaries shall have power to administer oaths and affirmations, according to law, in all matters belonging or incident to the exercise of their notarial office. Any person who shall be convicted of having wilfully and knowingly made or taken a false oath or affirmation before any notary in any matters within their official duties shall be guilty of perjury and shall be subject to the penalties in such case made and provided.

§ 163. **Power to take acknowledgment of instruments of writing relating to commerce or navigation and to make declarations.** Notaries shall have the power to receive the proof of acknowledgment of all instruments of writing relating to commerce or navigation, such as bills of sale, bottomries, mortgages and hypothecations of ships or vessels, charter parties of affreightment, letters of attorney, and such other writings as have been usually proved or acknowledged before notaries within this Commonwealth, and also to make declarations and testify the truth thereof, under their seals of office, concerning all matters by them done in virtue of their respective offices.

§ 164. Power to take depositions, affidavits and acknowledgment of writings relative to lands. Notaries shall have power to take depositions and affidavits, to take and receive the acknowledgment or proof of all deeds, conveyances, mortgages, or other instruments or writing touching or concerning any lands, tenements or hereditaments, situate, lying and being in any part of this State.

§ 165. Limitation on powers; fees. (a) No director or officer in any bank, banking institution or trust company, holding at the same time the office of notary public, shall do or perform any act or duty as notary public for any bank, banking institution or trust company in which he is a director or officer. Any act or duty performed by any such notary public for any such bank, banking institution or trust company is hereby declared invalid.

(b) No clerk in any bank, banking institution or trust company, holding at the same time the office of notary public, shall be authorized to protest checks, notes, drafts, bill of exchange, or any commercial paper, for any bank, banking institution or trust company in which he is employed.

(c) The fees of any such notary for other services rendered shall be the property of such notary and in no case belong to or be received by the corporation of which he is a director or clerk.

(d) No justice of the peace, magistrate or alderman, holding at the same time the office of notary public, shall have jurisdiction in cases arising on papers or documents containing acts by him done in the office of notary public.

(e) No notary public may act as such in any transaction in which he is a party directly or pecuniarily interested.

§ 166. Admissibility in evidence. The official acts, protests and attestations of all notaries public, certified, according to law, under their respective hands and seals of office, including the dishonor of all bills and promissory notes, and of notice to the drawers, acceptors or endorsers thereof, may be received and read in evidence, as proof of the facts therein stated, in all suits now pending or hereafter to be brought. Any party may be permitted to contradict by other evidence any such certificate.

PUERTO RICO

Oaths, Affidavits and Affirmations

[P.R. LAWS ANN.]

Tit. 4, § 881. Administration of oaths, affidavits, and affirmations —Mode; perjury. All oaths, affidavits and affirmations shall be administered in the mode most binding upon the conscience of the individual taking the same, and shall be taken subject to the pains and penalties of perjury.

§ 882. Officers authorized to administer, in Puerto Rico. All oaths, affidavits or affirmations, necessary or convenient or required by law, may be administered within Puerto Rico, and a certificate of the fact given, by any judge of the Supreme Court, or by any judge of the Superior Court, or by any secretary of either of the above mentioned courts, or by any justice of the peace or District Court judge, or by any notary public, or by any Commissioner of the United States for the District of Puerto Rico; Provided, That the prosecuting attorney of the Supreme Court of Puerto Rico is likewise authorized by this law to administer oaths in such cases in which the law permits prosecuting attorneys of the Superior Court to administer them, whenever by special delegation or substitution of any such prosecuting attorney of the Superior Court he shall conduct any investigation specially intrusted by law to said prosecuting attorneys of the Superior Court.

§ 883. Writing and signature of affidavits. All affidavits provided by sections 881-885 of this title shall be in writing and signed by the party making the same.

§ 884. Affidavits within and outside Puerto Rico. Affidavits may be made before either of the following officers who are authorized to take such affidavits and give a certificate thereof:

1.   If taken within Puerto Rico before the officers named in section 882 of this title.

2.   If taken without Puerto Rico and within the United States before any clerk of a court of record having a seal, any notary public, or any commissioner of deeds, duly appointed under the laws of Puerto Rico, within some state or territory.

3.   If without the United States, before any notary public, or any minister, commissioner, or charge d'affaires of the United States resident in, and accredited to, the country where the affidavit may be taken; or any consul general; vice consul general, consul, vice consul, commercial agent, vice commercial agent, deputy consul or consular agent of the United States in such country, or any commissioner of deeds, duly appointed under the laws of Puerto Rico, within such country.

§ 887. Registry of affidavits or declarations of authenticity — Definition. By affidavit or declaration of authenticity is meant the act and the document by means of which a notary or any other of the officers designated by sections 887-895 of this title certifies to, or witnesses the truth or recognition of a signature, an oath, or any other fact or contract affecting real or personal property not made in a public instrument.

§ 888. Inclusion of oath. Affidavits or declarations of authenticity may or may not include an oath, but in no case shall an oath be allowed in contracts, in accordance with the prohibition set forth in section 3377 of Title 31.

§ 889. **Form of affidavit or declaration; numbering.** The affidavit or declaration of authenticity shall be drawn in the following form. In the case of the recognition of a signature under oath:

"Sworn to and subscribed before me, by . . . . (name, age, trade or occupation and residence) personally known to me (or who has been identified to my satisfaction by the two witnesses, known to me, whose statement to that effect is also signed by them), this, the . . . . . . day of . . . . 19. . .

In the case of the recognition of a signature not made under oath, the same form shall be used, except that the words "sworn to" shall be stricken out.

A concise and simple form shall be used for all other cases and which shall include the authenticity of the act, but in all cases the officer authorizing same shall set forth that he knows personally the interested party; or knows the witnesses identifying such party.

Affidavits or declarations of authenticity shall be numbered in successive and continuous numbers and each declaration shall contain at its head the number corresponding to it and which shall be correlative with that of the entry in the Registry, referred to hereinafter.

§ 890. **Officers who may authorize affidavits or declarations.** All notaries, justices of the Supreme Court, judges of the Court of First Instance, justices of the peace, the Secretary of State, the heads of departments and the municipal treasurers may authorize affidavits or declarations; but only notaries may authorize such affidavits and declarations when they have reference to facts, acts or contracts of a purely private nature; Provided, however, That municipal treasurers shall be authorized only and exclusively to administer oaths in those cases where required under sections 621-639 of Title 21, with reference to certificates for industrial and commercial license taxes; And provided, further, That in towns where there is no notary with an open office, the district judges and justices of the peace may take affidavits, in which this fact shall appear, on recognition of signatures on instruments of credit and contracts of a private nature, the amount of which does not exceed two thousand five hundred (2,500) dollars.

The foregoing provisions shall not be so construed as to leave without effect any law in force under which authority is granted to other public officials, not mentioned in sections 887-895 of this title, to take affidavits, oaths and affirmations, which authorizations shall remain in full force.

§ 895. **Exemption of certain declarations.** There shall not be deemed to be included in sections 887-895 of this title any declarations in judicial, or administrative proceedings, made before judges or officers of any capacity, in matters under their jurisdiction.

General Provisions

§ 1001. Notaries only officers authorized to attest and certify extrajudicial instruments. Notaries are the only officers authorized to attest and certify to contracts and other extrajudicial instruments executed in their presence in accordance with law.

Editorial comment

It is the duty of a notary to report any change of residence or notarial office to the Secretary of the Supreme Court of Puerto Rico within five (5) days following such change. See *Appointment*, P.R. LAWS ANN. tit. 4, § 1002.

Tit. 4, § 1003. Practice throughout Commonwealth; fireproof safes. Notaries may practice throughout the Commonwealth of Puerto Rico. When located in a wooden building the office of a notary shall be provided with steel or iron fireproof safes in which to keep the protocols.

§ 1004. Substitute notary. A notary may appoint another notary residing in the same locality to act as his substitute, and whenever for any cause other than a permanent one, he should be unable to perform the duties of his office, said substitute shall act in his stead. Both the notary and his substitute shall notify such substitution in writing and over their signatures to the Secretary of the pertinent part of the Superior Court of Puerto Rico.

§ 1006. Instruments, copies, and protocols; internal revenue stamps; Bar Association stamps. Notaries shall draw up original instruments, issue copies thereof, and form their own protocols.* It shall be the duty of every notary to affix to and cancel on each original deed executed and on the copies thereof issued by him the proper internal revenue stamps and a stamp to be adopted and issued by the Bar Association of Puerto Rico of a value of twenty-five (25) cents, the proceeds of the sale of said stamp to be covered into the funds of said association. Any original instrument or copy thereof to which said stamp has not been affixed shall be considered null for all purposes.

It shall also be the duty of every notary before whom any conveyance of an ownership title is executed, whose amount exceeds twenty-five thousand (25,000) dollars, to remit to the Secretary of the Treasury, not later than the Monday immediately following the date of execution, a true and correct copy of said deed, with his signature and notarial certificate, and with each one of the folios marked and sealed, but without attaching thereto internal-revenue stamps or the notarial tax. The sending of such copy shall not be required when the title conveyance is made by the Commonwealth, its agencies, instrumentalities or municipalities, or by the Government of the United States or its agencies or instrumentalities.

(*) For the definition of "protocol", see *Records*, P.R. LAWS ANN. tit. 4, § 1028.

§ 1007. **Receipt on bail of documents, securities and sums.** Notaries may receive on bail any documents, securities and sums which private parties may desire to bail to them, as pledge for the performance of their contracts. Admission of such bail shall be optional and notaries may impose conditions upon such bailors, which conditions shall be recited in the receipt or voucher issued therefor by them.

§ 1008. **Disqualification by interest or relationship.** No notary shall authorize a contract to which he is a party or which contains any provision in his favor or in which any of the parties is related to him within the fourth degree of consanguinity or second degree of affinity. When a notary acts in the execution of any instrument to be recorded in a Registry of Property that is in charge of a relative within the degrees above stated, the Registrar of Property shall inhibit himself from passing upon such instrument.

Instruments

§ 1009. **Original instrument defined.** An original instrument is one drawn up by a notary upon the contract or writing submitted to him for authentication and which is signed by the parties and the witnesses, where this chapter requires or permits the appearance of the latter, and which is authorized by the notary before whom it is executed, with his signature, sign, seal and mark, no rubber-stamp signing being allowed.

§ 1010. **Matters which must be set forth in public instruments.** In all public instruments the notary shall set forth his name and residence and, where witnesses are required or permitted under this chapter, the name, majority, status, and residence of such witnesses, as well as the place, year and day of execution.

§ 1011. **Serial number.** Every instrument shall bear its corresponding serial number spelled at the beginning thereof.

§ 1012. **Size and margins of original instruments.** Original instruments shall be drawn up on sheets of paper or pages thirteen inches long by eight and one-half inches wide, and on the part left for binding there shall be a blank margin of twenty (20) millimeters, and besides, a margin of sixty (60) millimeters on the left side of each sheet or page of the instrument, where the notary shall affix his special mark, and on which the parties to the instrument shall affix their initials, and on the right, a margin of three (3) millimeters.

§ 1013. **Witnesses; time and place of signature by parties.** Every public instrument, except as provided for special cases in section 1027 of this title, may be authenticated by a notary without the presence of witnesses; and it shall not be required that the parties sign it in the same act. Contrariwise, the notary may personally take their signatures at any time provided it is done on the same calendar day of the execution of the instrument; Provided, That for all legal purposes, the place of execution shall be where the last of the parties initialed and signed the public instrument or deed, which place the notary shall set forth as such in the heading thereof.

§ 1014. **Parties unable to sign.** Should the parties to the instrument, or any of them, not know how or be unable to sign, the notary shall so state, and for those who do not sign a witness shall sign, but the notary shall set forth these facts in the instrument, indicating by his name and surname the witness who on request signed for such party or parties. In addition, beside the signature of the witness and on all the pages of the instrument shall be affixed the fingerprints of the thumbs and, in default thereof, of any of the fingers of the party or parties who do not know how or are unable to sign, and said witness shall affix his intials on each page of the instrument.

If the party or parties are fingerless the notary shall set forth this circumstance and at his behest two witnesses shall sign and initial the instrument as above expressed.

§ 1015. **Procedure for witnesses; disqualifications.** Where under sections 1014, 1016, and 1027 of this title witnesses are required or permitted for the execution of a public deed or instrument, the transaction shall be one sole act, and those who do not know how to sign, neither the employees or servants of the authorizing notary, nor the relatives within the fourth degree of consanguinity or second degree of affinity of the notary or of the parties concerned may serve as witnesses.

§ 1016. **Identification of parties.** In public instruments notaries shall certify that they know the parties to the instrument, or that they have assured themselves of their identity by the saying of witnesses. They shall also certify to the age, status, profession and residence of the parties, in accordance with their statements, and in case the person acquiring the right the object of the contract is married, the name and surname of the spouse absent at the execution shall appear. In those serious and extraordinary cases where it is impossible to set forth these circumstances in full, they shall state everything concerning such matters as are known to them of their own knowledge and as is stated by the witnesses. The identifying witness or witnesses must in all cases be persons well known to the notary, who shall certify to that effect in the instrument. If any such serious and extraordinary case it is impossible for a notary to certify to his knowledge of the parties, and the latter are unable to present any identifying witness or witnesses, the notary shall so express, designating the documents presented to him as proof of their name, status and residence, and stating also the cause of such serious and extraordinary case.

§ 1017. **Form of public instruments; language; notary's certification; instruments executed outside Puerto Rico.** Public instruments shall be drawn up in the Spanish language, but may be in English, provided the notary, the parties, and the witnesses, if required or solicited pursuant to sections 1014, 1016, and 1027 of this title, know said language. No abbreviations shall be used nor blank spaces left therein, and the originals may be either manuscript, printed, or typewritten, but in this latter case ribbons of indelible color shall be used, lest the notary be subject to a maximum fine of five hundred (500) dollars imposable by the Supreme Court on recommendation of the protocol inspectors. Dates and amounts shall not be expressed in figures unless spelled immediately after, and the notary shall certify that he has read the instrument to the parties and to the witnesses, where the latter are required or have been solicited, or that he allowed them to read same, at their option, before signing it. The notary need not state in each clause of the instrument that he certifies to the stipulations and statements contained therein or to the legal conditions or circumstances of the persons or things referred to; it shall be sufficient for him to state for once at the end of the instrument that he certifies to everything contained therein, and said statement shall be understood to apply to every word, stipulation, statement, and condition, real or personal, contained in the instrument, in accordance with law. No operation shall be carried out in the books of the Registry of Property in connection with a notarial instrument executed outside of Puerto Rico unless the same has been previously protocolized in Puerto Rico, and it shall be the duty of the notary to cancel the same scheduled fees as if the instrument had been originally executed in Puerto Rico. Provided, however, that it shall not be necessary to protocolize the certificates issued outside of Puerto Rico of resolutions adopted by the board of directors of a banking entity, corporation or trust; but same shall be duly authenticated before the notary; Provided, further, That the protocolization instrument and its certified copies of documents executed outside of Puerto Rico, of assignment to any United States or foreign banking institution not authorized to do business in Puerto Rico of any share in a loan made to the Commonwealth of Puerto Rico or any public corporation or government instrumentality or municipality of Puerto Rico, or that any such borrower has guaranteed or is liable for the payment thereof, shall be executed free from the payment of the scheduled fees above mentioned.

§ 1018. **Changes in instruments.** Any additions, annotations, interlineations, erasures or striking-out of words in original instruments shall be valueless unless mentioned at the foot thereof, with the express approval of the parties and the signatures of those who are to sign the instrument.

§ 1019. **Blank spaces.** A blank space at the end of a line shall not be considered as such when the next line begins with a paragraph, but in that case such blank space shall be filled in with a line drawn.

§ 1020. Public instruments which are void or voidable. The following public instruments shall be null and void:

1. Those in which the authorizing notary has intervened as a party thereto, or which contain any provision in his favor.

2. Where witnesses are required or solicited under sections 1014, 1016, and 1027 of this title and the same are covered by any of the limitations prescribed in section 1015 of this title.

3. Where the signatures of the parties, when required, the signature of the notary, and, in the cases to which sections 1014, 1016, and 1027 of this title refer, the signatures of the witnesses, do not appear.

Public instruments in which the notary fails to certify to his knowledge of the parties or to supply this deficiency with an identifying witness or witnesses shall be voidable, unless through a public deed or notarial instrument or by a memorandum following the signatures in the instrument the same notary who authorized the defective instrument attests to his knowledge of said parties at the time of executing same.

If on account of the death of the notary or of the parties, or because of the time elapsed, or for any other reason, it is not possible to make such reparation, it may be sought through judicial proceeding before the Superior Court of Puerto Rico.

Public documents in which the pertinent fees have not been affixed shall be voidable only if any of the parties thereto do not deliver to the proper official, for immediate cancellation, the full amount of said fees, all without prejudice to the provisions of section 1035 of this title.

The provisions of this section shall be applicable to all public deeds and instruments executed prior to the approval of this chapter and to those executed thereafter. Public deeds or instruments judicially challenged or held null by final judgment on the date this chapter is approved shall not be validated under the provisions of this section.

§ 1021. Provisions in favor of notary's relatives. Provisions in favor of relatives within the fourth degree of consanguinity or second degree of affinity of the notary certifying the instrument wherein said provisions are made shall be ineffective.

§ 1022. Wills and other dispositions causa mortis. The provisions hereof as to the form of public instruments and the qualifications of witnesses, where required, and as to the capacity to acquire property left or bequeathed by a testator, shall not apply to wills and other dispositions causa mortis, which shall be governed by the special law or laws on the matter.

Copies

§ 1023. Certified copy defined. By certified copy is understood the literal transcript of the whole or part of an instrument executed

before a notary, issued by him or by the person who is lawfully
in charge of the protocol,° on request of an interested party; Provided, That in the case of a partial certified copy, the notary shall
so state.

(°) For the definition of "protocol", see *Records*, P.R. LAWS ANN.
tit. 4, § 1028.

**§ 1025. Persons entitled to copies; memorandum of issue; electro-
mechanic reproduction.** The parties, their constituents and successors in interest under the contract, and any other interested person,
may request and obtain from the notary the pertinent certified copies
of the original instruments. Any other person may also obtain
certified copies of a notarial instrument upon justified request to the
Superior Court, which may in its reasonable discretion issue an
order to that effect.

Upon issuing a certified copy the notary shall state whether that
is the first copy he issues or the number appertaining to it according
to the copies already issued, and shall set forth this same fact
by a memorandum at the foot or on the margin of the original
instrument of which the certified copy is issued, stating also the
name of the person to whom issued and the date. This memorandum shall be signed by the notary.

Public notaries are hereby empowered to issue certified photographic or photostatic copies or copies reproduced by any other
electromechanic means of reproduction designed to obtain an exact
reproduction of an original, of original instruments in their protocols,
which copies shall be certified by the notary as if they were printed,
manuscript or typewritten copies of an instrument, affixing to the original of the instrument or deed the proper extraction note, upon
payment of the cost of reproduction of said copies, plus the fees
prescribed by law for the issuance of copies and payment of the
proper internal revenue tax fixed by law for the issuance of certified
copies. Said copies shall be held to be equivalent to a duly
certified copy and shall as such be admissible in evidence.

**§ 1026. Reports to Superior Court; certificates of wills to Supreme
Court; powers of attorney.** On and after the approval of this chapter
notaries shall forward to the part of the Superior Court to which
his notarial office appertains, not later than Monday of each week,
a report stating that no deeds or affidavits have been executed or
else giving the indices of the original deeds and the affidavits
executed by them during the preceding week, with the serial numbers thereof in the protocols, and with respect to each instrument,
the names of the parties thereto, the date of execution and the
purpose of the act or contract, and where witnesses are required
or permitted hereunder, the names of such witnesses. The protocol
inspectors shall see to the enforcement of the provisions of this
paragraph.

Likewise, notaries shall send the Secretary of the Supreme Court of Puerto Rico by registered mail, return receipt requested, within twenty-four hours after its execution, a certificate authorized by them with their signatures and notarial seals, of each original deed of constitution, modification, revocation, extension or protocolization of will executed by them, stating in said certificate the number of the deed, the date, place and time of execution, the name of the testator or testatrix with their personal circumstances, and the names of the witnesses; and it shall be the duty of the Secretary of the Supreme Court of Puerto Rico to acknowledge receipt of this certificate to the notary and to take note of the name and surname of the testator and all other data set forth in said notarial certificate, in order that the said Secretary may thereafter issue, as he is hereby authorized to issue, upon delivery of a fifty-cent internal revenue stamp which shall be cancelled by him, and on petition of an interested party or of his attorney, a certificate stating whether or not the execution of the will in question has been recorded. The Secretary of the Supreme Court shall have under his custody the certificate of the notaries as to the authorization of wills and shall bind same in the order of remittance. The Superior Court shall not admit or process any petition for a declaration of heirs which is not accompanied by a certificate from the Secretary of the Supreme Court of Puerto Rico stating over his signature and official seal that there is no record in his office that the person designated has executed a will. As to the execution of powers of attorney, the notary shall comply with the provisions of the Power of Attorney Registry Act, sections 921-927 of this title.

§ 1027. **When witnesses required; procedure.** In the execution of public deeds and instruments, the intervention of witnesses shall not be required except if requested by the authorizing notary or any of the parties, or when a blind person is involved therein, or when any of the parties does not know how or is unable to sign, as provided in section 1014 of this title, or where an identifying witness or witnesses is a requisite, as provided in section 1016 of this title.

Where witnesses are required, at least two persons shall appear in such capacity except in the cases provided in the first paragraph of section 1014 of this title or in the case provided in section 1016 of this title.

Where witnesses appear, the act of the execution shall be one sole act, but if witnesses do not intervene, the provisions of section 1013 of this title shall govern.

Where a party is blind, the instrument shall be read aloud twice, once by the notary and again by one of the witnesses or by other person designated by said party; and if, besides, said party does not know how or is unable to sign, then the provisions of section 1014 of this title shall govern.

Tit. 32, § 2248. Place of recording [of nuncupative will]; filing of certified copy by notary. The recording [of a nuncupative will] by the interested parties, or if they be not agreed as to the designation, the same shall be made by the judge of the court. Within the five (5) days following the date on which the recording is ordered, the notary designated to make such recording shall file with the Superior Court, free from the payment of scheduled fees on presentation of an order to that effect, to be issued by the judge on petition of the notary himself, a certified copy of the documents entrusted to his custody; Provided, That when said term lapses without the notary's having complied with that obligation, any of the parties on whose petition a nuncupative will may be reduced to a public instrument may appear in court to petition that said requisite be complied with.

Concerning the curing of defects in notarial instruments, see *Records*, P.R. LAWS ANN. tit. 4, § 1032.

[P.R. R. SUP. CT. 9]

Notaries. (a) ° ° ° [The notary] shall forward to [the Part of the Superior Court within his domicile] on Monday of every week his indices of deeds and affidavits. The notaries shall ° ° ° notify any change of residence or notarial office to the Secretary of the Supreme Court, the secretary of the corresponding Part of the Superior Court and to the protocol inspectors.

(b) [Omitted.]

(c) The notaries shall send by registered mail, receipt requested, to the secretary of this Court, within twenty-four hours after its execution, a certificate authorized by them under their notarial seal, of each matrix of a will executed or protocolized by them, stating in said certificate the number of the deed, the date of its execution, and the name of the testator or testatrix, as well as their personal description; and it shall be the duty of the secretary of the Supreme Court to acknowledge receipt of this certificate to the notary and to proceed immediately after receipt thereof to annotate it in the Register of Wills in order that the secretary may thereafter issue, after payment of the proper fees and on petition of an interested party or of his attorney, a certificate stating whether or not the execution of the will in question is annotated in said book; Provided, That no part of the Superior Court of Puerto Rico shall admit or take into consideration any petition for declaration of heirs if the petition is not accompanied by a certificate from the secretary of this Court, in which certificate he states under his signature and the seal of this Court, that it does not appear from the entries in the said Register that the person referred to has executed any will.

(d) It shall be the duty of every notary before whom a deed to constitute, modify, extend, substitute, renounce, revoke or protocolize a power of attorney is executed, to send to the secretary of this Court, by registered mail within seventy-two hours following the execution thereof, a notice certified under his seal, setting forth therein the name or names of the grantor or grantors and of the witnesses, and the date, number and nature of the deed, specifying the person to whom the power of attorney is granted, extended, modified, or revoked. In case of substitution of a power of attorney, the name of the person substituted and of the attorney-in-fact shall be stated in said notice, and in cases of renunciation of the power of attorney, the name of the constituent thereof shall be given. Where the protocolization of a power of attorney executed outside of Puerto Rico is sought, it shall be the duty of the notary to set forth also the date and place of the execution of the power protocolized, name of the attorney-in-fact and the constituent of the power, notary before whom the power protocolized was executed and the officer who attested to the signature of said notary. It shall be the duty of the secretary of this Court to acknowledge to the notaries receipt of said notice and to proceed immediately after receipt thereof to make the corresponding entry in the register prescribed by law.

RHODE ISLAND

[R.I. GEN. LAWS ANN.]

§ 19-4-4. Protests not to be made by bank officers. No protest of any note, draft or check shall be made by any notary public who is the president, cashier, director, or officer of any bank, savings bank, or trust company wherein such note, draft or check has been placed for collection or has been discounted.

§ 36-2-1. Officers with statewide power. The following persons may administer oaths anywhere within the state: The governor, lieutenant governor, secretary of state, attorney-general, assistant attorneys-general, general treasurer, justices of the supreme, superior, family and district courts, each member of the general assembly after he has filed his signature with the secretary of state, commissioners appointed by other states to take acknowledgments of deeds and depositions within this state and notaries public.

§ 42-30-7. Powers of notaries and justices. [Notaries public and justices of the peace] shall possess all the powers which now are or hereafter may be conferred by law upon justices of the peace or notaries public.

§ 42-30-8. Powers of notaries. Notaries public may, within this state act, transact, do and finish matters and things relating to protests and protesting bills of exchange and promissory notes, and all other matters within their office required by law; take depositions as prescribed by law, and acknowledgments of deeds and other instruments.

§ 42-30-11. Continuation of powers without reappointment. Every justice of the peace and notary public appointed by the governor and not reappointed, may continue to officiate for a space of thirty (30) days after the first day of July in the year in which his commission expires.

§ 42-30-12. Continuation of powers without new engagement. Every such officer who may be reappointed or continued in office, may continue to officiate for the same length of time without taking a new engagement.°

(°) The word "engaged" is construed to include either sworn or affirmed. See *Depositions*, R.I. GEN. LAWS ANN. § 43-3-11.

SOUTH CAROLINA

[S.C. CODE ANN.]

§ 12-1004. Acknowledgments. No person who is authorized to take acknowledgments under the laws of this State shall be disqualified from taking acknowledgments of instruments executed in favor of a cooperative or to which it is a party by reason of being an officer, director or member of such cooperative.

§ 49-6. Seal of office; notary to indicate date of expiration of commission. Each notary public shall have a seal of office, which shall be affixed to his instruments of publications and to his protestations. He shall indicate below his signature the date of expiration of his commission. But the absence of such seal or date prior to and after May 30, 1968 shall not render his acts invalid if his official title be affixed thereto.

§ 49-7. Jurisdiction. The jurisdiction of notaries public shall extend throughout the State.

§ 4918. Powers generally. A notary public may administer oaths, take depositions, affidavits, protests for nonpayment of bonds, notes, drafts and bills of exchange, acknowledgments and proof of deeds and other instruments required by law to be acknowledged and renunciations of dower and perform all other acts provided by law to be performed by notaries public.

§ 49-9. No jurisdiction in criminal cases. A notary public shall exercise no power or jurisdiction in criminal cases.

§ 49-10. Effect of employment as attorney. Any attorney at law who is a notary public may exercise all his powers as a notary notwithstanding the fact that he may be interested as counsel or attorney at law in any matter with respect to which he may so exercise any such power and may probate in any court in this State in which he may be counsel.

§ 49-11.   Not disqualified when stockholder, director, officer or employee of corporation.   A notary public who is a stockholder, director, officer or employee of a corporation may take renunciation of dower in any written instrument, take the acknowledgment or the oath of a subscribing witness of any party to a written instrument executed to or by such corporation, administer an oath to any stockholder, director, officer, employee or agent of such corporation or protest for nonacceptance or nonpayment bills of exchange, drafts, checks, notes and other negotiable instruments which may be owned or held for collection by such corporation.   But when a notary public is individually a party to an instrument it shall be unlawful for him to take the acknowledgment or probate to such instrument executed by or to a corporation of which he is a stockholder, director, officer or employee or to protest any such negotiable instrument owned or held for collection by such corporation.

§ 49-12.   Force of jurat of notaries public in other states.   All verifications of pleadings, affidavits and proofs of claims made before notaries public in other states shall have the same force and effect as they would have if sworn to before a commissioner of deeds for this State resident in another state.

§ 49-13.   Officers of Armed Forces or Merchant Marine to act as notaries public.   Beginning December 7, 1941 any commissioned officer of the Armed Forces of the United States or any officer of the United States Merchant Marine, serving either within or without the limits of the United States, is authorized to verify pleadings, probate deeds and mortgages, take renunciations of dower, proofs of claims and to otherwise act in the same capacity as a notary public.   When acting as such the officer shall sign his name, rank, serial number and organization and in such cases no official seal shall be necessary.

SOUTH DAKOTA

Notaries have authority anywhere in the state to administer oaths and perform all other duties required of them by law.   See *Appointment*, S.D. COMPILED LAWS ANN. § 18-1-1.

The commission issued to the notary by the secretary of state, or the duplicate thereof issued by the same officer, must be posted by the notary in a conspicuous place in his office for public inspection. See *Appointment*, S.D. COMPILED LAWS ANN. § 18-1-4.

Whenever a notary changes his place of residence from the county in which he was first appointed to another county, it is his duty to comply with the requirements of S.D. COMPILED LAWS § 18-1-5, concerning the recording of his commission and seal by the clerk of courts, before he again enters upon the duties of his office. See *Appointment*, S.D. COMPILED LAWS ANN. §§ 18-1-5, 18-1-6.

[S.D. COMPILED LAWS ANN.]

§ 18-1-7.   Notarial acts valid despite notary's agency for party to transaction.   A notary public who is personally interested directly or indirectly, or as a stockholder, officer, agent, attorney, or employee of any person or party to any transaction concerning which he is exercising any function of his office as such notary public, may make any certificates, take any acknowledgments, administer any oaths or do any other official acts as such notary public with the same legal force and effect as if he had no such interest except that he cannot do any of such things in connection with any instrument which shows upon its face that he is a principal party thereto.

§ 18-1-8.   Notice to parties when instrument protested by notary— Fee—Record of protests and notices.   It shall be the duty of each notary public when any bill of exchange, promissory note, or other written instrument shall be by him protested for nonacceptance or nonpayment, immediately after such protest shall have been made, to give notice in writing thereof to each and every party to such instrument whose liability in connection therewith would be affected by want of such notice.

It shall be the duty of every notary public personally to serve notice upon the person or persons protested against, or by properly folding the notice, directing it to the party to be charged at his place of residence, according to the best information that the person giving the notice can obtain, depositing it in the United States mail or post office most conveniently accessible from the place where the protest was made, and prepaying the postage thereon.

The officer making such protest shall receive the sum of twenty-five cents and postage for each and every notice so made out and served.

Each notary public shall keep a record of all such notices and of the time and manner in which the same shall have been served and of the names of all the parties to whom the same were directed, and the description and amount of the instrument protested, which record or a copy thereof certified by the notary under seal, shall at all times be competent evidence to prove such notice in any trial before any court in this state where proof of such notice may become requisite.

§ 18-1-10.   Faith and credit to notarial acts.   Full faith and credit shall be given to all the protestations, attestations, and other instruments of publication, of all notaries public now in office or hereafter to be appointed under the provisions of this chapter.

§ 18-3-1.   Officers authorized to administer oaths.   The following officers are authorized to administer oaths:

(1)   Supreme Court judges, circuit judges, notaries public, and

the clerk and deputy clerk of the Supreme Court, within the state;

o   o   o

§ 18-3-5. Affirmation in lieu of oath. Persons conscientiously opposed to swearing may affirm, and shall be subject to the penalties of perjury as in case of swearing.

TENNESSEE

[TENN. CODE ANN.]

§ 8-1608. Location of office. Every notary public shall keep his office in the county in which he shall be appointed.

§ 8-1609. Qualification in other counties. A notary public elected and commissioned for any county in the state, upon filing in the office of the clerk of the county court for any other county, his autograph signature and a certificate of the clerk of the county court for which he was elected, commissioned and qualified, setting forth the fact of his election, commission and date thereof and of qualifications as such notary public and paying to the clerk of the county court of said other county a fee of one dollar ($1.00), may exercise all the functions of his office in the county in which such autograph signature and certificate are filed, with the same effect as if same were executed in the county in which he resided and for which he was appointed.

§ 8-1610. Certificate of clerk of other county. The clerk of other county court of a county in whose office any notary public residing in another county has so filed his autograph signature and such certificate shall, when so requested, subjoin to any certificate of proof or acknowledgment signed by such notary public a certificate under his hand and seal, stating that such notary public has filed a certificate of his election, commission and qualification, with his autograph signature, in the office of said clerk, and was at the time of taking such proof or acknowledgment duly authorized to take the same; and that he is well acquainted with the handwriting of such notary public and believes that the signature to such proof or acknowledgment is genuine, and thereupon the instrument so proved or acknowledged and certified shall be entitled to be read in evidence or to be recorded in any of the counties of this state in respect to which a certificate of the clerk of the county court may be necessary for either purpose.

§ 8-1611. Certificate of qualification in other county. Whenever a notary public takes an affidavit, proof or acknowledgment in a county other than the county for which he was elected, commissioned and qualified, he shall add to his certificate, following his official signature and the date of expiration of his commission, a statement that he is qualified in such other county under the provisions of §§ 8-1609 and 8-1610.

§ 8-1612. Qualification as notary at large. Any notary public who has been duly elected by the county court of any county and who has otherwise qualified may, upon application to the secretary of state, be issued a certificate authorizing him to exercise the functions of a notary public in all the counties in Tennessee. He shall pay in to the secretary of state a fee of two dollars ($2.00) for such certificate and his name shall be registered in a book kept in the office of the secretary of state for that purpose, and the fees so collected by the secretary shall go into the same fund and be used for the same purposes that other fees in connection with the qualification of notaries public are used.

§ 8-1613. Powers of notary at large. The qualifications, powers, duties, fees and liabilities of such notaries shall be the same as those prescribed by law for notaries public elected by the county courts, except that they are authorized to act in any county in the state instead of only in the county of their residence and election; §§ 8-1612 — 8-1618 not being intended in any manner to repeal or modify the law with reference to notaries public elected by the county courts but to create another class of notaries public with power to act in any county in Tennessee.

§ 8-1616. Title of notary at large. Any notary public receiving the certificate, as provided in § 8-1612, shall be known as a notary public at large for the state of Tennessee, and his official signature shall so indicate.

§ 8-1620. Powers of notary. Notaries public shall have power to administer oaths, to take depositions, to qualify parties to bills in chancery, and to affidavits, in all cases; and in all such cases the notary's seal shall be affixed.

§ 8-1621. Expiration of commission indicated on instruments. All notaries public within this state shall be and they are required to have written, stamped, or printed on every certificate of acknowledgment, officially attached and affixed to any instrument, the true date of the expiration of their several commissions, when the same is attached and affixed to said instrument; provided, however, that the failure so to do shall not render void or invalidate such certificate of acknowledgment, but shall subject such notary public to the penalty below prescribed. A violation of the provisions of this section is a misdemeanor, and any person so offending shall pay a fine of not less than twenty-five dollars ($25.00) nor more than one hundred dollars ($100) for each offense.

§ 8-1622. Receipt of instruments in evidence. The attestations, protestations, and other instruments of publication or acknowledgment, made by any notary public under his seal, shall be received in evidence.

§ 8-1623. Notice of deposition of notary. The deposition of a notary may be taken, whether a suit be pending or not, on ten (10) days' notice to the opposite party, if resident in the state, and forty (40) days' notice out of it; to be read as evidence between the same parties in any suit then or afterward depending, should the notary die or remove out of the state before the trial.

§ 65-2518. Trustees, officers or members may take acknowledgments. No person who is authorized to take acknowledgments under the laws of this state shall be disqualified from taking acknowledgments of instruments executed in favor of a cooperative° or to which it is a party, by reason of being an officer, director, or member of such cooperative.

(°) As used in this section, a "cooperative" is a cooperative, non-profit membership corporation organized for the purpose of supplying electric energy and promoting and extending the use thereof. Electric Cooperative Law. TENN. CODE ANN. § 65-2503.

§ 65-2927. Acknowledgments by officers, directors or members. No person who is authorized to take acknowledgments under the laws of this state shall be disqualified from taking acknowledgments of instruments executed in favor of a cooperative°° or to which it is a party, by reason of being an officer, director, or member of such cooperative.

(°°) As used in this section, a "cooperative" is a cooperative, non-profit membership corporation organized for the purpose of furnishing telephone service in rural areas to the widest practical number of users of such service. Telephone Cooperatives. TENN. CODE ANN. § 65-2902.

TEXAS

[TEX. REV. CIV. STAT. ANN.]

Art. 5954. Authority of notary; printing or stamping of name under signature. Notaries Public shall have the same authority to take acknowledgments or proofs of written instruments, protests [sic] instruments permitted by law to be protested, administer oaths, and take depositions, as is now or may hereafter be conferred by law upon County Clerks, and provided further that all Notaries Public shall print or stamp their names under their signatures on all such written instruments, protests [sic] instruments, oaths, or depositions; provided that failure to so print or stamp their names under their signatures shall not invalidate such acknowledgment.

Art. 5956. Copies of records. Copies of all records, declarations, protests, and other official acts of notaries public may be certified by the county clerk with whom they are deposited, and shall have the same authority as if certified by the notary by whom they are originally made.

Various Special Provisions

Art. 852a.   [Savings and loan associations.]

✿   ✿   ✿

Acknowledgments by members and employees

Sec. 11.02.   No public officer qualified to take acknowledgments or proofs of written instruments shall be disqualified from taking the acknowledgments or proofs of any instrument in writing in which [a savings and loan] association or Federal [savings and loan] association is interested by reason of his membership in or stockholding in or employment by such an institution so interested, and any such acknowledgments or proofs heretofore taken are hereby validated.

✿   ✿   ✿

Art. 1528c.   Telephone Cooperative Act.

Short title

Section 1.   This Act may be cited as the "Telephone Cooperative Act."

Definitions

Sec. 2.   In this Act, unless the context otherwise requires:

(1)   "Corporation" means any corporation organized under this Act or which becomes subject to this Act in the manner hereinafter provided.

✿   ✿   ✿

Directors, officers or members—notaries

Sec. 27.   No person who is authorized to take acknowledgments under the laws of this State shall be disqualified from taking acknowledgments of instruments executed in favor of a corporation or to which it is a party, by reason of being an officer, director, or member of such corporation.

✿   ✿   ✿

Art. 342-509a.   Stockholders, Officers and Employees [of Banks]— Authority to Take Acknowledgments.

No Notary Public or other Public Officer qualified to take acknowledgments or proofs of written instruments shall be disqualified from taking the acknowledgment or proof of an instrument in writing in which a State bank, national bank or private bank is interested by reason of his ownership of stock in or employment by the State or national or private bank interested in such instrument, and any such acknowledgment heretofore taken is hereby validated.

UTAH

[UTAH CODE ANN.]

§ 7-13-50. Acknowledgments of instruments by public officer interested in [savings and loan] association. No public officer qualified to take acknowledgments or proofs of written instruments shall be disqualified from taking the acknowledgment or proof of any instrument, in writing, in which [a savings and loan] association is interested, by reason of his membership in or employment by an association so interested, and any such acknowledgments or proofs heretofore taken are hereby validated.

Note: See also § 46-1-10, below, concerning banks and other corporations.

Editorial comment

Notaries public shall be appointed for the state at large. See *Appointment*, UTAH CODE ANN. § 46-1-1.

§ 46-1-5. Powers. Notaries public may exercise the following powers within this state: Administer all oaths provided by law, acknowledge powers of attorney and all such instruments of writing conveying or affecting property in any part of this state, or elsewhere as may be lawful; take affidavits and depositions; make declarations and protests; and do all other acts usually done by notaries public.

§ 46-1-8. Affix to signature place of residence and date commission expires. To all acknowledgments, oaths, affirmations and instruments of every kind taken and certified by a notary public he shall affix to his signature his official title and his place of residence and the date on which his commission expires.

§ 46-1-10. Disqualification because of interest. Any notary public who is a stockholder, director, officer or employee of a bank or other corporation may take the acknowledgment of any party to any written instrument executed to or by such corporation, and may administer an oath to any other stockholder, director, officer, employee or agent of such corporation, and may protest for nonacceptance or nonpayment bills of exchange, drafts, checks, notes and other negotiable instruments which may be owned, or held for collection, by such corporation; but it shall be unlawful for any notary public to take the acknowledgment of any person to an instrument executed by or to a bank or other corporation of which he is a stockholder, director, officer or employee where he is a party to such instrument, either individually or as a representative of such corporation, or to protest any negotiable instrument owned or held for collection by such corporation where he is individually a party to such instrument.

Note: See also § 7-13-50, above, concerning savings and loan associations.

VERMONT

The jurisdiction of a notary public extends throughout the state. See *Appointment*, VT. STAT. ANN. tit. 24, § 441.

[VT. STAT. ANN]

Tit. 11, § 231.   Acknowledgments by stockholder or officer.   A person legally qualified to take acknowledgments shall not be disqualified to take such acknowledgments to an instrument in which a corporation is a party, by reason of his being a stockholder in or an officer or employee of such corporation.

Note: See also tit. 30, § 3036, below, concerning electric cooperatives.

Tit. 12, § 5852.   Oaths of office; by whom administered.   When other provision is not made by law, oaths of office may be administered by any justice of the supreme court, superior judge, justice of the peace, judge of the district court, notary public or the presiding officer, secretary or clerk of either house of the general assembly.

Tit. 12, § 5854.   Oaths, administering by court clerks, justices, notaries, etc.; certification.   The clerk of the supreme court, county clerks, justices of the peaces, judges and registers of probate, judges and clerks of the district court, notaries public and masters appointed by a county court under an order of referee may administer oaths in all cases where an oath is required, unless a different provision is expressly made by law; and a notary public need not affix his official seal to a certificate of an oath administered by him. County clerks and clerks of the district court may certify the oaths administered by them under the seal of the court.

Tit. 30, § 3036.   Acknowledgments, members [of electric cooperatives] authorized.   A person who is authorized to take acknowledgments under the laws of this state shall not be disqualified from taking acknowledgments of instruments executed in favor of [an electric cooperative] or to which it is a party, by reason of being an officer, trustee or member of such cooperative.

Note: See also tit. 11, § 231, above, concerning corporations.

VIRGIN ISLANDS

[V.I. CODE ANN.]

Tit. 3, § 777.   Powers; limitations.   (a)   Notaries public may take acknowledgments of deeds and other instruments, administer oaths and affirmations, and perform such other acts as may be authorized by law.

(b) No notary public shall certify, attest or take an oath or acknowledgment for or to an instrument to which he is an interested party.

Special Notaries Public

Tit. 3, § 802. Oath of office; records to be kept. Notaries public appointed and commissioned under section 801 of this title* shall take an official oath and keep an official record in which a memorandum of all official acts shall be noted.

(*) See *Qualifications*, "Special Notaries Public," V.I. CODE ANN. tit. 3, § 801.

Tit. 3, § 805. Restriction on powers; exception.°° (a) Except as otherwise provided in subsection (b) of this section, notaries public appointed and commissioned under section 801 of this title, shall not be permitted to take acknowledgments of deeds and administer oaths and affirmations except on matters of official business of the Government of the Virgin Islands or the Government of the United States, and no fees for such acknowledgments and oaths or affirmations shall be charged.

(b) Not to exceed four of the notaries public commissioned under subsection (a) of section 801 of this title for the Island of St. John, two for the area of Cruz Bay and two for the area of Coral Bay, shall be permitted, in addition to the powers granted in that section, to take acknowledgments of deeds, and administer oaths and affirmations in matters not connected with official business of the Government of the Virgin Islands, in which cases the regular fees for such acknowledgments, oaths and affirmations shall be charged and deposited in the General Fund of the Treasury.

(°°) For § 801 mentioned herein, see *Qualifications*, "Special Notaries Public," V.I. CODE ANN. tit. 3, § 801.

VIRGINIA

A notary or other officer returning affidavits or depositions shall state at the foot thereof the fees therefor, to whom charged and, if paid, by whom. See *Fees Chargeable*, VA. CODE ANN. § 14.1-98.

Notaries are authorized to exercise the powers and functions of conservators of the peace. The Governor may appoint the same person to serve for two or more counties and cities. A notary for a city also has authority to act as such in counties and cities contiguous thereto. A notary for a county also has authority to act as such in cities contiguous thereto. See *Appointment*, VA. CODE ANN. § 47-1 (1), (2), (3).

A notary appointed for the state at large may exercise the same powers and functions, and is subject to the same restrictions and regulations, as are prescribed by law for notaries for counties and cities, except that a notary at large is empowered to act as a notary in any county or city in the state. See *Appointment*, VA. CODE ANN. § 47-2.

[VA. CODE ANN.]

§ 49-4. **Justices and other officers who may administer oaths and take affidavits.** Any oath or affidavit required by law, which is not of such nature that it must be made in court, may be administered by or made before a justice of the peace and certified by him, unless otherwise provided, a notary, a commissioner in chancery, a commissioner appointed by the Governor, or a court or clerk of a court or deputy clerk of a court, or clerks of city councils, common councils, or boards of aldermen; or in case of a survey directed by a court in a cause therein pending, by or before the surveyor directed to execute the order of survey.

See also *Acknowledgments* and *Depositions*.

WASHINGTON

[WASH. REV. CODE ANN.]

§ 42.28.040. **Powers—General.** Every duly qualified notary public is authorized in any county in this state—(1) to transact and perform all matters and things relating to protests, protesting bills of exchange and promissory notes, and such other duties as pertain to that office by the custom and laws merchant; (2) to take acknowledgments of all deeds and other instruments of writing, and certify the same in the manner required by law; (3) to take depositions and affidavits, and administer all oaths required by law to be administered, and every attorney at law who is a notary public may administer any oath to his client, and no pleading or affidavit shall, on that account, be held by any court to be improperly verified.

§ 42.28.050. **Powers as to banks and corporations.** It shall be lawful for any notary public who is a stockholder, director, officer or employee of a bank or other corporation to take the acknowledgment of any party to any written instrument executed to or by such corporation, or to protest for nonacceptance or nonpayment bills of exchange, drafts, checks, notes and other negotiable instruments which may be owned or held for collection by such corporation: *Provided*, It shall be unlawful for any notary public to take the acknowledgment of an instrument by or to a bank or other corporation of which he is a stockholder, director, officer or employee, where such notary is a party to such instrument individually or to protest any negotiable instrument owned or held for collection by such corporation, where such notary is individually a party to such instrument.

WEST VIRGINIA

[W. VA. CODE ANN.]

§ 29-4-3. Power as to oaths, affidavits and depositions. When any oath may lawfully be administered, or affidavit or deposition taken, within any county, it may be done by a notary thereof, unless otherwise expressly provided by law.

§ 29-4-4. Power to take acknowledgments and as conservator of peace. A notary, under the regulations prescribed by law, may take, within his county, and the county or counties to which his commission has been extended, acknowledgments of deeds and other writings. He shall be a conservator of the peace within the county of his residence, and as such conservator shall exercise all the powers conferred by law upon justices of the peace.

§ 29-4-6. Powers as to protests and other matters. Notaries shall have authority to demand acceptance of foreign and inland bills of exchange, including checks, and to demand payment thereof, and of negotiable promissory notes, and protest the same for nonacceptance or nonpayment, as the case may require; and perform such other duties as by the law of nations or commercial usage may be performed by notaries public.

§ 29-4-7. Powers of notaries connected with banks or other corporations. It shall be lawful for any notary who is a stockholder, director, officer or employee of a banking institution, including national banking associations, or other corporation, to take the acknowledgment of any party to any written instrument executed to or by such corporation, or to administer an oath to any other stockholder, director, officer, employee or agent of such corporation, or to protest, for nonacceptance or nonpayment, bills of exchange, drafts, checks, notes and other negotiable instruments which may be owned or held for collection by such corporation; Provided, that it shall be unlawful for any notary public to take the acknowledgment of an instrument by or to a banking institution, including national banking association, or other corporation, of which he is a stockholder, director, officer, or employee, when such notary is a party to such instrument, either personally or as a representative of such corporation; or to protest any negotiable instrument owned or held for collection by such corporation, when such notary is personally a party to such instrument.

§ 29-4-8. Signature of notary to state date of expiration of commission. The official signature of any notary shall state the date of expiration of his commission, but a misstatement of such date shall not invalidate any official act of such notary, if his commission be at the time thereof in force.

Editorial comment

It is the duty of all ministerial officers, including among others, notaries public, to report to the prosecuting attorney of the county the names of all persons guilty of violating any of the provisions of W. VA. CODE ANN. article 7 (Dangerous Weapons) of Chapter 61 (Crimes and Their Punishment). There is a penalty for failure to report. See *Offenses*, W. VA. CODE ANN. § 61-7-13.

WISCONSIN

[WIS. STAT. ANN.]

§ 137.01. Notaries.

○   ○   ○

(4) **Attestation.** (a) Every official act of a notary public shall be attested by his written signature.

(4) (b) All certificates of acknowledgments of deeds and other conveyances, or any written instrument required or authorized by law to be acknowledged or sworn to before any notary public, within this state, shall be attested by a clear impression of the official seal or imprint of the rubber stamp of said officer, and in addition thereto shall be written or stamped either the day, month and year when the commission of said notary public will expire, or that such commission is permanent.

(c) The official certificate of any notary public, when attested and completed in the manner provided by this subsection, shall be presumptive evidence in all cases, and in all courts of the state, of the facts therein stated, in cases whereby law a notary public is authorized to certify such facts.

(5) **Powers.** Notaries public have power to act throughout the state. Notaries public have power to demand acceptance of foreign and inland bills of exchange and payment thereof, and payment of promissory notes, and may protest the same for nonacceptance or nonpayment, may administer oaths, take depositions and acknowledgments of deeds, and perform such other duties as by the law of nations, or according to commercial usage, may be exercised and performed by notaries public.

(6) **Authentication.**

(6) (a) The secretary of state may certify to the official qualifications of any notary public and to the genuineness of his signature and seal or rubber stamp.

(b) Whenever any notary public has filed in the office of the clerk of the circuit court of his county of residence his signature, an impression of his official seal or imprint of his official rubber stamp and a certificate of the secretary of state, such clerk may certify to the official qualifications of such notary public and the genuineness of his signature and seal or rubber stamp.

(c)   Any certificate specified under this subsection shall be presumptive evidence of the facts therein stated.

(6m)   Change of residence.   A notary public shall not vacate his office by reason of his change of residence within the state. Written notice of any change of address shall be given to the secretary of state within 5 days of such change.

◦   ◦   ◦

(8)   Misconduct.   If any notary public shall be guilty of any misconduct or neglect of duty in office he shall be liable to the party injured for all the damages thereby sustained.

◦   ◦   ◦

§ 220.18.   Bank or corporation notaries; permitted acts.   It shall be lawful for any notary public who is a stockholder, director, officer or employe of a bank or other corporation to take the acknowledgment of any party to any written instrument executed to or by such corporation, or to administer an oath to any other stockholder, director, officer, employe or agent of such corporation, or to protest for nonacceptance or nonpayment bills of exchange, drafts, checks, notes and other negotiable instruments which may be owned or held for collection by such corporation, if such notary is not a party to such instrument, either individually or as a representative of such corporation.

§ 409.403.   What constitutes filing; ° ° °.   (1) Presentation for filing of a financing statement and tender of the filing fee or acceptance of the statement by the filing officer constitutes filing under this chapter.   An accurate reproduction of the financing statement, certified to be a true copy by the secured party, public officer or notary public, or a carbon copy bearing signatures appearing by carbon impression, may be filed.

§ 887.01.   Oaths, who may administer.   (1)   Within the state.   (1)   An oath or affidavit required or authorized by law, except oaths to jurors and witnesses on a trial and such other oaths as are required by law to be taken before particular officers, may be taken before any judge, court commissioner, resident United States commissioner who has complied with s. 706.07, clerk, deputy clerk or calendar clerk of a court of record, notary public, town clerk, village clerk, city clerk, municipal justice, county clerk or his deputy within the territory in which such officer is authorized to act; and, when certified by such officer to have been taken before him, may be read and used in any court and before any officer, board or commission.   Oaths may be administered by any person mentioned in s. 885.01 (3) and (4) to any witness examined before him.

(2) **Without the state.** Any oath or affidavit required or authorized by law may be taken in any other state, territory or district of the United States before any judge or commissioner of a court of record, master in chancery, notary public, justice of the peace or other officer authorized by the laws thereof to administer oaths, and in case the same shall have been properly certified by any such officer to have been taken before him, and shall have attached thereto a certificate of the clerk of a court of record of the county or district within which such oath or affidavit was taken, under the seal of his office, that the person whose name is subscribed to the jurat was, at the date thereof, such officer as he is therein represented to be, was empowered by law as such officer to administer the oath or affidavit, and that he believes the name so subscribed is the signature of such officer, such oath or affidavit may be read or used in any court within this state and before any officer, board or commission authorized to use or consider the same. Whenever any such oath or affidavit is certified by any notary public or clerk of a court of record and an impression of his official seal is thereto affixed no further attestations shall be necessary.

(3) [Omitted].

WYOMING

[WYO. STAT. ANN.]

§ 1-9. Officers authorized to administer oaths. (a) The following officers are authorized to administer oaths, viz.: The chief justice and justices of the supreme court, the judges of the district courts, the judge of the district court of the United States, for the district of Wyoming, the clerks of the supreme and district courts of this state, and the clerk of the district court of the United States for Wyoming, and their deputies, United States commissioners, and United States magistrates appointed by or under the authority of the laws of the United States, or court commissioners appointed by or under the authority of the laws of this state, notaries public, county clerks and their deputies, county treasurers and their deputies, clerks of any school district, or of any city, town or village now or hereafter incorporated under the laws of this state, county commissioners within their respective counties, and county superintendents of schools, justices of the peace within their respective counties.

§ 32-5. Powers and jurisdiction. Every notary public so appointed, commissioned and qualified, is hereby authorized and empowered, within and throughout the state, to administer oaths and affirmations, to take depositions, to receive acknowledgments of deeds, mortgages and powers of attorney and other instruments in writing; to demand acceptance of payment of foreign and inland bills of exchange, promissory notes, and obligations in writing, and to protest the same for nonacceptance or nonpayment, as the case may require; and to exercise such other powers and duties as, by the law of nations and according to commercial usage, may be exercised and performed by notaries public.

§ 32-9. **Notary's certificate as presumptive evidence.** In all the courts within this state the certificate of a notary public over his hand and official seal, shall be received as presumptive evidence of the facts contained in such certificate; provided, that any person interested as a party to a suit may contradict, by other evidence, the certificate of a notary public.

§ 32-13. **When justice may protest paper in lieu of notary.** When the holder of any instrument desires it to be protested, and no notary public can be found, it shall be lawful for any justice of the peace of the county wherein said instrument is required to be protested, to perform the services herein required to be performed by notaries public, and to be entitled to the same fees as are hereinafter provided for notaries public for similar services.

§ 32-15. **Notary's interest in bank, etc., not disqualifying.** It shall be lawful for any notary public who is a stockholder, director, officer or employee of a bank or other corporation to take the acknowledgment of any party to any written instrument executed to or by said corporation, or to administer an oath to any other stockholder, director, officer, employee or agent of such corporation, or to protest for nonacceptance, or nonpayment, bills of exchange, drafts, checks, notes, and other negotiable instruments which may be owned or held for collection by any such bank or other corporation.

UNITED STATES

[5 U.S.C.]

§ 2903. **Oath; authority to administer.**

✿   ✿   ✿

(c) An oath authorized or required under the laws of the United States may be administered by —

(1) the Vice President; or

(2) an individual authorized by local law to administer oaths in the State, District, or territory or possession of the United States where the oath is administered.

[10 U.S.C.]

§ 936. **Authority to administer oaths and to act as notary.** (a) The following persons on active duty may administer oaths for the purposes of military administration, including military justice, and have the general powers of a notary public and of a consul of the United States, in the performance of all notarial acts to be executed by members of any of the armed forces, wherever they may be, by persons serving with, employed by, or accompanying the armed forces outside the United States and outside the Canal Zone, Puerto Rico, Guam, and the Virgin Islands, and by other persons subject to this chapter [§ 801 et seq. of this title] outside of the United States:

(1) All judge advocates of the Army and the Air Force.

(2) All law specialists.

(3) All summary courts-martial.

(4) All adjutants, assistant adjutants, acting adjutants, and personnel adjutants.

(5) All commanding officers of the Navy, Marine Corps, and Coast Guard.

(6) All staff judge advocates and legal officers, and acting or assistant staff judge advocates and legal officers.

(7) All other persons designated by regulations of the armed forces or by statute.

(b) The following persons on active duty may administer oaths necessary in the performance of their duties:

(1) The president, law officer, trial counsel, and assistant trial counsel for all general and special courts-martial.

(2) The president and the counsel for the court of any court of inquiry.

(3) All officers designated to take a deposition.

(4) All persons detailed to conduct an investigation.

(5) All recruiting officers.

(6) All other persons designated by regulations of the armed forces or by statute.

(c) No fee may be paid to or received by any person for the performance of any notarial act herein authorized.

(d) The signature without seal of any such person acting as notary, together with the title of his office, is prima facie evidence of his authority.

[12 U.S.C.]

§ 73. **Oath.** Each director, when appointed or elected, shall take an oath that he will, so far as the duty devolves on him, diligently and honestly administer the affairs of such association, and will not knowingly violate or willingly permit to be violated any of the provisions of this title, and that he is the owner in good faith, and in his own right, of the number of shares of stock required by this title, subscribed by him, or standing in his name on the books of the association, and that the same is not hypothecated, or in any way pledged, as security for any loan or debt. The oath shall be taken before a notary public, properly authorized and commissioned by the State in which he resides, or before any other officer having an official seal and authorized by the State to administer oaths, except that the oath shall not be taken before any such notary public or other officer who is an officer of the director's bank. The oath, subscribed by the director making it, and certified by the notary public or other officer before whom it is taken, shall be immediately transmitted to the Comptroller of the Currency and shall be filed and preserved in his office for a period of ten years.

[12 U.S.C.]

§ 131.   **Protest of notes—Waiver.**   Whenever any national banking association fails to redeem in the lawful money of the United States any of its circulating notes, upon demand of payment duly made during the usual hours of business, at the office of such association, or at its designated place of redemption, the holder may cause the same to be protested, in one package, by a notary public, unless the president or cashier of the association whose notes are presented for payment, or the president or cashier of the association at the place at which they are redeemable, offers to waive demand and notice of the protest, and, in pursuance of such offer, makes, signs, and delivers to the party making such demand an admission in writing, stating the time of the demand, the amount demanded, and the fact of the nonpayment thereof. The notary public, on making such protest, or upon receiving such admission, shall forthwith forward such admission or notice of protest to the Comptroller of the Currency, retaining a copy thereof. If, however, satisfactory proof is produced to the notary public that the payment of the notes demanded is restrained by order of any court of competent jurisdiction, he shall not protest the same. When the holder of any notes causes more than one note or package to be protested on the same day, he shall not receive pay for more than one protest.

[28 U.S.C.]

§ 636.   **Jurisdiction and powers.**   (a)   Each United States magistrate serving under this chapter shall have within the territorial jurisdiction prescribed by his appointment—

(1)   all powers and duties conferred or imposed upon United States commisisoners by law or by the Rules of Criminal Procedure for the United States District Courts;

(2)   the power to administer oaths and affirmations, impose conditions of release under section 3146 of title 18, and take acknowledgments, affidavits, and depositions; and

*   *   *

CHAPTER 6: SEAL

§ 6.1 Disqualifications.

In a number of states, there is a statute which declares that no banker, broker, cashier, director, teller, clerk, or other person holding an official relationship to a bank, banker or broker, shall be competent to act as a notary public in any matter in which the bank, banker, or broker is interested.

Contrary to the situation in those states, most states have adopted a more liberal attitude. They allow any notary public who is a stockholder, director, officer or employee of a bank or other corporation to take the acknowledgment of any party to any written instrument to or by such corporation, or to administer an oath to any other stockholder, director, officer, employee or agent of such corporation, or to protest for nonacceptance or nonpayment bills of exchange, drafts, checks, notes, or other negotiable instruments which may be owned or held for collection by such corporation. Such notary is disqualified from acting, however, if he is a party to the instrument, either individually or as a representative of the corporation, or has a financial interest in the subject thereof.

Readers interested in the statutory provisions in this regard, relative to any specific jurisdiction, should consult *Authority and Duties: State and Other Statutes*, page 127.

§ 6.2 Signature.

A notary public must sign his name to each official certificate. Some states require the notary's name to be en-

207

graved on his official seal or stamp, or printed, stamped or typewritten on the document. Concerning the statutory provisions in this regard for a jurisdiction, see *Authority and Duties: State and Other Statutes,* page 127.

§ 6.3   Expiration of commission.[1]

Perhaps for the purpose of preventing a notary public from performing a notarial act after his term of office expires, a large number of states and other jurisdictions require him to add to his jurat, or other certificate, the date of expiration of his commission. The usual form for such statement is:

My commission expires —— [date].

Some jurisdictions have statutes which provide that any act done by a notary after the expiration of his term is valid, but in addition impose a fine or other penalty for performing the act after his commission has expired. Some states also impose a fine or other penalty for the failure to state the date when the commission expires.[2]

Regardless of the formal requirements in the local state or other jurisdiction, it is good practice to always state the date of the expiration of the commission when the document is intended to be used in another state.

§ 6.4   Seal.[3]

Under the law merchant and the law of nations, notaries must attest their official certificates and other writings with their seal of office. This is also a requirement imposed by statute in most of the states and other jurisdictions. The statutes in a few jurisdictions provide that a seal is not necessary, or are silent concerning a seal. It is universal good practice, however, to affix an official seal to every certificate or affidavit.

---

[1] See *Authority and Duties: State and Other Statutes,* page 127.

[2] See *Offenses: State and Other Statutes,* page 283.

[3] For definition, see Glossary, page 862.

The requisites of a notary seal must be determined according to the statutes of the state or other jurisdiction from which the notary derives his authority. In states which prescribe the words and devices which the seal must contain, the statutory provisions in this regard must be strictly complied with.

See *Seal: State and Other Statutes*, which follows.

SEAL: STATE AND OTHER STATUTES

ALABAMA

[ALA. CODE]

Commercial Notaries

Tit. 40, § 6. Seal. For the authentication of his official acts, each notary must provide a seal of office, which must present, by its impression, his name, office, state, and county for which he was appointed.

Notaries Ex Officio Justices of the Peace

Such officers are vested with the powers of notary as defined by law. See *Appointment*, ALA. CODE tit. 40, § 15.

Notaries for State at Large

[ALA. CODE]

Tit. 40, § 23. Seal. For the authentication of his official acts each such notary must provide a seal of office which must present, by its impression, his name, office, and the state for which he was appointed.

ALASKA

[ALASKA STAT.]

§ 44.50.080. Seal. (a) A notary public shall provide and keep an official seal, upon which shall appear the words, "State of Alaska" and "Notary Public," together with the name of the notary. He shall authenticate all official acts with his seal.

(b) The seal of every notary public whose commission is issued on or after July 1, 1972 may be affixed by a seal press or stamp that will print or emboss a seal which legibly reproduces under photographic methods the words "State of Alaska" and "Notary Public" and the name of the notary. The seal may be circular not over two inches in diameter, or may be a rectangular form not more than an inch in width by two and one-half inches in length, and shall contain the information required by this section.

ARIZONA

Notary seals shall be engraved with the words "Notary Public," the name of the county for which commissioned, and the name of the notary. See *Authority and Duties,* ARIZ. REV. STAT. ANN. § 41-312.

ARKANSAS

[ARK. STAT. ANN.]

§ 12-1402. Seal. Every notary shall provide a seal of his office, which shall be engraved so as to present by its impression, such emblems and devices as he may deem proper, surrounded by the words "Notary Public: County of ———, Ark.;" and he shall authenticate all his official acts therewith, and until an official seal shall be procured, each notary may use his private seal, which shall be of the same force and effect as a public seal.

§ 5-106. Form of all official seals. All official seals, used in the State shall present the same impressions, emblems, and devices presented by the seal of State, except the surrounding words, which shall be such as to indicate the Office to which they may severally belong.

CALIFORNIA

[CAL. GOV'T CODE—West]

§ 8207. Seal. A notary public shall provide and keep an official seal, which shall clearly show, when embossed, stamped, impressed or affixed to a document, the name of the notary, the State Seal, the words "Notary Public" and the name of the county wherein his bond is filed. He shall authenticate with his official seal all official acts.

The seal of every notary public shall be affixed by a seal press or stamp that will print or emboss a seal which legibly reproduces under photographic methods the required elements of the seal. The seal may be circular not over two inches in diameter, or may be a rectangular form of not more than an inch in width by two inches and one-half in length, with a serrated or milled edged border, and shall contain the information required by this section.

The seal of every notary public whose commission is issued on or after January 1, 1968, shall also clearly show, and legibly reproduce, the date his commission expires.

COLORADO

[COLO. REV. STAT. ANN]

§ 12-55-105. Seal—expiration of commission. (1) Each official act of a notary shall be attested by his notarial seal, which shall consist of an impression upon the instrument, setting forth the name of the notary, the words "State of Colorado" and the words "Notary Public," and such notary shall also designate in writing on all official certificates signed by him, the date when his commission as such notary expires.

(2) Nothing in this section shall be construed to require any notary public appointed prior to July 1, 1959, to alter his notarial seal adopted before July 1, 1959.

DELAWARE

[DEL. CODE ANN.]

Tit. 29, § 4308. Engraving of seal; effect of use of non-conforming seal. The seals required by section 4307 of this title shall be used in the transaction of official business and shall have engraved thereon the name of the officer, either in full or using the initials of his Christian name; his official title, the date of his appointment, and anything additional which he may see fit to have engraved thereon.

If the official seal of any notary public is not engraved in conformity with the provisions of this section, it shall not invalidate his official act, but such act shall be as valid as though the seal had been engraved in conformity with the requirements of this section.

Any notary public failing to comply with the requirements of this section may be removed by the Governor for his neglect.

> *Editorial comment*
>
> Notaries are directed to have seals. See *Authority and Duties*, DEL. CODE ANN. tit. 29, § 4307.
>
> No official certificate of any notary shall be invalid or defective because the impression of the official seal of such officer upon the certificate does not strictly comport with the requirements of DEL. CODE ANN. tit. 29, § 4308. See *Acknowledgments*, DEL. CODE ANN. tit. 25, § 110.

DISTRICT OF COLUMBIA

[D.C. CODE ENCYCL. ANN.]

§ 1-505. Seal. Each notary public shall provide a notarial seal with which he shall authenticate all his official acts.

§ 1-506. Signature and impression of seal deposited. Each notary public shall file his signature and deposit an impression of his official seal with the Commissioners of the District of Columbia or their designated agent, and the Commissioners or their designated agent may certify to the authenticity of the signature and official seal of the notary public.

§ 1-507. Exemption. A notary's official seal and his official documents shall be exempt from execution.

FLORIDA

[FLA. STAT. ANN.]

§ 117.07. Must state time of expiration of commission; and affix seal. (1) Every notary public in the state shall add to his official signature to any certificate of acknowledgment made before him a statement of the time of expiration of his commission as notary public in words and figures as follows: "My commission expires ————" (Herein insert the date when the commission expires.)

(2) A notary seal shall be affixed to all documents notarized, which may be of the rubber stamp or impression type and shall include the words "Notary Public—State of Florida at Large." The seal may also include the name of the notary public.

GEORGIA

[GA. CODE ANN.]

§ 71-107. Notarial seal and register; scrawl; attestation of deeds. For the authentication of their notarial acts each notary must provide a seal of office, which shall have for its impression his name; the words, "Notary Public"; the name of the State and the county of his residence, or shall have for its impression his name and the words "Notary Public, Georgia, State at Large." A scrawl shall not be a sufficient notary seal. No seal is required to his attestation of deeds.

HAWAII

[HAWAII REV. STAT.]

§ 456-3. Seal. Every notary public shall constantly keep a seal of office, whereon shall be engraved his name, and the words, "notary public" and "State of Hawaii." He shall authenticate all of his official acts, attestations, certificates, and instruments therewith, and shall always add to his official signature a statement showing the circuit for which he is commissioned and the date of expiration of his commission as notary public. Upon resignation, death, expiration of term of office without reappointment, removal from or abandonment of office, or change of residence from the judicial circuit for which he is appointed, he shall immediately deliver his seal to the attorney general who shall deface or destroy the same. By a neglect of sixty days to comply with the above requisition, the notary public, his executor or administrator, shall forfeit to the State not more than $200, in the discretion of the court, to be recovered in an action to be brought by the attorney general on behalf of the State.

IDAHO

It is the duty of a notary to provide and keep an official seal, upon which must be engraved his name, the words "Notary Public" and "State of Idaho", and to authenticate with his official seal all official acts. See *Authority and Duties*, IDAHO CODE § 51-104(6), (7). An impress of the official seal must be filed in the office of the secretary of state. See *Appointment*, IDAHO CODE § 51-103.

ILLINOIS

[ILL. ANN. STAT.—Smith-Hurd]

Ch. 99, § 7. Notarial seal. Each notary public shall, upon entering upon the duties of his office, provide himself with a proper official seal, with which he shall authenticate his official acts, upon which shall be engraved words descriptive of his office; and the name of the place or county in which he resides.

INDIANA

[IND. CODE]

§ 33-16-2-4. Seal requisite. No notary shall be authorized to act until he shall have procured such a seal as will stamp upon paper a distinct impression, in words or letters, sufficiently indicating his official character, to which may be added such other device as he may choose, and all notarial acts not attested by such seal shall be void.

Note: The use of a rubber stamp as a seal complies with this provision. 1965 OP. ATT'Y GEN. (IND.) 44 (No. 10).

IOWA

[IOWA CODE ANN.]

§ 77.4. Conditions. Before any such commission is delivered to the person appointed, he shall:

1. Procure a seal, or an ink stamp of a size and design approved by the secretary of state, on which shall be included the words "Notarial Seal" and "Iowa," with his surname at length and at least the initials of his given name. The embossed impression made by the seal may be blackened, but permanent black ink shall be used

for fixing an impression with the official ink stamp. The seal or stamp may include the date of expiration of the notary's commission, but the date of expiration shall not be mandatory.

＊   ＊   ＊

KANSAS

[KAN. STAT. ANN.]

§ 53-105. Seal; expiration date of commission on authentication; seal press or rubber stamp, use. Every notary public shall provide a notarial seal containing his name and place of residence, and shall authenticate all his official acts, attestations and instruments therewith; and he shall add to his official signature the date of expiration of his commission as such notary public. The seal of every notary public who is appointed or commissioned on or after July 1, 1970, shall be affixed by a seal press and the impression thereof inked or blackened or the notarial seal provided for in this act may consist of a rubber stamp to be used with permanent ink so that any such seal may be legibly reproduced by photographic process. Any notary public commissioned prior to the effective date of this act, may use a rubber stamp seal as aforesaid upon filing an impression thereof in the same manner as his original seal was filed.

KENTUCKY

The statutes are vague concerning notary seals. In several statutes the seal is required for particular notarial acts, but little more is said concerning the seal or its requisites. For example, see *Records,* KY. REV. STAT. ANN. § 423.030.

LOUISIANA

The statutes are vague concerning notary seals. There is no statute requiring or defining a notary seal, except that in the case of a notary for the Parish of Orleans, before the governor issues the notary's commission, the impress of the notary's official seal must be deposited in the office of the Secretary of State. See *Appointment,* "Orleans Parish", LA. REV. STAT. § 35:255.

MAINE

[ME. REV. STAT. ANN.]

Tit. 4, § 951. Seal; authority to administer oaths. Every notary public shall constantly keep a seal of office, whereon is engraven his name and the words "Notary Public" and "Maine" or its abbreviation "Me.," with the arms of state or such other device as he chooses. When authorized by the laws of this State or of any other state or country to do any official act, he may administer any oath necessary to the completion or validity thereof.

MARYLAND

[MD. ANN. CODE]

Art. 68, § 6. Notary to have seal or stamp. Every notary shall provide a public notarial seal or stamp with which he shall authenticate his acts, instruments and attestations, on which seal or stamp shall be shown such device as he may think proper and for legend shall have the name, surname and office of the notary and the place of his residence, which shall be designated by the county of his residence or if the notary is a resident of the City of Baltimore, by the City of Baltimore.

MASSACHUSETTS

The statutes are vague concerning notary seals. In one section the seal is required for a particular notarial act, but nothing more is said in the statutes concerning notary seals or their requisites.

[MASS. ANN. LAWS]

Ch. 59, § 31. Lists to be verified by oath. The assessors shall in all cases require a person bringing in a list to make oath that it is true. The oath may be administered by any of the assessors or by their secretary or head clerk, or by any notary public, whose jurat shall be duly authenticated by his seal, or, in this commonwealth, by a justice of the peace. So much of this section as relates to administering the oath shall not apply to Boston.

MICHIGAN

The statutes are vague concerning notary seals. In all the courts of the state, the certificate of a notary under his hand and seal of office, of official acts done by him as such notary, must be received as presumptive evidence of the facts contained in the certificate, with certain specified exceptions. See *Authority and Duties*, MICH. COMP. LAWS ANN. § 55.113.

MINNESOTA

[MINN. STAT. ANN.]

§ 359.03. Seal; register. Subdivision 1. Every notary shall provide himself with an official seal, with which he shall authenticate his official acts, and upon which shall be engraved the arms of this state, the words "notarial seal," and the name of the county for which he was appointed. Such seal, with his official register, shall be exempt from execution, and, on his death or removal from office, such register shall be deposited with the clerk of the district court of his county.

Subd. 2. [omitted]

Subd. 3. The seal of every notary public after January 1, 1972, may be affixed by a stamp that will print a seal which legibly reproduces under photographic methods the seal of the state of Minnesota, the name of the notary, the words "Notary Public", the name of the county for which appointed, and the words "My commission expires ————", with the expiration date shown thereon. The seal shall be a rectangular form of not more than three fourths of an inch vertically by two and one half inches horizontally, with a serrated or milled edge border, and shall contain the information required by this subdivision.

MISSISSIPPI

[MISS. CODE ANN.]

§ 25-33-3. **To procure seals.** Every notary public hereafter appointed and commissioned shall, at his own expense, procure a suitable seal, having the name of the county for which he shall have been appointed and commissioned, with that of the state and his own name on the margin thereof, and the words "notary public" across the center; and his official acts shall be attested by his seal of office.

The failure of such seal to conform to the provisions of this section shall not invalidate any official act or certificate of such notary public.

It shall be the duty of the secretary of state to have printed a suitable number of copies of this section and to deliver to each notary public hereafter appointed a copy at the time of the issuance of his commission.

§ 25-33-19. **Common seal of [ex-officio notaries public].** The board of supervisors of every county which has not done so shall provide a notarial seal, with the inscription "notary public of the county of ————" around the margin and the image of an eagle in the center, which seal shall be kept in the office of the clerk of the circuit court; and all ex-officio notaries public may at all times have access to and use such seal for the authentication of any notarial act necessary to be so authenticated.

Note: See *Qualifications,* MISS. CODE ANN. § 25-33-17, concerning ex-officio notaries public.

MISSOURI

[MO. ANN. STAT.—Vernon]

§ 486.040. **Notarial seal, information required on—information required following notary's signature—effect of authentication.** Every notary public shall provide a notarial seal, on which shall be inscribed his name, the words "notary public," the name of the county or city, if appointed for such city, in which he resides and has his office, and the name of the state. Immediately below his signature in any certificate or acknowledgment which is to be recorded in the office of a recorder of deeds, he shall print, stamp or type his name, and he shall designate in writing, in any certificate signed by him, the date of the expiration of his commission. No notary public shall change his seal during the term for which he is appointed, and he shall authenticate therewith all his official acts, and the record and copies, certified by the proper custodian thereof, shall be received in evidence.

MONTANA

It is the duty of a notary public to provide and keep an official seal, upon which must be engraved the name of the state of Montana, and the words "Notarial Seal", with the surname of the notary, and at least the initials of his Christian name. It is also his duty to authenticate with his official seal all official acts. See *Authority and Duties,* MONT. REV. CODES ANN. § 56-104(5), (6).

NEBRASKA

[NEB. REV. STAT.]

§ 64-210. Seal; contents; ink stamp. (1) Each notary public, before performing any duties of his office, shall provide himself with an official seal on which shall appear the words State of Nebraska, General Notary or State of Nebraska, General Notarial, and his name, and in addition, at his option, the date of expiration of his commission; *Provided,* a notary public may use the initial letters of his first name and middle name. A notary public shall authenticate all his official acts with such seal. Under his official signature, on all certificates of authentication made by him, he shall write, stamp, or otherwise show the date when his term of office as such notary public will expire if such date of expiration is not engraved on the seal.

(2) The official seal of a notary public may be either an engraved or ink stamp seal with which he shall authenticate all of his official acts; *Provided,* that every notary who receives a commission, either new or renewal, on or after January 1, 1972, shall use an ink stamp seal to authenticate any instrument.

NEVADA

[NEV. REV. STAT.]

§ 240.040. Authentication of official acts; use of rubber, mechanical stamp. 1. Each notary public shall authenticate all his official acts, including any acknowledgment, jurat, verification or other certificate, by setting forth the following:

(a) The venue;

(b)   His signature; and

(c)   A statement imprinted in black ink with a rubber or other mechanical stamp setting forth his name, the phrase "Notary Public, State of Nevada" and the date on which his commission expires.

2.   After July 1, 1965, a notarial seal shall no longer be required on notarized documents, and all provisions or forms previously enacted in NRS or any other law of this state requiring the use of a notarial seal shall be construed to require, in place of the seal, the statement provided for in paragraph (c) of subsection 1.

NEW HAMPSHIRE

The statutes are vague concerning notary seals. Some of the notary fees established by statute make reference to the use of a seal as a part of the official act for which a specified charge may be made. See *Fees Chargeable*, N.H. REV. STAT. ANN. § 455:11.

NEW JERSEY

[N.J. STAT. ANN.]

§ 41:1-7.   **Seal not necessary to validity of oath or affidavit.** It shall not be necessary to the validity or sufficiency of any oath, affirmation or affidavit, made or taken before any of the persons named in section 41:2-1 of this title [which includes, among others, "Notaries public" and "Commissioners of deeds"], that the same shall be certified under the official seal of the officer before whom made.

§ 52:7-9.   **Affixation of name.** Each notary public, in addition to subscribing his autograph signature to any jurat upon the administration of any oath or the taking of any acknowledgment or proof, shall affix thereto his name in such a manner and by such means (including, but not limited to, printing, typing, or impressing by seal or mechanical stamp) as will enable the Secretary of State easily to read said name.

NEW MEXICO

[N.M. STAT. ANN]

§ 35-1-5.   **Seal.** Each notary public shall provide himself with a notarial seal containing his name and the words "NOTARY PUBLIC —STATE OF NEW MEXICO," and shall authenticate his official acts and acknowledgments with the seal.

NEW YORK

The statutes are vague concerning notary seals. Every notary public having a seal shall, except as otherwise provided, and when requested, affix his seal to protests free of expense. See *Fees Chargeable*, N.Y. EXEC. LAW § 135.

Concerning the manner of exercising the powers of a notary public, particularly with reference to the formalities of executing instruments and authenticating the notary's signature, see *Authority and Duties*, N.Y. EXEC. LAW § 137.

NORTH CAROLINA

[N.C. GEN. STAT.]

§ 10-10. **Notarial stamp or seal.** A notary public shall provide and keep an official stamp or seal which shall clearly show and legibly reproduce under photographic methods, when embossed, stamped, impressed or affixed to a document, the name of the notary, the name of the county in which appointed and qualified, the words "North Carolina" or an abbreviation thereof, and the words "Notary Public." It shall be the duty of a notary public to replace a seal which has become so worn that it can no longer clearly show or legibly reproduce under photographic methods the information required by this section. Provided, that a notary public appointed prior to July 1, 1973, who has adopted and is using a seal which does not meet the requirements of this section, shall be entitled to continue to use such seal until the expiration of his current commission.

NORTH DAKOTA

[N.D. CENT. CODE]

§ 44-06-04. **Filing of oath, bond, and impression of notarial seal.** Each notary public, before entering upon the duties of such office, shall provide himself with an official seal bearing his name and shall:

1. Deposit a legible impression of such seal, together with his oath and bond, in the office of the secretary of state; and

2. File his commission for record in the office of the clerk of the district court of the county of which he is a resident and deposit with such clerk an impression of his seal together with his official signature. The clerk shall record such information in a book to be kept for that purpose, and the person complying with the provisions of this subsection is a notary public during the time the commission is in force.

OHIO

[OHIO REV. CODE ANN. — Page]

§ 147.04. **Seal [and register].** Before entering upon the discharge of his duties, a notary public shall provide himself with the seal of a notary public. Said seal shall consist of the coat of arms of the state* within a circle one inch in diameter and shall be surrounded by the words "notary public," "notarial seal," or words to that effect, the name of such notary public and the counties for which he is commissioned, or if an attorney at law and commissioned for the whole state, the words for the "State of Ohio." The seal may be of either a type which will stamp ink onto a document or one which will emboss it. The name of the notary public and the limits of his jurisdiction may, instead of appearing on the seal, be printed, typewritten, or stamped in legible, printed letters near the signature of such notary public on each document signed by him.

✿   ✿   ✿

(°)   For the coat of arms of the state, see § 5.04, below.

Note: Concerning the register, see *Records,* OHIO REV. CODE ANN. § 147.04.

§ 5.04.   Coat of arms of state.

✿   ✿   ✿

The coat of arms of the state shall correspond substantially with the following design:

✿   ✿   ✿

OKLAHOMA

Concerning the requirement that every notary public, before entering upon the duties of his office, shall file in the office of the court clerk, in his capacity as clerk of the district court, of the county in which the notary resides, among other things, an impression of his official seal, see *Appointment,* OKLA. STAT. ANN. tit. 49, § 2.

[OKLA. STAT. ANN.]

Tit. 49, § 5.   Official acts—how authenticated—misdemeanor. Every notary shall provide a notarial seal containing his name and place of residence, and he shall authenticate all his official acts, attestations and instruments therewith; and he shall add to his official signature the date of expiration of his commission as such notary public. If any notary public shall neglect or refuse to attach to his official signature the date of expiration of his commission as provided in this act, he shall be deemed guilty of a misdemeanor, and upon conviction thereof shall be fined in any sum not exceeding fifty dollars.

OREGON

[ORE. REV. STAT.]

§ 194.031. Notarial seal or stamp; filing of sample imprint; effect of stamp; dating required. (1) Each notary public shall obtain an official seal or official stamp made of rubber or some other substance capable of making a legible imprint on paper in indelible black ink. The imprint must set out the name of the notary and the words "Notary Public—Oregon," and may set out the date on which the commission expires. The Secretary of State shall promulgate rules prescribing the size and form of the imprint required under this section to promote uniformity and legibility.

(2) Before he enters upon his duties, each notary public shall file a sample imprint of his official seal or official stamp, together with his oath and bond required by ORS 194.050,° with the Secretary of State.

(3) Notwithstanding any other law of this state, an impression made by an official stamp has the same force and effect as a seal.

(4) If the official stamp of the notary does not imprint the date on which his commission expires, the notary must indicate this date in some other manner as a part of each notarization or other official use of such stamp.

(°) See *Appointment*, ORE. REV. STAT. § 194.050.

PENNSYLVANIA

[PA. STAT. ANN.]

Tit. 57, § 158. Notarial seal. Every notary shall provide a public notarial seal with which he shall authenticate all his acts, instruments and attestations. There shall be engraved on such seal the words "Notary Public, Commonwealth of Pennsylvania," and the name and surname of the notary.

§ 160. Position of seal and date of expiration of commission. (a) The seal of a notary public shall be impressed opposite the jurat, and affixed in such manner as to make a legible impression on all documents executed.

(b) The date of expiration of a notary's commission and the location of his office shall be written, typed or stamped immediately below the signature of the notary.

PUERTO RICO

[P.R. LAWS ANN.]

Tit. 4, § 1005.° [Oath of office;] seal, signature, mark, and sign; registry in Department of State.

°   °   °

[Notaries] shall record in the register ad hoc kept in the Department of State the seal, signature, sign and mark to be used by them, which they shall not be permitted to alter unless as hereinafter provided. When a notary wishes to change the seal, it shall be his duty to impress same in the register kept in the Department of State and to surrender the useless seal to the Secretary of State for its destruction. ° ° °

(°) For the complete text of P.R. LAWS ANN. tit. 4, § 1005, see *Appointment.*

RHODE ISLAND

The statutes are vague concerning notary seals. There is no requirement that notaries have seals.

SOUTH CAROLINA

Each notary public must have a seal of office. It must be affixed to his instruments of publications and to his protestations. The absence of the seal will not render his acts invalid, if his official title is affixed. See *Authority and Duties,* S.C. CODE ANN. § 49-6.

SOUTH DAKOTA

[S.D. COMPILED LAWS ANN.]

§ 18-1-3.   **Seal, oath and bond filed with secretary of state.**   Every notary public before entering upon the duties of his office, shall provide an official seal and file an impression of the same, together with his oath and bond, in the office of the secretary of state.

Editorial comment

Before entering upon the duties of his office, a notary public must file with the clerk of courts of his county, among other things, an impression of his seal. The clerk shall record same in a book kept for that purpose. See *Appointment,* S.D. COMPILED LAWS ANN. § 18-1-5. Whenever a notary changes his place of residence from the county in which he was first appointed to another county, it is his duty to comply with the same requirement before he again enters upon the duties of his office. See *Appointment,* S.D. COMPILED LAWS ANN. § 18-1-6.

TENNESSEE

[TENN. CODE ANN.]

§ 8-1617.   **Seal of notary at large.**   The secretary of state shall prescribe and design an official seal to be used by a notary public at large for the state of Tennessee.

§ 8-1619. Seal of notaries generally. Every notary shall, at his own expense, procure a seal of office, which he shall surrender to the county court when he resigns, or at the expiration of his term of office, and which his representatives, in case of his death, shall likewise surrender, to be canceled, on pain of indictment as for a misdemeanor.

§ 39-105. Penalty for misdemeanor. Every person who is convicted of a misdemeanor, the punishment for which is not otherwise prescribed by a statute of this state, shall be punished by imprisonment in the county jail or workhouse not more than one (1) year, or by fine not exceeding one thousand dollars ($1,000), or by both, in the discretion of the court.

TEXAS

[TEX. REV. CIV. STAT. ANN.]

Art. 5960. Seal. Each notary public shall provide a seal of office, whereon shall be engraved in the center a star of five points, and the words, "Notary Public, County of ——————, Texas," around the margin (the blank to be filled with the name of the county for which the officer is appointed), and he shall authenticate all his official acts therewith.

Editorial comment

The seal of any notary vacating his office may be sold by the owner thereof to any qualified notary public in the county. See *Records*, TEX. REV. CIV. STAT. ANN. art. 5959.

UTAH

[UTAH CODE ANN.]

§ 46-1-7. Seal. Each notary public shall have an official seal, with which he shall authenticate all of his official acts. It must contain the words "State of Utah," and "Notary Public" or "Notarial Seal," with the surname and at least the initials of his Christian name.

VERMONT

[VT. STAT. ANN.]

Tit. 24, § 444. Seal. A notary public shall have a seal of office, which shall be affixed to papers officially signed by him, unless otherwise provided.

Editorial comment

A notary public need not affix his official seal to a certificate of an oath administered by him. See *Authority and Duties*, VT. STAT. ANN. tit. 12, § 5854.

VIRGIN ISLANDS

[V.I. CODE ANN.]

Tit. 3, § 776. Notarial seal. Each notary public shall keep an official impression seal bearing his name and the date of expiration of his commission.

Special Notaries Public

Tit. 3, § 804. Notarial seal. Notaries public appointed and commissioned under section 801 of this title,° shall keep an official impression seal which shall be furnished without cost by the government of the Virgin Islands.

(°) See *Qualifications*, "Special Notaries Public", V.I. CODE ANN. tit. 3, § 801.

VIRGINIA

There are no statutes which require a notary to have or use a seal in the performance of his duties in the state.

WASHINGTON

Before a commission is issued to a person appointed as a notary public, he shall procure a seal, on which is engraved the words "Notary Public" and "State of Washington," and the date of the expiration of his commission, with surname in full, and at least the initials of his Christian name. See *Appointment*, WASH. REV. CODE ANN. § 42.28.030(3).

[WASH. REV. CODE ANN.]

§ 42.28.060. Seal must be affixed—Judicial papers excepted. It shall not be necessary for a notary public in certifying an oath to be used in any of the courts in this state, to append an impression of his official seal, but in all other cases when the notary public shall sign any instrument officially, he shall, in addition to his name and the words "Notary Public," add his place of residence and affix his official seal.

WEST VIRGINIA

[W. VA. CODE ANN.]

§ 29-4-5. Necessity for seal. The certificate of a notary of this State, in cases specified [in §§ 29-4-3 and 29-4-4],° may be under his signature, without his notarial seal being affixed thereto: Provided, that a notary public who affixes his seal to any instrument or other writings shall affix his seal for the county in which the acknowledgment is taken and the certificate is made.

(°) See *Authority and Duties,* W. VA. CODE ANN. §§ 29-4-3, 29-4-4, concerning powers of notaries in relation to oaths, affidavits, depositions, acknowledgments and as conservators of the peace.

Editorial comment

A notary appointed for the entire state must have a seal containing the words, "State of West Virginia," instead of any particular county designation. See *Appointment,* W. VA. CODE ANN. § 29-4-2b.

WISCONSIN

Qualified applicants for appointment as notaries public, who are not attorneys, must file, among other things, an impression of their official seal, or imprint of their official rubber stamp with the secretary of state. See *Appointment,* WIS. STAT. ANN. § 137.01(1)(e). Applicants for appointment as notaries public, who are attorneys, must file with their application, among other things, an impression of their official seal, or imprint of their official rubber stamp. See *Appointment,* WIS. STAT. ANN. § 137.01(2)(a).

[*WIS. STAT. ANN.*]

§ 137.01. Notaries.

°   °   °

(3) Notarial Seal or Stamp. (a) Every notary public shall provide an engraved official seal which makes a distinct and legible impression or official rubber stamp which makes a distinct and legible imprint on paper. The impression of the seal or the imprint of the rubber stamp shall state, "Notary Public," "State of Wisconsin" and the name of the notary. But any notarial seal in use on August 1, 1959, shall be considered in compliance.

(b) The impression of the notarial seal upon any instrument or writing or upon wafer, wax or other adhesive substance and affixed to any instrument or writing shall be deemed an affixation of the seal, and the imprint of the notarial rubber stamp upon any instrument or writing shall be deemed an affixation of the rubber stamp.

°   °   °

Editorial comment

All certificates of acknowledgments of deeds and other conveyances, or any written instrument required or authorized by law to be acknowledged or sworn to before a notary public within the state, must be attested by a clear impression of the official seal, or imprint of the rubber stamp, of the officer. See *Authority and Duties,* WIS. STAT. ANN. § 137.01(4)(b).

WYOMING

[WYO. STAT. ANN.]

§ 32-6. **Official seal generally.** (a) Each notary public before entering upon the duties of his office, shall provide himself with an official seal with which he shall authenticate all his official acts, which seal shall clearly show, when embossed, stamped, impressed or affixed to a document, his name, the words "notary public," the name of the county wherein he resides, and the word "Wyoming," and the seal of a notary public shall not be levied upon or sold. If the notary public changes his county of residence to a different county than that shown on the seal, he shall have the seal altered to indicate such change.

(b) The seal of every notary public may be affixed by a seal press or stamp that will print or emboss a seal which legibly reproduces under the photographic methods the name of the notary, the words "notary public," the name of the county in which he resides and the word "Wyoming." The seal may be circular not over two inches in diameter or may be a rectangular form of not more than three-fourths of an inch in width by two and one-half inches in length, with a serrated or milled edged border, and shall contain the information required by this section.

CHAPTER 7: RECORDS

§ 7.1 Records of notaries.

In many of the states and other jurisdictions, the statutes require a notary public to keep a record or register of his official acts. This is particularly so concerning protests of commercial paper. Some states require a record of all instruments acknowledged, and of all depositions taken. Ordinarily, a notary must furnish a certified copy of any notarial record in his office to any person who applies therefor and pays the notary the necessary fee.

Statutes often provide that at the expiration of the notary's term of office, or upon his resignation, disqualification, death, removal from the county, or removal from office, his records must be deposited in some designated public office. A penalty is frequently imposed upon anyone who fails to so deposit the records.

Penalties are also often provided for destroying or defacing the records of a notary public.

See *Records: State and Other Statutes,* which follows.

RECORDS: STATE AND OTHER STATUTES

ALABAMA

[ALA. CODE]

Commercial Notaries

Tit. 40, § 7. To keep a register. Each notary public must keep a fair register of all his official acts, and give a certified copy therefrom, when required, and on payment of his legal fees.

§ 8. Disposition of register on death, etc. In case of the death, resignation, removal, or expiration of his term of office, the registers of any notary must, within thirty days thereafter, be delivered to the judge of probate of the county; and any person having the same in possession, and refusing to deliver them on demand to such judge, is liable to an action for the recovery thereof in the name of such judge.

227

§ 9. **Failure to deliver notary's register to probate judge on demand.** Any person who, after the death, resignation, removal, or expiration of the term of office of any notary public, having in possession the register kept by such notary public, refuses, on demand, to deliver the same to the judge of probate of the county, must, on conviction, be fined not less than one hundred dollars.

§ 10. **Certified copies of such registers.** The registers referred to in the preceding section may, by such judge, be delivered to any other notary of his county, who must give certified copies from the same to any person making application therefor, on payment of the legal fees. While the registers are in the possession of the judge of probate, he must give certified copies from the same on application, and the payment of the fees therefor, in the same manner as notaries public.

Notaries Ex Officio Justices of the Peace

§ 20. **Dockets and files to be delivered to successor.** On the vacation of the office, or expiration of the term of office of a notary public having the jurisdiction of a justice of the peace, the docket and all papers pertaining to his office, as justice, must be delivered to his successor, if he have a successor appointed, within thirty days, or if he have no successor, to a justice of the peace of the precinct; such successor or justice must complete all unfinished business pending before such notary, and must exercise all the powers and jurisdiction in reference to such unfinished business, and in the issue of a process upon judgments rendered, and in the certifying of such dockets and papers, which he can or may exercise in reference to business originally commenced before him, and in reference to his own judgments, dockets, and papers.

Notaries for State at Large

Notaries for State at Large shall perform all the acts and exercise all authority performed and exercised by notaries public under the general laws of the state. See *Appointment*, ALA. CODE tit. 40, § 21.

ALASKA

[ALASKA STAT.]

§ 44.50.100. **Return of papers to lieutenant governor.** If a notary public dies, resigns, is disqualified, removed from office, or removes from the state, all his public papers shall be delivered to the lieutenant governor.

ARIZONA

Notaries must keep a record of all their official acts, and a record of the parties to, date and character of every instrument acknowledged or proved before them, date of acknowledgment and description of the property affected by the instrument, and furnish, when requested, a certified copy of any record in their office. See *Authority and Duties*, ARIZ. REV. STAT. ANN. § 41-312.

[ARIZ. REV. STAT. ANN.]

§ 41-315. Depositing notarial records upon vacancy in office; failure to comply; storing of records; certified copies. A. When the office of a notary public becomes vacant, his records and official papers shall be deposited in the office of the county recorder, and a notary who neglects for three months thereafter to deposit such records and papers, or the personal representative of a deceased notary who neglects for three months after his appointment to deposit such records and papers, shall forfeit to the state not less than fifty nor more than five hundred dollars.

B. The recorder shall keep all records and papers of notaries public deposited in his office and give certified copies thereof when required, and for the copies he shall receive the same fees as are by law allowed to notaries public. Such copies shall be as valid and effectual as if given by a notary public.

§ 41-316. Wilful destruction of records; penalty. Any person who knowingly destroys, defaces or conceals any records or papers belonging to the office of a notary public, shall forfeit to the state an amount not exceeding five hundred dollars, and shall be liable for damages to any party injured thereby.

ARKANSAS

[ARK. STAT. ANN.]

§ 12-1408. Record book—Certified copies. Each notary shall keep a fair record of all his official acts in a book to be by him kept for that purpose, and when required, shall give a certified copy of any record in his office, to any person applying therefor, on the payment of the fees thereon.

§ 12-1410. Effect of death, resignation or removal. If any notary die, resign or remove from the county, or be removed from office, his record book and all his public papers shall be delivered to the clerk of the county court, to be delivered to his successor.

CALIFORNIA

[CAL. GOV'T CODE—West]

§ 8206. Records; certified copies. A notary public shall keep a record of all official acts done by him and a record of the parties to, date, and character of every instrument acknowledged or proved before him.

When requested, and upon payment of the fee therefor, a notary public shall make and give a certified copy of any record in his office.

§ 8209. Death, resignation, disqualification, or removal of notary. If any notary public dies, resigns, is disqualified, removed from office, or allows his appointment to expire without obtaining reappointment within 30 days, his records and all his public papers shall be delivered to the clerk of the county in which his principal place of business is located within 30 days. After 10 years from the date of deposit with the county clerk, if no request for, or reference to such records has been made, they may be destroyed upon order of court.

COLORADO

[COLO. REV. STAT. ANN.]

§ 12-55-103. Records—Liability. Every notary public shall keep a record of every acknowledgment taken by him to an instrument affecting the title to real property, and, if required, give a certified copy of, or a certificate as to any such record or any of his acts, upon payment of his fee therefor. Any notary who shall fail to keep such record shall be liable in an action upon his official bond, for any damages that may have been sustained, by any person, by reason of his failure to keep such record.

§ 96-1-4. Disposition of records. If any notary die, resign, become disqualified or remove from this state, his record and the official and public papers of his office, within thirty days, shall be delivered to the secretary of state.

DISTRICT OF COLUMBIA

[D.C. CODE ENCYCL. ANN.]

§ 1-512. Record of official acts—Certified copies. Each notary public shall keep a fair record of all his official acts, except such as are mentioned in the preceding section, [See *Authority and Duties,* D.C. CODE ENCYCL. ANN. § 1-511] and when required, shall give a certified copy of any record in his office to any person upon payment of the fees therefor.

§ 1-516. Vacation of office—Custody of records and papers. Upon the death, resignation, or removal from office of any notary public, his records, together with all his official papers, shall be deposited in the office of the Commissioners of the District of Columbia or their designated agent.

HAWAII

[HAWAII REV. STAT.]

§ 456-15. Record; copies as evidence. Every notary public shall record at length in a book of records all acts, protests, depositions, and other things, by him noted or done in his official capacity. All copies or certificates granted by him shall be under his hand and notarial seal, and shall be received as evidence of such transactions.

Note: A notary must keep a separate record for each judicial circuit. See *Qualifications,* HAWAII REV. STAT. § 456-2.

§ 456-16. Disposition of records, penalty. The records of each notary public shall each year on June 30 and upon the resignation, death, expiration of term of office, removal from or abandonment of office, or change of residence from the judicial circuit or circuits for which he is appointed, be deposited with the clerk of the circuit court of the judicial circuit for and in which the notary public was or is commissioned to act, or to which such records relate. By a neglect of sixty days to comply with the above requisition, the notary, his executor or administrator, shall forfeit to the State not less than $50 nor more than $500, in the discretion of the court, in an action brought therefor by the attorney general on behalf of the State.

IDAHO

It is the duty of a notary public to keep a record of all official acts done by him under IDAHO CODE § 51-104(1). See *Authority and Duties,* IDAHO CODE § 51-104.

[IDAHO CODE]

§ 51-106. Removal, death or resignation—Delivery of records to county recorder. If any notary die, resign, is disqualified or removed from office, his records and all his public papers, must within thirty days, be delivered to the recorder of the county in which he resided.

§ 51-107. Certified copies of predecessor's records. Every notary having in his possession the records and papers of his predecessor in office, may grant certificates or give certified copies of such records and papers, in like manner and with the same effect as such predecessor could have done.

ILLINOIS

[ILL. ANN. STAT.—Smith-Hurd]

Ch. 99, § 9. Deposit of records on expiration of office. On the expiration of the term of office of a notary public, he or in case of his decease, his legal representatives, shall deposit the records of his office in the office of the county clerk of his county: Provided, that when he is continued in office by reappointment, he may retain such records so long as he shall remain in office.

IOWA

[IOWA CODE ANN.]

§ 77.13. Record to be kept. Every notary public is required to keep a true record of all notices given or sent by him, with the time and manner in which the same were given or sent, and the names of all the parties to whom the same were given or sent, with a copy of the instrument in relation to which the notice is served, and of the notice itself.

§ 77.14. Death—resignation—removal. On the death, resignation, or removal from office of any notary, his records, with all his official papers, shall, within three months therefrom, be deposited in the office of the secretary of state.

Note: Concerning the penalty for the failure to deposit the records as required by § 77.14, see *Offenses,* IOWA CODE ANN. §§ 77.15, 77.16, 687.7.

§ 77.18. Duty of secretary of state as to records. The secretary of state shall receive and safely keep all such records and papers of the notary in the cases above-named, and shall give attested copies of them, under the seal of his office, for which he may demand such fees as by law may be allowed to the notaries, and such copies shall have the same effect as if certified by the notary.

KANSAS

[KAN. STAT. ANN.]

§ 53-110. Register of protests for banks. In cases of protest for banks or banking corporations, notaries shall keep a register thereof in a book provided for that purpose by the bank or banking corporation; and the notary shall not be required to deliver such register to his successor in office, but shall leave the same in the possession of such bank or banking corporation.

§ 53-111. Record of official acts; certified copies. Every notary shall keep a fair record of his official acts, and if required shall give a certified copy of any record in his office upon the payment of the fees therefor.

§ 53-112. Disposition of records and papers on termination of authority. If any notary die, resign, be disqualified, or remove from the county, his record and official and public papers of his office shall within thirty days be delivered to the clerk of the district court of the county, to be delivered to his successor when qualified.

KENTUCKY

[KY. REV. STAT. ANN.]

§ 423.030. **Protests to be recorded; copies as evidence.** The notaries public shall record in a well bound and properly indexed book, kept by them for that purpose, all protests made by them for the nonacceptance or nonpayment of all bills of exchange, checks or promissory notes placed on the footing of bills of exchange, and on which a protest is required by law, or of which protest is evidence of dishonor. A copy of such protest certified by the notary public under his notarial seal is prima facie evidence in all the courts of this state.

> *Editorial comment*
> Concerning the penalty for the failure to record the protest as required by the foregoing section, see *Offenses*, KY. REV. STAT. ANN. § 423.990.

§ 423.050. **Records of notary to be delivered to county clerk, when.** Upon the resignation of a notary public or the expiration of his term of office if he is not reappointed, he shall place his record book in the office of the county clerk in the county in which he was appointed, and if a notary dies, his representative shall deposit the record book with the clerk aforesaid. A copy of such record certified by the clerk in whose office it is filed shall be evidence in all the courts of this state.

LOUISIANA

Concerning records, see generally *Authority and Duties*. Concerning records of notaries in Orleans Parish, see *Authority and Duties*, "Orleans Parish".

MAINE

Concerning protests of losses, and records and copies, see *Authority and Duties*, ME. REV. STAT. ANN. tit. 4, § 952.

On the resignation or removal from office of any notary, his records must be deposited within three (3) months with the clerk of the judicial courts in the county for which he was appointed. See *Offenses*, ME. REV. STAT. ANN. tit. 4, § 956, wherein the penalty for violation is stated.

Concerning the penalty, and liability for damages, for knowingly destroying, defacing or concealing such records, see *Offenses*, ME. REV. STAT. ANN. tit. 4, § 957.

MARYLAND

[MD. ANN. CODE]

Art. 68, § 5. **Register; certified copies of record.** Each notary shall keep a fair register of all protests and other official acts by him done in virtue of his office and shall, when required, give a certified copy of any record in his office to any person applying for the same, the said person paying the usual fees therefor.

MASSACHUSETTS

Concerning the penalty for knowingly destroying, defacing, or concealing the records or official papers of a notary public, see *Offenses*, MASS. ANN. LAWS ch. 222, § 10.

MICHIGAN

[MICH. COMP. LAWS ANN.]

§ 55.114. Office vacated, disposition of records; penalty, neglect. Sec. 114. Whenever the office of any notary public shall become vacant, the records of such notary and all the papers relating to his office, shall be deposited in the office of the clerk of the proper county; and any notary, who, on his resignation or removal from office, shall neglect for the space of 3 months, to deposit such records and papers, and any executor or administrator of any deceased notary public, who shall neglect for the space of 3 months after his appointment, to deposit with said clerk all such records and papers as shall come to his hands, shall forfeit and pay a sum not less than 50 dollars, nor more than 200 dollars.

§ 55.115. Destruction or concealment of papers, penalty, civil liability. Sec. 115. If any person shall knowingly destroy, deface, or conceal any records or papers belonging to the office of a notary public, he shall forfeit and pay a sum not exceeding 500 dollars; and such person shall also be liable to an action for damages at the suit of the party injured.

§ 55.116. Records kept by county clerk; copies, fees. Sec. 116. The county clerk shall receive and safely keep all the records and papers of notaries public, directed to be deposited in his office, and shall give certified copies of such records and papers, under his hand and seal, when required; and for such copies he shall receive the same fees as are by law allowed to notaries public; and copies so given by said clerk shall be as valid and effectual as if given by a notary public.

MINNESOTA

A notary's official register shall be exempt from execution, and on his death or removal from office, such register shall be deposited with the clerk of the district court of his county. See *Seal*, MINN. STAT. ANN. § 359.03(1).

MISSISSIPPI

[MISS. CODE ANN.]

§ 25-33-5. Register of official acts. Every notary public shall keep a fair register of all his official acts, and shall give a certified copy of his record, or any part thereof, to any person applying for it and paying the legal fees therefor.

§ 25-33-7. Disposal of register and papers. In case of the death, resignation, disqualification, or expiration of the term of office of any notary public, his registers and other public papers shall, within thirty days, be lodged in the office of the clerk of the circuit court of the county where he resided; and the clerk may maintain an action for them.

§ 25-33-15. Record of protest of bill or note. When any notary public, justice of the peace, or clerk shall protest any bill of exchange or promissory note, he shall make a full and true record in his register or book kept for that purpose of all his proceedings in relation thereto, and shall note thereon whether demand of the sum of money therein mentioned was made, of whom, when, and where; whether he presented such bill or note; whether notices were given, to whom, and in what manner; where the same was mailed, and when and to whom and where directed; and of every other fact touching the same.

MISSOURI

[MO. ANN. STAT.—Vernon]

§ 486.030. Notary to keep a record, etc. Every notary shall keep a true and perfect record of his official acts, except those connected with judicial proceedings, and those for whose public record the law provides, and if required, shall give a certified copy of any record in his office, upon the payment of the fees therefor. Every notary shall make and keep an exact minute, in a book kept by him for that purpose, of each of his official acts, except as herein provided.

MONTANA

It is the duty of a notary public to keep a record of his acts concerning the demand for acceptance and payment of bills of exchange and promissory notes, the protest of same for nonacceptance or nonpayment, and the exercise of other powers and duties. It is also his duty, when requested, and upon payment of his fees therefor, to make and give a certified copy of any record in his office. See *Authority and Duties*, MONT. REV. CODES ANN. § 56-104(1), (4).

[MONT. REV. CODES ANN.]

§ 56-108. Records of, on death or resignation. It is the duty of every notary public, on his resignation or removal from office, and in case of his death, of his legal representative, or at the expiration of his term, to forthwith deposit all the records kept by him in the office of the county clerk of the county in which he was resident, and on failure to do so, the person so offending is liable to damages to any person injured thereby.

§ 56-109. Certified copies of records. It is the duty of each clerk aforesaid to receive and safely keep all such records and papers of the notary in the case above named, and to give attested copies of them under his seal, for which he may demand such fees as by law may be allowed to the notaries, and such copies shall have the same effect as if certified by the notary.

NEBRASKA

The statutes are vague concerning the keeping of records by notaries. See generally, *Authority and Duties*, NEB. REV. STAT. § 64-107.

NEVADA

Each notary public must keep a fee book in his office in which he shall enter the fees charged, in detail, and the title of the matter, proceeding or action on which they are charged. The fee book must be open to public inspection. There is a penalty for the violation of these provisions. See *Offenses*, NEV. REV. STAT. § 240.120.

Each officer authorized by law to take the proof or acknowledgment of the execution of conveyances of real property, or other instrument required by law to be proved or acknowledged, must keep a record of all his official acts in relation thereto in a book to be provided by him for that purpose. The statute specifies the information to be entered in the book. During business hours, the record must be open to public inspection without fee or reward. There are liabilities and penalties for the refusal or neglect to comply with these requirements. See *Acknowledgments*, NEV. REV. STAT. § 281.180, where the statute is quoted in full, including the specific information which must be entered in the book.

NEW HAMPSHIRE

[N.H. REV. STAT. ANN.]

§ 455:5. Deposit of Records. Whenever a notary shall remove from the state, resign or from any cause cease to act in that capacity, he shall within six months thereafter, deposit all his notarial records and all papers filed in his office in the office of the secretary of state.

§ 455:6. Notary's death or insanity. If a notary shall die or become insane it shall be the duty of his administrator, executor or guardian to deposit his records and papers in the manner aforesaid.

§ 455:7. Demand for records. The secretary of state may demand and receive any such records and papers of any person in whose possession the same may be.

§ 455:8. —Penalty for non-delivery.° If any person in whose possession any such records or papers may be shall neglect or refuse to deliver the same to the secretary, or upon his order on demand, or shall knowingly destroy or conceal any such records, he shall be guilty of a misdemeanor if a natural person, or guilty of a felony if any other person, and shall also be liable for damages to any person injured, in an action on the case.

(°) Concerning punishment, see *Offenses*, N.H. REV. STAT. ANN. § 651:2.

§ 455:9. Custody of records. All notarial records and papers shall be kept by the secretary of state safely and in such manner that reference thereto may easily be had, and shall be open to the examination of any person interested therein.

§ 455:10. Copies of records. The secretary of state shall make out and certify copies of any such records and papers, upon payment or tender of the fees therefor, and his certificate shall have the same validity as if made by such notary himself.

NEW MEXICO

[N.M. STAT. ANN.]

§ 35-1-11. Recording protest notices—use as evidence. Each notary public shall keep record of all protest notices and of the time and manner in which the same were served and of the names of all persons to whom the same were directed. Also the description and the amount of the instrument protested, which record, or a copy thereof certified by the notary public under seal, shall at all times be competent evidence to prove such notice in any court of this state.

NORTH DAKOTA

[N.D. CENT. CODE]

§ 44-06-05. Vacancy—disposition of records. Whenever the office of any notary public shall become vacant, the record of such notary together with all papers relating to the office shall be deposited in the office of the clerk of the district court of the county in which such notary public resides. Any notary public who, on resignation or removal from office, or any executor or administrator of the estate of any deceased notary public who neglects to deposit such records and papers as aforesaid for the space of three months, or any person who knowingly destroys, defaces, or conceals any records or papers of any notary public, shall forfeit and pay a sum of not less than fifty dollars nor more than five hundred dollars, and he also shall be liable in a civil action for damages to any party injured.

§ 44-06-08. Record of notices—certified copy—competent evidence. Each notary public shall keep a record of all notices, of the time and manner in which the same were served, the names of all the persons to whom the same were directed, and the description and amount of the instrument protested. Such record, or a copy thereof, certified by the notary under seal, at all times shall be competent evidence to prove such notice in any court of this state.

§ 44-06-09. Clerks of district courts—preservation of records. The clerk of the district court shall receive and keep safely all the records and papers directed by this chapter to be deposited in his office and shall furnish certified copies thereof when required. Such copies shall have the same force and effect as if the same were certified by the notary public by whom the record was made.

OHIO

[OHIO REV. CODE ANN.—Page]

§ 147.04. Seal and register.

o   o   o

[A] notary public shall also provide himself with an official register in which shall be recorded a copy of every certificate of protest and copy of note, which [seal and] record shall be exempt from execution. Upon the death, expiration of term without reappointment, or removal from office of any notary public, his official register shall be deposited in the office of the county recorder of the county in which such notary public resides.

OKLAHOMA

[OKLA. STAT. ANN.]

Tit. 49, § 7. Record of protests. In cases of protests for banks, notaries shall keep a register thereof in a book provided for that purpose by the bank, and the notary shall not be required to deliver such register to the county clerk, but shall leave the same in the possession of such bank.

§ 8. Official record—certified copy. Every notary shall keep a fair record of his official acts, and if required shall give a certified copy of any record in his office, upon the payment of the fees therefor.

§ 9. Vacancy. If any notary die, resign, be disqualified or remove from the county, his record and official and public papers of his office, shall, within thirty days be delivered to the clerk of the county.

OREGON

[ORE. REV. STAT.]

§ 194.090. Record of protests; effect as evidence. Each notary public shall cause a record to be kept of all protests of commercial paper made by him under ORS 73.5090. Such record is competent evidence to prove notice of dishonor for purposes of ORS 73.5100.

Note: ORE. REV. STAT. §§ 73.5090 and 73.5100, to which reference is made in the foregoing section, are part of the Uniform Commercial Code as enacted in Oregon. Concerning the Uniform Commercial Code, see Chapter 14, page 690.

Editorial comment

Whenever the office of a notary public becomes vacant, the record referred to in ORE. REV. STAT. § 194.090, above, kept by the notary public, together with all the papers relating to such record, must be deposited in the office of the Secretary of State. For the statute so providing, and for the penalty for failure to properly dispose of records or for destroying or altering records, see *Offenses*, ORE. REV. STAT. § 194.130.

§ 194.140. County clerks to keep records and papers and furnish attested copies; effect of copies. Each county clerk shall receive and keep safe all the records and papers directed by this chapter to be deposited in his office and shall give attested copies of any of the records or papers when required. Copies so given by the clerk are as valid as if given by the notaries public.

PENNSYLVANIA

[PA. STAT. ANN.]

Tit. 57, § 161. Register; copies of records. (a) Every notary public shall keep an accurate register of all official acts by him done by virtue of his office, and shall, when thereunto required, give a certified copy of any record in his office to any person applying for same. Said register shall contain the date of the act, the character of the act, and the date and parties to the instrument, and the amount of fee collected for the service.

(b) The register and other public papers of such notary shall not in any case be liable to be seized, attached or taken in execution for debt or for any demand whatsoever.

PUERTO RICO

[P.R. LAWS ANN.]

Tit. 4, § 891. Registries kept by notaries. Notaries shall keep a Registry of affidavits or declarations of authenticity, in brief entries, dated, numbered, sealed, and subscribed to by the notaries themselves, setting forth the names of the parties to the instrument, and the nature of the act, thereby authenticated.

These affidavits or declarations of authenticity shall be included in the indices referred to in section 836 of this title.

The registry of affidavits or declarations of authenticity, as soon as it shall contain two hundred folios shall be bound in the same manner as protocols of public instruments.

§ 894. Unrecorded affidavit or declaration void. Any affidavit or declaration not recorded in the Registry, or not included in the corresponding indice shall be null.

Protocols

Notaries are directed by statute to form their own protocols. See *Authority and Duties*, P.R. LAWS ANN. tit. 4, § 1006.

Tit. 4, § 1028. Protocol defined; secrecy. A protocol is the orderly collection of the original instruments authorized during a year by a notary. A protocol shall be secret and may be examined only as provided in this chapter or by judicial decree. Every original deed in a protocol shall be secret except for the parties concerned appearing therein or their heirs or legal representatives.

§ 1029. Numbering of folios of protocol. All the folios of a protocol shall be paged correlatively with the numbers expressed in words, but the corresponding figures may be added to.

§ 1030. Form of first page and closing memorandum of protocol. The first page of the first sheet of each protocol shall be captioned thus:

"Protocol of public instruments appertaining to the year . . . .
. . . ."

This caption shall be signed and marked by the notary.

In like manner shall every protocol be closed at the end of each calendar year, with the notary's authorizing the following memorandum immediately below the last instrument in the protocol:

"Here ends the protocol of the year . . . . which contains (so many) public instruments and (so many) folios authorized by me, the undersigned notary, to which I attest."

This memorandum shall be signed, marked, sealed and dated by the authorizing notary.

§ 1031. Binding of protocol; number of volumes. By the first month of each year all protocols with their indices must already be bound. When because of its bulkiness it shall become necessary, according to the notary's best judgment, to bind the protocol of a given year in more than one volume, the first shall be closed and the second opened with the notes expressed in section 1030 of this title, conveniently modified to designate the months comprised in each volume, none of which shall contain more than 500 folios. The various volumes, then, shall not be considered different protocols, wherefore the paging begun in the first volume shall not be interrupted and re-started in the second, and in the closing memorandum on the last volume of each protocol shall be stated, besides the number of instruments and folios of the volume, the aggregate number of instruments and folios constituting the protocol of the year.

§ 1032. **Curing defects in notarial instruments.** Defects in notarial instruments inter vivos may be cured without prejudice to third persons by the parties thereto through a public instrument setting forth the defect, its cause, and the curing statement.

§ 1033. **Removal of protocol from building where kept.** No protocol shall be taken out of the building where it is kept in custody except upon a judicial decree or by provision of law, and in such case it shall be presented to the court demanding it by the notary in charge of its custody.

§ 1034. **Protocols property of Commonwealth; custody and preservation.** Protocols belong to the Commonwealth of Puerto Rico but shall be kept in the custody and under the responsibility of the notaries pursuant to the provisions of this chapter.

Notaries are responsible for the integrity and preservation of protocols, and should said protocols become deteriorated through negligence, they shall be replaced at the expense of the notaries and the Supreme Court may reprimand the latter or impose on them a fine not to exceed five hundred (500) dollars, all by way of disciplinary measure, if there is reasonable ground to suspect that an offense has been committed, the proper charge shall be immediately filed in the competent court.

§ 1035. **Procedure when notary ceases to practice.** In case of the death or of the permanent mental or physical disability of a notary, or when he voluntarily or forcefully ceases in the discharge of his functions, or in the event that the surety company requests the termination of his bond, or when he accepts a permanent appointment to any judicial or executive office which under the laws of Puerto Rico is incompatible with the free exercise of the profession of law, it shall be the duty of the notary, his heirs, sucessors, or successors in interest, and of his sureties, to surrender within thirty (30) days thereafter his protocols and registers of affidavits, duly bound, and any other documents he may have in his possession as such notary, to any of the protocol inspectors whose offices are created by section 1038 of this title, in order that they may be examined and approved. If such surrender is not made voluntarily within the term specified the Chief Justice of the Supreme Court of Puerto Rico may issue the proper orders so that the marshal of said court may seize said protocols, registers of affidavits and documents. After the protocols, registers of affidavits and documents have been examined, they shall be delivered by the inspector who examined them to the general keeper of notarial protocols of the corresponding district. If from the inspection made it arises that the proper internal revenue stamps and bar stamps have not been affixed, the prosecuting attorney of the Supreme Court shall proceed to demand of the notary, his heirs, successors, successors in interest, or sureties reimbursement of the amount due, for the benefit of the Commonwealth of Puerto Rico or of the Bar Association of Puerto Rico, and he shall immediately report to the Chief Justice the outcome of the action taken by him. When the notary ceases to be disabled or to hold the judicial or executive office to which he was appointed, the general keeper of notarial protocols of the district shall return to him his protocols, if he resumes the practice of the notarial profession.

§ 1036. Notarial districts; general keepers of notarial protocols; notarial archives; certified copies. For the purposes of section 1035 of this title, the territory of the Commonwealth shall be divided into the following notarial districts comprising the demarcation appertaining to the parts of the Superior Court with seats at San Juan, Arecibo, Aguadilla, Mayaguez, Ponce, Guayama, Humacao, Caguas and Bayamon, and in each of said seats shall reside the respective general keeper of notarial protocols, who shall be a notary residing in each such locality and shall be appointed by the Secretary of Justice. The Secretary of Justice shall pass upon all matters concerning said notarial archives and upon the resignations and vacancies of the keepers of protocols, and shall take such measures as he may deem advisable in connection with the said general notarial archives.

General keepers of notarial protocols may issue literal, full or partial, manuscript, typewritten, photographic or photostatic copies or copies reproduced by any electromechanic means of reproduction designed to obtain an exact reproduction of an original, of the original instruments under his custody, upon payment of the reproduction cost of said copies, plus the scheduled fees prescribed for the issuance of copies and payment of the proper internal revenue stamps required by law.

Copies of any instrument so issued, duly certified by the general keeper of notarial protocols of the district shall be admissible in evidence.

Present incumbents in the office of general keeper of notarial protocols shall continue to hold office during good conduct, or until they resign or are removed for any reason.

§ 1036a.   Notarial protocols over 60 years old—transfer to General Archives of Puerto Rico.   (a)   Authorization is hereby granted for the transfer to the General Archives of Puerto Rico of those notarial protocols kept in the Archives of Notarial Protocols of Puerto Rico which are over sixty (60) years old on the effective date of this section and also for the transfer to the said General Archives of Puerto Rico, hereafter, of such protocols as, in the course of time, may reach that age limit.

(b)   The General Archivist of Puerto Rico shall be the custodian of the notarial protocols transferred to the General Archives of Puerto Rico pursuant to subd. (1) hereof.   It shall be the duty of the General Archivist to take the necessary measures to insure the proper conservation of the protocols placed under his custody, and always to keep them in their original format and orderly arrangement.   The protocols shall continue to be the property of the Commonwealth, pursuant to the Notarial Law in force [sections 1001-1040 of this title].

(c)   The protocols referred to in this section shall continue to be secret, according to the Notarial Law in force, except for the interested parties appearing in a deed or their heirs and legal representatives, and bona fide historical researchers.   With respect to the latter, the General Archivist of Puerto Rico shall, by regulations to that effect, prescribe the necessary rule to prove their status of bona fide researchers.

(d)   The Notarial Archivist of the District of San Juan is hereby empowered, to the exclusion of any other officer, to issue copies of the deeds included in the protocols referred to by this section, pursuant to the provisions of the Notarial Law, even in the case of protocols transferred to the General Archives of Puerto Rico from any of the other notarial districts of Puerto Rico.

§ 1037.   Restoration of destroyed or useless protocols.   In case a protocol is rendered useless or is lost in whole or in part, the notary shall report the fact to the Chief Justice of the Supreme Court, who shall direct a protocol inspector to institute the proper proceedings and summon the parties.   The indices and books shall be collated and all necessary data shall be looked into with a view to restoring in so far as practicable what has been destroyed or rendered useless. The record of the proceedings shall be approved by the Chief Justice on recommendation of the protocol inspector.

§ 1038.   Inspection of notarial offices; protocol inspectors; disciplinary fines and suspension.   The inspection of notarial offices and the examination of protocols shall be in charge of the Chief Justice of the Supreme Court of Puerto Rico.   The Chief Justice shall appoint a Director of Protocol Inspection and three or more experienced notaries as protocol inspectors all of whom shall be exempt from the provisions of sections 641-678 of Title 3, and shall hold office during good conduct.   The Director of Protocol Inspection shall receive a salary of fifteen thousand (15,000) dollars per annum, and each one of the protocol inspectors shall receive a salary of thirteen thousand six hundred (13,600) dollars per annum and all shall further receive the same per diem and compensation for travel expenses as all other employees of the Commonwealth of Puerto Rico receive when they leave San Juan, Ponce or the cities where they are assigned, in the discharge of their duties. One such protocol inspector shall reside in the district of San Juan, another in the district of Ponce, and the others shall reside where the Chief Justice may designate. The Supreme Court, through the Director of Protocol Inspection, shall allocate among the inspectors, as it may deem advisable, the work of examination of protocols in the different districts of the Commonwealth.

Protocol inspectors shall act under the direction of the Chief Justice and shall perform the duties and obligations he may assign to them, it being their duty to visit at least once a year all notarial offices, for which purpose notaries shall place their protocols and registers of affidavits at the disposal of any of them for examination in their notarial offices all working days from 8:00 a.m. to 12:00 noon and from 1:00 p.m. to 5:00 p.m. Upon inspecting the protocols of a notary, the inspector shall state in a brief memorandum over his signature and immediately following the last instrument in each volume of the protocols examined, the condition in which he has found them and the date of the inspection. Once through with said inspection, the inspector shall submit to the Chief Justice a written report setting forth the result of the examination, the state of preservation of the protocols, whether they are kept in accordance with law, whether the provisions of this chapter and of any other applicable law were complied with at the time of the execution of the instruments making up the protocols, and whether internal revenue stamps in the amount of the fees the Commonwealth of Puerto Rico should receive in accordance with the notarial tariff, as well as the proper bar stamps of the Bar Association of Puerto Rico, appear affixed to and cancelled on the original instruments in the protocols.

The power herein granted to protocol inspectors shall not extend to protocols already examined and approved by the former district judges.

If any disagreement should arise between the protocol inspector and the notary in the course of an inspection, as to the form and manner in which the latter keeps his protocols and register of affidavits, or with respect to the compliance with any other provisions of this chapter or of any other law of Puerto Rico, including those on notarial tariff, the inspector shall so state in his report, briefly reciting the facts and the grounds of the controversy, which report shall be submitted to the part of the Superior Court of the place where the notary practices his profession, so that said court may, upon hearing both the inspector and the notary, decide the controversy, which decision shall be reviewable by the Supreme Court through a writ of certiorari requested within ten days after service of notice.

The Supreme Court of Puerto Rico may, after giving the notary an opportunity to be heard in his defense, discipline him through a reprimand, a fine not to exceed five hundred (500) dollars, or a temporary or permanent suspension from office, for any violation of the provisions of this chapter or of any other law relative to the practice of the notarial profession.

§ 1039. **Bailment of protocols with general keeper of notarial protocols; copies.** Every notary public may in his discretion bail in custody to the general keeper of notarial protocols of his district any number of volumes of his protocol which he deems expedient and said officer is under obligation to give the notary proper receipt for the volumes so entrusted to him.

While the volumes of a protocol belonging to a practicing notary public are in the hands of the general keeper of notarial protocols of the district, this officer may issue certified literal, full or partial copies of the instruments contained in the volumes of said notary's protocol in his custody.

RHODE ISLAND

The statutes are vague concerning records. Specific fees are provided for recording protests. See *Fees Chargeable*, R.I. GEN. LAWS ANN. § 42-30-13.

SOUTH CAROLINA

The statutes are vague concerning records.

SOUTH DAKOTA

Each notary must keep a record of all notices to parties when instruments are protested by him, and of the time and manner in which the notices are served and of the names of all the parties to whom the same were directed, and the description and amount of the instrument protested. Such record or a copy thereof certified by the notary under seal shall at all times be competent evidence to prove the notice in any trial before any court in the state where proof of such notice may become requisite. See *Authority and Duties*, S.D. COMPILED LAWS ANN. § 18-1-8.

TENNESSEE

A notary must record in a well-bound book, to be kept by him for the purpose, each of his attestations, protestations, and other instruments of publication. See *Fees Chargeable*, TENN. CODE ANN. § 8-1624.

TEXAS

[TEX. REV. CIV. STAT. ANN.]

Art. 5955. Notaries' records. Each notary public shall keep a well bound book, in which shall be entered the date of all instruments acknowledged before him, the date of such acknowledgments, the name of the grantor or maker, the place of his residence or alleged residence, whether personally known or introduced, and, if introduced, the name and residence or alleged residence of the party introducing him; if the instrument be proved by a witness, the residence of such witness, whether such witness is personally known to him or introduced; if introduced, the name and residence of the party introducing him; the name and residence of the grantee; if land is conveyed or charged by such instrument, the name of the original grantee shall be kept, and the county where the land is situated. The book herein required to be kept, and the statements herein required to be entered shall be an original public record, open to inspection by any citizen at all reasonable times. Each notary public shall give a certified copy of any record in his office to any person applying therefor on payment of all fees thereon.

Note: Concerning records of acknowledgments, see also *Acknowledgments*, TEX. REV. CIV. STAT. ANN. art. 6619 to 6622.

Art. 5959. Effect of vacancy. Whenever the office of notary public shall be vacated by resignation, removal or death, the county clerk of the county where said notary resides shall obtain and deposit in his office the record books and all public papers belonging in the office of said notary. The seal of any notary vacating his office may be sold by the owner thereof to any qualified notary public in the county.

Editorial comment

See also *Offenses*, TEX. PENAL CODE ANN. § 37.10, Tampering with Governmental Record, and § 32.21, Forgery.

Records of Out of State Notaries

Art. 3731a. Official written instruments, certificates, records, returns and reports; foreign laws.

❋　　❋　　❋

Federal, Out of State, and Foreign Records

Sec. 2. Any written instrument which is permitted or required by law to be made, filed, kept or recorded (including but not limited to certificate, written statement, contract, deed, conveyance, lease, concession, covenant, grant, record, return, report or recorded event) by an officer or clerk of the United States or of another state or nation or of any governmental subdivision of any of the foregoing, or by his deputy or employee; or by any Notary Public of a foreign country in a protocol or similar book in the performance of the functions of his office, shall, so far as relevant, be admitted in the courts of this State as evidence of the matter stated therein, subject to the provisions in Section 3.

                         ○   ○   ○

UTAH

[UTAH CODE ANN.]

§ 46-1-6. Record of protests—evidence. Each notary public shall keep a fair record of all notices of protest made by him, noting the time and manner in which they were served, the names of all parties to whom they were directed and a description and the amount of the instrument protested. Such record shall be competent evidence to prove such notices. When required and the fees therefor are paid each notary public shall give a certified copy of any official record of paper in his office.

VERMONT

The statutes are vague concerning records.

VIRGIN ISLANDS

[V.I. CODE ANN.]

Tit. 3, § 775. Records to be kept; inspection by United States attorney; filing. (a) Each notary public shall keep an official record in which a memorandum of all official acts shall be noted.

(b) The United States attorney may inspect the official record of any notary public at any time.

(c) Upon the expiration of the term of office of each notary public, his official record shall be permanently filed in the office of the clerk of the district court in the judicial division in which the notary public resided.

Special Notaries Public

Government employees appointed as notaries public under tit. 3, § 801,° must keep an official record in which a memorandum of all official acts is noted. See *Authority and Duties,* "Special Notaries Public," V.I. CODE ANN. tit. 3, § 802.

(°) See *Qualifications,* "Special Notaries Public," V.I. CODE ANN. tit. 3, § 801.

WASHINGTON

[WASH. REV. CODE ANN.]

§ 42.28.070. Record of notices of protest. Every notary public is required to keep a true record of all notices of protest given or sent by him, with the time and manner in which the same were given or sent, and the names of all the parties to whom the same were given or sent, with the copy of the instrument in relation to which the notice is served, and of the notice itself; said record, or a copy thereof, duly certified under the hand and seal of the notary public, or county clerk having the custody of the original record, shall be competent evidence to prove the facts therein stated, but the same may be contradicted by other competent evidence.

WEST VIRGINIA

[W. VA. CODE ANN.]

§ 29-4-9. Disposition of records on death of notary or termination of office. On the death of a notary, or the termination of his office by resignation, removal from office or otherwise, his records and official papers shall be deposited in the office of the clerk of the county court of the county; and copies thereof certified by such clerk shall have the same effect as if certified by the notary.

Note: Concerning the penalty for the violation of the foregoing section, see *Offenses*, W. VA. CODE ANN. § 29-4-10.

WISCONSIN

[WIS. STAT. ANN.]

§ 137.01. Notaries.

o   o   o

(7) Official records to be filed. When any notary public ceases to hold office he, or in case of his death his executor or administrator, shall deposit his official records and papers in the office of the clerk of the circuit court of the county of his residence. If any such notary or any executor or administrator, after such records and papers come to his hands, neglects for 3 months to deposit them he shall forfeit not less than $50 nor more than $500.

o   o   o

Concerning the offense of knowingly destroying, defacing, or concealing the records or papers of a notary public, see *Offenses*, WIS. STAT. ANN. § 137.01(7).

WYOMING

Any officer or his deputy who has the custody of a record, book, document, paper, or proceeding, and steals or fraudulently takes away, secretes, withdraws or destroys any such record book [sic], document, paper, or proceeding, will be imprisoned in the penitentiary for not more than 10 years. See *Offenses,* WYO. STAT. ANN. § 6-173.

Any person who steals, takes and carries away the whole or any part of any record, record book, docket or journal authorized to be made by law, or belonging or pertaining to, among others, any state or county officer, will be imprisoned in the penitentiary for not more than 10 years. See *Offenses,* WYO. STAT. ANN. § 6-189.

Maliciously, mischievously or fraudulently altering, defacing, injuring, mutilating or destroying the whole or any part of a record authorized to be made by law belonging to or pertaining to, among others, any state or county officer, will be punished by imprisonment in the penitentiary for not more than 10 years. See *Offenses,* WYO. STAT. ANN. § 6-190.

[WYO. STAT. ANN.]

§ 32-7. Register to contain record of protests. Each notary public shall record in his official register, in a comprehensive manner, a copy of every bill of exchange, promissory note or obligation received by him for demand and protest, his official act, and the date thereof, stating specifically the name of each drawer or indorser or other person notified, and the place where notice was delivered, or to which notice was sent.

§ 32-8. Register to be deposited with county clerk upon expiration of term, etc.; failure to comply. Each person who has held the office of notary public shall, within thirty days after the expiration of his term of office, or his removal from office, or his removal from the county, deposit his official register with the register of deeds for the county [county clerk], who shall preserve the same and in case of death of a person holding the office of notary public, his executor or administrator shall, within thirty days after his decease, deposit his official register with the register of deeds [county clerk], and any person who shall neglect or fail to fulfill and perform the duty prescribed in this section, shall be liable in the penal sum of two hundred dollars, to be applied to the school fund of the county, which sum may be recovered by any citizen of the county suing therefor.

CHAPTER 8: FEES

§ 8.1 Compensation.

The compensation of a notary public for his services is received in the form of fees, the amount of which is usually fixed by statute in each state. As is shown in Fees Chargeable: State and Other Statutes, which follows, the statutes ordinarily prescribe precisely what a notary may charge for protesting commercial paper, administering an oath, taking a deposition or acknowledgment, or performing some other act.

In recent years several states have enacted laws prohibiting a notary from making a charge for any service to honorably discharged soldiers, sailors, airmen, or marines, in connection with applications for pensions.

FEES CHARGEABLE:
STATE AND OTHER STATUTES

ALABAMA

[ALA. CODE]

Tit. 40, § 14. Notary's fees. Notaries public are entitled to the following fees: The sum of one dollar and fifty cents and necessary postage for all services rendered in connection with the protest of any bill of exchange for acceptance, or of any bill of exchange, promissory note, check, or other writing for payment, and shall not charge any other fees therefor; for any oath, certificate, and seal, taken under subdivision 1 of section 5 of this title, fifty cents; for giving copies from register, twenty cents for each hundred words; for each certificate and seal to such copy, twenty-five cents; for giving any other certificate, and affixing seal of office, fifty cents.

ALASKA

[ALASKA STAT.]

§ 39.20.100. Fees, mileage or compensation. If a law requires or authorizes a service to be performed or an act to be done by an official or person within the state, and provides no compensation for

250

it, the attorney general may prescribe and adopt a schedule of fees, mileage, or other compensation considered by him to be proper for each judicial district. The attorney general may from time to time amend the schedule.

Editorial comment

The Attorney General of Alaska has not established a fee schedule for notaries. In Juneau the usual fee for acknowledgments or jurats is $1.00. In Anchorage and Fairbanks the fee for acknowledgments or jurats is likely to be around $2.00.

ARIZONA

[ARIZ. REV. STAT. ANN.]

§ 38-412. Posting schedule of fees. [Among other officers] notaries public shall keep posted at all times in a conspicuous place in their respective offices a complete list of the fees they are allowed to charge.

§ 41-314. Fees. Notaries public may receive the following fees:

1. Protesting a bill or note for nonacceptance or nonpayment, registering and affixing a seal, two dollars.

2. Each notice of protest, fifty cents.

3. Protest in all other cases, for each one hundred words, twenty cents.

4. Certificate and sale to such protest, seventy-five cents.

5. Taking the acknowledgment or proof of any deed or other instrument of writing for registration, including certificate and sale, seventy-five cents.

6. Taking the acknowledgment of a bill of sale of livestock, including certificate and seal, twenty-five cents.

7. Administering an oath or affirmation with the certificate and seal, seventy-five cents.

8. All certificates under seal not otherwise provided for, seventy-five cents.

9. Copies of all records and papers in their office, including certificate and seal, if less than two hundred words, seventy-five cents, or if more than two hundred words, for each one hundred words in excess of two hundred, in addition to the fee, twenty cents.

10. All notarial acts not otherwise provided for, fifty cents.

11. Taking the deposition of a witness, for each one hundred words, forty cents.

12. Swearing a witness to depositions, making certificate thereof with seal, and all other business connected with taking depositions, seventy-five cents.

Concerning the penalty for charging excessive fees, see *Offenses,* ARIZ. REV. STAT. ANN. § 38-413.

ARKANSAS

[ARK. STAT. ANN.]

§ 12-1733.   Notaries public.   Each Notary Public in this State shall charge and collect the following fees:

For protest and record of same	$1.00
For each notice of protest	.25
For each certificate and seal	1.50

Provided, that in no case of a protested item shall the entire fees charged exceed the sum of two dollars and seventy-five cents ($2.75).

CALIFORNIA

[CAL. GOV'T CODE—West]

§ 8211.   Fees; acknowledgment or proof of deed; administering oath or affirmation; change in immigration status.   The fees of a notary public are set forth in this section and in Sections 8211.5 and 8211.8.   The fee of a notary public for taking an acknowledgment or proof of a deed, or other instrument, to include the seal and the writing of the certificate, is, for the first two signatures, two dollars ($2) each, and for each additional signature, one dollar ($1).   The fee of a notary public for administering an oath or affirmation to one person and executing the jurat, including the seal, is two dollars ($2).   The fee of a notary public, exclusive of signature verification, shall not exceed ten dollars ($10) per individual for each set of forms relating to a change of that individual's immigration status.   This fee limitation shall apply whether the notary is acting in his capacity as a notary or not but shall not apply to an attorney, who is also a notary public, who is rendering professional services regarding immigration matters.

§ 8211.5.   Fees; depositions; notary public or reporter.   The fee of a notary public for all services rendered in connection with the taking of any deposition is the sum of five dollars ($5), and in addition thereto, the sum of one dollar ($1) for administering the oath to the witness and the sum of one dollar ($1) for the certificate to such deposition.

The fees herein provided for are exclusive of any fees for services rendered either by a notary public or another in connection with the reporting or transcription of depositions.

For his services transcribing a deposition the reporter shall receive from the party purchasing the original seventy-five cents ($0.75) per 100 words, and for each copy made at the same time ten cents ($0.10) per 100 words; from all other parties purchasing the same the reporter shall receive for each copy made at the same time as the original twenty-five cents ($0.25) per 100 words for the first copy, and ten cents ($0.10) per 100 words for additional copies.

In any county having a population of 5,000,000 or over, for services in reporting a deposition, a reporter shall receive not less than thirty-five dollars ($35) for one-half day nor more than the fees of a reporter pro tempore in the superior court of the county. For services in transcribing a deposition, the reporter shall receive from the party purchasing the original and one copy not less than two dollars ($2) per 28-line 8½- x 11-inch page, and, for each additional copy made at the same time or from all other parties purchasing a copy, the reporter shall receive not less than fifty cents ($0.50) per page.

If a deposition is transcribed, the reporter shall not receive the compensation provided in this section for reporting the deposition.

§ 8211.8. **Other fees.** Except as provided in Sections 8211 and 8211.5, the fees of a notary public are:

(a) For every protest for the nonpayment of a promissory note or for the nonpayment or nonacceptance of a bill of exchange, draft, or check, two dollars ($2).

(b) For serving every notice of nonpayment of a promissory note or of nonpayment or nonacceptance of a bill of exchange, order, draft, or check, one dollar ($1).

(c) For recording every protest, one dollar ($1).

(d) For copying an affidavit, or other paper for which provision is not made herein, ten cents ($0.10) for each folio.

COLORADO

[COLO. REV. STAT. ANN.]

§ 12-55-110. **Fees.** The fees of notaries public shall be as follows: For noting a bond, bill of exchange, or promissory note for protest, twenty-five cents; for each protest and record of the same, fifty cents; for each notice of protest, twenty cents; for each certificate and seal, twenty-five cents; for the acknowledgment of one party to a deed or other instrument, in writing, fifty cents; for each additional acknowledgment, twenty-five cents; for taking depositions, per folio of one hundred words, fifteen cents; for swearing any person to an affidavit, with certificate and seal, twenty-five cents; for all other service, the same fees as otherwise provided by law for like services.

CONNECTICUT

[CONN. GEN. STAT. ANN.]

§ 3-95. **Fees of notary.** The fees of notaries public shall be: For a marine protest, two dollars; for entering a protest of a bill or note, or noting without protest, fifty cents; for administering an oath to a pensioner, and taking the acknowledgment on his paper under the notarial seal, twenty-five cents; for noting a bill or note of protest, recording a protest, each notice to indorsers, makers, drawers or acceptors, affixing the notarial seal, or each certificate, twenty-five cents; for travel, ten cents a mile; for copies, the same as clerks of the superior court.

§ 52-262. **Fees for signing process, administering oaths, acknowledgments.** There shall be paid to the person legally authorized, except when otherwise provided and except to judges, prosecutors and clerks of court, for signing an attachment, summons, warrant or subpoena, taking a bond or recognizance, or an affidavit, or administering an oath out of court, ten cents; for taking the acknowledgment of any instrument, or signing and issuing a subpoena or capias, twenty-five cents; for causing notices of the seizure of intoxicating liquors to be posted, or issuing an order for their destruction, fifty cents.

DELAWARE

[DEL. CODE ANN.]

Tit. 29, § 4309. **Fees for services.** (a) The fees of a notary public, for the services specified, shall be as follows—

Taking and certifying an affidavit .... $ .25

For protest of a promissory note, bill of exchange, draft or cheque, and registering the same .... .80

Giving notice of a protest, personal or otherwise, and registering the notice and manner thereof, for each notice .... .20

For exemplification, under hand and notarial seal, of such protest .... .25

Protest of a foreign bill of exchange (to wit, a bill of exchange drawn beyond sea), and registering the same .. 1.00

Giving notice of such protest, personal or otherwise, and registering the notice and manner thereof, for each notice .... .37

Exemplification under hand and notarial seal of such protest .... .75

Registering a bill of exchange, promissory note, bank note, or cheque, where no fee for probate is charged ..... .20

Registering a common sea protest .... .75

Registering a foreign sea protest 1.00

Registering a protest against merchant, or other person, for detaining vessel beyond proper time, with answers and persistence to the protest 4.00

Exemplification under hand and notarial seal of either of said three last mentioned protests 1.00

And additionally two cents a line of ten words.

Registering an obligation, letter of attorney, bill of sale, or
other writing of similar length 1.00

Taking and certifying under hand and Notarial Seal, the
acknowledgment of a deed, letter of attorney, or other
instrument .... .50

Administering and certifying oaths to applicants for registration and titling of motor vehicles and operator's
licenses not to exceed fifty cents for first certificate
and twenty-five cents for each additional.

Drawing affidavit, or deposition, two cents a line of ten
words.

Taking depositions under order of court, a sum to be taxed
by the court.

Certicate under hand and notarial seal, when no other
service for which a fee is allowed is performed ...... .35

Taking depositions, a reasonable sum, to be taxed by the
court from which the commission issued.

(b)   The fees prescribed in this section shall be the minimum fees
to be charged by any notary public, and upon violation of this
provision the Governor may revoke the commission of such notary
and such notary shall not be re-appointed within a period of two
years.

(c)   Every notary public, who keeps a public office, shall always
keep hung up, in some convenient and conspicuous place therein,
a printed or written list of the fees prescribed in this section.

(d)   The provisions of this section shall be construed strictly and
no fee shall be allowed for any service, except where otherwise
expressly provided, until it has been actually performed.

(e)   Notary fees for affidavits in connection with the indigent
sick of Kent and Sussex Counties shall not be in excess of ten cents
for each such affidavit.

§ 4311.   Special fee provisions for certain services to members of
the armed forces and to veterans; penalties; jurisdiction of justices of
peace.   (a)   No notary public or other person who is authorized by
law to take the acknowledgment of instruments or to administer oaths
or affirmations shall charge any person serving in the armed forces
of the United States, or a veteran of any war, or the widow or
children of a soldier or soldier's parents or widower or other relative
of any person in the armed services the fee provided by law, when
an acknowledgment, oath or affirmation is taken in connection with
any paper or papers required to be executed by the Veterans Administration or in support of any claim or other papers connected
with or referring to the service of any male or female now serving
or who hereafter may serve or who, in the past, has served in the
armed forces of the United States.

(b)   Whoever violates subsection (a) of this section shall be fined not less than $10 nor more than $25, and, in default of the payment of such fine, shall be imprisoned for not more than 5 days.

(c)   Justices of the peace shall have jurisdiction of offenses under this section.

DISTRICT OF COLUMBIA

[D.C. CODE ENCYCL. ANN.]

§ 1-514.   Fees of notary.   The fees of notaries public shall be—
For each certificate and seal, fifty cents.

Taking depositions or other writings, for each one hundred words, ten cents.

Administering an oath, fifteen cents.

Taking acknowledgment of a deed or power of attorney, with certificate thereof, fifty cents.

Every protest of a bill of exchange or promissory note, and recording the same, one dollar and seventy-five cents.

Each notice of protest, ten cents.

Each demand for acceptance or payment, if accepted or paid, one dollar, to be paid by the party accepting or paying the same.

Each noting of protest, one dollar.   Mar. 3, 1901, ch. 854, § 571.

§ 1-515.   Penalties for taking higher fees.   Any notary public who shall take a higher fee than is prescribed by the preceding section shall pay a fine of one hundred dollars and be removed from office by the Superior Court of the District of Columbia.

FLORIDA

[FLA. STAT. ANN.]

§ 117.05.   Fees.   The fees of notaries public shall be as follows: For protesting bills of exchange, promissory notes, noting protest of captain of vessel and all other papers necessary to be protested, both for nonacceptance and nonpayment, including the entering and registering of same, issuing certificates with seal, all necessary notices and postage and each and every act necessary to perfect such protest, two dollars; administering each oath, ten cents; attending at a demand, tender or deposit and noting the same, one dollar; each certificate with seal thereto, fifty cents; each order for survey, fifty cents; copying any paper necessary to be copied, the same as allowed clerks of the circuit court.

§ 320.04.   License plates; service charge.

* * *

(2)   ° ° ° No tax collector, deputy tax collector or employee of the state or any county shall charge, collect or receive any fee or compensation as notary public in connection with or incidental to the issuance of license tags or titles.

GEORGIA

[GA. CODE ANN.]

§ 71-110. Fees. The fees of notaries public are as follows, to-wit:
Administering an oath in any case, $.30
Each attendance on any person to make proof as a notary public,
and certifying to same, $1.00
Every other certificate, $.50
It shall not be lawful for any notary public or other officer, whose
duty it is under the law to protest, note, or give notice to indorsers,
sureties, or makers of negotiable paper, mortgages, or other evidences
of debt, to charge for such service a greater sum than $1.50.
Registering shall be paid for by the party who has the service
performed. The fees for all official acts which the notary may
perform shall be the same as those prescribed for other officers who
are likewise permitted to perform them.

HAWAII

[HAWAII REV. STAT.]

§ 456-17. Fees. Subject to section 456-18, every notary public
is entitled to demand and receive the following fees:
For noting the protest of mercantile paper, $2;
For each notice and certified copy of protest, $2;
For noting any other protest, $3;
For every notice thereof, and certified copy of protest, $3;
For every deposition, or official certificate, $2;
For the administration of oath, including the certificate of the
oath, 50 cents; for affixing the certificate of the oath to every
duplicate original instrument beyond four, 25 cents;
For taking any acknowledgment, $1 for each party signing; for
affixing to every duplicate original beyond one of any instrument
acknowledged before him, his certificate of the acknowledgment, 50
cents for each person making the acknowledgment.

§ 456-18. Notaries in government service. Except as otherwise
provided for by law, the head of every department (which term as
used in this chapter includes any department, board, commission,
bureau, or establishment of the United States, or of the State, or
any political subdivision thereof) may designate one or more of his
subordinates to be a notary public who, upon duly qualifying and
receiving a commission as a notary public in government service,
shall perform, without charge, the services of a notary public in all
matters of business pertaining to the State, any political subdivision
thereof, or the United States.
Any provision of this chapter to the contrary notwithstanding, a
subordinate so designated and thus qualified and commissioned as a
notary public in government service shall:

(1)   Be authorized to perform the duties of a notary public in one or more of the judicial circuits of the State as the attorney general shall designate;

(2)   Not be required (A) to pay any fee to the clerk of any circuit court for filing a copy of his commission; (B) to pay any fee to the attorney general for the issuance of his commission or the renewal thereof; (C) to furnish and file an official bond unless such bond is required by the head of the department in which the notary is a subordinate, in which event, the expense of furnishing any such bond shall be borne by the department concerned;

(3)   Not demand or receive any fee for his service as a notary public; provided, that where the occasion, in the judgment of the head of the department, is deemed one of urgent necessity and convenience, the notary may, but shall not be compelled to, administer oaths or take acknowledgments in nongovernmental matters, for which services the prescribed fees shall be demanded and received as governmental realizations and covered into the general fund of the State; provided, further, that with the prior written approval of the attorney general, the notary public, upon paying the fees prescribed by law and upon executing, depositing, and filing at his own expense, the required official bond, may demand or receive the fees prescribed by law for services rendered by him in matters not pertaining to such public business.

IDAHO

[IDAHO CODE]

§ 51-108.   Fees of notaries.   The fees of notaries are as follows:

For drawing and copying every protest for nonpayment of a promissory note, or for the nonpayment or nonacceptance of a bill of exchange, draft or check, three dollars, said sum shall be in full payment of all fees for services of such notaries for drawing and serving every notice of nonpayment of a promissory note, or of the nonpayment or nonacceptance of a bill of exchange, order, draft or check, or for recording every protest, or for any other services necessary by such notaries in connection therewith.

For taking an acknowledgment or proof of a deed or other instrument, to include seal and the writing of the certificate, fifty cents.

For administering and certifying an oath, twenty-five cents.

For every certificate under seal, to include writing the same, fifty cents.

§ 65-301.   Performance without fee—Services enumerated.   Any state, county, city or public officer, or board, or body, acting in his or her or its official capacity on behalf of the state, county, or city, including notaries public, shall not collect, demand or receive any fee or compensation for recording or indexing the discharge papers of any male or female veteran who had active service in any war or conflict officially engaged in by the government of the United States; or for issuing certified copies thereof, or for any service whatever rendered by any such officer or officers, in the matter of a pension claim, application, affidavit, voucher, or in the matter of any claim to be presented to the United States veterans bureau or United States bureau of pensions for the purposes of securing any benefits under the World War Veterans Act of June 7, 1924 and other acts of congress providing pension benefits for honorably discharged veterans of any war, and all acts or parts of acts amendatory thereto, or for furnishing a certified copy of the public record of a marriage, death, birth, divorce, deed of trust, mortgage, or property assessment, or making a reasonable search for the same, wherein the same is to be used in a claim for pension, or a claim for allotment, allowance, compensation, insurance, automatic insurance, or otherwise provided for by the provisions of the World War Veterans Act and amendments thereto or any and all legislation by congress providing pension benefits for honorably discharged veterans of any war.

ILLINOIS

[ILL. ANN. STAT.—Smith-Hurd]

Ch. 53, § 46. Notaries public—Fees. For taking acknowledgment of a deed, mortgage, power of attorney, or other writing, with certificate under seal, 50 cents.

For noting a bond or promissory note, or bill of exchange for protest, 50 cents.

For protesting bond or bill of exchange, 75 cents.

For noting protest, 50 cents.

For noting marine protest and furnishing one copy thereof, $1.

For extending marine protest and furnishing one copy thereof, $4; for each additional copy furnished, $1.

For giving notice to drawees and indorsees, 50 cents each.

For any other certificate, under seal, 50 cents.

For administering oath to an affiant, 50 cents.

For filling out automobile applications and administering oath to affiant, 50 cents.

For taking depositions, for each 100 words, in counties of first and second classes, 15 cents; and in counties of the third class, 10 cents.

INDIANA

[IND. CODE]

§ 5-7-9-6. Fees of notaries public and commissioners of deeds. The fees of notaries public and commissioners of deeds shall be as follows, to wit:

For each certificate and seal ....50 cents

Taking depositions or other writing for each one hundred

[100] words ....25 cents

Administering an oath ....25 cents

For each protest ....50 cents

Each notice thereof ....25 cents.

§ 33-16-7-1. Protest fees. A notary public shall not, directly or indirectly, demand or receive for the protest for the nonpayment of any note or the nonacceptance or nonpayment of any bill of exchange, check or draft, and giving the requisite notices and certificates of such protest, including his notarial seal, any greater fee or reward than fifty cents (50¢) for such protest and twenty-five cents (25¢) for each notice on any bill, check, draft or note, and necessary postage, and, in event said notary public keeps a record of such protest, a fee of fifty cents (50¢) for such record.

IOWA

[IOWA CODE ANN.]

§ 77.19. Notary fees. Notaries public shall be entitled to the following fees:

1. For all services in connection with the legal protest of a bill or note, two dollars.

2. For being present at a demand, tender, or deposit and noting the same, seventy-five cents.

3. For administering an oath, ten cents.

4. For certifying to an oath under his official seal, twenty-five cents.

5. For any other certificate under seal, twenty-five cents.

KANSAS

[KAN. STAT. ANN.]

§ 28-131. Notary public fees. Notaries public shall receive for protest and record of the same, twenty-five cents; for each notice of protest, ten cents; for certificate and seal, twenty-five cents; for all other services, the same fees as are allowed to the clerk of the district court for like services.

§ 28-170. Fees of clerks of district courts. ° ° ° The clerks of the district court in each county of the state shall charge for services rendered by them as required by law to be performed by clerks of the district court the fees as hereinafter provided:

°   °   °

7. Administering any oath .... .50

8.   Making any record required to be made, or copying any
     record, per page 1.00

                   ◦   ◦   ◦

11.   Acknowledge a signature .... .50

                   ◦   ◦   ◦

§ 28-132.   Soldiers' compensation cases; fee allowed.   No judge
or clerk of any court, county clerk, notary public or any other person
authorized to administer oaths, shall be allowed to charge any
discharged soldier or seaman, or the widow, orphan, or legal representative thereof, more than fifteen cents (15¢) for administering any
oath, or giving any official certificate for the procuring of any pension, bounty or back pay, nor for administering any oath or oaths,
and giving the certificate required upon any voucher for collection
of periodical dues from the pension agent, nor more than fifteen
cents (15¢) for all services rendered in perfecting any one voucher.

§ 28-133.   Same; penalty.   Any such officer who may accept more
than fifteen cents for any such service shall be deemed guilty of a
misdemeanor, and fined in any sum not less than twenty-five dollars
nor more than fifty dollars.

   Editorial comment

   Notaries and other officers are required to post a list of
   their fees in their office in some conspicuous place, to give
   on demand a certified bill of fees charged specially stating
   the items of service and the charge therefor, and if required
   by the person paying fees charged, to give him a receipt
   therefor, setting forth the items and the date of each.   See
   Commissioners of Deeds, KAN. STAT. ANN. §§ 28-140,
   28-142, 28-143.

KENTUCKY

[KY. REV. STAT. ANN.]

§ 64.300.   Notaries public.   (1)   The fees of notaries public for
the following services shall be not more than set out in the following
schedule:

Every attestation, protestation, or taking acknowledgment
  of any instrument of writing, and certifying the same
  under seal including, but not limited to, the notarization
  of absentee ballots $0.50

Recording same in book to be kept for that purpose ...... .75

Each notice of protest .... .25

Administering oath and certicate thereof .... .20

   (2)   No fee or compensation shall be allowed or paid for affixing
the jurat of a notary public to any application, affidavit, certificate

or other paper necessary to be filed in support of any claim for the benefits of federal legislation for any person or his dependents who has served as a member of the Army, Navy, or Marine Corps of the United States.

LOUISIANA

The statutes are not definitive concerning notary fees.

[LA. REV. STAT.]

§ 9:1423. Fees of experts and appraisers. The fees allowed to experts, notary publics and appraisers appointed to assist in taking inventories of successions, tutorships, interdictions, and other proceedings requiring the taking of inventories, shall be fixed by the court appointing such experts, notary publics and appraisers, and shall be taxed as costs in those proceedings in which the taking of an inventory is required.

MAINE

[ME. REV. STAT. ANN.]

Tit. 4, § 958. Fees for protest ° ° °. For each protest of a bill or note, notifying parties, making his certificate thereof in due form and recording his proceedings, a notary public shall receive $1.50. ° ° °

MARYLAND

[MD. ANN. CODE]

Art. 36, § 23. Enumeration. Notaries public shall be entitled to demand and receive the following fees, to wit:

For protesting any note, draft, bill of exchange or check for nonacceptance or nonpayment $2.00

For drawing all proceedings, exceeding two sides ...... .50

For drawing all proceedings, exceeding two sides, per side .... .25

For registering or copying proceedings, for every side ... .10

For presenting a bill of exchange for acceptance, if accepted and not afterwards protested for nonpayment 1.00

For noting a bill for nonacceptance, if not protested for nonacceptance or nonpayment 1.00

For noting a marine protest 1.00

For affixing notarial seal .... .50

For every search where no copy is made .... .25

For administering an oath or taking an acknowledgment .12½

For all other acts and service, in proportion to the aforesaid fees, to be paid at the time of doing the same.

For going any distance more than three miles from his
residence, per mile .... .20
For every notice of protest, mailed or delivered .... .05
For presentation and demand of payment of a promissory
note, a bill of exchange, if payment of same be made
to the notary 1.00

MASSACHUSETTS

[MASS. ANN. LAWS]

Ch. 262, § 41. Notaries public. The fees of notaries public shall
be as follows:

For the protest of a bill of exchange, order, draft or check for
non-acceptance or non-payment, or of a promissory not for nonpayment, if the amount thereof is five hundred dollars or more, one
dollar; if it is less than five hundred dollars, fifty cents; for recording
the same, fifty cents; for noting the non-acceptance or non-payment
of a bill of exchange, order, draft or check or the non-payment of a
promissory note, seventy-five cents; and for each notice of the nonacceptance or non-payment of a bill, order, draft, check or note,
given to a party liable for the payment thereof, twenty-five cents;
but the whole cost of protest, including necessary notices and the
record, if the bill, order, draft, check or note is of the amount of
five hundred dollars or more, shall not exceed two dollars, and if
it is less than five hundred dollars, shall not exceed one dollar and
fifty cents; and the whole cost of noting, including recording and
notices, shall in no case exceed one dollar and twenty-five cents.

§ 43. Cases not specified. The fees of public officers for any
official duty or service shall, except as otherwise provided, be at the
rate prescribed in this chapter for like services. Neither justices of
the peace nor notaries public shall charge any fee for completing the
jurat on official absent voting ballot envelopes ° ° °.

MICHIGAN

[MICH. COMP. LAWS ANN.]

§ 35.51. Fees for oaths, certificates; to discharged soldier or sailor.
Sec. 1. That no judge of the probate, clerk of any court, justice
of the peace, notary public, or any person authorized to administer
oaths under and by the provisions of the laws of this state, shall be
allowed to charge any discharged soldier, seaman, or the legal representative of a discharged or deceased soldier or sailor more than 15
cents for administering any oath or giving any official certificate for
the procuring or obtaining payment of any pension, bounty or back
pay.

Note: For the penalty for the violation of the foregoing section,
see *Offenses*, MICH. COMP. LAWS ANN. § 35.53.

§ 35.52.   Same; to widow of deceased soldier or sailor.   Sec. 2. That no judge of probate, clerk of any court, justice of the peace, notary public, or any person authorized to administer oaths under and by the provisions of the laws of this state, shall be allowed to charge any widow of a deceased soldier, or guardian to minor children, or other legal representative of such deceased soldier or sailor, more than 25 cents for the oath or oaths of such widow, guardian, or legal representative and their witnesses; nor shall it be lawful for a judge of probate to charge more than 15 cents for a certificate of guardianship, administration, or of the death of a pensioner, or the widow, children, or other legal representatives of a pensioner, for the purpose of procuring the payment of any installment of pension.

Note: For the penalty for the violation of the foregoing section, see Offenses, MICH. COMP. LAWS ANN. § 35.53.

§ 600.2564.   Fees of notaries public.   Sec. 2564.   Notaries public shall be entitled to the following fees, which are not taxable as costs:

(1)   For drawing and copy of protest of the nonpayment of a promissory note or bill of exchange, or of the nonacceptance of such bill, 50 cents, in cases where by law, such protest is necessary, but in no other case.

(2)   For drawing and copy of every other protest, 25 cents.

(3)   For drawing, copy, and serving every notice of nonpayment of a note, or nonacceptance of a bill, 25 cents.

(4)   For drawing any affidavit, or other paper or proceeding, for which provision is not herein made, 20 cents for each folio, and for copying the same, 6 cents for each folio.

(5)   For taking the acknowledgment of deeds, and for other services authorized by law, the same fees as are allowed to other officers for similar services.   [In this regard see § 600.2573 below.]

§ 600.2573.   Fees of circuit court commissioners; allowance to other persons.   Sec. 2573.   Circuit court commissioners shall be entitled to the following fees:

      o   o   o

(18)   For administering an oath, 75 cents.

      o   o   o

(25)   For every deposition, for each day's attendance in taking testimony, $6.00, taxable as costs only in accordance with subsection (1) of section 2549.

      o   o   o

(29)   For taking the acknowledgment of any conveyance or mortgage of real estate or other instrument which may be recorded, 50 cents for the first person acknowledging, and 25 cents for each additional person; and when the execution of any conveyance or

mortgage of real estate or other instrument is proven by 2 witnesses, $1.00.

o   o   o

MINNESOTA

[MINN. STAT. ANN.]

§ 357.17. Notaries public. The fees to be charged and collected by a notary public shall be as follows, and no other or greater fees shall be charged:

(1) For protest of non-payment of note or bill of exchange or of non-acceptance of such bill, where protest is legally necessary, and copy thereof, $1;

(2) For every other protest and copy, 25 cents;

(3) For making and serving every notice of non-payment of note or non-acceptance of bill and copy thereof, 25 cents;

(4) For any affidavit or paper for which provision is not made herein, 20 cents per folio, and six cents per folio for copies;

(5) For each oath administered, 25 cents;

(6) For acknowledgments of deeds and for other services authorized by law, the legal fees allowed other officers for like services;

(7) For recording each instrument required by law to be recorded by him, ten cents per folio.

MISSISSIPPI

[MISS. CODE ANN.]

§ 25-7-29. Notaries public. Notaries public shall charge the following fees:

(a) For protesting bill or note for non-acceptance or non-payment, and giving notice $1.00

(b) Registering such protest and making record .... .50

(c) Attesting letters of attorney and seal .... .50

(d) Notarial affidavit to an account or other writing and seal .50

(e) Each oath or affirmation and seal .... .50

(f) Notarial procuration and seal 1.00

(g) Certifying sales at auction and seal .... .50

(h) Taking proof of debts to be sent abroad .... .50

(i) Protest in insurance cases and seal 1.00

(j) Copy of record and affidavit 1.00

MISSOURI

[MO. ANN. STAT.—Vernon]

§ 486.090. Fees of notaries. Notaries shall be allowed fees for their services as follows:

For noting a bill of exchange or note for protest $0.15

For noting without protest .... .35

For entering protest of same .... .35

For registering a protest .... .35

For notice to each indorser or other party .... .15

For travel, per mile .... .08

For taking acknowledgment of a deed or other instrument
with a certificate and seal .... .50

For a marine protest or fire insurance protest 5.00

For certificate, attested by seal .... .50

For taking the acknowledgment of parties to contract, attested
by seal .... .50

For all copies of records and papers, for every hundred words .15

For all other services, the same fees as are allowed by law to magistrates in like cases.

[MO. CONST.]

Art. 6, § 12. Officers compensated only by salaries in certain counties. All public officers in the city of St. Louis and all state and county officers in counties having 100,000 or more inhabitants, excepting public administrators and notaries public, shall be compensated for their services by salaries only.

MONTANA

[MONT. REV. CODES ANN.]

§25-112. Fees of notaries public. For drawing, copying, and recording each and every protest for the nonpayment of a promissory note, or for the nonpayment or nonacceptance of a bill of exchange, order, draft, or check, one dollar.

For drawing and serving every notice of nonpayment of a promissory note, or of the nonpayment or nonacceptance of a bill of exchange, order, draft, or check, twenty-five cents.

For drawing an affidavit, deposition, or other paper for which provision is not herein made, for each folio, unless otherwise prescribed, twenty cents.

For taking an acknowledgment or proof of a deed or other instrument, to include the seal and the writing of the certificate, for the first signature, one dollar.

For each additional signature, fifty cents.

For administering an oath or affirmation, twenty-five cents.

For certifying an affidavit, with or without seal, including oath, fifty cents.

Provided, the maximum fee that can be computed or charged for drawing, copying, and recording a protest, and for drawing and serving the notices of nonpayment or nonacceptance, shall be two dollars and fifty cents.

NEBRASKA

[NEB. REV. STAT.]

§ 33-133. Notaries public; fees. Notaries public may charge and collect fees as follows: For each protest, one dollar; for recording the same, fifty cents; for each notice of protest, twenty-five cents; for taking affidavits and seal, twenty-five cents; for administering oath or affirmation, five cents; for taking deposition, for each one hundred words contained in such deposition and in the certificate, ten cents and no more; for each certificate and seal, twenty-five cents; for taking acknowledgment of deed or other instrument, fifty cents; and for each mile traveled in serving notice, five cents.

NEVADA

[NEV. REV. STAT.]

§ 240.100. Fees.

1. The fees of notaries public in counties polling 800 votes or less and in counties polling over 800 votes at the last general election shall be as follows:

	800 Votes or Less	Over 800 Votes
For drawing and copying every protest for the nonpayment of a promissory note, or for the nonpayment or nonacceptance of a bill of exchange, draft or check . . .	$2.00	$2.00
For drawing and serving every notice of nonpayment of a promissory note, of the nonpayment or nonacceptance of a bill of exchange, order, draft or check	1.00	1.00
For drawing an affidavit, deposition or other paper, for which provision is not made in this chapter, for each folio	.30	.20
For taking an acknowledgment or proof of a deed or other instrument, to include the seal and the writing of the certificate, for the first signature	1.00	1.00
For each additional signature	.50	.50
For administering an oath or affirmation . .	.25	.25
For every certificate, to include writing the same and the seal	.50	.50

2. All fees prescribed in this section shall be payable in advance, if demanded.

Editorial comment

A notary must publish and set up in some conspicuous place in his office a table of his fees, for the inspection of all persons who have business in his office. There is a penalty for the failure to comply with this requirement. See *Offenses*, NEV. REV. STAT. § 240.110.

Each notary must keep a fee book in his office, in which he must enter the fees charged in detail, and the title of the matter, proceeding, or action on which they are charged. The fee book must be open to public inspection. There is a penalty for the violation of this requirement. See *Offenses*, NEV. REV. STAT. § 240.120.

No other fees may be charged than those specially set forth in the statutes, nor shall fees be charged for any other services than those mentioned in the statutes. There is a penalty for the violation of these requirements. See *Offenses*, NEV. REV. STAT. § 240.130. There is also a penalty for a notary public to take more or greater fees than are allowed by the statutes. See *Offenses*, NEV. REV. STAT. § 240.140.

NEW HAMPSHIRE

[N.H. REV. STAT. ANN.]

§ 455:11. Protests, Certificates, etc. Notaries public shall be entitled to the following fees:

For every protest under seal, fifty cents; every certificate under seal, twenty-five cents.

For waiting on a person to demand payment, or to witness any matter, and certifying the same under seal, fifty cents.

For every notice of nonpayment to any party to a bill or note, twenty-five cents.

For services relating to the taking of depositions, the same fees as justices are entitled to receive°

For administering and certifying oaths, except the oaths of office of town officers, one dollar.

(°) Concerning the specific fees chargeable for taking depositions, see *Depositions*, N.H. REV. STAT. ANN. §§ 517:19, 517:20.

Editorial comment

The fee for taking and certifying the acknowledgment of a deed or other instrument by one or more persons at one time is 17¢. See *Acknowledgments*, N.H. REV. STAT. ANN. § 477:6.

NEW JERSEY

[N.J. STAT. ANN.]

§ 22A:4-13. Demand or protest of negotiable instruments. A notary public for performing the services herein enumerated shall be entitled to receive the following fees:

For making demand for payment or acceptance of a promissory note, bill of exchange, draft or check, protesting the same and registering protest of the same, two dollars ($2.00).

For making and serving each and every notice of protest to be served on the persons entitled thereto, in addition to the cost of postage for each notice if sent by mail, for each of said notices so made and served, ten cents ($0.10).

If a notary charges any greater fees for the services mentioned than are herein allowed he shall forfeit and pay to the party from whom he has taken the same the sum of twenty-five dollars ($25.00), to be recovered in a civil action, with costs, before a court of competent jurisdiction.

§ 22A:4-14. Acknowledgments, proof, affidavits and oaths. For a service specified in this section, commissioners of deeds, foreign commissioners of deeds, notaries public, judges and other officers authorized by law to perform such service, shall receive a fee as follows:

For administering an oath or taking an affidavit $0.50.

For taking proof of a deed, $1.00.

For taking all acknowledgments, $1.00.

NEW MEXICO

[N.M. STAT. ANN.]

§ 35-1-23. Fees. A. Every notary public in this state shall be entitled to collect the following fees for his services:

(1) for each act of protest and certificate thereof $2.00

(2) for each notice of protest prepared and mailed to the parties in interest .... .25

(3) for any certificate under seal 1.00

(4) for each acknowledgment to deed or other document .. 1.00

(5) for administering or certifying to any oath 1.00

B. Whenever a notary shall be authorized by proper process to take testimony or depositions and report the same to the proper authority without making findings of fact or law, such notary public shall be entitled to collect the following fees for his services:

(1) for noting each meeting to take testimony 1.00

(2) for noting each adjournment from one day to another .. 1.00

(3) for swearing each witness .... .25

(4)   for certifying and transmitting the record 1.50

(5)   for transcribing or reducing to writing testimony, per folio of one hundred words, original .... .15

(6)   for each additional copy of same, per folio .... .05

And every notary in addition to collecting fees when called from his office shall be entitled to ten cents ($.10) per mile.

NEW YORK

[N.Y. EXEC. LAW]

§ 135. Powers and duties; in general; of notaries public who are attorneys at law.

                              ○   ○   ○

A notary public shall not, directly or indirectly, demand or receive for the protest for the non-payment of any note, or for the non-acceptance or non-payment of any bill of exchange, check or draft and giving the requisite notices and certificates of such protest, including his notarial seal, if affixed thereto, any greater fee or reward than seventy-five cents for such protest, and ten cents for each notice, not exceeding five, on any bill or note. Every notary public having a seal shall, except as otherwise provided, and when requested, affix his seal to such protest free of expense.

§ 136 Notarial fees. A notary public shall be entitled to the following fees:

1.   For administering an oath or affirmation, and certifying the same when required, except where another fee is specifically pre-scribed by statute, twenty-five cents.

2.   For taking and certifying the acknowledgment or proof of execution of a written instrument, by one person, twenty-five cents, and by each additional person, twenty-five cents, for swearing each witness thereto, twenty-five cents.

[N.Y. CIV. PRAC. LAW]

§ 8009.   Oaths; acknowledgments; certification or exemplification. Any authorized officer is entitled, for the services specified, to the following fees:

1.   for administering an oath or affirmation, and certifying it when required, except where another fee is specifically prescribed by statute, in the counties within the city of New York, one dollar, and in all other counties, twenty-five cents.

2.   for taking and certifying the acknowledgment or proof of the execution of a written instrument, twenty-five cents for one person and twenty-five cents for each additional person, and twenty-five cents for swearing each witness thereto; and

3.   for certifying or exemplifying a typewritten or printed copy

of any document, paper, book or record in his custody, except in the counties within the city of New York, three cents for each folio with a minimum fee of twenty-five cents.

Editorial comment

See also *Acknowledgments*, "Commissioners of Deeds," N.Y. PUB. OFFICERS LAW §§ 68-a, 69, concerning fees for oaths or acknowledgments, and the prohibition of fees for administering certain official oaths.

NORTH CAROLINA

[N.C. GEN. STAT.]

§ 10-8. Fees of notaries. Notaries public shall be allowed the following fees:

(1) Taking and certifying the acknowledgment or proof of the execution or signing of any instrument or writing $0.50
(2) Taking affidavits 0.50
(3) Administering oaths (except that oaths of office shall be administered to public officials without charge) .. 1.00

NORTH DAKOTA

[N.D. CENT. CODE]

§ 44-05-03. Fee for taking acknowledgment and administering an oath. Any officer authorized by law to take and certify acknowledgment of a deed or other instrument is entitled to charge and receive not more than one dollar.

Note: Compare § 44-06-14, below.

§ 44-06-14. Fees to be charged by notaries public. A notary public is entitled to charge and receive the following fees:

1. For each protest, fifty cents;
2. For recording the same, twenty-five cents;
3. For each notice of protest completed and served, twenty-five cents and postage for mailing the notice;
4. For taking affidavit and seal, twenty-five cents;
5. For administering an oath or affirmation, ten cents;
6. For taking a deposition, each ten words, one and one-half cents;
7. For each certificate and seal, twenty-five cents; and
8. For taking proof of acknowledgment, twenty-five cents.

Note: Compare § 44-05-03, above.

OHIO

[OHIO REV. CODE ANN.—Page]

§ 147.08. Fees. A notary public is entitled to the following fees:

(A) For the protest of a bill of exchange or promissory note, one dollar and actual necessary expenses in going beyond the corporate limits of a municipal corporation to make presentment or demand;

(B) For recording an instrument required to be recorded by a notary public, ten cents for each one hundred words;

(C) For taking and certifying acknowledgments of deeds, mortgages, liens, powers of attorney, and other instruments of writing, and for taking and certifying depositions and affidavits, administering oaths, and other official services, the same fees as are allowed by law to judges of county courts for like services.

§ 147.13. Removal for receiving excess fees. A notary public who charges or receives for an act or service done or rendered by him a fee greater than the amount prescribed by law, or who dishonestly or unfaithfully discharges any of his duties as notary public, shall be removed from his office by the court of common pleas of the county in which he resides, upon complaint filed and substantiated in such court, and the court shall thereupon certify such removal to the governor. The person so removed shall be ineligible for reappointment to the office of notary public.

OKLAHOMA

[OKLA. STAT. ANN.]

Tit. 28, § 47. Fees of notaries. Each notary public shall charge and collect the following fees:

For protest and record of same .... $ .50
For each notice of protest .... .10
For each certificate and seal .... .25

Provided, that he may charge, receive and collect the fees provided in this article for the clerks of the district court for like service and none other.

§ 31. Fees of court clerks. The clerk of the district court, or the clerk of any other court of record, shall charge and collect the following fees for services by them respectively rendered and none others, except as otherwise provided by law:

      ○   ○   ○

Swearing jurors and witnesses .... .20

      ○   ○   ○

Certifying to any instrument (each) .... .25

      ○   ○   ○

OREGON

[ORE. REV. STAT.]

§ 194.010.   [Appointment of notary public; term; qualifications;] office may be nonlucrative; [functions not official duties.]

○   ○   ○

(4)   Each notary public may file with the Secretary of State a statement waiving the fees prescribed in ORS 194.160; and in such case the office of notary public is considered nonlucrative.

○   ○   ○

§ 194.160.   Schedule of notary fees.   The fees of notaries public shall be as follows:

(1)   Attesting any written instrument, $1.

(2)   Certifying and taking an affidavit, and all certificates, $1.

(3)   Taking the acknowledgment of any deed or other instrument of writing, $1.

(4)   Making and taking proof of any legal instrument, for each page, 25 cents.

(5)   Taking depositions, each page, 25 cents.

(6)   Administering an oath, 25 cents.

(7)   Protesting commercial paper, $1; except that no fees shall be allowed for protesting a check because of the insolvency of the bank upon which the check was written.

§ 194.170.   Mileage of notaries public.   Every notary public whose fees are prescribed in ORS 194.160 who is required to travel in order to execute or perform his duties as a notary public, in addition to the fees prescribed in ORS 194.160, shall be entitled to mileage at the rate of eight cents a mile, and no more, in going to and returning from the place where the service is performed.

PENNSYLVANIA

The fees of a notary for services rendered shall be the property of the notary, and in no case shall they belong to or be received by a corporation of which the notary is a director or clerk.   See *Authority and Duties,* PA. STAT. ANN. tit. 57, § 165(c).

[PA. STAT. ANN.]

Tit. 57, § 167.   Fees of notaries public.   The fees of notaries public shall be fixed by the Secretary of the Commonwealth with the approval of the Attorney General.

Notary Public Fee Schedule

As provided by law, following is the schedule of fees you may charge for performing the various functions of your office:

Making demand for payment or acceptance of a promissory note, bill of exchange, draft, or check, ... $1.25

Protesting the same, ... 1.25

Registering protest of the same, ... 1.00

For first notice of protest, ... .35

and each additional notice, ... .15

Administering oaths or affidavits, writing out and certifying the same with seal, ... 1.00

Probate to bill or account and certifying the same with seal, ... 1.25

Certified copy of any record, ... .75

Comparing the same, for every hundred words, ... .10

Every acknowledgment or probate of deed or other instrument of writing, for the first name, ... .75

each additional name after the first, ... .25

Take depositions (first page folio cap), ... 1.25

each additional page, ... 1.00

Marine protest, including affidavits, certificate, seal, et cetera, ... 10.00

The Secretary of the Commonwealth

PUERTO RICO

[P.R. LAWS ANN.]

Tit. 4, § 847. Notarial tariff. Notaries shall receive for the execution of instruments made before them and for the copies thereof, the fees contained in the following tariff:

Notarial Tariff

Article 1. The execution of documents or deeds of arras, dowry, articles of marriage, wills, associations, dissolutions thereof, contracts of work, simple obligations, obligations guaranteed by mortgage or pledges, securities, mandates or trusts, powers of attorney, protest, protest of bills of exchange and promissory notes, donations, services, usufruct, use, dwelling, tenancy, antichresis, acquitance, cancellations, exchange, purchase and sales, cessions, deposits, promises, annuities, subrogations, acknowledgments, redemption of annuities, loans with or without mortgage, renouncement or substitution of powers of attorney, furnishing capital to estates, engagements, appointment of arbiters or friendly arbitrators, allotments, partitions, protocolizations, acceptance or repudiation of inheritance, recognitions of natural children, rescissions of contracts, retraction sales on reversion, receipts through a third party, subrogation of mortgages, leases, subleases, pledgings of property, judicial declarations, marital licenses, paternal counsel and consent emancipation and any other kind of recordable deed of objects not appraisable or involving objects or sums not exceeding one thousand dollars, shall pay for each folio one dollar.

Article 2. For the execution of the same deeds mentioned in the preceding article, that is, deeds of appraisable objects or deeds involving objects or sums, as the price thereof, exceeding one thousand dollars, the fee of one-half percent shall be charged.

Article 3. For authenticating each act of acknowledgment of signatures in private documents containing nothing recordable or inscribable in the registry of deeds, there shall be charged a fee of fifty cents.

Article 4. For making a copy of recorded deeds, appertaining to any year, or issued from others, or from any public or private document, fifty cents per folio shall be charged.

Article 5. For each notification or note of issuance of copies to the parties concerned, forty cents shall be charged.

Article 6. For searching documents in the registry of the notarial archives or record, thirty cents for each year shall be charged.

General Provisions

The imposing of fees for the searching of a document in the notarial offices of the Commonwealth shall not exceed double the amount of the fees collected for the making of a copy therefor: Provided, That such limitation shall not apply to the General Archive of Protocols for the searching of documents dated before the last thirty years.

§ 893. Fees. Notaries may charge the sum of fifty cents as fees, for every affidavit or declaration of authenticity.

Tit. 30, § 1770a. Exemption of United States Government from certain fees. The United States of America and its agencies and instrumentalities, including The Federal Land Bank of Baltimore, the Federal Intermediate Credit Bank of Baltimore, The Baltimore Bank of Cooperatives, The Federal Land Bank Association of San Juan and The Puerto Rico Production Credit Association, are hereby exempted from payment of all kinds of duties, taxes or fees prescribed by the laws of the Commonwealth of Puerto Rico for the authentication of documents before a notary or before any public officer and for the registration of documents and other operations in the registries of property.

RHODE ISLAND

[R.I. GEN. LAWS ANN.]

§ 36-2-4. Fees for acknowledgments and engagements. To all officers empowered to take acknowledgments of deeds and administer oaths of engagement° to office, there shall be allowed:

For taking acknowledgment of one or more parties to any instrument at one time ....$ .50

For engaging* every officer .... .25

(*) The word "engaged" is construed to include either sworn or affirmed. See *Depositions*, R.I. GEN. LAWS ANN. § 43-3-11.

§ 42-30-13. Fees of notaries. The fees of notaries public shall be as follows: For noting a marine protest, one dollar ($1.00); for drawing and extending such a protest and recording the same, one dollar and fifty cents ($1.50); for taking affidavits, twenty-five cents (25¢); for travel, per mile, ten cents (10¢); for taking acknowledgment of any instrument and affixing his seal, fifty cents (50¢); for the protest of a bill of exchange, order or draft, for nonacceptance or nonpayment, or of a promissory note or check for nonpayment, if the amount thereof is five hundred dollars ($500) or more, one dollar ($1.00), if it is less than five hundred dollars ($500), for recording the same, fifty cents (50¢); for noting the nonacceptance or nonpayment of a bill of exchange, order or draft, or the nonpayment of a promissory note or check, seventy-five cents (75¢); and for each notice of the nonacceptance or nonpayment of a bill, order, draft, check, or note, given to a party liable for the payment thereof, twenty-five cents (25¢); provided, that the whole cost of protest, including necessary notices and the record, shall not exceed two dollars ($2.00), and the whole cost of noting, including notices, shall in no case exceed one dollar and twenty-five cents ($1.25).

SOUTH CAROLINA

[S.C. CODE ANN.]

§ 27-506. Fees of notaries public. The fees of notaries public shall be as follows:

(1) For taking a deposition and swearing witnesses, twenty-five cents per copy sheet;

(2) For a duplicate of a deposition, protest and certificate, ten cents per copy sheet of one hundred words;

(3) For each attendance upon any person for proving a matter or thing and certifying the same, fifty cents;

(4) For every notarial certificate, with seal, fifty cents;

(5) For administering an oath for an affidavit, twenty-five cents;

(6) For taking a renunciation of dower or inheritance, one dollar; and

(7) For every protest, fifty cents, together with the cost of postage for transmitting notice thereof.

SOUTH DAKOTA

A notary who makes a protest of an instrument is entitled to receive the sum of 25¢ and postage for each and every notice made out and served.　See *Authority and Duties*, S. D. COMPILED LAWS ANN. § 18-1-8.

[S.D. COMPILED LAWS ANN.]

§ 18-1-9.　**Fees chargeable by notaries.**　Notaries public are entitled to charge and receive the following fees:

(1)　For each protest, one dollar and fifty cents;

(2)　For recording the same, fifty cents;

(3)　For taking affidavit and affixing seal, twenty-five cents;

(4)　For administering oath or affirmation, ten cents;°

(5)　For taking deposition, each ten words, one and a half cents;

(6)　For each certificate and seal, twenty-five cents;

(7)　For taking proof of acknowledgment, twenty-five cents.°

(°)　*Accord,* § 18-4-16.　See *Acknowledgments.*

TENNESSEE

[TENN. CODE ANN.]

§ 8-1624.　**Recording fee.**　A fee of one dollar ($1.00) and no more is allowed to a notary public for recording in a well-bound book, to be by him kept for the purpose, each of his attestations, protestations, and other instruments of publication.

§ 8-1625.　**Protest fee.**　The fee of the notary for the protestation of negotiable instruments shall be one dollar and fifty cents ($1.50) for each instrument protested, without regard to the number of parties on each instrument.

§ 8-2142.　**Notaries public.**　Notaries public are entitled to demand and receive the following fees and compensation for services:

(1)　For recording, in a well-bound book, to be kept by him for that purpose, each attestation, protestation, and other instrument of publication ....$ 1.00

(2)　For the protestation of negotiable instruments, for each instrument protested, without regard to the number of parties on each instrument 1.50

(3)　For every acknowledgment or probate of deed, or other instrument of writing, with seal attached, the same as county court clerks.

(4)　For acknowledgment of notes for advances on tobacco .. .25

(5)　For each deposition taken 1.00

(6)　For any other service legally performed by him, the same fees allowed other officers for like services.

TEXAS

[TEX. REV. CIV. STAT. ANN.]

Art. 3945. Notary public. Notaries public shall receive the following fees:

Protesting a bill or note for non-acceptance or non-payment, register and seal	$3.00
Each notice of protest	.50
Protesting in all other cases, for each 100 words	.50
Certificate and seal to such protest	.50
Taking the acknowledgment or proof of any deed or other instrument in writing, for registration, including certificate and seal	.50
Taking an acknowledgment of a married woman to any deed or other instrument of writing authorized to be executed by her, including certificate and seal	.50
Administering an oath or affirmation with certificate and seal	.50
All certificates under seal not otherwise provided for	.50
Copies of all records and papers in their office, including certificate and seal, if less than 200 words	.50
If more than 200 words, for each 100 words in excess of 200 words, in addition to the fee of fifty cents	.25
All notarial acts not provided for	.50
Taking the depositions of witnesses, for each 100 words	.15
Swearing a witness to depositions, making certificate therefor with seal, and all other business connected with taking such deposition	.50

UTAH

[UTAH CODE ANN.]

§ 21-4-1. Fees of notaries public. Every notary public may collect for his own use the following fees:

For protesting the nonpayment of a promissory note, or nonpayment or nonacceptance of a bill of exchange, draft or check, $2.00.

For drawing and serving each notice of nonpayment of a promissory note, or the nonpayment or nonacceptance of a bill of exchange, order, draft or check, $1.00.

For recording each protest, $1.00.

For drawing an affidavit, deposition or other paper, for which provision is not herein made, for first folio, $1.00; for each subsequent folio, 50 cents.

For taking an acknowledgment or proof of a deed or other instrument, to include the seal and writing of the certificate, for the first signature, 50 cents; for each additional signature, 25 cents.

For administering an oath or affirmation, 25 cents.
For every certificate, to include writing the same and the seal, 50 cents.

VERMONT

[VT. STAT. ANN.]

Tit. 32, § 1759. Notaries public. Notaries public shall receive for each protest under seal and the notices, $2.00; for each certificate under seal, $.50.

VIRGIN ISLANDS

[V.I. CODE ANN.]

Tit. 3, § 778. Fees; retention by notary. (a) Each notary public shall charge the fees prescribed in section 519 of Title 4.

(b) Each notary public shall retain the fees earned by him as notary public.

Tit. 4, § 519. Fees of notaries public. Subject to the provisions of section 778 of Title 3,° the following fees shall be charged by notaries public:

(1) Protest on notes and bills of exchange, when the note is issued in an amount—

    (A) Not over $500 .... $3.00

    (B) Over $500 and not over $1,500 .... 4.00

    (C) Over $1,500 and not over $3,000 .... 5.00

    (D) Over $3,000 and not over $5,000 .... 6.00

    (E) Over $5,000 .... 7.00

(2) Other protests, etc. 2.00

(3) Receiving marine note of protest 3.00

    (A) For copy of the proceedings, double the amount of ordinary fees for copies under section 882 of Title 3.

(4) Authorization of journals for American vessels 2.00

(5) Oaths, affirmations, and acknowledgments, as provided in section 520 of this title.°°

° For tit. 3, § 778, see above.
°° For § 520, see below.

Tit. 4, § 520. Fees for oaths, affirmations, and acknowledgments. The fee of any person who takes an oath, affirmation or acknowledgment shall be 50 cents, except that—

(1) if such service is performed outside the office in the town limits, the fee shall be $1.00; and

(2) if such service is performed outside the office in the country districts, the fee shall be $1.00 plus actual expenses.

Editorial comment

Concerning fees chargeable by government employees appointed as notaries public, see *Authority and Duties,* "Special Notaries Public", V.I. CODE ANN. tit. 3, § 805.

VIRGINIA

[VA. CODE ANN.]

§ 14.1-98. Officer to state fees, etc., on affidavit, deposition or report. A notary or other officer returning affidavits or depositions of witnesses and a commissioner returning a report shall state at the foot thereof the fees therefor, to whom charged and, if paid, by whom.

§ 14.1-134. Notaries. A notary may, for services performed by him by virtue of his office, charge the following fees, to wit:

(1) When there is a protest by a notary, for the record thereof, making out instrument of protest under his official seal, and notice of dishonor to one person besides the maker of a note or acceptor of a bill .. $1.00

(2) For every additional notice .... .10

(3) For taking and certifying the acknowledgment of any deed or other writing 1.00

(4) For administering and certifying an oath, unless it be the affidavit of a witness .... .50

(5) For taking and certifying affidavits or depositions of witnesses, when done in an hour .... .75

(6) If not done in an hour, for any additional time, at the rate per hour of .... .75

(7) For other services a notary shall have the same fees as the clerk of a circuit or city court for like services.

WASHINGTON

[WASH. REV. CODE ANN.]

§ 42.28.090. Fees of notary—Collection of fees by public officers. Notaries public may make but not exceed the following charges for their services:

Protest of a bill of exchange or promissory note, one dollar;

Attesting any instrument of writing with or without seal, one dollar;

Taking acknowledgment, two persons, with seal, one dollar;

Taking acknowledgment, each person over two, fifty cents;

Certifying affidavit, with or without seal, one dollar;

Registering protest of bill of exchange or promissory note for nonacceptance or nonpayment, fifty cents;

Being present at demand, tender, or deposit, and noting the same, beside mileage at the rate of ten cents per mile, fifty cents;

Noting a bill of exchange or promissory note, for nonacceptance or nonpayment, fifty cents;

For copying any instrument or record, per folio, besides certificate and seal, fifteen cents.

All public officers who are paid a salary in lieu of fees shall collect the prescribed fees for the use of the state or county as the case may be.

WEST VIRGINIA

[W. VA. CODE ANN.]

§ 59-1-7. **Fees to be charged by notaries public.** A notary public may charge the following fees:

When there is a protest by him, for the record thereof, making out instrument of protest under his official seal and notice of dishonor to one person besides the maker of a note or acceptor of a bill $1.00

For every additional notice 10

For taking and certifying the acknowledgment of any deed or writing 50

For administering and certifying an oath, unless it be the affidavit of a witness 25

For taking and certifying affidavits or depositions of witnesses, at the rate, for each hour actually employed in taking the same, of 75

For other services, where no specific fee is prescribed the same fees as are allowed by law to the clerk of the circuit court for similar services.

WISCONSIN

[WIS. STAT. ANN.]

§ 137.01. **Notaries.**

      ᵒ   •   ᵒ

(9) **Fees.**

(a) For drawing and copy of protest of the nonpayment of a promissory note or bill of exchange, or of the nonacceptance of such bill, $1 in the cases where by law such protest is necessary, but in no other case.

(b) For drawing and copy of every other protest, 50 cents.

(c) For drawing, copying and serving every notice of nonpayment of a note or bill, or nonacceptance of a bill, 50 cents.

(d) For drawing any affidavit, or other paper or proceeding for which provision is not herein made, 50 cents for each folio, and for copying the same 12 cents per folio.

(e) For taking the acknowledgment of deeds, and for other services authorized by law, the same fees as are allowed to other officers for similar services, but the fee per document shall not exceed 50 cents.

§ 887.02. **Duty to administer official and election oaths; no fees.** (1) Every person thereto authorized by law shall administer and certify, on demand, any official oath and any oath required on any nomination paper, petition or other instrument used in the nomination or election of any candidate for public office, or in the submission of any question to a vote of the people.

(2) No fee shall be charged by any officer for administering or certifying any official oath, or any oath to any person relative to his right to be registered or to vote.

WYOMING

[WYO. CONST.]

Art. 14, § 2. Fees. The legislature shall provide by law the fees which may be demanded by justices of the peace and constables in precincts having less than fifteen hundred population, and of court commissioners, boards of arbitration and notaries public, which fees the said officers shall accept as their full compensation. ° ° °

[WYO. STAT. ANN.]

§ 32-14. Fees. Notaries public shall be entitled to receive the following fees from the persons for whom the service is rendered: For any protest of bill of exchange, check, draft, promissory note or other negotiable instrument where protest is made at the request of any party, one dollar; for each notice of protest, fifty cents; for certificate and seal, fifty cents; for administering oath or affirmation, fifty cents; for taking acknowledgment of deed of one person, fifty cents; and twenty-five cents for each additional person; for taking depositions, fifteen cents per folio, and five dollars for all other services in taking, certifying, directing, endorsing and transmitting the same.

CHAPTER 9:   OFFENSES

§ 9.1   Civil liability.

A notary public must perform his duties honestly, skillfully, and with reasonable diligence. He owes these duties to anyone who officially employs him, and who relies on his certificates. Nominally the state, the governor, or some official is the obligee of the notary's bond, but the real beneficiaries of the bond are the persons who may incur a loss as a proximate result of a notary's misconduct.

Both the notary and the sureties on his official bond are liable for any loss which is the proximate result of the failure of the notary to perform his duties. Liability will arise from a notary's negligence in taking an acknowledgment or for making a false certificate of acknowledgment. If a notary certifies to an acknowledgment of an instrument without personal knowledge concerning the identity of the party acknowledging, and without a careful investigation, he is guilty of negligence and liable for all damage resulting therefrom. The public is entitled to rely upon the truth of a notary's certificate. The notary can therefore be held liable for falsely certifying that particular persons, such as grantors or mortgagors, personally appeared before him and acknowledged the execution of a deed or mortgage.

Concerning official bonds in specific states and other jurisdictions, see *Appointment: State and Other Statutes,* page 15.

§ 9.2   Offenses and penalties.

Notaries public, of course, are not above the law. When they perform their functions, they must observe the same laws as other persons. In addition to the ordinary statutory prohibitions which all persons, including notaries public, must observe, there are various statutes in many of the states and other jurisdictions which prohibit and punish specified wrongful acts by notaries and other public officials. Some states and other jurisdictions also have statutes which relate to persons who commit offenses against notaries or their records.

Concerning various offenses by and against notaries public under the statutes of specific states and other jurisdictions, see *Offenses: State and Other Statutes*, which follows.

OFFENSES: STATE AND OTHER STATUTES

ALABAMA

[ALA. CODE]

Tit. 40, § 14(1). Personating a notary. Any person who having been a commercial notary, a notary public for the state at large, or a notary public ex officio justice of the peace, willfully performs, assumes the authority to perform a notarial act after his commission expires, or any person who without a notary's commission assumes the authority and performs a notarial act, is guilty of a misdemeanor and upon conviction shall be punished by imprisonment for not more than one year.

ALASKA

[ALASKA STAT.]

§ 11.30.230. Receiving unauthorized fees; nonfeasance in office. An officer of the state, borough, city, or other municipal or public corporation, other than the governor or judge of the superior court, who (1) wilfully and knowingly charges, takes, or receives a fee or compensation, other than that authorized or permitted by law, for an official service or duty performed by him; (2) wilfully neglects or refuses to perform a duty or service pertaining to his office, with intent to injure or defraud; or (3) wilfully neglects or refuses to perform his duty or service to the injury of another, or the manifest hindrance or obstruction of public justice or business, whether intended or not, upon conviction, is punishable by imprisonment in the penitentiary for not less than six months nor more than one year, or by imprisonment in jail for not less than three months nor more than one year, or by a fine of not less than $50 nor more than $500, or by dismissal from office with or without imprisonment or fine.

ARIZONA

[ARIZ. REV. STAT. ANN.]

§ 38-413. Charging excessive fees; penalty. A. If an officer demands and receives a higher fee than prescribed by law, or any fee not so allowed, such officer shall be liable to the party aggrieved in an amount four times the fee unlawfully demanded and received by him.

B. An officer who violates this section is guilty of extortion and upon conviction shall be punished as provided by § 13-401.

Note: Extortion under color of official right, when a different punishment is not otherwise prescribed, is a misdemeanor. § 13-401(D). A misdemeanor is punishable by imprisonment in a county jail for not to exceed 6 months, by a fine not exceeding $300, or both. § 13-1645.

Editorial comment

The wilful destruction, defacement, or concealment of records or papers is prohibited. See *Records*, ARIZ. REV.

ARKANSAS

STAT. ANN. § 41-316.

The failure to attach the statement of the date on which the notary's commission will expire to a certificate of acknowledgment or jurat to an affidavit is a misdemeanor. See *Authority and Duties*, ARK. STAT. ANN. §§ 12-1406, 12-1407.

DELAWARE

The violation of the special fee provisions for certain services to members of the armed forces and to veterans is punishable by a fine, and in default of the payment of the fine, by imprisonment. See *Fees Chargeable*, DEL. CODE ANN. tit. 29, § 4311.

DISTRICT OF COLUMBIA

The taking of a higher fee than is prescribed by D.C. CODE ENCYCL. ANN. § 1-514 is prohibited. See *Fees Chargeable*, D.C. CODE ENCYCL. ANN. §§ 1-514, 1-515.

The failure to comply with a notary's duties concerning inland bills and notes is punishable by a fine. See *Authority and Duties*, D.C. CODE ENCYCL. ANN. § 1-509.

FLORIDA

Any person obtaining or using a notary public commission in other than his legal name shall be guilty of a felony of the third degree. See *Appointment*, FLA. STAT. ANN. § 117.01(5).

[FLA. STAT. ANN.]

§ 117.08. Notary public acting after expiration of commission.
Every notary public in this state who shall take any acknowledgment of any instrument as a notary public, or who makes any certificate as such, after the expiration of his commission, shall be guilty of a misdemeanor of the second degree, punishable as provided in § 775.082 or § 775.083.

§ 117.09. Penalties. (1) Every notary public in the state shall require reasonable proof of the identity of the person whose signature is being notarized and such person must be in the presence of the notary public at the time the signature is notarized. Any notary public violating the above provision shall be guilty of a misdemeanor of the second degree, punishable as provided in § 775.082 or § 775.083. It shall be no defense under this section that the notary public acted without intent to defraud.

(2) Any notary public in this state who shall falsely or fraudulently take any acknowledgment of any instrument as a notary public or who falsely or fraudulently makes any certificate as a notary public or who falsely takes or receives an acknowledgement of the signature on any written instrument shall be guilty of a felony of the third degree, punishable as provided in § 775.082, § 775.083, or § 775.084.

§ 775.082. Penalties for felonies and misdemeanors.

     ✿   ✿   ✿

(4) A person who has been convicted of any other designated felony may be punished as follows:

     ✿   ✿   ✿

(d) For a felony of the third degree, by a term of imprisonment in the state prison not exceeding five (5) years.

(5) A person who has been convicted of a designated misdemeanor may be sentenced as follows:

     ✿   ✿   ✿

(b) For a misdemeanor of the second degree, by a definite term of imprisonment in the county jail not exceeding sixty (60) days.

     ✿   ✿   ✿

§ 775.083. Fine in lieu of or in addition to other criminal penalty.
A person who has been convicted of a crime, other than a capital felony, may be sentenced, when specifically designated by statute, to pay a fine in lieu of or in addition to any punishment described in § 775.082. Fines for designated crimes shall not exceed:

     ✿   ✿   ✿

(2) $5,000, when the conviction is of a felony of the third degree;

     ✿   ✿   ✿

(4) $500, when the conviction is of a misdemeanor of the second degree;

(5) Any higher amount equal to double the pecuniary gain derived from the offense by the offender or double the pecuniary loss suffered by the victim.

ο   ο   ο

§ 775.084. Subsequent felony offenders; extended terms. [Text of statute omitted.]

HAWAII

[HAWAII REV. STAT.]

§ 456-7. Acts prohibited; penalty. No person shall be qualified to act as a notary public or shall enter upon any of the duties of the office or offer or assume to perform any such duties until he has fully complied with each of the requirements in each of the foregoing sections of this chapter. (§§ 456-1 to 456-6, incl.) Any person wilfully violating this section shall be fined not more than $500, or imprisoned not more than one year, or both. Nothing in this section shall be construed to restrict or to do away with any liability for civil damages.

Note: For the sections of the HAWAII REV. STAT. to which this section refers, see *Appointment* (§§ 456-1, 456-4 to 456-6, incl.), *Qualifications* (§ 456-2), and *Seal* (§ 456-3).

Concerning the penalty for neglecting to comply with the statute concerning disposition of records, see *Records*, HAWAII REV. STAT. § 456-16.

Concerning the penalty for knowingly incorporating in a certificate of acknowledgment false or misleading statements, see *Acknowledgments*, HAWAII REV. STAT. § 502-54.

ILLINOIS

[ILL. ANN. STAT.—Smith-Hurd]

Ch. 99, § 18.1. Attestation by persons not commissioned—attestation by persons with expired commissions—Punishment. Any person who attests to any document as a notary public without having been commissioned pursuant to the provisions of this Act, or who attests to any document as a notary public knowing his commission has expired, shall be guilty of a petty offense.

Ch. 38, § 1005-1-17. Petty offense. "Petty offense" means any offense for which a sentence to a fine only is provided.

Ch. 38, § 1005-9-1. Authorized fines. (a) An offender may be sentenced to pay a fine which shall not exceed for each offense:

ο   ο   ο

(4) for a petty offense, $500 or the amount specified in the offense, whichever is less;

ο   ο   ο

(c)   In determining the amount and method of payment of a fine, the court shall consider:

(1)   the financial resources and future ability of the offender to pay the fine; and

(2)   whether the fine will prevent the offender from making court ordered restitution or reparation to the victim of the offense.

(d)   The court may order the fine to be paid forthwith or within a specified period of time or in installments.

INDIANA

[IND. CODE]

§ 33-16-3-2.   **Certificate—date of commission—penalty.**   Any notary public, failing or omitting to make such statement as provided for in the foregoing section,* shall be guilty of a misdemeanor and shall be fined therefor in any sum not exceeding twenty-five dollars [$25.00].

* See *Authority and Duties,* IND. CODE § 33-16-3-1.   The section to which reference is made provides that a notary must append a true statement of the date of the expiration of his notary commission to all certificates of acknowledgment, jurats, and other official documents.

§ 35-1-95-4.   **Notaries public.**   Whoever, while holding any lucrative office, acts as a notary public, or whoever, being an officer in any bank, corporation or association possessed of banking powers, or of any trust company or building and loan association, acts as a notary public in the business of such bank, corporation, association, trust company or building and loan association, shall, on conviction, be fined not less than ten dollars [$10.00] nor more than one thousand dollars [$1,000], to which may be added imprisonment in the county jail for not less than ten [10] days nor more than six [6] months.

§ 35-1-95-5.   **Falsely attesting affidavit.**   Whoever, being a notary public or other officer or person authorized to administer oaths, certifies that any person was sworn or affirmed before him to any affidavit or other instrument or writing, when, in fact, such person was not so sworn or affirmed, shall, on conviction, be imprisoned in the state prison not less than one [1] year nor more than three [3] years, and fined not less than ten dollars [$10.00] nor more than one thousand dollars [$1,000].

§ 35-1-95-6.   **Falsely attesting acknowledgment.**   Whoever, being a notary public or other officer authorized to take and certify acknowledgments of conveyances, mortgages or other instruments of writing, shall append his signature as such officer when no official seal is required, or who shall append his signature or affix his official seal when such seal is required by law to be affixed to the certificate of acknowledgment of any conveyance, mortgage or other instrument of writing required to be recorded in this state, or which can not be legally recorded therein without acknowledgment and certificate thereof, when at the time of such signing or sealing, the grantor, mortgagor or other party executing such deed, mortgage or other instrument had not first acknowledged the execution thereof before such notary public or other officer as aforesaid, shall, on conviction, be imprisoned in the state prison not less than one [1] year nor more than three [3] years, and fined not less than ten dollars [$10.00] nor more than one thousand dollars [$1,000].

§ 35-1-95-7.　Officer not explaining instrument.　Whoever, being a notary public or other officer authorized to take the acknowledgment of deeds, mortgages and other instruments of writing, in any case where the party executing such deed, mortgage or other instrument of writing shall sign the same with his or her mark, or where such officer has good cause to believe that the contents and purport of such deed, mortgage or other instrument of writing are not fully known to the party executing the same, neglects or refuses to read and explain fully to such party so executing the same the contents and purport of such deed, mortgage or other instrument of writing before certifying to the acknowledgment thereof, shall, on conviction, be fined not less than five dollars [$5.00] nor more than five hundred dollars [$500], to which may be added imprisonment in the county jail not less than ten [10] days nor more than six [6] months.

§ 33-1-95-8.　Notary acting after term expires.　Whoever, having been appointed a notary public, does or performs any act as a notary public after the expiration of his term of office, knowing that such term of office has expired, shall, on conviction, be fined not less than twenty-five dollars [$25.00] nor more than five hundred dollars [$500].

Editorial comment

Concerning the penalty for notaries public and other officers who affix their name in blank, see *Acknowledgment*, IND. CODE § 35-1-125-1.

IOWA

[IOWA CODE ANN.]

§ 77.11.　Improperly acting as notary.　If any notary public exercises the duties of his office after the expiration of his commission, or when otherwise disqualified, or appends his official signature to documents when the parties have not appeared before him, he shall be fined not less than fifty dollars, and shall be removed from office by the secretary of state.

§ 77.15.   Neglect to deposit records.   If any notary, on his resignation or removal, neglects for three months so to deposit them [records]°, he shall be guilty of a misdemeanor and be liable in an action to any person injured by such neglect.

° This reference is to the records of a resigned or removed notary and his official papers, which must within three months of the notary's resignation or removal from office, be deposited in the office of the secretary of state.   See *Records,* IOWA CODE ANN. § 77.14.

§ 77.16.   Neglect of executor to deposit records.   If an executor or administrator of a deceased notary willfully neglects, for three months after his acceptance of that appointment, to deposit in the secretary of state's office the records and papers of a deceased notary which came into his hands, he shall be held guilty of a misdemeanor.

§ 687.7.   Punishment for indictable misdemeanors.   Every person who is convicted of a misdemeanor, the punishment of which is not otherwise prescribed by any statute of this state, shall be punished by imprisonment in the county jail not more than one year, or by fine not exceeding five hundred dollars, or by both such fine and imprisonment.

Editorial comment

Concerning the penalty for any officer, including a notary public, knowingly misstating a material fact in a certificate of acknowledgment, or proof of execution and delivery in lieu of acknowledgment, see *Acknowledgment,* IOWA CODE ANN. § 558.40.

KANSAS

[KAN. STAT. ANN.]

§ 53-106.   Penalty for failure to attach date of expiration of commission.   If any notary public shall neglect or refuse to attach to his official signature the date of expiration of his commission, as provided in section 1 [53-105] of this act, he shall be deemed guilty of a misdemeanor, and upon conviction thereof shall be fined in any sum not exceeding one hundred dollars.

Editorial comment

For § 53-105, mentioned above, see *Seal.*

Among other officers, any notary who accepts more than fifteen cents for particular services to any discharged soldier or seaman, or the widow, orphan, or legal representative thereof, is subject to a fine in any sum not less than $25.00 nor more than $50.00.   See *Fees Chargeable,* KAN. STAT. ANN. §§ 28-132, 28-133.

Notaries and other officers must post a list of their fees in their office in some conspicuous place under penalty of $3.00 for each day they shall neglect to do so. See *Commissioners of Deeds,* KAN. STAT. ANN. § 28-140.

KENTUCKY

[KY. REV. STAT. ANN.]

§ 62.990. Penalties. (1) Any person who violates ° ° ° or subsection (1) of KRS 62.050 [pertaining to when bonds are to be given] shall be fined not less than fifty nor more than one hundred dollars and removed from office by the judgment of conviction.

(2) If any person violates ° ° ° or subsection (2) or (3) of KRS 62.050 [pertaining to when bonds are to be given], his office shall be considered vacant and he shall not be eligible for the same office for two years.

Editorial comment

For KY. REV. STAT. ANN. § 62.050, mentioned in the foregoing section, see *Appointment.*

§ 423.990. Penalties. For each failure to record his protest as required by KRS 423.030, a notary public shall forfeit all his fees and shall be fined five dollars, to be recovered by warrant before any justice of the peace of the county where the failure occurs.

Editorial comment

For § 423.030, mentioned above, see *Records.*

§ 432.100. Forging or counterfeiting ° ° ° seals.

°   °   °

(2) Any person who fraudulently counterfeits any device for stamping an impression resembling the seal officially used by the United States, by any state, by any court or officer of the United States or of any state or by any notary public, or who has in his possession any such device and conceals it knowing it to be counterfeited, or who uses the false impression made by it and publishes it as true knowing it to be counterfeited, shall be confined in the penitentiary for not less than five nor more than fifteen years.

§ 432.160. False statement of notary public. Any notary public who falsely states in a protest made by him that notices were given or sent by him shall be confined in the penitentiary for not less than one nor more than five years.

§ 434.060. Obtaining money by false personation; personating another in legal acts; fraudulently displaying badge of organization. (1) Any person who fraudulently represents or personates another, and in such assumed character does any of the following acts, shall be confined in the penitentiary for not less than one nor more than five years:

         *   *   *

(c)   Acknowledge the execution of any conveyance of real property or of any other instrument which may be recorded;

         *   *   *

LOUISIANA

General Provisions

[LA. REV. STAT.]

§ 35:13.   Fine for violating preceding sections.   All notaries, or other persons acting as such, contravening the provisions of R.S. 35:11 (concerning the giving of the marital status of the parties) or 35:12 (concerning the giving of the parties' full Christian names and their permanent mailing addresses) shall be liable to a fine of one hundred dollars, to be recovered before any court of competent jurisdiction, one-half for the benefit of the informer.

Editorial comment

For LA. REV. STAT. §§ 35:11, 35:12, mentioned in the foregoing section, see *Authority and Duties.*

Orleans Parish

§ 35:257.   Office and office hours.   Every notary public in and for the Parish of Orleans shall keep his office in a building covered with tile, slates or terrace, and keep such office open, for the ready examination of his records, every day from the hour of 10 o'clock a.m. to 3 o'clock p.m., Sundays and holidays excepted.   Any notary public violating the provisions of this Section shall, on proof thereof before the Criminal District Court for the Parish of Orleans, be condemned to pay a fine of twenty-five dollars for each and every day he shall deprive the public from access to his records; and on his failure to pay such fine, and in case he should continue for a period of ten successive days in the violation of the provisions of this Section, he shall forfeit his commission and shall be required to turn over his archives to the Custodian of Notarial Records.

§ 35:284.   Violations.   Whoever violates the provisions of R.S. 35:281 or R.S. 35:282 (concerning the filing of copies of acts evidencing the transfer of real property and a duplicate copy of any sketch, blue-print or survey) shall be fined not more than fifty dollars or imprisoned in the parish jail for not more than sixty days, or both.

Editorial comment

For LA. REV. STAT. §§ 35:281, 35:282, mentioned in the foregoing section, see *Authority and Duties.*

§ 35:286. **Violations.** Notaries who contravene the provisions of R.S. 35:285 [concerning the deposit of original acts when the property affected is situated outside New Orleans] are liable to a fine of one hundred dollars for each infraction to be recovered before any court of competent jurisdiction, one-half for the benefit of the informer, as well as for all such damages as the parties may suffer thereby.

Editorial comment

For LA. REV. STAT. § 35:285 mentioned in the foregoing section, see *Authority and Duties.*

MAINE

[ME. REV. STAT. ANN.]

Tit. 4, § 956. Resignation or removal; deposit of records. On the resignation or removal from office of any notary public, his records shall be deposited with the clerk of the judicial courts in the county for which he was appointed. Any notary public who shall, for a period of 3 months, neglect to comply with such requirement and any administrator or executor representing a deceased notary public who shall, for a period of 3 months, neglect to comply with such requirement shall forfeit not less than $50 nor more than $500.

§ 957. Injury or concealment of records. Whoever knowingly destroys, defaces or conceals such record forfeits not less than $200 nor more than $1,000, and is liable for damages to any person injured in a civil action.

Tit. 17, § 1501. Forgery defined. Whoever, with intent to defraud, falsely makes, alters, forges or counterfeits any public record or proceeding filed or entered in any court; or process issued, or purporting to be issued by a competent court, magistrate or officer; or attestation or certificate of any person required by law or receivable as legal proof in relation to any matter; or any charter, deed, will, testament, bond, writing obligatory, power of attorney, letter of credit, policy of insurance, bill of lading, bill of exchange, promissory note, order or acceptance, or indorsement or assignment thereof, or of any debt or contract; or acquittance, discharge or accountable receipt for anything of value; or a motor vehicle operator's license or registration certificate; or any other written instrument of another, or purporting to be such, by which any pecuniary demand or obligation or any right in any property is or purports to be created, increased, conveyed, transferred, diminished or discharged; and whoever utters and publishes as true any instrument before-mentioned, knowing it to be false, forged or counterfeit, with like intent, shall be punished by imprisonment for not more than 10 years.

§ 1503.   **False certificates and fictitious signatures.**   If any person, legally authorized to take the proof or acknowledgment of any instrument that by law may be recorded, willfully and falsely certifies that such proof or acknowledgment was duly made, ° ° ° he is guilty of forgery and shall be punished as provided in section 1501.°

° For § 1501, see above.

MASSACHUSETTS

[MASS. ANN. LAWS]

Ch. 222, § 9.   **Penalty for acting as justice of the peace, etc., after expiration of commission.**   Whoever presumes to act as a justice of the peace or notary public after the expiration of his commission, and after receiving notice of such expiration, shall be punished by a fine of not less than one hundred nor more than five hundred dollars.

§ 10.   **Penalty for destroying records of notary public.**   Whoever knowingly destroys, defaces or conceals the records or official papers of a notary public shall forfeit not more than one thousand dollars and be liable for damages to any person injured thereby.

Ch. 267, § 1.   **Forgery of records, certificates, etc.**   Whoever, with intent to injure or defraud, falsely makes, alters, forges or counterfeits a public record, or a certificate, return or attestation of a clerk or register of a court, public register, notary public, justice of the peace, town clerk or any other public officer, in relation to a matter wherein such certificate, return or attestation may be received as legal proof; or a charter, deed, will, testament, bond or writing obligatory, power of attorney, policy of insurance, bill of lading, bill of exchange or promissory note; or an order, acquittance or discharge for money or other property; or an acceptance of a bill of exchange, or an endorsement or assignment of a bill of exchange or promissory note for the payment of money; or an accountable receipt for money, goods or other property; or a stock certificate, or any evidence or muniment of title to property; or a certificate of title, duplicate certificate of title, certificate issued in place of a duplicate certificate, the registration book, entry book, or any indexes provided for by chapter one hundred and eighty-five, or the docket of the recorder; shall be punished by imprisonment in the state prison for not more than ten years or in jail for not more than two years.

Ch. 268, § 33.   **Falsely assuming to be justice of the peace or certain other public officers.**   Whoever falsely assumes or pretends to be a ° ° ° notary public, ° ° ° and acts as such or requires a person to aid or assist him in a matter pertaining to the duty of such officer, shall be punished by a fine of not more than four hundred dollars or by imprisonment for not more than one year.

MICHIGAN

[MICH. COMP. LAWS ANN.]

§ 35.53. Penalty. Sec. 3. Any [notary public, among others,] who may ask or accept more than the fees enumerated in sections 1 and 2 of this act° for any such service, shall on conviction thereof be adjudged guilty of a misdemeanor.

° MICH. COMP. LAWS ANN. § 35.51 (concerning fees for oaths or certificates charged to discharged soldiers or sailors) and § 35.52 (concerning fees for oaths or certificates charged to widows of deceased soldiers or sailors). For the text of MICH. COMP. LAWS ANN. §§ 35.51, 35.52, see *Fees Chargeable.* Concerning the punishment of misdemeanors, see § 750.504 below.

§ 750.248. Forgery of records and other instruments, venue. Sec. 248. (1) Any person who shall falsely make, alter, forge or counterfeit any public record, or any certificate, return or attestation of any clerk of a court, public register, notary public, justice of the peace, township clerk, or any other public officer, in relation to any matter wherein such certificate, return or attestation may be received as legal proof, or any charter, deed, will, testament, bond or writing obligatory, letter of attorney, policy of insurance, bill of lading, bill of exchange, promissory note, or any order, acquittance of discharge for money or other property, or any waiver, release, claim or demand, or any acceptance of a bill of exchange, or indorsement, or assignment of a bill of exchange or promissory note for the payment of money, or any accountable receipt for money, goods or other property, with intent to injure or defraud any person, shall be guilty of a felony, punishable by imprisonment in the state prison not more than 14 years.

(2) The venue in a prosecution under this section may be either in the county in which the forgery was performed, or in a county in which any false, forged, altered or counterfeit record, deed, instrument or other writing is uttered and published with intent to injure or defraud.

§ 750.249. Same; uttering and publishing. Sec. 249. UTTERING AND PUBLISHING FORGED INSTRUMENTS—Any person who shall utter and publish as true, any false, forged, altered or counterfeit record, deed, instrument or other writing mentioned in the preceding section, knowing the same to be false, altered, forged or counterfeit, with intent to injure or defraud as aforesaid, shall be guilty of a felony, punishable by imprisonment in the state prison not more than 14 years.

§ 750.504. Punishment of misdemeanors when not fixed by statute. A person convicted of a crime declared in this or any other act of the state of Michigan to be a misdemeanor, for which no other punishment is specially prescribed by any statute in force at the time of the conviction and sentence, shall be punished by imprisonment in the county jail for not more than 90 days or by a fine of not more than 100 dollars, or by both such fine and imprisonment.

Editorial comment

Concerning the penalty for neglecting, for the space of three months, to deposit records and papers relating to the office of any notary which has become vacant in the office of the clerk of the proper county, see *Records*, MICH. COMP. LAWS ANN. § 55.114.

Concerning the penalty for knowingly destroying, defacing, or concealing records or papers belonging to the office of a notary, see *Records*, MICH. COMP. LAWS ANN. § 55.115.

MINNESOTA

[MINN. STAT. ANN.]

§ 359.08. **Misconduct.** Any notary who shall exercise the duties of his office after the expiration of his term, or when otherwise disqualified, shall be guilty of a misdemeanor.

§ 609.03. **Punishment when not otherwise fixed.** If a person is convicted of a crime for which no punishment is otherwise provided he may be sentenced as follows:

*   o   o

(3) If the crime is a misdemeanor, to imprisonment for not more than 90 days or to payment of a fine of not more than $300, or both;
o   o   o.

§ 609.65. **False certification by notary public.** Whoever, when acting or purporting to act as a notary public or other public officer, certifies falsely that an instrument has been acknowledged or that any other act was performed by a party appearing before him or that as such notary public or other public officer he performed any other official act may be sentenced as follows:

(1) If he so certifies with intent to injure or defraud, to imprisonment for not more than three years or to payment of a fine of not more than $3,000, or both; or

(2) In any other case, to imprisonment for not more than 90 days or to payment of a fine of not more than $300, or both.

MISSISSIPPI

[MISS. CODE ANN.]

§ 97-11-25. **Embezzlement—officers, trustees and public employees converting property to own use.** If ° ° ° a notary public [among others] ° ° ° shall unlawfully convert to his own use any

money or other valuable thing which comes to his hands or posse
by virtue of his office or employment, or shall not, when lawfu
required to turn over such money or deliver such thing, immediate
do so according to his legal obligation, he shall, on conviction, be
imprisoned in the penitentiary not more than twenty years, or be
fined not more than one thousand dollars, or imprisoned in the county jail not more than one year.

MISSOURI

[MO. ANN. STAT.—Vernon]

§ 561.011. Forgery, counterfeiting, possession and uttering forged instrument or plates, penalty. 1. It shall be unlawful:

(1) For any person with the intent to defraud to make or alter any writing of any kind having legal efficacy or commonly relied upon in business or commercial transactions, so that it purports to have been made by another, or at another time, or with different terms, or by authority of one who did not give such authority, or for any person with intent to defraud to totally erase, obliterate or destroy any such instrument;

(2) For any person with intent to defraud to make or alter anything other than a writing, so that it purports to have a genuineness, antiquity, rarity, ownership or authorship which it does not possess;

(3) For any person with intent to defraud to use as true, or to utter as true, or to possess with intent to utter as true or false, or to transfer with intent that it shall be uttered as true, any writing or other thing which said person knows has been made or altered in the manner described in either of subdivisions (1) or (2);

(4) For any person with the intent to use the same in violation of subdivisions (1) or (2), to make, engrave, or cause to be made, any plate, mold, instrument or device for making, altering or destroying any writing having any legal efficacy or commonly relied upon in business or commercial transactions, or any plate, mold, instrument or device for making or altering anything other than a writing in a way that would give such thing an appearance of genuineness, antiquity, rarity, ownership, or authorship which it does not possess;

(5) For any person with intent to use the same in violation of subdivisions (1) or (2) or with intent to cause or to permit the same to be so used, to have in his custody or possession any plate, mold, instrument or device, described in subdivision (4), or any raw ma terials for making or altering any writing or any thing;

(6) Any plate or mold forbidden by subdivisions (4) and (5) shall be deemed to be within the terms of those subdivisions whenever such plate or mold is partly finished and such parts resemble a genuine writing or other thing sought to be made, altered or de-stroyed or made to appear genuine, antique, rare, or have an owner-ship or authorship which it does not possess.

ing this section shall be deemed guilty of
\`tion thereof, shall be punished by impris-
\`or a term of not less than two years nor
\`imprisonment in the county jail for a
year or by fine of not more than one
\`oth such fine and imprisonment.

comment

\`cerning the penalty for willfully certifying a false
\`nowledgment of a deed, see *Acknowledgments,* MO.
ANN. STAT. § 561.060.

NEBRASKA

Concerning the penalty for various violations in relation to acknowledgment and recording of instruments, see *Acknowledgments,* NEB. REV. STAT. § 76-218.

NEVADA

[NEV. REV. STAT.]

§ 205.120. False certificate to certain instruments punishable as forgery. Every officer authorized to take a proof or acknowledgment of an instrument which by law may be recorded, who shall willfully certify falsely that the execution of such instrument was acknowledged by any party thereto, or that the execution thereof was proved, shall be guilty of a felony, and shall be punished the same as persons who are guilty of forgery.

Note: The penalty for forgery is punishment by imprisonment in the state prison for a term not less than 1 year nor more than 10 years, or by a fine of not more than $5,000, or by both fine and imprisonment. NEV. REV. STAT. § 205.090.

§ 240.110. Fee table to be posted; penalty. 1. Every notary public shall publish and set up in some conspicuous place in his office a table of his fees, according to this chapter, for the inspection of all persons who have business in his office.

2. For each day's failure to comply with the provisions of subsection 1, he shall forfeit a sum not exceeding $20 with costs, which may be recovered by any person by an action before any justice of the peace of the same county.

§ 240.120. Fee book; penalty. 1. Each notary public shall keep a fee book in his office in which he shall enter:

(a) The fees charged, in detail.

(b) The title of the matter, proceeding or action on which they are charged.

2. The fee book shall be open to public inspection.

3. Any notary public who shall violate any of the provisions of this section shall be fined not more than $1,000.

§ 240.130. **No other fees to be charged; penalty.** 1. No other fees shall be charged than those specially set forth in this chapter, nor shall fees be charged for any other services than those mentioned in this chapter.

2. Any notary public who shall violate any of the provisions of this section shall be fined not more than $1,000.

§ 240.140. **Penalty for taking larger fees than allowed by law.** If any notary public shall take more or greater fees than are allowed in this chapter, he shall be liable to indictment and on conviction shall be removed from office and fined in any sum not exceeding $1,000.

§ 240.150. **Penalties for misconduct or neglect.** For any misconduct or neglect in any of the cases in which any notary public appointed under the authority of this state, is authorized to act, either by the law of this state, or of any state, territory or country, or by the law of nations, or by commercial usage, he shall be liable on his official bond to the parties injured thereby, for all the damages sustained; and for any willful violation or neglect of duty, a notary public shall be subject to criminal prosecution, and may be punished by fine not exceeding $2,000, and removal from office.

Editorial comment

Concerning the liabilities and penalties for the refusal or neglect to comply with the statutory requirements regarding records of official acts of officers taking acknowledgments, see *Acknowledgments,* NEV. REV. STAT. § 281.180.

NEW HAMPSHIRE

[N.H. REV. STAT. ANN.]

§ 638:1. **Forgery.°** I. A person is guilty of forgery if, with purpose to defraud anyone, or with knowledge that he is facilitating a fraud to be perpetrated by anyone, he:

(a) Alters any writing of another without his authority or utters any such altered writing; or

(b) Makes, completes, executes, authenticates, issues, transfers, publishes or otherwise utters any writing so that it purports to be the act of another, or purports to have been executed at a time or place or in a numbered sequence other than was in fact the case, or to be a copy of an original when no such original existed.

II. As used in this section, "writing" includes printing or any other method of recording information, checks, tokens, stamps, seals, credit cards, badges, trademarks, and other symbols of value, right, privilege, or identification.

III.   Forgery is a class B felony if the writing is or purports to be

(a)   a security, revenue stamp, or any other instrument issued by a government, or any agency thereof; or

(b)   a check, an issue of stocks, bonds, or any other instrument representing an interest in or a claim against property, or a pecuniary interest in or claim against any person or enterprise.

IV.   All other forgery is a misdemeanor.

V.   A person is guilty of a misdemeanor if he knowingly possesses any writing that is a forgery under this section or any device for making any such writing.   It is an affirmative defense to prosecution under this paragraph that the possession was without an intent to defraud.

° Concerning penalties, see § 651:2 below.

§ 638:2.   Fraudulent handling of recordable writings.°   A person is guilty of a class B felony if, with a purpose to deceive or injure anyone, he falsifies, destroys, removes or conceals any will, deed, mortgage, security instrument or other writing for which the law provides public recording.

° Concerning penalties, see § 651:2 below.

Editorial comment

If a person who has possession of notarial records or papers neglects or refuses to deliver them to the secretary of state, or knowingly destroys or conceals any of them, he is subject to a penalty.   See *Records,* N.H. REV. STAT. ANN. § 455:8.

Concerning the offense of neglecting or refusing to appear or testify or give a deposition pursuant to a writ issued by a notary, see *Depositions,* N.H. REV. STAT. ANN. §§ 516:4, 516:7.

§ 651:2.   Sentences and limitations.   I.   A person convicted of a felony or misdemeanor may be sentenced to imprisonment, probation, conditional or unconditional discharge, or a fine.

II.   If a sentence of imprisonment is imposed, the court shall fix the maximum thereof which is not to exceed:

(a)   Fifteen years for a class A felony,

(b)   Seven years for a class B felony,

(c)   One year for a misdemeanor,

(d)   Life imprisonment for murder,

and, in the case of a felony only, a minimum which is not to exceed one-half of the maximum, or if the maximum is life imprisonment, such minimum term as the court may order.

III. A person convicted of a violation may be sentenced to probation, conditional or unconditional discharge, or a fine.

IV. A fine may be imposed in addition to any sentence of imprisonment, probation, or conditional discharge. The amount of any fine imposed on

(a) any individual may not exceed two thousand dollars for a felony, one thousand dollars for a misdemeanor, and one hundred dollars for a violation.

(b) a corporation or unincorporated association may not exceed fifty thousand dollars for a felony, ten thousand dollars for a misdemeanor and five hundred dollars for a violation. A writ of execution may be issued by the court against the corporation or unincorporated association to compel payment of the fine, together with costs and interest.

(c) If a defendant has gained property through the commission of any felony, then in lieu of the amounts authorized in paragraphs (a) and (b), the fine may be an amount not to exceed double the amount of that gain.

o   o   o

NEW JERSEY

[N.J. STAT. ANN.]

§ 2A:135-10. **Personating public officers or employees.°** Any person who, without authority, exercises the functions of, or holds himself out to anyone as, an officer or employee of the state or any agency or political subdivision thereof, not so being, is guilty of a misdemeanor.

° Concerning punishment, see § 2A:85-7, below.

§ 2A:135-11. **Unauthorized persons taking acknowledgments.°** Any person who, knowing that he is not authorized to take acknowledgments or proofs to deeds or other instruments in writing, takes an acknowledgment or proof to any deed or instrument in writing, and signs a certificate thereon certifying that the deed or instrument was acknowledged before him, is guilty of a misdemeanor.

° Concerning punishment, see § 2A:85-7, below.

§ 2A:85-7. **Misdemeanors; punishment.** Any person found guilty of a crime which by any statute is declared to be a misdemeanor, and for which no punishment is specifically provided, shall be punished by a fine of not more than $1,000, or by imprisonment for not more than 3 years, or both.

NEW MEXICO

[N.M. STAT. ANN.]

§ 35-1-21. Disqualified notary exercising powers—penalty. Any notary public who exercises the duties of his office with the knowledge that his commission has expired or that he is otherwise disqualified, is guilty of a misdemeanor, and upon conviction thereof shall be punished by a fine of one hundred dollars [$100] and shall be removed from office by the governor.

§ 35-1-22. False certificate—authenticating documents in absence of proper party—penalty. If any notary public, or any other officer authorized by law to make or give any certificate or other writing shall make or deliver as true any certificate or writing containing statements which he knows to be false, or appends his official signature to acknowledgments or other documents when the parties executing same have not appeared in person before him shall be deemed guilty of a misdemeanor and upon conviction shall be punished by a fine not exceeding two hundred dollars [$200], or by imprisonment for a period not exceeding three [3] months, or both such fine and imprisonment.

NEW YORK

[N.Y. EXEC. LAW]

§ 135-a. Notary public or commissioner of deeds; acting without appointment; fraud in office. 1. Any person who holds himself out to the public as being entitled to act as a notary public or commissioner of deeds, or who assumes, uses or advertises the title of notary public or commissioner of deeds, or equivalent terms in any language, in such a manner as to convey the impression that he is a notary public or commissioner of deeds without having first been appointed as notary public or commissioner of deeds, or

2. A notary public or commissioner of deeds, who in the exercise of the powers, or in the performance of the duties of such office shall practice any fraud or deceit, the punishment for which is not otherwise provided for by this act, shall be guilty of a misdemeanor.

[N.Y. PENAL LAW]

§ 55.10. Designation of offenses.

o o o

2. Misdemeanors.

o o o

(b) Any offense defined outside this chapter which is declared by law to be a misdemeanor without specification of the classification thereof or of the sentence therefor shall be deemed a class A misdemeanor.

o o o

**§ 70.15. Sentences of imprisonment for misdemeanors and viola-
tion. 1. Class A misdemeanor.** A sentence of imprisonment for a
class A misdemeanor shall be a definite sentence. When such a
sentence is imposed the term shall be fixed by the court, and shall
not exceed one year.

○   ○   ○

§ 80.05. Fines for misdemeanors and violation. 1. Class A misdemeanor. A sentence to pay a fine for a class A misdemeanor shall
be a sentence to pay an amount, fixed by the court, not exceeding
one thousand dollars.

○   ○   ○

NORTH CAROLINA

[N.C. GEN. STAT.]

**§ 10-1. Appointment and commission; term of office; revocation
of commission.**

○   ○   ○

Any person holding himself out to the public as a notary public,
or any person attempting to act in such capacity after his commission
shall have been revoked by the Secretary of State, shall be guilty
of a misdemeanor and upon conviction shall be fined or imprisoned,
or both, in the discretion of the court.°

° Concerning punishment, see § 14-3, below.

**§ 14-76. Larceny, mutilation, or destruction of public records and
papers.** If any person shall steal, or for any fraudulent purpose
shall take from its place of deposit for the time being, or from any
person having the lawful custody thereof, or shall unlawfully and
maliciously obliterate, injure or destroy any record, writ, return, panel,
process, interrogatory, deposition, affidavit, rule, order or warrant of
attorney or any original document whatsoever, of or belonging to
any court of record, or relating to any matter, civil or criminal, begun,
pending or terminated in any such court, or any bill, answer, interrogatory, deposition, affidavit, order or decree or any original document whatsoever, of or belonging to any court or relating to any
cause or matter begun, pending or terminated in any such court,
every such offender shall be guilty of a misdemeanor; and in any
indictment for such offense it shall not be necessary to allege that
the article, in respect to which the offense is committed, is the property of any person or that the same is of any value. If any person
shall steal or for any fraudulent purpose shall take from the register's
office, or from any person having the lawful custody thereof, or shall
unlawfully and willfully obliterate, injure or destroy any book wherein deeds or other instruments of writing are registered, or any other
book of registration or record required to be kept by the register
of deeds or shall unlawfully destroy, obliterate, deface or remove

any records of proceedings of the board of county commissioners, or unlawfully and fraudulently abstract any record, receipt, order or voucher or other paper writing required to be kept by the clerk of the board of commissioners of any county, he shall be guilty of a misdemeanor.°

° Concerning punishment, see § 14-3, below.

§ 14-3.   Punishment of misdemeanors, infamous offenses, offenses committed in secrecy and malice or with deceit and intent to defraud. (a)   Except as provided in subsection (b), every person who shall be convicted of any misdemeanor for which no specific punishment is prescribed by statute shall be punishable by fine, by imprisonment for a term not exceeding two years, or by both, in the discretion of the court.

(b)   If a misdemeanor offense as to which no specific punishment is prescribed be infamous, done in secrecy and malice, or with deceit and intent to defraud, the offender shall, except where the offense is a conspiracy to commit a misdemeanor, be guilty of a felony and punishable as prescribed in § 14-2.

NORTH DAKOTA

Any notary who, on resignation or removal from office, or any executor or administrator of the estate of a deceased notary, who neglects to deposit records and papers as required by statute for the space of three months, or any person who knowingly destroys, defaces, or conceals any records or papers of a notary, shall forfeit and pay a sum of not less than $50.00 nor more than $500.00. He also shall be liable in a civil action for damages to any party injured. See *Records*, N.D. CENT. CODE § 44-06-05.

[N.D. CENT. CODE]

§ 44-06-13.   Acting as notary when disqualified—penalty.   Any notary public who exercises the duties of his office with knowledge that his commission has expired or that he is disqualified otherwise, or who appends his official signature to any document when the parties thereto have not appeared before him, is guilty of a misdemeanor and shall be punished by a fine of one hundred dollars for each offense, and also shall be removed from office by the secretary of state.

OHIO

[OHIO REV. CODE ANN.—Page]

§ 147.10.   Notary public acting after commission expires.   No notary public shall do or perform any act as a notary public knowing that his term of office has expired.

§ 147.11.   Forfeiture.   A person appointed notary public who performs any act as such after expiration of his term of office, knowing that his term has expired, shall forfeit not more than five hundred dollars, to be recovered by an action in the name of the state. Such act shall render such person ineligible for reappointment.

§ 147.14. **Removal from office for certifying affidavit without administering oath.** No notary public shall certify to the affidavit of a person without administering the oath or affirmation to such person. A notary public who violates this section shall be removed from office by the court of common pleas of the county in which the conviction was had. The court shall thereupon certify such removal to the governor. The person so removed shall be ineligible to reappointment for a period of three years.

§ 2921.13. **Falsification.** (A) No person shall knowingly make a false statement, or knowingly swear or affirm the truth of a false statement previously made, when any of the following apply:
  (1) The statement is made in any official proceeding.

o   o   o

  (6) The statement is sworn or affirmed before a notary public or other person empowered to administer oaths.
  (7) The statement is in writing on or in connection with a report or return which is required or authorized by law.

o   o   o

  (C) Where contradictory statements relating to the same fact are made by the offender within the period of the statute of limitations for falsification, it is not necessary for the prosecution to prove which statement was false, but only that one or the other was false.
  (D) Whoever violates this section is guilty of falsification, a misdemeanor of the first degree.

§ 2929.21. **Penalties for misdemeanor.** (A) Whoever is convicted of or pleads guilty to a misdemeanor other than a minor misdemeanor shall be imprisoned for a definite term or fined, or both, which term of imprisonment and fine shall be fixed by the court as provided in this section.
  (B) Terms of imprisonment for misdemeanor shall be imposed as follows:
  (1) For a misdemeanor of the first degree, not more than six months;

o   o   o

  (C) Fines for misdemeanor shall be imposed as follows:
  (1) For a misdemeanor of the first degree, not more than one thousand dollars;

o   o   o

  Editorial comment
  Concerning the removal of a notary for receiving excess fees, or dishonestly or unfaithfully discharging his duties, see *Fees Chargeable*, OHIO REV. CODE ANN. § 147.13.

OKLAHOMA

[OKLA. STAT. ANN.]

Tit. 21, § 1561. Wills, deeds and certain other instruments, forgery of. Every person who, with intent to defraud, forges, counterfeits or falsely alters:

1st. Any will or codicil of real or personal property, or any deed or other instrument being or purporting to be the act of another, by which any right or interest in real property is, or purports to be, transferred, conveyed or in any way changed or affected; or,

2nd. Any certificate or indorsement of the acknowledgment by any person of any deed or other instrument which by law may be recorded or given in evidence, made or purporting to have been made by any officer duly authorized to make such certificate or indorsement; or,

3rd. Any certificate of the proof of any deed, will, codicil or other instrument which by law may be recorded or given in evidence, made or purporting to have been made by any court or officer duly authorized to make such certificate,

Is guilty of forgery in the first degree.

Note: Concerning punishment, see § 1621, below.

§ 1574. Making false certificate of acknowledgment. If any officer authorized to take the acknowledgment or proof of any conveyance of real property, or of any other instrument which by law may be recorded, knowingly and falsely certifies that any such conveyance or instrument was acknowledged by any party thereto, or was proved by any subscribing witness, when in truth such conveyance or instrument was not acknowledged or proved as certified, he is guilty of forgery in the second degree.

Note: Concerning punishment, see § 1621, below.

§ 1621. Punishment for forgery. Forgery is punishable by imprisonment in the penitentiary as follows:

1. Forgery in the first degree by imprisonment not less than seven years nor more than twenty.

2. Forgery in the second degree not exceeding seven years.

Editorial comment

If any notary shall neglect or refuse to attach to his official signature the date of expiration of his commission, as provided by law, he shall be deemed guilty of a misdemeanor, and upon conviction thereof shall be fined in any sum not exceeding $50.00. See *Seal*, OKLA. STAT. ANN. tit. 49, § 5.

Concerning the suspension from office upon conviction of a felony, see *Appointment*, OKLA. STAT. ANN. tit. 51, § 24.1.

OREGON

[ORE. REV. STAT.]

§ 194.130. Disposition of records on vacancy in office; penalty for failure to properly dispose of records or for destroying or altering records. (1) Whenever the office of a notary public becomes vacant, the record referred to in ORS 194.090 kept by the notary public, together with all the papers relating to such record, shall be deposited in the office of the Secretary of State. Any notary public neglecting for the space of three months after his resignation or removal from office to deposit such record and papers in the Secretary of State's office, or any executor or administrator of a deceased notary public neglecting for the space of three months after the acceptance of that trust to lodge in the Secretary of State's office such record and papers as come into his hands, shall forfeit not more than $500.

(2) If any person knowingly destroys, defaces, materially alters or conceals any record or paper of a notary public, he shall forfeit not more than $500, and shall be liable to an action for damages by the party injured.

§ 194.150. Recovery of forfeitures. All forfeitures under ORS 194.130 shall be recovered in a civil action in any court having jurisdiction of the same in the county where the notary public resides. One-half shall be paid to the person bringing the action and one-half shall be paid to the State Treasurer to be credited to the General Fund.

§ 194.310. False personation of notary or commissioner of deeds and fraud or false certificate in exercise of powers prohibited.° (1) No person shall represent to any person that he is, or hold himself out to the public as being entitled to act as, a notary public or commissioner of deeds, or assume, use or advertise the title of notary public or commissioner of deeds, or equivalent terms in any language, in such a manner as to convey the impression that he is a notary public or commissioner of deeds when he is not a duly appointed, qualified and acting notary public or commissioner of deeds.

(2) No notary public or commissioner of deeds, in the exercise of the powers or in the performance of his duties, shall practice any fraud or deceit, or wilfully make any false certificate, acknowledgment or jurat.

° Concerning the penalty for violation of this section, see § 194.990, below.

§ 194.320. Removal from office for committing prohibited acts. The clerk of the court in which a conviction for acts prohibited by ORS 194.310 is had shall forthwith transmit to the Governor of Oregon a duly certified copy of the judgment, which is sufficient grounds for the removal of the convicted notary public or commissioner of deeds.

§ 194.990. **Penalties.** If punishment therefor is not otherwise provided for, violation of ORS 194.310 [above] is a misdemeanor.

Punishment

§ 161.555. **Classification of misdemeanors.**

    o   o   o

(3) An offense defined by a statute of this state, but without specification as to its classification or as to the penalty authorized upon conviction, shall be considered a Class A misdemeanor.

§ 161.615. **Prison terms for misdemeanors.** Sentences for misdemeanors shall be for a definite term. The court shall fix the term of imprisonment within the following maximum limitations:

(1) For a Class A misdemeanor, 1 year.

    o   o   o

§ 161.635. **Fines for misdemeanors and violations.** (1) A sentence to pay a fine for a misdemeanor shall be a sentence to pay an amount, fixed by the court, not exceeding:

(a) $1,000 for a Class A misdemeanor.

    o   o   o

(4) If a person has gained money or property through the commission of a misdemeanor or violation, then upon conviction thereof the court, instead of imposing the fine authorized for the offense under subsection (1), (2) or (3) of this section, may sentence the defendant to pay an amount fixed by the court, not exceeding double the amount of the defendant's gain from the commission of the offense. ° ° °.

(5) This section shall not apply to corporations.

PENNSYLVANIA

[PA. STAT. ANN.]

Tit. 18, § 4101. **Forgery.** (a) Offense defined.—A person is guilty of forgery if, with intent to defraud or injure anyone, or with knowledge that he is facilitating a fraud or injury to be perpetrated by anyone, the actor:

(1) alters any writing of another without his authority;

(2) makes, completes, executes, authenticates, issues or transfers any writing so that it purports to be the act of another who did not authorize that act, or to have been executed at a time or place or in a numbered sequence other than was in fact the case, or to be a copy of an original when no such original existed; or

(3) utters any writing which he knows to be forged in a manner specified in paragraphs (1) or (2) of this subsection.

(b) Definition.—As used in this section the word "writing" includes printing or any other method of recording information, money, coins, tokens, stamps, seals, credit cards, badges, trademarks, and other symbols of value, right, privilege, or identification.

(c) Grading.—Forgery is a felony of the second degree if the writing is or purports to be part of an issue of money, securities, postage or revenue stamps, or other instruments 'issued by the government, or part of an issue of stock, bonds or other instruments representing interests in or claims against any property or enterprise. Forgery is a felony of the third degree if the writing is or purports to be a will, deed, contract, release, commercial instrument, or other document evidencing, creating, transferring, altering, terminating, or otherwise affecting legal relations. Otherwise forgery is a misdemeanor of the first degree.

§ 4103. **Fraudulent destruction, removal or concealment of recordable instruments.** A person commits a felony of the third degree if, with intent to deceive or injure anyone, he destroys, removes or conceals any will, deed, mortgage, security instrument or other writing for which the law provides public recording.

Editorial comment

Concerning the penalty for exercising incompatible offices or appointments, see *Qualifications*, PA. STAT. ANN. tit. 65, §§ 1, 1.1, 2, 3.

PUERTO RICO

In public instruments, no abbreviations may be used nor blank spaces left therein. The originals may be either manuscript, printed, or typewritten, but in the latter case ribbons of indelible color must be used. For a violation of these provisions a notary is subject to a maximum fine of $500.00 imposable by the Supreme Court on recommendation of the protocol inspectors. See *Authority and Duties*, P.R. LAWS ANN. tit. 4, § 1017.

Notaries are responsible for the integrity and preservation of protocols, and should the protocols become deteriorated through negligence, among other things, the Supreme Court may reprimand the notary or impose on the notary a fine not to exceed $500.00. If there is reasonable ground to suspect that an offense has been committed, the proper charge must be immediately filed in the competent court. See *Records*, P.R. LAWS ANN. tit. 4, § 1034.

SOUTH DAKOTA

[S.D. COMPILED LAWS ANN.]

§ 18-1-11. **Notarizing without appearance of parties unlawful.** It shall be unlawful for any notary public to affix his official signature to documents when the parties have not appeared before him.

Note: Concerning penalty, see § 18-1-13, below.

§ 18-1-12. Acting after expiration of term or disqualification unlawful. It shall be unlawful for any notary public to exercise the duties of his office after the expiration of his commission or when he is otherwise disqualified.

Note: Concerning penalty, see § 18-1-13, below.

§ 18-1-13. Unlawful acts of notary as misdemeanor—penalty—removal from office. Any notary public who shall violate any of the provisions of § 18-1-11 or § 18-1-12 shall be guilty of a misdemeanor and fined one hundred dollars for each offense. In addition to the penalty provided for violation of said sections, any notary public who violates the same shall be removed from office by the Governor.

§ 22-39-2. Forgery in first degree—wills, acknowledgments, and certificates. Every person is guilty of forgery in the first degree, who with intent to defraud forges, counterfeits, or falsely alters:

(1) Any will or codicil devising or bequeathing real or personal property, or any deed or other instrument being or purporting to be the act of another, by which any right or interest in real property is or purports to be transferred, conveyed, or in any way charged or affected;

(2) Any certificate or endorsement of the acknowledgment by any person of any deed or other instrument which by law may be recorded or given in evidence made or purporting to have been made by any officer duly authorized to make such certificate or endorsement; or

(3) Any certificate of the proof of any deed, will, codicil, or other instrument which by law may be recorded or given in evidence made or purporting to have been made by any court or officer duly authorized to make such certificate.

§ 22-39-3. Punishment for forgery in first degree. Forgery in the first degree is punishable by imprisonment in the state penitentiary not less than five years.

§ 22-39-4. Forgery in second degree—public seals and impressions. Every person who with intent to defraud forges or counterfeits the great seal of this state, the seal of any public office authorized by law, the seal of any court of record, or the seal of any corporation created by the laws of this state or of any state, government, or country, or any other public seal authorized or recognized by the laws of this state or of any other state, government, or country or who falsely makes, forges, or counterfeits any impression purporting to be the impression of any such seal, is guilty of forgery in the second degree.

§ 22-39-11. Punishment for forgery in second degree. Forgery in the second degree is punishable by imprisonment in the state penitentiary not less than three years nor more than ten years.

§ 22-40-1. Particular acts constituting false personation—punishment. Every person who falsely personates another, and in such assumed character:

(1) Marries or pretends to marry, or to sustain the marriage relation toward another, with or without the connivance of such other person;

(2) Becomes bail or surety for any party, in any proceeding, before any court or officer authorized to take such bail or surety;

(3) Subscribes, verifies, publishes, acknowledges, or proves, in the name of another person, any written instrument, with intent that the same may be delivered or used as true; or

(4) Does any other act whereby, if it were done by the person falsely personated, he might in any event become liable to any suit or prosecution, or to pay any sum of money, or to incur any charge, forfeiture, or penalty, or whereby any benefit might accrue to the party personating or to any other person;

is punishable by imprisonment in the state penitentiary not exceeding ten years.

TENNESSEE

Every notary must, at his own expense, procure a seal of office, which he shall surrender to the county court when he resigns, or at the expiration of his term of office, to be cancelled. His representatives, in case of death, shall likewise surrender it. The punishment for violation of these duties is indictment as for a misdemeanor. See *Seal*, TENN. CODE ANN. §§ 8-1619, 39-105.

A violation of the section concerning the indication on instruments of the notary's true date of expiration of commission is a misdemeanor. Any person so offending shall pay a fine of not less than $25.00 nor more than $100.00 for each offense. See *Authority and Duties*, TENN. CODE ANN. § 8-1621.

[TENN. CODE ANN.]

§ 8-1626. Acting after expiration of commission. It shall be unlawful for any person, who has been commissioned as a notary public, either as a result of his election or upon direct appointment by the governor, to take acknowledgments or otherwise act in an official capacity after the expiration of his commission; and any person violating this section shall be guilty of a misdemeanor and punishable by a fine of not less than one hundred dollars ($100) nor more than one thousand dollars ($1,000) for each offense.

§ 39-1939. False certificate of probate or acknowledgment—pen-

alty. If any officer authorized to take the proof and acknowledgment of any conveyance of real and personal property, or other instrument, willfully certifies that such conveyance or other instrument was duly proven or acknowledged by any party thereto, when no such acknowledgment or proof was made, or was not made at the time it was certified to have been made, with intent to injure or defraud, or enable any other person to injure or defraud, he is guilty of a felony, and shall be punished as provided in § 39-1721.°

§ 39-1940. **False registration or certification of conveyance or other instrument—penalty.** Any officer whose duty it is to record, register, note for registration, or certify for record or registration, any conveyance or other instrument, who willfully, with like intent, falsely notes, records, registers, or certifies such conveyance or other instrument, is guilty of felony, and shall be punished as provided in § 39-1721.°

° TENN. CODE ANN. § 39-1721, mentioned in §§ 39-1939 and 39-1940, states as follows: The punishment for a violation of ° ° ° or of §§ 39-1939, 39-1940, is imprisonment in the penitentiary not less than two (2) years nor more than fifteen (15) years. However, in cases involving the forgery of instruments representing monetary values, such as notes, due bills, bills of exchange, checks, etc., the punishment shall be as in case of larceny.

TEXAS

[TEX. PENAL CODE ANN.]

§ 32.21. **Forgery.** (a) For purposes of this section:
  (1) "Forge" means:
    (A) to alter, make, complete, execute, or authenticate any writing so that it purports:
      (i) to be the act of another who did not authorize that act;
      (ii) to have been executed at a time or place or in a numbered sequence other than was in fact the case; or
      (iii) to be a copy of an original when no such original existed;
    (B) to issue, transfer, register the transfer of, pass, publish, or otherwise utter a writing that is forged within the meaning of Paragraph (A) of this subdivision; or
    (C) to possess a writing that is forged within the meaning of Paragraph (A) with intent to utter it in a manner specified in Paragraph (B) of this subdivision.
  (2) "Writing" includes:
    (A) printing or any other method of recording information;

(B) money, coins, tokens, stamps, seals, credit cards, badges, and trademarks; and

(C) symbols of value, right, privilege, or identification.

(b) A person commits an offense if he forges a writing with intent to defraud or harm another.

(c) Except as provided in Subsections (d) and (e) of this section an offense under this section is a Class A misdemeanor.°

(d) An offense under this section is a felony of the third degree°° if the writing is or purports to be a will, codicil, deed, deed of trust, mortgage, security instrument, security agreement, credit card, check or similar sight order for payment of money, contract, release, or other commercial instrument.

(e) An offense under this section is a felony of the second degree† if the writing is or purports to be part of an issue of money, securities, postage or revenue stamps, or other instruments issued by a state or national government or by a subdivision of either, or part of an issue of stock, bonds, or other instruments representing interests in or claims against another person.

° Concerning the punishment for a Class A misdemeanor, see § 12.21, below.

°° Concerning the punishment for a felony of the third degree, see § 12.34, below.

† Concerning the punishment for a felony of the second degree, see § 12.33, below.

§ 37.10. Tampering with governmental record. (a) A person commits an offense if he:

(1) knowingly makes a false entry in, or false alteration of, a governmental record;°

(2) makes, presents, or uses any record, document, or thing with knowledge of its falsity and with intent that it be taken as a genuine governmental record;° or

(3) intentionally destroys, conceals, removes, or otherwise impairs the verity, legibility, or availability of a governmental record.°

(b) It is an exception to the application of Subsection (a)(3) of this section that the governmental record is destroyed pursuant to legal authorization.

(c) An offense under this section is a Class A misdemeanor°° unless the actor's intent is to defraud or harm another, in which event the offense is a felony of the third degree.†

° "Governmental record" means anything: (A) belonging to, received by, or kept by government for information; or (B) required by law to be kept by others for information of government. TEX. PENAL CODE ANN. § 37.01(1).

°° Concerning the punishment for a Class A misdemeanor, see § 12.21, below.

† Concerning the punishment for a felony of the third degree, see § 12.34, below.

Punishments

§ 12.21. **Class A misdemeanor.** An individual adjudged guilty of a Class A misdemeanor shall be punished by:

    (1)   a fine not to exceed $2,000;

    (2)   confinement in jail for a term not to exceed one year; or

    (3)   both such fine and imprisonment.

§ 12.33. **Second-degree felony punishment.** (a) An individual adjudged guilty of a felony of the second degree shall be punished by confinement in the Texas Department of Corrections for any term of not more than 20 years or less than 2 years.

(b) In addition to imprisonment, an individual adjudged guilty of a felony of the second degree may be punished by a fine not to exceed $10,000.

§ 12.34. **Third-degree felony punishment.** (a) An individual adjudged guilty of a felony of the third degree shall be punished by confinement in the Texas Department of Corrections for any term of not more than 10 years or less than 2 years.

(b) In addition to imprisonment, an individual adjudged guilty of a felony of the third degree may be punished by a fine not to exceed $5,000.

UTAH

[UTAH CODE ANN.]

§ 46-1-9. **Acting after commission expires—penalty.** Any person who willfully affixes his signature and seal as notary public to any instrument after the expiration of his commission as such notary public is guilty of a misdemeanor.

Note: Concerning punishment, see §§ 76-3-104, 76-3-204, 76-3-301, below.

§ 76-20-1. **Personating a public officer—assuming insignia of office.** Every person who falsely personates a public officer, civilian or military, or a policeman, or other peace officer of any character whatsoever, or who falsely personates a private individual having special authority by law to perform an act affecting the rights or interests of another, ° ° °; and every person who falsely assumes or pretends to be a justice of the peace, sheriff, deputy sheriff, coroner or notary public and takes upon himself to act as such;—is punishable by imprisonment in the county jail not less than sixty days and not to exceed one year, or by fine not less than $250 and not to exceed $1,000, or by both such imprisonment and fine.

§ 76-20-3. Other acts of false personation—penalty. Every person who falsely personates another, and in such assumed character either:

(1)   [Omitted]

(2)   Verifies, publishes, acknowledges or proves in the name of another person any written instrument, with intent that the same may be recorded, delivered and used as true; or,

(3)   Does any other act whereby, if it were done by the person falsely personated, he might, in any event, become liable to any suit or prosecution, or to pay any sum of money, or to incur any charge, forfeiture or penalty, or whereby any benefit might accrue to the party personating, or to any other person;—is punishable by imprisonment in the county jail not exceeding one year or by fine not exceeding $1,000, or by both.

Punishment

§ 76-3-104.   Misdemeanors classified.   (1)   Misdemeanors are classified into three categories:

(a)   Class A misdemeanors;

(b)   Class B misdemeanors;

(c)   Class C misdemeanors.

(2)   An offense designated a misdemeanor, either in this code or in another law, without specification as to punishment or category, is a class B misdemeanor.

§ 76-3-204.   Misdemeanor conviction—term of imprisonment. A person who has been convicted of a misdemeanor may be sentenced to imprisonment as follows:

✿   ✿   ✿

(2)   In the case of a class B misdemeanor, for a term not exceeding six months;

✿   ✿   ✿

§ 76-3-301.   Fines of persons.   A person who has been convicted of an offense may be sentenced to pay a fine not exceeding:

✿   ✿   ✿

(4) $299 when the conviction is of a class B or C misdemeanor or infraction.

(5)   Any higher amounts specifically authorized by statute.

This section shall not apply to a corporation, association, partnership, government, or government instrumentality.

WASHINGTON

[WASH. REV. CODE ANN.]

§ 9.34.010. **Falsely personating another.** Every person who shall falsely personate another, and in such assumed character shall—

°   °   °

(4) Subscribe, verify, publish, acknowledge or approve a written instrument which by law may be recorded, with intent that the same may be delivered or issued as true; or

°   °   °

(6) Do any other act in the course of any action or proceeding, wherein, if it were done by the person falsely personated such person might in any event become liable to an action or special proceeding, civil or criminal, or to pay a sum of money, or to incur a charge, forfeiture, or penalty, or whereby any benefit might accrue to the offender or to any other person.

Shall be punished by imprisonment in the state penitentiary for not more than ten years.

§ 9.44.020. **First degree.** Every person who, with intent to defraud, shall forge ° ° ° the seal of any public officer, court, notary public or corporation, or any public seal authorized or recognized by the laws of this or any other state or government, or any impression of any such seal; ° ° ° shall be guilty of forgery in the first degree, and shall be punished by imprisonment in the state penitentiary for not more than twenty years.

§ 9.44.030. **False certificate to certain instruments.** Every officer authorized to take a proof or acknowledgment of an instrument which by law may be recorded, who shall wilfully certify falsely that the execution of such instrument was acknowledged by any party thereto, or that the execution thereof was proved, shall be guilty of forgery in the first degree.

Note: Forgery in the first degree is punishable by imprisonment in the state penitentiary for not more than 20 years. WASH. REV. CODE ANN. § 9.44.020, above.

WEST VIRGINIA

[W. VA. CODE ANN.]

§ 29-4-10. **Violation of § 29-4-9°; penalty.** A notary who, for three months after the termination of his office, neglects so to deposit his records and official papers,° and the personal representative of a deceased notary who, for three months after his qualification as such representative, neglects so to deposit the records and official papers of the deceased which have come to his hands or control, shall be guilty of a misdemeanor, and, upon conviction thereof, shall be fined not exceeding five hundred dollars.

(°) See *Records,* W. VA. CODE ANN. § 29-4-9, concerning the disposition of records on the death of a notary or termination of his office.

§ 29-4-11. Destruction or defacement of notarial records; penalty. Whoever knowingly destroys, defaces or conceals the records or official papers of a notary shall be guilty of a misdemeanor, and, upon conviction thereof, shall be fined not exceeding one thousand dollars, and, whether convicted or not, he shall be liable in damages to any person injured thereby.

§ 61-4-1. Forgery of public record, certificate, return or attestation of court or officer; penalty. If any person forge a public record, or a certificate, return or attestation of a clerk of a court, notary public, judge, justice, or any public officer, in relation to any matter wherein such certificate, return, or attestation may be received as legal proof, or utter or attempt to employ as true such forged record, certificate, return or attestation, knowing the same to be forged, he shall be guilty of a felony, and, upon conviction, shall be confined in the penitentiary not less than two nor more than ten years.

§ 61-7-13. Duty of officers and other persons to report violations; penalty for failure to report. It shall be the duty of all ministerial officers, consisting of justices of the peace, notaries public and other conservators of the peace of this State, to report to the prosecuting attorney of the county the names of all persons guilty of violating any of the provisions of this article [article 7 (Dangerous Weapons) of Chapter 61 (Crimes and Their Punishment)], and any person wilfully failing so to do shall be guilty of a misdemeanor, and, upon conviction, shall be fined not exceeding two hundred dollars, and shall, moreover, be liable to removal from office for such wilful failure. It shall likewise be the duty of every person having knowledge of the violation of any of the provisions of this article to report the same to the prosecuting attorney, and to freely and fully give evidence concerning the same, and anyone failing so to do shall be guilty of a misdemeanor, and, upon conviction, shall be fined not exceeding one hundred dollars.

Editorial comment

See also *Appointment,* W. VA. CODE ANN. § 6-2-13, concerning the penalty for the failure of the officer in whose office the official bond of a notary is filed to send a copy of it to the state tax commissioner within two months after it is filed in his office.

See also *Acknowledgments,* W. VA. CODE ANN. § 39-1-7, concerning the penalty for wilfully making a false certificate of acknowledgment contrary to the true facts in the case, or certifying the acknowledgment of a person whom the officer does not personally know to be the person whose name is signed to the writing acknowledged.

WISCONSIN

When a notary public ceases to hold office, he, or if he is dead, his executor or administrator, must deposit his official records and papers in the office of the clerk of the circuit court of the county of his residence. If the notary or executor or administrator, after the records and papers come to his hands, neglects for three months to deposit them, he shall forfeit not less than $50 nor more than $500. See *Records*, WIS. STAT. ANN. § 137.01(7).

[WIS. STAT. ANN.]

§ 137.01. Notaries.

°   °   °

(7) **Official records to be filed.** ° ° ° If any person knowingly destroys, defaces or conceals any records or papers of any notary public he shall forfeit not less than $50 nor more than $500, and shall be liable to the party injured for all damages thereby sustained. The clerks of the circuit courts shall receive and safely keep all such papers and records in their office.

°   °   °

§ 943.39. **Fraudulent writings.** Whoever, with intent to injure or defraud, does any of the following may be fined not more than $2,500 or imprisoned not more than 3 years or both:

°   °   °

(3) By means of deceit obtains a signature to a writing which is the subject of forgery under § 943.38(1); or

(4) Makes a false written statement with knowledge that it is false and with intent that it shall ultimately appear to have been signed under oath.

WYOMING

[WYO. STAT. ANN.]

§ 6-153.1. **Perjury in judicial, legislative, or administrative proceeding.** Whoever, being under oath or affirmation lawfully administered, shall willfully, corruptly and falsely testify or make any false affidavit, certificate, declaration, deposition or statement in any judicial, legislative, or administrative proceeding in which an oath or affirmation may be required by law, touching a matter material to the point in question, is guilty of perjury, and shall be imprisoned in the penitentiary not more than 14 years.

§ 6-154.1. **False swearing other than in judicial or administrative proceeding; false claim or voucher.** Whoever, under oath or affirmation lawfully administered in any matter where an oath is authorized by law to be taken, shall willfully, corruptly and falsely make any false certificate, affidavit, acknowledgment, declaration or statement of any nature other than in a judicial or administrative proceeding, or whoever submits a false claim or voucher under penalty of perjury, shall be guilty of false swearing, and upon conviction shall be imprisoned in the penitentiary not more than five (5) years.

§ 6-168. **False personation generally.** Whoever falsely personates another person before any court or judge thereof, or before any justice of the peace, mayor of any city or town, clerk of any court, notary public, or any state or county officer who is authorized either to administer oaths or take the acknowledgment of deeds, powers or warrants of attorney, or other instruments, or to grant marriage licenses, with intent to defraud; or who falsely personates or represents another, and, in such assumed character, receives any property intended to be delivered to the party so personated, with intent to convert the same to his own use, shall be imprisoned in the penitentiary not more than fourteen (14) years.

§ 6-171. **False jurat.** Whoever, being a notary public or other officer or person authorized to administer oaths, certifies that any person was sworn or affirmed before him to any affidavit or other instrument of writing when, in fact, such person was not so affirmed or sworn, shall be imprisoned in the penitentiary not more than three years.

§ 6-172. **False certificate of acknowledgment.** Whoever, being a notary public, or other officer authorized to take and certify acknowledgments of conveyances, mortgages, or other instruments of writing, shall append his signature as such officer when no official seal is required, or shall append his signature and affix his official seal when such seal is required by law to be affixed to the certificate of acknowledgment of any conveyance, mortgage or other instrument of writing required to be recorded or filed in this state, or which cannot be legally recorded therein without acknowledgment and certificate thereof, when at the time of such signing and sealing, the grantor, mortgagor, or other party executing such deed, mortgage or other instrument had not first acknowledged the execution thereof before such notary public or other officer as aforesaid, shall be imprisoned in the penitentiary not more than three years.

§ 6-173. **Custodian stealing record.** Whoever, being an officer or his deputy, having the custody of any record, book, document, paper or proceeding specified in [§ 6-189],* steals or fraudulently takes away, secretes, withdraws or destroys any such record book, document, paper or proceeding, shall be imprisoned in the penitentiary not more than ten years.

* For § 6-189, see below.

§ 6-189. Stealing public records. Whoever steals, takes and carries away the whole or any part of any record, record book, docket or journal authorized to be made by law, or belonging or pertaining to any court of record, justice of the peace, or any state, district, county, municipal or legislative office or officer, shall be imprisoned in the penitentiary not more than ten years.

§ 6-190. Altering record. Whoever maliciously, mischievously or fraudulently alters, defaces, injures, mutilates or destroys the whole or any part of any record authorized to be made by law, belonging or pertaining to any court of record, justice of the peace, or any state, district, county, municipal or legislative office or officer, or any public record so authorized, or any paper, pleading, exhibit or other writing filed with, in, or by any such court, office, or officer, shall be imprisoned in the penitentiary not more than ten years.

Editorial comment

Any person who neglects or fails to fulfill and perform the duties concerning the deposit of a notary's official register with the county clerk, within 30 days, is liable in the penal sum of $200.00, to be applied to the school fund of the county. The sum may be recovered by any citizen of the county suing therefor. See *Records*, WYO. STAT. ANN. § 32-8.

§ 32-11. Notary acting after term expires. Whoever, having been appointed a notary public, does or performs any act as a notary public, after the expiration of his term of office, knowing that such term of office has expired, shall be fined not more than five hundred dollars nor less than twenty-five dollars.

§ 32-12. Failure of county clerk to perform duties imposed by chapter. If any register of deeds [county clerk] shall fail or neglect to fulfill and perform the duties imposed on him by this chapter [§§ 32-1 to 32-10, 32-12, 32-13], such person shall be liable in the penal sum of two hundred dollars, to be recovered and applied as provided in [§ 32-8].

Note: The provisions of §§ 32-1 to 32-10, 32-13, are variously located in the separate chapters, classified according to their subject matter. Concerning § 32-8, see comment above following § 6-190.

UNITED STATES

18 U.S.C. § 1016. Acknowledgment of appearance or oath. Whoever, being an officer authorized to administer oaths or to take and certify acknowledgments, knowingly makes any false acknowledgment, certificate, or statement concerning the appearance before him or the taking of an oath or affirmation by any person with respect

to any proposal, contract, bond, undertaking, or other matter submitted to, made with, or taken on behalf of the United States or any department or agency thereof, concerning which an oath or affirmation is required by law or lawful regulation, or with respect to the financial standing of any principal, surety, or other party to any such proposal, contract, bond, undertaking, or other instrument, shall be fined not more than $2,000 or imprisoned not more than two years, or both.

CHAPTER 10: SAFE DEPOSIT BOXES

In an increasing number of states and other jurisdictions, notaries public are being assigned duties concerning safe deposit boxes on which the rent has not been paid. Typically, the various statutes provide that when the rent due on a safe deposit box has remained unpaid for a specified number of months, the bank or other institution owning the box may give notice to the lessee of the box that the rent is unpaid and the contents will be removed if the rent is not paid within a certain specified period of time. If the rent is not paid within that period, the bank or other institution owning the box may open it in the presence of an officer of the bank and a notary public who is not in the general employment of the bank. The notary is authorized to remove the contents of the box, list them, and seal the contents in a package marked with a legend identifying the lessee of the box from which the contents were removed. A certificate by the notary public, listing the contents is mailed to the lessee of the box. The statutes usually provide additional details concerning how the contents of the package shall be stored and eventually liquidated by sale by the bank or other institution which owns the safe deposit box.

The statutes of the various states and other jurisdictions relevant to this function of a notary public are quoted below in *Safe Deposit Boxes: State and Other Statutes.*

SAFE DEPOSIT BOXES:
STATE AND OTHER STATUTES

MASSACHUSETTS

[MASS. ANN. LAWS]

Ch. 158, § 17. Proceedings if rent of safe deposit boxes not paid. As herein used, "bank" shall mean any bank as defined in section one of chapter one hundred and sixty-seven, any national banking association doing business in the commonwealth and any domestic corporation organized under general or special laws of the commonwealth for the purpose of carrying on the business of a safe deposit company; "safe deposit box" shall mean a box or safe in the vaults of any bank; "lessee" shall mean the person or persons in whose name or names a safe deposit box stands on the books of a bank; and "rent" shall mean the amount due to a bank for the rental or use of a safe deposit box.

If the rent for a safe deposit box in a bank has not been paid for two years after being due, the bank may mail, postpaid, to the lessee at his address shown on the books of said bank, a notice stating that if the rent for such safe deposit box is not paid within sixty days from the date of such notice, the bank may cause such safe deposit box to be opened and the contents disposed of in accordance with the terms of this section. Upon the expiration of sixty days from the date of such notice, if the lessee has failed to pay the rent for such safe deposit box in full to the date of such notice, all rights of the lessee in the safe deposit box and of access thereto shall cease, and such bank may, at any time thereafter in the presence of one of its officers and of a notary public not in the general employ of such bank, cause such safe deposit box to be opened, and such notary public shall remove the contents thereof, list the same and seal such contents in a package, marking thereon the name of the lessee and his address as shown on the books of the bank. An affidavit setting forth the facts concerning the entry, listing the contents of the safe deposit box and signed by the bank officer and the notary public shall be retained by the bank. Such affidavit shall be prima facie evidence of the facts therein set forth in all proceedings at law and equity wherein evidence of such facts would be competent.

The package containing the contents of any safe deposit box opened as aforesaid shall be retained on special deposit by the bank, subject to payment of rent due for such safe deposit box, all expenses incurred in connection with opening said safe deposit box and charges for safekeeping of such package. If such package remains unclaimed for seven years and the amounts due as above provided remain unpaid the bank may mail, postpaid, to the person or persons to whom, and at the address at which, the notice provided for above was mailed, a notice stating that if such amounts shall not be paid within sixty days from the date of such notice, the bank will turn over the contents less the rental charges to the commissioner of corporations and taxation as abandoned property, to be held by him subject to the provisions of chapter two hundred A. The bank may sell, assign or deliver so much of the contents of such package, at either public or private sale, as will enable it to realize such amount as will compensate for said charges.

The affidavit required by this section may be in the following form:

COMMONWEALTH OF MASSACHUSETTS

County of

We, ——— an authorized official of ——— and ——— a notary public not in the general employ of said bank, hereby certify that on the ——— day of ——— 19———, we were present and witnessed the forcible opening of Safe No. ——— leased in the name of ——— in the valuts of the ——— office of said bank; that the contents of said safe were removed, examined, listed and then enclosed in a package and sealed in our presence. We further certify that the following is a true and complete list of all the contents removed from said safe.

(Allow space here for listing of contents.)

_____   _____
Signature of officer.   Title.

_____
Name of Bank.

_____
Signature of notary public not in the general employ of said bank.

Ch. 167, § 32. Disposition of property deposited with bank. Should any bank, at the time when the commissioner takes possession thereof, have in its possession for safe keeping and storage, any jewelry, plate, money, securities, valuable papers or other valuable personal property, or should it have rented any box, safes or safe deposit boxes, or any part thereof, for the storage of property of any kind, the commissioner may at any time after taking possession as aforesaid cause to be mailed to the person claiming or appearing upon the books of the bank to the owner of such property, or to the person in whose name the safe, vault, or box stands, a written notice in a securely closed postpaid, registered letter, directed to such person at his post office address as recorded upon the books of the bank, notifying such person to remove, within a period fixed by said notice and not less than sixty days from the date thereof, all such personal property; and upon the date fixed by said notice, the contract, if any, between such persons and the bank for the storage of said property, or for the use of said safe, vault or box, shall cease and determine, and the amount of the unearned rent or charges, if any, paid by such person shall become a debt of the bank to such person. If the property be not removed within the time fixed by the notice, the commissioner may make such disposition of said property as the supreme judicial court, upon application thereto, may direct; and thereupon the commissioner may cause any safe, vault or box to be opened in his presence, or in the presence of one of his special

agents and of a notary public not an officer or in the employ of the
bank, or of the commissioner, and the contents thereof, if any, to
be sealed up by such notary public in a package upon which the
notary public shall distinctly mark the name and address of the person in whose name such safe, vault or box stands upon the books
of the bank, and shall attach thereto a list and description of the
property therein. The package so sealed and addressed, together
with the list and description, may be kept by the commissioner in
one of the general safes for boxes of the bank until delivered to the
person whose name it bears, or may otherwise be disposed of as
directed by the court.

MINNESOTA

[MINN. STAT. ANN.]

§ 55.14. **Safety deposit boxes; rental procedure.** If the amount
due for the use or rental of any safe deposit box of any licensed safe
deposit company shall have remained unpaid for a period of six
months, the safe deposit company may, at any time after the expiration of that period, cause to be sent by registered mail, addressed
to the renter or lessee of the safe deposit box, directed to the address
standing on its books, a written notice that, if the amount due for
the use or rental of the safe deposit box is not paid within 60
days after the date of the mailing of the notice, it will cause the
safe deposit box to be opened in the presence of its president or
vice-president or secretary or treasurer or assistant secretary or assistant treasurer or superintendent, and of a notary public not in its
employ, and the contents thereof, if any, to be placed in a sealed
package by the notary public, upon which he shall mark the name
of the renter or lessee as given upon its books and the estimated value
thereof, and that the package so sealed and marked will be placed
in one of the general safe deposit boxes of the safe deposit company.
Upon the expiration of 60 days from date of mailing the notice, as
aforesaid, and in default of payment within said 60 days of the
amount due for the use or rental of the safe deposit box, it may, in
the presence of a notary public not in its employ and one of its
officers heretofore named, cause the safe deposit box to be opened
and the contents thereof, if any, to be removed and sealed by
the notary public in a package, upon which he shall mark the name
of the renter or lessee and also the estimated value of the contents
of the safe deposit box and, in the presence of one of its officers
heretofore named, the notary public shall place in one of its general
safe deposit boxes this package; and the proceedings of the notary
public shall be set out in a certificate by him under his official seal,
which shall be delivered to the licensed safe deposit company. The
licensed safe deposit company shall have a lien upon the contents of
any such safe deposit box, which shall have been removed in the
manner provided, for the amount due to it for the use or rental of the

safe deposit box, up to the time of the removal of the contents, and for the costs and expenses, if any, incurred in the opening of the safe or box and its repair, or restoration for use. In case the lien of the licensed safe deposit company, for rental and expenses, shall not be paid and discharged within six months from the date of the opening of the safe deposit box and the removal of the contents therefrom, then the licensed safe deposit company may sell, or cause to be sold, at public auction, the contents of the safe deposit box, or so much thereof as is required to pay and discharge the lien and expenses of sale, having first caused to be sent by registered mail, addressed to the renter or lessee of the safe deposit box, directed to the address standing on its books, a written notice of the time and place of the sale, and also giving public notice of the time and place of the sale by advertisement in a legal newspaper published in the county in which the place of business of the licensed safe deposit company is located, at least once a week for two successive weeks, and from the proceeds of the sale it may retain for its own use the amount of its lien and the expenses of the sale; the balance of the proceeds of the sale and the contents remaining unsold, if any, being held to be paid over and delivered to those having ownership of the contents of the safe deposit box so sold, as aforesaid. Authority to place the contents of an opened safe deposit box in one of the general safe deposit boxes of the safe deposit company includes authority to place the contents of any number of opened boxes in one general box which is under the sole control of the safe deposit company. Any currency or other money found in any box opened under authority of this section may be applied by the safe deposit company toward the payment of rental and the costs and expenses referred to in this section.

MISSOURI

[MO. ANN. STAT.—Vernon]

§ 362.485. **Special remedies available to banks doing a safe deposit business.** 1. Every bank and trust company doing a safe deposit business and every safe deposit company owned by a bank or trust company shall be entitled to the following special remedies in enforcing the liabilities of depositors and of renters or lessees of boxes:

(1) Whenever any bank or trust company doing a safe deposit business receives personal property upon deposit, as bailee, and issues a receipt therefor, it is a warehouseman as to this property and all existing statutes and laws affecting warehousemen shall apply to these deposits, and the corporation shall have a lien on the deposit or the proceeds thereof to the same extent and with the same effect, and enforceable in the same manner, as provided by law with reference to warehousemen.

(2) (a) If the amount due for the rental of any safe or box in the vaults of any bank or trust company is not paid for one year, the

bank or trust company may, at the expiration thereof, send to the person or persons, partnerships or corporation in whose name the safe or box stands on its books a notice in writing in a securely closed postpaid, registered letter, directed to the renter or lessee at his, their or its post-office address, as recorded upon the books of the bank or trust company, notifying the renter or lessee that if the amount due for the rental of the safe or box shall not be paid within thirty days from date, the bank or trust company will then cause the safe or box to be opened, and the contents thereof to be inventoried, sealed, and placed in one of the general safes or boxes of the bank or trust company.

(b) Upon the expiration of thirty days from the date of mailing the notice, and the failure within the period of time of the renter or lessee in whose name the safe or box stands on the books of the bank or trust company to pay the amount due for the rental thereof to the date of notice, the bank or trust company may, in the presence of a notary public and of its president, secretary or cashier, cause the safe or box to be opened, and the contents thereof, if any, to be removed, inventoried and sealed up by the notary public in a package, upon which the notary public shall distinctly mark the name of the renter or lessee in whose name the safe or box stood on the books of the bank or trust company, and the date of removal of the property, and when the package has been so marked for identification by the notary public, it shall, in the presence of the president, secretary or cashier of the bank or trust company, be placed by the notary public in one of the general safes or boxes of the bank or trust company, at a rental not to exceed the original rental of the safe which was opened, and shall remain in the general safe or box for a period of not less than two years, unless sooner removed by the owner thereof, and the notary public shall thereupon file with the bank or trust company a certificate under seal, which shall fully set out the date of the opening of the safe or box, the name of the renter or lessee in whose name it stood and a list of the contents if any.

(c) A copy of the certificate shall within ten days thereafter be mailed to the renter or lessee in whose name the safe or box so opened stood on the books of the bank or trust company, at his, their or its last known post-office address, in a securely closed postpaid, registered letter, together with a notice that the contents will be kept, at the expense of such renter or lessee, in a general safe or box in the vaults of the bank or trust company for a period of not less than two years.

(d) At any time after the mailing of the certificate and notice, and before the expiration of two years, the renter or lessee may require the delivery of the contents of the safe as shown by the certificate upon the payment of all rentals due at the time of opening of the safe or box, the cost of opening the box, the fees of the notary public for issuing his certificate thereon, and the payment of all further charges accrued during the period the contents remained in the general safe or box of the bank or trust company.

o   o   o

NEVADA

[NEV. REV. STAT.]

§ 663.085.   Safe-deposit boxes: Unpaid rentals; notice to lessee; disposition of contents.   1.   If the rental due on a safe-deposit box has not been paid for 90 days, the lessor may send a notice by registered or certified mail to the last-known address of the lessee stating that the safe-deposit box will be opened and its contents stored at the expense of the lessee unless payment of the rental is made within 30 days.   If the rental is not paid within 30 days from the mailing of the notice, the box may be opened in the presence of any officer of the lessor and a notary public.   The contents shall be sealed in a package by the notary public, who shall write on the outside the name of the lessee and the date of the opening in the presence of the officer. The notary public and the officer shall execute a certificate reciting the name of the lessee, the date of the opening of the box and a list of its contents.   The certificate shall be included in the package and a copy of the certificate shall be sent by registered or certified mail to the last-known address of the lessee.   The package shall then be placed in the general vaults of the lessor at a rental not exceeding the rental previously charged for the box.

2.   Any documents or writings of a private nature, having little or no apparent value, need not be offered for sale, but shall be retained, unless claimed by the owner, for the period of 6 months, after which they may be destroyed.

3.   If the contents of the safe-deposit box have not been claimed within 6 months of the mailing of the certificate, the lessor may send a further notice to the last-known address of the lessee stating that, unless the accummulated charges are paid within 30 days, the contents of the box will be sold at public or private sale at a specified time and place, or, in the case of securities listed on a stock exchange, will be sold upon the exchange on or after a specified date and that unsalable items will be destroyed.   The time, place and manner of sale shall also be posted conspicuously on the premises of the lessor and advertised once in a newspaper of general circulation in the community.   If the articles are not claimed, they may then be sold in accordance with the notice.

4.   The balance of the proceeds, after deducting accumulated charges, including the expense of advertising and conducting the sale, together with any money discovered in the box shall be deposited to the credit of the lessee in any account maintained by him, or if none, shall be a deposit account with the bank operating the safe-deposit facility, or in the case of a subsidiary safe-deposit company,

a bank owning stock therein, and shall be identified on the books of the bank as arising from the sale of contents of a safe-deposit box. Any items remaining unsold may be destroyed.

NEW HAMPSHIRE

[N.H. REV. STAT. ANN.]

§ 385:1. **Rent unpaid, procedure.** If the amount due for the rent or use of a box or safe in the vaults of a domestic corporation authorized to engage in the business of letting vaults, safes, and other receptacles shall not have been paid for six months, such corporation may cause to be mailed, postpaid, to the person in whose name such safe or box stands upon the books of such corporation and at his address as stated on said books, a notice stating that if the amount then due for the use or rent of such safe or box shall not be paid within sixty days from the date of such notice such corporation will cause the safe or box to be opened in the presence of its president, treasurer, or superintendent and of a notary public, and the contents thereof, if any, to be sealed up in a package and placed in one of the storage vaults of such corporation.

§ 385:2. **Box to be opened, etc.** If, upon the expiration of said sixty days from the date of such notice, such person shall have failed to pay the amount due for the use or rent of such safe or box in full to the date of such notice, all right of such person in such safe or box and of access thereto shall cease, and such corporation may in the presence of its president, treasurer, or superintendent and of a notary public not an officer or in the general employ of such corporation, cause such safe or box to be opened, and such notary public shall remove the contents thereof, make a list of the same and shall seal up such contents in a package and shall mark thereon the name of the person in whose name such safe or box stood on the books of such corporation and his address as stated on said books, and such package shall in the presence of said notary public and of said president, treasurer, or superintendent be placed in one of the storage vaults of such corporation; and the proceedings of such notary public, including said list of the contents of said safe or box and his estimate of the total value of said contents, shall be set forth by him in his own handwriting and under his official seal in a book kept by such corporation for the purpose. The officer of such corporation who sent said written notice shall in the same book state his proceedings relative thereto, setting forth a copy of said notice. Both of said statements shall be sworn to by such notary public and officer, respectively, before a justice of the peace, who shall make certificate thereof in said book.

§ 385:3. **Statement of proceedings as evidence.** Said written statements shall be prima facie evidence of the facts therein set forth in all proceedings at law and in equity wherein evidence of such facts would be competent. The provisions hereof shall not impair any right relative to such safes or boxes or their contents which such corporation would otherwise have.

§ 385:4. **Delivery to state.** At the expiration of five years after the removal of the contents of such safe or box, the corporation shall sell all the property or articles of value set out in said written statements at public auction, provided that a notice of the time and place of sale has been published once weekly for three consecutive weeks, the last such publication being no less than ten days before said public auction, in a newspaper published in the place where the sale is held, or having a general circulation in such place.

§ 385:5. **Disposition of proceeds.** From the proceeds of said sale the corporation shall deduct all its charges for rental up to the time of opening said box or safe, the cost of opening, further cost of safekeeping all its contents and any costs of said public auction and shall hold the net cash proceeds from such public auction subject to the provisions of RSA 471-A. The corporation shall maintain a statement of all charges deducted from the proceeds of said auction which shall be signed by the president, treasurer or superintendent of said corporation and verified before a notary public or justice of the peace.

NEW YORK

[N.Y. BANKING LAW]

§ 335. **Special remedies where rental of safe deposit box is not paid or when safe deposit box is not vacated on termination of lease.** Every lessor shall be entitled to the following special remedies:

1. (a) If the amount due for the rental of any safe deposit box let by any lessor shall not have been paid for one year, or if the lessee thereof shall not have removed the contents thereof within thirty days from the termination of the lease therefor for any reason other than for nonpayment of rent, the lessor may, at the expiration of such period, send to the lessee of such safe deposit box; by registered or certified mail, return receipt requested, a notice in writing in a securely closed postpaid letter, directed to such person at his last known post-office address, as recorded upon the books of the lessor, notifying such lessee that if the amount due for the rental of such safe deposit box is not paid within thirty days from date, and/or if the contents thereof are not removed within thirty days from date, the lessor may, at any time thereafter, cause such safe deposit box to be opened, and the contents thereof to be inventoried and removed from such safe deposit box.

(b) At any time after the expiration of thirty days from the date of mailing such notice, and the failure of the lessee of the safe deposit box to pay the amount due for the rental thereof to the date of payment, and/or remove the contents thereof, the lessor may, in the presence of a notary public and of any officer of the lessor or any other employee of the lessor designated for such purpose by the lessor, cause such safe deposit box to be opened, and the contents thereof, if any, to be removed and inventoried. Such contents shall be retained by the lessor for safe-keeping for a period of not less than two years unless sooner removed by the lessee of the safe deposit box so opened. The charge for such safe-keeping shall not exceed the original rental of the safe deposit box so opened. The notary public shall file with the lessor a certificate under seal, which shall fully set out the date of the opening of such safe deposit box, the name of the lessee of such safe deposit box and a list of the contents, if any.

o   o   o

§ 605.   Voluntary liquidation; sale of assets; forfeiture of charter by non-user. 1.   Any corporate banking organization, the assets of which have a value at least equal to its liabilities, exclusive of any liability to shareholders or stockholders, as such, may voluntarily wind up its affairs; but no banking organization of which the superintendent has taken possession in accordance with the provisions of section six hundred six of this chapter shall take any steps for such voluntary dissolution until it has received the written approval of the superintendent.

2.   To effect a voluntary dissolution a meeting of the stockholders or shareholders of any corporation shall be held upon not less than twenty days' written notice to each such stockholder or shareholder, either served personally or mailed to him at the address appearing upon the books of the corporation, and containing a statement of the purpose for which such meeting is called. Proof by affidavit of due service of such notice shall be filed in the office of the corporation before or at the time of such meeting.

In the case of a savings bank, a meeting of its board of trustees shall be held upon like notice. Proof by affidavit of due service of such notice shall be filed in the office of the savings bank before or at the time of such meeting.

3.   At such a meeting of stockholders or shareholders, such stockholders or shareholders may, by a vote of the owners of at least two-thirds in amount of the entire capital stock or capital of such corporation, direct that the corporation be closed and its business wound up. The proceedings of such meeting shall be entered in the minutes of such corporation.

At such a meeting of the board of trustees of a savings bank, the trustees may by vote of not less than two-thirds of their whole number, direct by resolution that the savings bank be closed and its business wound up. The vote on such resolution shall be recorded with the resolution in the minutes of the board of trustees.

A copy of the minutes of such meeting of stockholders or shareholders or board of trustees, verified by the presiding officer and by the secretary of such meeting, shall be filed in the office of the superintendent within five days after the date of such meeting.

4. Within three months after the date of any such meeting, application may be made to the supreme court, after due notice to the superintendent, for an order declaring the business of such corporation closed. In a proper case the court shall make such order which shall prescribe the notice to be given to creditors and depositors to present their claims to the corporation for payment. Within five days after the making of such order, a certified copy thereof shall be filed in the office of the superintendent. Upon the entry of such order such corporation shall cease to do business and shall wind up its affairs, pay its creditors and depositors, if any, and, except in the case of a savings bank, distribute any remaining assets among its shareholders or stockholders according to their respective rights and interests. Any petition, application, or motion to vacate, set aside, modify or amend such order so as to permit the corporation to resume business shall have incorporated therein a certificate of the superintendent certifying that after investigation the superintendent has found, and the banking board by a three-fifths vote of all its members has found, that the public convenience and advantage will be promoted by the granting of said petition, application or motion.

4-a. (a) Such corporation may, at any time after entry of the order described in subdivision four of this section, cause to be mailed to each person claiming to be, or appearing upon the books of such corporation to be

(1) the owner of any personal property in the custody or possession of such corporation as bailee or depositary for hire or otherwise, including the contents of any safe, vault or box theretofore opened for non-payment of rental in accordance with the provisions of this chapter, or

(2) the lessee of any safe, vault or box, a notice in writing directed by registered mail to such person at his last address as the same appears on the books of such corporation or at his last known address if no address appears on such books, notifying such person to remove all such property or the contents of any such safe, vault or box, within a period stated in said notice, which period shall be not less than sixty days from the date of such notice, and further notifying such person of the terms and provisions of this subdivision. The contract of bailment or of deposit for hire, or lease of safe, vault or box, if any, between the person to whom such notice is mailed and such corporation shall cease and determine upon the date for removal fixed in such notice. Such person shall have a claim against such corporation for the amount of the unearned rent or charges, if any, paid by such person from the date fixed in such notice, if the property or contents is removed on or before such date, or from the date of actual removal, if the property or contents is removed after such date.

(b) If such property or contents shall not be removed, and all rent or storage and other charges theretofore accrued, if any, shall not be paid, within the time fixed by such notice, such corporation shall, within thirty days thereafter, cause such property to be inventoried, or such safe, vault or box, or any package, parcel or receptacle in the custody or possession of such corporation as bailee or depositary for hire or otherwise, to be opened and the contents, if any, to be removed and inventoried, in the presence of an officer of such corporation and of a notary public, not an officer or employee thereof. Such property or contents shall thereupon be sealed up by such notary public in a package distinctly marked by him with the name of the person in whose name such property or such safe, vault, box, package, parcel or receptacle stands upon the books of such corporation, and a copy of the inventory of the property therein shall be certified and attached thereto by such notary public. Such package may be kept in such place as the corporation, with the approval of the superintendent, may determine, at the expense and risk of the person in whose name it stands until delivered to such person or until sold, destroyed or otherwise disposed of as hereinafter provided. Such package may, from time to time, pending final disposition of its contents, be opened in the presence of an officer of such corporation and of a notary public, not an officer or employee thereof, for inspection or appraisal, or to enable such corporation to exercise any of the powers conferred or duties imposed by this article. Whenever such package is opened, the notary shall endorse on the outside thereof the date of opening and re-sealing, and shall certify and attach thereto a list of the articles, if any, removed therefrom, or placed or replaced therein, and an affidavit of the officer in whose presence it was opened showing the reason for opening the same.

(c) At any time prior to the sale, destruction or other disposition of the contents thereof, the person in whose name such package stands may require the delivery thereof upon payment of all rental or storage charges accrued, and all other charges or expenses paid or incurred to the date of delivery with respect to such package or the contents thereof, including the cost of inventorying or of opening and inventorying, the fees of the notary public, the cost of preparing and mailing the notice, and advertising, if any. If the principal of, or interest, income, or dividends on any bonds, stock certificates, promissory notes, choses in action or other securities contained in such package, is or becomes due and payable while it is in the possession of such corporation, it may at its election collect such principal, interest, income or dividends, and from the proceeds thereof may deduct all such sums due for rental and other charges, until the time of such collection. The balance, if any, of the amount or amounts so collected shall be disposed of as hereafter in paragraph (e) of this subdivision and in subdivision five hereof provided.

    * * *

NORTH CAROLINA

[N.C. GEN. STAT.]

§ 53-43.7.   Safe-deposit boxes; unpaid rentals; procedure; escheats.
(a)   If the rental due on a safe-deposit box has not been paid for one year, the lessor may send a notice by registered mail to the last known address of the lessee stating that the safe-deposit box will be opened and its contents stored at the expense of the lessee unless payment of the rental is made within 30 days.   If the rental is not paid within 30 days from the mailing of the notice, the box may be opened in the presence of an officer of the lessor and of a notary public who is not a director, officer, employee or stockholder of the lessor.   The contents shall be sealed in a package by the notary public who shall write on the outside the name of the lessee and the date of the opening.   The notary public shall execute a certificate reciting the name of the lessee, the date of the opening of the box and a list of its contents.   The certificate shall be included in the package and a copy of the certificate shall be sent by registered mail to the last known address of the lessee.   The package shall then be placed in the general vaults of the lessor at a rental not exceeding the rental previously charged for the box.

(b)   Any documents or writings of a private nature, and having little or no apparent value need not be offered for sale, but shall be retained, unless claimed by the owner, for the period specified for unclaimed deposits, after which they may be destroyed.

(c)   If the contents of the safe-deposit box have not been claimed within two years of the mailing of the certificate, the lessor may send a further notice to the last known address of the lessee stating that, unless the accumulated charges are paid within 30 days, the contents of the box will be sold at public auction at a specified time and place, or, in the case of securities listed on a stock exchange, will be sold upon the exchange on or after a specified date and that unsalable items will be destroyed.   The time, place and manner of sale shall also be posted conspicuously on the premises of the lessor and advertised once in a newspaper of general circulation in the community.   If the articles are not claimed, they may then be sold in accordance with the notice.

(d)   The balance of the proceeds, after deducting accumulated charges, including the expense of advertising and conducting the sale, together with any money discovered in the box shall be deposited to the credit of the lessee in any account maintained by him, or if none, shall be deemed a deposit account with the bank or trust company operating the safe-deposit facility, or in the case of a subsidiary safe-deposit company, a bank or trust company owning stock therein, and shall be identified on the books of the bank as arising from the sale of contents of a safe-deposit box.   When any such deposit is surrendered as unclaimed deposits, the lessor shall also send to the Commissioner a copy of the certificate and an itemized statement of the amount received and the deductions. Any items remaining unsold may be destroyed.

(e) The deposits or proceeds from sales referred to in the preceding paragraph shall be subject to all the provisions of G.S. 116A-6, relating to the escheat of bank deposits.

(f) A copy of this section shall be printed on every contract for rental of a safe-deposit box.

PENNSYLVANIA

[PA. STAT. ANN.]

Tit. 71, § 733-724. Property in safe deposit vault or held for safekeeping. The secretary° may, any time after taking possession of an institution as receiver, give written notice to anyone claiming or appearing on the books of such institution to be the owner, or to be entitled to the possession, of any personal property left with such institution as bailee for safe-keeping or depository for hire, and to anyone appearing on the books of the institution to be the lessee of any safe, vault, or safe deposit box, notifying such bailor or lessee respectively, to remove all such personal property within the period fixed by the notice, provided that such period shall in no case be less than sixty days after the date of the notice.

At the expiration of such period if the lessee of a safe, vault, or safe deposit box has not removed the contents thereof, the secretary may cause such safe, vault, or safe deposit box to be opened either in his presence or in the presence of the deputy receiver of the institution, and in the presence of a notary public not an officer or employee of the institution or of the department. The contents, if any, of such safe, vault, or safe deposit box shall then be sealed and marked by such notary with the name and address of the lessee in whose name such safe, vault, or safe deposit box appeared on the books of the institution and with a list and description of the property therein. The secretary shall take such action as he shall deem desirable to safeguard such property until it is delivered to the owner or is otherwise disposed of in accordance with law.

The secretary shall follow the same procedure and have the same powers with regard to the property left with the institution as bailee for safe-keeping or depository for hire and not called for within the period specified by the notice.

The contract of bailment or lease, if any, shall be considered at an end upon the date designated by the secretary for the removal of the property therein. The amount of unearned rent or charges, if any, paid by the bailor or lessee, shall become a debt of the institution.

° "Secretary" is defined by PA. STAT. ANN. tit. 71, § 733-2 as The Secretary of Banking of this Commonwealth or his duly authorized deputy or representative.

SOUTH CAROLINA

[S.C. CODE ANN.]

§ 8-507. Opening box when rental one year in default. If the rental due on a safe-deposit box has not been paid for one year, the lessor may send a notice by registered mail to the last known address of the lessee stating that the safe-deposit box will be opened and its contents stored at the expense of the lessee unless payment of the rental is made within thirty days. If the rental is not paid within thirty days from the mailing of the notice, the box may be opened in the presence of an officer, manager or assistant manager of the lessor and of a notary public who is not a director, officer, employee or stockholder of the lessor. The contents shall be sealed in a package by the notary public who shall write on the outside the name of the lessee and the date of the opening. The notary public shall execute a certificate reciting the name of the lessee, the date of the opening of the box and a list of its contents. The certificate shall be included in the package and a copy of the certificate shall be sent by registered mail to the last known address of the lessee. The package shall then be placed in the general vaults of the lessor at a rental not exceeding the rental previously charged for the box.

TEXAS

[TEX. REV. CIV. STAT. ANN.]

Art. 342-906. Safety Deposit Boxes—° ° °—opening—lien—sale of content. Any state, national or private bank may maintain safety deposit boxes and rent the same. ° ° ° If the box rental is delinquent for six (6) months, the bank after at least sixty (60) days' notice by mail addressed to the lessee at his address on the books of the bank, may, if the rent is not paid within the time specified in said notice, open the box in the presence of two (2) executive officers of the bank and a notary public and place the content of the box in a sealed envelope or container bearing the name of the lessee. The bank shall then hold the content of the box subject to a lien for its rental, the cost of opening the box and the damages in connection therewith. If such rental, cost and damages are not paid within two (2) years from the date of opening of such box, the bank may sell any part or all of the content at public auction in like manner and upon like notice as is prescribed for the sale of real property under deed of trust.

VIRGINIA

[VA. CODE ANN.]

§ 6.1-334. Opening box; marking contents. Upon the expiration of sixty days from the date of mailing the notice required by § 6.1-331 and the failure within such period of time of the renter or lessee in whose name the safe or box stands on the books of the company, bank, trust company, or other corporation to pay the amount due for the rental thereof to the time of payment, together with legal interest thereon, the company, bank, trust company, or other corporation may, in the presence of a notary public not in its employ, and of its president or any vice-president, assistant secretary, assistant treasurer, secretary, treasurer, cashier or assistant cashier, cause such safe or box to be opened, and the contents thereof, if any, to be removed, inventoried and sealed up by such notary public in a package, upon which the notary shall distinctly mark the name of the renter or lessee in whose name the safe or box stood on the books of the company, bank, trust company or other corporation, and the date of removal of the property.

§ 6.1-335. **Disposition of contents.** When a package has been marked for identification by a notary public as required under the provisions of the preceding section (§ 6.1-334), it shall, in the presence of any one of the above-named officers of the company, bank, trust company or other corporation, be placed by the notary public in one of the general safes or boxes of the company, at a rental not to exceed the original rental of the safe or box which was opened, and shall remain in such general safe or box for a period of not less than two years, unless sooner removed by such renter or lessee.

§ 6.1-336. **Certificate of notary.** The notary public who shall have placed a package as required under the provisions of the preceding section (§ 6.1-335) shall thereupon file with the company a certificate, under seal, which shall fully set out the date of the opening of such safe or box, the name of the renter or lessee in whose name it stood and a list of the contents, if any. Such certificate shall be sworn to by such notary public and shall be prima facie evidence of the facts therein set forth in all proceedings at law and in equity wherein evidence of such facts would be competent. A copy of such certificate shall, within ten days thereafter, be mailed to the renter or lessee in whose name the safe or box so opened stood on the books of the company, bank, trust company, or other corporation, at his last known post-office address, in a securely closed, post-paid, registered letter, together with a notice that the contents will be kept, at the expense of such renter or lessee, in a general safe or box in the vaults of the company, bank, trust company, or other corporation, for a period of not less than two years, unless sooner removed by such renter or lessee.

§ 6.1-337. **Subsequent right of lessee to contents.** At any time after the mailing of such notice as is required by the preceding section (§ 6.1-336) and before the expiration of two years, such renter or lessee may require the delivery of the contents of the safe or box as shown by the certificate, upon the payment of all rentals due at the time of opening the safe or box, the cost of opening the safe or box, the fees of the notary public for issuing his certificate thereon, and the payment of all charges accrued during the period the contents remained in the general safe or box of the company, bank, trust company, or other corporation, together with legal interest on such rentals, costs, fees, and charges.

WASHINGTON

[WASH. REV. CODE ANN.]

§ 22.28.040.   Procedure when rent is unpaid.   If the amount due for the rental of any safe or box in the vaults of any safe deposit company shall not have been paid for one year, it may, at the expiration thereof, send to the person in whose name such safe or box stands on its books a notice in writing in a securely closed, postpaid and registered letter, directed to such person at his postoffice address, as recorded upon the books of the safe deposit company, notifying such person that if the amount due for the rental of such safe or box is not paid within thirty days from date, the safe deposit company will then cause such safe or box to be opened, and the contents thereof to be inventoried, sealed, and placed in one of its general safes or boxes.

Upon the expiration of thirty days from the date of mailing such notice, and the failure of the person in whose name the safe or box stands on the books of the company to pay the amount due for the rental thereof to the date of notice, the corporation may, in the presence of a notary public and of its president or secretary, cashier or treasurer, cause such safe or box to be opened, and the contents thereof, if any, to be removed, inventoried and sealed up by such notary public in a package, upon which the notary public shall distinctly mark the name of the person in whose name the safe or box stood on the books of the company, and the date of removal of the property, and when such package has been so marked for identification by the notary public, it shall, in the presence of the president, secretary, treasurer or cashier of the company, be placed by the notary public in one of the general safes or boxes of the company at a rental not to exceed the original rental of the safe or box which was opened, and shall remain in such general safe or box for a period of not less than two years, unless sooner removed by the owner thereof, and the notary public shall thereupon file with the company a certificate under seal, which shall fully set out the date of the opening of such safe or box, the name of the person in whose name it stood and a list of the contents, if any.

A copy of such certificates shall within ten days thereafter be mailed to the person in whose name the safe or box so opened stood on the books of the company, at his last known postoffice address, in a securely closed, postpaid and registered letter, together with a notice that the contents will be kept, at the expense of such person, in a general safe or box in the vaults of the company, for a period of not less than two years.   At any time after the mailing of such certificate and notice, and before the expiration of two years, such person may require the delivery of the contents of the safe as shown by said certificate, upon the payment of all rentals due at the time of opening of the safe or box, the cost of opening the box, the fees of the notary public for issuing his certificate thereon, and the payment of all further charges accrued during the period the contents remained in the general safe or box of the company.

After the expiration of two years from the time of mailing the certificate herein provided for, the company shall mail in a securely closed postpaid registered letter, addressed to such person at his last known postoffice address, a notice stating that two years have elapsed since the opening of the safe or box and the mailing of the certificate thereof, and that the company will sell all the property or articles of value set out in said certificate, at a time and place to be stated in such notice, not less than thirty days after the time of mailing such notice, and stating the amount which shall have then become due for rental up to the time of opening such safe, the cost of opening thereof, and the further cost of safekeeping all of its contents for the period since the opening of the safe or box. Unless such person shall pay on or before the day mentioned all said sums, and all the charges accruing to the time of payment, including advertising, the company may sell all the property or articles of value set out in said certificate, at public auction, at the time and place stated in said notice, provided a notice of the time and place of sale has been published once within ten days prior to the sale in a newspaper published in the county where the sale is held.

From the proceeds of the sale, the company shall deduct all its charges as stated in said notice, together with any further charges that shall have accrued since the mailing thereof, including reasonable expenses for notices, advertising, and sale. The balance, if any, of such proceeds shall be deposited by the company within thirty days after the receipt of the same, with the county treasurer, of the county where the sale was held. The company shall file with such deposit a certificate stating the name and last known place of residence of the owner of the property sold, the articles sold, the price obtained therefor, and showing that the notices herein required were duly mailed and that the sale was advertised as required herein. The officer with whom such balance is deposited shall credit the same to the owner of the property, and pay the same to such owner, his assignee, or legal representative, on demand and satisfactory evidence of identity. If such balance remains in the possession of such officer for a period of ten years, unclaimed by the person legally entitled thereto, it shall be transferred to the state treasurer for the benefit of the permanent school fund of the state of Washington.

§ 22.28.060. Destruction of paper contents—Other remedies available. Whenever the contents of any such safe or box, so opened, shall consist either wholly or in part, of documents or letters or other papers of a private nature, such documents, letters, or papers shall not be sold, but shall be retained by the company for a period of five years from the time of the opening of the box, and, unless sooner claimed by the owner, may be thereafter destroyed in the presence of an officer of the corporation and a notary public not an officer or employee of the corporation.

The provision of this section shall not preclude any other remedy by action or otherwise now existing for the enforcement of the claims of a corporation against the person in whose name such safe or box stood, nor bar the right of a safe deposit company to recover so much of the debt due it as shall not be paid by the proceeds of the sale of the property deposited with it.

DIVISION THREE:
OATHS; ACKNOWLEDGMENT; DEPOSITION; COMMERCIAL PAPER (U.C.C.)

CHAPTER 11   OATHS AND AFFIDAVITS
CHAPTER 12   ACKNOWLEDGMENTS
CHAPTER 13   DEPOSITIONS
CHAPTER 14   COMMERCIAL PAPER (UNDER U.C.C.)
CHAPTER 15   COMMISSIONERS OF DEEDS

CHAPTER 11: OATHS AND AFFIDAVITS

OATHS

§ 11.1   General.

An oath is an outward pledge, given by the person taking it, that his attestation or promise is made under an immediate sense of his responsibility to God for the truth of what is stated or the faithful performance of what is undertaken.

341

An affirmation is a solemn declaration without oath. Generally, the term "oath" includes an affirmation, and whenever an oath is required or authorized by law, an affirmation may be taken in lieu of an oath by any person having conscientious scruples against taking an oath. The statutes in most states and other jurisdictions provide that an affirmation has the same force and effect as an oath.

See also the definitions in the Glossary, page 853.

§ 11.2   Manner of administering.

The form of administering an oath may be varied to conform to the religious belief of the individual, so as to make it binding on his conscience. One form consists of the person taking the oath or affirmation holding up his right hand while the officer repeats to him the words of the oath, which begins, "You do solemnly swear that ° ° °" and ends "so help you God" or "this you do as you shall answer unto God."

In the case of an affirmation, the officer's statement begins, "You do solemnly, sincerely and truly affirm and declare that ° ° °" and ends "this you do under the pains and penalties of perjury." The person being sworn or affirmed then gives an affirmative answer.

In the case of a public official taking an oath of office, a Christian may place his right hand on the Holy Bible, instead of raising his hand while the words are repeated by the officer administering the oath. A Jewish person should be sworn on the Old Testament; a Mohammedan on the Koran.

Occasionally these matters are specified in the state and other jurisdiction statutes. See Authority and Duties: State and Other Statutes, page 127.

§ 11.3   Forms of oath.

In addition to, and between, the introductory and closing clauses, the oath may contain a statement such as: "That the various matters and things set forth in this paper which you have here signed before me are true"; or "that the statements contained in the pleading you have just heard read are true"; or "that you will faithfully and diligently perform your duties as director of the —————— Company."

The form of oath which is ordinarily administered to a witness whose deposition is to be taken is as follows: "You do solemnly swear that you will testify the truth, the whole truth, and nothing but the truth in the deposition you are about to give in the case now pending in the —————— Court, wherein A B is plaintiff and C D is defendant, and this you do as you shall answer to God."

A common form of oath administered to a witness during a trial is: "You do solemnly swear that the evidence you are about to give in the cause now here pending shall be the truth, the whole truth, and nothing but the truth, so help you God."

The ordinary form of oath of office is as follows: "You do solemnly swear that you will support the Constitution of the United States, the constitution of the state of ——————, and that you will faithfully discharge the duties of the office of ——————, during the term for which you have been elected (or, appointed), so help you God."

§ 11.4 Who may administer.

In nearly every state and other jurisdiction the statutes authorize a notary public to administer an oath. In cases in which, under the laws of the United States, oaths are authorized or required to be administered, they may be administered by, among others, notaries public duly appointed in any state, district, territory, or possession of the United States.[1]

---

[1] See Authority and Duties: State and Other Statutes, 5 U.S.C. § 2903.

AFFIDAVITS

§ 11.5   General.

An affidavit is a declaration reduced to writing, signed by the affiant, and sworn to before an officer authorized by law to administer oaths. An affidavit is generally given or taken without notice to an adverse party, and without cross-examination, differing in this and other respects from a deposition.[2]

An affiant, occasionally called a deponent, is the person who swears or affirms that the matters contained in the affidavit are true.[3]

§ 11.6   Component parts.

An affidavit consists of: (1) the caption, which may include the title and venue; (2) the body of the affidavit, which includes the introductory statement and the allegations; and (3) the conclusion, being the signatures, seal and jurat.

§ 11.7   The caption.

In an affidavit which is not to be used in any proceeding in court, no title need be given. If, however, an affidavit is to be used in court, the title must show the court in which it is to be used, the names of the parties to the suit, the file number of the suit, and it must generally conform to the captions on pleadings, motions, and orders.

The venue, or name of the state and county where the affidavit is taken, must never be omitted. It precedes the body of the affidavit and fixes the place where the affidavit is made, to show that it is within the jurisdiction of the officer. The letters "ss." or "sct." frequently added to the venue, have no legal significance and are not essential.

---

[2] See Depositions, page 543.

[3] See also Glossary, page 853.

§ 11.8   Introductory statement.

The body of the affidavit usually begins with a formal statement, such as "Before me, G H, a notary public in and for said county, personally came E F, who, being duly sworn according to law, deposes and says that ° ° °." If desired, the phrase "authorized by law to administer oaths" may be inserted after the word "County." The affidavit may begin with a more simple introductory statement, such as, "E F, being duly sworn, says that ° ° °." Another form is, "E F, being first duly sworn, makes this his affidavit and states: ° ° °."

Where an agent or attorney makes an affidavit, it must expressly state that the affiant is such agent or attorney. One correct way is to say, "E F, being duly sworn, says that he is the agent of A B"; it is incorrect to begin the affidavit, "E F, agent of A B, being duly sworn, says that." Similarly, an affidavit for a partnership in proof of a claim due the partnership must be sworn by one of the partners as agent for the firm. Such an affidavit could begin: "E F, being duly sworn, says that he is a member of the firm of ————— Company."

Where it is necessary to show the residence of the affiant, the place of his residence should not be added as a matter of description to his name; instead the locality should be expressly stated and verified.

§ 11.9   Allegations.

The affiant's allegations may be classified as positive and not positive. Positive allegations are those that state facts and not opinions, and are not modified by any such phrase as "to the best of affiant's knowledge and belief," or "as he verily believes."

Allegations which are not positive may be described as: (1) allegations made upon knowledge and belief; (2) upon information and belief; or (3) upon belief.

It is common practice for the affiant to add, at the close of his statements the words, "to the best of his knowledge and belief," even when the matters stated are not merely matters of opinion but are clearly within his own knowledge, and could be positively averred, lest he might unwittingly make oath to an untruth by reason of the infirmity of his memory.

It is customary in some jurisdictions to close the allegations with the words "and further saith not," or "and further affiant saith not."

§ 11.10 Signatures.

Even in the absence of an express statutory requirement, the affiant should sign his name to the affidavit at the close of the allegations made by him.

To complete an affidavit taken before a notary public, it is essential that the notary sign his name thereto and comply with the various formalities specified by the appropriate statutes.

§ 11.11 Jurat.

The jurat is that part of an affidavit in which the notary states that it was sworn to before him.[4] The omission of words such as "before me," in the jurat may void the affidavit. A common form for the jurat is: "Sworn to before me and subscribed in my presence this ————— day of —————, 19 ——." Shorter forms, such as: "Subscribed and sworn to before me this [date]," are acceptable.

§ 11.12 Seal.

In most states requiring the notary public to have an official seal, he must further attest the affidavit by affixing his seal.[5]

---

[4] See also the definition in Glossary, page 859.

[5] See Seal: State and Other Statutes, page 862.

§ 11.13 General forms of affidavits.

State of ———,

County of ———, Sct.

E F, after being first duly sworn, makes this his affidavit and states: [allegations].

This [date]

[Signature of affiant]

The foregoing was subscribed and sworn to before me by E F this [date].

(SEAL)

G H, Notary Public

My commission expires [date].

Alternate Form

State of ———,

County of ———, ss.

E F, being first duly sworn, says that ——— [allegations.]

Sworn to before me and subscribed in my presence by E F this ——— day of ———, 19 ——.

(SEAL)

G H, Notary Public

My commission expires [date].

§ 11.14 Specimen form of affidavit in legal proceeding.

In the ——— Court of ———

Case No. ———

A B, Plaintiff

v.

C D, Defendant

Affidavit of E F

State of ————,

County of ————, Sct.

E F, being first duly sworn, makes this his affidavit and states: [allegations].

And further affiant saith not.

[Signature of affiant]

The foregoing was subscribed and sworn to before me by E F this ————— day of —————, 19——.

(SEAL)

G H, Notary Public

My commission expires [date].

§ 11.15   Before whom affidavits made.

When an affidavit is made in the state or other jurisdiction where it is to be used, it may be made before a notary public within the limits of his jurisdiction.[6] Usually, the statutes also authorize the following officers to take affidavits in the jurisdiction where they are to be used: justice of the peace, mayor, clerk of court, judge of any court of record, and court commissioner.

When an affidavit is made within the United States, but out of the jurisdiction where it is to be used, it may be made before a notary public in a majority of the states and other jurisdictions. The statutes also permit such affidavit to be taken by a commissioner of the state where it is to be used, or by anyone authorized to administer oaths or take depositions.[7]

When the affidavit is made out of the United States, it may usually be made before a notary public. The statutes of many states and other jurisdictions also authorize the following officers to take such affidavits: ambassador of the United States, consul, and consular agent.

---

[6] See Authority and Duties: State and Other Statutes, page 127.

[7] See Commissioners of Deeds, page 725.

CHAPTER 12: ACKNOWLEDGMENTS

ESSENTIAL REQUISITES

STATUTORY PROVISIONS AND FORMS
ESSENTIAL REQUISITES

§ 12.1 General.

Acknowledgment is a formal declaration before a public officer, by the person who has signed an instrument, that it is his or her voluntary act and deed. The term also includes the written certificate of the officer, as to the act of acknowledgment, upon the same sheet as the instrument or attached thereto. Acknowledgment must be distinguished from attestation, which is merely the act of witnessing the execution of a paper and subscribing one's name thereto as a witness.

349

The purpose of acknowledgment is to entitle the instrument to record, and to provide official evidence of its execution.[1]

§ 12.2   Instruments requiring acknowledgment.

An instrument need not be acknowledged unless required by statute, because acknowledgment was unknown to the common law. The statutory provisions of each state or other jurisdiction must be consulted to determine what particular instruments require acknowledgment.[2] Some idea of the scope of such statutes will be gained from the following list of instruments which, under the laws of various states, must be acknowledged: deeds, mortgages, land contracts and leases of any interest in real property; powers of attorney to convey, mortgage or lease the same; satisfactions and releases of mortgages, when not made on the original mortgage or on the margin of the record thereof; plats of towns, additions and subdivisions; deeds of sheriffs, master commissioners, and other officers selling real property in pursuance of an order of court; written agreements of owners of adjoining lands fixing the corners or boundary lines; certificates of limited partnerships; trade-marks of timber dealers.

Some statutes provide that certain instruments need not be acknowledged; for example, leases for a short term, releases of mortgages when made on the original mortgage, security agreements, and financing statements.

§ 12.3   Officers authorized to take.

Acknowledgments can be taken only by those officers specifically authorized by statute. Three different situations are recognized in the statutory provisions of most states and other jurisdictions, designating in separate lists what officers may take acknowledgments (1) within the state,

---

[1] For the definition of acknowledgment, see *Glossary*, page 853.

[2] See *Acknowledgments: State and Other Statutes*, below.

(2)elsewhere in the United States, and (3) outside the United States.[3] A notary public, among others, has authority under the laws of virtually every state and other jurisdiction to take acknowledgments in the three situations. Other officers frequently authorized by the various statutes are: justices of the peace, magistrates, mayors, judges of courts of record, clerks of courts, commissioners of deeds,[4] and consuls.

§ 12.4 Disqualification of officer.

The fact that the notary public is related to one of the parties signing the instrument does not usually disqualify him from taking the signer's acknowledgment. If, however, the notary is interested as grantor or grantee, or has some financial interest in the transaction, he is disqualified.

Several states have enacted laws permitting a notary public who is a stockholder, director, officer, or employee of a bank, savings and loan association, or other corporation to take the acknowledgment of any party to any written instrument to or by such corporation, provided such notary is not a party to the instrument, either individually or as a representative of the corporation.

§ 12.5 Manner of taking acknowledgment.

Before taking the acknowledgment of the person who is signing a deed or other instrument, a notary public should read to himself the certificate of acknowledgment. By doing this, he will be reminded of his responsibility to act only within the locality for which he has been appointed, and he also will be aware of the necessity of knowing the signer and having the signer personally appear before him. In addition, the wording of the certificate of acknowledgment will enable the notary to know what to say to the signer.

---

[3] See statutory provisions for each state, below.

[4] See Commissioners of Deeds, page 725.

After asking the signer to raise his right hand and be sworn, the notary ordinarily says: "Do you acknowledge the signing of this instrument to be your voluntary act and deed?" The signer should respond "I do" before the notary completes the certificate of acknowledgment by inserting the date, signing his name at the end of the certificate, affixing his notarial seal, and stating the date when his commission expires where that is required by law.

Some notaries have been tempted to accommodate various persons by taking acknowledgments over the telephone. Such a practice is hazardous, and should be scrupulously avoided. A majority of states and other jurisdictions hold that acknowledgments via telephone are invalid.[5] The pertinent statutes usually require the personal presence of the party "before" the officer taking the acknowledgment, and an acknowledgment given by a person via telephone when he or she is not in fact "before" or in the presence of the officer, is therefore void.[6] A notary's official acts as directed by legislation are not insignificant formalities "which may be smiled out of the law."[7] It has been held that a signing, which is not in fact acknowledged before the notary, is not properly executed, is not entitled to be recorded, and the recording in fact does not constitute constructive notice to a subsequent mortgagee.[8] "A notary public who affixes his name and seal to an acknowledgment or affidavit which states that the parties appeared before him when in effect they did not do so is himself making an untrue statement which may be followed by both civil and criminal liability," said the Court.[9]

---

[5] Charlton v. Richard Gill Co., 285 S.W.2d 801 (Tex. Civ. App. 1955).

[6] 1 C.J.S. Acknowledgment § 68 (1936 and supp.).

[7] Charlton v. Richard Gill Co., supra n. 5.

[8] Citizens Nat'l Bank v. Denison, 165 Ohio St. 89, 133 N.E.2d 329, 59 OhioOp. 96 (1956).

[9] Id. See also United States Auto. Ass'n v. Ratterree, 512 S.W.2d 30 (Tex. Civ. App. 1974) (oath to interrogatories), and In re Heaney,

§ 12.6   Corporate acknowledgment.

Corporate officers should swear that they are officers of the corporation; that the seal affixed to the instrument they have just signed is the seal of the corporation; that they have signed and sealed the instrument on behalf of the corporation and by authority of its board of directors; and that the signing of the instrument is their free act and deed individually and as such officers, and the free and corporate act of the corporation.

§ 12.7   Certificate of acknowledgment.

The certificate should be written on the same sheet with the instrument acknowledged. This requirement is mandatory under the laws of a number of states, although a few states allow it to be on a separate paper, attached to the instrument. In both printed forms and typewritten documents the certificate follows immediately after the signatures to be acknowledged.

§ 12.8   —Component parts.

The officer's certificate of acknowledgment may be analyzed as consisting of the following parts:

(1)   Venue, or statement of locality;

(2)   Body of certificate, which states:
    (a)   Introductory clause
    (b)   Date when acknowledged
    (c)   Name and identity of officer
    (d)   Presence of grantor
    (e)   Name of grantor
    (f)   Officer's knowledge of grantor's identity
    (g)   Voluntary nature of acknowledgment

---

75 Misc.2d 732, 347 N.Y.S.2d 922 (Nassau County Sur. Ct. 1973), aff'd mem., 44 App. Div. 2d 828, 355 N.Y.S.2d 569 (1974) (attesting witness to a will).

(3)   Testimonium clause

(4)   Officer's signature

(5)   Seal of officer

(6)   Date of expiration of officer's commission

§ 12.9   —General form.

With the exception of those states which have adopted the Uniform Acknowledgment Act, few states prescribe a form of certificate.   The figures and letters in parentheses in the following general form have been inserted only for the purpose of identifying the component parts as outlined in the preceding section.

(1)   State of ――――,

County of ――――, ss.

(2)   *(a)* Be it remembered that *(b)* on the ―――― day of ――――, 19 ―, *(c)* before me, G H, a notary public in and for said county, *(d)* personally came and appeared *(e)* A B, C D and E D, the grantors in the foregoing deed *(f)* to me known to be the same persons described in and who executed the foregoing instrument, *(g)* and acknowledged the signing thereof to be their voluntary act and deed, for the uses and purposes therein mentioned.

(3)   In testimony whereof, I have hereunto subscribed my name and affixed my notarial seal, on the day and year last above mentioned.

(4)   G H, Notary Public

(5)   (SEAL)

(6)   My commission expires ―――― (date).

§ 12.10   —Venue.

The state and county where the acknowledgment is made should appear at the beginning of each certificate.   It is then presumed that the officer acted within that locality.   This statement is important by reason of the fact that an acknowledgment can be taken by an officer only within the locality for which he has been appointed.

§ 12.11 —Introductory clause.

The phrase, "Be it remembered that," is of no legal significance and can be omitted if desired.

§ 12.12 —Date.

The date when the acknowledgment is taken should always be given in the certificate. It generally is the same as the date of signing the instrument. The date of acknowledgment cannot be earlier than the day of execution of the instrument.

There is no reason why an instrument may not be acknowledged years after its execution, or at different times and places by various grantors. If several persons acknowledge before the same officer, but on different days, he can state the facts as follows:

"Before me, G H, a notary public in and for said county, on the first day of June, 19 ——, personally came A B and C D, two of the grantors in the foregoing deed, and on the third day of June, 19 ——, personally came E D, another of said grantors."

§ 12.13 Name and identity of officer.

The certificate should contain the name and title of the officer before whom the acknowledgment is taken, together with a reference to the locality within which he is authorized to act. The words "in and for said county," or "within and for said county," are sufficient if the state and county are named in the venue at the beginning of the certificate.

§ 12.14 —Presence of grantor.

It is essential that the grantor personally appear before the notary public at the time of acknowledging the instrument. Acknowledgments should not be taken over a telephone. An officer who falsely certifies that a person has appeared before him, when in fact he has not, is guilty of misconduct and becomes liable on his bond.[10]

§ 12.15 —Name of grantor.

Usually, all the acknowledging grantors should be named in the certificate of acknowledgment. The name of the wife of each grantor should likewise be included, even if she joins in the execution of the deed for the sole purpose of relinquishing her right of dower. Care should be exercised that the name of the grantor as it appears in the certificate is the same as that in the instrument being acknowledged. Furthermore, the certificate should identify the party by showing that it was the grantor or other signer of the instrument who acknowledged it. A phrase such as "the grantors in the foregoing deed," or "the parties to the within lease," may be used immediately after the names of the parties in order to accomplish this purpose.

§ 12.16 —Knowledge of identity.

The certificate uniformly must state that the signer is known to the officer, or has been proved to him to be the person who signed. The phrase "known to me" or "proved to me on the oath of ———" precedes the general statement, "to be the same person whose name is subscribed to the foregoing instrument." It is not enough for the officer to say that he is "satisfied" as to the identity.

§ 12.17 —Voluntary nature of acknowledgment.

The fact that the person who has signed the instrument also acknowledges it must be stated in the certificate. The usual phrases are "acknowledged that he executed the same as his free act and deed," or "acknowledged the signing

---

[10] Concerning acknowledgments over the telephone, see § 12.5, above.

thereof to be his voluntary act and deed." Failure to include such statement will render the acknowledgment invalid.

In some states it is necessary to add the words "for the uses and purposes therein mentioned."[11]

§ 12.18　—Married woman.

Formerly, when a married woman was a party to a deed, the laws of some states required that the officer examine her separate and apart from her husband. Where this examination was required, the certificate had to show that, upon being examined separate and apart from her husband, and the contents of the instrument being explained to her, she declared that she signed and acknowledged the same voluntarily, and was still satisfied therewith.

Today, in virtually every state, however, a wife need not be examined separately.[12]

§ 12.19　—Testimonium clause.

The certificate of acknowledgment frequently contains a statement by the officer that the signature and seal to his certificate are his signature and seal. Instead of the long sentence, "In testimony whereof, I have hereunto subscribed my name and affixed my notarial seal, on the day and year last above mentioned," one of the following brief statements is often used: "Witness my hand and seal of office;" "Given under my hand and seal this —————— day of ——————, 19 ——;" or simply "Before me."

The forms of acknowledgments in a number of states omit the testimonium clause as being unnecessary.

§ 12.20　—Officer's signature.

The notary public must sign his name at the end of the certificate of acknowledgment. His mere personal signa-

---

[11] See Acknowledgments: State and Other Statutes, below.

[12] See Acknowledgments: State and Other Statutes, below.

ture is not sufficient; the words "Notary Public" should be added to his name. If the description of the officer in the body of the certificate has not already stated his locality, it is proper to sign, "G H, Notary Public, in and for ————— County, State of —————." The omission of the officer's signature renders the certificate of acknowledgment void.

§ 12.21   —Seal of officer.

Custom generally, and the statutes or decisions in many of the states, require that the certificate of acknowledgment should be authenticated by the officer's seal, if he be required by law to have a seal. In view of the well-known principle of law that a notary's seal proves itself, he should affix his seal to every acknowledgment taken by him.

§ 12.22   —Date of expiration of commission.

In those states which by statute require a notary public to add to his certificate the date of the expiration of his commission, a certificate of acknowledgment must conclude with the statement: "My commission expires ————— (date)."

§ 12.23   Authentication of officer's authority.

Unless required by a particular statute, no certificate of authentication need accompany an acknowledgment made before a notary public of another state, attested by his official seal.

When a justice of the peace, mayor, or similar officer takes the acknowledgment of a deed to land outside of his own state, there often must be affixed to his certificate of acknowledgment a certificate of the clerk of the court of his county, under the seal of the court, as to the official capacity of such justice or mayor, that he is authorized by law to take acknowledgments, that the clerk is acquainted with the handwriting of such justice, and that the signature to the certificate of acknowledgment is that of such justice.

§ 12.24   Proving deeds.

It is lawful and customary in some states and other jurisdictions to prove deeds as an alternative to acknowledging them. One or more of the subscribing witnesses goes before an officer authorized to administer oaths, and makes an affidavit that the grantor executed and acknowledged the instrument in the presence of the affiant and the other witness. The officer then prepares a certificate of this oath on the deed in the same manner as a certificate of acknowledgment is made. In some states this procedure is called probating the deed.

STATUTORY PROVISIONS AND FORMS

UNIFORM ACKNOWLEDGMENT ACT
TABLE OF JURISDICTIONS AND CITATIONS

Jurisdiction:	Local Citation:
Arizona	ARIZ. REV. STAT. ANN. §§ 33-511 to 33-516
Arkansas	ARK. STAT. ANN. §§ 49-101 to 49-114
Connecticut	CONN. GEN. STAT. ANN. §§ 1-28 to 1-41
Maryland	MD. ANN. CODE art. 18, §§ 1 to 14
New Hampshire	N.H. REV. STAT. ANN. §§ 456:1 to 456:15
Pennsylvania	PA. STAT. ANN. tit. 21, §§ 291.1 to 291.13
South Dakota	S.D. COMPILED LAWS ANN. §§ 18-5-1 to 18-5-18
Virgin Islands	V.I. CODE ANN. tit. 28, §§ 81 to 93. For selected portions of the act, as modified and adopted in the Virgin Islands, see *Acknowledgments*, V.I. CODE ANN. tit. 28, §§ 82 *et seq.*
Wisconsin	WIS. STAT. ANN. § 706.07

§ 1. **Acknowledgment of Instruments.** Any instrument may be acknowledged in the manner and form now provided by the laws of this State, or as provided by this Act.

§ 2. **Acknowledgment Within the State.** The acknowledgment of any instrument may be made in this State before: (1) A Judge of a court of record; (2) A Clerk or Deputy Clerk of a court having a seal; (3) A Commissioner or Register (or Recorder) of Deeds; (4) A Notary Public; (5) A Justice of the Peace; or (6) A Master in Chancery or Register in Chancery; (7) A duly licensed attorney at law.

§ 3. Acknowledgment Within the United States. The acknowledgment of any instrument may be made without the State but within the United States or a territory or insular possession of the United States and within the jurisdiction of the officer, before: (1) A Clerk or Deputy Clerk of any federal court; (2) A Clerk or Deputy Clerk of any court of record of any State or other jurisdiction; (3) A Notary Public; (4) A Commissioner of Deeds; (5) Any person authorized by the laws of such other jurisdiction to take acknowledgments.

§ 4. Acknowledgment Without the United States. The acknowledgment of any instrument may be made without the United States before: (1) An Ambassador, Minister, Charge d'Affaires, Counselor to or Secretary of a Legation, Consul General, Consul, Vice-Consul, Commercial Attache, or Consular Agent of the United States accredited to the country where the acknowledgment is made. (2) A Notary Public of the country where the acknowledgment is made. (3) A Judge or Clerk of a court of record of the country where the acknowledgment is made.

§ 5. Requisites of Acknowledgment. The officer taking the acknowledgment shall know or have satisfactory evidence that the person making the acknowledgment is the person described in and who executed the instrument.

§ 6. Acknowledgment by a Married Woman. An acknowledgment of a married woman may be made in the same form as though she were unmarried.

§ 7. Forms of Certificates. An officer taking the acknowledgment shall endorse thereon or attach thereto a certificate substantially in one of the following forms:

(1) By individuals:

State of ———

County of ———

On this the — day of ———, 19—, before me, ———, the undersigned officer, personally appeared ———, known to me (or satisfactorily proven) to be the person whose name ——— subscribed to the within instrument and acknowledged that ——— he ——— executed the same for the purposes therein contained.

In witness whereof I hereunto set my hand and official seal.

———

Title of Officer.

(2) By a Corporation:

State or ———

County of ———

On this the — day of ———, 19—, before me, ———, the

undersigned officer, personally appeared ———, who acknowledged himself to be the ——— of ———, corporation, and that he, as such ———, being authorized so to do, executed the foregoing instrument for the purposes therein contained, by signing the name of the corporation by himself as ———.

In witness whereof I hereunto set my hand and official seal.

————————
Title of Officer.

(3)   By an Attorney in Fact:

State of ———

County of ———

On this the — day of ———, 19—, before me, ———, the undersigned officer, personally appeared ———, known to me (or satisfactorily proven) to be the person whose name is subscribed as attorney in fact for ———, and acknowledged that he executed the same as the act of his principal for the purposes therein contained.

In witness whereof I hereunto set my hand and official seal.

————————
Title of Officer.

(4)   By any Public Officer or Deputy thereof, or by any Trustee, Administrator, Guardian, or Executor:

State of ———

County of ———

On this the — day of ———, 19—, before me, ———, the undersigned officer, personally appeared ———, of the State (County or City as the case may be) of ———, known to me (or satisfactorily proven) to be the person described in the foregoing instrument, and acknowledged that he executed the same in the capacity therein stated and for the purposes therein contained.

In witness whereof I hereunto set my hand and official seal.

————————
Title of Officer.

§ 8.   **Execution of Certificate.**   The certificate of the acknowledging officer shall be completed by his signature, his official seal if he has one, the title of his office, and if he is a Notary Public, the date his commission expires.

§ 9.   **Authentication of Acknowledgments.**

(1)   If the acknowledgment is taken within this State or is made without the United States by an officer of the United States no authentication shall be necessary.

(2) If the acknowledgment is taken without this State, but in the United States, or a territory or insular possession of the United States, the certificate shall be authenticated by a certificate as to the official character of such officer, executed, if the acknowledgment is taken by a Clerk or Deputy Clerk of a court, by the presiding judge of the court or, if the acknowledgment is taken by a Notary Public, or any other person authorized to take acknowledgments, by a Clerk of a Court of Record of the County, Parish or District in which the acknowledgment is taken. The signature to such authenticating certificate may be a facsimile printed, stamped, photographed or engraved thereon when the certificate bears the seal of the authenticating officer. A Judge or Clerk authenticating an acknowledgment shall endorse thereon or attach thereto a certificate in substantially the following form:

State of ———

County of ———

I ——— [judge or clerk] of the ——— in and for said county, which court is a court of record, having a seal, do hereby certify that ———, by and before whom the foregoing [or annexed] acknowledgment was taken, was at the time of taking the same a notary public [or other officer] residing [or authorized to act] in said county, and was authorized by the laws of said state to take and certify acknowledgments in said state, and, further, that I am acquainted with his handwriting and that I believe that the signature to the certificate of acknowledgment is genuine.

In testimony whereof I have hereunto set my hand and affixed the seal of the court this — day of ———, 19—.

(3) If the acknowledgment is taken without the United States and by a Notary Public or a Judge or Clerk of a Court of Record of the country where the acknowledgment is made, the certificate shall be authenticated by a certificate under the Great Seal of State of the country, affixed by the custodian of such Seal, or by a certificate of a diplomatic, consular or commercial officer of the United States accredited to that country, certifying as to the official character of such officer.

§ 10. **Acknowledgments Under Laws of Other States.** Notwithstanding any provision in this Act contained the acknowledgment of any instrument without this State in compliance with the manner and form prescribed by the laws of the place of its execution, if in a State, a Territory or insular possession of the United States, or in the District of Columbia, verified by the official seal of the officer before whom it is acknowledged, and authenticated in the manner provided by section 9 (subsection 2) hereof, shall have the same effect as an acknowledgment in the manner and form prescribed by the laws of this State for instruments executed within the State [except where the instrument is a deed by which a resident of this

State purports to convey his homestead in this State and the deed is not additionally acknowledged in the form prescribed by the law of this State for the validity of a conveyance of a homestead].

§ 11. **Acknowledgments by Persons Serving in or With the Armed Forces of the United States or their Dependents, Within or Without the United States.** In addition to the acknowledgment of instruments in the manner and form and as otherwise authorized by this Act, persons serving in or with the armed forces of the United States or their dependents, wherever located, may acknowledge the same wherever located before any commissioned officer in active service of the armed forces of the United States with the rank of Second Lieutenant or higher in the Army, Air Force, or Marine Corps, or Ensign or higher in the Navy or Coast Guard. The instrument shall not be rendered invalid by the failure to state therein the place of execution or acknowledgment. No authentication of the officer's certificate of acknowledgment shall be required but the officer taking the acknowledgment shall indorse thereon or attach thereto a certificate substantially in the following form:

On this the — day of ———, 19—, before me, ———, the undersigned officer, personally appeared ———, Serial No. (if any) ———, known to me (or satisfactorily proved) to be (serving in or with the armed forces of the United States) (a dependent of ———, Serial No. (if any) ———, a person serving in or with the armed forces of the United States) and to be the person whose name is subscribed to the within instrument and acknowledged that ——— he ——— executed the same for the purposes therein contained. And the undersigned does further certify that he is at the date of this certificate a commissioned officer of the rank stated below and is in the active service of the armed forces of the United States.

———————————

Signature of the Officer.

———————————

Rank and Serial No. of
Officer and Command to
which attached.

[§ 12. **Acknowledgments Not Affected by This Act.**] No acknowledgment heretofore taken shall be affected by anything contained herein.

[§ 13. **Uniformity of Interpretation.**] This Act shall be so interpreted as to make uniform the laws of those States which enact it.

[§ 14. **Name of Act.**] This Act may be cited as the Uniform Acknowledgment Act.

[§ 15. **Time of Taking Effect.**] This Act shall take effect ———.

UNIFORM RECOGNITION OF ACKNOWLEDGMENTS ACT
TABLE OF JURISDICTIONS AND CITATIONS

Jurisdiction:	Local Citation:
Arizona	ARIZ. REV. STAT. ANN. §§ 33-501 to 33-508
Colorado	COLO. REV. STAT. ANN. §§ 12-55-201 to 12-55-210
Connecticut	CONN. GEN. STAT. ANN. §§ 1-57 to 1-65
Illinois	ILL. ANN. STAT. ch. 30, §§ 221 to 230 (Smith-Hurd)
Kansas	KAN. STAT. ANN. §§ 53-301 to 53-309
Kentucky	KY. REV. STAT. ANN. §§ 423.110 to 423.190
Maine	ME. REV. STAT. ANN. tit. 4, §§ 1011 to 1019
Michigan	MICH. COMP. LAWS ANN. §§ 565.261 to 565.269
Minnesota	MINN. STAT. ANN. §§ 358.32 to 358.40
Nebraska	NEB. REV. STAT. §§ 64-201 to 64-209
New Hampshire	N.H. REV. STAT. ANN. §§ 456-A:1 to 456-A:9
North Dakota	N.D. CENT. CODE §§ 47-19-14.1 to 47-19-14.8
Ohio	OHIO REV. CODE ANN. §§ 147.51 to 147.57 (Page)
Oklahoma	OKLA. STAT. ANN. tit. 49, §§ 101 to 109
South Carolina	S.C. CODE ANN. §§ 49-61 to 49-69
Virginia	VA. CODE ANN. §§ 55-118.1 to 55-118.9
West Virginia	W. VA. CODE ANN. §§ 39-1A-1 to 39-1A-9
Wisconsin	WIS. STAT. ANN. § 706.065

§ 1. **Recognition of Notarial Acts Performed Outside This State.** —For the purposes of this Act "notarial acts" means acts which the laws and regulations of this State authorize notaries public of this State to perform, including the administering of oaths and affirmations, taking proof of execution and acknowledgments of instruments, and attesting documents. Notarial acts may be performed outside this State for use in this State with the same effect as if performed by a notary public of this State by the following persons authorized pursuant to the laws and regulations of other governments in addition to any other person authorized by the laws and regulations of this State:

(1) a notary public authorized to perform notarial acts in the place in which the act is performed;

(2) a judge, clerk, or deputy of any court of record in the place in which the notarial act is performed;

(3) an officer of the foreign service of the United States, a consular agent, or any other person authorized by regulation of

the United States Department of State to perform notarial acts in the place in which the act is performed;

(4) a commissioned officer in active service with the Armed Forces of the United States and any other person authorized by regulation of the Armed Forces to perform notarial acts if the notarial act is performed for one of the following or his dependents: a merchant seaman of the United States, a member of the Armed Forces of the United States, or any other person serving with or accompanying the Armed Forces of the United States; or

(5) any other person authorized to perform notarial acts in the place in which the act is performed.

§ 2. Authentication of Authority of Officer.—

(a) If the notarial act is performed by any of the persons described in paragraphs 1 to 4, inclusive of section 1, other than a person authorized to perform notarial acts by the laws or regulations of a foreign country, the signature, rank, or title and serial number, if any, of the person are sufficient proof of the authority of a holder of that rank or title to perform the act. Further proof of his authority is not required.

(b) If the notarial act is performed by a person authorized by the laws or regulations of a foreign country to perform the act, there is sufficient proof of the authority of that person to act if:

(1) either a foreign service officer of the United States resident in the country in which the act is performed or a diplomatic or consular officer of the foreign country resident in the United States certifies that a person holding that office is authorized to perform the act;

(2) the official seal of the person performing the notarial act is affixed to the document; or

(3) the title and indication of authority to perform notarial acts of the person appears either in a digest of foreign law or in a list customarily used as a source of such information.

(c) If the notarial act is performed by a person other than one described in subsections (a) and (b), there is sufficient proof of the authority of that person to act if the clerk of a court of record in the place in which the notarial act is performed certifies to the official character of that person and to his authority to perform the notarial act.

(d) The signature and title of the person performing the act are prima facie evidence that he is a person with the designated title and that the signature is genuine.

§ 3. Certificate of Person Taking Acknowledgment.—The person taking an acknowledgment shall certify that:

(1) the person acknowledging appeared before him and acknowledged he executed the instrument; and

(2) the person acknowledging was known to the person taking the acknowledgment or that the person taking the acknowledgment had satisfactory evidence that the person acknowledging was the person described in and who executed the instrument.

§ 4. **Recognition of Certificate of Acknowledgment.**—The form of a certificate of acknowledgment used by a person whose authority is recognized under section 1 shall be accepted in this state if:

(1) the certificate is in a form prescribed by the laws or regulations of this state;

(2) the certificate is in a form prescribed by the laws or regulations applicable in the place in which the acknowledgment is taken; or

(3) the certificate contains the words "acknowledged before me," or their substantial equivalent.

§ 5. **Certificate of Acknowledgment.**—The words "acknowledged before me" means

(1) that the person acknowledging appeared before the person taking the acknowledgment,

(2) that he acknowledged he executed the instrument,

(3) that, in the case of:

(i) a natural person, he executed the instrument for the purposes therein stated;

(ii) a corporation, the officer or agent acknowledged he held the position or title set forth in the instrument and certificate, he signed the instrument on behalf of the corporation by proper authority, and the instrument was the act of the corporation for the purpose therein stated;

(iii) a partnership, the partner or agent acknowledged he signed the instrument on behalf of the partnership by proper authority and he executed the instrument as the act of the partnership for the purposes therein stated;

(iv) a person acknowledging as principal by an attorney in fact, he executed the instrument by proper authority as the act of the principal for the purposes therein stated;

(v) a person acknowledging as a public officer, trustee, administrator, guardian, or other representative, he signed the instrument by proper authority and he executed the instrument in the capacity and for the purposes therein stated; and

(4) that the person taking the acknowledgment either knew or had satisfactory evidence that the person acknowledging was the person named in the instrument or certificate.

§ 6. **Short Forms of Acknowledgment.**—The forms of acknowledgment set forth in this section may be used and are sufficient for their

respective purposes under any law of this State. The forms shall
be known as "Statutory Short Forms of Acknowledgment" and may
be referred to by that name. The authorization of the forms in this
section does not preclude the use of other forms.

(1)   For an individual acting in his own right:

State of ―――
County of ―――

     The foregoing instrument was acknowledged before me this
(date) by (name of person acknowledged.)

         (Signature of Person Taking Acknowledgment)
         (Title or Rank)
         (Serial Number, if any)

(2)   For a corporation:

State of ―――
County of ―――

     The foregoing instrument was acknowledged before me this
(date) by (name of officer or agent, title of officer or agent) of
(name of corporation acknowledging) a (state or place of incorporation) corporation, on behalf of the corporation.

         (Signature of Person Taking Acknowledgment)
         (Title or Rank)
         (Serial Number, if any)

(3)   For a partnership:

State of ―――
County of ―――

     The foregoing instrument was acknowledged before me this
(date) by (name of acknowledging partner or agent), partner
(or agent) on behalf of (name of partnership), a partnership.

         (Signature of Person Taking Acknowledgment)
         (Title or Rank)
         (Serial Number, if any)

(4)   For an individual acting as principal by an attorney in fact:

State of ―――
County of ―――

     The foregoing instrument was acknowledged before me this
(date) by (name of attorney in fact) as attorney in fact on
behalf of (name of principal).

         (Signature of Person Taking Acknowledgment)
         (Title or Rank)
         (Serial Number, if any)

(5)   By any Public Officer, trustee, or personal representative:
State of ———
County of ———
The foregoing instrument was acknowledged before me this
(date) by (name and title of position).
(Signature of Person Taking Acknowledgment)
(Title or Rank)
(Serial Number, if any)

§ 7.   Acknowledgments Not Affected by This Act.—A notarial act performed prior to the effective date of this Act is not affected by this Act. This Act provides an additional method of proving notarial acts. Nothing in this Act diminishes or invalidates the recognition accorded to notarial acts by other laws or regulations of this State.

§ 8.   Uniformity of Interpretation.—This Act shall be so interpreted as to make uniform the laws of those states which enact it.

§ 9.   Short Title.—This Act may be cited as the Uniform Recognition of Acknowledgments Act.

§ 10.   Time of Taking Effect.—This Act shall take effect ———.

ACKNOWLEDGMENTS: STATE AND OTHER AUTHORITIES

ALABAMA

[ALA. CODE]

Tit. 47, § 25.   Officers authorized to take acknowledgments, etc., in this state.   Acknowledgments and proofs of conveyances may be taken by the following officers within this state: Judges of the supreme court, the court of appeals and circuit courts, and the clerks of such courts; registers of the circuit court, judges of the court of probate, justices of the peace, and notaries public.

§ 30.   Form of acknowledgment of conveyance.   The following are substantially the forms of acknowledgment to be used in this state, on conveyance and instruments of every description, admitted to record:

ACKNOWLEDGMENT FOR INDIVIDUAL
The State of ———
——— County
I (name and style of Officer) hereby certify that ——— whose name is signed to the foregoing conveyance, and who is known to me, acknowledged before me on this day that, being informed of the contents of the conveyance, he executed the same voluntarily on

the day the same bears date. Given under my hand this ——— day of ———, A. D. 19—.

A. B. Judge, etc. (or as the case may be)

ACKNOWLEDGMENT FOR CORPORATION

The State of ———

——— County

I, ———, a ——— in and for said county in said state, hereby certify that ——— whose name as ——— of the ———, a corporation, is signed to the foregoing conveyance, and who is known to me, acknowledged before me on this day that, being informed of the contents of the conveyance, he, is such officer and with full authority, executed the same voluntarily for and as the act of said corporation.

Given under my hand this the ——— day of ———, 19—.

(Style of Officer)

ACKNOWLEDGMENT FOR AN OFFICIAL, OR OTHER PERSON, IN REPRESENTATIVE CAPACITY

The State of ———

——— County

I, ———, a ———, in and for said County in said State, hereby certify that ———, whose name as ——— (here state representative capacity) is signed to the foregoing conveyance and who is known to me, acknowledged before me on this day that, being informed of the contents of the conveyance, he, in his capacity as such ———, executed the same voluntarily on the day the same bears date.

Given under my hand this the ——— day of ———, 19—.

(Style of Officer)

ACKNOWLEDGMENT FOR CORPORATION IN REPRESENTATIVE CAPACITY

The State of ———

——— County

I, ———, a ——— in and for said County, in said State, hereby certify that ——— whose name as ——— of ———, a corporation as ——— of the estate of ——— (or as the case may be) is signed to the foregoing ———, and who is known to me, acknowledged before me on this day, that being informed of the contents of said ———, he, as such officer, and with full authority, executed the same voluntarily for and as the act of said corporation, acting in its capacity as ——— as aforesaid.

Given under my hand this the ——— day of ———, 19—.

(Style of Officer)

ALASKA

[ALASKA STAT.]

§ 34.15.150. Execution of conveyances. (a) A conveyance executed in the state of land or an interest in land in the state shall be acknowledged before a judge, clerk of the superior court, notary public, postmaster, or commissioner in the state or proved in accordance with §§ 210 or 220 of this chapter. The officer taking an acknowledgment shall endorse on it a certificate of the acknowledgment of the conveyance and the date of making the acknowledgment.

(b) A conveyance executed before March 12, 1953, in due form but without two witnesses is validated, shall be received in evidence in all courts of the state, and is evidence of the title to the land or interest in land against the grantor, his heirs and assigns.

ARIZONA

[ARIZ. REV. STAT. ANN.]

§§ 33-501 to 33-508. The Uniform Recognition of Acknowledgments Act has been adopted. For text of Act, see page 349.

§§ 33-511 to 33-516. The Uniform Acknowledgment Act has been adopted. For text of act, see page 349.

§ 41-312. Duties. Notaries public shall, when requested:

o   o   o

2. Take acknowledgments and give a certificate of them endorsed on or attached to the instrument.

o   o   o

4. Keep a record of all their official acts, and a record of the parties to, date and character of every instrument acknowledged or proved before them, date of acknowledgment and description of the property affected by the instrument, and furnish, when requested, a certified copy of any record in their office.

o   o   o

ARKANSAS

[ARK. STAT. ANN.]

§§ 49-101 to 49-114. The Uniform Acknowledgment Act has been adopted. For text of act, see page 349.

§ 49-202. Officers authorized to take proof or acknowledgment of real estate conveyances. The proof or acknowledgment of every deed or instrument of writing for the conveyance of any real estate, shall be taken by some one of the following courts or officers:

First. When acknowledged or proven within this State before

the Supreme Court, the Circuit Court, the Chancery Court, or any Judges thereof, or the Clerk of any Court of record, or any County of [or] Probate Judge, or before any Justice of the Peace or Notary Public.

Second. When acknowledged or proved without this State, and within the United States or their Territories or the country known as the Indian Territory, or in any of the Colonies or Possessions or Dependencies of the United States, before any court of the United States, or of any State or Territory, or Indian Territory, or Colony or Possession or Dependency of the United States, having a seal, or a Clerk of any such Court, or before any Notary Public, or before the Mayor of any incorporated city or town, or the chief officer of any city or town having a seal, or before a Commissioner appointed by the Governor of this State.

Third. When acknowledged or proven without the United States, before any court of any State, kingdom or empire having a seal, or any Mayor or chief officer of any city or town having an official seal, or before any officer of any foreign country who by the laws of such country is authorized to take probate of the conveyance of real estate of his own country if such officer has, by law, an official seal.

CALIFORNIA

[CAL. GOV'T CODE]

§ 8205. **Duties.** It is the duty of a notary public:

o   o   o

(b) To take the acknowledgment or proof of powers of attorney, mortgages, deeds, grants, transfers, and other instruments of writing executed by any person, and to give a certificate of such proof or acknowledgment, endorsed on or attached to the instrument. Such certificate shall be signed by him in his own handwriting.

o   o   o

§ 8203.5. **Military and naval reservations, jurat.** In addition to the name of the State, the jurat shall also contain the name of the reservation in which the instrument is executed.

COLORADO

[COLO. REV. STAT. ANN.]

§§ 12-55-201 to 12-55-210. The Uniform Recognition of Acknowledgments Act has been adopted. For text of act, see page 349.

§ 24-12-104. **Officers in armed forces empowered to perform notarial acts.** (1) In addition to the acknowledgment of instruments and the performance of other notarial acts in the manner and form and as otherwise authorized by law, instruments may be acknowledged, documents attested, oaths and affirmations administered, depositions and affidavits executed, and other notarial acts performed before or by any commissioned officer in active service of the armed forces of the United States with the rank of second lieutenant or higher in the army or marine corps, or with the rank of ensign or higher in the navy or coast guard, or with equivalent rank in any other component part of the armed forces of the United States, by or for any person who is a member of the armed forces of the United States, or is serving as a merchant seaman outside the limits of the United States included within the fifty states and the District of Columbia, or is outside said limits by permission, assignment, or direction of any department or official of the United States government, in connection with any activity pertaining to the prosecution of any war in which the United States is then engaged.

(2) Such acknowledgment of instruments, attestation of documents, administration of oaths and affirmations, execution of depositions and affidavits, and performance of other notarial acts, whenever made or taken, are hereby declared legal, valid, and binding, and instruments and documents so acknowledged, authenticated, or sworn to shall be admissible in evidence and eligible to record in this state under the same circumstances and with the same force and effect as if such acknowledgment, attestation, oath, affirmation, deposition, affidavit, or other notarial act had been made or taken within this state before or by a duly qualified officer or official as otherwise provided by law.

(3) In the taking of acknowledgments and the performing of other notarial acts requiring certification, a certificate indorsed upon or attached to the instrument or document which shows the date of the notarial act and which states, in substance, that the person appearing before the officer acknowledged the instrument as his act or made or signed the instrument or document under oath, shall be sufficient for all intents and purposes. The instrument or document shall not be rendered invalid by the failure to state the place of execution or acknowledgment.

(4) If the signature, rank, and branch of service or subdivision thereof, of any such commissioned officer appears upon such instrument or document or certificate, no further proof of the authority of such officer so to act shall be required and such action by such commissioned officer shall be prima facie evidence that the person making such oath or acknowledgment is within the purview of this section.

(5) If any instrument is acknowledged substantially as provided in this section, whether such acknowledgment has been taken before or after February 27, 1943, such acknowledgment shall be prima facie evidence of proper execution of such instrument and shall carry with it the presumptions provided for by section 38-35-101, C.R.S. 1973.

§ 38-30-126. Acknowledgments, before whom taken. (1) Deeds, bonds and agreements in writing, conveying lands or any interest therein, or affecting title thereto, may be acknowledged or proved before the following officers:

(2) When executed within this state before any judge of any court of record, before the clerk of any such court of record, or the deputy of any such clerk, such judge, clerk or deputy clerk, certifying such acknowledgment under the seal of such court; before the clerk and recorder of any county, or his deputy, such clerk or deputy clerk certifying the same under the seal of such county; before any notary public, he certifying the same under his notarial seal; or, prior to the second Tuesday in January, 1965, before any justice of the peace within his county; provided, that if such deed, bond, or agreement be for the conveyance of lands situated beyond the county of such justice of the peace, there shall be affixed to his certificate of such acknowledgment a certificate of the county clerk and recorder of the proper county, under his hand and the seal of such county, to the official capacity of such justice of the peace, and that the signature to such certificate of acknowledgment is the true signature of such justice.

(3) When executed out of this state, and within the United States or any territory thereof, before the secretary of any such state or territory, he certifying such acknowledgment under the seal of such state or territory; before the clerk of any court of record of such state or territory, or of the United States within such state or territory, having a seal, such clerk certifying the acknowledgment under the seal of such court; before any notary public of such state or territory, he certifying the same under his notarial seal; before any commissioner of deeds for any such foreign state or territory appointed under the laws of this state, he certifying such acknowledgment under his hand and official seal; before any other officer authorized by the laws of any such state or territory to take and certify such acknowledgment; provided, there shall be affixed to the certificate of such officer, other than those above enumerated, a certificate by the clerk of some court of record of the county, city or district, wherein such officer resides, under the seal of such court, that the person certifying such acknowledgment is the officer he assumes to be; that he has the authority, by the laws of such state or territory, to take and certify such acknowledgment, and that the signature of such officer to the certificate of acknowledgment is the true signature of such officer.

(4) When executed or acknowledged out of the United States before any judge or clerk or deputy clerk of any court of record of any foreign kingdom, empire, republic, state, principality, province, colony, island possession or bailiwick, such judge, clerk or deputy clerk certifying such acknowledgment under the seal of such court; or before the chief magistrate or other chief executive officer of any province, colony, island possession or bailiwick, or before the mayor or the chief executive officer of any city, town, borough, county or municipal corporation having a seal, of such foreign kingdom, em-

pire, republic, state, principality, province, colony, island possession or bailiwick, such chief magistrate or other chief executive officer of such mayor certifying such acknowledgment under such seal; or before any ambassador, minister, consul, vice-consul, consular agent, vice-consular agent, charge d'affaires, vice-charge d'affaires, commercial agent, vice-commercial agent, or any diplomatic, consular or commercial agent or representative, or duly constituted deputy of any thereof of the United States, or of any other government or country appointed to reside in the foreign country or place where the proof of acknowledgment is made, he certifying the same under the seal of his office.

(5) When executed or acknowledged out of the state, and within any colony, island possession or bailiwick, such judge, clerk, or deputy clerk certifying such acknowledgment under the seal of such court; or before the chief magistrate or other chief executive officer of any such colony, island possession or bailiwick belonging to or under the control of the United States, before any judge or clerk or deputy clerk of any court of record of such colony, island possession or baliwick, he certifying the same under his official seal, or before the mayor or the chief executive officer of any city, town, borough, county or municipal corporation having a seal, of such colony, island possession or bailiwick, such mayor or other chief officer certifying such acknowledgment under his official seal; or before any notary public within such colony, island possession or bailiwick, having a seal, such notary public certifying such acknowledgment under his seal.

§ 38-30-127. **Acknowledgments by persons in armed forces.** In addition to the acknowledgment of instruments as provided by this chapter, instruments may be acknowledged by members of the armed forces of the United States, and certain other persons, as provided by section 24-12-104.

§ 38-30-129. **Clerk of U. S. courts may take acknowledgments.** Deeds, bonds, and agreements in writing, conveying lands or any interest therein, or affecting title thereto, may be acknowledged or proved before any clerk of the circuit or district court of the United States, for the district of Colorado, or any deputy of such clerk; such clerk certifying such acknowledgment under the seal of such court respectively.

§ 38-30-135. **Officer shall subscribe certificate.** Every certificate of the acknowledgment or proof of any deed, bond, agreement, power of attorney or other writing for the conveyance of real estate, or any interest therein, or affecting title thereto, shall be subscribed by the officer certifying the same, with his proper hand, and shall be endorsed upon or attached to such deed or other writing.

§ 38-30-136. Subsequent proof of execution — proof or acknowledgment of copy. (1) When any deed or instrument of writing has
been executed and not acknowledged according to law at the time
of the execution thereof, such deed or instrument of writing may at
any subsequent time be acknowledged by the makers thereof in
the manner provided in this article, or proof may be made of the
execution thereof before any officer authorized to take acknowledgments of deeds in the manner provided in this section. Such officer,
when the fact is not within his own knowledge, shall ascertain from
the testimony of at least one competent, credible witness, to be sworn
and examined by him, that the person offering to prove the execution
of such deed or writing is a subscribing witness thereto. Thereupon
such officer shall examine such subscribing witness upon oath or
affirmation, and shall reduce his testimony to writing and require
the witness to subscribe the same, endorsed upon or attached to such
deed or other writing, and shall thereupon grant a certificate that
such witness was personally known or was proved to him by the
testimony of at least one witness (who shall be named in such
certificate) to be a subscribing witness to the deed or instrument of
writing to be proved, that such subscribing witness was lawfully
sworn and examined by him, and that the testimony of the said officer
was reduced to writing and by said subscribing witness subscribed
in his presence.

(2) If by the testimony it appears that such witness saw the
person, whose name is subscribed to such instrument of writing, sign,
seal, and deliver the same or that such person afterwards acknowledged the same to the said witness to be his free and voluntary act
or deed and that such witness subscribed the said deed or instrument
of writing in attestation thereof, in the presence and with the consent of the person so executing the same, such proof if attested
and the authority of the officer to take the same duly proved in the
same manner as required in the case of acknowledgment, shall have
the same force and effect as an acknowledgment of said deed or
instrument of writing by the person executing the same, and duly
certified.

(3) When any such deed or instrument of writing has been
executed and recorded without due proof, attestation or acknowledgment as required by law, a certified copy from such record may be
proved or acknowledged in the same manner and with like effect as
the original thereof. No person shall be permitted to use such
certified copy so proved as evidence except upon satisfactory proof
that the original thereof has been lost or destroyed or is beyond his
power to produce.

§ 38-35-103. Acknowledgment before notary. In addition to the
officers now empowered by law to take acknowledgments within or
without the United States, deeds and other instruments in writing
may be acknowledged before any notary public having a notarial seal.

CONNECTICUT

[CONN. GEN. STAT. ANN.]

§§ 1-28 to 1-41. The Uniform Acknowledgment Act has been adopted. For text of act, see page 349.

§§ 1-57 to 1-65. The Uniform Recognition of Acknowledgments Act has been adopted. For text of act, see page 349.

§ 47-7. Conveyances and releases executed outside of this state. Notwithstanding the provisions of section 1-36,° any conveyance of real estate situated in this state, any mortgage or release of mortgage or lien upon any real estate situated in this state, and any power of attorney authorizing another to convey any interest in real estate situated in this state, executed and acknowledged in any other state or territory in conformity with the laws of such state or territory relating to the conveyance of real estate therein situated or of any interest therein or with the laws of this state, shall be valid, and no county clerk's certificate or other authenticating certificate shall be required for such deed to be valid, provided the officer taking such acknowledgment shall have indicated thereon the date, if any, on which his current commission expires.

° Uniform Acknowledgment Act.

DELAWARE

[DEL. CODE ANN.]

Tit. 25, § 110. Certificates of notaries public; validity. No official certificate of any notary public shall be invalid or defective because the impression of the official seal of such officer upon the certificate does not strictly comport with the requirements of section 4308 of Title 29.° All such certificates shall be valid in all respect; and in all cases where such certificates are annexed to papers proper to be recorded, the several recorders shall admit such papers to record. The record of the same, or a duly certified copy thereof, shall be competent evidence, and every such paper shall be as good and effectual in law as though the seal used by the officer certifying the acknowledgment of the same had been engraved in exact conformity with the provisions of the law.

° For tit. 29, § 4308, see *Seal.*

§ 123. Certification of acknowledgment or proof. Acknowledgment or proof shall be certified under the hand and seal of office of the clerk, or prothonotary, of the court in which, or under the hand of the judge, notary public or justices of the peace before whom, the acknowledgment or proof is taken, in a certificate endorsed upon, or annexed to the deed.

§ 128. Certification of acknowledgments by Mayor of Wilmington; fee. The Mayor of Wilmington may take and certify under his hand and seal of office, the acknowledgment of deeds, and letters of attorney in like manner as a judge or notary public may. For such service he shall receive a fee of 75 cents, and no more, whether there is one or more parties to the deed.

§ 129. Acknowledgment or proof outside state. (a) A deed, concerning lands, tenements, or hereditaments within this State, may be acknowledged or proved, or may be taken out of the State before any consul general, consul, vice-consul, consular agent, or commercial agent of the United States, duly appointed in any foreign country, at the places of their respective official residence, the judge of any United States district court or United States court of appeals, or any judge of a court of record of any State, territory, or country, or the mayor, or chief officer of any city, or borough, and certified under the hands of such judge, mayor or officer, and the seal of his office, court, city, or borough, by certificate indorsed upon, or annexed to the deed; or such acknowledgment, or proof, may be taken in such court, and certified, under the hand of the clerk, or other officer of the court, and the seal of the court in like manner. If certified by a judge, the seal of his court may be affixed to his certificate, or to a certificate of attestation of the clerk, or keeper of the seal.

(b) Acknowledgment and proof of a deed may also be taken out of this State by any commissioner of deeds, appointed by the Governor in any of the States, or territories, of the United States, or in the District of Columbia, or in the possessions of the United States, or in foreign countries, the deed to be certified, in like manner, under the hand and seal of the Commissioner.

(c) Any deed concerning lands, tenements, or hereditaments, within this State, any other instrument of writing whatsoever, or any affidavit, or other statement requiring acknowledgment or proof, may be so acknowledged and proved out of this State before a notary public of any State, or territory or of the District of Columbia. The provisions of this paragraph shall extend to affidavits of demand and defense as provided for in § 3901 of Title 10.

DISTRICT OF COLUMBIA

[D.C. CODE ENCYCL. ANN.]

§ 45-401. Acknowledgment by attorney. No deeds of conveyance of either real or personal estate by individuals shall be executed or acknowledged by attorney.

§ 45-402. Acknowledgment in the district. Acknowledgment of deeds may be made in the District of Columbia before any judge of any of the courts of said District, the clerk of the United States District Court for the District of Columbia, or any notary public, or the recorder of deeds of said District, and the certificate of the officer taking the acknowledgment shall be to the following effect:

I, A B, a notary public (or other officer authorized) in and for the District of Columbia, do hereby certify that C D, party to a certain deed bearing date on the ——— day of ———, and hereto annexed, personally appeared before me in said District, the said C D being personally well known to me as (or proved by the oath of credible witnesses to be) the person who executed the said deed, and acknowledged the same to be his act and deed.

Given under my hand and seal this ——— day of ———.

A. B. [Seal.]

§ 45-403. **Acknowledgment out of District.** When any deed or contract under seal is to be acknowledged out of the District of Columbia, but within the United States, the acknowledgment may be made before any judge of a court of record and of law, or any chancellor of a State, any judge or justice of the Supreme, District, or Territorial courts of the United States, any justice of the peace or notary public: *Provided,* That the certificate of acknowledgment aforesaid, made by any officer of the State or Territory not having a seal, shall be accompanied by the certificate of the register, clerk, or other public officer that the officer taking said acknowledgment was in fact the officer he professed to be.

§ 45-404. **Acknowledgment in foreign country.** Deeds made in a foreign country may be acknowledged before any judge or notary public, or before any secretary of legation or consular officer, or acting consular officer of the United States, as such consular officer is described in section 51 of title 22, U. S. Code; and when the acknowledgment is made before any other officer than a secretary of legation or consular officer or acting consular officer of the United States, the official character of the person taking the acknowledgment shall be certified in the manner prescribed in section 45-403.

§ 45-405. **Acknowledgments in Guam, Samoa, and Canal Zone.** Deeds and other instruments affecting land situate in the District of Columbia may be acknowledged in the islands of Guam and Samoa or in the Canal Zone before any notary public or judge, appointed therein by proper authority, or by any officer therein who has ex officio the powers of a notary public: *Provided,* That the certificate by such notary in Guam, Samoa, or the Canal Zone, as the case may be, shall be accompanied by the certificate of the governor or acting governor of such place to the effect that the notary taking said acknowledgment was in fact the officer he purported to be; and any deeds or other instruments affecting lands so situate, so acknowledged since the 1st day of January, 1905, and accompanied by such certificate shall have the same effect as such deeds or other instruments hereafter so acknowledged and certified.

§ 45-406. Acknowledgments in Phillippine Islands and Puerto Rico. Deeds and other instruments affecting land situate in the District of Columbia may be acknowledged in the Phillippine Islands and Puerto Rico before any notary public appointed therein by proper authority, or any officer therein who has ex officio the powers of a notary public: *Provided,* That the certificate by such notary in the Phillippine Islands or in Puerto Rico, as the case may be, shall be accompanied by the certificate of the executive secretary of Puerto Rico, or the governor or Attorney-General of the Phillippine Islands to the effect that the notary taking said acknowledgment was in fact the officer he purported to be.

FLORIDA

[FLA. STAT. ANN.]

§ 695.03. Acknowledgment and proof; validation of certain acknowledgments. To entitle any instrument concerning real property to be recorded, the execution must be acknowledged by the party executing it; or the execution must be proved by a subscribing witness to it before the officers and in the form and manner following:

(1) In this state. An acknowledgment or proof made within this state may be made before any judge, clerk, or deputy clerk of any court, a United States commissioner or magistrate, or a notary public, and the certificate of acknowledgment or proof shall be under the seal of the court or officer, as the case may be. All affidavits and acknowledgments heretofore made or taken in this manner are hereby validated.

(2) Without this state but within the United States. An acknowledgment or proof made out of this state but within the United States may be made before a commissioner of deeds appointed by the governor of this state; a judge or clerk of any court of the United States or of any state, territory, or district; a United States commissioner or magistrate; or a notary public, justice of the peace, master in chancery, or registrar or recorder of deeds of any state, territory, or district having a seal, and the certificate of acknowledgment or proof shall be under the seal of the court or officer, as the case may be. If the acknowledgment or proof is made before a notary public who does not have or does not affix a seal, the instrument shall have affixed a certificate by the clerk of a court having a seal under the seal to the effect that the notary public was duly authorized by the laws of the state to take the acknowledgment or proof of the instrument to which the certificate is affixed. All affidavits and acknowledgments heretofore made or taken in this manner are hereby validated.

(3) In foreign countries. If the acknowledgment or proof be made in any foreign country, it may be made before any commissioner of deeds appointed by the governor of this state to reside in such country, or before any notary public of such foreign country having

an official seal, or before any ambassador, envoy extraordinary, minister plenipotentiary, minister, commissioner, charge d'affaires, consul general, consul, vice-consul, consular agent, or any other diplomatic or consular officer of the United States appointed to reside in such country, military or naval officer authorized by the laws or articles of war of the United States to perform the duties of notary public, and the certificate of acknowledgment or proof shall be under the seal of the officer.

All affidavits and acknowledgments heretofore made or taken in the manner set forth above are hereby validated.

§ 695.05.   Certain defects cured as to acknowledgments and witnesses.   All deeds, conveyances, bills of sale, mortgages or other transfers of real or personal property within the limits of this state, heretofore or hereafter made and received bona fide and upon good consideration by any corporation, and acknowledged for record before some officer, stockholder or other person interested in the corporation, grantee, or mortgagee as a notary public or other officer authorized to take acknowledgments of instruments for record within this state, shall be held, deemed and taken as valid as if acknowledged by the proper notary public or other officer authorized to take acknowledgments of instruments for record in this state not so interested in said corporation, grantee or mortgagee; and said instrument whenever recorded shall be deemed notice to all persons; provided, however, that this section shall not apply to any instrument heretofore made, the validity of which shall be contested by suit commenced within one year of the effective date of this law.

§ 695.09.   Identity of grantor.   No acknowledgment or proof shall be taken by any officer within or without the United States unless he shall know, or have satisfactory proof, that the person making the acknowledgment is the individual described in and who executed such instrument, or that the person offering to make proof is one of the subscribing witnesses to such instrument.

GEORGIA

[GA. CODE ANN.]

§ 29-406.   Officers authorized to attest registrable instruments. Any such instrument may be attested by a judge of a court of record (including a judge of a municipal court), or by a justice of the peace, or notary public, or clerk or deputy clerk of the superior court or of a city court created by special Act of the General Assembly.   Such officers, except notaries public and judges of courts of record, may attest such instruments only in the county in which they respectively hold their offices.

§ 29-408.   Acknowledgment by officer subsequent to execution. If, subsequently to its execution, any registrable instrument is acknowledged in the presence of either of the officers referred to in section 29-406, that fact certified on the deed by such officer shall entitle it to be recorded.

§ 29-409. If executed out of this State. To authorize the record of a deed to realty or personalty, when executed out of this State, the deed must be attested by or acknowledged before a commissioner of deeds for the State of Georgia, or a consul or vice consul of the United States (the certificate of these officers under their seal being evidence of the fact), or by a judge of a court of record in the State or Country where executed, with a certificate of the clerk under the seal of such court of the genuineness of the signature of such judge, or by a clerk of a court of record under the seal of the court, or by a notary public or justice of the peace of the State or State and county, city or Country where executed, with his seal of office attached; and if such notary public or justice of the peace has no seal, then his official character shall be certified by a clerk of any court of record in the county, city, or Country of the residence of such notary or justice of the peace. A deed to realty must be attested by two witnesses, one of whom may be one of the officials aforesaid. Wherever any such instrument appears by the caption only to be executed in one State and county, and the official attesting witness appears to be an officer of another State or county not having jurisdiction to witness such instruments in the State and county named in the caption, the same shall be conclusively considered and construed to have been attested by the officer in the State and county in which he had authority to act, the caption to the contrary notwithstanding: Provided, this section shall not apply to transactions covered by Title 109A, Article 9, Uniform Commercial Code.

HAWAII

[HAWAII REV. STAT.]

§ 502-41. Certificate of acknowledgment; natural persons, corporations. Except as otherwise provided by sections 502-50 to 502-52, to entitle any conveyance or other instrument to be recorded there shall be endorsed, subjoined, or attached thereto an acknowledgment in the form provided or authorized in any of sections 502-42, 502-43, or 502-45, or in substantially the following form:

(Begin in all cases by a caption specifying the state or territory and the place where the acknowledgment is taken.)

1. In the case of natural persons acting in their own right:

On this —— day of ——, 19—, before me personally appeared A.B. (or A.B. and C.D.), to me known to be the person (or persons) described in and who executed the foregoing instrument, and acknowledged that he (or they) executed the same as his (or their) free act and deed.

2. In the case of natural persons acting by attorney:

On this ———— day of ————, 19—, before me personally appeared A.B., to me known to be the person who executed the foregoing instrument in behalf of C.D. and acknowledged that he executed the same as the free act and deed of said C.D.

3. In the case of corporations or joint stock associations:

On this ———— day of ————, 19—, before me appeared A.B., to me personally known, who, being by me duly sworn (or affirmed), did say that he is the president (or other officer or agent of the corporation or association) of (describing the corporation or association) and that the seal affixed to the instrument is the corporate seal of the corporation (or association), and that the instrument was signed and sealed in behalf of the corporation (or association) by authority of its board of directors (or trustees), and A.B. acknowledged the instrument to be the free act and deed of the corporation (or association).

In case the corporation or association has no corporate seal, omit "the seal affixed to the instrument is the corporate seal of the corporation (or association), and that" and add, at the end of the affidavit clause, "and that the corporation (or association) has no corporate seal."

4. In the case of a corporation or joint stock company acknowledging by an individual as its attorney, where the enabling power of attorney has previously been recorded, the acknowledgment of the instrument executed under the power of attorney shall be substantially in the following form:

On this ———— day of ————, 19—, before me personally appeared A.B., to me personally known, who being by me duly sworn (or affirmed) did say that he is the attorney in fact of C.D. (here name the corporation) duly appointed under power of attorney dated the ———— day of ————, 19—, recorded in book ————, at page ————; and that the foregoing instrument was executed in the name and behalf of said C.D. by A.B. as its attorney in fact; and A.B. acknowledged the instrument to be the free act and deed of C.D.

In case the enabling power of attorney has not previously been recorded, omit the reference to its place of record and insert in lieu thereof the words "which power of attorney is now in full force and effect."

5. In the case of a corporation or joint stock company acknowledging by another corporation or joint stock company as its attorney, where the enabling power of attorney has previously been recorded, the acknowledgment of the instrument executed under the power of attorney shall be substantially in the following form:

On this ———— day of ————, 19—, before me personally appeared A.B., to me personally known, who, being by me duly sworn (or affirmed) did say that he is the president (or other officer or agent of the corporation or joint stock company acting as attorney) of

C.D. (here name the corporation or joint stock company acting as attorney) and that C.D. is the attorney in fact of E.F. (here name the corporation or joint stock company in whose behalf the attorney is acting) duly appointed under power of attorney dated the ——— day of ———, 19—, recorded in book ———, at page ———; that the foregoing instrument was executed in the name and behalf of E.F. by C.D. as its attorney-in-fact; that the seal affixed to the foregoing instrument is the corporate seal of C.D., and the instrument was so executed by C.D. by authority of its board of directors; and A.B. acknowledged the instrument to be the free act and deed of E.F.

In case the corporation acting as attorney has no corporate seal, or no seal within the State, omit the words "the seal affixed to the foregoing instrument is the corporate seal of C.D." and insert in lieu thereof, "C.D. has no corporate seal," or "C.D. has no corporate seal within the State of Hawaii." In case the enabling power of attorney has not previously been recorded, omit the reference to its place of record and insert in lieu thereof the words "which power of attorney is now in full force and effect."

In all cases add signature and title of the officer taking the acknowledgment.

§ 502-42. **Certificate, contents.** The certificate of acknowledgment shall state in substance that the person who executed the instrument appeared before the officer granting the certificate and acknowledged or stated that he executed the same, and that such person was personally known to the officer granting such certificate to be the person whose name is subscribed to the instrument as a party thereto, or was proved to be such by the oath or affirmation of a credible witness known to the officer whose name shall be inserted in the certificate. It shall not be ground for the rejection of any such certificate, or for refusing to accept such instrument for record or in evidence, that the certificate fails to state that the person making the acknowledgment stated or acknowledged that the instrument was executed freely or voluntarily by him or as his free act and deed.

§ 502-43. **Form when person unknown.** When the person offering the acknowledgment is unknown to the officer taking the acknowledgment, the certificate may be substantially in the following form, to-wit:

State of Hawaii,
County of ——— ss.

On this ——— day of ———, 19—, personally appeared before me A.B., satisfactorily proved to me to be the person described in and who executed the within instrument, by the oath of C.D., a credible witness for that purpose, to me known and by me duly sworn, and he, A.B., acknowledged that he executed the same freely and voluntarily for the uses and purposes therein set forth.

§ 502-44. Married women. The acknowledgment of a married woman when required by law may be taken in the same form as if she were sole and without any examination separate and apart from her husband.

§ 502-45. Acknowledgments without the State. The proof or acknowledgment of any deed or other written instrument required to be proved or acknowledged in order to enable the same to be recorded or read in evidence, when made by any person without the State and within any other state, territory, district, or dependency of the United States, may be made before any officer of the state, territory, district, or dependency authorized by the laws thereof to take proof and acknowledgment of deeds and when so taken, and when the certificate of acknowledgment is in a form sufficient to entitle deeds of real property to be recorded in the appropriate office for recording in such state, territory, district, or dependency or in the form provided or permitted by any of sections 502-41 to 502-43, shall be entitled to be recorded and may be read in evidence in the State. The signature of such officer constitutes prima facie evidence that the acknowledgment is taken in accordance with the laws of the place where made and of the authority of the officer to take the acknowledgment. If the record of any such instrument, or a transcript thereof, is used in evidence in any proceeding the burden shall be on the party relying on such record to prove that the instrument was duly executed, in any proceeding where such fact is asserted by such party and is in dispute. The burden may be met by proof made in the manner provided in section 502-46.

§ 502-46. Same; certificate of authority of officer. The burden of proving due execution of any conveyance or written instrument, acknowledged or proved under section 502-45, may be met by any admissible evidence sufficient for that purpose and shall also be met if at the time of recording or thereafter there is indorsed, subjoined, or attached to the certificate of proof or acknowledgment, signed by such officer, a certificate of the secretary of state of the state or territory in which such officer resides, under the seal of the state or territory, or a certificate of the clerk of a court of record of the state, territory, or district in the county in which the officer resides or in which he took such proof or acknowledgment, under the seal of the court, or a certificate of the executive officer or clerk of a court of record of such dependency, authorized to make such certificate, stating that the officer was, at the time of taking the proof or acknowledgment, duly authorized to take acknowledgments and proofs of deeds of lands in the state, territory, district, or dependency, and that the secretary of state, or other authorized executive officer, or clerk of court, is well acquainted with the handwriting of the officer taking the acknowledgment or proof, and that he verily believes that the signature affixed to the certificate of proof or acknowledgment is genuine.

The authentication of the proof of acknowledgment of a deed or other written instrument when taken without the State and within any other state, territory, or district of the United States, shall be in substantially the following form:

(Begin with a caption specifying the state, territory, or district, and county or place, where the authentication is made.)

I, ——— clerk of the ——— in and for said county which court is a court of record, having a seal (or I, ——— the secretary of state of said state or territory) do hereby certify that ——— by and before whom the foregoing acknowledgment (or proof) was taken, was at the time of taking the same, a notary public (or other officer) residing (or authorized to act) in the county, and was duly authorized by the laws of the state (territory or district) to take and certify acknowledgments or proofs of deeds of land in the state (territory or district), and further that I am well acquainted with the handwriting of ———, and that I verily believe that the signature to the certificate of acknowledgment (or proof) is genuine. In testimony whereof, I have hereunto set my hand and affixed the seal of the court (or state) this ——— day of ———, 19—.

§ 502-47. **Acknowledgment without the United States; by members of the armed forces; recordation where no official authorized to take proof.** (a) The proof or acknowledgment of any deed or other instrument required to be proved or acknowledged in order to entitle the same to be recorded or read in evidence, when made by any person without the United States may be made by:

(1) Any officer now authorized thereto by the laws of the State;

(2) Any officer of the United States diplomatic or consular service, resident in any foreign country or port, when certified by him under his seal of office; and

(3) Any person authorized by the law of any foreign country to take such acknowledgment or proof, when such acknowledgment or proof is accompanied by a certificate to the effect that the person taking the same is duly authorized thereto and that such acknowledgment or proof is in the manner prescribed by the laws of the foreign country. The certificate may be made by a diplomatic or consular officer of the United States under the seal of his office, or by a diplomatic or consular officer of the foreign country, resident in the State, under the seal of his office.

For the purposes of this section diplomatic or consular officer includes any minister, consul, vice-consul, charge d'affaires, consular, or commercial agent, or vice-consular or vice-commercial agent.

(b) Proof or acknowledgment may be made by any person in the armed forces of the United States, or by any person without the United States, before any officer of the armed forces authorized by Congress to exercise the powers of a notary public. The signature without seal of any officer acting as such notary public is prima facie evidence of his authority.

(c) Where it is established to the satisfaction of any judge of a circuit court of the state that any instrument required to be acknowledged or proved has been executed by a person then permanently or temporarily resident at some place where acknowledgment or proof cannot be made as hereinabove provided, such instrument shall be declared acceptable for recordation by order of the judge issued upon such testimony and evidence as are sufficient in the judgment of the judge to establish the genuineness and authenticity thereof, and a certified copy of the order shall be recorded together with and attached to any instrument so ordered acceptable for recordation.

(d) Any instrument so proved, acknowledged, or ordered acceptable for recordation is entitled to be recorded in the State, and may be read in evidence in any court of the State in the same manner and with like effect as if therein duly recorded or acknowledged.

§ 502-48. **Identification of person making.** No acknowledgment of any conveyance or other instrument, except as provided by this chapter, whereby any real estate is conveyed or may be affected, shall be taken, unless the person offering to make the acknowledgment is personally known to the officer taking the same to be the person whose name is subscribed to the conveyance or instrument as a party thereto, or is proved to be such by the oath or affirmation of a credible witness known to the officer.

§ 502-49. **Certificate of officer, or judge, necessary.** Every officer who takes the acknowledgment of any instrument shall indorse, subjoin, or attach a certificate thereof, signed by himself, on the instrument.

Every judge who takes the proof of any instrument shall indorse, subjoin, or attach a certificate thereof, signed by himself, on the instrument, giving the names of the witnesses examined before him, their places of residence, and the substance of the evidence by them given.

§ 502-50. **How made; proof if not made.** (a) Except as otherwise provided, to entitle any conveyance or other instrument to be recorded, it shall be acknowledged by the person or persons executing the same, before the registrar of conveyances, or his deputy or before a judge of a court of record or a notary public of the State. If any person having executed an instrument within the State, dies, or departs from the State, without having acknowledged the instrument, or refuses to acknowledge it, or if the person has acknowledged it but such acknowledgment has not been duly certified by the officer before whom made and for any reason neither proper certification nor a new acknowledgment can be secured, the instrument may be entered as of record on proof of its execution by a subscribing witness thereto before the judge of the land court or a judge of a circuit court of the State. If all the subscribing witnesses to the conveyance or other instrument are dead or out of the State, the same may be proved before any court in the State by proving the handwriting of the person executing the same and any subscribing witness. For the purposes of this section a notary public or person who wrongfully undertakes to act as such, may be deemed a subscribing witness.

(b) If there is any interlineation, erasure, or other change in an instrument, not initialed as required by section 502-61, and for any reason compliance with section 502-61 cannot be secured, the instrument may be proved as provided in subsection (c), or, without the bringing of the proceeding therein provided for, the judge of the land court or a judge of a circuit court may certify that the instrument is entitled to be recorded, if it is established to his satisfaction that such change was made before execution of the instrument, and the instrument thereupon shall be received for record notwithstanding section 502-63. If the record of any such instrument, received for record by reason of such certificate, or a transcript thereof, is used in evidence in any proceeding, the burden shall be on the party relying on such record to prove that such change was made before execution of the instrument, in any proceeding where such fact is asserted by the party and is in dispute.

(c) Any person interested under an instrument which if properly proved or acknowledged would be entitled to record, may institute a proceeding against the proper parties to obtain a judgment proving such instrument. The proceeding shall be brought in a circuit court or the land court. If the instrument affects the title to real property the proceeding shall be brought in the judicial circuit where the property is located. If judgment is obtained a certified copy thereof shall be appended to the instrument.

§ 502-53. **No certificate of acknowledgment contrary hereto valid in court or entitled to be recorded; exception.** No certificate of acknowledgment contrary to this chapter is valid in any court of the State, nor is it entitled to be recorded in the bureau of conveyances, but no certificate of acknowledgment executed before July 29, 1872, shall in consequence of anything in this chapter contained be deemed invalid.

§ 502-54. **Penalty for false certificate.** Any officer authorized to take acknowledgments to instruments who knowingly incorporates in the certificate of acknowledgment any false or misleading statement as to the facts therein contained, shall be fined not more than $1,000 or imprisoned not more than one year, or both. Nothing in this section shall be construed to do away with the liability for civil damages for such act.

§ 502-61. **Changes noted in instrument.** Every notary public or the officer authorized to take acknowledgments to instruments, before taking any acknowledgment, shall first carefully inspect any instrument proposed to be acknowledged before him, and ascertain whether there are any interlineations, erasures, or changes in the instrument. If there are any interlineations, erasures, or changes, he shall call the attention thereto of the person offering to acknowledge the instrument. If they are approved, the acknowledging officer shall place his initials in the margin of the instrument opposite each interlineation, erasure, or change. The initialing by the officer taking the acknowledgment is prima facie evidence of the extent of the interlineations, erasures, or changes and of the fact that the same were made prior to acknowledgment of the instrument, but does not preclude proof to the contrary.

IDAHO

[IDAHO CODE]

§ 55-701. **By whom [acknowledgments] taken—any place within state.** The proof or acknowledgment of an instrument may be made at any place within this state, before a justice or clerk of the Supreme Court, or a notary public, of the secretary of state, or United States commissioner.

§ 55-702. **By whom taken—within limited territory.** The proof or acknowledgment of an instrument may be made in this state within the city, county or district for which the officer was elected or appointed, before either:

1. A judge or a clerk of a court of record; or,

2. A county recorder; or,

3. A justice of the peace.

§ 55-703. **By whom taken—outside of state.** The proof or acknowledgment of an instrument may be made without this state, but within the United States, and within the jurisdiction of the officer, before either:

1. A justice, judge or clerk of any court of record of the United States; or,

2. A justice, judge or clerk of any court of record of any state or territory; or,

3. A commissioner appointed by the governor of this state for that purpose; or,

4. A notary public; or,

5. Any other officer of the state or territory where the acknowledgment is made, authorized by its laws to take such proof or acknowledgment.

§ 55-704. **By whom taken—outside United States.** The proof of acknowledgment of an instrument may be made without the United States, before either:

1. A minister, commissioner or charge d'affaires of the United States, resident and accredited in the country where the proof or acknowledgment is made; or,

2. A consul or vice consul of the United States resident in the country where the proof or acknowledgment is made; or,

3. A judge of a court of record of the country where the proof or acknowledgment is made; or,

4. Commissioners appointed for such purposes by the governor of the state pursuant to statute; or,

5. A notary public.

§ 55-705. **By whom taken—members of the armed forces.** Any officer of any component of the army of the United States on active duty in federal service commissioned in or assigned or detailed to duty with the judge advocate general's department, any staff judge advocate or acting staff judge advocate, the president of a general or special court-martial, any summary court-martial, the trial judge advocate or any assistant trial judge advocate of a general or special court-martial, any officer designated to take a deposition, and the adjutant, assistant adjutant or personnel adjutant of any command; all commanders in chief of naval squadrons, commandants of navy yards and stations, officers commanding vessels of the navy, and recruiting officers of the navy, the adjutant and inspector, assistants adjutants and inspector(s), commanding officers, and recruiting officers of the marine corps, and such officers of the regular navy and marine corps, of the naval reserves, and of the marine corps reserve, as may be designated to take a deposition; shall have the general powers of a notary public in the administration of oaths, the execution and acknowledgment of legal instruments, the attestation of documents and all other forms of notarial acts to be executed by persons in any of the armed forces of the United States or subject to military or naval law;

Such an acknowledgment or oath, whether so taken within or without the state of Idaho or the United States and whether with or without seal or stamp, shall have the same force and effect as an acknowledgment or oath before a notary public duly commissioned by and residing in the state of Idaho. Recital in the certificate of such officer that he holds the office stated in the certificate and that the affiant is a member of the armed forces or subject to military or naval law shall be prima facia (facie) evidence of such facts.

§ 55-706. **Acknowledgment before deputies.** When any of the officers mentioned in the four preceding sections are authorized by law to appoint a deputy, the acknowledgment or proof may be taken by such deputy, in the name of his principal.

§ 55-707.   Requisites of acknowledgment. The acknowledgment of an instrument must not be taken, unless the officer taking it knows, or has satisfactory evidence, on the oath or affirmation of a credible witness, that the person making such acknowledgment is the individual who is described in, and who executed, the instrument; or, if executed by a corporation, that the person making such acknowledgment is the president or vice-president or secretary or assistant secretary of such corporation; or other person who executed on its behalf; or if executed in the name of the state of Idaho or that of any county, political subdivision, municipal or quasi-municipal or public corporation, that the person making such acknowledgment is one of its officers executing the same; or if executed in a partnership name, that the person making the acknowledgment is the partner or one of the partners subscribing the partnership name to such instrument.

§ 55-708.   Acknowledgment by married woman. The acknowledgment of a married woman to any instrument in writing shall be taken and certified to in the same manner and form as that of a single person, and must be substantially in the form prescribed by section 55-710.

§ 55-709.   Certificate of acknowledgment. An officer taking the acknowledgment of an instrument must indorse thereon a certificate substantially in the forms hereinafter prescribed.

§ 55-710.   Form of certificate. The certificate of acknowledgment, unless it is otherwise in this chapter provided, must be substantially in the following form:

State of Idaho, county of ———, ss.

On this ——— day of ———, in the year of ———, before me (here insert the name and quality of the officer), personally appeared ———, known to me (or proved to me on the oath of ———), to be the person whose name is subscribed to the within instrument, and acknowledged to me that he (or they) executed the same.

§ 55-711.   Form of certificate—acknowledgment by corporation. The certificate of acknowledgment of an instrument executed by a corporation must be substantially in the following form:

State of Idaho, county of ———, ss.

On this ——— day of ———, in the year ———, before me (here insert the name and quality of the officer), personally appeared ——— known to me (or proved to me on the oath of ———) to be the president, or vice-president, or secretary or assistant secretary, of the corporation that executed the instrument or the person who executed the instrument on behalf of said corporation, and acknowledged to me that such corporation executed the same.

§ 55-712. Form of certificate—acknowledgment by attorney. The certificate of acknowledgment by an attorney in fact must be substantially in the following form:

State of Idaho, county of ———, ss.

On this ——— day of ———, in the year ———, before me (here insert the name and quality of the officer), personally appeared ———, known to me (or proved to me on the oath of ———) to be the person whose name is subscribed to the within instrument as the attorney in fact of ———, and acknowledged to me that he subscribed the name of ——— thereto as principal, and his own name as attorney in fact.

§ 55-713. Form of certificate—acknowledgment by official or fiduciary. The certificate of acknowledgment of an instrument which is executed by a person in his own name as trustee or as executor, administrator, guardian, sheriff, receiver or other official or representative capacity, shall be substantially in the following form:

State of Idaho, county of ———, ss.

On this ——— day of ———, in the year ———, before me (here insert the name and quality of the officer) personally appeared ———, known to me (or proved to me on the oath of ———), to be the person whose name is subscribed to the within instrument as (here insert the official or representative capacity in which the instrument is executed) and acknowledged to me that he (or they) executed the same as such (here insert again the official or representative capacity in which the instrument is executed).

§ 55-714. Form of certificate—acknowledgment by partnership. The certificate of acknowledgment of an instrument executed in a partnership name must be substantially in the following form:

State of Idaho, county of ———, ss.

On this ——— day of ———, in the year ———, before me (here insert the name and quality of the officer), personally appeared ———, known to me (or proved to me on the oath of ———), to be one of the partners in the partnership of (here insert partnership name signed to instrument), and the partner or one of the partners who subscribed said partnership name to the foregoing instrument, and acknowledged to me that he executed the same in said partnership name.

§ 55-715. Form of certificate—acknowledgment by state or political subdivision. The certificate of acknowledgment of an instrument executed in the name of the state of Idaho or any county, political subdivision, municipal, quasi-municipal or public corporation, must be substantially in the following form:

On this ——— day of ———, in the year ———, before me State of Idaho, county of ———, ss.

(here insert the name and quality of the officer), personally appeared ———, known to me (or proved to me on the oath of ———), to be the (here insert the official capacity of the officer making the acknowledgment) of the (here insert the name of state, county, subdivision or corporation executing the instrument) that executed the said instrument, and acknowledged to me that such (here insert name of state, county, political subdivision, municipal or public corporation executing the instrument) executed the same.

§ 55-716. **Authentication of certificate.** Officers taking and certifying acknowledgments or proof of instruments for record must authenticate their certificates by affixing thereto their signatures, followed by the names of their offices; also their seals of office, if by the laws of the territory, state or country where the acknowledgment or proof is taken, or by authority of which they are acting, they are required to have official seals.

§ 55-717. **Certificate of justice—authentication.** The certificate of proof or acknowledgment, if made before a justice of the peace, when used in any county other than that in which he resides, must be accompanied by a certificate under the hand and seal of the recorder of the county in which the justice resides, setting forth that such justice, at the time of taking such proof or acknowledgment, was authorized to take the same, and that the recorder is acquainted with his handwriting, and believes that the signature to the original certificate is genuine.

§ 55-718. **Proof of execution.** Proof of the execution of an instrument, when not acknowledged, may be made either:

1. By the parties executing it, or either of them; or,

2. By subscribing witness; or,

3. By other witnesses in the cases hereinafter mentioned.

§ 55-719. **Identity of witness must be known or proved.** If by a subscribing witness such witness must be personally known to the officer taking the proof, to be the person whose name is subscribed to the instrument, as a witness, or must be proved to be such by the oath of a credible witness.

§ 55-720. **Proof of identity of grantor.** The subscribing witness must prove that the person whose name is subscribed to the instrument as a party is the person described in it, and that such person executed it, and that the witness subscribed his name thereto as a witness.

§ 55-805. **Acknowledgment necessary to authorize recording.** Before an instrument may be recorded, unless it is otherwise expressly provided, its execution must be acknowledged by the person executing it, or if executed by a corporation, by its president or vice-president, or secretary or assistant secretary, or other person executing the same on behalf of the corporation, or if executed in name of the state of Idaho or any county, political subdivision, municipal, quasi-municipal, or public corporation, by one or more of the officers of such state, county, political subdivision, municipal, quasi-municipal, or public corporation executing the same, or if executed in a partnership name, by one or more of the partners who subscribed the partnership name thereto, or the execution must be proved and the acknowledgment or proof, certified in the manner prescribed by chapter 7 of this title; provided, that if such instrument shall have been executed and acknowledged in any other state or territory of the United States, or in any foreign country, according to the laws of the state, territory or country wherein such acknowledgment was taken, the same shall be entitled to record, and a certificate of acknowledgement indorsed upon or attached to any such instrument purporting to have been made in any such state, territory or foreign country, shall be prima facie sufficient to entitle the same to such record.

ILLINOIS

[ILL. ANN. STAT.]

Ch. 30, § 18. Acknowledgment by married woman. The acknowledgment or proof of any deed, mortgage, conveyance, power of attorney, or other writing of or relating to the sale, conveyance, or other disposition of lands or real estate, or any interest therein, by a married woman, may be made and certified the same as if she were a feme sole, and shall have the same effect.

§ 19. Acknowledgment or proof of deeds, mortgages, conveyances, releases, etc.—courts or officers authorized to take—attestation—persons serving with armed forces—validating provision. Deeds, mortgages, conveyances, releases, powers of attorney or other writings of or relating to the sale, conveyance or other disposition of real estate or any interest therein whereby the rights of any person may be affected in law or in equity, may be acknowledged or proven before some one of the following courts or officers, namely:

First—When acknowledged or proven within this State, before a notary public, United States commissioner, county clerk, or any court or any judge, clerk or deputy clerk of any such court. When taken before a notary public or United States commissioner, the same shall be attested by his official seal; when taken before a court or the clerk thereof, or a deputy clerk thereof, the same shall be attested by the seal of such court.

Second—When acknowledged or proven without this State and within the United States or any of its territories or dependencies or the District of Columbia, before a justice of the peace, notary public, master in chancery, United States commissioner, commissioner to take acknowledgments of deeds, mayor of city, clerk of a county, or before any judge, justice, clerk or deputy clerk of the supreme, circuit or district court of the United States, or before any judge, justice, clerk or deputy clerk, prothonotary, surrogate, or registrar of the supreme, circuit, superior, district, county, common pleas, probate, orphan's or surrogate's court of any of the states, territories or dependencies of the United States. In any dependency of the United States such acknowledgment or proof may also be taken or made before any commissioned officer in the military service of the United States. When such acknowledgment or proof is made before a notary public, United States commissioner or commissioner of deeds, it shall be certified under his seal of office. If taken before a mayor of a city it shall be certified under the seal of the city; if before a clerk, deputy clerk, prothonotary, registrar or surrogate, then under the seal of his court; if before a justice of the peace or a master in chancery there shall be added a certificate of the proper clerk under the seal of his office setting forth that the person before whom such proof or acknowledgment was made was a justice of the peace or master in chancery at the time of taking such acknowledgment or proof. As acknowledgment or proof of execution of any instrument aforesaid, may be made in conformity with the laws of the State, territory, dependency or district where it is made: Provided, that if any clerk of any court of record within such state, territory, dependency or district shall, under his hand and the seal of such court, certify that such acknowledgment or proof was made in conformity with the laws of such state, territory, dependency or district, or it shall so appear by the laws of such state, territory, dependency or district such instrument or a duly proved or certified copy of the record of such deed, mortgage or other instrument relating to real estate heretofore or hereafter made and recorded in the proper county may be read in evidence as in other cases of such certified copies.

Third—When acknowledged or proven without the United States, then before any court of any republic, dominion, state, kingdom, empire, colony, territory, or dependency having a seal, or before any judge, justice or clerk thereof or before any mayor or chief officer of any city or town having a seal, or before a notary public or commissioner of deeds, or any ambassador, minister or secretary of legation or consul of the United States or vice consul, deputy consul, commercial agent or consular agent of the United States in any foreign republic, dominion, state, kingdom, empire, colony, territory or dependency attested by his official seal or before any officer authorized by the laws of the place where such acknowledgment or proof is made to take acknowledgments of conveyances of real estate or to administer oaths in proof of the execution of conveyances of real estate. Such acknowledgment to be attested by the official seal, if any, of such court or officer, and in case such acknowledgment or proof is taken or made before a court or officer having no official seal, a certificate shall be added by some ambassador, minister, secretary of legation, consul, vice consul, deputy consul, commercial agent or consular agent of the United States residing in such republic, dominion, state, kingdom, empire, colony, territory, or dependency under his official seal, showing that such court or officer was duly elected, appointed or created and acting at the time such acknowledgment or proof was made.

Fourth—Any person serving in or with the armed forces of the United States, within or without the United States, and the spouse or former spouse of any such person, may acknowledge the instruments wherever located before any commissioned officer in active service of the armed forces of the United States with the rank of Second Lieutenant or higher in the Army, Air Force or Marine Corps, or Ensign or higher in the Navy or United States Coast Guard. The instrument shall not be rendered invalid by the failure to state therein the place of execution or acknowledgment. No authentication of the officer's certificate of acknowledgment shall be required and such certificate need not be attested by any seal but the officer taking the acknowledgment shall indorse thereon or attach thereto a certificate substantially in the following form:

On this the ——— day of ———, 19— before me, ———, the undersigned officer, personally appeared ———, known to me (or satisfactorily proven) to be serving in or with the armed forces of the United States (and/or the spouse or former spouse of a person so serving) and to be the person whose name is subscribed to the within instrument and acknowledgment that ——— he ——— executed the same as ——— free and voluntary act for the purposes therein contained. And the undersigned does further certify that he is at the date of this certificate a commissioned officer of the rank stated below and is in the active service of the armed forces of the United States.

———————

Signature of Officer

———————

Rank of Officer and Command
to which attached.

Fifth—All deeds or other instruments or copies of the record thereof duly certified or proven which have been acknowledged or proven prior to August 30, 1963, before either of the courts or officers in this act mentioned and in the manner herein provided, shall be deemed to be good and effectual in law and the same may be read in evidence without further proof of their execution, with the same effect as if this amendatory Act of 1963 had been in force at the date of such acknowledgment or proof.

§ 21. **Foreign acknowledgment—certificate of conformity.** Where any deed, conveyance or power of attorney has been or may be acknowledged or proved in any foreign state, kingdom, empire or country, the certificate of any consul or minister of the United States in said country, under his official seal, that the said deed, conveyance, or power of attorney is executed in conformity with such foreign law shall be deemed and taken as prima facie evidence thereof: Provided, that any other legal mode of proving that the same is executed in conformity with such foreign law may be resorted to in any court in which the question of such execution or acknowledgment may arise.

§ 22. **Foreign acknowledgment—effect.** All deeds, conveyances and powers of attorney, for the conveyance of lands lying in this state, which have been or may be acknowledged or proved and authenticated as aforesaid or in conformity with the laws of any foreign state, kingdom, empire or country, shall be deemed as good and valid in law as though acknowledged or proved in conformity with the existing laws of this state.

§ 23. **Duty of officer taking acknowledgment.** No judge or other officer shall take the acknowledgment of any person to any deed or instrument of writing, as aforesaid, unless the person offering to make such acknowledgment shall be personally known to him to be the real person who and in whose name such acknowledgment is proposed to be made, or shall be proved to be such by a credible witness, and the judge or officer taking such acknowledgment shall, in his certificate thereof, state that such person was personally known to him to be the person whose name is subscribed to such deed or writing, as having executed the same, or that he was proved to be such by a credible witness (naming him), and on taking proof of any deed or instrument of writing, by the testimony of any subscribing witnesses, the judge or officer shall ascertain that the person who offers to prove the same is a subscribing witness, either from his own knowledge, or from the testimony of a credible witness; and if it shall appear from the testimony of such subscribing witness that the person whose name appears subscribed to such deed or writing is the real person who executed the same, and that the witness subscribed his name as such, in his presence and at his request, the judge or officer shall grant a certificate, stating that the person testifying as subscribing witness was personally known to him to be the person whose name appears subscribed to such deed, as a witness of the execution thereof, or that he was proved to be such by a credible witness (naming him), and stating the proof made by him; and where any grantor or person executing such deed or writing, and the subscribing witnesses, are deceased or cannot be had, the judge or officer, as aforesaid, may take proof of the handwriting of such deceased party and subscribing witness or witnesses (if any); and the examination of a competent and credible witness, who shall state on oath or affirmation that he personally knew the person whose handwriting he is called to prove, and well knew his signature (stating his means of knowledge), and that he believes the name of such person subscribed to such deed or writing, as party or witness (as the case may be), was thereto subscribed by such person; and when the handwriting of the grantor or person executing such deed or writing, and of one subscribing witness (if any there be), shall have been proved, as aforesaid, or by proof of signature of grantor where there is no subscribing witness, the judge or officer shall grant a certificate thereof stating the proof aforesaid.

§ 25. **Form of acknowledgment.** A certificate of acknowledgment, substantially in the following form, shall be sufficient:

State of (name of state),

ss:

County of (name of county),

I (here give name of officer and his official title) do hereby certify that (name of grantor, and if acknowledged by wife, her name, and add "his wife") personally known to me to be the same person whose name is (or are) subscribed to the foregoing instrument, appeared before me this day in person, and acknowledged that he (she or they) ——— signed and delivered the said instrument as his (her or their) free and voluntary act, for the uses and purposes therein set forth.

Given under my hand and official seal, this (day of the month) day of (month) A.D. (year).

(Signature of officer.) (Seal.)

§ 34c. **Deeds and instruments of conveyances—inclusion—effect of absence or neglect.** Whenever any deed or instrument of conveyance or other instrument to be made a matter of record is executed there shall be typed or printed to the side or below all signatures the names of the parties signing such instruments including the witnesses thereto, if any, and the names of the parties or officers taking the acknowledgments. The absence or neglect to print or type the names of the parties under the signatures shall not invalidate the instrument.

                    ◦   ◦   ◦

§§ 221 to 230. The Uniform Recognition of Acknowledgments Act has been adopted. For text of act, see page 349.

Ch. 32, § 804. Acknowledgments. No acknowledgment of a deed, mortgage, or other instrument shall be invalid because such acknowledgment was taken before an officer authorized by the laws of this State to acknowledge conveyances, who is also a member, director, employee, or officer of an association which is a party to such deed, mortgage, or other instrument.

INDIANA

[IND. CODE]

§ 17-3-42-1. **Essential requirements for recording of instruments.** No instrument executed after the effective date of this act ° ° ° shall be received for record by the county recorder of any county of the state unless the same complies with each of the following requirements:

(a) The name of each person who executed such instrument shall be legibly printed, typewritten or stamped upon such instrument immediately beneath the signature of such person;

(b) No discrepancy shall exist between the name of such person as it appears either in the body of such instrument, the acknowledgment or jurat, as printed, typewritten or stamped upon such instrument by the signature, or in the signature of such person;

(c) The name of each witness to such instrument shall be legibly printed, typewritten or stamped upon such instrument immediately beneath the signature of such witness;

(d) The name of any notary public whose signature appears upon such instrument shall be legibly printed, typewritten or stamped upon such instrument immediately beneath the signature of such notary public;

(e) Wherever in this act it is required that the name of a person shall be "printed, typewritten or stamped upon such instrument immediately beneath the signature" of such person, it is the intent of the legislature to require that such signature be written upon such instrument directly preceding such name so "printed, typewritten or stamped." Such signature shall not, however, be superimposed upon such name so as to render either illegible. Such instrument shall, however, be entitled to be received for record if such name and signature are in the discretion of the county recorder so placed upon such instrument as to render the connection between the two apparent. Any instrument received and recorded by a county recorder shall be conclusively presumed to comply with the requirements of this act. The requirements contained in this act shall be cumulative to the requirements imposed by any other act relating to the recording of instruments.

§ 32-1-2-18. **Acknowledgment or proof.** To entitle any conveyance, mortgage, or instrument of writing to be recorded, it shall be acknowledged by the grantor, or proved before any judge, or clerk of a court of record, justice of the peace, auditor, recorder, notary public, or mayor of a city in this or any other state; or before any commissioner appointed in another state by the governor of this state; or before any minister, charge d'affaires, or consul of the United States in any foreign country.

§ 32-1-2-19. Acknowledgment in another county. When any conveyance, mortgage, or other instrument required to be recorded, is acknowledged in any county in this state, other than the one in which the same is required to be recorded, the acknowledgment shall be certified by the clerk of the circuit court of the county in which such officer resides, and attested by the seal of said court; but an acknowledgment before an officer, having an official seal, if attested by such official seal, shall be sufficient without such certificate.

§ 32-1-2-20. Acknowledgment in another state. To entitle to record, in this state, conveyances acknowledged out of this state and within the United States, the same must be certified by the clerk of any court of record of the county in which the officer receiving the acknowledgment resides, and attested by the seal of said court; but an acknowledgment before an officer having an official seal, attested by his official seal, shall be sufficient without such certificate.

§ 32-1-2-21. Manner of proof. All deeds may be proved according to the rules of the common law, before any officer authorized to take acknowledgments, and being so proved, shall be entitled to record.

§ 32-1-2-22. Wife's acknowledgment. It shall not be necessary for a married woman to acknowledge her deed in any form other than that required by unmarried persons.

§ 32-1-2-23. Form of acknowledgment. The following or any other form substantially the same, shall be a good or sufficient form of acknowledgment of any deed or mortgage:

"Before me, E. F. [a judge or justice, as the case may be] this ———— day of ————, ————, A. B. acknowledged the execution of the annexed deed, [or mortgage, as the case may be]."

§ 32-1-2-24. Acknowledgment when grantor signs by mark. Whenever before any public officer duly authorized to receive acknowledgment of deeds, the grantor of any deed shall sign the same with his or her mark, and also in all other cases in which the said public officer shall have good cause to believe that the contents and purport of said deed are not fully known to the grantor thereof, it shall be the duty of the said public officer before signature, fully to explain to him or her, the contents and purport of the within deed. But the failure of such officer so to do shall not affect the validity of any deed.

§ 32-1-2-25. Power of attorney—wife may join. A married woman may join in a power of attorney with her husband for the conveyance or mortgage of lands, or of any interest therein, and said power of attorney shall be duly acknowledged, and shall be entitled to record.

§ 32-1-2-26. Certificate of acknowledgment. A certificate of the acknowledgment of the conveyance or other instrument in writing, required to be recorded, under the hand and seal of the officer taking the same, shall be written on or attached to such deed; and in all cases where, by law, the certificate of the clerk of the proper county is required to accompany the acknowledgment, the said certificate shall set forth that the officer before whom such acknowledgment was taken, was at the time, lawfully acting as such, and that his signature to the certificate of acknowledgment, is genuine.

§ 32-2-4-1. Acknowledgment in foreign country. Conveyances, mortgages and other instruments in writing, of a character to admit them to record under the recording laws of this state, when executed in a foreign country, shall be acknowledged by the grantor or person executing the same, and proved before any diplomatic or consular officer of the United States, duly accredited, or before any officer of such country who, by the laws thereof, is authorized to take acknowledgments or proof of conveyances; and if such acknowledgment or proof is in the English language, and attested by the official seal of such officer, it shall be sufficient to admit such instrument to record; but if in some other language or not attested by such official seal, then such instrument must be accompanied by a certificate of an officer of the United States, as aforesaid, to the effect that it is duly executed according to the laws of such foreign country; that the officer certifying to the acknowledgment or proof had legal authority so to do, and the meaning of his certificate, if the same is made in a foreign language.

§ 35-1-125-1. Acknowledgment—affixing name to blank. If any justice of the peace, notary public or other officer authorized to administer oaths or take acknowledgments, affixes his name to any blank form of affidavit or certificate of acknowledgment of any instrument proper to be acknowledged, and delivers the same so signed to any other person with intent that such blank form shall be afterwards filled up and used as an affidavit or acknowledgment, such justice, notary public or other officer as aforesaid, and such persons so filling up or using such affidavit or acknowledgment, shall, on conviction, be imprisoned in the state prison not less than two [2] years nor more than fourteen [14] years, and be fined not less than ten dollars [$10.00] nor more than one thousand dollars [$1,000].

IOWA

[IOWA CODE ANN.]

§ 534.65. Acknowledgments by employees. No public officer qualified to take acknowledgments or proofs of execution of written instruments shall by reason of his membership in or being an officer of or employment by a savings and loan association interested in such instrument be disqualified from taking and certifying to the acknowledgment or proof of execution of any written instrument in which such association is interested, and any such acknowledgment or proof heretofore taken or certified is hereby legalized and declared valid.

§ 558.20. Acknowledgments within state. The acknowledgment of any deed, conveyance, or other instrument in writing by which real estate in this state is conveyed or encumbered, if made within this state, must be before some court having a seal, or some judge or clerk thereof, or some county auditor, or judicial magistrate or district associate judge within the county, or notary public within the state. Each of the officers above named is authorized to take and certify acknowledgments of all written instruments, authorized or required by law to be acknowledged.

§ 558.21. Acknowledgments outside of state. When made out of the state but within the United States, it shall be before a judge of a court of record, or officer holding the seal thereof, or a commissioner appointed by the governor of this state to take the acknowledgment of deeds, or some notary public, or justice of the peace.

§ 558.22. Certificate of authenticity. When made out of the state but within the United States and before a judge, or justice of the peace, a certificate, under the official seal of the clerk or other proper certifying officer of a court of record of the county or district, or of the secretary of state of the state or territory within which such acknowledgment was taken, under the seal of his office, of the official character of said judge, or justice, and of the genuineness of his signature, shall accompany said certificate of acknowledgment.

§ 558.23. Authorized foreign officials. The proof or acknowledgment of any deed or other written instrument required to be proved or acknowledged in order to entitle the same to be recorded or read in evidence, when made by any person without this state and within any other state, territory, or district of the United States, may also be made before any officer of such state, territory, or district authorized by the laws thereof to take the proof and acknowledgment of deeds; and when so taken and certified as provided in section 558.24, may be recorded in this state, and read in evidence in the same manner and with like effect as proofs and acknowledgments taken before any of the officers named in section 558.21.

§ 558.24. Certificate of authenticity. To entitle any conveyance or written instrument, acknowledged or proved under section 558.23, to be read in evidence or recorded in this state, there shall be subjoined or attached to the certificate of proof or acknowledgment signed by such officer a certificate of the secretary of state of the state or territory in which such officer resides, under the seal of such state or territory, or a certificate of the clerk of a court of record of such state, territory, or district in the county in which said officer resides or in which he took such proof or acknowledgment, under the seal of such court.   Such certificate shall comply substantially with section 558.25.

§ 558.25.   Form of authentication.   The following form of authentication of the proof or acknowledgment of a deed or other written instrument, when taken without this state and within any other state, territory, or district of the United States, or any form substantially in compliance with the foregoing provisions of this chapter, shall be used:

(Begin with a caption specifying the state, territory, or district, and county or place where the authentication is made.)

"I, ———, clerk of the ——— court in and for said county, which court is a court of record, having a seal (or I, ———, secretary of state of such state or territory), do hereby certify that ———, by and before whom the foregoing acnkowledgment or proof was taken, was at the time of taking the same ——— residing or authorized to act in said county, and (Name of office held) was duly authorized by the laws of said state, territory, or district to take and certify acknowledgments or proofs of deeds of land in said state, territory, or district, and that said conveyance and the acknowledgment thereof are in due form of law; and, further, that I am well acquainted with the handwriting of said ———, and that I verily believe that the signature to said certificate of acknowledgment or proof is genuine.   In testimony whereof, I have hereunto set my hand and affixed the seal of the said court or state this ——— day of ———, A.D. 19—."

§ 558.26.   Acknowledgments by military or naval officers.   In addition to the acknowledgment of instruments in the manner and form and as otherwise authorized by law, any person serving in or with the armed forces of the United States may acknowledge the same wherever located before any commissioned officer in active service of the armed forces of the United States with the rank of second lieutenant or higher in the army or marine corps, or ensign or higher in the navy or United States coast guard.   Neither the instrument nor the acknowledgment shall be rendered invalid by the failure to state therein the place of execution or acknowledgment. No authentication of the officer's certificate of acknowledgment shall be required, but the officer taking the acknowledgment shall indorse thereon or attach thereto a certificate substantially in the following form:

On this the ——— day of ———, 19—, before me, ———, the undersigned commissioned officer, personally appeared ———, known to me, or satisfactorily proven) to be serving in or with the armed forces of the United States and to be the person whose name is subscribed to the within instrument and acknowledged that

———— he —————— executed the same as —————— voluntary act and deed.

————————

Signature of officer.

————————

Rank of officer and command to which attached.

Such acknowledgments executed according to the above provisions shall be deemed of the same force and effect as acknowledgments executed before officers authorized to accept acknowledgments.

Any acknowledgments heretofore made by any person serving in or with the armed forces of the United States in the manner as prescribed by this section, or substantially so, are hereby legalized and considered sufficient.

§ 558.27. **Acknowledgments outside United States.** When the acknowledgment is made without the United States, it may be before any ambassador, minister, secretary of legation, consul, vice-consul, charge d'affaires, consular agent, or any other officer of the United States in a foreign country who is authorized to issue certificates under the seal of the United States.

§ 558.28. **Authorized foreign officials.** Said instruments may also be acknowledged or proved without the United States before any officer of a foreign country who is authorized by the laws thereof to certify to the acknowledgments of written documents.

§ 558.29. **Certificate of authenticity.** The certificate of acknowledgment by a foreign officer must be authenticated by one of the above-named officers of the United States, whose official written statement that full faith and credit is due to the certificate of such foreign officer shall be deemed sufficient evidence of the qualification of said officer to take acknowledgments and certify thereto, and of the genuineness of his signature, and seal if he have any.

§ 558.30. **Certificate of acknowledgment.** The court or officer taking the acknowledgment must indorse upon the deed or instrument a certificate setting forth the following particulars:

1. The title of the court or person before whom the acknowledgment was made.

2. That the person making the acknowledgment was known to the officer taking the acknowledgment to be the identical person whose name is affixed to the deed as grantor, or that such identity was proved by at least one credible witness, naming him.

3. That such person acknowledged the execution of the instrument to be his voluntary act and deed.

§ 558.31. **Proof of execution and delivery in lieu of acknowledgment.** Proof of the due and voluntary execution and delivery of a deed or other instrument may be made before any officer authorized to take acknowledgments, by one competent person other than the vendee or other person to whom the instrument is executed, in the following cases:

1. If the grantor dies before making the acknowledgment.

2. If his attendance cannot be procured.

3. If, having appeared, he refuses to acknowledge the execution of the instrument.

§ 558.32. **Contents of certificate.** The certificate indorsed by the officer upon a deed or other instrument thus proved must state:

1. The title of the officer taking the proof.

2. That it was satisfactorily proved that the grantor was dead, or that for some other reason his attendance could not be procured in order to make the acknowledgment, or that, having appeared, he refused to acknowledge the same.

3. The name of the witness by whom proof was made, and that it was proved by him that the instrument was executed and delivered by the person whose name is thereunto subscribed as a party.

§ 558.33. **Subpoenas.** An officer having power to take the proof hereinbefore contemplated may issue the necessary subpoenas, and compel the attendance of witnesses residing within the county, in the manner provided for the taking of depositions.

§ 558.34. **Use of seal.** The certificate of proof or acknowledgment may be given under seal or otherwise, according to the mode by which the officer making the same usually authenticates his formal acts.

§ 558.35. **Married women.** The acknowledgment of a married woman, when required by law, may be taken in the same form as if she were sole, and without any examination separate and apart from her husband.

§ 558.38. **Officers of corporation.** If the acknowledgment is made by the officers of a corporation, the certificate shall show that such persons as such officers, naming the office of each person, acknowledged the execution of the instrument as provided in section 558.39.

§ 558.39. **Forms of acknowledgment.** The following forms of acknowledgment shall be sufficient in the cases to which they are respectively applicable. In each case where one of these forms is used, the name of the state and county where the acknowledgment is taken shall precede the body of the certificate, and the signature and official title of the officer shall follow it as indicated in the first form and shall constitute a part of the certificate, and the seal of the officer shall be attached when necessary under the provisions of this chapter. No certificate of acknowledgment shall be held to be defective on account of the failure to show the official title of the officer making the certificate if such title appears either in the body of such certificate or in connection therewith, or with the signature thereto.

1. In the case of natural persons acting in their own right:

State of ———

ss.

County of ———

On this ——— day of ———, A.D. 19—, before me ———, (Insert title of acknowledging officer) personally appeared ———, to me known to be the person ——— named in and who executed the foregoing instrument, and acknowledged that ——— executed the same as ——— voluntary act and deed.

Notary Public in the state of Iowa.

2. In the case of natural persons acting by attorney:

On this ——— day of ———, A.D. 19—, before me ———, (Insert title of acknowledging officer) personally appeared ———, to me known to be the person who executed the foregoing instrument in behalf of ———, and acknowledged that he executed the same as the voluntary act and deed of said ———.

3. In the case of corporations or joint-stock associations:

On this ——— day of ———, A.D. 19—, before me, a ———, (Insert title of acknowledging officer) in and for said county, personally appeared ———, to me personally known, who being by me duly [sworn or affirmed] did say that he is ——— (Insert title of acknowledging officer) (Insert title of executing officer) ——— (Insert title of executing officer) of said [corporation/association], that [the seal affixed to said instrument is the seal of said/no seal has been procured by the said] [corporation/association] and that said instrument was signed and sealed on behalf of the said [corporation/ association] by authority of its board of [directors/trustees] and the said ——— acknowledged the execution of said instrument to be the voluntary act and deed of said [corporation/association] by it voluntarily executed.

(In all cases add signature and title of the officer taking the acknowledgment, and strike from between the parentheses the word or clause not used, as the case may be.)

Any instrument affecting real estate situated in this state which has been or may be acknowledged or proved in a foreign state or country and in conformity with the laws of that foreign state or country, shall be deemed as good and valid in law as though acknowledged or proved in conformity with the existing laws of this state.

§ 558.40. **Liability of officer.** Any officer, who knowingly misstates a material fact in either of the certificates mentioned in this chapter,° shall be liable for all damages caused thereby, and shall be guilty of a misdemeanor, and fined any sum not exceeding the value of the property conveyed or otherwise affected by the instrument on which such certificate is indorsed.

° Includes a certificate of acknowledgment and proof of execution and delivery in lieu of acknowledgment.

KANSAS

[KAN. STAT. ANN.]

§§ 53-301 to 53-309. The Uniform Recognition of Acknowledgments Act has been adopted. For text of act, see page 349.

§ 58-2211. **Acknowledgment within state.** All conveyances, and other instruments affecting real estate, acknowledged within this state, must be acknowledged before some court having a seal, or some judge, justice, or clerk thereof, or some notary public, county clerk, or register of deeds, or mayor or clerk of an incorporated city.

§ 58-2212. **Acknowledgment out of state.** If acknowledged out of this state, it must be before some court of record, or clerk or officer holding the seal thereof, or before some commissioner to take the acknowledgments of deeds, appointed by the governor of this state, or before some notary public or any consul of the United States, resident in any foreign port or country.

§ 58-2228. **Validity of instruments acknowledged in other states.** All deeds, mortgages, powers of attorney and other instruments of writing for the conveyance or encumbrance of any lands, tenements or hereditaments situate within this state, executed and acknowledged or proved in any other state, territory, or country, in conformity with the laws of such state, territory, or country, or in conformity with the laws of this state, shall be as valid as if executed within this state in conformity with the provisions of this act.

§ 58-2229. **Instruments as evidence.** Every instrument in writing, conveying or affecting real estate, which shall be acknowledged or proved and certified as hereinbefore prescribed, may, together with the certificates of acknowledgment or proof, be read in evidence without further proof.

KENTUCKY

[KY. REV. STAT. ANN.]

§ 382.130. **When deeds executed in this state to be admitted to record.** Deeds executed in this state may be admitted to record:

(1) On the acknowledgment, before the proper clerk, by the party making the deed;

(2)   By the proof of two subscribing witnesses, or by the proof of one subscribing witness, who also proves the attestation of the other;

(3)   By the proof of two witnesses that the subscribing witnesses are both dead; and also like proof of the signature of one of them and of the grantor;

(4)   By like proof that both of the subscribing witnesses are out of the state, or that one is so absent and the other is dead; and also like proof of the signature of one of the witnesses and of the grantor; or

(5)   On the certificate of a county clerk of this state, or any notary public, that the deed has been acknowledged before him by the party making the deed or proved before him in the manner required by subsection (2), (3) or (4).

§ 382.140.   Recording of deeds executed out of state.   Deeds executed out of this state and within the United States or any of its dependencies may be admitted to record when certified, under the seal of his office or court, by a judge, clerk or deputy clerk of a court, or by a notary public, mayor of a city, secretary of state, commissioner authorized to take acknowledgment of deeds or justice of the peace, to have been acknowledged or proved before him in the manner required by KRS 382.130.

§ 382.150.   Recording of deeds executed in foreign country. Deeds not executed within the United States or any of its dependencies, may be admitted to record when certified, under his seal of office, by any foreign minister, officer in the consular service of the United States, secretary of legation of the United States, or by the secretary of foreign affairs or a notary public of the nation in which the acknowledgment is made, or by the judge or clerk of a superior court of the nation where the deed is executed, to have been acknowledged or proven before him in the manner prescribed by law.

§ 382.160.   Certificate of acknowledgment or proof of deed.   (1) Where the acknowledgment of a deed is taken by an officer of this state or by an officer residing out of this state, he may simply certify that it was acknowledged before him, and when it was done.

(2)   Where a deed is proved by persons other than the subscribing witnesses, the officer shall state the name and residence of each person in his certificate.

§§ 423.110 to 423.190.   The Uniform Recognition of Acknowledgments Act has been adopted.   For text of act, see page 349.

LOUISIANA

[LA. REV. STAT.]

§ 6:787.   Directors, employees and members not disqualified to make acknowledgments.   No public officer qualified to take acknowledgments or proofs of written instruments shall be disqualified from taking the acknowledgment or proof of any instrument in writing in which an association is interested by reason of his membership in or employment by an association so interested, and any such acknowledgments or proofs heretofore taken are hereby validated.

§ 35:5.   Foreign notaries; oaths and acknowledgments, effect. In all cases in which, under the laws of Louisiana, oaths or acknowledgments may be taken or made before any Louisiana commissioner residing in any other state or territory of the United States, or in the District of Columbia, the same may be taken or made by or before any notary public, duly appointed in any such state, territory, or District; and when certified under the hand and official seal of the notary shall have the same force and effect without further proof of the signature, seal, and official character of the notary as if taken or made by or before a Louisiana commissioner residing in such state, territory, or district.

§ 35:6.   Foreign notaries; acts and other instruments, effect. All acts passed before any notary public and two witnesses in the District of Columbia, or any state of the United States other than Louisiana shall be authentic acts and shall have the same force and effect as if passed before a notary public in Louisiana.

Within State

§ 35:511.   Forms of acknowledgment. Either the forms of acknowledgment now in use in this State, or the following, may be used in the case of conveyances or other written instruments, whenever such acknowledgment is required or authorized by law for any purpose:

(Begin in all cases by a caption specifying the state and place where the acknowledgment is taken.)

1.   In the case of natural persons acting in their own right:

On this ——— day of ———, 19—, ——— before me personally appeared A B (or A B and C D), to me known to be the person (or persons) described in and who executed the foregoing instrument, and acknowledged that he (or they) executed it as his (or their) free act and deed.

2.   In the case of natural persons acting by attorney:

On this ——— day of ———, 19—, before me personally appeared A B, to me known to be the person who executed the foregoing instrument in behalf of C D, and acknowledged that he executed it as the free act and deed of said C D.

3.   In the case of corporations or joint stock associations:

On this ——— day of ———, 19—, before me appeared A B, to me personally known, who, being by me duly sworn (or affirmed) did say that he is the president (or other officer or agent of the corporation or association), of (describing the corporation or association), and that the seal affixed to said instrument is the corporate seal of said corporation (or association) and that the instrument was signed and sealed in behalf of the corporation (or association) by authority of its Board of Directors (or trustees) and that A B acknowledged the instrument to be the free act and deed of the corporation (or association).

(In case the corporation or association has no corporate seal, omit the words "the seal affixed to said instrument is the corporate seal of the corporation (or association), and that" and add, at the end of the affidavit clause, the words "and that the corporation (or association) has no corporate seal").

(In all cases add signature and title of the officer taking the acknowledgment.)

§ 35:512. Married women, acknowledgment by. The acknowledgment of a married woman when required by law may be taken in the same form as if she were sole and without any examination separate and apart from her husband.

§ 35:513. Officers before whom proof or acknowledgment taken in other states. The proof or acknowledgment of any deed or other written instrument required to be proved or acknowledged in order to enable the same to be recorded or read in evidence, when made by any person without this state and within any other state, territory, or district of the United States, may be made before any officer of such state, territory or district, authorized by the laws thereof to take the proof and acknowledgment of deeds, and when so taken and certified under his official seal, shall be entitled to be recorded in this state, and may be read in evidence in the same manner and with like effect as proofs and acknowledgments taken before any of the officers now authorized by law to take such proofs and acknowledgments, and whose authority so to do is not intended to be hereby affected.

Foreign

§ 35:551. Officers before whom made. All instruments requiring acknowledgment, if acknowledged without the United States, shall be acknowledged before an ambassador, minister, envoy or charge d'affaires of the United States, in the country to which he is accredited, or before one of the following officers commissioned or accredited to act at the place where the acknowledgment is taken, and having an official seal, viz.:—any officer of the United States; a notary public; or a commissioner or other agent of this state having power to take acknowledgments.

§ 35:552. Form of certificate of acknowledgment. Every certificate of acknowledgment, made without the United States, shall contain the name or names of the person or persons making the acknowledgment, the date when and the place where made, a statement of the fact that the person or persons making the acknowledgment knew the contents of the instrument, and acknowledged it to be his, her or their act; the certificate shall also contain the name of the person before whom made, his official title, and be sealed with his official seal and may be substantially in the following form:

———— (name of country).

———— (name of city, province or other political subdivision). Before the undersigned ———— (naming the officer and designating his official title) duly commissioned (or appointed) and qualified, this day personally appeared at the place above named ———— (naming the person or persons acknowledging) who declared that he (she or they) knew the contents of the foregoing instrument, and acknowledged it to be his (her or their) act.

Witness my hand and official seal this ———— day of ———— 19—

———— (name of officer).

(seal)   ———— (official title).

When the seal affixed shall contain the names or the official style of the officer, any error in stating, or failure to state otherwise the name or the official style of the officer, shall not render the certificate defective.

§ 35:553. **Acknowledgments in form used in state.** A certificate of acknowledgment of a deed or other instrument acknowledged without the United States before any officer mentioned in R.S. 35:551 shall also be valid if in the same form as now is or hereafter may be required by law, for an acknowledgment within this state.

§ 35:554. **Interpretation and construction.** This Part shall be so interpreted and construed as to effectuate its general purpose to make uniform the law of those states which enact it.

§ 35:555. **Force and effect.** Every acknowledgment or proof of any legal instrument and any oath or affirmation, taken or made before a commissioner, ambassador, minister, charge d'affaires, secretary of legation, consul general, consul, or vice consul, and every attestation or authentication made by them, when duly certified as above provided, shall have the force and effect of an authentic act executed in this state.

MAINE

[ME. REV. STAT. ANN.]

Tit. 4, §§ 1011 to 1019. The Uniform Recognition of Acknowledgments Act has been adopted. For text of act, see page 349.

Tit. 33, § 203. Need for acknowledgment. Deeds and all other written instruments before recording in the registries of deeds, except those issued by a court of competent jurisdiction and duly attested by the proper officer thereof, and excepting plans and notices of foreclosure of mortgages and certain financing statements as provided in Title 11, section 9-401, and excepting notices of liens for internal revenue taxes and certificates discharging such liens as provided in section 664, shall be acknowledged by the grantors, or by the persons executing any such written instruments, or by one of them, or by their attorney executing the same, or by the lessor in a lease or one of the lessors or his attorney executing the same, before a justice of the peace or notary public having a seal, in the State, or before an attorney-at-law duly admitted and eligible to practice in the courts of the State, if within the State; or before any clerk of a court of record having a seal, notary public, justice of the peace or commissioner appointed by the Governor of this State for the purpose, or a commissioner authorized in the state where the acknowledgment is taken, within the United States or before a minister, vice-consul or consul of the United States or notary public in any foreign country. The seal of such court or the official seal of such notary public or commissioner, if he has one, shall be affixed to the certificate of acknowledgment, but if such acknowledgment is taken outside the State before a justice of the peace, notary public not having a seal or commissioner, a certificate under seal from the secretary of state, or clerk of a court of record in the county where the officer resides or took the acknowledgment, authenticating the authority of the officer taking such acknowledgment and the genuineness of his signature, must be annexed thereto.

* * *

Tit. 33, § 207. Recording master form. An instrument containing a form or forms of covenants, conditions, obligations, powers and other clauses of a mortgage, or deed of trust, may be recorded in the registry of deeds of any county and the recorder of such county, upon the request of any person, on tender of the lawful fees therefor, shall record the same in his registry. Every such instrument shall be entitled on the face thereof as a "Master form recorded by —————" (name of person causing the instrument to be recorded). Such instrument need not be acknowledged to be entitled to record.

Tit. 33, § 306. Indorsement of certificate of acknowledgment. A certificate of acknowledgment or proof of execution must be indorsed on or annexed to the deed, and then the deed and certificate may be recorded in the registry of deeds. No deed can be recorded without such certificate.

Tit. 33, § 351. Acknowledgments after commission expired. When a person authorized to take acknowledgments takes and certifies one in good faith after the expiration of his commission, not being aware of it, such acknowledgment is as valid as if done before such expiration.

MARYLAND

[MD. ANN. CODE]

Art. 18, §§ 1 to 14. The Uniform Acknowledgment Act has been adopted. For text of act, see page 349.

Art. 23, § 123. Acknowledgments. A corporation may acknowledge any instrument by law to be acknowledged, by its appointed attorney, and such appointment may be embodied in the deed, or such instrument may be acknowledged by the president or any vice-president of such corporation without such appointment.

MASSACHUSETTS

[MASS. ANN. LAWS]

Ch. 183, § 30. Acknowledgment, how made. The acknowledgment of a deed or other written instrument required to be acknowledged shall be by one or more of the grantors or by the attorney executing it. The officer before whom the acknowledgment is made shall endorse upon or annex to the instrument a certificate thereof. Such acknowledgment may be made—

(a) If within the commonwealth, before a justice of the peace or notary public.

(b) If without the commonwealth, in any state, territory, district or dependency of the United States, before a justice of the peace, notary public, magistrate or commissioner appointed therefor by the governor of this commonwealth, or, if a certificate of authority in the form prescribed by section thirty-three is attached thereto, before any other officer therein authorized to take acknowledgment of deeds.

(c) If without the United States or any dependency thereof, before a justice of the peace, notary, magistrate or commissioner as above provided, or before an ambassador, minister, consul, vice consul, charge d'affaires or consular officer or agent of the United States accredited to the country where the acknowledgment is made; if made before an ambassador or other official of the United States, it shall be certified by him under his seal of office.

Ch. 183, § 31. Acknowledgment by married woman. The acknowledgment by a married woman may be taken in the same form as if she were sole, and without any examination separate and apart from her husband.

Ch. 183, § 32. Acknowledgment of powers of attorney to convey real estate. The law relative to the acknowledgment and recording of deeds shall apply to letters of attorney for the conveyance of real estate.

Ch. 183, § 33. Certificate of authority of officer. Whenever, under clause (b) of section thirty or under section forty-one, a certificate of authority is required to be attached, there shall be subjoined or attached to the certificate of proof or acknowledgment a certificate of the secretary of state of the state where the officer taking the acknowledgment resides, under the seal of such state, or a certificate of the clerk of a court of record of such state in the county where said officer resides or where he took such proof or acknowledgment, under the seal of the court, stating that said officer was, at the time of taking such proof or acknowledgment, duly authorized thereto in said state, and that said secretary of state or clerk of court is well acquainted with his handwriting and verily believes the signature affixed to such certificate of proof or acknowledgment is genuine.

Ch. 183, § 34. Proof of execution if grantor is dead or non-resident. If the grantor dies or removes from the commonwealth without having acknowledged his deed, the due execution thereof may be proved before any court of record in this commonwealth by the testimony of a subscribing witness thereto.

Ch. 183, § 35. Proof if witnesses are dead or non-resident. If all the subscribing witnesses to the deed are also dead or out of the commonwealth, the due execution thereof may be proved before such court by proving the handwriting of the grantor and of a subscribing witness.

Ch. 183, § 39. Unwitnessed deeds not to be so proved. The execution of a deed shall not be proved in the manner before provided unless it has at least one subscribing witness.

Ch. 183, § 40. Endorsement of certificate of proof. A certificate of proof of the execution of a deed shall be endorsed upon it or annexed thereto by the clerk or register of the court or by the judge before whom such proof is made, and the certificate shall state whether the grantor was present at the hearing.

Ch. 183, § 41. Proof of deed outside the commonwealth. The proof of a deed or other instrument, if made without the commonwealth in some state, territory, district or dependency of the United States, may be made before any of the persons enumerated in clause (b) of section thirty; provided, however, that a certificate of authority as provided in section thirty-three shall be attached thereto; if without the United States or any dependency thereof, such may be made before any of the persons enumerated in clause (c) of said section thirty.

Ch. 183, § 42. Forms of acknowledgment, etc. The forms set forth in the appendix to this chapter for taking acknowledgments to deeds and other instruments and for certifying the authority of officers taking proofs for acknowledgments may be used; but shall not prevent the use of any other form heretofore lawfully used.

Ch. 183, § 56.   ° ° °

FORMS OF ACKNOWLEDGMENTS, ETC.

(13)   *Acknowledgment of Individual acting in his Own Right*

(Caption specifying the state and place where the
acknowledgment is taken.)

On this ———— day of ———— 19—, before me personally appeared A B (or A B and C D), to me known to be the person (or persons) described in and who executed the foregoing instrument, and acknowledged that he (or they) executed the same as his (or their) free act and deed.

(Signature and title of officer taking acknowledgment.   Seal,
if required.)

(14)   *Acknowledgment of Individual acting by Attorney*

(Caption specifying the state and place where the
acknowledgment is taken.)

On this ———— day of ———— 19—, before me personally appeared A B, to me known to be the person who executed the foregoing instrument in behalf of C D, and acknowledged that he executed the same as the free act and deed of said C D.

(Signature and title of officer taking acknowledgment.   Seal,
if required.)

(15)   *Acknowledgment of a Corporation or Joint Stock Association*

(Caption specifying the state and place where the
acknowledgment is taken.)

On this ———— day of ———— 19—, before me appeared A B, to me personally known, who, being by me duly sworn (or affirmed), did say that he is the president (or other officer or agent of the corporation or association) of (describing the corporation or association) and that the seal affixed to said instrument is the corporate seal of said corporation (or association), and that said instrument was signed and sealed in behalf of said corporation (or association) by authority of its board of directors (or trustees), and said A B acknowledged said instrument to the free act and deed of said corporation (or association).

(Signature and title of officer taking acknowledgment.   Seal,
if required.)

[If the corporation or association has no corporate seal, the words "the seal affixed to said instrument is the corporate seal of said corporation (or association), and that" shall be omitted, and at the end of the affidavit shall be added the words "and that said corporation (or association) has no corporate seal".]

(16)   *Certificate of Authority of Officer taking Acknowledgment*

(Caption specifying the state, county or place where the authentication is made.)

I, ———, clerk of the ——— in and for said county, which court is a court of record having a seal (or, I, ———, the secretary of state of such state or territory), do hereby certify that ———, by and before whom the foregoing acknowledgment (or proof) was taken, was, at the time of taking the same, a notary public (or other officer) residing (or authorized to act) in said county, and was duly authorized by the laws of said state (territory or district) to take and certify acknowledgments or proofs of deeds of land in said state (territory or district), and further that I am well acquainted with the handwriting of said ———, and that I verily believe that the signature to said certificate of acknowledgment (or proof) is genuine. In testimony whereof, I have hereunto set my hand and affixed the seal of the said court (or state) this ——— day of ———, 19—.

(Signature and title of officer certifying.   Seal.)

Ch. 222, § 11.   Acknowledgment of written instruments by persons serving in or with the armed forces of the United States or their dependents.   Persons serving in or with the armed forces of the United States or their dependents, wherever located, may acknowledge any instrument, in the manner and form required by the laws of this commonwealth, before any commissioned officer in the active service of the armed forces of the United States with the rank of second lieutenant or higher in the army, air force or marine corps, or ensign or higher in the navy or United States Coast Guard. Any such instrument shall contain a statement that the person executing the instrument is serving in or with the armed forces of the United States or is a dependent of a person serving in or with the armed forces of the United States, and in either case the statement shall include the serial number of the person so serving. No such instrument shall be rendered invalid by the failure to state therein the place of execution or acknowledgment.

No authentication of the officer's certificate of acknowledgment shall be required.

Instruments so acknowledged outside of the commonwealth, if otherwise in accordance with law, shall be received and may be used in evidence, or for any other purpose, in the same manner as if taken before a commissioner of the commonwealth appointed to take depositions in other states.

MICHIGAN

[MICH. COMP. LAWS ANN.]

§ 565.8.   Execution of deed; witnesses, acknowledgment; validation of certain acknowledgments; deeds not properly witnessed, use

in evidence.   Sec. 8.   Deeds executed within this state of lands, or any interest in lands therein, shall be executed in the presence of 2 witnesses, who shall subscribe their names to the same as such, and the persons executing such deeds may acknowledge the execution thereof before any judge, clerk or commissioner of a court of record, or before any notary public, justice of the peace, or master in chancery, within the state, and the officer taking such acknowledgment shall endorse thereon a certificate of the acknowledgment thereof, and the true date of making the same, under his hand.

⁘   ⁘   ⁘

§ 565.9.   Execution of deed in another state; governing law, acknowledgment.   Sec. 9.   If any such deed shall be executed in any other state, territory or district of the United States, such deed may be executed according to the laws of such state, territory or district, and the execution thereof may be acknowledged before any judge of a court of record, notary public, justice of the peace, master in chancery or other officer authorized by the laws of such state, territory or district to take the acknowledgment of deeds therein, or before any commissioner appointed by the governor of this state for such purpose.

§ 565.10.   Same; acknowledgment; seal of officer, certificate; record of prior deeds as evidence.   Sec. 10.   In the cases provided for in the last preceding section unless the acknowledgment be taken before a commissioner appointed by the governor of this state for that purpose the officer taking such acknowledgment shall attach thereto the seal of his office, and if such acknowledgment be taken before a justice of the peace or other officer having no seal of office, such deed or other conveyance or instrument shall have attached thereto a certificate of the clerk or other proper certifying officer of a court of record of the county or district, or of the secretary of state of the state or territory within which such acknowledgment was taken under the seal of his office, that the person whose name is subscribed to the certificate of acknowledgment was, at the date thereof, such officer as he is therein represented to be, and that he believes the signature of such person to such certificate of acknowledgment to be genuine, and that the deed is executed and acknowledged according to the laws of such state, territory or district. Whenever any deed or other instrument affecting the title to land, executed, acknowledged and authenticated in accordance with this section and the last preceding section, has been heretofore recorded in the proper county, such record, or a certified transcript thereof shall be prima facie evidence of the due execution of such instrument to the same extent as if it had been authenticated as required by the statute in force at the time such instrument was recorded.

§ 565.11.   Execution of deed in foreign country; governing law; acknowledgment; certificate, seal; validation of certain deeds, record

as evidence. Sec. 11. If such deed be executed in any foreign country it may be executed according to the laws of such country, and the execution thereof may be acknowledged before any notary public therein or before any minister plenipotentiary, minister extraordinary, minister resident, charge d'affaires, commissioner, or consul of the United States, appointed to reside therein; which acknowledgment shall be certified thereon by the officer taking the same under his hand, and if taken before a notary public his seal of office shall be affixed to such certificate: Provided, That all deeds of land situated within this state, heretofore or hereafter made in any foreign country, and executed in the presence of 2 witnesses, who shall have subscribed their names to the same as such, and the execution thereof shall have been acknowledged by the persons executing the same before any 1 of the officers authorized by this section to take such acknowledgment, and such acknowledgment shall have been certified thereon, as above required, shall be deemed between the parties thereto and all parties claiming under or through them, as valid and effectual to convey the legal estate of the premises therein described; and whenever such deed has been recorded in the office of the register of deeds of the proper county such rcord shall be effectual for all purposes of a legal record, and the record of such deed, or a transcript thereof, may be given in evidence as in other cases: Provided, That nothing herein contained shall impair the rights of any person under a purchase heretofore made in good faith and on valuable consideration.

§ 565.16. Refusal to acknowledge deed; application to justice, summons to grantor. Sec. 16. If any grantor residing in this state, shall refuse to acknowledge his deed, the grantee or any person claiming under him, may apply to any justice of the peace in the county where the land lies, or where the grantor or any subscribing witness to the deed resides, who shall thereupon issue a summons to the grantor to appear at a certain time and place before the said justice, to hear the testimony of the subscribing witnesses to the deed; and the said summons with a copy of the deed annexed, shall be served at least 7 days before the time therein assigned for proving the deed.

§§ 565.261 to 565.269. The Uniform Recognition of Acknowledgments Act has been adopted. For text of act, see page 349.

MINNESOTA

[MINN. STAT. ANN.]

§ 358.14. Married persons. No separate examination of a married woman shall be required, but if husband and wife join in and acknowledge the execution of any instrument, they shall be described in the certificate of acknowledgment as husband and wife; and, if they acknowledge it before different officers, or before the same officer at different times, each shall be described in the certificate as the spouse of the other.

§ 358.15. **By whom taken in this state.** The following named officers shall have power to take and certify acknowledgments within the state:

(1) Every member of the legislature, so long as he shall remain such and continue to reside in the district from which he was elected; but he shall receive no fee or compensation for so doing. The form of his official signature in such cases shall be: "A.B., Representative (or Senator), ———— District, Minnesota. My term expires January 1, 19—;"

(2) The judges and clerks and deputy clerks of all courts of record, residing within the state, including those of the circuit and district courts of the United States, and resident United States commissioners;

(3) Notaries public, justices of the peace, and the clerks or recorders of towns, villages, boroughs, and cities; and

(4) Court commissioners, registers of deeds, and county auditors, and their several deputies, and county commissioners, all within their respective counties.

§§ 358.32 to 358.40. The Uniform Recognition of Acknowledgments Act has been adopted. For text of act, see page 349.

MISSISSIPPI

[MISS. CODE ANN.]

§ 89-3-3. **Acknowledgment and proof.** Every conveyance, contract, or agreement proper to be recorded, may be acknowledged or proved before any judge of a United States court, any judge of the supreme court, any judge of the circuit court, or any chancellor, or any judge of the county court, or before any clerk of a court of record or notary public, who shall certify such acknowledgment or proof under the seal of his office, or before any justice of the peace, or police justice, or mayor of any city, town, or village, or member of the board of supervisors, whether the property conveyed be within his county or not.

§ 89-3-5. **Acknowledgments before commissioned officers of United States armed forces.** In all cases where a conveyance, contract, agreement or other instrument of writing has heretofore been acknowledged or proved before any commissioned officer in the services of the United States armed forces, such acknowledgment or affidavit is hereby declared to be good, valid and binding to the same extent and with like effect as though such conveyance, contract, agreement, or other instrument of writing had been acknowledged or proved before any officer authorized by law to take acknowledgments in the State of Mississippi.

Accord, § 25-33-23. See *Armed Forces* below.

§ 89-3-7. Forms of acknowledgment. The following forms of acknowledgment may be used in the case of conveyances or other written instruments affecting real estate or personal property; and any acknowledgment so taken and certified shall be sufficient to satisfy all requirements of law:

[Begin in all cases by a caption specifying the state and county, and it would be well to state the place, where the acknowledgment is taken.]

1.—In the case of natural persons acting in their own right.

"Personally appeared before me, ———, a judge of the Supreme Court of said state [or a judge of the circuit court, chancellor, clerk of the ——— court of the county of ———, or a justice of the peace of the county of ———, or a member of the board of supervisors of the county of ———, as the case may be], the within named A B, who acknowledged that he signed and delivered the foregoing instrument on the day and year therein mentioned.

"Given under my hand, this the ——— day of ———, A. D. ———."

2.—In case of witnesses.

And in case the proof of execution of the instrument be made by a subscribing witness, follow the above form to and including the word "appeared," and then as follows, to wit:

"C D, one of the subscribing witnesses to the foregoing instrument, who, being first duly sworn, deposeth and saith that he saw the within [or above] named A B, whose name is subscribed thereto, sign and deliver the same to the said E F [or that he heard the said A B acknowledge that he signed and delivered the same to the said E F]; that he, this affiant, subscribed his name as a witness thereto in the presence of the said A B."

[In all cases add signature and title of the officer taking the acknowledgment; and if he have an official seal, affix it.]

3.—Directions for married woman's acknowledgment.

When a married woman unites with her husband in the execution of an instrument, and acknowledges the same in one of the forms above sanctioned, she should be described in the acknowledgment as his wife; but in all other respects, and when she executes any instrument affecting her separate property, real or personal, her acknowledgment shall be taken and certified as if she were sole; and a separate examination of a married woman in respect to the execution of any instrument affecting real estate or other property shall not be required, nor shall the failure to describe her as the wife of a grantor affect the acknowledgment.

§ 89-3-9. **Acknowledgment or proof in another state.** If the party who shall execute any conveyance of lands or person property situated in this state, or if the witnesses thereto reside or be in some other state, territory in the Union, the District of Columbia, or in any possession of the United States, or land over which the United States has sovereign power, then the acknowledgment or proof may be made before and certified by the chief justice of the United States, or an associate justice of the Supreme Court of the United States, or a circuit or district judge of the United States, or any other United States judge, or any judge or justice of the supreme or superior court of any such state, territory, District of Columbia, or possession of the United States, or land over which the United States has sovereign power, or any justice of the peace of such state, territory, District of Columbia, possession, or land over which the United States has sovereign power, whose official character shall be certified under the seal of some court of record in his country, parish or other named official jurisdiction, or before any commissioner residing in such state, territory, District of Columbia, possession, or land over which the United States has sovereign power, who may be appointed by the governor of this state to take acknowledgments and proof of conveyances, or any notary public or a clerk of a court of record having a seal of office in said state, territory, District of Columbia, possession, or land over which the United States has sovereign power, and shall be as good and effectual as if the certificate of acknowledgment or proof had been made by a competent officer in this state.

§ 89-3-13. **Acknowledgment or proof in foreign country.** If the party who shall execute any conveyance of lands or personal property situated in this state, or if the witnesses thereto, reside or be in a foreign country, the acknowledgment or proof of the execution of such conveyance may be made before any court of record, or the mayor or chief magistrate of any city, borough, or corporation of such foreign country in which the party or witness resides or may be; or before any commissioner residing in such country who may be appointed by the governor, or before any ambassador, foreign minister, secretary of legation, or consul of the United States to the foreign country in which the party or witness may reside or be; but the certificate shall show that the party, or the party and witness, were identified before the officer, and that the party acknowledged the execution of the instrument, or that the execution was duly proved by the witness, and it shall be as good and effectual as if made and certified by a competent officer of this state.

§ 89-3-15. **Grantor and witness dead or absent, how proved.** If the grantor and witness or witnesses of any instrument of writing be dead or absent, so that the personal attendance of neither can be had, it may be established by the oath of any person who, on examination before an officer competent to take acknowledgments, can prove the handwriting of the deceased or absent witness or witnesses; or when such proof cannot be had, then the handwriting of the grantor may be proved, and the officer before whom such proof is made shall certify accordingly, and such certificate shall be deemed equivalent to an acknowledgment by the grantor or proof by a subscribing witness, and entitle the instrument to be recorded.

Armed Forces

§ 25-33-23. Notarial acts of commissioned officers of United States armed forces. In addition to the acknowledgment of instruments and the performance of other notarial acts in the manner and form and as otherwise authorized by law, instruments may be acknowledged, documents attested, oaths and affirmations administered, depositions and affidavits executed, and other notarial acts performed before or by any commissioned officer in active service of the armed forces of the United States with the rank of second lieutenant or higher in the army or marine corps, or with the rank of ensign or higher in the navy or coast guard, or with equivalent rank in any other component part of the armed forces of the United States, by any person who either (a) is a member of the armed forces of the United States or the husband or wife of a member of the armed forces of the United States; or (b) is serving as a merchant seaman outside the limits of the United States included within the 48 states and the District of Columbia; or (c) is outside said limits by permission, assignment, or direction of any department or official of the United States government, in connection with any activity pertaining to the prosecution of any war in which the United States is then engaged.

Such acknowledgments of instruments, attestation of documents, administration of oaths and affirmations, executions of depositions and affidavits, and performance of other notarial acts, heretofore or hereafter made or taken, are hereby declared legal, valid, and binding, and instruments and documents so acknowledged, authenticated, or sworn to shall be admissible in evidence and eligible to record in this state under the same circumstances and with the same force and effect as if such acknowledgment, attestation, oath, affirmation, deposition, affidavit, or other notarial act had been made or taken within this state before or by a duly qualified officer or official as otherwise provided by law.

In the taking of acknowledgments and the performing of other notarial acts requiring certification, a certificate endorsed upon or attached to the instrument or documents, which shows the date of the notarial act and which state, in substance, that the person appearing before the officer acknowledged the instrument as his act or made or signed the instrument or document under oath, shall be sufficient for all intents and purposes. The instrument or document shall not be rendered invalid by the failure to state the place of execution or acknowledgment.

If the signature, rank, and branch of service or subdivision thereof, of any such commissioned officer appear upon such instrument or document or certificate, no further proof of the authority of such officer so to act shall be required, and such action by such commissioned officer shall be prima facie evidence that the person making such oath or acknowledgment is within the purview of this section.

Accord, § 89-3-5, above.

MISSOURI

[MO. ANN. STAT.—Vernon]

§ 442.150. **Proof or acknowledgment, by whom taken.** The proof or acknowledgment of every conveyance or instrument in writing affecting real estate in law or equity, including deeds of married women, shall be taken by some one of the following courts or officers:

(1) If acknowledged or proved within this state, by some court having a seal, or some judge, justice or clerk thereof, or a notary public; or

(2) If acknowledged or proved without this state and within the United States, by any notary public or by any court of the United States, or of any state or territory, having a seal, or the clerk of any such court or any commissioner appointed by the governor of this state to take the acknowledgment of deeds;

(3) If acknowledged or proved without the United States, by any court of any state, kingdom or empire having a seal or the mayor or chief officer of any city or town having an official seal or by any minister or consular officer of the United States or notary public having a seal.

§ 442.180. **Certificate to be endorsed on conveyance.** Every court or officer taking the proof or acknowledgment of any conveyance or instrument of writing affecting real estate, or the relinquishment of the dower of a married woman, shall grant a certificate thereof, and cause the same to be endorsed on such conveyance or instrument or writing.

§ 442.190. **Certificate, how made.** Such certificate shall be

(1) When granted by a court, under the seal of the court;

(2) When granted by the clerk of the court, under the hand of the clerk and seal of the court of which he is clerk;

(3) When granted by an officer who has a seal of office, under the hand and official seal of such officer;

(4) When granted by an officer who has no seal of office, under the hand of such officer.

§ 442.200. **Identity of persons making acknowledgments, how ascertained.** No acknowledgment of any instrument in writing conveying real estate, or whereby any real estate may be affected, shall be taken, unless the persons offering to make such acknowledgment shall be personally known to at least one judge of the court, or to the officer taking the same, to be the person whose name is subscribed to such instrument as a party thereto, or shall be proved to be such by at least two credible witnesses.

§ 442.210. **Certificate of acknowledgment—contents. 1.** The certificate of acknowledgment shall state the act of acknowledgment, and that the person making the same was personally known to at least one judge of the court, or to the officer granting the certificate, to be the person whose name is subscribed to the instrument as a party thereto, or was proved to be such by at least two witnesses, whose names and places or residence shall be inserted in the certificate; and the following forms of acknowledgment may be used in the case of conveyances or other written instruments affecting real estate; and any acknowledgment so taken and certified shall be sufficient to satisfy all requirements of law relating to the execution or recording of such instruments (begin in all cases by a caption, specifying the state and place where the acknowledgment is taken):

(1)   In case of natural persons acting in their own right

On this ——— day of ———, 19—, before me personally appeared A B (or A B and C D), to me known to be the person (or persons) described in and who executed the foregoing instrument, and acknowledged that he (or they) executed the same as his (or their) free act and deed.

(2)   In the case of natural persons acting by attorney

On this ——— day of ———, 19—, before me personally appeared A B, to me known to be the person who executed the foregoing instrument in behalf of C D, and acknowledged that he executed the same as the free act and deed of C D.

(3)   In the case of corporations or joint stock associations

On this ——— day of ——— 19—, before me appeared A B, to me personally known, who, being by me duly sworn (or affirmed) did say that he is the president (or other officer or agent of the corporation or association), of (describing the corporation or association), and that the seal affixed to foregoing instrument is the corporate seal of said corporation (or association), and that said instrument was signed and sealed in behalf of said corporation (or association) by authority of its board of directors (or trustees), and said A B acknowledged said instrument to be the free act and deed of said corporation (or association).

2.   In case the corporation or association has no corporate seal, omit the words "the seal affixed to said instrument is the corporate seal of said corporation (or association), and that," and add at the end of the affidavit clause the words "and that said corporation (or association) has no corporate seal."

3.   (In all cases add signature and title of the officer taking the acknowledgment.)

4. When a married woman unites with her husband in the execution of any such instrument, and acknowledges the same in one of the forms above sanctioned, she shall be described in the acknowledgment as his wife, but in all other respects her acknowledgment shall be taken and certified as if she were sole; and no separate examination of a married woman in respect to the execution of any release or dower, or other instrument affecting real estate, shall be required.

§ 561.060. False acknowledgment of deed—penalty. 1. It shall be unlawful for any person authorized by law to take proof or acknowledgment of any instrument which by law may be recorded to:

(1) Willfully certify that any such instrument was acknowledged by any party when no such acknowledgment was made;

(2) Willfully certify that any such instrument was proved when no such proof was made;

(3) Willfully certify falsely in any material matter contained in any certificate being or purporting to be a certificate of acknowledgment or proof of any such instrument; or

(4) Willfully sign or sign and seal, and place or leave in the hands of possession of another, any blank certificate of acknowledgment of any conveyance, with the design or intent that such other, or any other person, without any acknowledgment of such instrument having been made before such officer, shall insert in such blank certificate any name, date or any matter whatever.

2. Any person violating any of the provisions of this section shall be deemed guilty of a felony and upon conviction shall be punished by imprisonment in the penitentiary for not less than two nor more than ten years or by imprisonment in the county jail for a term of not more than one year or by a fine of one thousand dollars or by both such fine and imprisonment.

MONTANA

[MONT. REV. CODES ANN.]

§ 14-525. Trustees, officers or members [of co-operatives]—notaries. No person who is authorized to take acknowledgments under the laws of this state shall be disqualified from taking acknowledgments of instruments executed in favor of a co-operative or to which it is a party, by reason of being an officer, director or member of such co-operative.

§ 39-101. By whom acknowledgments may be taken in this state. The proof of acknowledgment of an instrument may be made at any place within this state before a justice or clerk of the supreme court, or a judge of this district court.

§ 39-102. Same—where and by whom acknowledgments may be taken. The proof of acknowledgment of an instrument may be made in this state within the city, county, or district for which the officer was elected or appointed, before either:

1. A clerk of a court of record; or,

2. A county clerk; or,

3. A notary public; or,

4. A justice of the peace; or,

5. A United States commissioner.

§ 39-103. By whom taken without the state. The proof of acknowledgment of an instrument may be made without this state, but within the United States, and within the jurisdiction of the officer, before either:

1. A justice, judge, or clerk of any court of record of the United States; or,

2. A justice, judge, or clerk of any court of record of any state or territory; or,

3. A commissioner appointed by the governor of this state for that purpose; or,

4. A notary public; or,

5. Any other officer of the state or territory where the acknowledgment is made authorized by its laws to take such proof or acknowledgment.

§ 39-103.1. Effect of acknowledgment outside state in accordance with other state's law. Notwithstanding any provision contained in Title 39 of the Revised Codes of Montana of 1947, the acknowledgment of any instrument without this state in compliance with the manner and form prescribed by the laws of the place of its execution, if in a state, a territory or insular possession of the United States, or in the District of Columbia, verified by the official seal of the officer before whom it is acknowledged, shall have the same effect as an acknowledgment in the manner and form prescribed by the laws of this state for instruments executed within the state.

§ 39-104. By whom taken without the United States. The proof or acknowledgment of an instrument may be made without the United States, before either:

1. A minister, commissioner, or charge d'affaires of the United States, resident and accredited in the country where the proof or acknowledgment is made; or,

2. A consul, vice-consul, or consular agent of the United States, resident in the country where the proof or acknowledgment is made; or,

3. A judge of a court of record of the country where the proof or acknowledgment is made; or,

4. Commissioners appointed for such purposes by the governor of the state, pursuant to special statutes; or,

5. A notary public.

§ 39-105. Deputy can take acknowledgment. When any of the officers mentioned in the four preceding sections are authorized by law to appoint a deputy, the acknowledgment or proof may be taken by such deputy, in the name of his principal.

§ 39-107. Officer taking acknowledgment must know person— corporations. The acknowledgment of an instrument must not be taken unless the officer taking it knows or has satisfactory evidence that the person making such acknowledgment is the individual who is described in and who executed the instrument; or, if executed by a corporation, that the person making such acknowledgment is the president, or vice-president, or secretary, or assistant secretary of such corporation, or other person duly authorized by resolution of such corporation, who executed it on its behalf.

§ 39-108. Acknowledgment by married women. The acknowledgment of a married woman to an instrument purporting to be executed by her must be taken the same as that of any other person.

§ 39-109. Conveyance by married woman—acknowledgment. A conveyance by a married woman has the same effect as if she were unmarried, and may be acknowledged in the same manner.

§ 39-110. Officer must endorse certificate. An officer taking the acknowledgment of an instrument must endorse thereon, or attach thereto, a certificate substantially in the forms hereinafter prescribed.

§ 39-111. General form of certificate. The certificate of acknowledgment, unless it is otherwise in this chapter provided, must be substantially in the following form:

State of ——

ss.

County of ——

On this —— day of ——, in the year ——, before me (here insert the name and quality of the officer), personally appeared ——, known to me (or proved to me on the oath of ——), to be the person whose name is subscribed to the within instrument, and acknowledged to me that he (she or they) executed the same.

§ 39-112. Certificate of acknowledgment by corporation. The certificate of acknowledgment of an instrument executed by a corporation must be substantially in the following form:

State of ———

           ss.

County of ———

On this ——— day of ———, in the year ———, before me (here insert the name and quality of the officer), personally appeared ——— known to me (or proved to me on the oath of ———) to be the president (or vice-president) or the secretary (or the assistant secretary) of the corporation that executed the within instrument (where, however, the instrument is executed in behalf of the corporation by some one other than the president, or vice-president, or secretary, or assistant secretary), insert: known to me (or proved to me on the oath of ———) to be the person who executed the within instrument on behalf of the corporation therein named, and acknowledged to me that such corporation executed the same.

§ 39-113. Form of certificate of acknowledgment by married woman. The certificate of acknowledgment by a married woman must be substantially in the form prescribed in section 39-111.

§ 39-114. Form of certificate of acknowledgment by attorney in fact. The certificate of acknowledgment by an attorney in fact must be substantially in the following form:

State of ———

           ss.

County of ———

On this ——— day of ———, in the year ———, before me (here insert the name and quality of the officer), personally appeared ———, known to me (or proved to me on the oath of ———), to be the person whose name is subscribed to the within instrument as the attorney in fact of ———, and acknowledged to me that he subscribed the name of ——— thereto as principal, and his own name as attorney in fact.

§ 39-115. Officers must affix their signatures. Officers taking and certifying acknowledgments or proof of instruments for record must authenticate their certificates by affixing their signatures, following by the names of their offices; also, their seals of office, if by the laws of the state or country where the acknowledgment or proof is taken, or by authority of which they are acting, they are required to have official seals.

§ 39-116. Certificate of authority of justices in certain cases. The certificate of proof or acknowledgment, if made before a justice of the peace, when used in any county other than that in which he resides, must be accompanied by a certificate, under the hand and seal of the clerk of the county in which the justice resides, setting forth that such justice, at the time of making such proof or acknowledgment, was authorized to take the same, and that the clerk is acquainted with his handwriting, and believes that the signature to the original certificate is genuine.

§ 39-117.   **Proof of execution—how made.**   Proof of the execution of an instrument, when not acknowledged, may be made either:

1.   By the party executing it, or either of them; or,
2.   By a subscribing witness; or,
3.   By other witnesses, in cases mentioned in section 39-120.

§ 39-120.   **Handwriting may be proved, when.**   The execution of an instrument may be established by proof of the handwriting of the party and of a subscribing witness, if there is one, in the following cases:

1.   When the parties and all the subscribing witnesses are dead; or,
2.   When the parties and all the subscribing witnesses are nonresidents of the state; or,
3.   When the place of their residence is unknown to the party desiring the proof, and cannot be ascertained by the exercise of due diligence; or,
4.   When the subscribing witness conceals himself, or cannot be found by the officer by the exercise of due diligence in attempting to serve the subpoena or attachment; or,
5.   In case of the continued failure or refusal of the witness to testify for the space of one hour, after his appearance.

§ 39-121.   **What facts must be proved by evidence of handwriting.** The evidence taken under the preceding section must satisfactorily prove to the officer the following facts:

1.   The existence of one or more of the conditions mentioned therein; and,
2.   That the witness testifying knew the person whose name purports to be subscribed to the instrument as a party, and is well acquainted with his signature, and that it is genuine; and,
3.   That the witness testifying personally knew the person who subscribed the instrument as a witness, and is well acquainted with his signature, and that it is genuine; and,
4.   The place of residence of the witness.

§ 39-122.   **Certificate of proof.**   An officer taking proof of the execution of any instrument must, in his certificate endorsed thereon or attached thereto, set forth all the matters required by law to be done or known by him, or proved before him on the proceeding, together with the names of all the witnesses examined before him, their places of residence respectively, and the substance of their testimony.

§ 39-123.   **Officers authorized to do certain things.**   Officers authorized to take the proof of instruments are authorized in such proceedings:

1. To administer oaths or affirmations, as prescribed in the Code of Civil Procedure;

2. To employ and swear interpreters;

3. To issue subpoenas, as prescribed in the Code of Civil Procedure;

4. To punish for contempt, as prescribed in the Code of Civil Procedure.

The civil damages and forfeiture to the party aggrieved are prescribed in the Code of Civil Procedure.

§ 39-124. **Instrument improperly certified—how corrected.** When the acknowledgment or proof of the execution of an instrument is properly made, but defectively certified, any party interested may have an action in the district court to obtain a judgment correcting the certificate.

§ 39-125. **Judgment proving instrument.** Any person interested under an instrument entitled to be proved for record may institute an action in the district court against the proper parties to obtain a judgment proving such instrument.

§ 39-126. **Effect of judgment in such action.** A certified copy of the judgment in a proceeding instituted under either of the two preceding sections, showing the proof of the instrument, and attached thereto, entitles such instrument to record, with the like effect as if acknowledged.

§ 67-1603. **Grant by married woman—how acknowledged.** No estate in the real property of a married woman passes by any grant purporting to be executed or acknowledged by her, unless the grant or instrument is acknowledged by her in the manner prescribed by sections 39-108 and 39-113.

§ 67-1604. **Power of attorney of married woman—how acknowledged.** A power of attorney of a married woman, authorizing the execution of an instrument transferring an estate in her separate real property, has no validity for that purpose unless acknowledged by her in the manner provided in sections 39-108 and 39-113.

§ 67-1605. **Attorney in fact—how must execute for principal.** When an attorney in fact executes an instrument transferring an estate in real property, he must subscribe the name of his principal to it, and his own name as attorney in fact.

§ 93-1101-9. **Private writings—how proved.** Every private writing, except last wills and testaments, may be acknowledged or proved and certified in the manner provided for the acknowledgment or proved and certified in the manner provided for the acknowledgment or proof of conveyances of real property, and the certificate of such acknowledgment or proof is prima-facie evidence of the execution of the writing in the same manner as if it were a conveyance of real property.

NEBRASKA

[NEB. REV. STAT.]

§ 25-1222. Private writing; when admissible without proof. Every private writing, except a last will and testament, after being acknowledged or proved and certified in the manner prescribed for the proof or acknowledgment of conveyances of real property, may be read in evidence without further proof.

§§ 64-201 to 64-209. The Uniform Recognition of Acknowledgments Act has been adopted.   For text of act, see page 349.

§ 76-217.01. Acknowledgment; defective seal; validity. No deed, mortgage, affidavit, power of attorney or other instrument in writing shall be invalidated because of any defects in the wording of the seal of the notary public attached thereto.

§ 76-217.02. Acknowledgment; insurance companies; cooperative credit associations; credit unions; by officers, agents and servants; authorized. It shall be lawful for a member or shareholder, an appointive officer, agent, or employee of an insurance company, a cooperative credit association, or a credit union who is a notary public and is not a director or elected officer of such association, insurance company, or credit union, to take the acknowledgment of any person to any written instrument executed to or by said association, insurance company, or credit union and to administer an oath to any shareholder, director, elected or appointive officer, employee, or agent of such association, insurance company, or credit union.

§ 76-217.04. Acknowledgments; banks; by stockholders, officers and directors; authorized. (1) It shall be lawful for any stockholder, officer, or director of a bank, who is a notary public, to take the acknowledgment of any person to any written instrument given to or by the bank and to administer an oath to any other stockholder, director, officer, employee or agent of the bank.

(2)   * * *.

§ 76-217.05. Acknowledgments; savings and loan associations; industrial loan and investment companies; by shareholders, directors, officers, agents, and servants; authorized; prior acknowledgments validated. It shall be lawful for any shareholder, director, employee, agent, or any elected or appointed officer of a savings and loan association or industrial loan and investment company, who is a notary public, (1) to take the acknowledgment of any person to any written instrument given to or by the savings and loan association or instrument given to or by the savings and loan association or industrial loan and investment company and (2) to administer an oath to any other shareholder, director, officer, employee, or agent of the savings and loan association or industrial loan and investment company. ° ° °.

§ 76-218. Acknowledgment and recording of instruments; violations; penalty. Every officer within this state authorized to take the acknowledgment or proof of any conveyance, and every county clerk, who shall be guilty of knowingly stating an untruth, or guilty of any malfeasance or fraudulent practice in the execution of the duties prescribed for them by law, in relation to the taking or the certifying of the proof or acknowledgment, or the recording or certifying of any record of any such conveyance, mortgage or instrument in writing, or in relation to the canceling of any mortgage, shall upon conviction be adjudged guilty of a misdemeanor, and be subject to punishment by fine not exceeding five hundred dollars, and imprisonment not exceeding one year, and shall also be liable in damages to the party injured.

§ 76-219. Acknowledgment; before whom taken in any other state or territory. If the instrument is executed and acknowledged or proved in any other state, territory or district of the United States, it must be executed and acknowledged or proved either according to the laws of such state, territory or district or in accordance with the law of this state, and if acknowledged out of this state it must be before some court of record or clerk or officer holding the seal thereof, or before some commissioner to take the acknowledgment of deeds, appointed by the Governor of this state, or before some notary public or justice of the peace. If taken before a justice of the peace, the acknowledgment shall be accompanied by a certificate of his official character under the hand of the clerk of some court of record, to which the seal of such court shall be affixed.

Note: See also § 76-242 below.

§ 76-226. Deeds; execution in foreign country; laws governing; acknowledgment. If such deed be executed in a foreign country, it may be executed according to the laws of such country, and the execution thereof may be acknowledged before any notary public therein, or before any minister plenipotentiary, minister extraordinary, minister resident, charge d'affaires, commissioner, commercial agent, or consul of the United States appointed to reside therein, which acknowledgment shall be certified thereon by the officer taking the same, under his hand, and if taken before a notary public, his seal of office shall be affixed to such certificate.

§ 76-227. Acknowledgment before army officers; validity. The acknowledgment of legal instruments, the attestation of documents, the administration of oaths and other notarial acts, heretofore or hereafter taken before any duly commissioned officer of the army, navy, marine corps, coast guard, or any other component part of the armed forces of the United States are hereby declared legal, valid and binding, and such instrument and documents shall be admissible in evidence and eligible to record in this state under the same circumstances, and with the same force and effect as if such acknowledgment, attestation, oath, affidavit, or other notarial act had been made or taken before a notary public within this state. If the signature, rank and branch of service of any such officer appear upon such instrument or document, no further proof of the authority of such officer to so act shall be required.

§ 76-241. Deeds and other instruments; when not lawfully recorded. All deeds, mortgages and other instruments of writing shall not be deemed lawfully recorded unless they have been previously acknowledged or proved in the manner prescribed by statute.

§ 76-242. Conveyances; acknowledged in another state; recording; what constitutes sufficient authentication. In all cases provided for in section 76-219,° if such acknowledgment or proof is taken before a notary public or other officer using an official seal, except a commissioner appointed by the Governor of this state, the instrument thus acknowledged or proved shall be entitled to be recorded without further authentication. In all other cases the deed or other instrument shall have attached thereto a certificate of the clerk of a court of record, or other proper certifying officer of the county, district or state within which the acknowledgment or proof was taken, under the seal of his office, showing that the person, whose name is subscribed to the certificate of acknowledgment, was at the date thereof such officer as he is therein represented to be; that he is well acquainted with the handwriting of such officer; that he believes the signature of such officer to be genuine; and that the deed or other instrument is executed and acknowledged according to the laws of such state, district or territory.

° For § 76-219, see above.

NEVADA

[NEV. REV. STAT.]

§ 1.180. Documents to which seal affixed. The seal of [a] court need not be affixed to any proceedings therein except:

1. To a summons, writ or commission to take testimony.

°   °   °

4. To certificate of acknowledgment and all final process.

§ 111.240. Acknowledgment of conveyances. Every conveyance in writing whereby any real property is conveyed or may be affected shall be acknowledged or proved and certified in the manner provided in this chapter.

§ 111.245. Acknowledgment of married woman. Any officer authorized by this chapter to take the proof or acknowledgment of any conveyance whereby any real property is conveyed, or may be affected, may take and certify the acknowledgment of a married woman to any such conveyance of real property.

§ 111.250. Endorsement or annexation of certificate by officer. 1. Every officer who shall take the proof or acknowledgment of any conveyance affecting any real property shall grant a certificate thereof and cause the certificate to be endorsed or annexed to the conveyance.

2. The certificate shall be:

(a) When granted by any judge or clerk, under the hand of the judge or clerk, and the seal of the court.

(b) When granted by an officer who has a seal of office, under the hand and official seal of the officer.

§ 111.255. Proof of identity of person making acknowledgment required. No acknowledgment of any conveyance whereby any real property is conveyed, or may be affected, shall be taken unless the person offering to make the acknowledgment shall be personally known to the officer taking the same to be the person whose name is subscribed to the conveyance as a party thereto, or shall be proved to be such by the oath or affirmation of a credible witness.

§ 111.260. Contents of certificate of acknowledgment. The certificate of such acknowledgment shall state the fact of acknowledgment, and that the person making the same was personally known to the officer granting the certificate to be the person whose name is subscribed to the conveyance as a party thereto, or was proved to be such by the oath or affirmation of a credible witness, whose name shall be inserted in the certificate.

§ 111.265. Who may take acknowledgment or proof within the state. 1. The proof or acknowledgment of every conveyance affecting any real property, if acknowledged or proved within this state, shall be taken by some one of the following officers:

(a) By a judge or a clerk of a court having a seal.

(b) By a notary public.

(c) By a justice of the peace.

2. When the acknowledgment is taken before a justice of the peace in any other county than that in which the real property is situated, the same shall be accompanied with the certificate of the clerk of the district court of the county, as to the official character of the justice of the peace taking the proof or acknowledgment, and the authenticity of his signature.

§ 111.270. Form of certificate made within state for individual, corporation, partnership. 1. A certificate, when made for an acknowledgment by an individual, corporation or partnership, shall be in substantially the following form:

STATE OF NEVADA

ss.

COUNTY OF ———

On ——— (date) personally appeared before me, a notary public (or judge or other officer, as the case may be), ———, who acknowledged that he executed the above instrument.

———————
(signature)

2. ° ° °

§ 111.280. **Form of certificate made within the state for attorney in fact.** A certificate, when made for an acknowledgment by an attorney in fact, shall be in substantially the following form:

STATE OF NEVADA

ss.

COUNTY OF ———

On this ——— day of ———, A.D. ———, personally appeared before me, a notary public (or judge or other officer, as the case may be), in and for ——— County, A.B., known (or proved) to me to be the person whose name is subscribed to the within instrument as the attorney in fact of ———, and acknowledged to me that he subscribed the name of ——— thereto as principal, and his own name as attorney in fact, freely and voluntarily and for the uses and purposes therein mentioned.

§ 111.285. **Form of certificate made within the state when grantor is unknown to officer.** When the grantor is unknown to the court or officer taking the acknowledgment, the certificate shall be in the following form:

STATE OF NEVADA

ss.

COUNTY OF ———

On this ——— day of ———, A.D. ———, personally appeared before me, a notary public (or judge or other officer as the case may be), in and for ——— County, A.B., satisfactorily proved to me to be the person described in and who executed the within conveyance, by the oath of C.D., a competent and credible witness, for that purpose by me duly sworn, and he, A.B., acknowledged that he executed the same freely and voluntarily and for the uses and purposes therein mentioned.

§ 111.290. **Who may take acknowledgment or proof without the state.** 1. The proof or acknowledgment of every conveyance affecting any real property, taken without this state but within the United States, shall be taken by some one of the following officers:

(a)   A judge or a clerk of a court having a seal.

(b)   A notary public.

(c)   A justice of the peace.

(d)   A commissioner appointed by the governor of this state for that purpose.

2.   When the acknowledgment is taken by a justice of the peace, the same shall be accompanied with the certificate of the clerk of a court of record of the county having a seal as to the official character of the justice of the peace and the authenticity of his signature.

3.   ° ° °.

§ 111.295.   **Form of acknowledgment certificate made without state: when sufficient.**   Any acknowledgment heretofore or hereafter taken, or certificate thereof made, without this state, either in accordance with the laws of this state or in accordance with the laws of the place where the acknowledgment is taken, shall be sufficient in this state.

§ 111.300.   **Who may take acknowledgment without the United States: form of certificate.**   1.   All deeds or other instruments requiring acknowledgment, if acknowledged without the United States, shall be acknowledged:

(a)   Before an ambassador, minister, envoy or charge d'affaires of the United States, in the country to which he is accredited; or

(b)   Before one of the following officers commissioned or credited to act at the place where the acknowledgment is taken, and having an official seal:

(1)   Any consular officer of the United States.

(2)   A notary public.

(3)   A commissioner or other agent of this state having power to take acknowledgments to deeds.

2.   Every certificate of acknowledgment made without the United States shall contain:

(a)   The name or names of the person or persons making the acknowledgment.

(b)   The date when and the place where made.

(c)   A statement of the fact that the person or persons making the acknowledgment knew the contents of the instrument and acknowledged the same to be his, her or their act.

(d)   The name of the person before whom made, his official title, and be sealed with his official seal.   When the seal affixed shall contain the name or the official style of the officer, any error in stating, or failure to state otherwise the name or the official style of the officer, shall not render the certificate defective.

3. The certificate may be substantially in the following form:

―――― (Name of country)

―――― (Name of city, province or other political subdivision)

Before the undersigned, ―――― (naming the officer and designating his official title), duly commissioned (or appointed) and qualified, this day personally appeared at the place above named ―――― (naming the person or persons acknowledging), who declared that he (she or they) knew the contents of the foregoing instrument, and acknowledged the same to be his (her or their) act.

Witness my hand and official seal this ―――― day of ――――, 19―.

(Seal)

                         ―――― (Name of officer)

                         ―――― (Official title)

4. A certificate of acknowledgment of a deed or other instrument acknowledged without the United States before any officer mentioned in subsection 1 shall also be valid if in the same form as now is or hereafter may be required by law, for an acknowledgment within this state.

§ 111.305. **Acknowledgments of members of and persons present with the armed forces: form of certificate; retroactive provisions.**
1. In addition to the acknowledgment of instruments in the manner and form and as otherwise authorized by the laws of the State of Nevada, any person serving in or with the armed forces of the United States or any person whose duties require his presence with the armed forces of the United States may acknowledge the same wherever located, whether within or without the United States, before any commissioned officer in active service of the armed forces of the United States with the rank of second lieutenant or higher in the army, air force or marine corps, or ensign or higher in the navy or United States Coast Guard. The instrument shall not be rendered invalid by the failure to state therein the place of execution or acknowledgment.

2. No authentication of the officer's certificate of acknowledgment shall be required, but the officer taking the acknowledgment shall endorse thereon or attach thereto a certificate substantially in the following form:

On this, the ―――― day of ――――, 19―, before me, ――――, the undersigned officer, personally appeared ――――, known to me (or satisfactorily proven) to be serving in or with the armed forces of the United States, or known to me (or satisfactorily proven) to be a person whose duties require his presence with the armed forces of the United States, and to be the person whose name is subscribed to the within instrument, and acknowledged that ―he― executed the same freely and voluntarily for the purposes therein mentioned. And the undersigned does further certify that he is at the date of this certificate a commissioned officer of the rank stated below and is in the active service of the armed forces of the United States.

Signature of officer.

Rank of officer and command to which attached.

3. Any officer mentioned in subsection 1 shall have power to administer oaths or affirmations to any person serving in or with the armed forces of the United States, or to any person whose duties require his presence with the armed forces of the United States, wherever located, whether within or without the United States, with the same force and effect as if the same were administered by any other officer now authorized by the laws of the State of Nevada to administer oaths or affirmations.

4. ° ° °.

§ 111.310. **Instruments entitled to recordation; patents need not be acknowledged.** 1. A certificate of the acknowledgment of any conveyance or other instrument in any way affecting the title to real or personal property, or the proof of the execution thereof, as provided in this chapter, signed by the officer taking the same, and under the seal or stamp of such officer, if such officer is required by law to have a seal or stamp, shall entitle such conveyance or instrument, with the certificate or certificates, to be recorded in the office of the recorder of any county in this state.

2. Any state or United States contract or patent for land may be recorded without any acknowledgment or proof.

§ 281.180. **Records of official acts of officers taking acknowledgments; liabilities and penalties.** 1. Each officer authorized by law to take the proof or acknowledgment of the execution of conveyances of real property, or other instrument required by law to be proved or acknowledged, shall keep a record of all his official acts in relation thereto in a book to be provided by him for that purpose. There shall be entered in the book:

(a) The date of the proof or acknowledgment thereof.

(b) The date of the instrument.

(c) The name or character of the instrument proved or acknowledged.

(d) The names of each of the parties thereto, as grantor, grantee or otherwise.

During business hours, the record shall be open to public inspection without fee or reward.

2. Any officer mentioned in subsection 1 who refuses or neglects to comply with the requirements of this section shall:

(a) Be punished by a fine of not more than $500; and

(b)   Be liable on his official bond in damages to any person injured by such refusal or neglect to the extent of the injury sustained by reason of the refusal or neglect mentioned in this subsection.

NEW HAMPSHIRE

[N.H. REV. STAT. ANN.]

§§ 456:1 to 456:15.   The Uniform Acknowledgment Act has been adopted.   For text of act, see page 349.

§§ 456-A:1 to 456-A:9.   The Uniform Recognition of Acknowledgments Act has been adopted.   For text of act, see page 349.

§ 477:3.   **Execution; Record.**   Every deed or other conveyance of real estate shall be signed and sealed by the party granting the same, attested by one or more witnesses, acknowledged by the grantor before a justice, notary public or commissioner, showing the mailing address of the grantee, and shall be recorded at length in the registry of deeds in the county in which the land lies, except that the recording of a notice of lease as provided for in RSA 477:7-a,° shall be sufficient compliance with this section.

° See below.

§ 477:4.   **Acknowledgments.**   Acknowledgments may be taken outside the United States before an ambassador, minister, envoy or charge d'affaires of the United States, in the country to which he is accredited, or before any consular officer of the United States, a notary public, or a commissioner or other agent of this state having an official seal and power to take acknowledgments at such place.

§ 477:5.   **Certificate of acknowledgment.**   A certificate of an acknowledgment taken outside the United States before any authorized officer shall be valid if in the form required by law for an acknowledgment taken within the state.

§ 477:6.   **—Fee for certificate.**   The fee for taking and certifying the acknowledgment of a deed or other instrument by one or more persons at one time shall be seventeen cents.

§ 477:7.   **Validity.**   No deed of bargain and sale, mortgage nor other conveyance of real estate, nor any lease for more than seven years from the making thereof, shall be valid to hold the same against any person but the grantor and his heirs only, unless such deed or lease be attested, acknowledged and recorded, according to the provisions of this chapter.

§ 477:7-a.   **Notice of lease.**   Notwithstanding the provisions of RSA 477:7 a notice of lease consisting of an instrument in writing executed, witnessed, acknowledged and sealed by all persons who are parties to the lease, and containing the following information with reference to such lease shall be sufficient compliance with the provisions of this chapter:

(1) The names and addresses of each party to the lease;

(2) The date of execution of the lease;

(3) A description of the demised premises as it appears in the lease;

(4) The term of such lease; and

(5) The date of commencement of such term and all rights of extension or renewal.

Note: Reference to this section is made in § 477:3, above.

NEW JERSEY

Notaries public, among others, are authorized to take and certify acknowledgments. See *Authority and Duties*, N.J. STAT. ANN. § 52:7-4. See also § 46:14-6 below.

[N.J. STAT. ANN.]

§ 2A:82-17. Certificates of acknowledgment or proof of instruments as evidence of execution thereof. If any instrument heretofore made and executed or hereafter to be made and executed shall have been acknowledged, by any party who shall have executed it, or the execution thereof by such party shall have been proved by one or more of the subscribing witnesses to such instrument, in the manner and before one of the officers provided and required by law for the acknowledgment or proof of instruments in order to entitle them to be recorded, and, when a certificate of such acknowledgment or proof shall be written upon or under, or be annexed to such instrument and signed by such officer in the manner prescribed by law, such certificate of acknowledgment or proof shall be and constitute prima facie evidence of the due execution of such instrument by such party. Such instrument shall be received in evidence in any court or proceeding in this state in the same manner and to the same effect as though the execution of such instrument by such party had been proved by other evidence.

§ 46:14-1. Acknowledgments by married women. From and after March seventeenth, one thousand nine hundred and sixteen, any instrument of the nature or description set forth in section 46:16-1 of this title, may be executed and delivered by any married woman of the age of twenty-one years without a private examination apart from her husband, and without an acknowledgment made by her that she signed, sealed and delivered the same as her voluntary act and deed, freely, without any fear, threats or compulsion of her husband; and any such deed or instrument shall be sufficiently acknowledged by such married woman if she shall acknowledge the same manner as if she were a feme sole, and to which the officer taking such acknowledgment shall certify in like manner as in the case of a feme sole.

§ 46:14-2. Acknowledgment by corporation. Whenever any president, vice-president or other presiding officer, or any secretary, assistant secretary or other recording officer, or any treasurer or assistant treasurer of any corporation, or in the case of a corporation dissolved in any manner, the trustee or trustees in dissolution thereof, who shall have signed the same as such officer or as such trustee or trustees shall acknowledge that any deed, paper or other instrument in writing, made by any corporation and sealed with its corporate seal, is the voluntary act and deed of such corporation, made by virtue of authority from its board of directors, board of trustees, or other similar body, and such acknowledgment is made before any officer authorized by the laws of this State to take acknowledgment of deeds for real estate in this State, in order to entitle the same to be recorded, and there shall be indorsed on or attached to such deed, paper or other instrument in writing a certificate of such acknowledgment signed by the officer before whom the same was made, it shall be as good and effectual in law as if it had been made, executed and acknowledged by a natural person.

§ 46:14-4. Proof of instruments not acknowledged or proved when witnesses dead, insane or nonresident; application to County Court; notice; certificate of proof. If the grantor or any of the grantors of any deed or instrument of the nature or description set forth in section 46:16-1 of this Title, made and executed, but not acknowledged or proved according to law, and the subscribing witnesses thereto are dead, of unsound mind or resident without the United States, such deed or instrument may be proved before the County Court of the county in which the real estate or property affected thereby, or some part thereof, is situate, by proving the handwriting of such grantor or grantors, to the full satisfaction of such court, which proof may be made by affidavits in writing, taken before any officer in this State authorized by law to take the acknowledgment and proof of deeds, and annexed to such deed or instrument. The proofs shall be certified on or under such deed or instrument in open court by the judge holding such court.

Before any proof shall be taken as herein provided, notice of the application to the County Court for that purpose, describing the deed or instrument and the real estate or property contained therein or affected thereby, of assignment may be proved before a judge of the Superior Court, by and the time and place of such application, shall be given by advertisements, signed by the person making the application, and set up in at least five of the public places in the county, one of which such places shall be in the municipality in which such real estate or property is situate at least four weeks before making the application, and also by a publication four times during four consecutive calendar weeks, once in each week, in a newspaper printed in such county, if any be printed therein, and, if not, in a newspaper circulating in such county and printed in an adjacent county. Due proof, by affidavit annexed to such deed or instrument, of the notice herein required shall be made to the court, and certified by the judge thereof in the certificate of proof herein required.

§ 46:14-5. Proof of assignments of mortgages not acknowledged or proved; record thereof. If the assignor of any mortgage upon real estate in this State, heretofore or hereafter made and executed but not acknowledged or proved according to law and the subscribing witnesses thereto be dead, of unsound mind, nonresidents of this State or not to be found within this State, the deed proving the handwriting of such witnesses to the satisfaction of the judge, and, upon the certificate of such judge indorsed on or annexed to such assignment that such proof has been made before him, such assignment may be recorded the same as if it were acknowledged according to law.

§ 46:14-6. Officers of state before whom deeds or instruments may be acknowledged or proved; methods; certificates. If any deed or instrument of the nature or description set forth in section 46:16-1 of this Title shall have been or shall be acknowledged by a party executing the same, such party being in this State, whether residing in this State or elsewhere, before any one of the officers herein named, whether such officer was or is appointed for, or whether he was or is in the county where the affected real estate is situate or where such acknowledgment was or is taken, or not, such officer being satisfied that such party is the grantor, vendor, vendee, lessor or lessee in such deed or instrument, of all of which such officer shall make his certificate on, under or annexed to such deed or instrument, or if such deed or instrument shall have been or shall be proved before any such officer anywhere in this State by one or more of the subscribing witnesses thereto, such witness or witnesses being within this State, whether residing in this State or elsewhere, that such party (the grantor, vendor, vendee, lessor or lessee), signed, sealed and delivered such deed or instrument as his act and deed, and a certificate of such proof signed by such officer, shall be written upon, or under or be annexed to, such deed or instrument, every such deed or instrument, so acknowledged or proved, shall be deemed to be duly acknowledged or proved.

The officers of this State authorized to take acknowledgments or proofs in this State under authority of this section are a justice of the Supreme Court; a judge of the Superior Court; a judge of the County Court of any county; a master of the Superior Court by such designation, or by the designation of master-in-chancery or master of the court of chancery of New Jersey; an attorney-at-law; a counsellor-at-law; a notary public; a commissioner of deeds appointed for any county; a county clerk of any county; a deputy county clerk; a surrogate or deputy surrogate of any county; and a register of deeds and mortgages or deputy register of any county.

§ 46:14-7. Officers without state but within United States before whom deeds or instruments may be acknowledged or proved; methods; certificates. If the party who shall have executed or who shall execute any deed or instrument of the description or nature set forth in section 46:16-1 of this Title, or the witnesses thereto, shall have happened or shall happen to be in some other State of the United States or territory thereof, or in the District of Columbia, whether resident in this State, or in such State, territory or district, or elsewhere, an acknowledgment or proof of such as is prescribed by section 46:14-6 of this Title, made before and certified by any one of the officers herein named, shall be as good and effectual as if the same had been made in this State before an officer authorized to take acknowledgments or proofs within the State and had been certified by him, as provided in section 46:16-6.

The officers authorized to take acknowledgments and proofs under authority of this section are:

(a) The Chief Justice or any associate justice of the Supreme Court of the United States, or a master of the Superior Court of New Jersey or attorney-at-law of New Jersey, at any place without the State but within the territorial limits of the United States.

(b) At any place without this State but within the territorial limits of the United States and within the territorial limits of the jurisdiction of such officer or of his court, by

(1) A judge of any of the United States courts other than the Supreme Court;

(2) The Chancellor of any State of the United States or territory thereof;

(3) Any judge or justice of the Supreme or Superior Courts of any State of the United States or territory thereof, or the District of Columbia;

(4) Any foreign commissioner of deeds for New Jersey, when his certificate of acknowledgment or proof is duly certified under his official seal;

(5) The mayor or other chief magistrate of any city, borough or corporation, when his certificate of acknowledgment or proof is duly certified under the seal of the city, borough or corporation of which he was or is the mayor or chief magistrate;

(6) A judge of a court of record of any State of the United States or territory thereof, or of the District of Columbia when his certificate of acknowledgment or proof is duly certified that he was or is such judge under the great seal of such State, territory or district, or under the seal of a court of record of the State,

county, city or district in which the acknowledgment or proof was or is made and in and for which he was or is such judge; or

(7) Any notary public of any such State, territory or district, then residing or being anywhere therein, and a recital in his certificate of acknowledgment or proof that he is such notary with his official designation annexed to his signature and attested under his official seal, shall be sufficient proof that the person before or by whom such acknowledgment or proof was taken is such notary.

(8) Any officer of any such State, territory, or district, then residing and being anywhere in such State, territory or district, authorized at the time of such acknowledgment or proof by the laws of such State, territory or district to take acknowledgments and proofs, when his certificate of acknowledgment or proof is accompanied by a certificate under the great seal of such State, territory or district, or under the seal of some court of record in or county clerk of the State, county, city or district in which the acknowledgment or proof was or shall be made, and that such officer was, at the time of the taking of such acknowledgments or proofs, authorized by the laws of such State, territory or district to take acknowledgments and proofs.

§ 46:14-8. **Officers without United States before whom deeds or instruments may be acknowledged or proved: methods; certificates; proof of authority.** If the party who shall have executed or who shall execute any deed or instrument of the description or nature set forth in section 46-16-1 of this Title, or the witnesses thereto, shall have happened or shall happen to be in any foreign kingdom, State, nation or colony, whether resident in this State, or in such foreign kingdom, State, nation or colony, or elsewhere, an acknowledgment or proof such as is prescribed by section 46:14-6 of this Title, made before and certified by any one of the officers herein named, shall be as good and effectual as if the same had been made within this State before an officer authorized to take acknowledgments or proofs within the State and had been certified by him, as provided in section 46:14-6.

The officers authorized to take acknowledgments or proofs under authority of this section are:

(a) Any master of the Superior Court or attorney-at-law of New Jersey;

(b) Any public ambassador, minister, consul, vice-consul, consular agent, charge d'affaires or other representative of the United States for the time being, to or at any such foreign kingdom, State, nation or colony;

(c) Any court of law of such foreign kingdom, State, nation or colony;

(d) Any notary, notary public, commissioner for oaths, mayor or other chief magistrate, of and then having been or being within any city, borough, or corporation of such foreign kingdom, State, nation or colony, in which city, borough or corporation such party or witnesses may have happened or may happen to be.

Acknowledgments or proofs taken or made by a court of law, a notary, notary public, commissioner for oaths, or a mayor or other chief magistrate under authority of this section shall be certified if taken by said court under the official seal of said court, and the hand of the judge or clerk thereof, or under the official seal, if any, and the hand of any other person hereby authorized to take acknowledgments or proofs; and such certificate of acknowledgment or proof shall be sufficient proof as to the existence and authority of said court, mayor, notary or other officer.

Commissioners of Deeds

§ 52:6-1. Appointment by senate and general assembly; number. The senate and general assembly in joint meeting shall appoint as many fit and proper persons for each of the counties of the state as may be deemed necessary, each of whom shall be designated a "commissioner of deeds".

Note: The office of commissioner of deeds should not be confused with the office of foreign commissioner of deeds. New Jersey law provides for both offices. Concerning foreign commissioners of deeds, see *Commissioners of Deeds,* N.J. STAT. ANN. §§ 52:6-12 to 52:6-22.

§ 52:6-2. Commissions and terms of office. The commissioners appointed under authority of section 52:6-1 of this title shall be commissioned by the governor and hold office for a term of five years. The commissions issued by the governor shall be dated as of the dates of the appointments by the legislature, and the terms of office shall begin on the first day of May next following such dates.

§ 52:6-3. Notice of appointments to secretary of state. The secretary of the joint meeting of the legislature shall, within three days after the date of appointments of commissioners of deeds made thereat, notify the secretary of state of all such appointments, stating therein the municipality in which the appointees shall reside.

§ 52:6-4. Notice of appointments to county clerks. The secretary of state shall, within three days after receiving the notice mentioned in section 52:6-3 of this title, notify the county clerk of each county of all appointments of commissioners of deeds for his county.

§ 52:6-5. Notice to appointees of appointment; oath; fees; commissions delivered. The county clerk shall, within three days after receiving from the secretary of state the notice mentioned in section 52:6-4 of this title, notify each person appointed a commissioner of deeds, by mail or otherwise, of his appointment, advising him to qualify on or before the first day of May next following the date of his appointment, by taking and subscribing before the clerk of the county for which he has been appointed an oath to perform well and faithfully the duties required of him by law as such commissioner, and by paying to the clerk and to the secretary of state the fees required by section 22:2-19 of the title Fees and Costs.*

Each appointee shall affix to a copy of his oath, on blanks provided for that purpose, his personal signature and post-office address, all of which shall, on or before the fifth day of said May, be forwarded by the clerk to the secretary of state, who shall, on or before the twentieth day of said May, forward to the clerks of the respective counties the commissions issued pursuant to section 52:6-2 of this title to all persons who have qualified as herein provided. Thereupon the clerks shall deliver such commissions to the proper persons upon proper request therefor.

* § 22:2-19 was amended and is now codified as § 22A:2-29. Insofar as it is relevant here, § 22A:2-29 provides:

> Upon the filing, indexing, entering or recording of the following documents or papers in the office of the county clerk or clerk of the law division of the County Court, such parties, filing or having the same recorded or indexed in the county clerk's office or with the clerk of the law division of the County Court of the various counties in this State shall pay the following fees in lieu of the fees heretofore provided for the filing, recording or entering of such documents or papers.
>
> ⚬   ⚬   ⚬
>
> Commissions and oaths—
>   Administering oaths to notaries public and
>   commissioners of deeds 3.00
>
> ⚬   ⚬   ⚬

§ 52:6-6. **Commission vacated by removal from county of residence.** If a commissioner of deeds removes out of the county in which he resides at the time of his appointment his commission shall be void.

§ 52:6-7. **Removal from office.** The governor may, for misconduct in office, remove from office any commissioner of deeds.

§ 52:6-8. **Resignation of office.** A commissioner of deeds may resign his office by sending his resignation to the governor, who, upon accepting it, shall file it with the secretary of state.

§ 52:6-9. **Additional appointments by governor during recess of legislature.** When the governor shall, during a recess of the legislature, deem it desirable to have additional commissioners of deeds appointed for a county, he may make such appointments for terms to expire on the first day of May next following the dates thereof.

Appointees under this section shall qualify in the manner provided by section 52:6-5 of this title.

§ 52:6-10. Vacancies filled by appointments by governor. When a vacancy, from whatever cause, occurs in the office of a commissioner of deeds and the legislature is not in session, the governor may fill the vacancy by appointment for a term to cease upon the filling of the vacancy by the legislature in joint session. A person so appointed shall qualify as provided by section 52:6-5 of this title.

§ 52:6-11. Acknowledgment or proof before commissioner after removal from county of appointment. An acknowledgment or proof taken before a commissioner of deeds during his term of office, but after his removal from the county for which he was appointed, into another county, shall be valid and effectual notwithstanding such removal and the consequent vacation of his commission.

Editorial comment

Concerning the fees which commissioners of deeds may charge, see *Fees Chargeable*, N.J. STAT. ANN. § 22A:4-14.

NEW MEXICO

[N.M. STAT. ANN.]

§ 43-1-4. Officers authorized to take acknowledgments. The acknowledgment of any instrument of writing may be made within this state before either:

1. A clerk of the district court.

2. A judge or clerk of the probate court, using the probate seal.

3. A notary public.

4. A justice of the peace.

5. A county clerk, using the county clerk seal.

§ 43-1-5. Acknowledgments outside state. The acknowledgment of any instrument of writing may be made without this state, but within the United States or their territories, before either:

1. A clerk of some court of record having a seal.

2. A commissioner of deeds duly appointed under the laws of this state.

3. A notary public having a seal.

§ 43-1-6. Acknowledgments in foreign countries. The acknowledgment of any instrument of writing may be made without the United States before either:

1. A minister, commissioner or charge d'affaires of the United States, resident and accredited in the country where the acknowledgment is made.

2. A consul-general, consul, vice-consul, deputy-consul, or consular agent of the United States resident in the country where the acknowledgment is made, having a seal.

3. A notary public having a seal.

4. A commissioner of deeds duly appointed under the laws of this state.

§ 43-1-7. **Military officers—power to take acknowledgments and administer oaths.** In addition to the acknowledgment of instruments and the performance of other notarial acts in the manner and form as otherwise authorized by law, instruments may be acknowledged, documents attested, oaths and affirmations administered, depositions and affidavits executed, and all notarial acts, authorized under the laws of the state of New Mexico to be performed by notaries public, may be performed before or by any commissioned officer in active service of the armed forces of the United States with the rank of second lieutenant or higher in the army or marine corps, or with the rank of ensign or higher in the navy or coast guard, or with equivalent rank in any other component part of the armed forces of the United States, for any person who either—

(a) is a member of the armed forces of the United States; or

(b) is serving as a merchant seaman outside the limits of the United States included within the 48 states and the District of Columbia; or

(c) is outside said limits by permission, assignment or direction of any department or official of the United States government, in connection with any activity pertaining to the prosecution of any war in which the United States is then engaged.

Such acknowledgment of instruments, attestation of documents, administration of oaths and affirmations, execution of depositions and affidavits, and performance of other notarial acts, heretofore or hereafter made or taken, are hereby declared legal, valid and binding, and instruments and documents so acknowledged, authenticated, or sworn to shall be admissible in evidence and eligible to record in this state under the same circumstances, and with the same force and effect as if such acknowledgment, attestation, oath, affirmation, deposition, affidavit, or other notarial act, had been made or taken within this state before or by a duly qualified officer or official as otherwise provided by law.

In the taking of acknowledgments and the performing of other notarial acts requiring certification, a certificate endorsed upon or attached to the instrument or documents, which shows the date of the notarial act and which states, in substance, that the person appearing before the officer acknowledged the instrument as his act or made or signed the instrument or document under oath, shall be sufficient for all intents and purposes. The instrument or document shall not be rendered invalid by the failure to state the place of execution or acknowledgment.

If the signature, rank, and branch of service or subdivision thereof, of any such commissioned officer appear upon such instrument or document or certificate, no further proof of the authority of such officer so to act shall be required and such action by such commissioned officer shall be prima facie evidence that the person making such oath or acknowledgment is within the purview of this act [43-1-7], and that the signature of such person is genuine.

§ 43-1-8.   **Contents of certificate of acknowledgment.** The certificate of acknowledgment shall express the fact of the acknowledgment being made, and also, that the person making the same was personally known to at least one [1] of the judges of the court, or to the officer granting the certificate, to be the person whose name is subscribed to the writing or a party to it, or that it was proven to be such person by the testimony of at least two [2] reliable witnesses.

§ 43-1-9.   **Forms—instruments affecting real estate.** The following forms of acknowledgment may be used in the case of conveyances or other written instruments affecting real estate, and any acknowledgment so taken and certified shall be sufficient to satisfy all requirements of law relating to the execution or recording of such instruments:

First.   In case of natural persons acting in their own right:

State of New Mexico,
County of ———

On this ——— day of ——— 19—, before me personally appeared A. B. (or A.B. and C. D.) to me known to be the person (or persons) described in and who executed the foregoing instrument, and acknowledged that he (or they) executed the same as his (or their) free act and deed.

Second.   In the case of natural persons acting by attorney:

State of New Mexico,
County of ———

On this ——— day of ——— 19—, before me personally appeared A. B., to me known to be the person who executed the foregoing instrument in behalf of C. D., and acknowledged that he executed the same as the free act and deed of said C. D.

Third.   In case of corporations or joint stock associations:

State of New Mexico,
County of ———

On this ——— day of ——— 19—, before me appeared A. B., to me personally known, who, being by me duly sworn (or affirmed) did say that he is the president (or other officer or agent of the corporation or association) of (describing the corporation or association), and that the seal affixed to said instrument is the corporate seal of said corporation (or association) and that said instrument was signed and sealed in behalf of said corporation (or association) by authority of its board of directors, (or trustees), and said A. B. acknowledged said instrument to be the free act and deed of said corporation (or association).

In case the corporation or association has no corporate seal, omit the words: "The seal affixed to said instrument is the corporate seal of such corporation, (or association), and that," and add at the end of the affidavit clause the words: "And that said corporation, (or association), has no corporate seal."

In all cases add signature and title of the officer taking the acknowledgment.

§ 43-1-10. **Acknowledgment by married woman.** When a married woman unites with her husband in the execution of any such instrument and acknowledges the same in one of the forms sanctioned, she shall be described in the acknowledgment as his wife, but in all other respects her acknowledgment shall be taken and certified as if she were sole.

§ 43-1-15. **Short forms for acknowledgments authorized.** The forms of acknowledgment set forth in the appendix to this act [43-1-19] may be used and shall be sufficient for their respective purposes. They shall be known as "Statutory Forms of Acknowledgment" and may be referred to as such. They may be altered as circumstances require; and the authorization of such forms shall not prevent the use of other forms. Marital status or other status of a person or persons may be shown if desired after the name of such person or persons.

§ 43-1-16. **Application of act.** For the purpose of avoiding the unnecessary use of words in acknowledgments whether said statutory form or other form is used, the rules and definitions contained in this act [43-1-15 to 43-1-19] shall apply to all instruments executed or delivered on or after the effective date of this act.

§ 43-1-17. **"Was acknowledged" defined.** In the forms of acknowledgment provided by this act [43-1-15 to 43-1-19] or any modification thereof, the words "was acknowledged" shall mean:

(a) In the case of a natural person acknowledging that such person personally appeared before the officer taking the acknowledgment and acknowledged that he executed the acknowledged instrument as his free act and deed for the uses and purposes therein set forth.

(b) In the case of a person acknowledging as principal by an attorney in fact, that such attorney in fact appeared personally before the officer taking the acknowledgment and that said attorney in fact acknowledged that he executed the acknowledged instrument as the free act and deed of the principal for the uses and purposes therein set forth.

(c) In the case of a partnership acknowledging by a partner or partners, that such partner or partners personally appeared before the officer taking the acknowledgment and that he or they acknowledged that he or they executed the acknowledged instrument as the free act and deed of the partnership for the uses and purposes therein set forth.

(d) In the case of a corporation or incorporated association acknowledging by an officer or agent of said corporation or incorporated association, that such acknowledging officer or agent personally appeared before the officer taking the acknowledgment; that the seal affixed to the instrument is the corporate seal of the corporation or association, that the instrument was signed and sealed on behalf of the corporation or association by authority of its board of directors, and that said acknowledging officer or agent acknowledged that the acknowledged instrument was the free act and deed of such corporation or association for the uses and purposes therein set forth. In case a corporation or association has no corporate seal, this fact can be indicated by adding to the form provided for in the Fourth Form in the appendix to this act [43-1-19], the words "Said corporation (or association) has no corporate seal."

§ 43-1-18. **Prima facie evidence of execution.** Any acknowledgment taken and certified as provided by law shall be prima facie evidence of the execution of the instrument by the parties acknowledging the same, in all of the courts of this state.

§ 43-1-19. **Appendix—short forms of acknowledgment.** (1) For a natural person acting in his own right:

State of ———

County of ———

The foregoing instrument was acknowledged before me this (date) by (name or names of person or persons acknowledging).

Signature of officer

———————————————

(Title of Officer)

My commission expires:

(2) For a natural person as principal acting by attorney in fact:

State of ———

County of ———

The foregoing instrument was acknowledged before me this (date) by (name of attorney in fact) as attorney in fact on behalf of (name of principal).

Signature of officer

———————————————

(Title of Officer)

My commission expires:

(3) For a partnership acting by one or more partners:

State of ———

County of ———

The foregoing instrument was acknowledged before me this (date) by (name of acknowledging partner or partners), partner(s) on behalf of (name of partnership), a partnership.

Signature of officer

_____

(Title of Officer)

My commission expires:

(4) For a corporation or incorporated association:

State of ———

County of ———

The foregoing instrument was acknowledged before me this (date) by (name of officer), (title of officer) of (name of corporation acknowledging), a (state or county of incorporation) corporation, on behalf of said corporation.

Signature of Officer

_____

(Title of Officer)

My commission expires:

§ 45-4-25. Trustees, officers or members—notaries. No person who is authorized to take acknowledgments under the laws of this state shall be disqualified from taking acknowledgments of instruments executed in favor of a co-operative or to which it is a party, by reason of being an officer, director or member of such co-operative.

NEW YORK

[N.Y. REAL PROP. LAW]

§ 298. Acknowledgments and proofs within the state. The acknowledgment or proof, within this state, of a conveyance of real property situate in this state may be made: 1. At any place within the state, before (a) a justice of the supreme court; (b) an official examiner of title; (c) an official referee; or (d) a notary public.

2. Within the district wherein such officer is authorized to perform official duties, before (a) a judge or clerk of any court of record; (b) a commissioner of deeds outside of the city of New York, or a commissioner of deeds of the city of New York within the five counties comprising the city of New York; (c) the mayor or recorder of a city; (d) a surrogate, special surrogate, or special county judge; or (e) the county clerk or other recording officer of a county.

3. Before a justice of the peace, town councilman, village police

justice or a judge of any court of inferior local jurisdiction, anywhere within the county containing the town, village or city in which he is authorized to perform official duties.

§ 299. **Acknowledgments and proofs without the state, but within the United States or any territory, possession, or dependency thereof.** The acknowledgment or proof of a conveyance of real property situate in this state, if made (a) without the state but within the United States, (b) within any territory, possession, or dependency of the United States, or (c) within any place over which the United States, at the time when such acknowledgment or proof is taken, has or exercises jurisdiction, sovereignty, control, or a protectorate, may be made before any of the following officers acting within his territorial jurisdiction or within that of the court of which he is an officer: 1. A judge or other presiding officer of any court having a seal, or the clerk or other certifying officer thereof.

2. A mayor or other chief civil officer of any city or other political subdivision.

3. A notary public.

4. A commissioner of deeds appointed pursuant to the laws of this state to take acknowledgments or proofs without this state.

5. Any person authorized, by the laws of the state, District of Columbia, territory, possession, dependency, or other place where the acknowledgment or proof is made, to take the acknowledgment or proof of deeds to be recorded therein.

§ 299-a. **Acknowledgment to conform to law of New York or of place where taken; certificate of conformity.** 1. An acknowledgment or proof made pursuant to the provisions of section two hundred ninety-nine of this chapter may be taken in the manner prescribed either by the laws of the state of New York or by the laws of the state, District of Columbia, territory, possession, dependency, or other place where the acknowledgment or proof is taken. The acknowledgment or proof, if taken in the manner prescribed by such state, District of Columbia, territory, possession, dependency, or other place, must be accompanied by a certificate to the effect that it conforms with such laws. Such certificate may be made by

(a) An attorney-at-law admitted to practice in the state of New York, resident in the place where the acknowledgment or proof is taken, or by

(b) An attorney-at-law admitted to practice in the state, District of Columbia, territory, possession, dependency, or other place where the acknowledgment or proof is taken, or by

(c) Any other person deemed qualified by any court of the state of New York, if, in any action, proceeding, or other matter pending before such court, it be necessary to determine that such acknowledgment or proof conforms with the laws of such state, District of Columbia, territory, possession, dependency, or other place; or by the supreme court of the state of New York, on application for such determination. The justice, judge, surrogate, or other presiding judicial officer shall append to the instrument so acknowledged or proved his signed statement that he deemed such person qualified to make such certificate.

2. (a) The signature to such a certificate of conformity shall be presumptively genuine, and the qualification of the person whose name is so signed as a person authorized to make such certificate shall be presumptively established by the recital thereof in the certificate.

(b) The statement of a judicial officer appended to the instrument that he deemed the person making such certificate qualified shall establish the qualification of the person designated therein to make such certificate; and the recording, filing, registering or use as evidence of the instrument shall not depend on the power of the court to make the statement and proof shall not be required of any action, proceeding, matter or application in which or in connection with which the statement is made.

(c) When an instrument so acknowledged or proved is accompanied by the certificate of conformity and the statement of a judicial officer, if any be required, the acknowledgment or proof of the instrument, for the purpose of recording, filing or registering in any recording or filing office in this state or for use as evidence, shall be equivalent to one taken or made in the form prescribed by law for use in this state; and if the acknowledgment or proof is properly authenticated, where authentication is required by law, and if the instrument be otherwise entitled to record, filing or registering, such instrument, together with the acknowledgment or proof, the certificate of conformity and any certificate of authentication or statement of a judicial officer, may be recorded, filed or registered in any recording or filing office in this state, and shall be so recorded, filed or registered upon payment or tender of lawful fees therefor. In fixing the fees of a recording, filing or registering officer, the certificate of conformity and the statement of a judicial officer appended, if any, shall be treated as certificates of authentication required by other provisions of this chapter.

§ 300. **Acknowledgments and proofs by persons in or with the armed forces of the United States.** The acknowledgment or proof of a conveyance of real property situate in this state, if made by a person enlisted or commissioned in or serving in or with the armed forces of the United States or by a dependent of any such person, wherever located, or by a person attached to or accompanying the armed forces of the United States, whether made within or without the United States, may be made before any commissioned officer in active service of the armed forces of the United States with the rank of second lieutenant or higher in the Army, Air Force or Marine Corps, or ensign or higher in the Navy or Coast Guard, or with equivalent rank in any other component part of the armed forces of the United States.

In addition to the requirements of sections three hundred and three, three hundred and four, and three hundred and six of this chapter, the certificate of an acknowledgment or proof taken under this section shall state (a) the rank and serial number of the officer taking the same, and the command to which he is attached, (b) that the person making such acknowledgment or proof was, at the time of making the same, enlisted or commissioned in or serving in or with the armed forces of the United States or the dependent of such a person, or a person attached to or accompanying the armed forces of the United States, and (c) the serial number of the person who makes, or whose dependent makes the acknowledgment or proof if such person is enlisted or commissioned in the armed forces of the United States. The place where such acknowledgment or proof is taken need not be disclosed.

No authentication of the officer's certificate of acknowledgment or proof shall be required.

Notwithstanding any of the provisions of this section, the acknowledgment or proof of a conveyance of real property situate in this state may also be made as provided in sections two hundred ninety-eight, two hundred ninety-nine, two hundred ninety-nine-a, three hundred one, and three hundred one-a, of this chapter.

§ 301. Acknowledgments and proofs in foreign countries. The acknowledgment or proof of a conveyance of real property situate in this state may be made in foreign countries before any of the following officers acting within his territorial jurisdiction or within that of the court of which he is an officer: 1. An ambassador, envoy, minister, charge d'affaires, secretary of legation, consul-general, consul, vice-consul, consular agent, vice-consular agent, or any other diplomatic or consular agent or representative of the United States, appointed or accredited to, and residing within, the country where the acknowledgment or proof is taken.

2. A judge or other presiding officer of any court having a seal, or the clerk or other certifying officer thereof.

3. A mayor or other chief civil officer of any city or other political subdivision.

4. A notary public.

5. A commissioner of deeds appointed pursuant to the laws of this state to take acknowledgments or proofs without this state.

6. A person residing in, or going to, the country where the acknowledgment or proof is to be taken, and specially authorized for that purpose by a commission issued to him under the seal of the supreme court of the state of New York.

7. Any person authorized, by the laws of the country where the acknowledgment or proof is made, to take acknowledgments

of conveyances of real estate or to administer oaths in proof of the execution thereof.

§ 301-a. Acknowledgment to conform to law of New York or of foreign country; certificate of conformity. 1. An acknowledgment or proof made pursuant to the provisions of section three hundred one of this chapter may be taken in the manner prescribed either by the laws of the state of New York or by the laws of the country where the acknowledgment or proof is taken. The acknowledgment or proof, if taken in the manner prescribed by the laws of such foreign country, must be accompanied by a certificate to the effect that it conforms with such laws. Such certificate may be made by

(a) An attorney-at-law admitted to practice in the state of New York, resident in such foreign country, or by

(b) A consular officer of the United States, resident in such foreign country, under the seal of his office, or by

(c) A consular officer of such foreign country, resident in the state of New York, under the seal of his office, or by

(d) Any other person deemed qualified by any court of the state of New York, if, in any action, proceeding, or other matter pending before such court, it be necessary to determine that such acknowledgment or proof conforms with the laws of such foreign country; or by the supreme court of the state of New York, on application for such determination.

The justice, judge, surrogate, or other presiding judicial officer shall append to the instrument so acknowledged or proved his signed statement that he deemed such person qualified to make such certificate.

2. (a) The signature to such a certificate of conformity shall be presumptively genuine, and the qualification of the person whose name is so signed as a person authorized to make such certificate shall be presumptively established by the recital thereof in the certificate.

(b) The statement of a judicial officer appended to the instrument that he deemed the person making such certificate qualified shall establish the qualification of the person designated therein to make such certificate; and the recording, filing, registering or use as evidence of the instrument shall not depend on the power of the court to make the statement and proof shall not be required of any action, proceeding, matter or application in which or in connection with which the statement is made.

(c) When an instrument so acknowledged or proved is accompanied by the certificate of conformity and the statement of a judicial officer, if any be required, the acknowledgment or proof of the instrument, for the purpose of recording, filing or registering in any recording or filing office in this state or for use as evidence, shall be equivalent to one taken or made in the form prescribed by law for use in this state; and if the acknowledgment or proof is properly authenticated, where authentication is required by law, and if the instrument be otherwise entitled to record, filing or registering, such instrument, together with the acknowledgment or proof, the certificate of conformity and any certificate of authentication or statement of a judicial officer, may be recorded, filed or registered in any recording or filing office in this state, and shall be so recorded, filed or registered upon payment or tender of lawful fees therefor. In fixing the fees of a recording, filing or registering officer, the certificate of conformity and the statement of a judicial officer appended, if any, shall be treated as certificates of authentication required by other provisions of this chapter.

§ 302. **Acknowledgments and proofs by married women.** The acknowledgment or proof of a conveyance of real property, within the state, or of any other written instrument, may be made by a married woman the same as if unmarried.

§ 303. **Requisites of acknowledgments.** An acknowledgment must not be taken by any officer unless he knows or has satisfactory evidence, that the person making it is the person described in and who executed such instrument.

§ 304. **Proof by subscribing witness.** When the execution of a conveyance is proved by a subscribing witness, such witness must state his own place of residence, and if his place of residence is in a city, the street and street number, if any thereof, and that he knew the person described in and who executed the conveyance. The proof must not be taken unless the officer is personally acquainted with such witness, or has satisfactory evidence that he is the same person, who was a subscribing witness to the conveyance.

§ 305. **Compelling witnesses to testify.** On the application of a grantee in a conveyance, his heir or personal representative, or a person claiming under either of them, verified by the oath of the applicant, stating that a witness to the conveyance, residing in the county where the application is made, refuses to appear and testify concerning its execution, and that such conveyance can not be proved without his testimony, any officer authorized to take, within the state, acknowledgment or proof of conveyance of real property may issue a subpoena, requiring such witness to attend and testify before him concerning the execution of the conveyance. A subpoena issued under this section shall be regulated by the civil practice law and rules.

§ 306. **Certificate of acknowledgment or proof.** A person taking the acknowledgment or proof of a conveyance must indorse thereupon or attach thereto, a certificate, signed by himself, stating all the matters required to be done, known, or proved on the taking of such acknowledgment or proof; together with the name and substance of the testimony of each witness examined before him, and if a subscribing witness, his place of residence.

*   *   *

§ 308. **When certificate must be under seal.** 1. When a certificate of acknowledgment or proof is made without this state, whether within or without the United States, (a) if made by a judge or other presiding officer of a court having a seal, or by the clerk or other certifying officer thereof, such certificate must be under the seal of such court; (b) if made by a commissioner of deeds appointed pursuant to the laws of this state to take acknowledgments or proofs without this state, such certificate must be under his seal of office; (c) if made by any officer specified in subdivision one of section three hundred one of this chapter, such certificate must be under the seal of the legation or consulate to which such officer is attached.

2. Any certificate, required by the provisions of section three hundred eleven of this chapter to be authenticated, must be so authenticated, in addition to being under seal as provided in this section.

§ 309. **Acknowledgment by corporation and form of certificate.** The acknowledgment of a conveyance or other instrument by a corporation, must be made by some officer, or in case of a dissolved corporation, by some officer or director thereof authorized to execute the same by the board of directors of said corporation. The certificate of acknowledgment must be in substantially the following form, the blanks being properly filled:

State of New York
ss.:
County of ———

On the ——— day of ——— in the year ——— before me personally came ——— to me known, who, being by me duly sworn, did depose and say that he resides in ——— (if the place of residence is in a city, include the street and street number, if any, thereof); that he is the (president or other officer or director) of the (name of corporation), the corporation described in and which executed the above instrument; that he knows the seal of said corporation; that the seal affixed to said instrument is such corporate seal; that it was so affixed by order of the board of directors of said corporation, and that he signed his name thereto by like order.

(Signature and office of person taking acknowledgment.)

If such corporation have no seal, that fact must be stated in place of the statements required respecting the seal.

§ 310. **Authentication of acknowledgments and proofs made within the state.** 1. When a certificate of acknowledgment or proof is

made, within this state, by a commissioner of deeds, a justice of the
peace, town councilman, village police justice, or a judge of any
court of inferior local jurisdiction, such certificate does not entitle
the conveyance so acknowledged or proved to be read in evidence
or recorded in any county of this state except a county in which
the officer making such certificate is authorized to act at the time
of making the same, unless such certificate is authenticated by a
certificate of the clerk of such county; provided, however, that all
certificates of acknowledgment or proof, made by a commissioner
of deeds of the city of New York residing in any part therein,
shall be authenticated by the clerk of any county within said city,
in whose office such commissioner of deeds shall have filed a certificate under the hand and seal of the city clerk of said city, showing
the appointment and term of office of such commissioner; and no
other certificates shall be required from any other officer to entitle
such conveyance to be read in evidence or recorded in any county
of this state.

2.   Except as provided in this section, no certificate of authentication shall be required to entitle a conveyance to be read in
evidence or recorded in this state when acknowledged or proved
before any officer designated in section two hundred ninety-eight of
this article to take such acknowledgment or proof, nor shall such
authentication be required for recording in the office of the city
register of the city of New York of such acknowledgment or proof
by a commissioner of deeds of the city of New York.

§ 311.   Authentication of acknowledgments and proofs made without the state.   1.   When a certificate of acknowledgment or proof
is made, either within or without the United States, by a commissioner of deeds appointed pursuant to the laws of this state to
take acknowledgments or proofs without this state, the conveyance
so acknowledged or proved is not entitled to be read in evidence
or recorded in this state, except as provided in [§ 142(6)] of the
executive law, unless such certificate is authenticated by the certificate of the secretary of state of the state of New York.

2.   When a certificate of acknowledgment or proof is made by
a notary public within the United States, or within any territory,
possession, or dependency of the United States, or within any place
over which the United States, at the time when such acknowledgment or proof is taken, has or exercises jurisdiction, sovereignty,
control, or a protectorate, the conveyance so acknowledged or proved
is not entitled to be read in evidence or recorded in this state unless
such certificate is authenticated (a) by the certificate of the clerk
or other certifying officer of a court in the district in which such
acknowledgment or proof was made, under the seal of such court,
or (b) by the certificate of the clerk, register, recorder, or other
recording officer of the district in which such acknowledgment or
proof was made, or (c) by the certificate of the officer having charge

of the official records of the appointment of such notary, or having a record of the signature of such notary.

When a certificate of acknowledgment or proof is made by a notary public in a foreign country, the conveyance so acknowledged or proved is not entitled to be read in evidence or recorded in this state unless such certificate is authenticated either by the certificate of an officer designated in (a), (b), or (c) of this subdivision, or by the certificate of a consular officer of the United States resident in such country.

3. When a certificate of acknowledgment or proof, made by the mayor or other chief civil officer of a city or other political subdivision, is not under the seal of such city or other political subdivision, the conveyance so acknowledged or proved is not entitled to be read in evidence or recorded in this state unless such certificate is authenticated by the certificate of the clerk of such city or other political subdivision, or by the certificate of a consular officer of the United States resident in the country where the acknowledgment or proof was made.

4. When a certificate of acknowledgment or proof is made pursuant to the provisions of subdivision five of section two hundred ninety-nine or of subdivision seven of section three hundred one of this chapter by an officer or person not elsewhere in either of said sections specifically designated to take acknowledgments or proofs, the conveyance so acknowledged or proved is not entitled to be read in evidence or recorded within this state unless such certificate is authenticated (a) by the certificate of the secretary of state of a state, or of the secretary of a territory, of the United States, or (b) by the certificate of any officer designated in subdivision three of this section to authenticate certificates of acknowledgment or proof, or (c) by the certificate of any officer designated in clause (a) or (b) of subdivision two of this section to authenticate certificates of acknowledgment or proof, or (d) by the certificate of the officer having charge of the official records showing that the person taking the acknowledgment or proof is such officer as he purports to be, or having a record of the signature of such person.

5. Except as provided in this section, no certificate of authentication shall be required to entitle a conveyance to be read in evidence or recorded in this state when acknowledged or proved before any officer designated in section two hundred ninety-nine or in section three hundred one of this chapter to take such acknowledgment or proof.

§ 312. **Contents of certificate of authentication.** 1. An officer authenticating a certificate of acknowledgment or proof must subjoin or attach to the original certificate a certificate under his hand.

2. When the certificate of acknowledgment or proof is made by a notary public, without the state but within the United States or within any territory, possession, or dependency of the United

States, or within any place over which the United States, at the time when such acknowledgment or proof is taken, has or exercises jurisdiction, sovereignty, control, or a protectorate, the certificate of authentication must state in substance that, at the time when such original certificate purports to have been made, the person whose name is subscribed to the certificate was such officer as he is therein represented to be.

In every other case the certificate of authentication must state in substance (a) that, at the time when such original certificate purports to have been made, the person whose name is subscribed to the original certificate was such officer as he is therein represented to be; (b) that the authenticating officer is acquainted with the handwriting of the officer making the original certificate, or has compared the signature of such officer upon the original certificate with a specimen of his signature filed or deposited in the office of such authenticating officer, or recorded, filed, or deposited, pursuant to law, in any other place, and believes the signature upon the original certificate is genuine; and (c), if the original certificate is required to be under seal, that the authenticating officer has compared the impression of the seal affixed thereto with a specimen impression thereof filed or deposited in his office, or recorded, filed, or deposited, pursuant to law, in any other place, and believes the impression of the seal upon the original certificate is genuine.

3. When such original certificate is made pursuant to subdivision five of section two hundred ninety-nine of this chapter, such certificate of authentication must also specify that the person making such original certificate, at the time when it purports to have been made, was authorized, by the laws of the state, District of Columbia, territory, possession, dependency, or other place where the acknowledgment or proof was made, to take the acknowledgment or proof of deeds to be recorded therein.

4. When such original certificate is made pursuant to subdivision seven of section three hundred one of this chapter, such certificate of authentication must also specify that the person making such original certificate, at the time when it purports to have been made, was authorized, by the laws of the country where the acknowledgment or prof was made, to take acknowledgments of conveyances of real estate or to administer oaths in proof of the execution thereof.

§ 330. **Officers guilty of malfeasance liable for damages.** An officer authorized to take the acknowledgment or proof of a conveyance or other instrument, or to certify such proof or acknowledgment, or to record the same, who is guilty of malfeasance or fraudulent practice in the execution of any duty prescribed by law in relation thereto, is liable in damages to the person injured.

Editorial comment

Concerning the taking of acknowledgments or proof of written instruments by officers who are stockholders, directors, officers or employees of a corporation, when the corporation is a party to the instrument, see *Authority and Duties*, N.Y. EXEC. LAW § 138.

Commissioners of Deeds within the State

[N.Y. EXEC. LAW]

§ 139. **Commissioners of deeds within the state.** 1. Commissioners of deeds in the cities of this state shall be appointed by the common councils of such cities respectively, and shall hold office for the term of two years from the date of their appointment, and until others are appointed in their places. A vacancy occurring during the term for which any commissioner shall be appointed, shall be filled by the common council. The common council of the several cities of this state, except in cities of this state situate in a county which has a population of not less than one hundred and eighty thousand, and not more than six hundred and fifty thousand, according to the last state or federal enumeration, shall at the end of every even numbered year, by resolution of the board, determine the number of commissioners of deeds to be appointed for such cities respectively.

2. The term of office of each commissioner of deeds appointed by the common council in cities of this state situate in a county which has a population of not less than one hundred and eighty thousand, and not more than six hundred and fifty thousand, according to the last state or federal enumeration, shall expire on the thirty-first of December of the even numbered year next after he shall be appointed. The common council of any such city shall in the month of November in every even numbered year, by resolution, determine the number of commissioners of deeds to be appointed in such cities, respectively, for the next succeeding two years.

3. Any person who resides in or maintains an office or other place of business in any such city and who resides in the county in which said city is situated shall be eligible to appointment. Such commissioners of deeds may be appointed by the common council by resolution, and the city clerk shall immediately after such appointment, file a certificate thereof with the county clerk of the county in which such city is situate, specifying the term for which the said commissioners of deeds shall have been appointed; the county clerk shall thereupon notify such persons of their appointment, and such persons so appointed shall qualify by filing with him his oath of office, duly executed before such county clerk or before any person authorized to administer an oath, together with his official signature, within thirty days from the date of such notice.

4. The county clerk shall make a proper index of certificates of appointment and official signatures filed with him. For filing and indexing the certificate of appointment and official signature, the

county clerk shall be paid a fee of one dollar by the appointee, which fee shall include the administration of the oath by the county clerk, should he administer the same.

5. If a person appointed commissioner of deeds shall not file his oath of office as such commissioner of deeds, in the office of the clerk of the county of his residence, within thirty days after the notice of his appointment as above provided, his appointment is deemed revoked and the fee filed with his application forfeited.

6. A commissioner of deeds may file his autograph signature and certificate of appointment in the office of any county clerk, and the county clerk of the county in which such city is located, upon request of any commissioner appointed under the provisions of this section and upon payment of twenty-five cents for each certificate, must make and deliver to such commissioner such number of certificates as may be required. Such certificates shall be issued under the hand and seal of the county clerk of the county in which such city is located, showing the appointment and term of office of such commissioner and stating the county in which he resides. Such a certificate may be filed in the office of any county clerk upon the payment of one dollar for such filing in each office. The clerks of the counties outside the city of New York, shall each keep a book or card index file in which shall be registered the signature of the commissioners so filing such certificates.

7. The county clerk of the county in which said city is located shall, upon demand and upon payment of the sum of fifty cents, authenticate a certificate of acknowledgment or proof of oath taken before such commissioner of deeds within such city, by subjoining or attaching to the original certificate of acknowledgment or proof of oath a certificate under his hand and official seal specifying that at the time of taking the acknowledgment or proof of oath the officer taking it was duly authorized to take the same; that the authenticating officer is acquainted with the former's handwriting, or has compared the signature on the certificate of acknowledgment or proof of oath with the autograph signature deposited in his office by such officer, and that he verily believes the signature is genuine.

8. Any instrument or paper sworn to, proved or acknowledged before a commissioner of deeds within a city and authenticated as hereinbefore provided by the clerk of a county within which such city is located shall be recorded and read in evidence in any county in this state without further proof; provided, however, that a county clerk's certificate of authentication shall not be necessary to entitle any deed or other instrument or paper so proved or acknowledged to be recorded in any office where such commissioner has filed his autograph signature and certificate of appointment or to be read in evidence in any county in which such commissioner has filed with the county clerk his autograph signature and certificate of appointment, as herein provided.

9. The foregoing provisions of this section shall not apply in the city of New York.

Note: The office of commissioner of deeds within the state should not be confused with the office of commissioner of deeds in other states, territories and foreign countries. New York law provides for both offices. Concerning commissioners of deeds in other states, territories and foreign countries, see *Commissioners of Deeds*, N.Y. EXEC. LAW §§ 96, 141 to 143.

§ 140. Commissioners of deeds in the city of New York. 1. The council of the city of New York is hereby authorized and is empowered to appoint commissioners of deeds in such city from time to time, who shall hold their offices for two years from the date of their appointment.

2. No person shall be appointed a commissioner of deeds except an attorney-at-law unless such person shall have submitted with his application proof of his ability to perform the duties of the office. Applicants serving clerkships in the offices of attorneys, and whose clerkship certificates is on file with the proper officials, shall submit an affidavit to that effect. Other employees of attorneys shall submit an affidavit sworn to by a member of the firm of such attorneys that the applicant is a proper and competent person to perform the duties of a commissioner of deeds. Every other applicant shall furnish a certificate of the city clerk of such city stating that he has examined the applicant and believes such applicant to be competent to perform the duties of a commissioner of deeds; provided, however, that where a commissioner of deeds applies, before the expiration of his term, for a reappointment or where a person whose term as commissioner of deeds shall have expired applies within six months after such expiration for appointment as a commissioner of deeds, such examination shall not be required. Upon any such application for such renewal the city clerk shall furnish the applicant with a certificate stating that the applicant has theretofore qualified for appointment and indicate the date of the applicant's original appointment thereon. The fee for issuing each such certificate shall be fifty cents.

3. Such appointment shall not require the approval of the mayor, and hereafter, at the time of subscribing or filing the oath of office, the city clerk shall collect from each person appointed a commissioner of deeds the sum of seven dollars and fifty cents, and he shall not administer or file such oath unless such fee has been paid.

4. The city clerk shall designate a commissioner of deeds clerk, whose duties shall be to enter the names of commissioners of deeds appointed in a book kept for that purpose, make out certificates of appointment and discharge such other duties as the city clerk may designate.

5. Any person hereafter appointed to the office of commissioner of deeds in and for the city of New York by the council, before entering upon the discharge of the duties of such office and within thirty days after such appointment, shall take and subscribe before the commissioner of deeds clerk in the office of the city clerk or before any person authorized to administer oaths the following oath of office: that the applicant is a citizen of the United States, and a resident of the State of New York, the city of New York and the county of (naming the county); that he will support the constitution of the United States and the constitution of the state of New York and faithfully discharge the duties of the office of commissioner of deeds. A person regularly admitted to practice as an attorney and counsellor in the courts of record of this state, whose office for the practice of law is within the city of New York, may be appointed a commissioner of deeds in and for the city of New York and may retain his office as such commissioner of deeds although he resides in or removes to another city in this state or to an adjoining state. For the purposes of this and the following sections of this article such person shall be deemed a resident of the county where he maintains such office.

5-a. A person regularly admitted to practice as an attorney and counsellor in the courts of record of this state, whose office for the practice of law is within the city of New York, may be appointed a commissioner of deeds in and for the city of New York and may retain his office as such commissioner of deeds although he resides in or removes to any other county in this state or to an adjoining state. For the purposes of this article such person shall be deemed a resident of the county where he maintains such office.

6. Any commissioner of deeds who may remove from the city of New York during his term of office vacates his office and is hereby required to notify the city clerk of such removal, and immediately upon the receipt of such notice of removal the city clerk shall cause the name of such commissioner to be stricken from the roll of commissioners of deeds of the city.

7. Any person appointed to the office of commissioner of deeds under the provisions of this section, upon qualifying as above provided, may administer oaths and take acknowledgments or proofs of deeds and other instruments in any part of the city of New York.

8. A commissioner of deeds may file his autograph signature and certificate of appointment in the office of any county clerk in the city; and the city clerk, upon request of any commissioner appointed under the provisions of this section and upon payment of twenty-five cents for each certificate, must make and deliver to such commissioner such number of certificates as such commissioner may require. Such certificates shall be issued under the hand and official seal of the city clerk, showing the appointment and term of office of such commissioner and stating the county in which he resides, which

certificates may be filed in the offices of the several county clerks in the city upon payment of one dollar in each office for filing.

9. The clerks of the counties of New York, Kings, Queens, Richmond and Bronx shall each keep a book or card index file in which shall be registered the signature of the commissioners so filing such certificates; and the county clerk of any county in the city with whom such commissioner has filed a certificate of appointment shall, upon demand and upon payment of the sum of fifty cents, authenticate a certificate of acknowledgment or proof of oath taken before such commissioner of deeds, without regard to the county in the city in which such acknowledgment or proof was taken or oath administered, by subjoining or attaching to the original certificate of acknowledgment or proof or oath a certificate under his hand and official seal specifying that at the time of taking the acknowledgment or proof or oath the officer taking it was duly authorized to take the same; that the authenticating officer is acquainted with the former's handwriting, or has compared the signature on the certificate of acknowledgment, proof or oath with the autograph signature deposited in his office by such officer, and that he verily believes the signature is genuine.

10. Any instrument or paper sworn to, proved or acknowledged before a commissioner of deeds within the city of New York and authenticated as hereinbefore provided by the clerk of any county within the city with whom such commissioner has filed his autograph signature and certificate of appointment shall be recorded and read in evidence in any county in this state without further proof; provided, however, that a county clerk's certificate of authentication shall not be necessary to entitle any deed or other instrument or paper so proved or acknowledged to be recorded or read in evidence in any office of the county clerks within the city of New York or the office of the register of the city of New York.

11. A commissioner of deeds must affix, in black ink, to each instrument sworn to, acknowledged or proved, in addition to his signature, the date when his term expires and his official number as given to him by the city clerk, and must print, typewrite or stamp his name in black ink beneath his signature.

12. The mayor of the city of New York may remove any commissioner of deeds appointed under the provisions of this section for cause shown; but no such commissioner shall be removed until charges have been duly made against him to the mayor and the commissioner shall have had an opportunity to answer the same. At any proceedings held before the mayor for the removal of such commissioner of deeds the mayor shall have power to subpoena witnesses and to compel the attendance of the same, and to administer oaths, and to compel the production of books and papers, and upon the termination of such proceedings shall make his decision thereon in writing, and cause the same to be filed in the office of

the city clerk of the city of New York, provided, however, that the mayor may, whenever a hearing is granted by him on complaint against a commissioner of deeds, designate an assistant corporation counsel to preside who shall have power to subpoena witnesses and to compel the attendance of the same, administer oaths, compel the production of books and papers and receive exhibits; such assistant shall, upon the termination of such proceedings, certify a copy of the stenographer's minutes of such hearing and such exhibits as may be received in evidence, together with his recommendations on the issues presented, whereupon the mayor shall render a decision on all matters presented on such hearing.

13.   In case such commissioner shall be removed from office the city clerk, immediately upon the receipt by him of the order of removal signed by the mayor, shall cause the name of such commissioner so removed to be stricken from the roll of commissioners of deeds of the city.

14.   No person who has been removed from office as a commissioner of deeds for the city of New York, as hereinbefore provided, shall thereafter be eligible again to be appointed as such commissioner nor, shall he be eligible thereafter to appointment to the office of notary public.

15.   Any person who has been removed from office as aforesaid, who shall, after knowledge of such removal, sign or execute any instrument as a commissioner of deeds or notary public shall be deemed guilty of a misdemeanor.

16.   In case of the removal for cause, or removal from the city or resignation of a commissioner of deeds, the city clerk shall immediately notify each county clerk and the register of the city of New York of such removal or resignation.

[N.Y. PUB. OFFICERS LAW]

§ 3.   Qualifications for holding office.

¤   ¤   ¤

3-a.   Nothing herein contained shall operate to prevent a person regularly admitted to practice as an attorney and consellor in the courts of record of this state, whose office for the practice of law is within the city of New York, from accepting or retaining an appointment as a commissioner of deeds in and for the city of New York, as provided in section one hundred forty of the executive law, although he resides in or removes to another city in this state or to an adjoining state.   For the purposes of accepting and retaining an appointment as a commissioner of deeds in and for the city of New York, such person shall be deemed a resident of the county where he maintains such office.

¤   ¤   ¤

7.   Nothing herein contained shall operate to prevent a person

regularly admitted to practice as an attorney and counsellor in the
courts of record of this state, whose office for the practice of law
is within the state, from accepting or retaining an appointment as a
commissioner of deeds in and for the city of New York, as provided
in section one hundred forty of the executive law, although he resides in or removes to any other county in the state or an adjoining
state. For the purposes of accepting and retaining an appointment
as a commissioner of deeds such person shall be deemed a resident
of the county where he maintains such office for the practice of law.

o   o   o

§ 68-a. Fees for oath or acknowledgment. Any officer, authorized
to perform the services specified in this section, and to receive fees
therefor, is entitled to the following fees:

1. For administering an oath or affirmation, and certifying the
same when required, except where another fee is specially prescribed
by statute, twenty-five cents.

2. For taking and certifying the acknowledgment or proof of
the execution of a written instrument; by one person, twenty-five
cents; and by each additional person, twenty-five cents; for swearing
each witness thereto, twenty-five cents.

§ 69. Fee for administering certain official oaths prohibited. An
officer is not entitled to a fee, for administering the oath of office
to a member of the legislature, to any military officer, to an inspector
of election, clerk of the poll, or to any other public officer or public
employee.

Editorial comment

Concerning offenses committed by, among others, commissioners of deeds, and punishments therefor, see *Offenses,*
N.Y. EXEC. LAW § 135-a, and N.Y. PENAL LAW §§ 55.10,
70.15, 80.05.

NORTH CAROLINA

[N.C. GEN. STAT.]

§ 47-1. Officials of State authorized to take probate. The execution of all deeds of conveyance, contracts to buy, sell or convey
lands, mortgages, deeds of trust, instruments modifying or extending
the terms of mortgages or deeds of trust, assignments, powers of
attorney, covenants to stand seized to the use of another, leases for
more than three years, releases, affidavits concerning land titles
or family history, any instruments pertaining to real property, and
any and all instruments and writings of whatever nature and kind
which are required or allowed by law to be registered in the office
of the register of deeds or which may hereafter be required or
allowed by law to be so registered, may be proved or acknowledged

before any one of the following officials of this State: The justices, judges, magistrates, clerks, assistant clerks, and deputy clerks of the General Court of Justice, and notaries public.

§ 47-2. **Officials of the United States, foreign countries, and sister states.** The execution of all such instruments and writings as are permitted or required by law to be registered may be proved or acknowledged before any one of the following officials of the United States, of the District of Columbia, of the several states and territories of the United States, of countries under the dominion of the United States and of foreign countries: Any judge of a court of record, any clerk of a court of record, any notary public, any commissioner of deeds, any commissioner of oaths, any mayor or chief magistrate of an incorporated town or city, any ambassador, minister, consul, vice-consul, consul general, vice-consul general, or commercial agent of the United States, any justice of the peace of any state or territory of the United States, any officer of the army or air force of the United States or United States marine corps having the rank of warrant officer or higher, any officer of the United States navy or coast guard having the rank of warrant officer, or higher, or any officer of the United States merchant marine having the rank of warrant officer, or higher. No official seal shall be required of said military, naval or merchant marine official, but he shall sign his name, designate his rank, and give the name of his ship or military organization and the date, and for the purpose of certifying said acknowledgment, he shall use a form in substance as follows:

On this the ——— day of ———, 19—, before me ———, the undersigned officer, personally appeared ———, known to me (or satisfactorily proven) to be accompanying or serving in or with the armed forces of the United States (or to be the spouse of a person accompanying or serving in or with the armed forces of the United States) and to be the person whose name is subscribed to the within instruments and acknowledged that ——— he ——— executed the same for the purposes therein contained. And the undersigned does further certify that he is at the date of this certificate a commissioned officer of the rank stated below and is in the active service of the armed forces of the United States.

———

Signature of Officer

———

Rank of Officer and command to which attached.

If the proof or acknowledgment of the execution of an instrument is had before a justice of the peace of any state of the United States other than this State or of any territory of the United States, the certificate of such justice of the peace shall be accompanied by a certificate of the clerk of some court of record of the county in which such justice of the peace resides, which certificate of the clerk shall be under his hand and official seal, to the effect that such justice of the peace was at the time the certificate of such justice bears date an acting justice of the peace of such county and state or territory and that the genuine signature of such justice of the peace is set to such certificate.

§ 47-5. **When seal of officer necessary to probate.** When proof or acknowledgment of the execution of any instrument by any maker of such instrument, whether a married woman or other person or corporation, is had before any official authorized by law to take such proof and acknowledgment, and such official has an official seal, he shall set his official seal to his certificate. If the official before whom the instrument is proved or acknowledged has no official seal he shall certify under his hand, and his private seal shall not be essential. When the instrument is proved or acknowledged before the register of deeds of the county in which the instrument is to be registered, the official seal shall not be necessary.

§ 47-7. **Probate where clerk is a party.** All instruments required or permitted by law to be registered to which clerks of the superior court are parties, or in which such clerks are interested, may be proved or acknowledged and the acknowledgment of any married woman may be taken before any magistrate or notary public of the county of said clerk which clerk may then under his hand and official seal certify to the genuineness thereof. Such proofs and acknowledgments may also be taken before any justice or judge of the General Court of Justice, and the instruments may be probated and ordered to be registered by such judge or justice, in like manner as is provided by law for probates by clerks of the superior court in other cases. Provided, that nothing contained herein shall prevent the clerk of the superior court who is a party to any instrument, or who is a stockholder or officer of any bank or other corporation which is a party to any instrument, from adjudicating and ordering such instruments for registration as have been acknowledged or proved before some magistrate or notary public.

o   o   o

§ 47-9. **Probates before stockholders in building and loan associations.** No acknowledgment or proof of execution, including the privy examination of any married woman, of any mortgage or deed of trust executed to secure the payment of any indebtness to any building and loan association shall hereafter be held invalid by reason of the fact that the officer taking such acknowledgment, proof or privy examination, is a stockholder in said building and loan association. This section does not authorize any officer or director of a building and loan association to take acknowledgments, proofs and privy examinations. The provisions of this section shall apply to federal savings and loan associations having their principal offices in this State.

o   o   o

§ 47-14.1. Repeal of laws requiring private examination of married women. All deeds, contracts, conveyances, leaseholds or other instruments executed from and after February 7, 1945, shall be valid for all purposes without the separate, privy, or private examination of a married woman where she is a party to or a grantor in such deed, contract, conveyance, leasehold or other instrument, and it shall not be necessary nor required that the separate or privy examination of such married woman be taken by the certifying officer. From and after February 7, 1945, all laws and clauses of laws contained in any section of the General Statutes requiring the privy or private examination of a married woman are hereby repealed.

§ 47-38. Acknowledgment by grantor. Where the instrument is acknowledged by the grantor or maker, or where a married woman is a grantor or maker, the form of acknowledgment shall be in substance as follows:

North Carolina, ———— County.

I (here give the name of the official and his official title), do hereby certify that (here give the name of the grantor or maker) personally appeared before me this day and acknowledged the due execution of the foregoing instrument. Witness my hand and (where an official seal is required by law) official seal this the ———— day of ————
(year).

(Official seal.)

_____

(Signature of officer.)

§ 47-39. Form of acknowledgment of conveyances and contracts between husband and wife. When an instrument or contract purports to be signed by a married woman and such instrument or contract comes within the provisions of G.S. 52-6,* the form of certificate of her acknowledgment before any officer authorized to take the same shall be in substance as follows:

North Carolina, ———— County.

I (here give name of the official and his official title), do hereby certify that (here give name of the married woman who executed the instrument), wife of (here give husband's name), personally appeared before me this day and acknowledged the due execution of the foregoing (or annexed) instrument; and the said (here give married woman's name), being by me privately examined, separate and apart from her said husband, touching her voluntary execution of the same, does state that she signed the same freely and voluntarily, without fear or compulsion of her said husband or any other person, and that she does still voluntarily assent thereto.

And I do further certify that it has been made to appear to my satisfaction, and I do find as a fact, that the same is not unreasonable or injurious to her.

Witness my hand and (when an official seal is required by law) official seal, this ———— (day of month), A.D. ———— (year). (Official seal)

———————

(Signature of officer.)

* For § 52-6 see below.

§ 47-40. Husband's acknowledgment and wife's acknowledgment before the same officer. Where the instrument is acknowledged by both husband and wife or by other grantor before the same officer the form of acknowledgment shall be in substance as follows:

I (here give name of official and his official title), do hereby certify that (here give names of the grantors whose acknowledgment is being taken) personally appeared before me this day and acknowledged the due execution of the foregoing (or annexed) instrument.

§ 47-41. Corporate conveyances. The following forms of probate for deeds and other conveyances executed by a corporation shall be deemed sufficient, but shall not exclude other forms of probate which would be deemed sufficient in law. If the deed or other instrument is executed by the president or vice-president of the corporation, is sealed with its common, or corporate seal, and is attested by its secretary or assistant secretary, or, in case of a bank, by its secretary, assistant secretary, cashier or assistant cashier, the following form of acknowledgment is sufficient:

———————————————

(State and county, or other description of place where acknowledgment is taken)

I, ————, (Name of officer taking acknowledgment) ————, (Official title of officer taking acknowledgment) certify that ———— (Name of secretary, assistant secretary, cashier or assistant cashier) personally came before me this day and acknowledged that he (or she) is ———— (Secretary, assitant secretary, cashier or assistant cashier) of ———— (Name of corporation, a corporation, and that by authority duly given and as the act of the corporation, the foregoing instrument was signed in its name by its ———— (President or vice-president), sealed with its corporate seal, and attested by himself (or herself) as its ———— (Secretary, assistant secretary, cashier or assistant cashier).

My commission expires ———— (Date of expiration of commission as notary public).

Witness my hand and official seal, this the ———— day of ———— (Month), ———— (Year).

———————————————

(Signature of officer taking acknowledgment) (Official seal, if officer taking acknowledgment has one)

(1) The words "a corporation" following the blank for the name of the corporation may be omitted when the name of the corporation ends with the word "Corporation" or "Incorporated."

(2) The words "My commission expires" and the date of expiration of the notary public's commission may be omitted except when a notary public is the officer taking the acknowledgment.

(3) The words "and official seal" and the seal itself may be omitted when the officer taking the acknowledgment has no seal or when such officer is the clerk, assistant clerk or deputy clerk of the superior court of the county in which the deed or other instrument acknowledged is to be registered.

If the instrument is executed by the president or presiding member or trustee and two other members of the corporation, and sealed with the common seal, the following form shall be sufficient:

North Carolina, ———— County.

This ———— day of ————, A.D. ————, personally came before me (here give the name and official title of the officer who signs this certificate), A. B. (here give the name of the subscribing witness), who, being by me duly sworn, says that he knows the common seal of the (here give the name of the corporation), and is also acquainted with C. D., who is the president (or presiding member or trustee), and also with E. F. and G. H., two other members of said corporation; and that he, the said A. B., saw the said president (or presiding member or trustee) and the two said other members sign the said instrument, and saw the said president (or presiding member or trustee) affix the said common seal of said corporation thereto, and that he, the said subscribing witness, signed his name as such subscribing witness thereto in their presence. Witness my hand and (when an official seal is required by law) official seal, this ———— day of ———— (year).

(Official seal.)

                                    _____

                                    (Signature of officer.)

If the deed or other instrument is executed by the president, presiding member or trustee of the corporation, and sealed with its common seal, and attested by its secretary or assistant secretary, either of the following forms of proof and certificate thereof shall be deemed sufficient:

North Carolina, ———— County.

This ———— day of ————, A.D. ————, personally came before me (here give name and official title of the officer who signs the certificate) A. B. (here give the name of the attesting secretary or assistant secretary), who, being by me duly sworn, says that he knows the common seal of (here give the name of the corporation), and is acquainted with C. D., who is the president of said corporation, and that he, the said A. B., is the secretary (or assistant secretary) of the said corporation, and saw the said president sign the foregoing (or annexed) instrument, and saw the said common seal of said corporation affixed to said instrument by said president (or that he, the said A. B., secretary or assistant secretary as aforesaid, affixed said seal to said instrument), and that he, the said A. B., signed his name in attestation of the execution of said instrument in the presence of said president of said corporation. Witness my hand and (when an official seal is required by law) official seal, this the —————— day of —————— (year).

(Official seal.)

_____

(Signature of officer.)

North Carolina, —————— County.

This is to certify that on the —————— day of ——————, 19 —, before me personally came —————— (president, vice-president, secretary or assistant secretary, as the case may be), with whom I am personally acquainted, who, being by me duly sworn, says that —————— is the president (or vice-president), and —————— is the secretary (or assistant secretary) of the ——————, the corporation described in and which executed the foregoing instrument; that he knows the common seal of said corporation; that the seal affixed to the foregoing instrument is said common seal, and the name of the corporation was subscribed thereto by the said president (or vice-president), and that said president (or vice-president) and secretary (or assistant secretary) subscribed their names thereto, and said common seal was affixed, all by order of the board of directors of said corporation, and that the said instrument is the act and deed of said corporation. Witness my hand and (when an official seal is required by law) official seal, this the —————— day of —————— (year).

(Official seal.)

_____

(Signature of officer.)

If the deed or other instrument is executed by the signature of the president, vice-president, presiding member or trustee of the corporation, and sealed with its common seal and attested by its secretary or assistant secretary, the following form of proof and certificate thereof shall be deemed sufficient:

This —————— day of —————— A.D. ——————, personally came before me (here give name and official title of officer who signs the certificate) A. B., who, being by me duly sworn, says that he is president (vice-president, presiding member or trustee) of the —————— Company, and that the seal affixed to the foregoing (or annexed) instrument in writing is the corporate seal of said company, and that said writing was signed and sealed by him in behalf of said corporation by its authority duly given. And the said A. B. acknowledged the said writing to be the act and deed of said corporation.

(Official seal.)

_____

(Signature of officer.)

If the officer before whom the same is proven be the clerk or deputy clerk of the superior court of the county in which the instrument is offered for registration, he shall add to the foregoing certificate the following: "Let the instrument with the certificate be registered."

✿   ✿   ✿

The following forms of probate for contracts in writing for the purchase of personal property by corporations providing for a lien on the property or the retention of a title thereto by the vendor as security for the purchase price or any part thereof, or chattel mortgages, chattel deeds of trust and conditional sales of personal property executed by a corporation shall be deemed sufficient but shall not exclude other forms of probate which would be deemed sufficient in law:

_____

(Name of state)

_____

(County)

I, ——— (Name of officer taking proof), ——— (Official title of officer taking proof), of ——— (County), ——— (Name of state), certify that ——— (Name of subscribing witness), personally appeared before me, and being duly sworn, stated that in his presence ———.

(Name of president, secretary or treasurer of maker)

(signed the foregoing instrument) (acknowledged the execution of the foregoing instrument.) (Strike out the words not applicable.)

WITNESS my hand and official seal, this ——— day of ——— (Month), 19— (Year).

_____

(Signature of official taking proof)

_____

(Official title of official taking proof)

My commission expires ——— (Date of expiration of official's commission).

§ 47-42. Attestation of bank conveyances by secretary or cashier. (a) In all forms of proof and certificates for deeds and conveyances executed by banking corporations, either the secretary or the cashier of said banking corporation shall attest such instruments.

* * *

§ 47-43. Form of certificate of acknowledgment of instrument executed by attorney in fact. When an instrument purports to be signed by parties acting through another by virtue of the execution of a power of attorney, the following form of certificate shall be deemed sufficient, but shall not exclude other forms which would be deemed sufficient in law:

North Carolina, ———— County.

I (here give name of the official and his official title), do hereby certify that (here give name of attorney in fact), attorney in fact for (here give names of parties who executed the instrument through attorney in fact), personally appeared before me this day, and being by me duly sworn, says that he executed the foregoing and annexed instrument for and in behalf of (here give names of parties who executed the instrument through attorney in fact), and that his authority to execute and acknowledge said instrument is contained in an instrument duly executed, acknowledged, and recorded in the office of (here insert name of official in whose office power of attorney is recorded, and the county and state of recordation), on the (day of month, month, and year of recordation), and that this instrument was executed under and by virtue of the authority given by said instrument granting him power of attorney; that the said (here give name of attorney in fact) acknowledged the due execution of the foregoing and annexed instrument for the purposes therein expressed for and in behalf of the said (here give names of parties who executed the instrument through attorney in fact).

WITNESS my hand and official seal, this ———— day of ————, (year) ————.

(Official seal.)

_____

Signature of Officer

§ 47-43.1. Execution and acknowledgment of instruments by attorneys or attorneys in fact. When an instrument purports to be executed by parties acting through another by virtue of a power of attorney, it shall be sufficient if the attorney or attorney in fact signs such instrument either in the name of the principal by the attorney or attorney in fact or signs as attorney or attorney in fact for the principal; and if such instrument purports to be under seal, the seal of the attorney in fact shall be sufficient. For such instrument to be executed under seal, the power of attorney must have been executed under seal.

§ 47-43.2. Officer's certificate upon proof of instrument by subscribing witness. When the execution of an instrument is proved by a subscribing witness as provided by G.S. 47-12, the certificate required by G.S. 47-13.1 shall be in substantially the following form:

STATE OF ——— (Name of state)

——— COUNTY

I, ——— (Name of officer taking proof), a ——— (Official title of officer taking proof) of ——— COUNTY, ——— (Name of state), certify that ——— (Name of subscribing witness) personally appeared before me this day, and being duly sworn, stated that in his presence ——— (Name of maker) (signed the foregoing instrument) (acknowledged the execution of the foregoing instrument.) (Strike out the words not applicable.)

WITNESS my hand and official seal, this the ——— day of ——— (Month), 19— (Year).

———————————————————————
(Signature of officer taking proof)

———————————————————————
(Official title of officer taking proof)

My commission expires ——— (Date of expiration of officer's commission).

o   o   o

§ 47-43.3. Officer's certificate upon proof of instrument by proof of signature of maker. When the execution of an instrument is proved by proof of the signature of the maker as provided by G.S. 47-12.1 or as provided by G.S. 47-13, the certificate required by G.S. 47-13.1 shall be in substantially the following form:

STATE OF ——— (Name of state)

——— COUNTY

I, ——— (Name of officer taking proof), a ——— (Official title of officer taking proof) of ——— COUNTY, ——— (Name of state), certify that ——— (Name of person familiar with maker's handwriting) personally appeared before me this day, and being duly sworn, stated that he knows the handwriting of ——— (Name of maker) and that the signature to the foregoing instrument is the signature of ——— (Name of maker).

WITNESS my hand and official seal, this the ——— day of ——— (Month), 19— (Year).

———————————————————————
(Signature of officer taking proof)

_____
(Official title of officer taking proof)

My commission expires ——— (Date of expiration of officer's commission).

§ 47-43.4. **Officer's certificate upon proof of instrument by proof of signature of subscribing witness.** When the execution of an instrument is proved by proof of the signature of a subscribing witness as provided by G.S. 47-12.1, the certificate required by G.S. 47-13.1 shall be in substantially the following form:

STATE OF ——— (Name of state)

——— COUNTY

I, ——— (Name of officer taking proof), a ——— (Official title of officer taking proof) of ——— COUNTY, ——— (Name of state), certify that ——— (Name of person familiar with handwriting of subscribing witness) personally appeared before me this day, and being duly sworn, stated that he knows the handwriting of ——— (Name of subscribing witness), and that the signature of ——— (Name of subscribing witness), as a subscribing witness to the foregoing instrument is the signature of ——— (Name of subscribing witness).

WITNESS my hand and official seal, this the ——— day of ——— (Month), 19— (Year).

_____
(Signature of officer taking proof)

_____
(Official title of officer taking proof)

My commission expires ——— (Date of expiration of officer's commission).

§ 47-44. **Clerk's certificate upon probate by justice of peace or magistrate.** When the proof or acknowledgment of any instrument is had before a justice of the peace of some other state or territory of the United States, or before a magistrate of this State, but of a county different from that in which the instrument is offered for registration, the form of certificate as to his official position and signature shall be substantially as follows:

North Carolina ——— County.

I, A. B. (here give name and official title of a clerk of a court of record), do hereby certify that C. D. (here give the name of the justice of the peace or magistrate taking the proof, etc.), was at the time of signing the foregoing (or annexed) certificate an acting justice of the peace or magistrate in and for the county of ——— and State (or territory) of ———, and that his signature thereto is in his own proper handwriting.

In witness whereof, I hereunto set my hand and official seal, this ―――― day of ――――, A.D. ――――.

(Official seal.)

_____

(Signature of officer.)

§ 47-63. **Probates before officer of interested corporation.** In all cases when acknowledgment or proof of any conveyance has been taken before a clerk of superior court, magistrate or notary public, who was at the time a stockholder or officer in any corporation, bank or other institution which was a party to such instrument, the certificates of such clerk, magistrate, or notary public shall be held valid, and are so declared.

§ 52-6. **Contracts of wife with husband affecting corpus or income of estate; authority, duties and qualifications of certifying officer; certain conveyances by married women of their separate property.** (a) No contract between husband and wife made during their coverture shall be valid to affect or change any part of the real estate of the wife, or the accruing income thereof for a longer time than three years next ensuing the making of such contract, nor shall any separation agreement between husband and wife be valid for any purpose, unless such contract or separation agreement is in writing, and is acknowledged before a certifying officer who shall make a private examination of the wife according to the requirements formerly prevailing for conveyance of land.

(b) The certifying officer examining the wife shall incorporate in his certificate a statement of his conclusions and findings of fact as to whether or not said contract is unreasonable or injurious to the wife. The certificate of the officer shall be conclusive of the facts therein stated but may be impeached for fraud as other judgments may be.

(c) Such certifying officer must be a justice, judge, magistrate, clerk, assistant clerk or deputy clerk of the General Court of Justice or the equivalent or corresponding officers of the state, territory or foreign country where the acknowledgment and examination are made and such officer must not be a party to the contract.

(d) This section shall not apply to any judgment of the superior court or other State court of competent jurisdiction, which, by reason of its being consented to by a husband and his wife, or their attorneys, may be construed to constitute a contract between such husband and wife.

(e) Any other provisions of this section to the contrary notwithstanding, in all cases where a married woman owning property as an individual joins with her husband in execution of a deed conveying her real property to a third party and said third party reconveys said real property to said wife and her husband as tenants by the entirety and in the deed to the third party the acknowledgment as herein provided was not complied with, but in all other respects the acknowledgment of the execution of said deed and the probate and registration thereof are regular, such conveyances shall not be void but shall be voidable only, and any action, the purpose of which is to have said conveyances set aside or declared invalid shall be commenced within seven (7) years after the recordation of such deed in the office of the register of deeds of the county or counties in which said real property is located. If no such action is or has been brought then the effect of the conveyances shall be to create an estate by the entirety.

Note: § 47-39, above, makes reference to this section.

NORTH DAKOTA

[N.D. CENT. CODE]

§ **12-39-04. Certifying false acknowledgment is forgery.** If any officer authorized to take the acknowledgment or proof of any conveyance of real property or of any other instrument which by law may be recorded, knowingly and falsely certifies that any such conveyance or instrument was acknowledged by any party thereto or was proved by any subscribing witness, when in truth such conveyance or instrument was not acknowledged or proved as certified, he is guilty of forgery.

Note: Forgery is punishable by imprisonment in the county jail for not more than one year, or by imprisonment in the penitentiary for not more than ten years. N.D. CENT. CODE § 12-39-27.

§ **47-19-13. Acknowledgment and proof—persons authorized to make—state-wide jurisdiction.** The proof or acknowledgment of an instrument may be made at any place within this state before a judge, or the clerk, of the supreme court, or a notary public.

§ **47-19-14. Acknowledgment and proof—Limited to district of officer.** The proof or acknowledgment of an instrument may be made in this state within the judicial district, county, subdivision, or city for which the officer was elected or appointed, before:

1. A judge or clerk of a court of record;
2. A mayor of a city;
3. A register of deeds;
4. A county justice;
5. A United States commissioner;
6. A county auditor; or
7. A township clerk or a city auditor.

§§ **47-19-14.1 to 47-19-14.8.** The Uniform Recognition of Acknowledgments Act has been adopted. For text of act, see page 349.

§ 47-19-20. Identity of person acknowledging—proof required. The acknowledgment of an instrument must not be taken unless the officer taking it knows or has satisfactory evidence on the oath or affirmation of a credible witness that the person making such acknowledgment is the individual who is described in and who executed the instrument, or if executed by a corporation, that the officer making such acknowledgment is authorized to make it as provided in sections 10-07-01 and 10-07-02.

§ 47-19-21. Proof of an unacknowledged instrument—method. Proof of the execution of an instrument when not acknowledged may be made:

1. By the party executing it;
2. By a subscribing witness; or
3. By other witnesses in cases mentioned in sections 47-19-23 and 47-19-24.

§ 47-19-22. Knowledge required by officer of subscribing witness in taking proof. If proof of the execution of an instrument is made by a subscribing witness, such witness must be known personally to the officer taking the proof to be the person whose name is subscribed to the instrument as a witness or must be proved to be such by the oath of a credible witness. The subscribing witness must prove that the person whose name is subscribed to the instrument as a party is the person described in it, that such person executed it, and that the witness subscribed his name thereto as a witness.

Forms

§ 47-19-26. Certificate of acknowledgment—forms. An officer taking an acknowledgment of an instrument within this state must endorse thereon or attach thereto a certificate substantially in the forms prescribed in sections 47-19-27, 47-19-28, 47-19-29, and 47-19-30.

§ 47-19-27. General certificate of acknowledgment. A certificate of acknowledgment, unless otherwise provided in this chapter, must be in substantially the following form:

STATE OF NORTH DAKOTA
County of ———

On this ——— day of ———, in the year ——— before me personally appeared ———, known to me (or proved to me on oath of ———) to be the person who is described in and who executed the within instrument, and acknowledged to me that he (or they) executed the same.

§ 47-19-28. Certificate of acknowledgment executed by a corporation. The certificate of acknowledgment of an instrument executed by a corporation must be substantially in the following form:

STATE OF NORTH DAKOTA
County of ———

On this ——— day of ———, in the year ——— before me (here insert the name and quality of the officer), personally appeared ———, known to me (or proved to me on oath of ———) to be the president (or other officer or person) of the corporation that is described in and that executed the within instrument, and acknowledged to me that such corporation executed the same.

§ 47-19-29. Certificate of acknowledgment by an attorney in fact. The certificate of acknowledgment by an attorney in fact must be substantially in the following form:

STATE OF NORTH DAKOTA
County of ———

On this ——— day of ———, in the year——— before me (here insert the name and quality of the officer), personally appeared ———, known to me (or proved to me on the oath of ———) to be the person who is described in and whose name is subscribed to the within instrument as the attorney in fact of ——— and acknowledged to me that he subscribed the name of ——— thereto as principal and his own name as attorney in fact.

§ 47-19-30. Certificate of acknowledgment by deputy sheriff. All acknowledgments of deeds or other instruments in writing made by any deputy sheriff of this state shall be made substantially in the following form:

STATE OF NORTH DAKOTA
County of ———

On this ——— day of ———, in the year ——— before me, a ———, in and for said county, personally appeared ———, known to me to be the person who is described in and whose name is subscribed to the within instrument as deputy sheriff of said county and acknowledged to me that he subscribed the name of ——— thereto as sheriff of said county and his own name as deputy sheriff.

§ 47-19-32. Certification of acknowledgments or proof of instruments—officer's certificate—how authenticated. An officer taking and certifying an acknowledgment or proof of an instrument for record must authenticate his certificate by affixing thereto:

1. His signature followed by the name of his office; and
2. His seal of office, if by the laws of the territory, state, or country where the acknowledgment or proof is taken, or by authority of which he is acting, he is required to have an official seal.

A judge or clerk of a court of record must authenticate his certificate by affixing thereto the seal of his court. A mayor of a city must authenticate his certificate by affixing thereto the seal of his city.

§ 47-19-33. Who shall not execute acknowledgments and affidavits. No person heretofore or hereafter authorized by law to take or receive the proof or acknowledgment of the execution of an instrument or affidavit and to certify thereto shall take or receive such proof, acknowledgment, or affidavit or certify to the same, if he shall be a party to such instrument, or a member of any partnership which shall or may be a party to such instrument, nor if the husband or wife of such person or officer shall be a party to such instrument.

§ 47-19-34. Proof and acknowledgment of instruments as to corporations. No provision in any of the laws of this state, relating to the proof and acknowledgment of instruments and the taking of affidavits, shall be construed to invalidate or affect the proof or acknowledgment, affidavit, or the certificate thereof, of any instrument to which a corporation may be a party and which shall have been or may be proven, acknowledged, sworn to before, or certified to by, an officer or person authorized by law, who may be an officer, director, employee, or stockholder of such corporation. No person otherwise qualified or authorized by law to take and receive the proof or acknowledgment of an instrument or affidavit and to certify thereto shall be disqualified by reason of being an officer, director, employee, or stockholder of any corporation which is a party to such instrument, and such proof, acknowledgment, and certificate thereof shall be valid for all purposes.

§ 47-19-35. Persons authorized to take acknowledgments and affidavits. All officers and persons, authorized by law to take the proof or acknowledgment of an instrument or affidavit and to certify thereto, may take such proof or acknowledgment and certify to the same in any case not prohibited by this chapter.

§ 47-19-36. Authority of officers in taking proof. Officers authorized to take the proof of instruments are authorized in such proceedings:

1. To administer oaths or affirmations;
2. To employ and swear interpreters; and
3. To issue subpoenas, obedience to which may be enforced as provided by title 28, Judicial Procedure, Civil.

§ 47-19-37. Acknowledgment before justice—certificate of clerk of court. The certificate of proof or acknowledgment, if made before a county justice when used in any county other than that in which he resides, must be accompanied by a certificate under the hand and seal of the clerk of the district court of the county in which the justice resides, setting forth:

1. That such justice, at the time of taking such proof or acknowledgment, was authorized to take the same;

2. That the clerk is acquainted with his handwriting; and
3. That the clerk believes that the signature to the original certificate is genuine.

OHIO

[OHIO REV. CODE ANN.—Page]

§§ 147.51 to 147.57. The Uniform Recognition of Acknowledgments Act has been adopted. For text of act, see page 349.

§ 5301.01. **Acknowledgment of deeds, mortgages, and leases.** A deed, mortgage, land contract ° ° °, or lease of any interest in real property must be signed by the grantor, mortgagor, vendor, or lessor, and such signing must be acknowledged by the grantor, mortgagor, vendor, or lessor in the presence of two witnesses, who shall attest the signing and subscribe their names to the attestation. Such signing must be acknowledged by the grantor, mortgagor, vendor, or lessor before a judge of a court of record in this state or a clerk thereof, a county auditor, county engineer, notary public, mayor, or county court judge, who shall certify the acknowledgment and subscribe his name to the certificate of such acknowledgment.

§ 5301.05. **Acknowledgment of deeds made out of state.** The acknowledgment of an instrument for the conveyance or encumbrance of lands, tenements, or hereditaments situated, within this state, may be made outside this state before a commissioner appointed by the governor of this state for that purpose, a consul general, vice-consul general, deputy consul general, consul, vice-consul, deputy consul, commercial agent, or consular agent of the United States resident in any foreign country.

§ 5301.06. **Instruments executed according to law of place where made.** All deeds, mortgages, powers of attorney, and other instruments of writing for the conveyance or encumbrance of lands, tenements, or hereditaments situated within this state, executed and acknowledged, or proved, in any other state, territory, or country in conformity with the laws of such state, territory, or country, or in conformity with the laws of this state, are as valid as if executed within this state, in conformity with ° ° ° the Revised Code.

OKLAHOMA

[OKLA. STAT. ANN.]

Tit. 16, § 27. **Instruments or copies, when received as evidence.** All instruments affecting real estate and executed and acknowledged in substantial compliance herewith shall be received in evidence in all courts without further proof of their execution; ° ° °

Tit. 16, § 33. Form of acknowledgment. An acknowledgment by individuals of any instrument affecting real estate must be substantially in the following form, to-wit:

State of Oklahoma,

                  ss.

———— County.

Before me, ———— in and for said county and State, on this ———— day of ———— 19—, personally appeared ———— and ———— to me known to be the identical person—who executed the within and foregoing instrument, and acknowledged to me that ———— executed the same as ———— free and voluntary act and deed for the uses and purposes therein set forth.

Tit. 16, § 34. Execution by mark. When real estate is conveyed or encumbered by an instrument in writing by a person who cannot write his name, he shall execute the same by his mark, and his name shall be written near such mark by one of two persons who saw such mark made, who shall write their names on such instrument as witnesses. In case such instrument is acknowledged, then the officer taking the acknowledgment shall, in addition to the other necessary recitals in the acknowledgment, state that the grantor executed the instrument, by inserting in the ordinary form of acknowledgment by individuals after the words "foregoing instrument" the words "by his mark, in my presence and in the presence of ———— and ———— as witness."

Tit. 16, § 35. Acknowledgment to be under seal—before whom taken. Every acknowledgment must be under seal of the officer taking the same; and when taken in this State, it may be taken before any Notary Public, County Clerk, Clerk of the District Court, Clerk of the County Court, or County Judge; and when taken elsewhere in the United States, or United States possessions, or Canada (including Newfoundland), it may be taken before any Notary Public, Clerk of a Court of Record, or Commissioner of Deeds duly appointed by the Governor of the State for the County, State or Territory where the same is taken; and when taken in any other foreign country, it may be taken before any Court of Record or Clerk of such Court, or before any Consul of the United States, provided, that acknowledgments relating to military business of the State may be taken before an officer in charge of any summary Court-Martial ° ° ° a certified copy of whose appointment is placed of record in the office of the Secretary of State by the Adjutant General.

Tit. 16, § 37b. Foreign execution and acknowledgments validated —exceptions. All deeds, mortgages, releases, oil and gas leases, powers of attorney and other instruments of writing for the conveyance or incumbrance of any lands, tenements or hereditaments situated within this state, now of record or hereafter recorded which are executed and acknowledged or proved in any state, territory, District of Columbia or foreign country, in conformity with the law of such state, territory, District of Columbia or foreign country, or in conformity with the Federal Statutes, shall be as valid as to execution and acknowledgment thereof, only, as if executed and acknowledged within this state in conformity with the provisions of the laws of this state. Provided this act shall not validate any deed, mortgage, releases, oil and gas leases, powers of attorney, and other instruments of writing for the conveyance of any lands, tenements, or hereditaments the validity of which is in litigation upon the effective date of this act. Provided this act shall not validate any execution or acknowledgment fraudulently obtained.

Tit. 16, § 95. Acknowledgment by corporation—form. Every deed or other instrument affecting real estate, executed by a corporation, must be acknowledged by the officer or person subscribing the name of the corporation thereto, which acknowledgment must be substantially in the following form, to-wit:

State of Oklahoma,

                    ss.

———— County.

Before me, a ———— in and for said county and State, on this ———— day of ———— 19—, personally appeared ————, to me known to be the identical person who subscribed the name of the maker thereof to the foregoing instrument as its (attorney in fact, president, vice-president, or mayor, as the case may be) and acknowledged to me that he executed the same as his free and voluntary act and deed, and as the free and voluntary act and deed of such corporation, for the uses and purposes therein set forth.

Tit. 16, ch. 1, App.   Title Examination Standards.

о   о   о

§ 6.2.   Omissions and inconsistencies in instruments and acknowledgments. Omission of the date of execution from a conveyance or other instrument affecting the title does not, in itself, impair marketability. Even if the date of execution is of peculiar significance, an undated instrument will be presumed to have been timely executed if the dates of acknowledgment and recordation, and other circumstances of record, support that presumption.

An acknowledgment taken by a notary public in another state which does not show the expiration of the notary's commission is not invalid for that reason.

Inconsistencies in recitals or indication of dates, as between dates of execution, attestation, acknowledgment, or recordation, do not, in themselves, impair marketability. Absent a peculiar significance of one of the dates, a proper sequence of formalities will be presumed notwithstanding such inconsistencies.

о   о   о

Tit. 18, § 438.28. Acknowledgment of instruments. No person who is authorized to take acknowledgments under the laws of this State shall be disqualified from taking acknowledgments of instruments executed in favor of a cooperative or to which it is a party, by reason of being an officer, trustee, member, or shareholder of such cooperative.

Tit. 49, §§ 101 to 109. The Uniform Recognition of Acknowledgments Act has been adopted. For text of act, see page 349.

Tit. 84, § 55. Formal requisites in execution—self-proved wills. Every will, other than a nuncupative will, must be in writing; and every will, other than a holographic will and a nuncupative will, must be executed and attested as follows:

1. It must be subscribed at the end thereof by the testator himself, or some person, in his presence and by his direction, must subscribe his name thereto.

2. The subscription must be made in the presence of the attesting witnesses, or be acknowledged by the testator to them, to have been made by him or by his authority.

3. The testator must, at the time of subscribing or acknowledging the same, declare to the attesting witnesses that the instrument is his will.

4. There must be two attesting witnesses, each of whom must sign his name as a witness at the end of the will at the testator's request and in his presence.

5. Such a will or testament may, at the time of its execution or at any subsequent date during the lifetimes of the testator and the witnesses, be made self-proved, and the testimony of the witnesses in the probate thereof may be made unnecessary by the acknowledgment thereof by the testator and the affidavits of the attesting witnesses, each made before an officer authorized to take acknowledgments to deeds of conveyance and to administer oaths under the laws of this State, such acknowledgments and affidavits being evidenced by the certificate, with official seal affixed, of such officer attached or annexed to such will or testament in form and contents substantially as follows:

THE STATE OF OKLAHOMA
COUNTY OF ———

Before me, the undersigned authority, on this day personally appeared ———, ———, and ———, known to me to be the testator and the witnesses, respectively, whose names are subscribed to the annexed or foregoing instrument in their respective capacities, and, all of said persons being by me first duly sworn, said ———, testator, declared to me and to the said witnesses in my presence that said instrument is his last will and testament, and that he had willingly made and executed it as his free and voluntary act and deed for the purposes therein expressed; and the said witnesses, each on his oath stated to me, in the presence and hearing of the said testator, that the said testator had declared to them that said instrument is his last will and testament, and that he executed same as such and wanted each of them to sign it as a witness; and upon their oaths each witness stated further that they did sign the same as witnesses in the presence of the said testator and at his request and that said testator was at that time eighteen years of age or over and was of sound mind.

_____
Testator

_____
Witness

_____
Witness

Subscribed and acknowledged before me by the said ———, testator, and subscribed and sworn, before me by the said ———, and ——— witnesses, this ——— day of ———, A.D., ———.

(SEAL) (SIGNED) ———.

(OFFICIAL CAPACITY OF OFFICER)
_____

A self-proved will shall be admitted to probate without the testimony of any subscribing witness, but otherwise it shall be treated no differently than a will not self-proved. In particular and without limiting the generality of the foregoing, a self-proved will may be contested, revoked, or amended by a codicil in exactly the same fashion as a will not self-proved.

OREGON

[ORE. REV. STAT.]

§ 93.410. **Execution and acknowledgment of deeds.** Deeds executed within this state, of lands or any interest in lands therein, shall be signed by the grantors and may be acknowledged before any judge of the Supreme Court, circuit judge, county judge, justice of the peace or notary public within the state. No seal of the grantor, corporate or otherwise, shall be required on the deed. The officer taking the acknowledgment shall indorse thereon under his hand a certificate of the acknowledgment thereof, and the date of making it.

§ 93.415. **Acknowledgment by married woman.** All acknowledgments of married women to conveyances of real property in this state shall be taken in the same manner as if they were unmarried.

§ 93.430. Officer taking acknowledgment must know grantor. No acknowledgment of any executed conveyance shall be taken by any officer unless he knows or has satisfactory evidence that the person making the acknowledgment is the individual described in and who executed the conveyance.

§ 93.440. Proof of execution by subscribing witness. Proof of the execution of any conveyance may be made before any officer authorized to take acknowledgments of deeds, and shall be made by a subscribing witness thereto, who shall state his own place of residence, and that he knew the person described in and who executed the conveyance. Such proof shall not be taken unless the officer is personally acquainted with the subscribing witness, or has satisfactory evidence that he is the same person who was a subscribing witness to the instrument.

§ 93.460. Subp[o]ena to compel witness to testify to execution of deed. Upon the application of any grantee, or any person claiming under him, verified by the oath of the applicant setting forth that the grantor is dead, out of the state, or refuses to acknowledge his deed, and that any witness to the conveyance residing in the county where the application is made refuses to appear and testify touching its execution and that the conveyance cannot be proven without his evidence, any officer authorized to take the acknowledgment or proof of conveyances, except a commissioner of deeds, may issue a subp[o]ena requiring the witness to appear and testify before him touching the execution of the conveyance.

§ 93.470. Indorsement of certificate of proof. Every officer who takes the proof of any conveyance shall indorse a certificate thereof, signed by himself, on the conveyance. In the certificate he shall set forth those matters required by ORS 93.440 to 93.460 to be done, known or proved, together with the names of the witnesses examined before the officer, and their places of residence, and the substance of the evidence given by them.

§ 93.480. Deed acknowledged or proved as evidence; recordability. Every conveyance acknowledged, proved or certified in the manner prescribed by law by any of the authorized officers may be read in evidence without further proof thereof and is entitled to be recorded in the county where the land is situated.

§ 93.490. Form of acknowledgments. Certificates of acknowledgment need not be in any particular form. A certificate substantially in the following form is sufficient:

(1) By individuals:

State of Oregon, County of ———, ss.
——— A.D. 19—.

Personally appeared the above-named ——— and acknowledged

the foregoing instrument to be ——— voluntary act and deed.
Before me:
——— (Signature) ——— (Title of Officer)   (Official Seal)

(2) By a corporation:
State of Oregon, County of ———, ss.
——— A.D. 19—.
Personally appeared ———, who, being duly sworn (or affirmed),
did say that he is the president (or other officer) of ——— (naming
the corporation) and that the seal affixed to the foregoing instrument
is the corporate seal of said corporation and that said instrument
was signed and sealed in behalf of said corporation by authority of
its board of directors; and he acknowledged said instrument to be
its voluntary act and deed.   Before me:
——— (Signature) ——— (Title of Officer)   (Official Seal)

(3) By an attorney in fact:
State of Oregon, County of ———, ss.
——— A.D. 19—.
Personally appeared ———, who, being duly sworn (or affirmed),
did say that he is the attorney in fact for ——— and that he
executed the foregoing instrument by authority of and in behalf of
said principal; and he acknowledged said instrument to be the act
and deed of said principal.   Before me:
——— (Signature) ——— (Title of Officer)   (Official Seal)

§ 93.500.   **Execution and acknowledgment of deed in other states.**
If any deed is executed in any other state, territory or district of the
United States, it may be executed according to the laws of that
place or of the State of Oregon.   The execution may be acknowledged either according to the laws of such other place or the State
of Oregon, before any judge of a court of record, justice of peace,
notary public or other officer authorized by the laws of the state,
territory or district to take acknowledgment of deeds therein, or
before any commissioner appointed by the Governor of this state
for that purpose.

§ 93.510.   **Necessity for certificate acknowledging officer's authority in another state.**   In the cases provided for in ORS 93.500, unless
the acknowledgment is taken before a commissioner appointed by
the Governor of this state for that purpose, or before a notary public
certified under his notarial seal, or before the clerk of a court of
record certified under the seal of the court, the deed shall have
attached thereto a certificate of the clerk or other proper certifying
officer of a court of record of the county or district within which the
acknowledgment was taken, under the seal of his office that the
person whose name is subscribed to the certificate of acknowledgment was at the date thereof such officer as he is therein represented

to be, that he believes the signature of such person subscribed thereto to be genuine and that the deed is executed and acknowledged according to the laws of such state, territory or district.

§ 93.520.   **Execution and acknowledgment of deeds in foreign countries.**   If a deed is executed in any foreign country, it may be executed according to the laws of that country or of the State of Oregon.   Its execution may be acknowledged either according to the laws of the foreign country or of the State of Oregon, before any notary public therein, or before any minister plenipotentiary, minister extraordinary, minister resident, charge d'affaires, commissioner, consul, vice consul or consul general of the United States appointed to reside therein.   The acknowledgment shall be certified thereon by the officer taking it, under his hand, and if taken before a notary public his seal of office shall be affixed to the certificate. It is not necessary for any of such persons to state in the certificate that the deed or instrument is executed according to the laws of such country.

§ 93.530.   **Execution, acknowledgment and recordation of assignments of sheriffs' certificates of sale.**   All assignments of sheriffs' certificates of sale.   All assignments of sheriffs' certificates of sale of real property on execution or mortgage foreclosure shall be executed and acknowledged and recorded in the same manner as deeds of real property.

Armed Forces

§ 194.410.   **Notarial acts before or by commissioned officers in Armed Forces.**   (1)   In addition to acknowledgment of instruments and performance of other notarial acts in the manner and form as otherwise authorized by law, instruments may be acknowledged, documents attested, oaths and affirmations administered, depositions and affidavits executed, and other notarial acts performed, before or by any commissioned officer in active service of the Armed Forces of the United States for any person who is a member of the category described in subsection (2) of this section and who is serving outside the boundaries of any of the 50 states and the District of Columbia.

(2)   A member of the Armed Forces of the United States is described as follows:

(a)   A member of the Army, Navy, Air Force, Marine Corps or Coast Guard on active duty, or

(b)   A member of the Merchant Marine of the United States, or

(c)   As a civilian employe of the United States, in whatever category, outside the boundaries of the 50 states and the District of Columbia, whether or not the employe is subject to Civil Service or federal administrative Acts, and whether or not paid from funds appropriated by the Congress of the United States, or

(d)   As a member of a religious group or welfare agency assisting members of the Armed Forces of the United States and officially attached to and serving with the Armed Forces, or

(e)   The spouse of any individual listed in this subsection.

§ 194.420.   Validation of acts; admissibility in evidence.   Such acknowledgment of instruments, attestation of documents, administration of oaths and affirmations, execution of depositions and affidavits, and performance of other notarial acts, heretofore or hereafter made or taken, hereby are declared legal, valid and binding, and instruments and documents so acknowledged, authenticated, or sworn to are admissible in evidence and eligible to record in this state under the same circumstances and with the same force and effect as if made or taken within this state before or by a duly qualified officer or official as otherwise provided by law.

§ 194.430.   Formalities of executing documents before commissioned officers.   (1) In taking acknowledgments and performing other notarial acts requiring certification, a certificate indorsed upon or attached to the instrument or documents, which shows the date of the notarial act and which states, in substance, that the person appearing before the commissioned officer acknowledged the instrument as his act or made or signed the instrument or document under oath, is sufficient for all intents and purposes.

(2)   The instrument or document is not rendered invalid by failure to state the place of execution or acknowledgment.

(3)   If the signature, rank and branch of service, or subdivision thereof, of any commissioned officer described in ORS 194.410 appears upon the instrument, document or certificate, no further proof of the authority of such officer so to act is required and such action by the commissioned officer is prima facie evidence that the person making the oath or acknowledgment is within the purview of ORS 194.410 to 194.430.

Savings and Loan Associations

§ 722.250.   Employees, members or shareholders who are public officers may take certain acknowledgments.   No public officer qualified to take acknowledgment or proof of written instruments shall be disqualified from taking the acknowledgment or proof of an instrument in writing in which a savings and loan association is interested by reason of his employment by, or his being a member or shareholder in the savings and loan association interested in such instrument.

Note: For similar provisions concerning banks, trust companies and other corporations, see *Authority and Duties,* ORE. REV. STAT. § 194.100.

PENNSYLVANIA

[PA. STAT. ANN.]

Tit. 12, § 2549. Form of deed and of acknowledgment. [S]her-iff's and coroner's deeds shall be made in the following words:

Know all men by these presents, That I, ———, sheriff (or coroner) of the county of ———, in the state of Pennsylvania, for and in consideration of the sum of ——— dollars, to me in hand paid, do hereby grant and convey to (here describe the grantee or grantees, and the property conveyed, with the recital of title if desired) the same having been sold by me to the said grantee, ———, on the ——— day of ———, Anno Domini one thousand nine hundred ———, after due advertisement according to law, under and by virtue of a writ (here name the writ), issued on the ——— day of ———, Anno Domini, ———, out of the (here name the court) as of ——— term, one thousand nine hundred —— ——, number ———, at the suit of (here name the plaintiff or plaintiffs) against (here name the defendant or defendants, and terre tenant or terre tenants if any).

In witness whereof, I have hereunto affixed my signature, this ——— day of ———, Anno Domini ———.

Commonwealth of Pennsylvania, ss.:

Before the undersigned, (prothonotary or clerk, or deputy, as the case may be) of the (here name the court), personally appeared, ——— sheriff (or coroner), of ——— county aforesaid, and in due form of law declared that the facts set forth in the foregoing deed are true, and that he acknowledged the same in order that said deed might be recorded.

Witness my hand and the seal of said court, this ——— day of ———, Anno Domini ———.

Tit. 21, § 81. Form of certificate of acknowledgment. The form of certificate of acknowledgment of individuals (single or married) of any deed may be in the following words:—

Commonwealth of Pennsylvania,

ss:

County of ———

On this ——— day of ——— A.D. 19—, before me, a ——— in and for ———, came the above named ——— and acknowledged the foregoing deed to be ——— act and deed, and desired the same to be recorded as such.

Witness my hand and ——— seal, the day and year aforesaid.

(Seal)

_____

_____

(Official character.)

My commission expires ———.

Tit. 21, § 82. Acknowledgments by married women. Acknowledgments of any married woman of any deeds, mortgages or other instruments of writing, required by law to be acknowledged, shall be taken by any judge, justice of the peace, notary public, or other person authorized by law to take acknowledgments of deeds, et cetera, in same manner and form as though said married woman were feme-sole; said acknowledgment to have the same force and effect as if taken separate and apart from the husband of said married woman.

Tit. 21, § 181. Judges of the federal courts and of the courts of other states may take acknowledgments of deeds made out of this state. All bargains and sales, deeds, conveyances and other instruments of writing, concerning any lands, tenements or hereditaments within this state, that may hereafter be made out of this state, the execution whereof, being duly acknowledged by the party or parties executing the same, or proved by the oath or affirmation of one or more of the subscribing witnesses thereto, before one of the judges of the supreme court of the United States, or before a judge of the district court of the United States, or before any one of the judges or justices of the supreme or superior courts or courts of common pleas, of any state or territory within the United States, and so certified under the hand of the said judge and seal of the court, shall be as valid, to all intents and purposes, and shall have the like effect, and be in like manner entitled to be recorded, as if the same had been made, acknowledged or proved, and certified in conformity with any law of this commonwealth. And in the case of a feme covert the said judges and justices, respectively, shall be, and they are hereby authorized to take her acknowledgment and separate examination, and to certify the same, with the same effect as any judge, justice or officer, now authorized by law to that effect may or can do.

Tit. 21, § 182. Acknowledgments duly taken in other states valid. The bargains and sales, deeds, conveyances and other instruments of writing, concerning any lands, tenements or hereditaments within this state, that have been or may hereafter be made out of this state, the execution, whereof being duly acknowledged by the party or parties executing the sale, or proved by the oath or affirmation of one or more of the subscribing witnesses thereto, before any one of the judges or justices of a court of probate, or court of record of any state or territory within the United States, and so certified under the hand of the said judge and seal of the court, shall be as valid to all intents and purposes, and shall have the like effect, and be in like manner entitled to be recorded, as if the same had been made, acknowledged or proved, and certified in conformity with any law of this commonwealth; and in the case of a feme covert, the said judges and justices respectively shall be and they are hereby authorized to take her acknowledgment and separate examination, and to certify the same with the same effect as any judge, justice or officer now authorized by law to that effect may or can do.

Tit. 21, § 183. Acknowledgments may be taken in any of the United States or territories. Any deed, conveyance, or other instrument of writing, of and concerning any lands, tenements, hereditaments, or any estate or interest therein, lying and being within this commonwealth, heretofore acknowledged or proved, or hereafter to be acknowledged or proved, before any judge of any court of record in any state or territory within these United States, and otherwise, according to the forms now provided by the laws of this state, relative to such acknowledgments or probates, and duly certified under the hand of the said judges, and the seal of the said court, shall be as valid, to all intents and purposes, and be in like manner entitled to be recorded, as if the same had been duly acknowledged or proved in conformity with the present law of this commonwealth.

Tit. 21, § 185. Acknowledgments in territories of United States. The provisions of the third section of the act of assembly of this commonwealth, approved December 14, 1854, authorizing acknowledgments, in certain cases, to be taken before any officer or magistrate of the state wherein such deeds, powers of attorney, or other instruments of writing, therein mentioned, are executed, be and are hereby extended so as to authorize such acknowledgments to be taken before any officer or magistrate of any territory of the United States, created and organized by act of Congress, authorized by the laws of such territory to take acknowledgments of such deeds, powers of attorney, or other instruments of writing; and all deeds, powers of attorney or other instruments of writing, which have been executed prior to the passage of this act, in any territory, created by act of Congress, and acknowledged before any officer or magistrate of such territory, authorized by the laws of such territory to take acknowledgments of deeds, powers of attorney, or other instruments of writing, shall be as valid, to all intents and purposes, as if such territory had been one of the states of this Union.

Tit. 21, § 186. May be taken in the District of Columbia. The provisions of the third section of the act of assembly entitled "An act relating to the authentication of letters of attorney, protests of notaries public and assignments made out of the state, and to the acknowledgment of deeds," approved December 14, 1854, for taking and certifying acknowledgments of deeds and other instruments of writing, executed in any of the United States, are hereby extended to the District of Columbia, with like effect as if the said district had been therein specially mentioned and included; and all such acknowledgments heretofore taken and certified in the said district, in the manner provided in said section, are hereby validated and confirmed, and the deeds and other instruments so acknowledged, and the records thereof when recorded, shall be deemed as valid and effectual as if said district had been mentioned and included in the provisions of said section.

Tit. 21, § 187. Acknowledgments in Cuba, and the island possessions, valid. All deeds, mortgages or other instruments of writing, heretofore made or which may hereafter be made by any person or corporation, concerning lands, tenements, hereditaments or property, or any estate or interest therein, lying or being within this commonwealth, heretofore acknowledged or proved, or which may hereafter be acknowledged or proved, in the manner directed and provided by the laws of this commonwealth, before any person holding the rank of major or any higher rank in the military service of the United States in Cuba, or in Puerto Rico, the Phillippine Islands, or other possessions of the United States, whether in the regular or volunteer service, or before any civil officer in the service of the United States in any of the said places hereinbefore referred to, shall be valid to all intents and purposes, and be in like manner entitled to be recorded as if the same had been duly acknowledged and proven before a notary public or other officer within this commonwealth having authority to take such proofs or acknowledgments according to the existing laws of this commonwealth.

Tit. 21, § 190. Proof of official character of person taking acknowledgment. And provided further, That the proof of the official character of the person taking such acknowledgment shall be his official seal, if he have one; and if not, then a certificate under the seal of any officer, of the United States who has an official seal, in any of said places.

Tit. 21, § 191. Acknowledgments of married women made in any other of the United States. In all cases of the sale, conveyance, mortgage or transfer of any lands, tenements or hereditaments of any married woman, or of any interest of any married woman in any lands, tenements or hereditaments in this commonwealth, and in all cases of any power or powers of attorney to make and execute such sale, conveyance, mortgage or transfer made, or that may be made and executed by such married woman in any other of the United States, the acknowledgment or written consent of such married women, as required by the act relating to the rights of married women, or any other law of this commonwealth, may be taken or acknowledged by and before any judge of any court of record in such state; and such acknowledgment so made, or to be made, shall be as valid and effectual as if made by said married woman before a judge of a court of common pleas of this commonwealth.

Tit. 21, § 221. Acknowledgments before consul or vice-consul of the United States. All deeds and conveyances, whether of femes covert or otherwise, made, granted and executed out of the United States, and brought into this commonwealth to be recorded, in the county where the lands lie, and all letters of attorney and instruments of writing made and executed out of the United States, and intended to have effect in this commonwealth, the execution of such deeds, conveyances, letters of attorney or instruments of writing, being first proved, or the acknowledgment thereof being first duly taken and made, in the manner directed and provided by the laws of this commonwealth, before any consul or vice-consul of the United States, duly appointed for and exercising consular functions in the state, kingdom, country or place where such deeds or conveyances, letters of attorney or instruments of writing may or shall be made and executed, and certified under the public official seal of such consul or vice-consul of the United States, shall be as valid and effectual in law as if the same had been made and duly proved or acknowledged before a justice of the peace or other officer within this commonwealth having authority to take such proof or acknowledgments, according to the existing laws of this commonwealth.

Tit. 21, § 222. **Ambassadors, public ministers, etc.** All ambassadors, ministers plenipotentiary, charges d'affaires, or other persons exercising public ministerial functions, duly appointed by the United States of America, shall have full power and authority to take all acknowledgments and proofs of any deeds, conveyances, settlements, mortgages, agreements, powers of attorney, or other instruments under seal relating to real or personal estate, made or executed in any foreign country or state, by any person or persons, or by husband and wife, in the manner and according to the forms required by the laws of this commonwealth, and to administer all oaths or affirmations necessary or required for the purposes aforesaid; and that all acknowledgments and proofs heretofore made by any or either of the persons aforesaid, before any of the officers aforesaid, in the manner and according to the forms aforesaid, are hereby ratified and confirmed, and the same, and the records of the instruments aforesaid, if the said instruments have been heretofore recorded, are declared to be as valid and effectual as if the said acknowledgments, proofs and records had been respectively made, taken and recorded under the provisions hereof.

Tit. 21, § 223. **Deputy consuls and commercial agents, etc., of United States.** All conveyances, mortgages or other instruments of writing, heretofore made, or which may hereafter be made by any person or corporation, concerning any lands, tenements, hereditaments or property, or any estate or interest therein, lying or being within this commonwealth, heretofore acknowledged or proved, or hereafter acknowledged or proved, in the manner directed and provided by the laws of this commonwealth, before any deputy consul, commercial agents, vice and deputy commercial agents, or consular agents of the United States, duly appointed for and exercising the functions of his office, in the place where such acknowledgment has been or may be taken, and certified under the public official seal of such deputy consul, commercial agents, vice and deputy commercial agents or consular agents, shall be valid to all intents and purposes, and be in like manner entitled to be recorded, as if the same had been duly acknowledged and proven before a notary public, or other officer, within this commonwealth, having authority to take such proofs or acknowledgments according to the existing laws of this commonwealth, and where any such instruments so acknowledged before such consular officers have heretofore been admitted to record in the proper office in this commonwealth, the record thereof shall be as good and valid as if they had been recorded subsequent to the passage of this act: Provided, That this act shall not apply to any case in which an action is now pending or has been heretofore judicially decided.

Tit. 21, § 224. Acknowledgments taken before commissioners in chancery in foreign countries. In all cases of the sale, conveyance, mortgage or other instrument of writing, heretofore made or which may be hereafter made by any person, or husband and wife, concerning any lands, tenements or hereditaments, or any estate or interest therein, lying or being within this commonwealth, and heretofore ackowledged or proved, or hereafter acknowledged or proved, before any commissioner in chancery in any foreign country, according to the forms now or hereafter required by the laws of this state relative to such acknowledgment or probate, duly certified under the seal of office of such commissioner in chancery, shall be valid to all intents and purposes, and be in like manner entitled to be recorded, as if the same had been duly acknowledged or proven according to the existing laws of this commonwealth: Provided, That no case heretofore decided judicially shall be affected by this act.

Tit. 21, § 225. Acknowledgments by married women out of United States. In all cases of the sale, conveyance, mortgage or transfer of the property of any married woman, or of any powers of attorney to make and execute such sale, conveyance, mortgage or transfer, made and executed out of the United States, the written consent of such married woman, as required by the act relating to the rights of married women, may be acknowledged before any minister, ambassador, charge d'affaires, consul or vice-consul of the United States; and such acknowledgment so made shall be equally valid as if made before a judge of a court of common pleas of this commonwealth.

Tit. 21, § 289. Records of legal instruments having defective acknowledgments. The records of all legal instruments which, by law, are directed to be recorded or are entitled to be recorded, and which have been duly executed by the proper party or parties, and which have been acknowledged to and certified by a qualified officer without this State but in the United States, a territory or insular possession of the United States or the District of Columbia, notwithstanding the absence of any authentication, affirming the official character of such officer in conformity with the laws of this Commonwealth in force at the time such instrument was acknowledged, are hereby severally made as valid and effective in law as if each such instrument had been fully acknowledged, certified and authenticated. The record of each such instrument, or the original of such instrument itself, shall be admitted as evidence in all courts of this Commonwealth, and shall be as valid and conclusive evidence as if such instrument had been in all respects acknowledged and the acknowledgment certified and authenticated in accordance with the then existing law.

Tit. 21, §§ 291.1 to 291.13. The Uniform Acknowledgment Act has been adopted. For text of act, see page 349.

PUERTO RICO

Cross-Reference

See also *Authority and Duties*, "Instruments," P.R. LAWS ANN. tit. 4, §§ 1009 *et seq.*

[P.R. LAWS ANN.]

"Federal Relations Act"

§ 54. Acknowledgment of deeds and instruments. That deeds and other instruments affecting land situate in the District of Columbia, or any other territory or possession of the United States, may be acknowledged in Puerto Rico before any notary public appointed therein by proper authority, or any officer therein who has ex officio the powers of any notary public; Provided, That the certificate by such notary shall be accompanied by the certificate of the Executive Secretary of Puerto Rico to the effect that the notary taking such acknowledgment is in fact such notarial officer.

RHODE ISLAND

[R.I. GEN. LAWS ANN.]

§ 15-4-5. Acknowledgment of deeds and letters of attorney. The deed of a married woman, conveying her separate interest in any lands, tenements or hereditaments, shall be acknowledged by her in the same manner as if she were single and unmarried. If any deed affecting her right of dower in any estate of her husband during his life, be executed by attorney of the wife, the letter of attorney shall be acknowledged in the same manner as if she were single and unmarried.

§ 34-12-1. Form of acknowledgment—foreign acknowledgments. Acknowledgment of any deed hereafter made need not be in any set form, but shall be made by all the parties grantors, including married women, even though releasing dower only, and the certificate thereof shall express the ideas that the grantors respectively making the acknowledgment were each and all known to the magistrate taking the acknowledgment, and known by the magistrate to be the parties executing the instrument, and that they acknowledged said instrument to be their free act and deed; provided, however, that in case of any such deed executed without this state, and within the limits of the United States or of any dependency thereof, if the deed is acknowledged or proved in the manner prescribed by the law of the state, District of Columbia, territory or such dependency, where executed, it shall be deemed to be legally executed, and shall have the same effect as if executed in the mode above prescribed. No other acknowledgment shall be required of married women.

§ 34-12-2. **Officers authorized to take acknowledgments.** Acknowledgment of any instrument required by any statute of this state to be acknowledged shall be made:

1. Within this state, before any state senator, any state representative, judge, justice of the peace, clerk or assistant clerk of the superior court, mayor, notary public, town clerk or recorder of deeds.

2. Without this state and within the limits of United States or any dependency thereof, before any judge or justice of a court of record or other court, justice of the peace, mayor or notary public, of the state, District of Columbia, territory or such dependency, in which such acknowledgment is made, or before any commissioner appointed by the governor of this state, or before any officer authorized by law to take acknowledgments of deeds in the place in which the acknowledgment is made.

3. Without the limits of the United States, before any of the following officers acting within his territorial jurisdiction or within that of the court of which he is an officer: (a) An ambassador, envoy, minister, charge d'affaires, secretary of legation, consul-general, consul, vice-consul, consular agent, vice-consular agent, or any other diplomatic or consular agent or representative of the United States, appointed or accredited to, and residing within the country where the acknowledgment or proof is taken.

(b) A judge or other presiding officer of any court having a seal or the clerk or other certifying officer thereof.

(c) A mayor or other chief civil officer of any city or other political subdivision.

(d) A notary public.

(e) A person residing in, or going to, the country where the acknowledgment or proof is to be taken, and specially authorized for that purpose by a commission issued to him under the seal of the superior court.

(f) Any person authorized, by the laws of the country where the acknowledgment or proof is made, to take acknowledgments of conveyances of real estate or to administer oaths in proof of the execution thereof.

§ 34-12-3. Acknowledgments in good faith before person claiming to be authorized—penalty for misrepresentation. Any acknowledgment made in good faith before a person claiming to be one of the foregoing officials authorized to take acknowledgments within the respective jurisdictions as above, shall be valid, although the official before whom the same is made was not duly qualified in such office; but every person who shall, within this state, wilfully take and certify to the taking of any such acknowledgment, without being lawfully qualified thereunto, shall be liable in a criminal proceeding to a fine not exceeding fifty dollars ($50.00), one-half to the use of the complainant and the other half thereto to the use of this state.

§ 34-12-4. Instruments executed by diplomatic officials outside United States. Every instrument requiring acknowledgment, executed without the limits of the United States, concerning lands lying within this state, in which instrument any ambassador, minister, charge d'affaires, consul general, vice-consul general, consul, vice-consul, consular agent, commercial agent, of the United States, or commissioner appointed by the governor of this state, shall be grantor, may be executed in the presence of two (2) witnesses; and when so executed, an official certificate under the hand and official seal of the grantor that such instrument is his act and deed shall be equivalent to an acknowledgment of such instrument in the manner required by law.

§ 34-12-5. Power of armed forces officers to take acknowledgments. In addition to the acknowledgment of instruments and the performance of other notarial acts in the manner and form and as otherwise authorized by law, instruments may be acknowledged, documents attested, oaths and affirmations administered, depositions and affidavits executed, and other notarial acts performed, before or by any commissioned officer in active service of the armed forces of the United States with the rank of second lieutenant or higher in the army, air force, or marine corps, or with the rank of ensign or higher in the navy or coast guard, or with equivalent rank in any other component part of the armed forces of the United States, by any person without the limits of the United States, and to any person who is a member of the armed forces who is within or without the limits of the United States and their lawful dependents.

SOUTH CAROLINA

A notary public may, among other things, take acknowledgments and proofs of deeds and other instruments required by law to be acknowledged, and renunciations of dower. See *Authority and Duties*, S.C. CODE ANN. § 49-8.

Dower

[S.C. CODE ANN.]

§ 19-111. Renunciation of dower. Any woman who has an inchoate right of dower in any lands in this State, whether she be of lawful age or minor, may renounce and relinquish her right of dower by acknowledging it in writing before any officer of this State, or of the state in which the renunciation is executed, or of the United States, who is authorized by law to administer oaths. The officer shall append to the writing his certificate in the form prescribed by § 19-114. No renunciation of the right of dower, heretofore or hereafter made, shall be held invalid because of the absence of the official seal of the person administering the oath.

When recorded in the county where the real estate is located, the renunciation shall be effective to convey away, bar and terminate the dower right of the woman, although she has executed no deed of conveyances for that purpose.

§ 19-114. Certificate to be endorsed on release; form; recordation. A certificate, under the hand of the woman and the hand and seal of the officer or officers aforesaid, shall be endorsed upon such release or a separate instrument of writing to the same effect, in the form or to the purport hereafter following, and be recorded in the office of register of mesne conveyances or clerk of court in the county where the land lies:

"The State of South Carolina, ———— County.

"I, F G (————, judge, magistrate or other officer, as the case may be), do hereby certify unto all whom it may concern that E B, the wife of the within named A B, did this day appear before me and, upon being privately and separately examined by me, did declare that she does freely, voluntarily and without any compulsion, dread or fear of any person or persons whomsoever, renounce, release and forever relinquish unto the within named C D, his heirs and assigns, all her interest and estate and also all her right and claim of dower of, in or to, all and singular the premises within mentioned and released.

"Given under my hand and seal this ———— day of ————, Anno Domini ————.

(Signed)   E ———— B————
(L. S.) F ———— G ————."

§§ 49-61 to 49-69. The Uniform Recognition of Acknowledgments Act has been adopted. For text of act, see page 349.

§ 60-51. Prerequisites to recording. Before any deed or other instrument in writing can be recorded in this State:

(1) The execution thereof shall be first proved by the affidavit of a subscribing witness to such instrument, taken before some officer

within this State competent to administer an oath. If the affidavit be taken without the limits of this State, it may be taken before:

(a) A commissioner appointed by dedimus issued by the clerk of the court of common pleas of the county in which the instrument is to be recorded,

(b) A commissioner of deeds of this State,

(c) A clerk of a court of record who shall make certificate thereof under his official seal,

(d) A justice of the peace who must append to the certificate his official seal,

(e) A notary public who shall affix thereto his official seal within the State of his appointment, which shall be a sufficient authentication of his signature, residence and official character,

(f) Before a minister, ambassador, consul general, consul or vice-consul or consular agent of the United States of America, or

(g) In the case of any officer or enlisted man of the United States Army, Air Force, Navy, Marine Corps or Coast Guard on active duty outside the State or any civilian employee of any such organization on active duty outside the continental confines of the United States, any commissioned officer of said Army, Air Force, Navy, Marine Corps or Coast Guard, if such probating officer shall state his rank, branch and organization;

(2) The Uniform Recognition of Acknowledgments Act° shall be complied with; or

(3) The person executing it shall submit an affidavit subscribed to before a person authorized to perform notarial acts herein or by the Uniform Recognition of Acknowledgments Act that the signature on the deed or other instrument is his signature and that the instrument was executed for the uses and purposes stated therein.

° See §§ 49-61 to 49-69 above.

SOUTH DAKOTA

[S.D. COMPILED LAWS ANN.]

§ 18-4-1. **Officers authorized to take proof or acknowledgment within state.** The proof or acknowledgment of an instrument may be made at any place within this state before a judge or the clerk of the Supreme Court or a notary public.

§ 18-4-2. **Officers authorized to take proof or acknowledgment within circuit, county or city.** The proof or acknowledgment of an instrument may be made in this state within the judicial circuit, county, or city for which the officer was elected or appointed, before either:

(1) A judge of the circuit, municipal, or county court;

(2) A clerk of circuit, county, or municipal court;

(3) A county auditor;

(4) A register of deeds;

(5) A mayor of a city;

(6) A justice of the peace; or

(7) A United States district court commissioner.

§ 18-4-3. **Indian agents authorized to take acknowledgment or proof in Indian country—recording of certificate of appointment.** Indian agents or superintendents are authorized to take acknowledgments or proofs of deeds or other instruments in writing, in Indian country, and acknowledgments or proofs so taken shall have the same force and effect as if taken before a notary public. To qualify for taking such acknowledgments or proofs, such Indian agent or superintendent shall file for record in the office of the register of deeds of the county in which he is stationed, or the county to which said county is attached for judicial purposes, a certificate signed by the secretary of the interior of the United States showing his appointment and authority as such Indian agent or superintendent.

§ 18-4-4. **Officers authorized to take proof or acknowledgment within United States.** The proof or acknowledgment of an instrument may be made without the state, but within the United States, and within the jurisdiction of the officer, before either:

(1) A justice, judge, or clerk of any court of record of the United States;

(2) A justice, judge, or clerk of any court of record of any state or territory;

(3) A notary public;

(4) Any officer of the state or territory where the acknowledgment is made, authorized by its laws to take such proof or acknowledgment; or

(5) A commissioner appointed for the purpose by the Governor of this state.

§ 18-4-5. **Officers authorized to take proof or acknowledgment in foreign countries.** The proof or acknowledgment of an instrument may be made without the United States, before either:

(1) An ambassador, a minister, commissioner, or charge d'affaires of the United States, resident and accredited in the country where the proof or acknowledgment is made;

(2) A consul, vice consul, or consular agent of the United States, resident in the country where the proof or acknowledgment is made;

(3) A judge, clerk, register, or commissioner of a court of record of the country where the proof or acknowledgment is made;

(4) A notary public of such country;

(5) An officer authorized by the laws of the country where the proof of acknowledgment is taken to take proof or acknowledgment; or

(6) When any of the officers mentioned in this chapter are authorized to appoint a deputy, the acknowledgment or proof may be taken before such deputy.

All proofs or acknowledgments heretofore taken according to the provisions of this section are hereby declared to be sufficiently authenticated and to be entitled to record, and any such record hereafter made shall be notice of the contents of the instrument so recorded.

§ 18-4-6. Acknowledgment before commissioned officer of armed forces—place of execution need not be shown. In addition to the acknowledgment of instruments in the manner and form and as otherwise authorized by the laws of South Dakota, any person serving in or with the armed forces of the United States may acknowledge the execution of an instrument, wherever located, before any commissioned officer in active service of the armed forces of the United States with the rank of second lieutenant or higher in the army, air force or marine corps, or ensign or higher in the navy or United States coast guard. The instrument shall not be rendered invalid by the failure to state therein the place of execution or acknowledgment.

§ 18-4-7. Authentication of military certificate not required—form of certificate attached. No authentication of the officer's certificate of acknowledgment taken pursuant to § 18-4-6 shall be required but the officer taking the acknowledgment shall endorse thereon or attach thereto a certificate substantially in the following form:

On this the ———— day of ————, 19—, before me ————, the undersigned officer personally appeared ————, known to me (or satisfactorily proven) to be serving in or with the armed forces of the United States and to be the person whose name is subscribed to the within instrument and acknowledged that—he executed the same for the purposes therein contained. And the undersigned does further certify that he is at the date of this certificate a commissioned officer of the rank stated below and is in the active service of the armed forces of the United States.

_____

Signature of officer.

_____

Rank of officer and command to which attached.

§ 18-4-10. Identity of person making acknowledgment to be known or proved to officer. The acknowledgment of an instrument must not be taken unless the officer taking it knows or has satisfactory evidence on the oath or affirmation of a credible witness, that the person making such acknowledgment is the individual who is described in and who executed the instrument; or, if executed by a corporation, that the person making such acknowledgment is an officer of the corporation authorized to execute the instrument.

§ 18-4-11. Certificate of officer taking acknowledgment to be attached. An officer taking the acknowledgment of an instrument must endorse thereon or attach thereto a certificate substantially in the forms prescribed in §§ 18-4-12 to 18-4-15, inclusive.

§ 18-4-12. Form of general certificate of acknowledgment. The certificate of acknowledgment of an instrument unless it is otherwise in this chapter provided must be substantially in the following form:

Territory of ―――― or State of ――――
County of ―――― ss

On this ―――― day of ――――, in the year ――――, before me personally appeared ――――, known to me (or proved to me on the oath of ――――) to be the person who is described in, and who executed the within instrument and acknowledged to me that he (or they) executed the same.

§ 18-4-13. Form of certificate of corporate acknowledgment. The certificate of acknowledgment of an instrument executed by a corporation must be substantially in the following form:

Territory of ―――― or State of ――――
County of ―――― ss

On this ―――― day of ――――, in the year ――――, before me ――――, personally appeared ――――, known to me (or proved to me on the oath of ――――) to be the ―――― of the corporation that is described in and that executed the within instrument and acknowledged to me that such corporation executed the same.

§ 18-4-14. Form of certificate of acknowledgment by attorney. The certificate of acknowledgment by an attorney in fact must be substantially in the following form:

Territory of ―――― or State of ――――
County of ―――― ss

On this ―――― day of ――――, in the year ――――, before me personally appeared ――――, known to me (or proved to me on the oath of ――――) to be the person who is described in and whose name is subscribed to the within instrument as the attorney in fact of ――――, and acknowledged to me that he subscribed the name of ―――― thereto as principal and his own name as attorney in fact.

§ 18-4-15. Form of certificate of acknowledgment by deputy sheriff. The certificate of acknowledgment by any deputy sheriff of South Dakota must be substantially in the following form:

State of South Dakota,

ss

County of ———

On this ——— day of ———, in the year ———, before me personally appeared ———, known to me (or proved to me on the oath of ———) to be the person who is described in and whose name is subscribed to the within instrument as deputy sheriff of said county and acknowledged to me that he subscribed the name of ——— thereto as sheriff of said county and his own name as deputy sheriff.

§ 18-4-16. Fees chargeable for acknowledgments. Officers authorized by law to take and certify acknowledgment of deeds and other instruments are entitled to charge and receive twenty-five cents each therefor, and for administering oaths and certifying the same, ten cents.

§ 18-4-17. Means of proving instrument not acknowledged. Proof of the execution of an instrument, when not acknowledged, may be made either:

(1) By the party executing it, or either of them;

(2) By a subscribing witness; or

(3) By other witnesses, in cases mentioned in §§ 18-4-19 and 18-4-20, relating to proof of handwriting.

§ 18-4-18. Proof of instrument by subscribing witness. If proof of the execution of an instrument is made by a subscribing witness, such witness must be personally known to the officer taking the proof to be the person whose name is subscribed to the instrument as a witness or must be proved to be such by the oath of a credible witness. The subscribing witness must prove that the person whose name is subscribed to the instrument as a party is the person described in it and that such person executed it and that the witness subscribed his name thereto as a witness.

§ 18-4-19. Circumstances permitting proof of instrument by handwriting. The execution of an instrument may be established by proof of the handwriting of the party and of a subscribing witness, if there is one, in the following cases:

(1) When the parties and all the subscribing witnesses are dead;

(2) When the parties and all the subscribing witnesses are nonresidents of the state;

(3) When the place of their residence is unknown to the party

desiring the proof and cannot be ascertained by the exercise of due diligence;

(4) When the subscribing witness conceals himself or cannot be found by the officer by the exercise of due diligence in attempting to serve the subpoena or attachment; or

(5) In case of the continued failure or refusal of the witness to testify for the space of one hour after his appearance.

§ 18-4-20. **Facts to be established for proof by handwriting.** The evidence taken under § 18-4-19 must satisfactorily prove to the officer the following facts:

(1) The existence of one or more of the conditions mentioned therein;

(2) That the witness testifying knew the person whose name purports to be subscribed to the instrument as a party and is well acquainted with his signature and that it is genuine;

(3) That the witness testifying personally knew the person who subscribed the instrument as a witness and is well acquainted with his signature and that it is genuine; and

(4) The place of residence of the witness.

§ 18-4-21. **Powers of officers authorized to take proof of instruments.** Officers authorized to take the proof of instruments are authorized in such proceedings:

(1) To administer oaths or affirmations;

(2) To employ and swear interpreters;

(3) To issue subpoenas and to punish for contempt as provided in title 19 in regard to the means of producing witnesses.

§ 18-4-22. **Contents of certificate of officer taking proof of instrument.** An officer taking proof of the execution of an instrument must in his certificate endorsed thereon or attached thereto set forth all the matters required by law to be done or known by him or proved before him on the proceeding, together with the names of all the witnesses examined before him, their places of residence respectively, and the substance of their evidence.

§ 18-4-23. **Authentication of certificates of acknowledgment or proof.** Officers taking and certifying acknowledgments or proof of instruments for record must authenticate their certificates by affixing thereto their signatures, followed by the names of their offices; also their seals of office, if by the laws of the state, territory, or country where the acknowledgment or proof is taken or by authority of which they are acting, they are required to have official seals. Judges and clerks of courts of record must authenticate their certificates as aforesaid by affixing thereto the seal of the proper court; and mayors of cities, by the seal thereof.

§ 18-4-24.   Clerk's certificate to accompany proof or acknowledgment taken by magistrate.   The certificate of proof or acknowledgment, if made before a magistrate, when used in any county other than that in which he resides, must be accompanied by a certificate under the hand and seal of the clerk of courts of the county in which the magistrate resides, setting forth that such magistrate at the time of taking such proof or acknowledgment was authorized to take the same, and that the clerk is acquainted with his handwriting and believes that the signature to the original certificate is genuine.

§ 18-4-25.   False certification of acknowledgment or proof as forgery.   If any officer authorized to take the acknowledgment or proof of any conveyance of real property or of any other instrument which by law may be recorded, knowingly and falsely certifies that any such conveyance or instrument was acknowledged by any party thereto or was proved by any subscribing witness, when in truth such conveyance or instrument was not acknowledged or proved as certified, he is guilty of forgery in the second degree.

Note: Forgery in the second degree is punishable by imprisonment in the state penitentiary not less than 3 years nor more than 10 years. See *Offenses*, S.D. COMPILED LAWS ANN. § 22-39-11.

§§ 18-5-1 to 18-5-18.   The Uniform Acknowledgment Act has been adopted.   For text of act, see page 349.

TENNESSEE

[TENN. CODE ANN.]

§ 64-2202.   Persons authorized to take acknowledgments within state.   If the person executing the instrument resides or is within the state, the acknowledgment shall be made before the clerk, or legally appointed deputy clerk, of the county court, or clerk and master of chancery court of some county in the state or before a notary public of some county in this state.

§ 64-2203.   Acknowledgment in other states or territories.   If the person executing the instrument resides or is beyond or without the limits of the state, but within the union or its territories or districts the acknowledgment may be made:

(1)   Before any court of record, or before the clerk of any court of record; or, before a commissioner for Tennessee, appointed by the governor; or before a notary public authorized there to take proof or acknowledgments.   If the acknowledgment be made before a court of record, a copy of the entry of the acknowledgment on the record shall be certified by the clerk, under his seal of office;

and the judge, chief justice, or presiding magistrate of the court shall certify as to the official character of the clerk.

(2) Or, before any other officer of such state, territory or district, authorized by the laws there to take the proof and acknowledgment of deed. There shall in cases under this paragraph be subjoined or attached to the certificate of proof or acknowledgment, signed by such other officer, a certificate of the secretary of state of the state or territory in which such officer resides, under the seal of such state, territory, or a certificate of the clerk of a court of record of such state, territory, or district, in the county in which said officer resides or in which he took such proof or acknowledgment under the seal of such court, stating that such officer was, at the time of taking such proof or acknowledgment duly authorized to take acknowledgments and proof of deeds of lands in said state, territory, or district, and that said secretary of state, or clerk of court is well acquainted with the handwriting of such officer, and that he verily believes that the signature affixed to such certificate of proof or acknowledgment is genuine.

§ 64-2207. **Form of certificate of acknowledgment.** If the acknowledgment be made before a clerk or deputy of the county court, or clerk and master, or notary public, or before any of the officers out of the state who are commissioned or accredited to act at the place where the acknowledgment is taken, and having an official seal, viz: those named in §§ 64-2203 and ° ° ° and, also, any consular officer of the United States having an official seal, such officer shall write upon or annex to the instrument the following certificate, in which he shall set forth his official capacity:

State of Tennessee,

County of ———

Personally appeared before me, (name of clerk or deputy) clerk (or deputy clerk) of the county court of said county, (bargainor's name), the within named bargainor, with whom I am personally acquainted, and who acknowledged that he executed the within instrument for the purposes therein contained. Witness my hand, at office, this ——— day of ———, 19—.

Or, in the alternative, the following certificate, in case of natural persons acting in their own right:

State of Tennessee,

County of ———

On this ——— day of ———, 19—, before me personally appeared ———, to me known to be the person (or persons) described in and who executed the foregoing instrument, and acknowledged that he (or they) executed the same as his (or their) free act and deed.

Or, in case of natural persons acting by attorney:

State of Tennessee,
County of ———

On this ——— day of ———, 19—, before me personally appeared ———, to me known to be the person who executed the foregoing instrument in behalf of ——— and acknowledged that he executed the same as the free act and deed of said ———.

§ 64-2208. Form for authentication of corporate instrument. The authentication or acknowledgment for record of a deed or other instrument in writing executed by a corporation, whether it has a seal or not, shall be good and sufficient, when made in substantially the following form:

State of ———, County of ———.

Before me, ——— of the state and county aforesaid, personally appeared ———, with whom I am personally acquainted, and who, upon oath, acknowledged himself to be president (or other officer authorized to execute the instrument) of the ———, the within named bargainor, a corporation, and that he as such ———, being authorized so to do, executed the foregoing instrument for the purpose therein contained, by signing the name of the corporation by himself as ———.

Witness my hand and seal, at office in ———, this ——— day of ———.

Or, alternatively as follows:

State of ———, County of ———.

On this ——— day of ———, 19—, before me appeared A. B., to me personally known, who, being by me duly sworn (or affirmed) did say that he is the president (or other officer or agent of the corporation or association) of (describing the corporation or association), and that the seal affixed to said instrument is the corporate seal of said corporation (or association), and that said instrument was signed and sealed in behalf of said corporation (or association), by authority of its Board of Directors (or Trustees) and said A. B. acknowledged said instrument to be the free act and deed of said corporation (or association).

(In case the corporation or association has no corporate seal omit the words "the seal affixed to said instrument is the corporate seal of said corporation or association and that," and add at the end of the affidavit clause, the words "and that said corporation (or association) has no corporate seal"). (In all cases add signature and title of officer taking the acknowledgment.)

§ 64-2209. Acknowledgment of married woman. The acknowledgment of a married woman, when required by law, may be taken in the same form as if she were sole and without any examination separate and apart from her husband.

§ 64-2210. Acknowledgments under seal. All acknowledgments shall be under the seal of office of the officer taking same.

TEXAS

[TEX. REV. CIV. STAT. ANN.]

Art. 3905. Fee for acknowledgment. Officers authorized by law to take acknowledgment or proof of deeds or other instruments of writing shall receive the same fees for taking such acknowledgment or proof as are allowed notaries public for the same services.°

° Concerning the fees allowed notaries public, see *Fees Chargeable,* TEX. REV. CIV. STAT. ANN. art. 3945.

Art. 6602. Persons before whom acknowledgments or proof made; members of armed forces; presumption; absence of seal. 1. The acknowledgment or proof of an instrument of writing for record may be made within this state before:

    a.   A Clerk of the District Court.

    b.   A Judge or Clerk of the County Court.

    c.   A Notary Public.

    2.   The acknowledgment or proof of such instrument may be made without this state, but within the physical limits of the United States of America or its territories before:

    a.   A Clerk of some court of record having a seal.

    b.   A Commissioner of Deeds duly appointed under the laws of this state.

    c.   A Notary Public.

    3.   The acknowledgment or proof of such instrument may be made without the physical limits of the United States and its territories before:

    a.   A Minister, a Commissioner or Charge D'affaires of the United States, resident and accredited in the country where the proof or acknowledgment is made.

    b.   A Consul-General, Consul, Vice-Consul, Commercial Agent, Vice-Commercial Agent, Deputy Consul or Consular Agent of the United States, resident in the country where proof of acknowledgment is made.

    c.   A Notary Public.

    4.   In addition to the methods above provided, the acknowledgment or proof of an instrument of writing for record may be made by a member of the Armed Forces of the United States or any auxiliary thereto, or by the husband or wife of a member of the

Armed Forces of the United States or any auxiliary thereto, before any Commissioned Officer in the Armed Forces of the United States of America or the auxiliaries thereto.

In the absence of pleading and proof to the contrary, it shall be presumed when any such acknowledgment is offered in evidence that the person signing such as a Commissioned Officer was such on the date signed, and that the person whose acknowledgment he took was one of those with respect to whom such action is hereby authorized.

No certificate of acknowledgment or proof of instrument taken in accordance with the provisions of this Subsection 4 of this Article shall be held invalid by reason of the failure of the officer certifying to such acknowledgment or proof of instrument to attach an official seal thereto.

Art. 6603. Acknowledgment, how made. The acknowledgment of an instrument of writing for the purpose of being recorded shall be by the grantor or person who executed the same appearing before some officer authorized to take such acknowledgment, and stating that he had executed the same for the consideration and purposes therein stated; and the officer taking such acknowledgment shall make a certificate thereof, sign and seal the same with his seal of office.

Art. 6604. Party must be known or proven. No acknowledgment of any instrument of writing shall be taken unless the officer taking it knows or has satisfactory evidence on the oath or affirmation of a credible witness, which shall be noted in his certificate, that the person making such acknowledgment is the individual who executed and is described in the instrument.

Art. 6606. Certificate of officer. An officer taking the acknowledgment of a deed, or other instrument of writing, must place thereon his official certificate, singed by him and given under his seal of office, substantially in form as hereinafter prescribed.

Art. 6607. Form of certificate. The form of an ordinary certificate of acknowledgment must be substantially as follows:

"The State of ———,

"County of ———,

"Before me ——— (here insert the name and character of the officer) on this day personally appeared ———, known to me (or proved to me on the oath of ———) to be the person whose name is subscribed to the foregoing instrument and acknowledged to me that he executed the same for the purposes and consideration therein expressed.

(Seal) "Given under my hand and seal of office this ——— day of ———, A.D., ———.""

Art. 6609. Proof by witness. The proof of any instrument of writing for the purpose of being recorded shall be by one or more of the subscribing witnesses personally appearing before some officer authorized to take such proof, and stating on oath that he or they saw the grantor or person who executed such instrument of writing subscribe the same or that the grantor or person who executed such instrument of writing acknowledged in his or their presence that he had executed the same for the purposes and consideration therein stated; and that he or they had signed the same as witnesses at the request of the grantor or person who executed such instrument; and the officer taking such proof shall make a certificate thereof, sign and seal the same with his official seal.

Art. 6610. Witness must be personally known. The proof by a subscribing witness must be by some one peronally known to the officer taking the proof to be the person whose name is subscribed to the instrument as a witness, or must be proved to be such by the oath of a credible witness, which fact shall be noted in the certificate.

Art. 6611. Form of certificate. The certificate of the officer, where the execution of the instrument is proved by a witness, must be substantially in the following form:

"The State of ———,

"County of ———.

"Before me, ——— (here insert the name and character of the officer), on this day personally appeared ———, known to me (or proved to me on the oath of ———), to be the person whose name is subscribed as a witness to the foregoing instrument of writing, and after being duly sworn by me stated on oath that he saw ———, the grantor or person who executed the foregoing instrument, subscribe the same (or that the grantor or person who executed such instrument of writing acknowledged in his presence that he had executed the same for the purposes and consideration therein expressed), and that he had signed the same as a witness at the request of the grantor (or person who executed the same.)

(Seal) "Given under my hand and seal of office this ——— day of ———, A.D., ———.' "

Art. 6612. Handwriting may be proved, when. The execution of an instrument may be established for record by proof of the handwriting of the grantor and of at least one of the subscribing witnesses in the following cases:

1. When the grantor and all the subscribing witnesses are dead.

2. When the grantor and all the subscribing witnesses are non-residents of this State.

3. When the place of their residence is unknown to the party desiring the proof, and cannot be ascertained.

4. When the subscribing witnesses have been convicted of felony, or have become of unsound mind, or have otherwise become incompetent to testify.

5. When all the subscribing witnesses to an instrument are dead or are non-residents of this State, or when their residence is unknown, or when they are incompetent to testify, and the grantor in such instrument refuses to acknowledge the execution of the same for record.

Art. 6613. Evidence must prove what. The evidence taken under the preceding article must satisfactorily prove to the officer the following facts:

1. The existence of one or more of the conditions mentioned therein; and,

2. That the witness testifying knew the person whose name purports to be subscribed to the instrument as a party, and is well acquainted with his signature, and that it is genuine; and,

3. That the witness testifying personally knew the person who subscribed the instrument as a witness, and is well acquainted with his signature, and that it is genuine; and,

4. The place of residence of the witness testifying.

Art. 6614. When grantor made his mark. When the grantor or person who executed the instrument signed the same by making his mark, and when also any one or more of the conditions mentioned in Article 6612 exists, the execution of any such instrument may be established by proof of the handwriting of two subscribing witnesses and of the place of residence of such witnesses testifying.

Art. 6615. Proofs how made and certified. The proof mentioned in the three preceding articles must be made by the deposition or affidavit of two or more disinterested persons in writing; and the officer taking such proof shall make a certificate thereof, and sign and seal the same with his official seal; which proofs and certificate shall be attached to such instrument.

Art. 6616. Officers' authority. Officers authorized to take the proof of instruments of writing under the provisions of this chapter are also authorized in such proceedings:

1. To administer oaths or affirmations.

2. To employ and swear interpreters.

3. To issue subpoenas.

4. To punish for contempt as hereinafter provided.

Records

Art. 6619. Record of acknowledgment. All officers authorized or permitted by law to take the acknowledgment or proof of any deed, bond, mortgage, bill of sale or any other written instrument required or permitted by law to be placed on record shall procure a well bound book, in which they shall enter and record a short statement of each acknowledgment or proof taken by them, which statement shall be by them signed officially.

Art. 6620. Contents of statement. Such statement shall recite the true date on which such acknowledgment or proof was taken, the name of the grantor and grantee of such instrument, its date, if proved by a subscribing witness, the name of the witness, the known or alleged residence of the witness and whether personally known or unknown to the officer; if personally unknown, this fact shall be stated, and by whom such person was introduced to such officer, if by any one, and the known or alleged residence of such person.

Art. 6621. Shall further recite. Such statement shall also recite, if the instrument is acknowledged by the grantor, his then place of residence, if known to the officer; if unknown, his alleged residence, and whether such grantor is personally known to the officer; if personally unknown, by whom such grantor was introduced, if by any one, and his place of residence. If land is conveyed or charged by the instrument, the name of the original grantee shall be mentioned, and the county where the same is situated.

Art. 6622. The book a public record. The book herein required to be procured and kept, and the statements herein required to be recorded in the same shall be an original public record, and shall be delivered to his successor, and the same shall be open to the inspection and examination of any citizen at all reasonable times.

Damages

Art. 6623. Action for damages. Any person injured by the failure, refusal or neglect of any officer whose duty it is to comply with any provision of this chapter shall have a right of action against such officer so failing, refusing or neglecting, before any court of competent jurisdiction, for the recovery of all damages resulting from such neglect, failure or refusal.

UTAH

[UTAH CODE ANN.]

§ 57-2-1. Manner of acknowledging or proving conveyances. Every conveyance in writing whereby any real estate is conveyed or may be affected shall be acknowledged or proved and certified in the manner hereinafter provided.

§ 57-2-2. Who authorized to take acknowledgments. The proof or acknowledgment of every conveyance whereby any real estate is conveyed or may be affected shall be taken by some one of the following officers:

(1) If acknowledged or proved within this state, by a judge or clerk of a court having a seal, or a notary public, county clerk or county recorder.

(2) If acknowledged or proved without this state and within any state or territory of the United States, by a judge or clerk of any court of the United States, or of any state or territory, having a seal, or by a notary public, or by a commissioner appointed by the governor of this state for that purpose.

(3) If acknowledged or proved without the United States, by a judge or clerk of any court of any state, kingdom or empire having a seal, or any notary public therein, or any ambassador, minister, commissioner or consul of the United States appointed to reside therein.

§ 57-2-3. **Acknowledgment by deputy.** When any of the officers above mentioned are authorized by law to appoint a deputy, such acknowledgment or proof may be taken by any such deputy in the name of his principal.

§ 57-2-4. **Taking acknowledgments of persons with United States armed forces.** In addition to the acknowledgment of instruments in the manner and form and as otherwise authorized by this chapter, any person serving in or with the armed forces of the United States may acknowledge the same wherever located before any commissioned officer in the active service of the armed forces of the United States with the rank of second lieutenant or higher in the Army or Marine Corps, or ensign or higher in the Navy or United States Coast Guard. The instrument shall not be rendered invalid by the failure to state therein the place of execution or acknowledgment. No authentication of the officer's certificate of acknowledgment shall be required, but the officer taking the acknowledgment shall endorse thereon or attach thereto a certificate substantially in the following form:

On this ———— day of ————, 19—, before me ————, the undersigned officer, personally appeared ————, known to me (or satisfactorily proven) to be serving in or with the armed forces of the United States and to be the person whose name is subscribed to the within instrument and acknowledged that — he — executed the same for the purposes therein contained. And the undersigned does further certify that he is at the date of this certificate a commissioned officer of the rank stated below and is in the active service of the armed forces of the United States.

———————————————————
Signature of Officer

———————————————————
Rank of Officer and Command to Which Attached

§ 57-2-5. Certificate of acknowledgment. Every officer who shall take the proof or acknowledgment of any conveyance affecting any real estate shall make a certificate thereof, and cause such certificate to be endorsed on or annexed to such conveyance. Such certificate shall be:

(1) When made by any judge or clerk, under the hand of such judge or clerk, and the seal of the court.

(2) When made by any other officer, under the hand and official seal of such officer.

§ 57-2-6. Party must be known or identified. No acknowledgment of any conveyance whereby any real estate is conveyed or may be affected shall be taken unless the person offering to make such acknowledgment shall be personally known to the officer taking the same to be the person whose name is subscribed to such conveyance as a party thereto, or shall be proved to be such by the oath or affirmation of a credible witness personally known to the officer taking the acknowledgment.

§ 57-2-7. Form of certificate of acknowledgment. A certificate of acknowledgment to any instrument in writing affecting the title to any real property in this state may be substantially in the following form:

State of Utah, County of ———

On the ——— day of ———, 19—, personally appeared before me ———, the signer of the above instrument, who duly acknowledged to me that he executed the same.

The certificate of acknowledgment of an instrument executed by a corporation must be substantially in the following form:

State of Utah, County of ———

On the ——— day of ———, 19—, personally appeared before me ———, who being by me duly sworn (or affirmed), did say that he is the president (or other officer or agent, as the case may be) of (naming the corporation), and that said instrument was signed in behalf of said corporation by authority of its bylaws (or of a resolution of its board of directors, as the case may be), and said ——— acknowledged to me that said corporation executed the same.

§ 57-2-8. When grantor unknown to officer. When the grantor is unknown to the officer taking the acknowledgment, the certificate shall be substantially in the following form, to wit:

State of Utah, County of ———

On this ——— day of ———, 19—, personally appeared before me ———, satisfactorily proved to me to be the signer of the above instrument by the oath of ———, a competent and credible witness for that purpose, by me duly sworn, and he, the said ——— acknowledged that he executed the same.

Such certificate when properly executed by an officer authorized to take acknowledgments to instruments in writing affecting the title to real property in this state, and attached to a conveyance in writing, shall be a sufficient acknowledgment and certificate that such conveyance was executed as required by law.

§ 57-2-9. When executed by attorney in fact. The certificate of acknowledgment of an instrument executed by an attorney in fact must be substantially in the following form:

State of Utah, County of ———

On the ——— day of ———, 19—, personally appeared before me ———, who, being by me duly sworn (or affirmed) did say that he is the attorney in fact of ——— (naming the grantor), and that said instrument was signed in behalf of said grantor by authority, and said ——— acknowledged to me that he as such attorney in fact executed the same.

§ 57-2-10. Proof of execution—how made. The proof of the execution of any conveyance whereby real estate is conveyed or may be affected shall be:

(1) By the testimony of a subscribing witness, if there is one; or,

(2) When all the subscribing witnesses are dead, or cannot be had, by evidence of the handwriting of the party, and of a subscribing witness, if there is one, given by a credible witness to each signature.

§ 57-2-11. Witness must be known or identified. No proof by a subscribing witness shall be taken unless such witness shall be personally known to the officer taking the proof to be the person whose name is subscribed to the conveyance as a witness thereto, or shall be proved to be such by the oath or affirmation of a credible witness personally known to such officer.

§ 57-2-12. What must be proven. No certificate of such proof shall be made unless such subscribing witness shall prove that the person whose name is subscribed thereto as a party is the person described in, and who executed, the same; that such person executed the conveyance, and that such person subscribed his name thereto as a witness thereof at the request of the maker of such instrument.

§ 57-2-13. Form of certificate. The certificate of such proof shall be substantially in the following form, to wit:

State of Utah, County of ———

On this ——— day of ———, 19—, before me personally appeared ———, personally known to me (or satisfactorily proved to me by the oath of ———, a competent and credible witness for that purpose, by me duly sworn) to be the same person whose name is subscribed to the above instrument as a witness thereto, who, being by me duly sworn, deposed and said that he resides in ———, county of ———, and state of Utah; that he was present and saw ———, personally known to him to be the signer of the above instrument as a party thereto, sign and deliver the same, and heard him acknowledge that he executed the same, and that he, the deponent, thereupon signed his name as a subscribing witness thereto at the request of said ———.

§ 57-2-14.   When subscribing witness dead—proof of handwriting. No proof by evidence of the handwriting of a party, or of the subscribing witness or witnesses, shall be taken unless the officer taking the same shall be satisfied that all the subscribing witnesses to such conveyance are dead, out of the jurisdiction, or cannot be had to prove the execution thereof.

§ 57-2-15.   What evidence required. No certificate of any such proof shall be made unless a competent and credible witness shall state on oath or affirmation that he personally knew the person whose name is subscribed thereto as a party, well knows his signature, stating his means of knowledge, and believes the name of the party subscribed thereto as a party was subscribed by such person; nor unless a competent and credible witness shall in like manner state that he personally knew the person whose name is subscribed to such conveyance as a witness, well knows his signature, stating his means of knowledge, and believes the name subscribed thereto as a witness was thereto subscribed by such person.

§ 57-2-16.   Subpoena to subscribing witness. Upon the application of any grantee in any conveyance required by law to be recorded, or of any person claiming under such grantee, verified under the oath of the applicant, that any witness to such conveyance residing in the county where such application is made refuses to appear and testify touching the execution thereof, and that such conveyance cannot be proved without his evidence, any officer authorized to take the acknowledgment or proof of such conveyance may issue a subpoena requiring such witness to appear before such officer and testify touching the execution thereof.

§ 57-2-17.   Disobedience—contempt—proof aliunde. Every person who, being served with a subpoena, shall without reasonable cause refuse or neglect to appear, or, appearing, shall refuse to answer upon oath touching the matters aforesaid, shall be liable to the party injured for such damages as may be sustained by him on account of such neglect or refusal, and may also be dealt with for contempt as provided by law; but no person shall be required to attend who resides out of the county in which the proof is to be taken, nor unless his reasonable expenses shall have first been tendered to him; provided, that if it shall appear to the satisfaction of the officer so authorized to take such acknowledgment that such subscribing witness purposely conceals himself, or keeps out of the way, so that he cannot be served with a subpoena or taken on attachment after the use of due diligence to that end, or in case of his continued failure or refusal to testify for the space of one hour after his appearance shall have been compelled by process, then said conveyance or other instrument may be proved and admitted to record in the same manner as if such subscribing witness thereto were dead.

§ 57-3-1.   Certificate of acknowledgment or of proof of execution a prerequisite.   A certificate of the acknowledgment of any conveyance, or of the proof of the execution thereof as provided in this title, signed and certified by the officer taking the same as provided in this title, shall entitle such conveyance, with the certificate or certificates aforesaid, to be recorded in the office of the recorder of the county in which the real estate is situated.

Telegraphic and Telephonic Transmittal

§ 69-1-2.   Transmitting written instruments by, authorized—entitled to record—force and effect of copies.   Any power of attorney or other instrument in writing duly proved or acknowledged and certified so as to be entitled to record may, together with the certificate of its proof or acknowledgment, be sent by telegraph or telephone, and the telegraphic or telephonic copy shall prima facie have the same force and effect in all respects, and may be admitted to record and recorded in the same manner and with the same effect, as the original.

§ 69-1-4.   Transmitting certified instruments—burden of proof.   Except as hereinbefore otherwise provided, any instrument in writing, duly certified under his hand and official seal by a notary public, commissioner of deeds or clerk of a court of record to be genuine to the personal knowledge of such officer, may, together with such certificate, be sent by telegraph or telephone.   The telegraphic or telephonic copy thereof shall, prima facie only, have the same force, effect and validity in all respects as the original, and the burden of proof shall be on the party denying the genuineness or due execution of the original.

Evidence of Execution

§ 78-25-7.   Certificate of acknowledgment as evidence of execution.   Every private writing, except last wills and testaments, may be acknowledged or proved, and certified in the manner provided for the acknowledgment or proof of conveyances of real property, and the certificate of such acknowledgment or proof is prima facie evidence of the execution of the writing in the same manner as if it were a conveyance of real property.

VERMONT

[VT. STAT. ANN.]

Tit. 27, § 341. Requirements generally; recording. Deeds and other conveyances of lands, or of an estate or interest therein, shall be signed by the party granting the same and signed by two or more witnesses and acknowledged by the grantor before a town clerk, notary public, master in chancery, county clerk or judge or register of probate and recorded at length in the clerk's office of the town in which such lands lie. Such acknowledgment before a notary public shall be valid without his official seal being affixed to his signature.

Tit. 27, § 379. Acknowledgment out of state. If deeds and other conveyances, and powers of attorney for the conveyance of lands, the acknowledgment or proof of which is taken without the state, are certified agreeably to the laws of the state, province or kingdom in which such acknowledgment or proof is taken, they shall be as valid as though the same were taken before a proper officer or court in this state. The proof of the same may be taken, and the same acknowledged with like effect before a justice, magistrate or notary public within the United States or in a foreign country, before a commissioner appointed for that purpose by the governor of this state, or before a minister, charge d'affaires, consul or vice consul of the United States in a foreign country.

VIRGIN ISLANDS

[V.I. CODE ANN.]

Tit. 28, § 81 to 93.

Editorial comment

In large part, the Uniform Acknowledgment Act has been adopted. For text of the act, see page 349. Certain sections of the act, as adopted in the Virgin Islands, however, have been modified to a material extent. For that reason, selected portions of the act, as adopted in the Virgin Islands, are published below.

Tit. 28, § 82. Acknowledgment within the Virgin Islands. The acknowledgment of any instrument may be made in the Virgin Islands before—

(1) a judge of a court of record;

(2) a clerk or deputy clerk of a court having a seal;

(3) a commissioner or recorder of deeds; or

(4) a notary public.

Tit. 28, § 83. Acknowledgment within the United States. The acknowledgment of any instrument may be made without the Virgin

Islands but within the United States and within the jurisdiction of the officer, before—

(1) a clerk or deputy clerk of any federal court;

(2) a clerk or deputy clerk of any court of record of any State;

(3) a notary public;

(4) a commissioner of deeds; or

(5) any person authorized by the laws of such State to take acknowledgments.

Tit. 28, § 87. Forms of certificates. An officer taking the acknowledgment shall endorse thereon or attach thereto a certificate substantially in one of the following forms:

(1) By Individuals:

Territory of the Virgin Islands

Judicial Division of ———

On this the ——— day of ———, 19—, before me ———, the undersigned officer, personally appeared ———, known to me (or satisfactorily proven) to be the person whose name ——— subscribed to the within instrument and acknowledged that ——— he ——— executed the same for the purposes therein contained.

In witness whereof I hereunto set my hand and official seal.

_____

_____

Title of Officer.

(2) By a Corporation:

Territory of the Virgin Islands

Judicial Division of ———

On this the ——— day of ———, 19—, before me ———, the undersigned officer, personally appeared ——— who acknowledged himself to be the ——— of ———, a corporation, and that he, as such ———, being authorized so to do, executed the foregoing instrument for the purposes therein contained, by signing the name of the corporation by himself as ———.

In witness whereof I hereunto set my hand and official seal.

_____

_____

Title of Officer.

(3) By an Attorney in Fact:

Territory of the Virgin Islands

Judicial Division of ———

On this the ——— day of ———, 19—, before me, ———,

the undersigned officer, personally appeared ———, known to me (or satisfactorily proven) to be the person whose name is subscribed as attorney in fact for ———, and acknowledged that he executed the same as the act of his principal for the purposes therein contained.

In witness whereof I hereunto set my hand and official seal.

———————————————

Title of Officer.

(4)   By any Public Officer or Deputy thereof, or by any Trustee, Administrator, Guardian, or Executor:

Territory of the Virgin Islands
Judicial Division of ———

On this the ——— day of ———, 19—, before me, ———, the undersigned officer, personally appeared ———, of the Territory (State, County or City as the case may be) of ———, known to me (or satisfactorily proven) to be the person described in the foregoing instrument, and acknowledged that he executed the same in the capacity therein stated and for the purposes therein contained.

In witness whereof I hereunto set my hand and official seal.

———————————————

Title of Officer.

Tit. 28, § 89.   Authentication of acknowledgments.   (1)   If the acknowledgment is taken within the Virgin Islands or is made without the United States by an officer of the United States no authentication shall be necessary.

(2)   If the acknowledgment is taken without the Virgin Islands, but in the United States, the certificate shall be authenticated by a certificate as to the official character of such officer, executed, if the acknowledgment is taken by a clerk or deputy clerk of a court, by the presiding judge of the court or, if the acknowledgment is taken by a notary public, or any other person authorized to take acknowledgments, by a clerk of a court of record of the county, parish or district in which the acknowledgment is taken.   The signature to such authenticating certificate may a facsimile printed, stamped, photographed or engraved thereon when the certificate bears the seal of the authenticating officer.   A judge or clerk authenticating an acknowledgment shall endorse thereon or attach thereto a certificate in substantially the following form:

State of ———
County of ———

I ——— [judge or clerk] of the ——— in and for said county,

which court is a court of record, having a seal, do hereby certify
that ——— by and before whom the foregoing [or annexed]
acknowledgment was taken, was at the time of taking the same a
notary public [or other officer] residing [or authorized to act] in said
county, and was authorized by the laws of said state to take and
certify acknowledgments in said state, and, further, that I am acquainted with his handwriting and that I believe that the signature
to the certificate of acknowledgment is genuine.

In testimony whereof I have hereunto set my hand and affixed
the seal of the court this ——— day of ———, 19—.

(3) If the acknowledgment is taken without the United States
and by a notary public or a judge or clerk of a court of record of
the country where the acknowledgment is taken, the certificate shall
be authenticated by a certificate under the Great Seal of State of
the country, affixed by the custodian of such Seal, or by a certificate
of a diplomatic, consular or commercial officer of the United States
accredited to that country, certifying as to the official character of
such officer. The officer authenticating an acknowledgment shall
endorse thereon or attach thereto a certificate in substantially the
form prescribed in paragraph (2) of this section.

Tit. 28, § 90. Acknowledgments under laws of other states. Notwithstanding any provision in this chapter contained the acknowledgment of any instrument without the Virgin Islands in compliance with
the manner and form prescribed by the laws of the place of its
execution, if in a State of the United States, verified by the official
seal of the officer before whom it is acknowledged, and authenticated
in the manner provided by paragraph (2) of section 89 of this title,
shall have the same effect as an acknowledgment in the manner and
form prescribed by the laws of the Virgin Islands for instruments
executed within the Virgin Islands.

VIRGINIA

[VA. CODE ANN.]

**§ 55-113. Acknowledgment within the United States or its depen-
dencies.** [The] court or clerk ° ° ° shall admit any such writing
to record as to any person whose name is signed thereto, except
acknowledgment of contracts for the sale of real property shall
require the seller or grantor of such real property to acknowledge his
signature as herein provided, except for contracts recorded after the
death of the seller pursuant to § 64.1-148 of the Code of Virginia.

(1) Upon the certificate of such clerk or his deputy, a notary
public, a commissioner in chancery, or a clerk of any court of record
within the United States or in Puerto Rico, or any territory or other
dependency or possession of the United States that such writing had
been acknowledged before him by such person. Such certificate shall
be written upon or annexed to such writing and shall be substantially
to the following effect, to wit:

I, ———, clerk (or deputy clerk, or a commissioner in chancery) of the ——— court, (or a notary public) for the county (or corporation) aforesaid, in the State (or territory, or district) of ———, do certify that E.F., or E.F. and G.H., and so forth, whose name (or names) is (or are) signed to the writing above (or hereto annexed) bearing date on the ——— day of ———, has (or have) acknowledged the same before me in my county (or corporation) aforesaid.

Given under my hand this ——— day of ———.

(2) Upon the certificate of acknowledgment of such person before any commissioner appointed by the Governor, within the United States, so written or annexed, substantially to the following effect, to wit:

State (or territory, or district) of ——— to wit:

I, ———, a commissioner appointed by the Governor of the State of Virginia, for said State (or territory or district) of ———, do certify that E.F. (or E.F. and G.H., and so forth) whose name (or names) is (or are) signed to the writing above (or hereto annexed) bearing date on the ——— day of ——— has (or have) acknowledged the same before me in my State (or territory or district) aforesaid.

Given under my hand this ——— day of ———.

(3) Or upon the certificate of such clerk or his deputy, a notary public, a commissioner in chancery, or a clerk of any court of record within the United States, or in Puerto Rico, or any territory or other possession or dependency of the United States, or of a commissioner appointed by the Governor, within the United States, that such writing was proved as to such person, before him, by two subscribing witnesses thereto. Such certificate shall be written upon or annexed to such writing and shall be substantially to the following effect, to wit:

State (or territory, or district) of ———; county (or corporation) of ———, to wit: I, ———, clerk (or deputy clerk, or a commissioner in chancery) of the ——— court, (or a notary public) for the county (or corporation) aforesaid, in the State (or territory or district) of ——— (or a commissioner appointed by the Governor of the State of Virginia for said State, or territory, or district of ———), do certify that the execution of the writing above (or hereto annexed) bearing date on the ——— day of ———, by A.B. (or A.B. and C.D., and so forth), whose name (or names) is (or are) signed thereto, was proved before me in my county (or corporation, or State) aforesaid, by the evidence on oath of E.F. and G.H., subscribing witnesses to said writing.

Given under my hand this ——— day of ———.

When authority is given in § 55-106 or in this section to the clerk of a court in or out of this State, but within the United States, such authority may be exercised by his duly qualified deputy.

§ 55-114. Acknowledgments outside of the United States and its dependencies. Such court or clerk shall also admit any such writing to record as to any person whose name is signed thereto upon the certificate under the official seal of any ambassador, minister plenipotentiary, minister resident, charge d'affaires, consul-general, consul, vice-consul or commercial agent appointed by the government of the United States to any foreign country, or of the proper officer of any court of record of such country or of the mayor or other chief magistrate of any city, town or corporation therein, that such writing was acknowledged by such person or proved as to him by two witnesses before any person having such appointment or before such court, mayor or chief magistrate.

§ 55-114.1. Acknowledgments by persons subject to Uniform Code of Military Justice; validation of certain acknowledgments. Such court or clerk shall also admit any such writing to record as to any person whose name is signed thereto and who at the time of such acknowledgment:

(1) Was a member of any of the armed forces of the United States, wherever they may have been, or

(2) Was employed by, or accompanying such armed forces outside the United States and outside the Canal Zone, Puerto Rico, Guam and the Virgin Islands, or

(3) Was subject to the Uniform Code of Military Justice of the United States outside of the United States, upon the certificate of any person authorized to take acknowledgments under § 936 (a) of Title 10 of United States Code Annotated as that section existed on October thirty, nineteen hundred sixty-three.

Such certification shall be in substantially the same form as required by § 55-115 of this Code.

Any acknowledgment heretofore taken which is in substantial conformity with this section is hereby ratified, validated and confirmed.

§ 55-115. Acknowledgments taken before commissioned officers in military service. Such court or clerk shall also admit any such writing to record as to any person whose name is signed thereto who at the time of such acknowledgment was in active service in the armed forces of the United States, or as to the consort of such person, upon the certificate of any commissioned officer of the army, navy, marine corps, coast guard, any state national guard that is federally recognized or other branch of the service of which such person is a member, that such writing had been acknowledged before him by such person. Such certificate shall be written upon or annexed to such writing and shall be substantially to the following effect:

In the army (or navy, etc.) of the United States.

I, ——, a commissioned officer of the army (or navy, marine corps, coast guard or other branch of service) of the United States with the rank of lieutenant (or ensign or other appropriate rank) whose home address is ————, do certify that E.F. (or E.F. and G.H., and so forth), whose name (or names) is (or are) signed to the writing above (or hereto annexed), bearing date on the ———— day of ————, ————, and who, or whose consort, is a private (corporal, seaman, captain or other grade or rank) in the army (or navy, etc.) of the United States, and whose home address is ————, has (or have) acknowledged the same before me.

Given under my hand this ———— day of ————.

Such acknowledgment may be taken at any place where the officer taking the acknowledgment and the person whose name is signed to the writing may be. Such commissioned officer may take the acknowledgment of any person in any branch of the armed forces of the United States, or the consort of such person.

Every acknowledgment executed prior to January one, nineteen hundred seventy-two, in substantial compliance with the provisions of this section is hereby validated, ratified and confirmed, notwithstanding any error or omission with respect to any address, grade or rank.

§ 55-116. **Notaries to affix date when their term of office expires.** Upon every certificate of acknowledgment taken by a notary within this State to any writing there shall be written in, or annexed to, such certificate the words following: "My term of office expires on the ———— day of ————," or words plainly showing when the term of such notary shall expire.

§ 55-117. **Change of name of notary.** Any duly appointed notary public in this State who shall legally change his name during his term of office as such notary shall, after such change of name, when taking acknowledgments or doing other acts as such notary, write or have written or printed in or annexed to his certificate the words: "I was commissioned notary as ————," or the equivalent.

§ 55-118. **Violation of preceding sections.** Any notary who shall fail to comply with the provisions of § 55-116 or 55-117 shall forfeit not less than five nor more than twenty dollars, but any such failure shall not invalidate the certificate of acknowledgment.

§§ 55-118.1 to 55-118.9. The Uniform Recognition of Acknowledgments Act has been adopted. For text of act, see page 349.

§ 55-119. **Deeds of corporations; how to be executed and acknowledged.** All deeds made by corporations shall be signed in the name of the corporation by the president or acting president, or any vice-president, or by such other person as may be authorized thereunto by the board of directors of such corporation, and the seal of the corporation shall be affixed and attested by the secretary or assistant secretary, acting treasurer or treasurer of such corporation or by such other person as may be authorized thereunto by the board of directors of such corporation and, if such deed is to be recorded, the person signing the name of the corporation shall acknowledge the same in the manner provided by § 55-120.

§ 55-120. Acknowledgments on behalf of corporations and others. When any writing purports to have been signed in behalf or by authority of any person or corporation, or in any representative capacity whatsoever, the certificate of the acknowledgment by the person so signing the writing shall be sufficient for the purposes of this and §§ ° ° °, 55-113, 55-114, and 55-115, and for the admission of such writing to record as to the person or corporation on whose behalf it is signed, or as to the representative character of the person so signing the same, as the case may be, without expressing that such acknowledgment was in behalf or by authority of such other person or corporation or was in a representative capacity. In the case of a writing signed in behalf or by authority of any person or corporation or in any representative capacity a certificate to the following effect shall be sufficient:

State (or territory or district) of ————, county (or corporation) of ————, to wit: I, ————, a ———— (here insert the official title of the person certifying the acknowledgment) in and for the State (or territory or district) and county (or corporation) aforesaid, do certify that ———— (here insert the name or names of the persons signing the writing on behalf of the person or corporation, or the name of the person signing the writing in a representative capacity), whose name (or names) is (or are) signed to the writing above, bearing date on the ———— day of ————, has (or have) acknowledged the same before me in my county (or corporation) aforesaid. Given under my hand this ———— day of ————.

§ 55-121. Corporate acknowledgment taken before officer or stockholder. Any notary or other officer duly authorized to take acknowledgments may take the acknowledgment to any deed or other writing, executed by a company, or to a company or for the benefit of a company, although he may be a stockholder, an officer, or both, in such company; provided he is not otherwise interested in the property conveyed or disposed of by such deed or other writing; and nothing herein shall be construed to authorize any officer to take an acknowledgment to any deed or other writing executed by such company by and through him as an officer or stockholder thereof, or to him for the benefit of such company.

§ 64.1-87.1. How will may be made self-proved. A will may at the time of its execution or at any subsequent date be made self-proved, by the acknowledgment thereof by the testator and the affidavits of the attesting witnesses, each made before an officer authorized to administer oaths under the laws of this State, and evidenced by the officer's certificate, under official seal, attached or annexed to the will in form and content substantially as follows:

STATE OF VIRGINIA
COUNTY/CITY OF ———

Before me, the undersigned authority, on this day personally appeared ———, ———, ———, and ———, known to me to be the testator and the witnesses, respectively, whose names are signed to the attached or foregoing instrument and, all of these persons being by me first duly sworn, ———, the testator, declared to me and to the witnesses in my presence that said instrument is his last will and testament and that he had willingly signed or directed another to sign the same for him, and executed it in the presence of said witnesses as his free and voluntary act for the purposes therein expressed; that said witnesses stated before me that the foregoing will was executed and acknowledged by the testator as his last will and testament in the presence of said witnesses who, in his presence and at his request, and in the presence of each other, did subscribe their names thereto as attesting witnesses on the day of the date of said will, and that the testator, at the time of the execution of said will, was over the age of 18 years and of sound and disposing mind and memory.

_____
Testator

_____
Witness

_____
Witness

_____
Witness

Subscribed, sworn and acknowledged before me by ———, the testator, subscribed and sworn before me by ———, ———, and ——— witness, this ——— day of ———, A.D., ———.

SIGNED _____

(OFFICIAL CAPACITY OF OFFICER)

The sworn statement of any such witnesses taken as herein provided shall be accepted by the court as if it had been taken ore-tenus before such court.

WASHINGTON

Telegraphic Transmittal

[WASH. REV. CODE ANN.]

§ 5.52.030. **Instrument transmitted by telegraph—effect.** Any power of attorney, or other instrument in writing, duly proved or acknowledged, and certified so as to be entitled to record may, together with the certificate of its proof or acknowledgment, be sent by telegraph, and telegraphic copy, or duplicate thereof, shall, prima facie, have the same force and effect, in all respects, and may be admitted to record and recorded in the same manner and with like effect as the original.

Acknowledgments

§ 64.08.010. **Who may take acknowledgments.** Acknowledgments of deeds, mortgages and other instruments in writing, required to be acknowledged may be taken in this state before a justice of the supreme court, or the clerk thereof, or the deputy of such clerk, before a judge of the court of appeals, or the clerk thereof, before a judge of the superior court, or qualified court commissioner thereof, or the clerk thereof, or the deputy of such clerk, or a county auditor, or the deputy of such auditor, or a qualified notary public, or a qualified United States commissioner appointed by any district court of the United States for this state, and all said instruments heretofore executed and acknowledged according to the provisions of this section are hereby declared legal and valid.

§ 64.08.020. **Acknowledgments out of state—certificate.** Acknowledgments of deeds conveying or encumbering real estate situated in this state, or any interest therein, and other instruments in writing, required to be acknowledged, may be taken in any other state or territory of the United States, the District of Columbia, or in any possession of the United States, before any person authorized to take the acknowledgments of deeds by the laws of the state, territory, district or possession wherein the acknowledgment is taken, or before any commissioner appointed by the governor of this state, for that purpose, but unless such acknowledgment is taken before a commissioner so appointed by the governor, or before the clerk of a court of record of such state, territory, district or possession, or before a notary public or other officer having a seal of office, the instrument shall have attached thereto a certificate of the clerk of a court of record of the county, parish, or other political subdivision of such state, territory, district or possession wherein the acknowledgment was taken, under the seal of said court, certifying that the person who took the acknowledgment, and whose name is subscribed to the certificate thereof, was at the date thereof such officer as he represented himself to be, authorized by law to take acknowledgments of deeds, and that the clerk verily believes the signature of the person subscribed to the certificate of acknowledgment to be genuine.

§ 64.08.040. **Foreign acknowledgments, who may take.** Acknowledgments of deeds conveying or encumbering real estate situated in this state, or any interest therein and other instruments in writing, required to be acknowledged, may be taken in any foreign country before any minister, plenipotentiary, secretary of legation, charge d'affaires, consul general, consul, vice consul, consular agent, or commercial agent appointed by the United States government, or before any notary public, or before the judge, clerk, or other proper officer of any court of said country, or before the mayor or other chief magistrate of any city, town or other municipal corporation therein.

§ 64.08.050. **Certificate of acknowledgment—evidence.** The officer, or person, taking an acknowledgment as in this act provided, shall certify the same by a certificate written upon or annexed to the instrument acknowledged and signed by him and sealed with his official seal, if any he has, and reciting in substance that the person, or persons, known to him as the person, or persons, whose name, or names, are signed to the instrument as executing the same, acknowledged before him that he or they, executed the same freely and voluntarily, on the date stated in the certificate. Such certificate shall be prima facie evidence of the facts therein recited.

§ 64.08.060. **Form of certificate for individual.** A certificate of acknowledgment, substantially in the following form shall be sufficient:

County of ——————

               ss.

State of ——————

On this day personally appeared before me (here insert the name of grantor or grantors) to me known to be the individual, or individuals described in and who executed the within and foregoing instrument, and acknowledged that he (she or they) signed the same as his (her or their) free and voluntary act and deed, for the uses and purposes therein mentioned. Given under my hand and official seal this ——— day of ———, 19—. (Signature of officer and official seal)

If acknowledgment is taken before a notary public of this state the signature shall be followed by substantially the following: Notary Public in and for the state of Washington, residing at ———, (giving place of residence).

§ 64.08.070. **Form of certificate for corporation.** Certificates of acknowledgment of an instrument acknowledged by a corporation shall be substantially the following form:

State of ———

               ss.

County of ———

On this ——— day of ———, 19—, before me personally appeared ———, to me known to be the (president, vice president, secretary, treasurer, or other authorized officer or agent, as the case may be) of the corporation that executed the within and foregoing instrument, and acknowledged said instrument to be the free and voluntary act and deed of said corporation, for the uses and purposes therein mentioned, and an oath stated that he was authorized to execute said instrument and that the seal affixed is the corporate seal of said corporation.

In Witness Whereof I have hereunto set my hand and affixed my official seal the day and year first above written. (Signature and title of officer with place of residence of notary public.)

§ 64.08.090. **Authority of superintendents, business managers and officers of correctional institutions to take acknowledgments and administer oaths—procedure.** The superintendent, associate and assistant superintendents, business managers, records officers and camp superintendents of any correctional institution or facility operated by the state of Washington are hereby authorized and empowered to take acknowledgments on any instruments of writing, and certify the same in the manner required by law, and to administer all oaths required by law to be administered, all of the foregoing acts to have the same effects as if performed by a notary public: *Provided,* That such authority shall only extend to taking acknowledgments for and administering oaths to officers, employees and residents of such institutions and facilities. None of the individuals herein empowered to take acknowledgments and administer oaths shall demand or accept any fee or compensation whatsoever for administering or taking any oath, affirmation, or acknowledgment under the authority conferred by this act.

In certifying any oath or in signing any instrument officially, an individual empowered to do so under this act shall, in addition to his name, state in writing his place of residence, the date of his action, and affix the seal of the institution where he is employed: *Provided,* That in certifying any oath to be used in any of the courts of this state, it shall not be necessary to append an impression of the official seal of the institution.

§ 73.20.010. **Acknowledgments.** In addition to the acknowledgment of instruments and the performance of other notarial acts in the manner and form and as otherwise authorized by law, instruments may be acknowledged, documents attested, oaths and affirmations administered, depositions and affidavits executed, and other notarial acts performed, before or by any commissioned officer in active service of the armed forces of the United States with the rank of second lieutenant or higher in the army or marine corps, or with the rank of ensign or higher in the navy or coast guard, or with equivalent rank in any other component part of the armed forces of the United States, by any person who either

(1) is a member of the armed forces of the United States, or

(2) is serving as a merchant seaman outside the limits of the United States included within the fifty states and the District of Columbia; or

(3) is outside said limits by permission, assignment or direction of any department or official of the United States government, in connection with any activity pertaining to the prosecution of any war in which the United States is then engaged.

Such acknowledgment of instruments, attestation of documents, administration of oaths and affirmations, execution of depositions and affidavits, and performance of other notarial acts, heretofore or hereafter made or taken, are hereby declared legal, valid and binding, and instruments and documents so acknowledged, authenticated, or sworn to shall be admissible in evidence and eligible to record in this state under the same circumstances, and with the same force and effect as if such acknowledgment, attestation, oath, affirmation, deposition, affidavit, or other notarial act, had been made or taken within this state before or by a duly qualified officer or official as otherwise provided by law.

In the taking of acknowledgments and the performing of other notarial acts requiring certification, a certificate endorsed upon or attached to the instrument or documents, which shows the date of the notarial act and which states, in substance, that the person appearing before the officer acknowledged the instrument as his act or made or signed the instrument or document under oath, shall be sufficient for all intents and purposes. The instrument or document shall not be rendered invalid by the failure to state the place of execution or acknowledgment.

If the signature, rank, and branch of service or subdivision thereof, of any such commissioned officer appear upon such instrument or document or certificate, no further proof of the authority of such officer so to act shall be required and such action by such commissioned officer shall be prima facie evidence that the person making such oath or acknowledgment is within the purview of this section.

Editorial comment

County and judicial district court commissioners, appointed by judges of superior courts, have the authority, among other things, to take acknowledgments and proofs of deeds, mortgages, and all other instruments requiring acknowledgment under the laws of the state. See *Depositions*, WASH. REV. CODE ANN. § 2.24.040(10).

WEST VIRGINIA

[W. VA. CODE ANN.]

§ 31-1-74. **Corporate acknowledgments.** A corporation may acknowledge any instrument required by law to be acknowledged by its attorney appointed under seal, and such appointment may be embodied in the deed or instrument to be acknowledged, or be made by a separate instrument; or such deed or other instrument may be acknowledged by the president or any vice president of such corporation without such appointment.

Note: Concerning the form of certificate of acknowledgment by attorney in fact, see § 39-1-8, below. Concerning acknowledgment by corporations, see also § 39-1-9, below.

§ 39-1-2. Conditions under which county clerk shall admit deeds, contracts, etc., to record. The clerk of the county court of any county in which any deed, contract, power of attorney, or other writing is to be, or may be, recorded, shall admit the same to record in his office, as to any person whose name is signed thereto, when it shall have been acknowledged by him, or proved by two witnesses as to him, before such clerk of the county court.

❂   ❂   ❂

§ 39-1-3. Who may take acknowledgment. Upon the request of any person interested therein, such clerk of the county court shall also admit any such writing to record, as to any person whose name is signed thereto, upon a certificate of his acknowledgment before the president of a county court, a justice of the peace, notary public, recorder, prothonotary or clerk of any court, within the United States, the Philippine Islands, Island of Porto [*sic*] Rico, Territory of Alaska, Territory of Hawaii, or any other territory, possession or dependency of the United States, or a commissioner appointed within the same by the governor of this State, written or annexed to the same; or upon a certificate so written or annexed under the official seal of any ambassador, minister plenipotentiary, minister resident, charge d'affaires, consul general, consul, deputy consul, vice consul, consular agent, vice consular agent, commercial agent, or vice commercial agent, appointed by the government of the United States to any foreign country, or of the proper officer of any court of record of such country, or of the mayor or other chief magistrate of any city, town or corporation therein, that such writing was acknowledged by such person, or proved as to him by two witnesses, before any person having such appointment, or before such court, mayor, or chief magistrate.

§ 39-1-4. Form of certificate of acknowledgment. The certificate of acknowledgment mentioned in the preceding section [§ 39-1-3] may be in form or effect as follows:

State (territory or district) of ———, county of ———, to-wit:

I, ———, a commissioner, appointed by the governor of the State of West Virginia, for the said State (or territory or district) of ———; or I, ———, a justice of the peace of the county aforesaid; or I, ———, recorder of said county; or I, ———, a notary public of said county; or I, ———, a prothonotary (or clerk) of the ——— court of said county; (or other officer or person authorized to take acknowledgments by section three of this article, as the case may be), do certify that ———, whose name (or names) is (or are) signed to the writing above (or hereto annexed) bearing date on the ———

day of ———, 19—, has (or have) this day acknowledged the same before me, in my said ———.

Given under my hand this ——— day of ———, 19—.

§ 39-1-4a. Acknowledgment of persons in the military service of the United States of America. Upon the request of any person interested therein, the clerk of the county court of any county in which any deed, contract, power of attorney, or other writing is to be, or may be, recorded, shall admit the same to record as to any person whose name is signed thereto who is in the military service of the United States (including the Women's Army Auxiliary Corps, Women's Appointed Volunteers for Emergency Service, Army Nurse Corps, "Spars," Women's Reserve, or similar women's auxiliary unit officially connected with the military service of the United States) or who is the spouse of any one in the military service of the United States (including the aforesaid components and auxiliary units officially connected therewith), upon the certificate of acknowledgment of such person before any commissioned officer of any branch of the military service of the United States, or auxiliary unit officially connected with such military service. Such acknowledgment may be taken at any place either within or outside of the United States of America, or any territory, possession or dependency thereof. The certificate of such acknowledgment need not state the place where same is taken and shall require no seal to be affixed thereto. The officer certifying such acknowledgment must state his rank, branch of military service, and identification number; and such certificate of acknowledgment may be in form and effect as follows:

IN THE MILITARY SERVICE OF THE UNITED STATES:

I, ———, a commissioned officer in the military service of the United States, do certify that ———, who is a member of the military service of the United States (or of ———, an auxiliary to the military forces of the United States), and/or ———, husband (or wife) of ———, a member of the military service of the United States (or of ———, an auxiliary to the military forces of the United States), whose name(s) is (are) signed to the foregoing writing bearing date on the ——— day of ———, 19—, has (have) this day acknowledged the same before me; and I further certify that I am a ——— (state rank) in the ——— of the United States and my identification number is ———.

Given under my hand this ——— day of — —, 19—.

_____

(Signature of Officer)

_____

(Official Title)

§ 39-1-5. Acknowledgment by husband and wife. When a husband and wife have signed a writing purporting to sell or convey real estate, the wife may acknowledge the same together with, or separately from her husband. Either the husband or the wife may sign and acknowledge such writing before the other has signed or acknowledged it. If both acknowledge such writing at the same time, the certificate of such acknowledgments may be in form or effect as follows:

State (territory or district) of ——— county of ———, to-wit:

I, ———, a commissioner appointed by the governor of the State of West Virginia for the said State of ———, (or territory or district of ———); or I, ———, a justice of the peace of the said county of ———; or I, ———, a notary public of the said county of ———; or I, ———, prothonotary (or clerk) of the ——— court or county of ———; (or other officer or person authorized to take acknowledgments by section three of this article, as the case may be),° do certify ——— and ———, his wife whose names are signed to the writing above (or hereto annexed) bearing date the ——— day of ———, 19—, have this day acknowledged the same before me in my said ———.

Given under my hand this ——— day of ———, 19—.

If the husband or wife acknowledge a deed or other writing separately from the other, the certificate of acknowledgment after the star in the foregoing form shall be in form or effect as follows: do certify that ———, the wife of ———, (or the husband of ———, as the case may be), whose name is signed to the writing above (or hereto annexed) bearing date the ——— day of ———, 19—, has this day acknowledged the same before me in my said ———.

Given under my hand this ——— day of ———, 19—.

§ 39-1-7. **False certificate of acknowledgment.** If any person shall in any case wilfully make any false certificate of acknowledgment, contrary to the true facts in the case, or shall certify the acknowledgment of any person whom he does not personally know to be the person whose name is signed to the writing acknowledged, he shall be guilty of a misdemeanor, and, upon conviction thereof, be fined not more than five hundred dollars, and imprisoned not more than sixty days, at the discretion of the court.

§ 39-1-8. **Form of certificate of acknowledgment by attorney in fact.** When any writing has been executed by an attorney in fact, and an acknowledgment of the execution thereof is required or authorized for any purpose, the certificate of acknowledgment may be in form or effect as provided in section four [§ 39-1-4] of this article as far as the words "do certify," and thence as follows: do certify that ———, whose name is signed to the writing above (or hereto annexed) bearing date the ——— day of ———, 19—, as attorney in fact for ———, has this day acknowledged the same before me in my said ———.

Given under my hand this ——— day of ———, 19—.

§ 39-1-9. **Acknowledgment by corporations.**[°] The certificate of acknowledgment of a corporation may be in form or effect as prescribed in section four [§ 39-1-4] of this article as far as the words "do certify" and thence as follows: do certify that ———, who signed the writing above (or hereto annexed), bearing date the ——— day of ———, 19 ———, for ——— (name of corporation), has this day in my said county, before me, acknowledged the said writing to be the act and deed of said corporation.

Given under my hand this ——— day of ———, 19—.

° See also § 31-1-74, above.

§§ 39-1A-1 to 39-1A-9. The Uniform Recognition of Acknowledgments Act has been adopted. For text of act, see page 349.

§ 39-1-10. **When certificate to be under official seal.** If any acknowledgment be before a notary without this State, he shall certify the same under his official seal.

WISCONSIN

[WIS. STAT. ANN.]

§ 706.06. **Authentication.** (1) Any instrument may be acknowledged, or its execution otherwise authenticated by its signators, as provided by the laws of this state; or as provided in this section s. 706.065[°°] or 706.07.[°°°]

(2) Any public officer entitled by virtue of his office to administer oaths, and any member in good standing of the state bar of Wisconsin, may authenticate one or more of the signatures on an instrument relating to lands in this state, by indorsing the instrument "Acknowledge," "Authenticated" or "Signatures Guaranteed", or other words to similar effect, adding the date of authentication, his own signature, and his official or professional title. Such indorsement, unless expressly limited, shall operate as an authentication of all signatures on the instrument; and shall constitute a certification that each authenticated signature is the genuine signature of the person represented; and, as to signatures made in a representative capacity, that the signor purported, and was believed, to be such representative.

(3) Affidavits shall be authenticated by jurat, executed by a person entitled to administer oaths.

(4) In addition to any criminal penalty or civil remedy otherwise provided by law, knowingly false authentication of an instrument shall subject the authenticator to liability in tort for compensatory and punitive damages caused thereby to any person.

°° See *Uniform Recognition of Acknowledgments Act,* page 349.
°°° See *Uniform Acknowledgment Act,* page 349.

§ 706.065. The Uniform Recognition of Acknowledgments Act has been adopted. For text of act, see page 349.

§ 706.07. The Uniform Acknowledgment Act has been adopted. For text of act, see page 349.

WYOMING

[WYO. STAT. ANN.]

§ 19-5. **Acknowledgment of instrument by members of armed forces and their dependents before commissioned officer; form of certificate.** In addition to the acknowledgment of instruments in the manner and form and as otherwise authorized by law, persons serving in or with the armed forces of the United States or their dependents, wherever located, may acknowledge the same before any commissioned officer in active service of the armed forces of the United States with the rank of second lieutenant or higher in the army, air force or marine corps, or ensign or higher in the navy or coast guard. The instrument shall not be rendered invalid by the failure to state therein the place of execution or acknowledgment. No authentication of the officer's certificate of acknowledgment shall be required, but the officer taking the acknowledgment shall endorse thereon or attach thereto a certificate substantially in the following form:

On this ———— day of ————, 19—, before me, ———— the undersigned officer, personally appeared ————, Serial No. (If any) ————, known to me (or satisfactorily proven) to be serving in or with the armed forces of the United States (A dependent of ————, Serial No. (If any) ————, a person serving in or with the armed forces of the United States) and to be the person whose name is subscribed to the within instrument and acknowledged that ———— he ———— executed the same for the purposes therein contained, and the undersigned does further certify that he is, at the date of this certificate, a commissioned officer of the rank stated below and is in the active service of the armed forces of the United States.

—————————————————————
Signature of the officer

—————————————————————
Rank and Serial No. of officer
and command to which attached.

§ 34-13. **Acknowledgment of conveyances; generally.** Execution of deeds, mortgages or other conveyances of lands, or any interest in lands, shall be acknowledged by the party or parties executing same, before any judge or clerk of a court of record, or before any United States magistrate appointed under and by authority of the laws of the United States, or any county clerk, justice of the peace, district court commissioner, notary public, or other officer authorized under the laws of the State of Wyoming to take such acknowledgments, and the officer taking such acknowledgment shall endorse thereon a certificate of the acknowledgment thereof, and the true date of making the same, under his hand and seal of office, if there be one.

§ 34-14. Same—notary, etc., to state date of expiration of term of office, etc. Every notary public, justice of the peace, and commissioner of deeds for Wyoming, who takes an acknowledgment to any written instrument to be recorded in any public office in Wyoming shall add to his certificate the date when commission or term of office expires.

§ 34-15. Same—execution out of state. Any deed, mortgage, conveyance, power of attorney or instrument in writing requiring an acknowledgment executed outside of this state, may be acknowledged before any officer authorized by law to take acknowledgments at the place where such acknowledgment is taken. Whenever the officer taking such acknowledgment has no seal the certificate of such officer shall have attached thereto the certificate of the clerk of the court of record, or a county clerk, of the same place, having a seal, certifying that the officer taking the acknowledgment is authorized to take the same and that he believes that the signature appended to the acknowledgment is genuine. Each instrument of writing as aforesaid executed and acknowledged as aforesaid shall be as valid and have the same force and effect as if executed in Wyoming according to the provisions of [§ 34-13].

§ 34-16. Effect of conveyance executed in another state. Any deed, mortgage or conveyance executed in any other state, territory, district or country, which shall be executed according to the laws of this state, and acknowledged before a clerk of a 'court of record, county clerk, or a commissioner appointed as aforesaid, shall have the same effect as if executed and acknowledged within this state.

§ 34-17. Execution, etc., in foreign countries; powers of attorney. If any deeds, mortgages or conveyances of lands, or of any interest in lands, be executed in any foreign country, government, kingdom or empire, such deed, mortgage, or conveyance of land may be executed according to the laws of this state, and may be acknowledged before a consul general, consul or vice-consul of the United States; and when so acknowledged the officer taking the acknowledgment shall certify the same over his hand and official seal or the seal of the consulate to which he is attached, if there be any such seal; and in case he has no official seal, and there be no seal of his consulate, that fact shall be stated in the certificate; and no other or further authentication shall be required to entitle such instrument to record in this state. This section shall also apply to powers of attorney executed in any such foreign country, government, kingdom or empire.

§ 34-18. Where conveyance, etc., to be recorded. A certificate of the acknowledgment of any deed, mortgage or conveyance, or proof of the execution thereof, before a court of record or a justice of the peace, signed by the clerk of such court, (or by the justice) before whom the same was taken, as provided in this act, and in the cases where the same is necessary, the certificate required by [§ 34-15], shall entitle such deed, mortgage or conveyance, certificate or certificates aforesaid, to be recorded in the office of the register of deeds [county clerk] in the county where the land lies.

Wyoming Acknowledgment Act

§ 34-50-1. Acknowledgment Act—citation of act. This act [§§ 34-50.1 to 34-50.5] shall be known as the "Wyoming Acknowledgment Act."

§ 34-50.2. Same; form of acknowledgment. A certificate of acknowlegment substantially in the following form shall be sufficient for all instruments conveying, mortgaging or otherwise disposing of or encumbering real estate, including homestead property, and shall be sufficient for all other instruments affecting title to real estate and all other instruments required by the laws of this state to be acknowledged:

State of ———
               ss.
County of ———

The foregoing instrument was acknowledged before me by ———,
———, this ——— day of ———, 19—.
Witness my hand and official seal.

———————————————
Title of officer
My Commission Expires: ———

§ 34-50.3. Same—requirements for implied acknowledgment. Every certificate of acknowledgment substantially in the form provided for in [§ 34-50.2] shall for all purposes be deemed to be a certification by the officer making the certificate that

(a) If the instrument to which the same is affixed was executed by natural persons acting in their own right, that such person or persons personally appeared before such officer, were known to him to be the person or persons described in and who executed such instrument, and that such person or persons acknowledged that the same was executed and acknowledged freely and voluntarily.

(b) If the instrument to which the certificate is affixed was executed by an attorney-in-fact acting for a natural person: that such attorney personally appeared before such officer, was known by such officer to be the party who executed such instrument on behalf of such natural person, and that such attorney acknowledged that such instrument was executed and acknowledged as the free and voluntary act of such natural person.

(c) If the instrument to which the certificate is affixed was executed by a corporation or a joint-stock association: that the president or other official who signed such instrument on behalf of such corporation or association appeared before and was personally known to the officer making the certificate, and was by him duly sworn and upon oath represented that he was the president or other officer or agent of such corporation or association, that the seal affixed to the instrument is the corporate seal of such corporation or association, that the instrument was signed and sealed on behalf of such corporation or association by the authority of the board of directors or trustees thereof, and that the officer who executed such instrument on behalf of the corporation or association acknowledged said instrument to be the free act and deed of the corporation or association. If such corporation or association has no corporate seal a recital to that effect shall be inserted at the end of the certificate by the officer making the same.

§ 34-50.4. Same—Acknowledgment of real estate transactions prior to January 1, 1966. [Omitted.]

§ 34-50.5. Same—out-of-state transactions. Any instrument conveying, mortgaging, or otherwise disposing of or encumbering real estate, excluding, however, homestead property, and any other instrument affecting title to real estate, and any other instrument required by the laws of this state to be acknowledged, which, prior to or after the effective date of this act [§§ 34-50.1 to 34-50.5], shall have been acknowledged out of this state before an officers empowered to take acknowledgments by the laws of the state, territory, or foreign country where the certificate of acknowledgment was made, if the form of such certificate of acknowledgment be in substantial compliance with the laws of the state, territory, or foreign country where taken or with the requirements of the laws of this state, shall for all purposes be conclusively deemed and regarded to be properly acknowledged.

UNITED STATES

22 U.S.C. § 1195. Notarial acts, oaths, affirmations, affidavits, and depositions—fees. Every consular officer of the United States is hereby required, whenever application is made to him therefor, within the limits of his consulate, to administer to or take from any person any oath, affirmation, affidavit, or deposition, and to perform any other notarial act which any notary public is required or

authorized by law to do within the United States; and for every such notarial act performed he shall charge in each instance the appropriate fee prescribed by the President under [22 U.S.C. § 1201].

In Puerto Rico

48 U.S.C. § 742. Acknowledgment of deeds. Deeds and other instruments affecting land situate in the District of Columbia, or any other territory or possession of the United States, may be acknowledged in Puerto Rico before any notary public appointed therein by proper authority, or any officer therein who has ex officio the powers of a notary public: Provided, that the certificate by such notary shall be accompanied by the certificate of the executive secretary of Puerto Rico to the effect that the notary taking such acknowledgment is in fact such notarial officer.

In Guam, Samoa and Canal Zone

48 U.S.C. § 1421f-1. Acknowledgment of deeds. Deeds and other instruments affecting land situate in the District of Columbia or any Territory of the United States may be acknowledged in the island of Guam and Samoa or in the Canal Zone before any notary public or judge appointed therein by proper authority, or by any officer therein who has ex officio the powers of a notary public: Provided, That the certificate by such notary in Guam, Samoa, or the Canal Zone, as the case may be, shall be accompanied by the certificate of the governor or acting governor of such place to the effect that the notary taking said acknowledgment was in fact the officer he purported to be; and any deeds or other instruments affecting lands so situate, so acknowledged since the 1st day of January nineteen hundred and five and accompanied by such certificate shall have the same effect as such deeds or other instruments ° ° ° so acknowledged and certified.

In Guam and Samoa

48 U.S.C. § 1663. Acknowledgment of deeds. Deeds and other instruments affecting land situate in the District of Columbia or any Territory of the United States may be acknowledged in the islands of Guam and Samoa before any notary public or judge, appointed therein by proper authority, or by any officer therein who has ex officio the powers of a notary public: Provided, That the certificate by such notary in Guam or Samoa, as the case may be, shall be accompanied by the certificate of the governor or acting governor of such place to the effect that the notary taking said acknowledgment was in fact the officer he purported to be; and any deeds or other instruments affecting lands so situate, so acknowledged since the 1st day of January, 1905, and accompanied by such certificate shall have the same effect as such deeds or other instruments hereafter so acknowledged and certified.

CHAPTER 13: DEPOSITIONS

STATUTORY PROVISIONS AND FORMS

§ 13.1 General.

A deposition is the testimony of a witness which is reduced to writing by a notary public or other public officer for various purposes incident to a lawsuit. It is made under oath and upon notice to the adverse party, who may attend and cross-examine the witness.[1]

§ 13.2 Right to take depositions.

The use of depositions was not permitted in the early common law courts, except by consent of the parties. Courts

---

[1] See the various definitions in the Glossary, page 853.

of equity, however, had power to obtain testimony by deposition, having created three different forms of relief: (1) A bill to take testimony de bene esse; (2) a bill to perpetuate testimony; and (3) a bill of discovery. To correct these limitations, most states and other jurisdictions have enacted statutes, and most courts have adopted rules of procedure, which now permit the use of depositions and prescribe the manner in which they are to be taken. Strict compliance with these statutory provisions and rules of procedure is necessary. The Federal Rules of Civil Procedure (Fed. R. Civ. P.) incorporate and broaden the former provisions of the United States statutes concerning depositions, and have served as a model for various state rules of civil procedure which has been closely followed by a large number of state courts.[2]

§ 13.3 Classification.

Depositions are frequently mentioned under different names and phrases in the various statutory provisions, with references chiefly to the manner, authorization, purpose, and time of their taking. They may be classified accordingly:

1. Deposition taken in reply to (a) oral interrogatories or questions, and (b) written interrogatories or questions.

2. Depositions taken (a) on notice; (b) under commission, or dedimus potestatem;[3] (c) under notice and commission; (d) by stipulation or agreement; (e) under letters rogatory.

3. Depositions taken (a) de bene esse[4] (conditionally); (b) to perpetuate testimony.

---

[2] For selected portions of FED. R. CIV. P., see Depositions: State and Other Statutes, "United States," below.

[3] For definition, see Glossary, page 857.

[4] For definition, see Glossary, page 856.

§ 13.4 Who may take depositions.

Statutes or rules of procedure, or both, usually identify the officers before whom depositions may be taken. Not only notaries public, but frequently the clerk of a court, a judge of a court, a justice of the peace, and various commissioners are authorized to take depositions. Some statutes and rules of procedure confer such power generally upon any officer authorized to administer an oath.

If the witness whose deposition is to be taken resides out of the state, a commission may be issued by the clerk of the court in which the suit is pending, to any person agreed upon by the parties to the suit, or to a notary public selected by the officer issuing the commission, or to a commissioner appointed by the governor to take depositions in other states.

The statutes of many states, and the rules of procedure of many courts, expressly provide that the officer before whom the deposition is taken must not be related to, or the attorney or agent of, either of the parties, or interested in the result of the law suit.

§ 13.5 Notice of intention to take.

The written notice of intention to take a deposition, given to the adverse party, usually contains the following information: (1) Names of the parties to the lawsuit; (2) court in which the deposition is to be used; (e) date, time, and place where it will be taken; (4) name of the witness or witnesses; (5) name or identity of officer who will take; (6) purpose of the deposition; (7) whether the examination is to be adjourned from day to day; (8) occasionally, the matters upon which the witness is to be examined; and (9) signature of the attorney of the party giving notice.

The manner and time of serving such notice are regulated by the statutes of the various states and other jurisdictions, and the rules of procedure of the various courts.

Depositions taken on notice are generally taken in answer to oral questions propounded by the attorneys of the parties, the notice being the only writing which comes to the notary public as evidence of his right to take the deposition. He must, therefore, be an officer expressly authorized by statute to take depositions.

§ 13.6 Manner of taking depositions — in general.

Depositions in reply to oral questions are ordinarily taken pursuant to notice or agreement, before a duly authorized officer, with whom the parties have arranged to be present and to have the witnesses present, at the time and place mentioned in the notice or agreement. Either or both parties have the right to be present at such taking, by attorney or in person, or both. The officer, after having written out the proper caption and preamble, records the names of the attorneys, parties, and witnesses present. This is often listed under the title, "Appearances." The officer proceeds to write, or to have written, the questions submitted orally to the witnesses by the attorneys, and the answers of each witness.

Depositions in reply to written interrogatories are taken under a commission, at which taking neither party to the lawsuit has a right to be present or to be represented by attorney or agent, the interrogatories being put to the witness by the officer, and the answers thereto written by him or some authorized person. In addition to the interrogatories prepared by the attorney of the party desiring the deposition, cross-interrogatories may be submitted by the opposing attorney. Both the interrogatories and cross-interrogatories are attached to the commission. The law of the state or other jurisdiction whence the commission issues governs such depositions and the manner of their taking.

§ 13.7 Taken under agreement or stipulation.

The parties to a lawsuit may agree or stipulate that the deposition of a witness or witnesses may be taken before a certain officer, at a designated date, time and place, and waive some of the strict formalities as to adjournments or other particulars. Such agreement or stipulation is usually reduced to writing, and takes the place of a commission or similar authority. As to matters not provided for in the agreement, the statutes and rules of procedure in the state or other jurisdiction where the deposition is to be used should be carefully observed.

§ 13.8 Swearing the witness.

The witness must be sworn before he gives his testimony. The usual form of oath to the witness is as follows:

"You do solemnly swear that you will testify the truth, the whole truth, and nothing but the truth in answer to the several questions (or interrogatories and cross-interrogatories) about to be put to you in the case now pending in the ——— Court, wherein A B is plaintiff and C D is defendant, and this you do as you shall answer unto God?"

§ 13.9 Writing of depositions.

Under the statutes and rules of procedure of most states and other jurisdictions, only the officer, or the witness who is deposing, or some disinterested third person, is allowed to write the answers to the questions put to the witness. They often provide that the officer before whom the deposition is taken shall personally, or by some one acting under his direction and in his presence, record the testimony of the witness. Usually, depositions may be taken stenographically and transcribed. When the testimony is fully transcribed, the deposition is submitted to the witness for examination and will be read to or by him for his correction or approval. Any changes in form or substance which the witness desires to make should be noted upon the deposition by the notary public with a statement of the reasons given by the witness for making them.

§ 13.10 Signing the deposition.

Unless the requirement is waived by the witness and by the parties, the deposition must be signed by the witness at the end thereof. Such waivers are often given. Some states and other jurisdictions require the witness to sign the deposition not only at the end, but also upon each piece of paper upon which any portion of his testimony is written. If, from ignorance, disability, or illness, the witness is unable to write his signature at the end of the deposition, the notary public may write the witness' name for him as follows: "William Brown, by George Houston;" or: "William (his x mark) Brown," the mark x being made by the witness, or by the notary public while the witness is touching the pen.

In some states, the officer must certify, after the signature of each witness, as follows: "Sworn to and subscribed before me, by the said E F, this ––– day of ––––, 19–, at the place and within the hours above mentioned. G H, Notary Public."

§ 13.11   Caption, preamble, and appearances.

The introductory portion of the deposition should show: (1) Name and title of officer before whom taken; (2) date and time when, and (3) place where taken; (4) by what authority taken; (5) in what court to be used; (6) names of the parties to suit; (7) names and residences of witnesses; (8) in whose behalf taken; (9) who was present in behalf of each party; and (10) that the witness was duly sworn.

§ 13.12   Form of deposition.

The statutes and rules of procedure of a few states and other jurisdictions prescribe the form of a deposition. In the absence of specific contrary directions in the appropriate statutes and rules of procedure,[5] the following general form may be used:

Deposition of E F taken before me, G H, a notary public in and for ––– County, State of ––––, pursuant to the annexed notice (*or*, commission; *or*, agreement) at the time

---

[5] See Depositions: State and Other Statutes, below.

and place therein specified, to be read in evidence on behalf of the plaintiff (*or,* defendant), in an action pending in the ――― Court of ――― County, State of ―――, in which A B is plaintiff, and C D is defendant. L M appeared as attorney for the plaintiff and R S appeared as attorney for the defendant.

E F, of lawful age, being first duly sworn, deposes and says as follows:

Question.[6]

Answer.

Q.

A.

[And so continue until the direct examination is finished. If the deposition is taken under written interrogatories, the officer or stenographer writes, not the interrogatory, but only: "To the first interrogatory he says:" and "To the second interrogatory he says:" etc.]

Cross-examination of E F, by ―――, in behalf of ―――:

Q.

A. (and so proceed to the close of the cross-examination).

Re-direct examination of E F by ―――:

Q.

A. (and so to the end of his testimony).

(Signature) E F

Witness

§ 13.13   Officer's certificate.

After the testimony of all the witnesses has been taken, the officer usually must add to the deposition a certificate stating: (1) That the witness was first sworn to testify the truth, the whole truth, and nothing but the truth; (2) by whom the deposition was written, and if written by deponent or some disinterested person, that it was written in the

---

[6] The questions and answers are often identified by the abbreviations "Q." and "A.", respectively.

presence and under the direction of the officer; (3) the date, time and place of taking the deposition; (4) that the witness signed it, or that the signing by the witness was waived; (5) that the officer is not counsel, attorney or relative of either party, or otherwise interested in the result of the lawsuit; (6) that the deposition is a true record of the evidence and testimony given by deponent. The officer must sign the certificate and affix his seal.

§ 13.14   Interpreters.

Even in the absence of express statutory authority, the right to take testimony would imply the power to employ an interpreter when the witness does not understand English, or cannot intelligently testify in that language. If the officer taking the deposition understands the witness' language, he may interpret the testimony.

An oath, in substantially the following form, should be administered to the interpreter: "You do solemnly swear that you know the English and the ――― languages, and can interpret from either of them into the other; and that you will truly and impartially interpret from the English language into the ――― language to E F, the witness, the oath that shall be administered to him, and the questions that shall be put to him as a witness, and that you will truly and impartially interpret from the ――― language into the English language the answers that said witness shall give; and this you do as you shall answer unto God."[7]

An interpreter also must sign the deposition with the witness whose testimony he interprets. The following statement should be inserted in the deposition, just preceding the testimony: "It appearing that the witness, E F, could not understand the English language (or, could not intelligently testify in the English language), and did understand the ――― language, one L M, who also well understands said

---

[7] See, however, the various provisions in *Depositions: State and Other Statutes,* below.

—— language, was employed as interpreter and sworn to impartially interpret the oath, questions and answers."

§ 13.15 Adjournments.

Ordinarily, when the deposition has not been finished and the closing hour of the day has come, or for other good reason an adjournment is necessary, the further taking of the deposition should be adjourned to the next day unless it be Sunday or a legal holiday. A notice to take depositions usually provides for adjournment from day to day.

The adjournment should be to the same place, unless the parties agree to some other place. The taking of a deposition under commission, at which the parties cannot be present, may be adjourned to such times and places as will suit the convenience of the officer and the witnesses.

There being more testimony than can be taken conveniently in one day, or a witness in attendance becoming sick and unable to attend longer on that day, or a witness duly subpoenaed failing to attend, are good reasons for an adjournment to the next day.

The adjournment may be noted by the officer as follows: "The taking of said deposition not being finished at —— o'clock of said —— day of ——, 19–, the further taking thereof was adjourned to —— o'clock of the —— day of ——, 19– [the next business day, omitting Sundays and legal holidays]."

The resumption of taking testimony, after adjournment, may be noted: "The taking of said E F's deposition commenced on the —— day of ——, 19–, was resumed on —— ——, 19–, at —— o'clock –M."

§ 13.16 Objections.

The adverse party or his attorney may object to questions, and occasionally answers, for various reasons. The objections should be recorded by the officer. At the appropriate place in the record of the examination, the officer writes, "The plaintiff (or, defendant) objects to this question (or, answer) as [state the reason given]," and then, nevertheless, writes the answer. The court before which the lawsuit is pending will rule on the objections when the deposition is filed in court.

§ 13.17   Exhibits.

If a letter, telegram, or other paper is introduced in evidence during the taking of a deposition, it should be marked for identification as required by the statutes or custom of the state or other jurisdiction in which the deposition is to be used. In many jurisdictions, such papers are described carefully in the deposition, the witness then adding such words as "which letter is hereto attached, marked Exhibit A." The next one is called "Exhibit B," the next one "Exhibit C," and they are all fastened to the deposition.

In other jurisdictions, such exhibits must be annexed to the deposition, subscribed by the witness, and endorsed by the officer as follows:

"At the execution of a commission for the examination of witnesses in a suit between A B, plaintiff, and C D, defendant, the paper writing was produced and shown to E F and by him deposed unto at the time of the examination before

G H
Commissioner"

§ 13.18   Filing of deposition.[8]

After the deposition has been completed, it must be fastened together with the notice, commission, or ageement, written interrogatories, if any, and exhibits into one package. All of these papers, including each page of the deposition, may be held firmly together by means of a fastener run through holes placed near the top of all the sheets or along one side of the sheets. To prevent any one from

---

[8] See the various provisions in Depositions: State and Other Statutes, below.

tampering with the package, a seal may be placed over the ends of the fastener and an impression of the officer's seal made on it.

The deposition must be enclosed in some suitable cover such as a large envelope, and sealed. The package, so sealed, ordinarily must be addressed to the clerk of the court in which the lawsuit is pending, as follows:

A B, Plaintiff   No. ――――
v.   Pending in
C D, Defendant   ―――― Court

Deposition of E F, taken in behalf of the plaintiff (or, defendant), before G H, Notary Public

To the Clerk of the ―――― Court
(name of postoffice),
―――― County,
(State)

Across the back of the envelope, or sealed place of the cover, the officer should write:

Deposition taken
before me, and
sealed, addressed
and transmitted
by me.
G H,
Notary Public in
and for ――――
County, State of
――――.

The object of this is to identify the deposition without opening it, and prevent its being opened by the wrong parties. The endorsements should, therefore, not be omitted even where not required by statute.

§ 13.19   Compelling attendance of witness.

In many states and other jurisdictions, the various officers authorized to take depositions are empowered to subpoena witnesses to attend and to testify, and to compel them to do so in case of their neglect or refusal to do either. In several jurisdictions, however, compulsory measures to secure attendance, answers, and signatures of witnesses at the taking of depositions must be secured through the court. In some jurisdictions, both provisions exist, and the persons taking the deposition may choose either alternative. Often, the proof of service of a notice to take a deposition constitutes a sufficient authorization for the issuance by the clerk of the court of subpoenas for the persons named or described therein. A subpoena commanding the production of documentary evidence on the taking of a deposition ordinarily cannot be used without an order of the court.

§ 13.20   Punishment for contempt.

Disobedience of a subpoena, a refusal to be sworn, a refusal to answer as a witness, or to subscribe a deposition, may be punished as a contempt of the court or officer by whom the attendance or testimony of the witness is required. The statutes of several states and other jurisdictions authorize the officer to impose a fine or commit the witness to jail.

If a party or other deponent refuses to answer a question propounded upon oral examination, or an interrogatory, the examination should be completed on other matters or adjourned, as the proponent of the question may prefer. Thereafter, on reasonable notice to all persons affected thereby, the proponent of the question may apply to the court for an order compelling an answer. The failure to comply with such an order would be considered a contempt of court.

STATUTORY PROVISIONS AND FORMS

DEPOSITIONS: STATE
AND OTHER STATUTES

ALABAMA

[ALA. R. CIV. P. 28]

Persons Before Whom Depositions May Be Taken

(a) **Depositions to be Used in This State.** The depositions provided for herein shall be taken before an officer authorized to administer oaths by the laws of the United States, or of the State of Alabama, or of the state or other place where the examination is held, or before a person appointed by the court in which the action is pending. A person so appointed has power to administer oaths and take testimony.

(b) **Depositions to be Used Outside This State.** A person desiring to take depositions in this state to be used in proceedings pending in the courts of any other state or country may produce to a judge of the circuit court where the witness resides a commission authorizing the taking of such depositions or proof of notice duly served, whereupon it shall be the duty of the judge to issue, pursuant to Rule 45, the necessary subpoenas. Orders of the character provided in Rules 30(d), 37(a)(1), 37(b)(1) and 45(b) may be made upon proper application therefor by the person to whom such a subpoena is directed. Failure by any person without adequate excuse to obey a subpoena served upon him pursuant to this rule may be deemed a contempt of the court from which the subpoena issued.

(c) **Disqualification for Interest.** No deposition shall be taken before a person who is a relative or employee or attorney or counsel of any of the parties, or is a relative or employee of such attorney or counsel, or is financially interested in the action.

ALASKA

[ALASKA STAT.]

§ 09.65.010. **Officers authorized to administer oaths or affirmations.** Every justice, judge, magistrate, clerk of a court, notary public, United States postmaster, and the commanding officer of a vessel of the United States Coast Guard may administer oaths or affirmations.

[ALASKA R. CIV. P. 28]

Persons Before Whom Depositions May Be Taken

(a) **Within the State.** Within the state, depositions shall be taken before an officer authorized by the laws of this state to administer oaths, or before a person appointed by the court in which the action is pending. A person appointed has power to administer oaths and take testimony.

(b) **Without the State but Within the United States.** Without the state but within the United States, or within a territory or insular possession subject to the dominion of the United States, depositions shall be taken before an officer authorized to administer oaths by the laws of the United States or of the place where the examination is held.

(c) **In Foreign Countries.** In a foreign state or country depositions shall be taken (1) on notice before a secretary of embassy or legation, consul general, consul, vice consul or consular agent of the United States, or (2) before such person or officer as may be appointed by commission or under letters rogatory. A commission or letters rogatory shall be issued only when necessary or convenient, on application and notice, and on such terms and with such directions as are just and appropriate. Officers may be designated in notices or commissions either by name or descriptive title and letters rogatory may be addressed "To the Appropriate Judicial Authority in (here name the country)."

(d) **Disqualification for Interest.** No deposition shall be taken before a person who is a relative or employee or attorney or counsel of any of the parties, or is a relative or employee of such attorney or counsel, or is financially interested in the action.

ARIZONA

[ARIZ. REV. STAT. ANN.]

§ 41-312. **Duties.** Notaries public shall, when requested:

o   o   o

3. Take depositions and administer oaths and affirmations.

o   o   o

[ARIZ. R. CIV. P. 28]

Persons Before Whom Depositions May Be Taken

28(a) **Within the United States; commission or letters rogatory.** Within the United States or within a territory or insular possession subject to the dominion of the United States, depositions shall be taken before an officer authorized to administer oaths by the laws of the United States or of the place where the examination is held, or before a person appointed by the court in which the action is pending. A person so appointed has power to administer oaths and take testimony. Depositions may be taken in this state or anywhere upon notice provided by these Rules without a commission, letters rogatory or other writ.

Upon proof that the notice to take a deposition outside this state has been given as provided by these Rules, the party seeking such deposition may, but is not required, after one full day's notice to the other parties, have issued by the clerk, in the form given in such notice, a commission or letters rogatory or other like writ either in lieu of the notice to take the deposition or supplementary thereto. Failure to file written objections to such form before or at the time of its issuance shall be a waiver of any objection thereto. Any objection shall be heard and determined forthwith by the court or judge thereof.

28(b) In foreign countries. In a foreign country, depositions may be taken (1) on notice before a person authorized to administer oaths in the place in which the examination is held, either by the law thereof or by the law of the United States, or (2) before a person commissioned by the court, and a person so commissioned shall have the power by virtue of his commission to administer any necessary oath and take testimony, or (3) pursuant to a letter rogatory. A commission or a letter rogatory shall be issued on application and notice and on terms that are just and appropriate. It is not requisite to the issuance of a commission or a letter rogatory that the taking of the deposition in any other manner is impracticable or inconvenient; and both a commission and a letter rogatory may be issued in proper cases. A notice or commission may designate the person before whom the deposition is to be taken either by name or descriptive title. A letter rogatory may be addressed "To the Appropriate Authority in (here name the country)." Evidence obtained in response to a letter rogatory need not be excluded merely for the reason that it is not a verbatim transcript or that the testimony was not taken under oath or for any similar departure from the requirements for depositions taken within the United States under these rules.

28(c) Disqualification for interest. No deposition shall be taken before a person who is a relative or employee or attorney or counsel of any of the parties, or is a relative or employee of such attorney or counsel, or is financially interested in the action.

ARKANSAS

[ARK. STAT. ANN.]

§ 12-1714. **Officers taking depositions.** The fees allowed an officer for taking depositions shall be two dollars [$2.00] for each deposition and five cents [5¢] per mile for each mile that an officer may have have to travel in going to and returning from the place of the taking, the distance to be estimated from his office, but whatever the number of depositions taken in one [1] day for the same party in any action, the fees thereof shall not exceed five dollars [$5.00], and if the officer shall be engaged more than one day in taking a deposition, he shall receive two dollars [$2.00] per day for each day he may be engaged in taking one [1] deposition.

§ 28-350. **Persons before whom depositions may be taken.** (a) WITHIN THE UNITED STATES. Within the United States or within a territory or insular possession subject to the dominion of the United States, a deposition shall be taken before an officer authorized to administer oaths by the laws of the United States or of the places where the examination is held, or before a person appointed by the court in which the action is pending. A person so appointed has power to administer oaths and take testimony.

(b) IN FOREIGN COUNTRIES. In a foreign state or country depositions shall be taken (1) on notice before a secretary of embassy or legation, consul general, consul, vice consul, or consular agent of the United States, or (2) before such person or officer as may be appointed by commission or under letters rogatory. A commission or letters rogatory shall be issued only when necessary or convenient, on application and notice, and on such terms and with such directions as are just and appropriate. Officers may be designated in notices or commissions either by name or descriptive title and letters rogatory may be addressed "To the Appropriate Judicial Authority in (here name the country)."

(c) DISQUALIFICATION FOR INTEREST. No deposition shall be taken before a person who is a relative or employee or attorney or counsel of any of the parties, or is a relative or employee of such attorney or counsel, or is financially interested in the action.

CALIFORNIA

[CAL. EVID. CODE—West]

Persons Before Whom Depositions May Be Taken

§ 2018. (a) **In United States or territory.** Within the United States or within a territory or insular possession subject to the dominion of the United States, depositions shall be taken before any notary public or a judge or officer authorized to administer oaths by the laws of the United States or of the place where the examination is held, or before a person appointed by the court in which the action is pending. A person so appointed has power to administer oaths and take testimony.

(b) **In foreign states or countries.** In a foreign state or country depositions shall be taken on notice before anyone agreed to by the parties, a secretary of embassy or legation, consul general, consul, vice-consul or consular agent of the United States, or before such person or officer as may be appointed by commission or under letters rogatory. A commission or letters rogatory shall be issued by the court in which the action is pending when necessary or convenient on motion and notice and upon such terms and with such directions as are just and appropriate. The person before whom the deposition is to be taken may be designated in notices or commissions either by name or descriptive title and letters rogatory may be addressed "to the appropriate judicial authority in [here name the country]."

(c) **Disqualification for interest.** No deposition shall be taken before a person who is a relative or employee or attorney or counsel of any of the parties, or is a relative or employee of such attorney or counsel, or is financially interested in the action.

§ 2093. Officers authorized to administer oaths or affirmations. JUDICIAL AND CERTAIN OFFICERS AUTHORIZED TO ADMINISTER OATHS. Every Court, every Judge, or Clerk of any Court, every Justice, and every Notary Public, and every officer or person authorized to take testimony in any action or proceeding, or to decide upon evidence, has power to administer oaths or affirmations.

§ 2094. Oath to witness; form. An oath, or affirmation, in an action or proceeding, may be administered as follows, the person who swears, or affirms, expressing his assent when addressed in the following form: "You do solemnly swear (or affirm, as the case may be), that the evidence you shall give in this issue (or matter), pending between ———— and ————, shall be the truth, the whole truth, and nothing but the truth, so help you God."

§ 2095. Oath to witness; variation to suit belief of witness. FORM MAY BE VARIED TO SUIT WITNESS' BELIEF. Whenever the Court before which a person is offered as a witness is satisfied that he has a peculiar mode of swearing, connected with or in addition to the usual form of administration, which, in his opinion, is more solemn or obligatory, the Court may, in its discretion, adopt that mode.

§ 2096. Oath to witness; administration according to ceremonies of his religion. SAME. When a person is sworn who believes in any other than the Christian religion, he may be sworn according to the peculiar ceremonies of his religion, if there be any such.

§ 2097. Oath to witness; option to declare or affirm. ANY PERSON WHO PREFERS IT MAY DECLARE OR AFFIRM. Any person who desires it may, at his option, instead of taking an oath make his solemn affirmation or declaration, by assenting, when addressed, in the following form: "You do solemnly affirm (or declare) that," etc., as in Section 2094.°

° For § 2094, see above.

Concerning the duties of a notary public when taking depositions, see also *Authority and Duties,* CAL. GOV'T CODE § 8205(c) (West).

COLORADO

A notary public, at any place in the state, has authority to administer oaths or affirmations and take depositions. See *Authority and Duties,* COLO. REV. STAT. ANN. § 12-55-102.

[COLO. R. CIV. P. 28]

Persons Before Whom Depositions May Be Taken

(a) **Within the United States.** Within the United States or within a territory or possession subject to the dominion of the United States, depositions shall be taken before an officer authorized to administer oaths by the laws of this state or of the United States or of the place where the examination is held, or before a person appointed by the court in which the action is pending. A person so appointed has power to administer oaths and take testimony.

(b) **In Foreign Countries.** In a foreign state or country depositions shall be taken: (1) On notice before a secretary of embassy or legation, consul general, consul, vice consul, or consular agent of the United States; or (2) before such person or officer as may be appointed by commission or under letters rogatory. A commission or letters rogatory shall be issued only when necessary or convenient, on application and notice, and on such terms and with such directions as are just and appropriate. Officers may be designated in notices or commissions either by name or descriptive title and letters rogatory may be addressed "To the Appropriate Judicial Authority in (here name the country)." Evidence obtained in response to a letter rogatory need not be excluded merely for the reason that it is not a verbatim transcript or that the testimony was not taken under oath or for any similar departure from the requirements for depositions taken within the United States under these rules.

(c) **Disqualification for Interest.** No deposition shall be taken before a person who is a relative or employee or attorney or counsel of any of the parties, or is financially interested in the action.

(d) **Outside Colorado.** Upon proof that the notice to take a deposition outside the state of Colorado has been given as provided in these rules, the clerk shall issue a commission or letters rogatory in the form prescribed by the state in which the deposition is to be taken, such form to be presented by the party seeking the deposition. Any error in the form or in the commission or letters is waived unless objection thereto be filed and served on or before the time fixed in the notice.

CONNECTICUT

[CONN. GEN. STAT. ANN.]

§ 1-23. **When affirmation may be used.** When any person, required to take an oath, from scruples of conscience declines to take it in the usual form or when the court is satisfied that any person called as a witness does not believe in the existence of a Supreme Being, a solemn affirmation may be administered to him in the form of the oath prescribed, except that instead of the word "swear" the words "solemnly and sincerely affirm and declare" shall be used and instead of the words "so help you God" the words "upon the pains and penalities of perjury or false statement" shall be used.

§ 1-24. Who may administer oaths. The following officers may administer oaths: ° ° ° [Among others] ° ° ° judges and clerks of any court, justices of the peace, commissioners of the superior court, notaries public, commissioners appointed by the governor to take acknowledgment of deeds, town clerks and assistant town clerks, in all cases where an oath may be administered, except in a case where the law otherwise requires; ° ° ° commissioners, appointed by governors of other states to take the acknowledgment of deeds, in the discharge of their official duty; ° ° °

§ 1-25. Forms of oaths. The forms of oaths shall be as follows, to-wit:

°   °   °

For Witnesses

You solemnly swear that the evidence you shall give, concerning the case now in question, shall be the truth, the whole truth and nothing but the truth; so help you God.

°   °   °

§ 52-148. Depositions in civil actions and probate proceedings. If any witness or party in a civil action or probate proceeding lives out of the state or more than twenty miles from the place of trial, is going to sea or out of the state, or, by reason of age or infirmity, is unable to travel to court, or is confined in jail, his deposition may be taken by a judge or clerk of any court, justice of the peace, notary public or commissioner of the superior court; provided reasonable notice shall have been given to each adverse party or his known agent or attorney by written notice served by an indifferent person at his usual place of abode or by mailing such notice to him by certified mail, to be present at the time of taking such deposition. Depositions may be taken in any other state or country by a notary public, a commissioner appointed by the governor of this state or any magistrate having power to administer oaths and, if taken out of the United States, before any foreign minister, secretary of legation, consul or vice consul, appointed by the United States, or any person by him appointed for the purpose and having authority under the laws of the country where the deposition is to be taken; and the official character of any such person may be proved by a certificate from the secretary of state of the United States. All witnesses or parties giving depositions shall be cautioned to speak the whole truth and shall be carefully examined, and shall subscribe their depositions, and make oath before the authority taking the same, who shall attest the same and certify whether or not each adverse party or his agent was present, and whether or not he was notified, and shall also certify the reason of taking such [deposition], seal it, direct it to the court where it is to be used and deliver it if desired to the party at whose request it was taken. The party on whose behalf the deposition of an adverse party is taken shall be subject to having his deposition taken on behalf of such adverse party.

DELAWARE

[DEL. R. CIV. P. 28]

Persons Before Whom Depositions May Be Taken

(a) **Within the United States.** Within the United States or within a territory or insular possession subject to the dominion of the United States, depositions shall be taken (1) before an officer authorized to administer oaths by the laws of the place where the examination is held, or (2) before such person or officer as may be appointed by commission or under letters rogatory.

(b) **In Foreign Countries.** In a foreign country, depositions may be taken (1) on notice before a person authorized to administer oaths in the place in which the examination is held, either by the law thereof or by the law of the United States, or (2) before a person commissioned by the court, and a person so commissioned shall have the power by virtue of his commission to administer any necessary oath and take testimony, or (3) pursuant to a letters rogatory. A commission or a letters rogatory shall be issued on application and notice and on terms that are just and appropriate. It is not requisite to the issuance of a commission or a letter rogatory that the taking of the deposition in any other manner is impracticable or inconvenient; and both a commission and a letter rogatory may be issued in proper cases. A notice or commission may designate the person before whom the deposition is to be taken either by name or descriptive title. A letters rogatory may be addressed "To the Appropriate Authority in [here name the country]." Evidence obtained in response to a letter rogatory need not be excluded merely for the reason that it is not a verbatim transcript or that the testimony was not taken under oath or for any similar departure from the requirements for depositions taken within the United States under these rules.

(c) **Disqualification for Interest.** No deposition shall be taken before a person who is a relative or employee or attorney or counsel of any of the parties, or is a relative or employee of such attorney or counsel, or is financially interested in the action.

(d) **Designation of Officers.** The officers referred to in paragraphs (a) and (b) hereof may be designated in notices or commissions either by name or descriptive title and letters rogatory may be addressed "To the Appropriate Judicial Authority in (here name the State or Country)."

DISTRICT OF COLUMBIA

Notaries have the power to take depositions, administer oaths and affirmations, and take affidavits to be used before any court, judge, or officer within the District. See *Authority and Duties,* D.C. CODE ENCYCL. ANN. § 1-511.

[D.C. SUPER. CT. R. CIV. P. 28]

Persons Before Whom Depositions May Be Taken

(a) **Within the United States.** Within the United States or within a territory or insular possession subject to the dominion of the United States, depositions shall be taken before an officer authorized to administer oaths by the laws of the United States or of the place where the examination is held, or before a person appointed by the court. A person so appointed has power to administer oaths and take testimony.

(b) **In Foreign Countries.** In a foreign country, depositions may be taken (1) on notice before a person authorized to administer oaths in the place in which the examination is held, either by the law thereof or by the law of the United States, or (2) before a person commissioned by the court, and a person so commissioned shall have the power by virtue of his commission to administer any necessary oath and take testimony, or (3) pursuant to a letter rogatory. A commission or a letter rogatory shall be issued on application and notice and on terms that are just and appropriate. It is not requisite to the issuance of a commission or a letter rogatory that the taking of the deposition in any other manner is impracticable or inconvenient; and both a commission and a letter rogatory may be issued in proper cases. A notice or commission may designate the person before whom the deposition is to be taken either by name or descriptive title. A letter rogatory may be addressed "To the Appropriate Authority in [here name the country]." Evidence obtained in response to a letter rogatory need not be excluded merely for the reason that it is not a verbatim transcript or that the testimony was not taken under oath or for any similar departure from the requirements for depositions taken within the United States under these rules.

(c) **Disqualification for Interest.** No deposition shall be taken before a person who is a relative or employee or attorney or counsel of any of the parties, or is a relative or employee of such attorney or counsel, or is financially interested in the action.

Rule 28-1.   Persons Commissioned to Take Depositions

(a)   **By This Court.**   Any party to a civil action pending in this court may file with the court a motion for appointment of an examiner to take the testimony of a witness who resides outside the District of Columbia.   The motion shall state the name and address of each witness sought to be deposed and the reasons why the testimony of such witness is required in the action.   The motion shall be served on all other parties to the action who may within five days file opposition to the motion as prescribed in Rule 12.   If the motion is granted, the court shall appoint an examiner to take the testimony of such witnesses as are designated in the order of appointment and shall issue a commission to the examiner who shall take the testimony in the manner prescribed in these rules.

(b)   **By Another Court.**   Any person appointed by a court of a state, territory, commonwealth, possession, or place under the jurisdiction of the United States to take the testimony of a witness found within the District of Columbia for use in an action pending in such court may cause to be filed with this court a copy of his commission or other evidence of authority together with a motion for leave of court to take the designated testimony.   If the motion and evidence of authority so filed are in order, the court shall grant the motion and may, upon application, issue a subpoena compelling the designated witness to present himself for deposition at a specified time and place.   Testimony taken under this section shall be taken in the manner prescribed in these rules and the court may entertain any motion, including motions for quashing service of a subpoena and for issuance of protective orders, in the same manner as if the action were pending in this court.

FLORIDA

[FLA. R. CIV. P. 1.300]

Persons Before Whom Depositions May Be Taken

(a)   **Persons Authorized.**   Depositions may be taken before any notary public or judicial officer or before any officer authorized by the statutes of Florida to take acknowledgments or proof of executions of deeds or by any person appointed by the court in which the action is pending.

(b)   **In Foreign Countries.**   In a foreign country depositions may be taken (1) on notice before a person authorized to administer oaths in the place in which the examination is held, either by the law thereof or by the law of Florida or of the United States or (2) before a person commissioned by the court, and a person so commissioned shall have the power by virtue of his commission to administer any necessary oath and take testimony or (3) pursuant to a letter rogatory. A commission or a letter rogatory shall be issued on application and notice and on terms that are just and appropriate. It is not requisite to the issuance of a commission or a letter rogatory that the taking of the deposition in any other manner is impracticable or inconvenient and both a commission and a letter rogatory may be issued in proper cases. A notice or commission may designate the person before whom the deposition is to be taken either by name or descriptive title. A letter rogatory may be addressed "To the Appropriate Authority in (herein name the country)." Evidence obtained in response to a letter rogatory need not be excluded merely for the reason that it is not a verbatim transcript or that the testimony was not taken under oath or any similar departure from the requirements for depositions taken within Florida under these rules.

(c) **Selection by Stipulation.** If the parties so stipulate in writing, depositions may be taken before any person at any time or place upon any notice and in any manner and when so taken may be used like other depositions.

(d) **Persons Disqualified.** Unless so stipulated by the parties no deposition shall be taken before a person who is a relative or employee or attorney or counsel of any of the parties or is a relative or employee of such attorney or counsel or is financially interested in the action.

GEORGIA

[GA. CODE ANN.]

§ 81-407. **Before whom oath to plea, answer, or defense may be made.** All answers, pleas or defenses in any court of this State, which have to be filed under oath, shall be held to be sufficiently verified when the same are sworn to before any notary public, justice of the peace, judge of a court of law, or chancellor, commissioner, or master of any court of equity of the State or county where the oath is made, or before any other officer of such State or county who is authorized by the laws thereof to administer oaths; and such oath so made shall have the same force and effect as if it had been made before an officer of this State authorized to administer the same. The official attestation of the officer before whom the oath or affidavit may be made shall be prima facie evidence of the official character of such officer and that he was authorized by law to administer oaths.

§ 81-408. **Verification by nonresident.** When a petition, answer, or other proceeding is required to be verified by a petition or defendant who resides or is temporarily beyond the limits of this State, an affidavit made before any commissioner of this State, or any commissioner, or master, or judge of any court of the State where made, authorized to administer an oath, or before a notary public or justice of the peace of the State and county where the oath is made, shall be a sufficient verification. The official attestation of the officer, before whom the oath or affidavit shall be made, shall be prima facie evidence of the official character of such officer and that he was authorized by law to administer oaths.

§ 81-409. **Affidavits made out of this State.** An affidavit made out of this State, before a notary public, justice of the peace, judge of a court of law, or chancellor, commissioner, or master of any court of equity of the State or county where the oath is made, or before any other officer of such State or county who is authorized by the laws thereof to administer oaths, shall have the same force and effect, and be recognized in like manner, as if it had been made before an officer of this State authorized to administer the same. The official attestation of the officer before whom the oath or affidavit may be made shall be prima facie evidence of the official character of such officer, and that he was authorized by law to administer oaths: Provided, that this section shall not apply to such affidavits as are expressly required by statute to be made before some particular officer within the State.

§ 81A-128. **Persons before whom depositions may be taken.** (a) **Within the United States or within a territory or insular possession subject to the dominion of the United States,** depositions shall be taken before an officer authorized to administer oaths by the laws of the United States or of the place where the examination is held, or before a person appointed by the court in which action is pending. A person so appointed has power to administer oaths and take testimony.

(b) **In foreign countries.** In a foreign State or Country depositions shall be taken (1) on notice before a secretary of embassy or legation, consul general, consul, vice-consul, or consular agent of the United States, or (2) before such person or officer as may be appointed by commission or under letters rogatory. A commission or letters rogatory shall be issued only when necessary or convenient, on application and notice, and on such terms and with such directions as are just and appropriate. Officers may be designated in notices or commissions either by name or descriptive title and letters rogatory may be addressed "To the Appropriate Judicial Authority in (here name the Country)."

(c) **Disqualification for interest.** No deposition shall be taken before a person who is a relative or employee or attorney or counsel of any of the parties, or is a relative or employee of such attorney or counsel, or is financially interested in the action, unless such disqualification is waived in writing by all parties to the action.

HAWAII

Every notary public may administer oaths in all cases in which oaths are by law authorized or required to be taken or administered, or in which the administering of an oath may be proper. See *Authority and Duties,* HAWAII REV. STAT. § 456-13. Notaries public are required to record at length in a book of records, among other things, all depositions noted or done in their official capacity. See *Records,* HAWAII REV. STAT. § 456-15.

[HAWAII R. CIV. P. 28]

Persons Before Whom Depositions May Be Taken

(a) **Within the United States.** Within the United States or within a territory or insular possession subject to the dominion of the United States, depositions shall be taken before an officer authorized to administer oaths by the laws of this State or of the United States or of the place where the examination is held, or before a person appointed by the court in which the action is pending. A person so appointed has power to administer oaths and take testimony.

(b) **In Foreign Countries.** In a foreign country, depositions may be taken (1) on notice before a person authorized to administer oaths in the place in which the examination is held, either by the law thereof or by the law of the United States, or (2) before a person commissioned by the court, and a person so commissioned shall have the power by virtue of his commission to administer any necessary oath and take testimony, or (3) pursuant to a letter rogatory. A commission or a letter rogatory shall be issued on application and notice and on terms that are just and appropriate. It is not requisite to the issuance of a commission or a letter rogatory that the taking of the deposition in any other manner is impracticable or inconvenient; and both a commission and a letter rogatory may be issued in proper cases. A notice or commission may designate the person before whom the deposition is to be taken either by name or descriptive title. A letter rogatory may be addressed "To the Appropriate Authority in [here name the country]." Evidence obtained in response to a letter rogatory need not be excluded merely for the reason that it is not a verbatim transcript or that the testimony was not taken under oath or for any similar departure from the requirements for depositions taken within the United States under these rules.

(c) **Disqualification for Interest.** No deposition shall be taken before a person who is a relative or employee or attorney or counsel of any of the parties, or is a relative or employee of such attorney or counsel, or is financially interested in the action.

IDAHO
Affidavits

[IDAHO CODE]

§ 9-804. **Affidavit—before whom taken.** An affidavit to be used before any court, judge or officer of this state, may be taken before any judge or clerk of any court, or notary public in this state, or United States commissioner.

§ 9-805. **Affidavits in other states—before whom taken.** An affidavit taken in another state or territory of the United States, to be used in this state, may be taken before a commissioner appointed by the governor of this state to take affidavits and depositions in such state or territory, or before any notary public in such state or territory, or before any judge or clerk of a court of record having a seal.

§ 9-806. **Affidavits in foreign country—before whom taken.** An affidavit taken in a foreign country to be used in this state, may be taken before an ambassador, minister, consul, vice consul or consular agent of the United States, or before any judge of a court of record having a seal, in such foreign country.

§ 9-807. **Affidavits taken outside of state—certificate of clerk.** When an affidavit is taken before a judge or a court in another state or territory, or in a foreign country, the genuineness of the signature of the judge, the existence of the court, and the fact that such judge is a member thereof, must be certified by the clerk of the court, under the seal thereof.

Depositions

§ 9-901. **Depositions within or without state—fees—amount—Taxation as costs.** Depositions of witnesses, taken within or without the state, may be taken according to the regulations hereinafter provided, before any judge, justice of the peace, notary public, clerk or a court of record, or commissioner appointed by the court to take depositions; but depositions shall not be taken before any person or the kin of any person interested in the action. The officer taking such deposition shall charge and collect a fee of five dollars, and when such deposition shall exceed twenty-five folios of one hundred words each written or transcribed in the taking thereof, then he shall charge and collect a further fee of twenty cents for each such folio, in excess of twenty-five folios, in addition thereto, including the certificate and seal and such fees shall be taxed as a part of the costs in the action.

§ 9-909. **Powers of officer taking deposition—contempt.** The officer taking the deposition shall have power to summon and compel the attendance of witnesses. In case of the refusal of a witness to attend or testify, such fact shall be reported by the officer to any probate or district court of the county, or the judge thereof, and such court or judge shall order such witness to attend and testify; and on the failure or refusal to obey such order, such witness shall be dealt with as for a contempt.

§ 9-910. **Application of preceding section.** The provisions of the last section shall extend to all officers and commissioners authorized to take depositions in this state to be read in the courts of other states or countries.

§ 9-911. **Swearing and examination of witness.** The deponent shall first be sworn by the officer to testify to the truth, the whole truth, and nothing but the truth relating to the cause or matter for which the deposition is to be taken; and he shall then be examined by the party producing him, and then by the adverse party, and by the officer or parties afterward if they see cause.

§ 9-912. **Writing, reading and signing depositions.** The deposition shall be written down by the officer, or by the deponent, or by some disinterested person, in the presence and under the direction of the officer; and after the same has been carefully read to or by the deponent, it shall be subscribed by him.

§ 9-913. **Certificate of officer.** The officer shall annex his certificate to the deposition stating the following facts:

1. That the deponent was sworn according to law.

2. By whom the deposition was written, and if written by the deponent or some disinterested person, that it was written in the presence and under the direction of the officer.

3. Whether or not the adverse party attended.

4. The time and place of taking the deposition, and the hours between which the same was taken. And the officer shall sign and attest the certificate, and seal the same, if he have a seal of office.

§ 9-914. **Transmission of deposition to clerk.** The officer taking the deposition shall seal up the same in a secure envelope, and direct the same to the clerk of the court in which the action is pending, indorsing upon the envelope the names of the parties and of the witnesses whose deposition are inclosed.

§ 9-916. **Commission to take deposition.** When a deposition is to be taken within or without the state, but within the United States, no commission shall be necessary for taking the deposition. When taken out of the United States, the clerk shall, upon the request of the party taking the deposition, issue a commission to the officer or commissioner designated to take the deposition. No order of the court or affidavit shall be necessary to authorize the issuing of the commission.

§ 9-917. **Authentication of commissioner's certificate.** When the commission contains the name of the officer before whom the deposition is to be taken, his attestation, officially certifying the same, shall be sufficient; but if the commission do not specify the name of the officer, and he have no official seal, his certificate shall be authenticated by the certificate and seal of the clerk prothonotary of any court of record of the county in which the officer exercises the duties of his office.

§ 9-918. Filing of deposition. Every deposition intended to be read in evidence must be filed in the court at least one day before the time at which the cause in which the deposition is to be used stands on the docket for trial; or, if filed afterward and claimed to be used on the trial, the adverse party shall be entitled to a continuance, at the cost of the party filing the deposition, upon showing good cause by affidavit.

§ 9-927. Commission issued—subpoenas for witnesses. If a commission to take such testimony has been issued from the court or judge before whom such action or proceeding is pending, on producing the commission to a judge, with an affidavit satisfactory to him of the materiality of the testimony, he may issue a subpoena to the witness, requiring him to appear and testify before the commissioner named in the commission, at a specified time and place.

§ 9-928. Commission not issued—subpoena for witnesses. If a commission has not been issued, and it appears to a judge by affidavit satisfactory to him:

1.   That the testimony of the witness is material to either party;

2.   That a commission to take the testimony of such witness has not been issued;

3.   That according to the law of the state or territory where the action or special proceeding is pending, the deposition of a witness taken under such circumstances, and before such judge, will be received in the action or proceeding;

He must issue his subpoena, requiring the witness to appear and testify before him at a specified time and place.

Oaths and Affirmations

§ 9-1401. Who may administer oaths. Every court, every judge or clerk of any court, every justice and every notary public, the secretary of state, and every officer or person authorized to take testimony in any action or proceeding, or to decide upon evidence, has power to administer oaths or affirmations.

§ 9-1402. Form of oath. An oath or affirmation in an action or proceeding, may be administered as follows, the person who swears or affirms, expressing his assent when addressed, in the following form:

You do solemnly swear (or affirm, as the case may be), that the evidence you shall give in the issue (or matter), pending between ———— and ————, shall be the truth, the whole truth, and nothing but the truth, so help you God.

§ 9-1403. Peculiar forms of oaths. Whenever the court before which a person is offered as a witness is satisfied that he has a peculiar mode of swearing, connected with, or in addition to, the usual form of administration, which, in his opinion, is more solemn or obligatory, the court may, in its discretion, adopt that mode.

§ 9-1404. **Peculiar forms of oath—religions other than Christian.** When a person is sworn who believes in any other than the Christian religion, he may be sworn according to the peculiar ceremonies of his religion, if there be any such.

§ 9-1405. **Affirmation in place of oath.** Any person who desires it, may, at his option, instead of taking an oath, make his solemn affirmation or declaration, by assenting when addressed, in the following form: "You do solemnly affirm (or declare), that," etc., as above provided.

Commissions to Examine Witnesses

§ 19-3201. **Examination of nonresident witness.** When an issue of fact is joined upon an indictment the defendant may have any material witness, residing out of the state, examined in his behalf, as prescribed in this chapter, and not otherwise.

§ 19-3202. **Application for order.** When a material witness for the defendant resides out of the state the defendant may apply for an order that the witness be examined on a commission.

§ 19-3203. **Commission defined.** A commission is a process issued under the seal of the court and the signature of the clerk, directed to some person designated as commissioner, authorizing him to examine the witness upon oath or interrogatories annexed thereto, to take and certify the deposition of the witness, and to return it according to the directions given with the commission.

§ 19-3209. **Execution of commission.** The commissioner, unless otherwise specially directed, may execute the commission as follows:

1. He must publicly administer an oath to the witness, that his answers given to the interrogatories shall be the truth, the whole truth and nothing but the truth.

2. He must cause the examination of the witness to be reduced to writing, and subscribed by him.

3. He must write the answers of the witness as near as possible in the language in which he gives them, and read to him each answer as it is taken down, and correct or add to it until it conforms to what he declares is the truth.

4. If the witness decline answering a question, that fact, with the reason assigned by him for declining, must be stated.

5. If any papers or documents are produced before him and proved by the witness, they, or copies of them, must be annexed to the deposition subscribed by the witness and certified by the commissioner.

6. The commissioner must subscribe his name to each sheet of the deposition, and annex the deposition, with the papers and documents, proved by the witness, to the commission, and must close it up under seal, and address it as directed by the indorsement thereon.

7. If there is a direction on the commission to return it by mail, the commissioner must immediately deposit it in the nearest post-office. If any other direction is made by the written consent of the parties, or by the court or judge, on the commission, as to its return, he must comply with the direction. A copy of this section must be annexed to the commission.

Rules of Civil Procedure

[IDAHO R. CIV. P. 28]

(a). **Persons before whom depositions may be taken—within the United States.** Within the state of Idaho, depositions shall be taken before a person authorized by the laws of this state to administer oaths; without the state, but within the United States, or within a territory or insular possession subject to the dominion of the United States, depositions shall be taken before a person authorized to administer oaths by the laws of this state, by the United States, or of the place where the examination is held; within or without the state of Idaho, depositions may also be taken before a person appointed by the court in which the action is pending, which person so appointed shall have the power to administer oaths and take testimony.

(b). **Taking in foreign countries.** In a foreign state or country depositions shall be taken (1) before a secretary of embassy or legation, consul, vice consul, or consular agent of the United States, or any officer authorized to administer oaths under the laws of this state, or of the United States or (2) before a person appointed by the court. The officer or person is empowered to administer oaths and take testimony. A commission shall be issued only when necessary or convenient, on application and notice, and on such terms and with such directions as are just and appropriate. Officers may be designated in notices or commissions either by name or descriptive title.

(c). **Disqualification for interest.** No deposition shall be taken before a person who is a relative or employee or attorney or counsel of any of the parties, or is a relative or employee of such attorney or counsel, or is financially interested in the action.

ILLINOIS

[ILL. ANN. STAT.—Smith-Hurd]

Ch. 101, § 1. Administration of oaths to witnesses and others— persons empowered. All courts, and all judges and the clerk thereof, the county clerk, deputy county clerk, and notaries public, have power to administer oaths and affirmations to witnesses and others, concerning anything commenced or to be commenced, or pending before them respectively.

§ 2. Administration of oath of office—affidavits and depositions— persons empowered. All courts, and judges, and the clerks thereof, the county clerk, deputy county clerk, the Secretary of State and notaries public, may, in their respective districts, circuits, counties or jurisdictions, administer all oaths of office and all other oaths authorized or required of any officer or other person, and take affidavits and depositions concerning any matter or thing, process or proceeding commenced or to be commenced, or pending in any court or before them, or on any occasion wherein any affidavit or deposition is authorized or required by law to be taken.

The same functions may be performed by any commissioned officer in active service of the armed forces of the United States, within or without the United States. Oaths, affidavits or depositions taken by or affirmations made before such officers need not be authenticated nor attested by any seal nor shall any instruments executed or proceedings had before such officers be invalid because the place of the proceedings or of the execution is not stated.

Ch. 110A, § 205. Persons before whom depositions may be taken.

(a) **Within the United States.** Within the United States or within a territory or insular possession subject to the dominion of the United States, depositions shall be taken (1) before an officer authorized to administer oaths by the laws of this state or of the United States or of the place where the examination is held, or (2) before a person appointed by the court. The officer or person is empowered to administer oaths and take testimony. Whenever the term "officer" is used in these rules, it includes a person appointed by the court unless the context indicates otherwise.

(b) **In foreign countries.** In a foreign state or country depositions shall be taken (1) before a secretary of embassy, consul general, consul, vice consul, or consular agent of the United States, or any officer authorized to administer oaths under the laws of this state, or of the United States, or of the place where the examination is held, or (2) before a person appointed by the court. The officer or person is empowered to administer oaths and take testimony.

(c) **Issuance of Commissions and Letters Rogatory.** A commission, dedimus potestatem, or letter rogatory is not required but if desired shall be issued by the clerk without notice. An officer may be designated in a commission either by name or descriptive title and a letter rogatory may be addressed "To the Appropriate Authority in (here name the country)."

(d) **Disqualification for Interest.** No deposition shall be taken before a person who is a relative of or attorney for any of the parties, a relative of the attorney, or financially interested in the action.

INDIANA

[IND. CODE]

§ 33-15-24-1. Court reporters administering oaths—bond—seal. Every official reporter appointed under "An act concerning the appointment of shorthand court reporters, regulating their duties, fixing their compensation, and providing that the original longhand manuscript may be used on appeal, and repealing all laws in conflict therewith, and declaring an emergency," approved March 3, 1899, and the acts amendatory thereto, which reporter receives a fixed annual salary, is hereby authorized and empowered to take and certify all acknowledgments of deeds, mortgages, or other instruments of writing required or authorized by law to be acknowledged, to administer oaths generally, take and certify affidavits, examinations and depositions, and perform any duty now conferred upon a notary public by the statutes of the state of Indiana. Any such official reporter taking such examinations and depositions shall have the right to take them in shorthand, the same to be afterwards transcribed by him into typewriting or longhand, and signed by the deposing witness. Before performing any official duty as hereinbefore authorized, such official reporter shall provide a bond as is now required by law for notary publics, and shall procure a seal which will stamp upon paper a distinct impression in words and letters indicating his official character, to which may be added such other device as he may choose.

[IND. TRIAL RULE 28]

Persons before whom depositions may be taken; ° ° °

(A) Within the United States. Within the United States or within a territory or insular possession subject to the dominion of the United States, depositions shall be taken before an officer authorized to administer oaths by the laws of the United States, or of the state of Indiana, or of the place where the examination is held, or before a person appointed by the court in which the action is pending. A person so appointed has power to administer oaths and take testimony.

(B) In foreign countries. In a foreign country, depositions may be taken:

(1) on notice before a person authorized to administer oaths in the place in which the examination is held, either by the law thereof or by the law of the United States; or

(2) before a person commissioned by the court, and a person so commissioned shall have the power by virtue of his commission to administer any necessary oath and take testimony; or

(3) pursuant to a letter rogatory.

A commission or a letter rogatory shall be issued on application and notice and on terms that are just and appropriate. It is not requisite to the issuance of a commission or a letter rogatory that the taking of the deposition in any other manner is impracticable or inconvenient; and both a commission and a letter rogatory may be issued in proper cases. A notice or commission may designate the person before whom the deposition is to be taken either by name or descriptive title. A letter rogatory may be addressed "To the Appropriate Authority in (here name the country)." Evidence obtained in response to a letter rogatory need not be excluded merely for the reason that it is not a verbatim transcript or that the testimony was not taken under oath or for any similar departure from the requirements for depositions taken within the United States under these rules.

(C) **Disqualification for interest.** Unless otherwise permitted by these rules, no deposition shall be taken before a person who is a relative or employee or attorney or counsel of any of the parties, or is a relative or employee of such attorney or counsel, or is financially interested in the action.

o   o   o

IOWA

[IOWA CODE ANN.]

§ 622.84. **Subpoenas—enforcing obedience.** When, by the laws of this or any other state or country, testimony may be taken in the form of depositions to be used in any of the courts thereof, the person authorized to take such depositions may issue subpoenas for witnesses, which must be served by the same officers and returned in the same manner as is required in district court, and obedience thereto may be enforced in the same way and to the same extent, or he may report the matter to the district court who may enforce obedience as though the action was pending in said court.

§ 622.102. **Refusal to appear or testify.** Any witness who refuses to obey such subpoena or after appearance refuses to testify shall be reported by the officer or commissioner to the district court of the county where the subpoena was issued.

Interpreters

§ 622A.1. **Definition.** As used in this chapter, "legal proceeding" means any action before any court, or any legal action preparatory to appearing before any court, whether civil or criminal in nature; and any administrative proceeding before any state agency or governmental subdivision which is quasi-judicial in nature and which has direct legal implications to any person.

§ 622A.2. **Who entitled to interpreter.** Every person who cannot speak or understand the English language, or every person who because of hearing, speaking or other impairment has difficulty in communicating with other persons, and who is a party to any legal proceeding or a witness therein, shall be entitled to an interpreter to assist such person throughout the proceeding.

Court Rules

[IOWA R. CIV. P. 148]

Conduct of Oral Examination

(a) **Examination and cross-examination; record of examination; oath; objections.** Examination and cross-examination of witnesses may proceed as permitted at the trial. The officer before whom the deposition is to be taken shall put the witness on oath and shall personally, or by someone acting under his direction and in his presence, record the testimony of the witness. The testimony shall be taken stenographically or recorded by any other means ordered in accordance with rule 140 "b" (4). If requested by one of the parties, the testimony shall be transcribed. All objections made at the time of the examination to the qualifications of the officer taking the deposition, or to the manner of taking it, or to the evidence presented, or to the conduct of any party, and any other objection to the proceedings, shall be noted by the officer upon the deposition. Evidence objected to shall be taken subject to the objections. In lieu of participating in the oral examination, parties may serve written questions in a sealed envelope on the party taking the deposition and he shall transmit them to the officer, who shall propound them to the witness and record the answers verbatim.

(b) **Motion to terminate or limit examination.** At any time during the taking of the deposition, on motion of a party or of the deponent and upon a showing that the examination is being conducted in bad faith or in such manner as unreasonably to annoy, embarrass, or oppress the deponent or party, the court in which the action is pending or the court in the district where the deposition is being taken may order the officer conducting the examination to cease forthwith from taking the deposition, or may limit the scope and manner of the taking of the deposition as provided in rule 123. If the order made terminates the examination, it shall be resumed thereafter only upon the order of the court in which the action is pending. Upon demand of the objecting party or deponent, the taking of the deposition shall be suspended for the time necessary to make a motion for an order. The provisions of rule 134 "a" (4) apply to the award of expenses incurred in relation to the motion.

Rule 149. Reading and Signing

(a) No oral deposition reported and transcribed by an official court reporter or certified shorthand reporter of Iowa need be submitted to, read or signed by the deponent.

(b) Submission to witness—changes, signing. In other cases, when the testimony is fully transcribed the deposition shall be submitted to the witness for examination and shall be read to or by him, unless such examination and reading are waived by the witness and by the parties. Any changes in form or substance which the witness desires to make shall be entered upon the deposition by the officer with a statement of the reasons given by the witness for making them. If rule 149 "a" is not applicable, the deposition shall then be signed by the witness, unless the parties by stipulation waive the signing or the witness is ill or dead or cannot be found or refuses to sign. If the deposition is not signed by the witness within 30 days of its submission to him, the officer shall sign it and state on the record the fact of the waiver or of the illness, death, or absence of the witness or the fact of the refusal to sign together with the reason, if any, given therefor; and the deposition may then be used as fully as though signed unless on a motion to suppress under rule 158 "f" the court holds that the reasons given for the refusal to sign require rejection of the deposition in whole or in part.

Rule 151. Answers to Interrogatories

The party taking a deposition on written interrogatories shall promptly transmit a copy of the notice and all interrogatories to the officer designated in the notice. The officer shall promptly take deponent's answers thereto and complete the deposition, all as provided in rules 148 and 149, except that answers need not be taken stenographically.

Rule 152. Certification and Return—Copies

(a) The officer shall certify on the deposition that the witness was duly sworn by him and that the deposition is a true record of the testimony given by the witness. He shall then securely seal the deposition in an envelope endorsed with the title of the action and marked "Deposition of (here insert name of witness)" and shall promptly file it with the court in which the action is pending or send it by registered or certified mail to the clerk thereof for filing. Documents and things produced for inspection during the examination of the witness shall, upon the request of a party, be marked for identification and annexed to and returned with the deposition, and may be inspected and copied by any party, except that

(1) the person producing the materials may substitute copies to be marked for identification, if he affords to all parties fair opportunity to verify the copies by comparison with the originals, and

(2) if the person producing the materials requests their return, the officer shall mark them, give each party an opportunity to inspect

and copy them, and return them to the person producing them, and the materials may then be used in the same manner as if annexed to and returned with the deposition. Any party may move for an order that the original be annexed to and returned with the deposition to the court, pending final disposition of the case.

(b) The clerk shall immediately give notice of the filing of all depositions to all parties who have appeared in the action.

(c) Upon payment of reasonable charges therefor, the officer shall furnish a copy of the deposition to any party or to the deponent.

Rule 153. Before Whom Taken

(a) No deposition shall be taken before any party, or any person financially interested in the action, or an attorney or employee of any party, or any person related by consanguinity or affinity within the fourth degree to any party, his attorney, or an employee of either of them.

(b) Depositions within the United States or a territory or insular possession thereof may be taken before any person authorized to administer oaths, by the laws of the United States or of the place where the examination is held.

(c) Depositions in a foreign land may be taken before a secretary of embassy or legation, or a consul, vice-consul, consul-general or consular agent of the United States, or under rule 154.

(d) When the witness is in the military or naval service of the United States, his deposition may be taken before any commissioned officer under whose command he is serving, or any commissioned officer in the judge advocate general's department.

Rule 154. Letters Rogatory

A commission or letters rogatory to take depositions in a foreign land shall be issued only when convenient or necessary, on application and notice, and on such terms and with such directions as are just and appropriate. They shall specify the officer to take the deposition, by name or descriptive title, and may be addressed: "To the Appropriate Judicial Authority of (country)."

Rule 155. Subpoena

(a) On application of any party, or proof of service of a notice to take depositions under rule 147 or rule 150, the clerk of court where the action is pending shall issue subpoenas for persons named in and described in said notice or application. Subpoenas may also be issued as provided by statute:

(b) No resident of Iowa shall be thus subpoenaed to attend out of the county where he resides, or is employed, or transacts his business in person.

(c) A subpoena may also command the person to whom it is directed to produce the books, papers, documents or tangible things designated therein; but the court, upon motion promptly made by the person to whom the subpoena is directed, or by any other person stating an interest in the documents affected, and in any event at or before the time specified in the subpoena for compliance therewith, may

(1) Quash or modify the subpoena if it is unreasonable and oppressive or

(2) Condition denial of the motion upon the advancement by the person in whose behalf the subpoena is issued of the reasonable cost of producing the books, papers, documents or tangible things.

KANSAS

[KAN. STAT. ANN.]

§ 54-101. Officers authorized to administer oaths. Notaries public, judges of courts in their respective jurisdictions, mayors of cities and towns in their respective cities and towns, clerks of courts of record, county clerks, and registers of deeds, are hereby authorized to administer oaths pertaining to all matters wherein an oath is required.

§ 54-102. How administered. All oaths shall be administered by laying the right hand upon the Holy Bible, or by the uplifted right hand.

§ 54-103. Persons having conscientious scruples may affirm. Any person having conscientious scruples against taking an oath, may affirm with like effect.

§ 54-104. Form of commencement and conclusion of oaths. All oaths shall commence and conclude as follows: "You do solemnly swear," etc.; "So help you God."

Affirmation shall commence and conclude as follows: "You do solemnly, sincerely and truly declare and affirm," etc.; "And this you do under the pains and penalties of perjury."

§ 54-105. Falsifying oaths or affirmations. All oaths and affirmations alike subject the party who shall falsify them to the pains and penalties of perjury.

Rules of Civil Procedure

§ 60-228. Persons before whom depositions may be taken. *(a) Within the United States.* (1) Depositions may be taken in this state before any officer or person authorized to administer oaths by the laws of this state. (2) Without the state but within the United States, or within a territory or insular possession subject to the dominion of the United States, depositions shall be taken before an officer authorized to administer oaths by the laws of the place where the examination is held, or before a person appointed by the court in which the action is pending. A person so appointed has power to administer oaths and take testimony. (3) Any court of record of this state, or any judge thereof, before whom an action or proceeding is pending, is authorized to grant a commission to take depositions within or without the state. The commission may be issued by the clerk to a person or persons therein named, under the seal of the court granting the same.

(b) *In foreign countries.* In a foreign country, depositions may be taken (1) on notice before a person authorized to administer oaths in the place where the examination is held, either by the law of the United States or the law of that place, or (2) before a person appointed by commission, or (3) under letters rogatory. A person appointed by commission has power by virtue of his appointment to administer oaths and take testimony. A commission or letters rogatory shall be issued on application and notice, and on terms and directions that are just and appropriate. It is not requisite to the issuance of letters rogatory that the taking of the deposition by commission or on notice is impracticable or inconvenient; and both a commission and letters rogatory may be issued in proper cases. A notice or commission may designate the person before whom the deposition is to be taken either by name or descriptive title. Letters rogatory may be addressed "To the Appropriate Judicial Authority in (here name the country)." Evidence obtained under letters rogatory shall not be excluded on the ground that it is not in the form of questions and answers or is not a verbatim transcript of the testimony.

(c) *Disqualification for interest.* No deposition shall be taken before a person who is a relative or employee or attorney or counsel of any of the parties, or is a relative or employee of such attorney or counsel, or is financially interested in the action.

(d) *Depositions for use in foreign jurisdictions.* Whenever the deposition of any person is to be taken in this state pursuant to the laws of another state or of the United States or of another country for use in proceedings there, the district court in the county where the deponent resides or is employed or transacts his business in person may, upon *ex parte* petition, make an order directing issuance of a subpoena as provided in section 60-245, in aid of the taking of the deposition, and may make any order in accordance with sections 60-230 (d), 60-237 (a) or 60-237 (b) (1).

KENTUCKY

[KY. R. CIV. P. 28]

PERSONS BEFORE WHOM DEPOSITIONS MAY BE TAKEN

Rule 28.01. Within the state. Depositions taken in this State, to be used in its courts, shall be taken before an examiner; a

judge, clerk, commissioner or official reporter of a court; a justice of the peace; a notary public; or before such other persons
and under such other circumstances as shall be authorized by law.

Rule 28.02. Without the state. Depositions may be taken out
of this State before a commissioner appointed by the Governor of the state where taken; or before any person empowered
by a commission directed to him by consent of the parties or
by order of the court; or before a judge of a court, a justice
of the peace, mayor of a city, or notary public; or before such
persons and under such other circumstances as shall be authorized
by the law of this State or the place where the deposition is taken.

Rule 28.03. Deposition to be used in other states. A party
desiring to take depositions in this State to be used in proceedings
outside this State, may produce to a judge of the county court
of the county where the witness resides a commission authorizing
the taking of such depositions or proof of notice duly served;
whereupon it shall be the duty of the judge to issue, pursuant to
Rule 45, the necessary subpoenas. Orders of the character provided in Rule 45.02 may be made upon proper application therefor
by the person to whom such a subpoena is directed. Failure by any
person without adequate excuse to obey a subpoena served upon
him pursuant to this rule may be deemed a contempt of the court
from which the subpoena issued.

LOUISIANA

[LA. CODE CIV. PRO. ANN.—West]

Art. 1423. Person before whom deposition taken. A deposition shall be taken before an officer authorized to administer
oaths, who is not an employee or attorney of any of the parties
or otherwise interested in the outcome of the case.

Certified Shorthand Reporters

[LA. REV. STAT.]

§ 37:2554. Qualifications; examinations; certificates A. The board
[of examiners] shall determine the qualifications of persons applying for examination under this Chapter, make rules for the examination of applicants and the issuance of certificates herein
provided for, and shall grant certificates to such applicants as may,
upon examination, be qualified in professional shorthand reporting and
in such other subjects as the board may deem advisable.

B. The board may, at its discretion, waive regular examination
of any person duly holding a comparable C.S.R. certificate from
another state and desiring to move to Louisiana as a verbatim
reporter.

C. No certificate holder shall be restricted from changing to any other shorthand system as defined in R.S. 37:2555, if he has at least five years previous experience as a verbatim shorthand reporter.

D. The board shall in no way restrict the use of electronic equipment to certificate holders hereunder in the performance of their duties, but shall exclude the use of all electronic recording equipment, including stenomask, to all applicants at the time and place of examination.

E. Every certificate holder hereunder shall be deemed a certified shorthand reporter, entitled to use the abbreviation "C.S.R." after his name, and without extra charge shall receive from the board, and may keep while his certificate remains in effect, a metal seal imprinting his name and "Certified Shorthand Reporter of the parish of ————, Louisiana," being the parish having the population of over four hundred fifty thousand in which said holder is certified to practice. Such certificate and seal shall authorize the holder thereof to issue affidavits with respect to his regular duties, to subpoena witnesses for depositions, to administer oaths and affirmations and to take depositions and sworn statements throughout such parish.

F. ° ° °

§ 37:2555. **Shorthand reporting defined.** The practice of shorthand is defined as the making, by written symbols or abbreviations in shorthand or machine writing, or stenomask voice recording, of a verbatim record of any oral court proceeding, public hearing, deposition or proceeding.

MAINE

[ME. REV. STAT. ANN.]

Tit. 4, § 202. **Oaths and acknowledgments; nominations of guardians.** All oaths required to be taken by executors, administrators, trustees or guardians, and all oaths required of commissioners of insolvency, appraisers and dividers of estates, or of any other persons in relation to any proceeding in the probate court, or to perpetuate the evidence of the publication of any order of notice, or of any notice of the time and place of sale of real estate by license of a judicial or probate court, may be administered by the judge or register of probate, by any justice of the peace or notary public. A certificate thereof, when taken out of court, shall be returned into the registry of probate and there filed. When any person of whom such oath is required, including any person making an affidavit in support of a claim against an estate, or any parent acknowledging consent to an adoption, or any child over 14 years of age nominating his guardian, resides temporarily or permanently without the State, the oath or acknowledgment may be taken before and said nomination may be certified by a notary public without the State, a commissioner for the State of Maine or a United States Consul.

[ME. R. CIV. P. 28]

PERSONS BEFORE WHOM DEPOSITIONS MAY BE TAKEN

(a) **Within the State.** Within the state depositions shall be taken before a justice of the peace or notary public or a person appointed by the court. A person so appointed has power to administer oaths and take testimony.

(b) **Outside the State.** Within another state, or within a territory or insular possession subject to the dominion of the United States, or in a foreign country, depositions may be taken (1) on notice before a person authorized to administer oaths in the place in which the examination is held, either by the law thereof or by the law of the United States, or (2) before a person appointed or commissioned by the court, and such a person shall have the power by virtue of his appointment or commission to administer any necessary oath and take testimony, or (3) pursuant to a letter rogatory. A commission or a letter rogatory shall be issued on application and notice and on terms that are just and appropriate. It is not requisite to the issuance of a commission or a letter rogatory that the taking of the deposition in any other manner is impracticable or inconvenient; and both a commission and a letter rogatory may be issued in proper cases. A notice or commission may designate the person before whom the deposition is to be taken either by name or descriptive title. A letter rogatory may be addressed "To the Appropriate Authority in (here name the state, territory or country)." Evidence obtained in a foreign country in response to a letter rogatory need not be excluded merely for the reason that it is not a verbatim transcript or that the testimony was not taken under oath or for any similar departure from the requirements for depositions taken within the United States under these rules.

(c) **Disqualification for Interest.** No deposition shall be taken before a person who is a relative or employee or attorney or counsel of any of the parties, or is a relative or employee of such attorney or counsel, or is financially interested in the action.

(d) **Depositions for Use in Foreign Jurisdictions.** Whenever the deposition of any person is to be taken in this state pursuant to the laws of another state or of the United States or of another country for use in proceedings there, the Superior Court in the county where the deponent resides or is employed or transacts his business in person may, upon petition, make an order directing issuance of a subpoena as provided in Rule 45, in aid of the taking of the deposition, and may make any order in accordance with Rule 30(d), 37(a) or 37(b)(1).

MARYLAND

[MD. ANN. CODE]

Commissioners to Take Depositions

Art. 35, § 23.   Standing commissioners.   Each of the circuit courts, or the judge thereof, shall appoint not more than three commissioners for the county in which such court is held, and each of the courts of civil jurisdiction in the City of Baltimore shall appoint two commissioners to take the depositions of witnesses.

§ 24.   Oath of commissioner.   Every commissioner so appointed, before he proceeds to act as such, shall take an oath before some judge or justice "that he will faithfully and impartially execute the duties of commissioner aforesaid, according to the best of his judgment"; a certificate of which oath shall be recorded among the records of the court by which such commissioner is appointed.

§ 25.   Fees of commissioners.   The several courts of law in this State shall from time to time prescribe what fees, shall be allowed to the commissioners for the services authorized herein, which shall be paid by the party requiring the performance of the service and taxed as other costs in the action.

§ 26.   Where and by whom depositions taken.   Any commissioner appointed by a court having common law and equity jurisdiction, whether such commissioner be appointed to take depositions in chancery or depositions to be used at law, may take depositions under this article; but no commissioner shall take depositions out of the county or city for which he was appointed, except by consent of the parties in writing, to be returned with the commission.

Commissions to Take Evidence From Other States

§ 31.   Manner of obtaining testimony and production of books and papers.   A party to any civil action, suit or special proceeding, pending in a court without this State, either in any state, district or territory of the United States or in a foreign country, may obtain in the following manner, the testimony of a witness or witnesses, and in connection therewith, the production of books and papers within this State, to be used in such action or special proceeding.

Whenever any commission, or process in the nature of a commission, to take the testimony of a witness or witnesses named therein within this State shall be issued by any court without the State, either in any state, district or territory of the United States, or in a foreign country, directed to any person designated by name, title or office or otherwise, in this State, the person so designated as commissioner shall serve notice on the witness or witnesses to be examined under said commission, of the time and place appointed for the execution of said commission at least five days before the day so appointed; and whenever the judge of the court, wherein such action, suit or special proceeding is pending, is satisfied by the affidavit of either party thereto or otherwise, and it be stated in such commission or process in the nature of a commission, that any witness to be examined under such commission or process, has in his possession or control any paper, writing, written instrument, book or other document, which if produced, would be competent and material evidence for the parties to such suit or action, or either of them, and said paper, writing, written instrument, book or other document be sufficiently described for identification in said commission or process in the nature of a commission, the said commissioner therein appointed shall serve notice as aforesaid of the time and place appointed for the execution of said commission, and therein require said witness to bring with him and produce to said commissioner any such paper, writing, written instrument, book or other document, supposed to be in his possession or control, the same to be described or identified in said notice as in said commission.

If any witness, who shall have been duly notified so to do, as hereinbefore prescribed, shall fail to attend at the execution of said commission, or refuse to testify or to answer such questions as may be propounded to him under such commission, or shall fail to produce, pursuant to said notice, any book, paper or instrument of writing in his possession or control, or shall refuse to subscribe his deposition, it shall be the duty of the commissioner named in said commission, at the request of the court issuing the same, to certify such failure to attend or refusal to testify or subscribe, or to produce books, papers or written instruments, to the circuit court for the county or to any judge of the Supreme Bench of Baltimore City, as the case may be, where said commission is to be executed; and the said court or judge, on receiving the said certificate, shall forthwith issue his order commanding the said delinquent witness on some day and at some place therein appointed to appear before him and show cause why he, the said witness, has so failed to attend or refused to testify or subscribe, or refused to produce books or papers in his possession or control, a copy of which order shall be served upon said delinquent witness at least five days before the day therein appointed; and if the said witness, after having had such notice of said order, shall neglect or refuse to appear before said judge, or appearing, shall fail to show good and sufficient cause why he, the said witness, has so failed to attend or refused to testify or subscribe his deposition, or refuse to produce said books or papers before said commissioner, then and not otherwise, the said court or judge may issue an attachment in the name of the State and compel the appearance and answer of such witness in the same manner as any court in this State would be authorized to do if such witness had been summoned to appear before such court and had failed to attend or refused to answer; provided, that the said court or judge may extend the time for hearing before him if deemed by him necessary or important.

Uniform Foreign Depositions Act

§ 32. Authority to act. Whenever any mandate, writ or commission is issued out of any court of record in any other state, territory, district or foreign jurisdiction, or whenever upon notice or agreement it is required to take the testimony of a witness or witnesses in this State, witnesses may be compelled to appear and testify in the same manner and by the same process and proceeding as may be employed for the purpose of taking testimony in proceedings pending in this State.

§ 33. Uniformity of interpretation. This act [§§ 32 to 34] shall be so interpreted and construed as to effectuate its general purposes to make uniform the law of those states which enact it.

§ 34. Short title. This act [§§ 32 to 34] may be cited as the Uniform Foreign Depositions Act.

Rules of Procedure

MD. RULES PROCEDURE 403

Before Whom [Deposition May Be] Taken Gen'l.

a. *Within This State.*

Within this State, depositions shall be taken before any standing commissioner or equity examiner or before any notary public of this State.

b. *In Other State.*

Within any other state of the United States or within a territory, district, or possession of the United States, depositions shall be taken before any officer authorized to administer oaths by the laws of the United States or of the place where the examination is held, or before a person appointed by the court in which the action is pending. A person so appointed shall have power to administer oaths and take testimony.

c. *In Foreign Country.*

In a foreign state or country depositions shall be taken (1) on notice before a secretary of embassy or legation, counsel general, consul, vice consul, or consular agent of the United States, or (2) before such person or officer as may be appointed by commission or under letters rogatory, or otherwise by the court in which the action is pending. A commission or letters rogatory shall be issued only when necessary or convenient, on application and notice, and on such terms and with such directions as are just and appropriate. Officers may be designated in notices or commissions either by name or descriptive title and letters rogatory may be addressed "To the Appropriate Judicial Authority in (here name the country)."

d. *Disqualification for Interest.*

A deposition shall not be taken before a person who is a relative or employee or attorney of any of the parties, or is a relative or employee of such attorney, or is financially interested in the action, unless the parties agree thereto.

MASSACHUSETTS

[MASS. ANN. LAWS]

State Administrative Procedure

Ch. 30A, § 12. Subpoenas in Adjudicatory Proceedings. In conducting adjudicatory proceedings, [state administrative] agencies shall issue, vacate, modify and enforce subpoenas in accordance with the following provisions:—

o   o   o

(3) Any party to an adjudicatory proceeding shall be entitled as of right to the issue of subpoenas in the name of the agency conducting the proceeding. The party may have such subpoenas issued by a notary public or justice of the peace, or he may make written application to the agency, which shall forthwith issue the subpoenas requested. However issued, the subpoena shall show on its face the name and address of the party at whose request the subpoena was issued. Unless otherwise provided by any law, the agency need not pay fees for attendance and travel to witnesses summoned by a party.

o   o   o

Depositions Taken Outside of State

Ch. 223A, § 10. Taking of Depositions Outside of Commonwealth to Obtain Evidence in Action Pending in Commonwealth; Issuance of Commission or Letter Rogatory. (a) A deposition to obtain testimony or documents or other things in an action pending in this commonwealth may be taken outside this commonwealth:

(1) On reasonable notice in writing to all parties, setting forth the time and place for taking the deposition, the name and address of each person to be examined, if known, and if not known, a general description sufficient to identify him or the particular class or group to which he belongs and the name or descriptive title of the person before whom the deposition will be taken. The deposition may be taken before a person authorized to administer oaths in the place in which the deposition is taken by the law thereof or by the law of this commonwealth or the United States.

(2) Before a person commissioned by the court. The person so commissioned shall have the power by virtue of his commission to administer any necessary oath.

(3)   Pursuant to a letter rogatory issued by the court.   A letter rogatory may be addressed "To the Appropriate Authority in (here name the sate or country)."

(4)   In any manner before any person, at any time or place, or upon any notice stipulated by the parties.   A person designated by the stipulation shall have the power by virtue of his designation to administer any necessary oath.

(b)   A commission or a letter rogatory shall be issued after notice and application to the court, and on terms that are just and appropriate.   It shall not be requisite to the issuance of a commission or a letter rogatory that the taking of the deposition in any other manner is impracticable or inconvenient, and both a commission and a letter rogatory may be issued in proper cases.   Evidence obtained in a foreign country in response to a letter rogatory need not be excluded merely for the reason that it is not a verbatim transcript or that the testimony was not taken under oath or for any similar departure from the requirements for depositions taken within this commonwealth.

Depositions for Foreign Proceedings

Ch. 223A, § 11.   Compelling Production of Evidence to Be Used in Proceeding in Tribunal Outside of Commonwealth; Application for Order; Practice and Procedure.   A court of this commonwealth may order a person who is domiciled or is found within this commonwealth to give his testimony or statement or to produce documents or other things for use in a proceeding in a tribunal outside this commonwealth.   The order may be made upon the application of any interested person or in response to a letter rogatory and may prescribe the practice and procedure, which may be wholly or in part the practice and procedure of the tribunal outside this commonwealth, for taking the testimony or statement or producing the documents or other things.   To the extent that the order does not prescribe otherwise, the practice and procedure shall be in accordance with that of the court of this commonwealth issuing the order. The order may direct that the testimony or statement be given, or document or other thing produced, before a person appointed by the court.   The person appointed shall have power to administer any necessary oath.

Witnesses

Ch. 233, § 1.   Witnesses, How Summoned.   A clerk of a court of record, a notary public or a justice of the peace may issue summonses for witnesses in all cases pending before courts, magistrates, auditors, referees, arbitrators or other persons authorized to examine witnesses, and at all hearings upon applications for complaints wherein a person may be charged with the commission of a crime; but a notary public or a justice of the peace shall not issue summonses for witnesses in criminal cases except upon request of the attorney general, district attorney or other person who acts in the case in behalf of the commonwealth or of the defendant. If the summons is issued at the request of the defendant that fact shall be stated therein. The summons shall be in the form heretofore adopted and commonly used, but may be altered from time to time like other writs.

Ch. 223, § 30. Deponent, How Sworn and Examined. The deponent shall be sworn or affirmed to testify the truth, the whole truth and nothing but the truth, relative to the cause for which the deposition is taken. He shall then be examined by the justice or notary, and the parties if they think fit, and his testimony shall be taken in writing.

Ch. 233, § 31. Order of Examination. The party producing the deponent shall be allowed first to examine him, either upon verbal or written interrogatories, on all the points which he considers material; the adverse party may then examine him in like manner, after which either party may propose further interrogatories.

Ch. 233, § 32. Manner of Taking Depositions. The deposition shall be written by the justice or notary or deponent or by a disinterested person in the presence and under the direction of the justice or notary, shall be carefully read to or by the deponent, and then subscribed by him.

Ch. 233, § 33. Certificate to Be Annexed. The justice or notary shall annex to the deposition a certificate of the time and manner of taking it, the person at whose request and the cause in which it was taken, the reason for taking it, and that the adverse party attended, or if he did not attend what notice was given to him.

Ch. 233, § 34. Depositions to Be Delivered to Court, etc. The deposition shall be delivered by the justice or notary to the court, arbitrators, referees or other persons before whom the cause is pending, or shall be enclosed and sealed by him and directed to it or them, and shall remain sealed until opened by it or them.

Ch. 233, § 40. Courts May Make Rules for Depositions. The courts may make rules regulating the time and manner of opening, filing and safe keeping of depositions, and the taking and use thereof.

Ch. 233, § 41. Depositions of Persons Outside Commonwealth. The deposition of a person without the commonwealth may be taken under a commission issued to one or more competent persons in another state or country by the court in which the cause is pending, or it may be taken before a commissioner appointed by the governor for that purpose, and in either case the deposition may be used in the same manner and subject to the same conditions and objections as if it had been taken in the commonwealth.

Ch. 233, § 42. Written Interrogatories, etc. Unless the court otherwise orders, a deposition taken before commissioners shall be taken upon written interrogatories, which shall be filed in the clerk's office and notice thereof given to the adverse party or his attorney, and upon cross interrogatories, if any are filed by him. But if the defendant does not enter his appearance in the action within the time required by law, no notice to him shall be required. The court may in any case order depositions to be taken before commissioners, in the manner provided by law for taking the depositions of witnesses within the commonwealth in actions at law, or in such manner as the court orders, and in such cases shall determine what notice shall be given to the adverse party, his agent or attorney, and the manner of service thereof, may authorize the taking of depositions of witnesses not specifically named in the commission, and may limit the extent of the inquiry. The court may order the production before the commissioner of any books, instruments or papers relative to any matter in issue.

Ch. 233, § 73. Oaths before a Notary of Another State or Country. All oaths and affidavits administered or taken by a notary public, duly commissioned and qualified by authority of any other state or government, within the jurisdiction for which he is commissioned, and certified under his official seal, shall be as effectual in this commonwealth as if administered or taken and certified by a justice of the peace therein.

Commissions to Take Depositions

Ch. 266, § 2. Fees of Clerks of District Courts in Civil Actions. The fees of the clerks of district courts, in civil actions, shall be in the following amounts, payable in advance:—

٭   ٭   ٭

(e) For a commission to take deposition, one dollar and fifty cents.

٭   ٭   ٭

Ch. 277, § 76. Commission to Examine Witnesses. If an issue of fact is joined upon an indictment, the court may, upon application of the defendant, grant a commission to examine any material witnesses residing out of the commonwealth, in the same manner as in civil causes; and the prosecuting officer may join in such commission, and may name any material witnesses to be examined on the part of the commonwealth.

Ch. 277, § 77. Commission, How Executed; Deposition, How Used. When such commission is issued, the interrogatories to be annexed thereto shall be settled and the commission executed and returned as is provided in relation to commissions in civil cases, and the depositions taken thereon and returned shall be read in the same manner and with the like effect, and subject to the same exceptions, as in civil cases; but if the defendant on his trial declines to use the deposition so taken, the prosecuting officer shall not, without the defendant's consent, make use of any deposition taken on behalf of the commonwealth.

Civil Procedure

[MASS. R. CIV. P. 28]

PERSONS BEFORE WHOM DEPOSITIONS MAY BE TAKEN

(a) Within the United States. Within the United States or within a territory or insular possession subject to the dominion of the United States, depositions shall be taken before an officer authorized to administer oaths by the laws of the United States or of the place where the examination is held, or before a person appointed by the court in which the action is pending. A person so appointed has power to administer oaths and take testimony.

(b) In Foreign Countries. In a foreign country, depositions may be taken (1) on notice before a person authorized to administer oaths in the place in which the examination is held, either by the law thereof or by the laws of the United States, or (2) before a person commissioned by the court, and a person so commissioned shall have the power by virtue of his commission to administer any necessary oath and take testimony, or (3) pursuant to a letter rogatory. A commission or a letter rogatory shall be issued on application and notice and on terms that are just and appropriate. It is not requisite to the issuance of a commission or a letter rogatory that the taking of the deposition in any other manner is impracticable ' or inconvenient; and both a commission and a letter rogatory may be issued in proper cases. A notice or commission may designate the person before whom the deposition is to be taken either by name or descriptive title. A letter rogatory may be addressed "To the Appropriate Authority in [here name the country]." Evidence obtained in response to a letter rogatory need not be excluded merely for the reason that it is not a verbatim transcript or that the testimony was not taken under oath or for any similar departure from the requirements for depositions taken within the United States under these rules.

(c) Disqualification for Interest. No deposition shall be taken before a person who is a relative or employee or attorney or counsel of any of the parties, or is a relative or employee of such attorney or counsel, or is financially interested in the action.

MICHIGAN

[MICH. COMP. LAWS ANN.]

§ 600.1432. Oath, mode of administration. Sec. 1432. The usual mode of administrating oaths now practiced in this state, by the person who swears holding up the right hand, shall be observed in all cases in which an oath may be administered by law except in the cases herein otherwise provided. The oath should commence, "You do solemnly swear or affirm."

§ 600.1442. ° ° ° **court appointee; stipulation.** Sec. 1442. Oaths, affidavits and depositions, in any cause, matter or proceeding in any court of record, may ° ° ° be taken before any person appointed by the court for that purpose or before any person upon whom the parties agree by stipulation in writing or on the record.

§ 600.1725. Witness, refusal to testify, penalty. Sec. 1725. If any witness attending pursuant to a subpoena, or brought before any court, judge, officer, commissioner, or before any person before whom depositions may be taken, refuses without reasonable cause

(1) to be examined, or

(2) to answer any legal and pertinent question, or

(3) to subscribe his deposition after it has been reduced to writing, the officer issuing the subpoena shall commit him, by warrant, to the common jail of the county in which he resides. He shall remain there until he submits to be examined, or to answer, or to subscribe his deposition, as the case may be, or until he is discharged according to law.

Note: This section may be misleading. A witness who is summoned for a deposition cannot be punished for contempt until he disobeys a court order requiring him to answer a specific question or do some other specific act.

§ 600.1852. Foreign proceedings; service of process; letters rogatory; foreign orders, judgments, or decrees, recognition or enforcement; orders to testify or produce documents; procedure. Sec. 1852. (1) Any court of record of this state as provided in subsection (2) may order service upon any person who is domiciled or can be found within this state of any document issued in connection with a proceeding in a tribunal outside this state. The order may be made upon application of any interested person or in response to a letter rogatory issued by a tribunal outside this state and shall direct the manner of service. Service in connection with a proceeding in a tribunal outside this state may be made within this state without an order of court. Service under this section does not, of itself, require the recognition or enforcement of an order, judgment or decree rendered outside this state.

(2) Any court of record of this state may order a person who is domiciled or is found within this state to give his testimony or statement or to produce documents or other things for use in a proceeding in a tribunal outside this state. The order may be made upon the application of any interested person or in response to a letter rogatory and may prescribe the practice and procedure, which may be wholly or in part the practice and procedure of the tribunal outside this state, for taking the testimony or statement or producing the documents or other things. The order shall be issued upon petition to a court of record in the county in which the deponent resides or is employed or transacts his business in person or is

found for a subpoena to compel the giving of testimony by him. The court may hear and act upon the petition with or without notice as the court directs. To the extent that the order does not prescribe otherwise, the practice and procedure shall be in accordance with that of the court of this state issuing the order. The order may direct that the testimony or statement be given, or document or other thing produced, before a person appointed by the court. The person appointed shall have power to administer any necessary oath. A person within this state may voluntarily give his testimony or statement or produce documents or other things for use in a proceeding before a tribunal outside this state.

§ 767.77. **Commission to examine out-of-state witness; granting on application of defendant.** Sec. 77. When an issue of fact shall be joined upon any indictment, the court in which the same is pending may, on application of the defendant, grant a commission to examine any material .witnesses residing out of this state, in the same manner as in civil cases.

§ 767.78. **Same; interrogatories, reading of deposition.** Sec. 78. Interrogatories to be annexed to such commission shall be settled and such commission shall be issued, executed and returned in the manner prescribed by law in respect to commissions in civil cases, and the deposition taken thereon and returned shall be read in the same cases, and with like effect in all respects, as in civil suits.

[MICH. GEN. CT. R. (1963) 304]

Persons Before Whom Depositions May Be Taken.

.1 **Within the United States.** Within the United States or within a territory or insular possession subject to the dominion of the United States, depositions shall be taken (1) before a person authorized to administer oaths by the laws of this state or of the United States or of the place where the examination is held, or (2) before such person as may be appointed by the court in which the action is pending, or (3) before any person upon whom the parties agree by stipulation in writing or on the record. A person so appointed or agreed to shall have the power to administer oaths, take testimony, and do all other acts necessary to take an effective deposition.

.2 **In Foreign Countries.** In a foreign state or country depositions shall be taken (1) before a secretary of embassy or legation, consul general, consul, vice consul, or consular agent of the United States, or (2) before such person as may be appointed by commission or under letters rogatory, or (3) before any person upon whom the parties agree by stipulation in writing or on the record. Such persons have the power to administer oaths, take testimony, and do all other acts necessary to take an effective deposition. A commission or letters rogatory shall be issued only when necessary or convenient, on application or notice, and on such terms and with such directions as are just and appropriate. Persons may be designated in notices or commissions either by name or descriptive title and letters rogatory may be addressed "To the Appropriate Judicial Authority in (here name the country)."

.3 **Disqualifications for Interest.** No deposition shall be taken before a person who is a relative or employee or attorney or counsel of any of the parties, or is a relative or employee of such attorney or counsel, or is financially interested in the action unless the parties agree by stipulation in writing or on the record to the contrary.

MINNESOTA

[MINN. STAT. ANN.]

§ 358.07. **Forms of oath in various cases.** An oath substantially in the following forms shall be administered to the respective officers and persons hereinafter named:

○   ○   ○

(7) To witnesses:
"You do swear that the evidence you shall give relative to the cause now under consideration shall be the whole truth, and nothing but the truth. So help you God."

(8) To interpreters:
"You do swear that you will truly and impartially interpret to this witness the oath about to be administered to him, and the testimony he shall give relative to the cause now under consideration. So help you God."

○   ○   ○

Concerning an affirmation in lieu of an oath, see *Authority and Duties,* MINN. STAT. ANN. § 358.08. Concerning by whom and how oaths are to be administered, see *Authority and Duties,* MINN. STAT. ANN. § 358.09.

§ 359.11. **Taking depositions.** In taking depositions, the notary shall have the same power to compel the attendance of and to punish witnesses for refusing to testify as may be vested by law in justices of the peace, and all sheriffs and constables shall serve and return all process issued by any notary in taking depositions.

Civil Procedure in District Courts

[MINN. R. CIV. P. (DIST. CT.) 28]

PERSONS BEFORE WHOM DEPOSITIONS MAY BE TAKEN

28.01. Within the United States. Within the United States or within a territory or insular possession subject to the dominion of the United States, depositions shall be taken before an officer authorized to administer oaths by the laws of the United States or of the place where the examination is held, or before a person appointed by the court in which the action is pending. A person so appointed has power to administer oaths and take testimony.

28.02. In Foreign Countries. In a foreign country, depositions may be taken (1) on notice before a person authorized to administer oaths in the place in which the examination is held, either by the law thereof or by the law of the United States, or (2) before a person commissioned by the court, and a person so commissioned shall have the power by virtue of his commission to administer any necessary oath and take testimony, or (3) pursuant to a letter rogatory. A commission or a letter rogatory shall be issued on application and notice, and on terms that are just and appropriate. It is not requisite to the issuance of a commission or a letter rogatory that the taking of the deposition in any other manner is impracticable or inconvenient; and both a commission and a letter rogatory may be issued in proper cases. A notice or commission may designate the person before whom the deposition is to be taken either by name or descriptive title. A letter rogatory may be addressed "To the Appropriate Authority in (here name the country)." Evidence obtained in response to a letter rogatory need not be excluded merely for the reason that it is not a verbatim transcript or that the testimony was not taken under oath or for any similar departure from the requirements for depositions taken within the United States under these Rules.

28.03. Disqualification for Interest. No deposition shall be taken before a person who is a relative or employe or attorney or counsel of any of the parties, or is a relative or employe of such attorney or counsel, or is financially interested in the action.

Civil Procedure in Municipal Courts

[MINN. R. CIV. P. (MUN. CT.) 28]

PERSONS BEFORE WHOM DEPOSITIONS MAY BE TAKEN

28.01. Within the United States. Within the United States or within a territory or insular possession subject to the dominion of the United States, depositions shall be taken before an officer authorized to administer oaths by the laws of the United States or of the place where the examination is held, or before a person appointed by the court in which the action is pending. A person so appointed has power to administer oaths and take testimony.

28.02. In Foreign Countries. In a foreign country, depositions may be taken (1) on notice before a person authorized to administer oaths in the place in which the examination is held, either by the law thereof or by the law of the United States, or (2) before a person commissioned by the court, and a person so commissioned shall have the power by virtue of his commission to administer any necessary oath and take testimony, or (3) pursuant to a letter rogatory. A commission or a letter rogatory shall be issued on application and notice, and on terms that are just and appropriate. It is not requisite to the issuance of a commission or a letter rogatory that the taking of the deposition in any other manner is impracticable or inconvenient; and both a commission and a letter rogatory may be issued in proper cases. A notice or commission may designate the person before whom the deposition is to be taken either by name or descriptive title. A letter rogatory may be addressed "To the Appropriate Authority in (here name the country)." Evidence obtained in response to a letter rogatory need not be excluded merely for the reason that it is not a verbatim transcript or that the testimony was not taken under oath or for any similar departure from the requirements for depositions taken within the United States under these Rules.

28.03. Disqualification for Interest. No deposition shall be taken before a person who is a relative or employe or attorney or counsel of any of the parties, or is a relative or employe of such attorney or counsel, or is financially interested in the action.

MISSISSIPPI

[MISS. CODE ANN.]

§ 13-1-33. Depositions of witnesses in state; before whom taken; notice. Depositions of witnesses in this state may be taken before any officer authorized to administer oaths and before any official court reporter, on ten (10) days notice to the opposite party or his attorney of the time and place of taking such deposition. In cases of emergency, to be expressed in the notice, shorter notice shall be sufficient. Depositions of witnesses in this state in civil suits may likewise be taken in the same manner provided for taking the depositions of witnesses absent from or residing out of the state.

Note: Every notary public has the power of administering oaths and affirmations in all matters incident his notarial office. See *Authority and Duties,* MISS. CODE ANN. § 25-33-9.

§ 13-1-35. Interrogatories to nonresident witness filed. The deposition of any witness absent from or residing out of the state may be taken by any party to the cause. When any party shall desire to take the deposition of any such witness he shall file interrogatories in the clerk's office, or with the justice of the peace in cases before them, and serve the opposite party or his attorney with a copy thereof ten days before issuing the commission, in which time the opposite party shall file his cross-interrogatories. The clerk or justice shall thereupon issue a commission, and shall annex thereto the interrogatories and such cross-interrogatories as may be filed, and the witness shall be examined by the commissioner thereon.

The witness may be cross-examined by the adverse party if he see proper to attend the examination, and the party at whose instance the deposition is taken may, in that event, further examine the witness in rebuttal.

§ 13-1-37. Persons to whom commissions may be directed. A commission to take depositions of a witness out of the state may be directed to one commissioner or to several commissioners in the alternative, by name, to a commissioner appointed by the governor of this state, or to any judge of a court of record, justice of the peace, mayor, or chief magistrate of a city or town, or other person authorized to administer oaths by the law of the place where the deposition is to be taken.

§ 13-1-43. Taking, returning, and opening depositions. The witnesses shall be sworn or affirmed by the commissioner to testify the truth, the whole truth, and nothing but the truth, and the commissioner shall carefully and impartially examine the witnesses on the interrogatories and cross-interrogatories; or, if the deposition be taken within the state, the officer shall so swear and examine the witnesses upon such interrogatories as may be put, verbally or in writing, by the parties, and, in either event, the officer shall cause the testimony to be fairly written down, either by himself, or by the witness, or some disinterested person in his presence, and subscribed by the witness. The testimony so taken down, with the commission, if any, and interrogatories, and every exhibit and voucher relating thereto, and also a certificate by the commissioner or officer of all his proceedings therein, shall be sealed up and directed to the clerk of the court or justice, as the case may be, where the action is pending, and transmitted in a safe and convenient manner. The clerk or justice shall open the same, and, having indorsed thereon the time of the receipt and opening thereof, shall deposit the same among the papers in the cause.

§ 13-1-45. Examination from day to day. The commissioner or officer shall have power to continue the taking of depositions from day to day, and may adjourn the taking thereof from time to time, giving notice to the parties unless they be present when such adjournment is made.

MISSOURI

[MO. ANN. STAT.—Vernon]

§ 485.140. Reporters, St. Louis court of criminal correction—appointment—compensation. 1. The judge of each division of the St. Louis court of criminal correction shall appoint a reporter of such division who shall hold his office from month to month during the pleasure of the judge. Each of such reporters shall receive an annual salary of twelve thousand dollars, payable in equal monthly installments on the certificate of the judge of the court certifying as to the time served by the reporter to be payable sixty-five hundred dollars out of the city treasury and fifty-five hundred dollars out of the state treasury.

2. Each reporter shall take oath to faithfully discharge the duties of reporter of the division to which he was appointed and to take accurate shorthand notes of the evidence in all cases and proceedings in the division, and when directed by the judge of the division, shall furnish the circuit attorney of the city of St. Louis a complete transcript of his notes of all evidence and proceedings in cases of preliminary examination of felonies in legible English for use of the circuit attorney without additional cost to the state.

3. In the absence of the reporter of a division, the judge of such division may appoint a temporary reporter who shall perform the same duties and receive the same compensation as provided for the regular reporter for the time served by the temporary reporter, to be paid upon the certification of the judge of the division, limited, however, to a maximum of thirty court days within any calendar year.

§ 492.090. **Officers authorized to take depositions.** Depositions may be taken by some one of the following officers:

(1) If taken within this state, by some judge, justice, magistrate, notary public or clerk of any court having a seal, in vacation of court, mayor or chief officer of a city or town having a seal of office;

(2) If taken without this state, by some officer out of this state appointed by authority of the laws of this state to take depositions, or by some consul or commercial or diplomatic representative of the United States, having a seal, or mayor or chief officer of any city, town or borough, having a seal of office, or by some judge, justice of the peace, or other judicial officer, or by some notary public, within the government where the witness may be found.

§ 492.290. **Witnesses to be examined on oath.** Every witness examined, in pursuance of sections 492.080 to 492.400 shall be sworn or affirmed to testify the whole truth, and his examination shall be reduced to writing, or taken in shorthand and transcribed, in writing, in the presence of the person or officer before whom the same shall be taken.

§ 492.320. **Residence of witness certified by officer.** When the officer taking depositions in virtue of this law shall, in his certificate, state the place of residence of the witness, such statement shall be prima facie evidence of the facts.

§ 492.340. **Deposition shall be submitted to witness for examination—signing of deposition.** When the testimony is fully transcribed the deposition shall be submitted to the witness for examination and shall be read to or by him, unless such examination and reading are waived by the witness and by the parties. Any changes in form or substance which the witness desires to make shall be entered upon the deposition by the officer with a statement of the reasons given by the witness for making them. The deposition shall then be signed by the witness, unless the parties by stipulation waive the signing or the witness is ill or cannot be found, or is dead or refuses to sign. If the deposition is not signed by the witness, the officer shall sign it and state on the record the fact of the waiver or of the illness, or death or absence of the witness or the fact of the refusal to sign together with the reason, if any, given therefor; and the deposition may then be used as fully as though signed, unless on a motion to suppress the court holds that the reasons given for the refusal to sign requires rejection of the deposition in whole or in part.

§ 492.350. Certificate of officer taking depositions. To every deposition or examination, taken by virtue of sections 492.080 to 492.400 shall be appended the certificate of the person or officer by or before whom the same shall be taken, showing that the deposition or examination was reduced to writing in his presence, and was subscribed and sworn to by the witnesses, and the place at which, and the days, and within the hours, when the same was taken.

§ 492.360. Exhibits to be enclosed with depositions and directed to clerk. Depositions or examinations taken by virtue of any of the provisions of sections 492.080 to 492.400 and all exhibits produced to the person or officer taking such examinations or depositions, and proved or referred to by any witness, together with the commission and interrogatories, if any, shall be enclosed, sealed up, and directed to the clerk of the court in which or the magistrate before whom the action is pending.

Civil Procedure

[MO. R. CIV. P. 57.02]

57.02. **Witness Residing Out of This State, Commission to Issue.** When the witness resides out of this state, the party desiring his testimony may sue out of the court in which the suit is pending, or out of the office of the clerk thereof, a commission to take the deposition of the witness.

57.03. **Officers Authorized to Take Depositions.** Depositions may be taken by someone of the following officers: (1) if taken within this state, by some judge (including a magistrate), notary public or clerk of any court having a seal, in vacation of court, mayor or chief officer of a city or town having a seal of office; (2) if taken without this state, by some officer out of this state appointed by authority of the laws of this state to take depositions, or by some consul or commercial or diplomatic representative of the United States, having a seal of office, or mayor or chief officer of any city, town or borough, having a seal of office, or by some judge, including a magistrate, justice of the peace or other judicial officer, or by some notary public, within the territorial jurisdiction of the government where the witness may be found.

57.04. Commission, How Issued, to Whom Directed. The commission shall be under the seal of the court, and shall be directed to any officer herein authorized to take depositions within the territorial jurisdiction of the government where the witness may be found.

57.05. Power and Duty of the Officer Under the Commission. The commission shall authorize such officer to cause to come before him such person or persons as shall be named to him by the party suing for the same, and shall command such officer to examine such person touching his knowledge of anything relating to the matter in controversy, and to reduce such examination to writing, and return the same, annexed to the Commission, to the court wherein, or the magistrate before whom the action is pending, with all convenient speed.

57.06. Witness found in this state—no commission necessary— special commissioner for deposition on oral interrogatories. (a) Commission not necessary—but special commissioner may be appointed— qualifications—time and place of taking.** When the witness is found in this state, the deposition may be taken by the proper officer without any commission or order of the court or clerk except that whenever a notice is given, as required by law, in a cause pending in any circuit or common pleas court of any county or of the City of St. Louis to take such deposition, the party upon whom such notice is served, as provided by law, may, at any time after the service of such notice and before the taking of such depositions shall be commenced, after having given the party or his attorney of record on whose behalf such notice was served, one day's written notice by delivering a copy thereof to all adverse parties or their attorneys of record, of his intention to apply for the appointment of a special commissioner to take such deposition and of the time and place of making such application, make an application, accompanied by a service copy of the notice of application, to the court or to the judge thereof to appoint a special commissioner to take and make an order affirming or reversing it.   In the event the ruling is reversed, the court shall enter an order of record directing the special commissioner to admit the testimony or evidence so excluded.

(g) Adjournment and further proceedings by commissioner. Whenever the special commissioner reports his ruling to the court, he shall adjourn the taking of depositions to such time and place as he may direct and enforce the attendance of any witness thereat by attachment or otherwise, so as to enable a party to have any question answered which he has ruled out and which the court may direct to be answered, together with such other questions as may appear proper under the ruling of the court reversing the special commissioner.

57.07.   What officers out of this state may take depositions without commission.   Depositions may be taken by any officer appointed out of this state, by authority of the laws of this state to take depositions without any commission or order from any court or clerk.

57.19.   Officer may compel attendance of witness—if witness imprisoned, on what terms discharged.   Every person, judge or other officer of the state required to take the depositions or examination of witnesses, in pursuance of this Rule, or by virtue of any commission issuing out of any court of record in this or any other government, shall have power to issue subpoenas for witnesses to appear and testify, and to compel their attendance in the same manner and under like penalties as any court of record of this state. Any person summoned as a witness by virtue of the provisions of this rule, and attending, who shall refuse to give evidence which may be lawfully required to be given by him, an oath or affirmation, or who shall refuse to produce documentary evidence or tangible things, in compliance with a court order or subpoena, may be committed to prison by the officer or person authorized to take his deposition or testimony, or by the judge of the court in which the cause is pending, there to remain without bail until he gives such evidence, or until he be discharged by due course of law; provided that in case such person be discharged from such commitment or imprisonment upon habeas corpus sued therefor, the party or parties litigant, in whose behalf the refused evidence shall have been required, shall be liable to pay such person the costs by him incurred in effecting such discharge; and the judge or court hearing the application for discharge may, in its discretion, at the time of such discharge allow a further sum of not exceeding twenty-five dollars for an attorney's fee for prosecuting the proceedings on habeas corpus, to be paid by such party or parties litigant to the person so discharged; and provided further, that until such costs and attorney's fee, if one be allowed, are paid or tendered to such person, he shall not be required further to depose or testify in the cause in which he was so summoned.

57.21.   Witness to be examined on oath.   Every witness whose deposition is taken in pursuance of these Rules, shall be sworn or affirmed to testify the whole truth by the person, judge or other officer before whom the deposition is taken.   The examination shall be recorded by a reporter (or recording device) and shall be reduced to writing or typewriting.

57.22.   Depositions shall be submitted to witness for examination—signing of deposition.   When the testimony is fully transcribed the deposition shall be submitted to the witness for examination and shall be read to or by him, unless such examination and reading are waived by the witness and by the parties. Any changes in form or substance which the witness desires to make shall be entered upon the deposition by the officer with a statement of the reasons given by the witness for making them; provided, however, that the answers or responses as originally given, together with the changes made and reasons given therefor, shall be considered as a part of the deposition. The deposition shall then be signed by the witness, unless the parties by stipulation waive the signing or the witness is ill or cannot be found, or is dead or refuses to sign. If the deposition is not signed by the witness, the officer shall sign it and state on the record the fact of the waiver or of the illness, or death or absence of the witness or the fact of the refusal to sign together with the reasons, if any, given therefor; and the deposition may then be used as fully as though signed, unless, on a motion to suppress, the court holds that the reasons given for the refusal to sign require rejection of the deposition in whole or in part.

57.23. Certificate of officer taking depositions. To every deposition or examination, taken or made by virtue of these Rules, shall be appended the certificate of the person, judge or other officer by or before whom the same shall be taken, showing that the deposition or examination was taken in his presence and was subscribed and sworn to by the witness, and the place at which, and the days, and within the hours, when the same was taken.

57.24. What sufficient evidence of the authentication of deposition. Depositions or examinations taken by any person or officer in this state authorized by these Rules, or by any person or officer out of this state appointed by authority of the laws of this state, to take depositions, or by any consul, commercial or diplomatic representative of the United States, or mayor or chief officer of any city, town or borough, having a seal of office, or by any notary public, and certified by such person or officer in his official character, and accompanied by his seal of office, if there be one, shall, to all intents and purposes, be sufficient evidence of the authentication of such depositions or examinations.

MONTANA

[MONT. REV. CODES ANN.]

§ 93-1601-3. A deposition defined. A deposition is a written declaration under oath, made upon notice to the adverse party for the purpose of enabling him to attend and cross-examine.

§ 93-1601-5. Depositions—how taken. Depositions must be taken in the form of questions and answers, and the words of the witness must be written down, unless the parties agree to a different mode.

§ 93-1701-1. **Affidavits—for what purposes may be used.** An affidavit may be used to verify a pleading or a paper in a special proceeding, to prove the service of a summons, notice, or other paper in an action or special proceeding, to obtain a provisional remedy, the examination of a witness, or a stay of proceedings, or upon a motion, and in any other cases expressly permitted by some other provision of this code.

§ 93-2401-1. **Judicial and certain officers authorized to administer oaths.** Every court, every judge, or clerk of any court, every justice, and every notary public, and every officer or person authorized to take testimony in any action or proceeding, or to decide upon evidence, has power to administer oaths or affirmations.

§ 93-2401-2. **Form of ordinary oath to witness.** An oath, or affirmation, in an action or proceeding, may be administered as follows, the person who swears, or affirms, expressing his assent when addressed in the following form: "You do solemnly swear (or affirm, as the case may be) that the evidence you shall give in this issue (or matter), pending between ———— and ————, shall be the truth, the whole truth, and nothing but the truth, so help you God."

§ 93-2401-3. **Form may be varied to suit witness' belief.** Whenever the court before which a person is offered as a witness is satisfied that he has a peculiar mode of swearing, connected with or in addition to the usual form of administration, which, in his opinion, is more solemn or obligatory, the court may, in its discretion, adopt that mode.

§ 93-2401-4. **Form of oath—witness not a Christian.** When a person is sworn who believes in any other than the Christian religion, he may be sworn according to the peculiar ceremonies of his religion, if there be any such.

§ 93-2401-5. **Any person who prefers it may declare or affirm.** Any person who desires it may, at his option, instead of taking an oath, make his solemn affirmation or declaration by assenting, when addressed in the following form: "You do solemnly affirm (or declare)," etc., as in section 93-2401-2.

[MONT. R. CIV. P. 28]

Persons Before Whom Depositions May Be Taken

(a) WITHIN THE UNITED STATES. Within the state of Montana, depositions shall be taken before a person authorized by the laws of this state to administer oaths; without the state, but within the United States, or within a territory or insular possession subject to the dominion of the United States, depositions shall be taken before a person authorized to administer oaths by the laws of this state, the United States, or of the place where the examination is held; within or without the state of Montana, depositions may also be taken before a person appointed by the court in which the action is pending, which persons so appointed shall have the power to administer oaths and take testimony.

(b) IN FOREIGN COUNTRIES. In a foreign country, depositions may be taken (1) on notice before a person authorized to administer oaths in the place in which the examination is held, either by the law thereof or by the law of the United States, or (2) before a person commissioned by the court, and a person so commissioned shall have the power by virtue of his commission to administer any necessary oath and take testimony, or (3) pursuant to letter rogatory. A commission or a letter rogatory shall be issued on application and notice, and on terms that are just and appropriate. It is not requisite to the issuance of a commission or a letter rogatory that the taking of the deposition in any other manner is impracticable or inconvenient; and both a commission and a letter rogatory may be issued in proper cases. A notice or commission may designate the person before whom the deposition is to be taken either by name or descriptive title. A letter rogatory may be addressed "To the Appropriate Authority in [here name the country]." Evidence obtained in response to a letter rogatory need not be excluded merely for the reason that it is not a verbatim transcript or that the testimony was not taken under oath or for any similar departure from the requirements for depositions taken within the United States under these Rules.

(c) DISQUALIFICATION FOR INTEREST. No deposition shall be taken before a person who is a relative or employee or attorney or counsel of any of the parties, or is a relative or employee of such attorney or counsel, or is financially interested in the action.

(d) DEPOSITIONS TO BE USED IN OTHER STATES. Whenever the deposition of any person is to be taken in this state pursuant to the laws of another state or the United States or of another country for use in proceedings there, the district court of the county where the witness is to be served, upon proof that notice has been duly served, may issue, pursuant to Rule 45(d), the necessary subpoenas.

(e) DEPOSITION TO BE TAKEN IN SISTER STATES AND FOREIGN COUNTRIES FOR USE IN THIS STATE. Whenever the deposition of any person is to be taken in a sister state or a foreign country, or any other jurisdiction, foreign or domestic, for use in this state, pursuant either to notice or stipulation, the Clerk or equivalent officer of any Court having jurisdiction at the place where the witness is to be served or the deposition taken, upon proof that notice has been duly served for taking of the deposition or that the parties have stipulated to such taking, may issue the necessary subpoenas or equivalent court instruments to require such witness to attend for the taking of the deposition at the time and place in the sister state or foreign country, or any other jurisdiction, foreign or domestic, designated in the notice or stipulation.

NEBRASKA

[NEB. REV. STAT.]

§ 25-1229. Subpoena; disobedience; refusal to testify or sign deposition; contempt. Disobedience of a subpoena, or a refusal to be sworn, or to answer as a witness, or to subscribe a deposition, when lawfully ordered, may be punished as a contempt of the court or officer by whom his attendance or testimony is required.

Note: § 64-108 provides as follows:

Summons; issuance, when authorized; contempt, power to punish. Every notary public, when notice by a party to any civil suit pending in any court of this state upon any adverse party for the taking of any testimony of witnesses by deposition, or any commission to take testimony of witnesses to be preserved for use in any suit thereafter to be commenced, has been deposited with him, or when a special commission issued out of any court of any state or country without this state, together with notice for the taking of testimony by depositions or commissions, has been deposited with him, is empowered to issue summons and command the presence before him of witnesses, and to punish witnesses for neglect or refusal to obey such summons, or for refusal to testify when present, by commitment to the jail of the county for contempt. All sheriffs and constables in this state are required to serve and return all process issued by notaries public in the taking of testimony of witnesses by commission or deposition.

§ 25-1231. Subpoena; disobedience; refusal to testify or sign deposition; punishment of witness for contempt. The punishment for the contempt mentioned in section 25-1229 shall be as follows: When the witness fails to attend in obedience to the subpoena, except in case of a demand and failure to pay his fees, the court or officer may fine the witness in a sum not exceeding fifty dollars. In other cases, the court or officer may fine the witness in a sum not exceeding fifty dollars nor less than five dollars, or may imprison him in the county jail, there to remain until he shall submit to be sworn, to testify or give his deposition. The fine imposed by the court shall be paid into the county treasurer, and that imposed by the officer shall be for the use of the party for whom the witness was subpoenaed. The witness shall also be liable to the party injured for any damages occasioned by his failure to attend, or his refusal to be sworn, to testify or give his deposition.

§ 25-1242. Deposition, defined. A deposition is a written declaration under oath or a videotape° taken under oath in accordance with procedures provided by law, made upon notice to the adverse party for the purpose of enabling him to attend and cross-examine, or made upon written interrogatories.

° Concerning videotape depositions, see § 25-1267.45, below.

§ 25-1267.14. Deposition; within state; person before whom taken. Depositions may be taken in this state before a judge or clerk of the Supreme Court or district court, or before a county judge, justice of the peace, notary public, mayor or chief magistrate of any city or town corporate, or before a master commissioner, or any person empowered by a special commission; but depositions taken in this state, to be used therein, must be taken by an officer or person whose authority is derived within the state.

§ 25-1267.15. Deposition; outside of state; person before whom taken. Depositions may be taken out of the state by a judge, justice, or chancellor of any court of record, a justice of the peace, notary public, mayor or chief magistrate of any city or town corporate, a commissioner appointed by the Governor of this state to take depositions, or any person authorized by a special commission from this state.

§ 25-1267.16. Deposition; commission ° granted; conditions. Any court of record of this state, or any judge thereof, is authorized to grant a commission to take depositions within or without the state. The commission must be issued to a person or persons therein named, by the clerk, under the seal of the court granting the same, and depositions under it must be taken upon written interrogatories, unless the parties otherwise agree.

§ 25-1267.17. Deposition; person before whom taken; disqualification. The officer before whom depositions are taken and the person recording the testimony taken at depositions must not be related to nor attorney for either party, nor employed by either party or any attorney in the case, except for the limited purpose of the taking of the deposition, nor otherwise interested in the event of the action or proceeding.

§ 25-1267.18. Deposition; order of court outside of state; witnesses within state; subpoena. Whenever under any mandate, writ, or commission issued out of any court of record in any other state, territory, district, or foreign jurisdiction, or whenever upon notice or agreement, it is required to take the testimony of a witness or witnesses in this state, witnesses may be compelled to appear and testify in the same manner and by the same process and proceedings as may be employed for the purpose of taking testimony in proceedings pending in this state.

§ 25-1267.19. Deposition; stipulations for taking. If the parties so stipulate in writing, depositions may be taken before any person,

at any time or place, upon any notice, and in any manner and when
so taken may be used like other depositions.

§ 25-1267.23.   **Deposition; record of examination; oath; objections
to qualifications of officer; objections to evidence; noted by officer;
written interrogatories.**   The officer before whom the deposition is
to be taken shall put the witness on oath and shall personally, or by
someone acting under his direction and in his presence, record the
testimony of the witness.   The testimony shall be taken stenographically and transcribed unless the parties agree otherwise; *Provided*, that such testimony may be taken by videotape upon compliance with the requirements of law relating thereto.   All objections
made at the time of the examination to the qualifications of the officer taking the deposition, or to the qualifications of the person
recording the testimony, or to the manner of taking the deposition,
or to the evidence presented, or to the conduct of any party, and
any other objection to the proceedings, shall be noted by the officer
upon the deposition.   Evidence objected to shall be taken subject
to the objections.   In lieu of participating in the oral examination,
parties served with notice of taking a deposition may transmit written
interrogatories to the officer, who shall propound them to the witness
and record the answers verbatim.

§ 25-1267.25.   **Deposition; submission to witness; changes; signing.**   (1)   If the testimony is fully transcribed the deposition shall
be submitted to the witness for examination and shall be read to or
by him, unless such examination and reading are waived by the witness and by the parties.   Any changes in form or substance which
the witness desires to make shall be entered upon the deposition by
the officer with a statement of the reasons given by the witness for
making them.   The deposition shall then be signed by the witness,
unless the parties by stipulation waive the signing or the witness is
ill or cannot be found or refuses to sign.   If the deposition is not
signed by the witness, the officer shall sign it and state on the record
the fact of the waiver or of the illness or absence of the witness or
the fact of the refusal to sign together with the reason, if any,
given therefor; and the deposition may then be used as fully as
though signed, unless on a motion to suppress ° ° ° the court holds
that the reasons given for the refusal to sign require rejection of the
deposition in whole or in part.

(2)   If the testimony is taken by other than stenographic means,
the court authorizing the taking of such testimony in such manner
shall make reasonable provisions for making such testimony available
to the parties and the witness.

§ 25-1267.26.   **Deposition; certification; filing; notice of filing.**
(1)   The officer shall certify on the deposition that the witness was
duly sworn by him and that the deposition is a true record of the
testimony given by the witness.   He shall then securely seal the

deposition in an envelope endorsed with the title of the action and marked Deposition of (here insert name of witness) and shall promptly file it with the court in which the action is pending or send it by either registered or certified mail to the clerk thereof for filing.

(2)   Upon payment of reasonable charges therefor, the officer shall furnish a copy of the deposition to any party or to the deponent.

(3)   ° ° °

§ 25-1267.29.   Deposition; written interrogatories; officer; duties. A copy of the notice and copies of all interrogatories served shall be delivered by the party taking the deposition to the officer designated in the notice, who shall proceed promptly, in the manner provided by sections 25-1267.23, 25-1267.25, and 25-1267.26,† to take the testimony of the witness in response to the interrogatories and to prepare, certify, and file or mail the deposition, attaching thereto a copy of the notice and the interrogatories received by him.

† See above.

Videotape Depositions

§ 25-1267.45.   Act; applicable to all courts; videotape; recording; objections.   (1)   The provisions of this act shall apply to all trial courts of record in Nebraska in the reception and utilization of testimony and other evidence recorded on videotape.

(2)(a)   A party taking a deposition may have the testimony recorded by videotape by complying with the provisions of this section.

(b)   The taking of a videotape deposition is subject to the requirements of this act and existing law regarding notice specifying the manner of recording, preserving, and filing of the videotape deposition, but it shall be sufficient in this regard if the notice specifies that the videotape deposition is to be taken pursuant to the provisions of this section regarding the recording, preserving, and filing of the videotape deposition.

(c)   The officer before whom a videotape deposition is taken shall be subject to the provisions enumerated in sections 25-1267.14 to 25-1267.18.°   Upon the request of any of the parties, the officer shall provide, at the cost of the party making the request, a copy of the deposition in the form of a videotape, an audio recording, or a written transcript.

(d)   When the videotape deposition has been taken, the videotape shall be shown immediately to the witness for examination, unless such showing and examination are waived by the witness and the parties.   Any changes in form or substance which the witness desires to make shall be recorded on the videotape with a statement by the witness on such tape of the reasons given by him for making such changes.

(e)   The officer before whom the videotape deposition is taken shall cause to be attached to the original videotape recording a certification that the witness was fully sworn or affirmed by him and that the videotape recording is a true record of the testimony given by the witness. If the witness has not waived his right to a showing and examination of the videotape deposition, the witness shall also sign the certification.

(f)(i) If no objections have been made by any of the parties during the course of the deposition, the videotape deposition, with the certification, shall be filed by the officer with the clerk of the trial court in accordance with subsection (1) of section 25-1267.26° and notice of its filing shall be given ° ° °.

(ii) If objections have been made by any of the parties during the course of the deposition, the videotape deposition, with the certification, shall be submitted by the officer to the trial judge upon the request of any of the parties within ten days after its recording or within such other period of time as the parties may stipulate, for the purpose of obtaining rulings on the objections. An audio copy of the sound track may be submitted in lieu of the videotape for this purpose. For the purpose of ruling on the objections, the trial judge may view the entire videotape recording, view only those parts made, or he may listen to an audio-tape recording submitted in lieu of the videotape recording. The trial judge shall rule on the objections prior to the date set for the trial of the action and shall return the recording to the officer with notice to the parties of his rulings and of his instructions as to editing. The editing shall reflect the rulings of the trial judge and shall then remove all references to the objections. The officer shall then cause the videotape to be edited in accordance with the court's instructions and shall cause both the original videotape recording and the edited version of that recording, each clearly identified, to be filed with the clerk of the trial court.

(g) Each trial court shall provide secure and adequate facilities for the storage of videotape recordings.

(h) Except upon order of the trial judge and upon such terms as he may provide, the videotape recordings on file with the clerk of the trial court shall not be available for inspection or viewing after their filing and prior to their use at the trial of the cause or their disposition in accordance with this section. The clerk may release the videotape to the officer taking the deposition, without the order of the trial judge, for the purpose of preparing a copy at the request of a party as provided in subdivision (2)(c) of this section.

(i) The effectiveness of a videotape deposition will be greatly increased when all of the objections have been ruled upon, following the procedures set forth in this section, prior to the time of trial. If an objection is made at the time of trial, which objection has not previously been waived ° ° ° or previously raised and ruled upon, such objection shall be made before the videotape deposition is presented and shall be ruled upon by the trial judge in advance of that presentation. If such objection is sustained, that portion of the videotape deposition containing the objectionable testimony shall not be presented to the jury.

* See above.

NEVADA

The seal of the court must be affixed to, among other things, a commission to take testimony. See *Acknowledgments*, NEV. REV. STAT. § 1.180.

Affidavits

[NEV. REV. STAT.]

§ 53.010. Officers before whom affidavits may be taken for use in this state. An affidavit to be used before any court, judge or officer of this state may be taken before any justice, judge or clerk of any court, or any justice of the peace or notary public in this state.

§ 53.020. Taking of affidavits in other states and territories for use in this state. An affidavit taken in another state or in a territory of the United States to be used in this state shall be taken before a commissioner appointed by the governor of this state to take affidavits and depositions in such other state or territory, or before any notary public or judge of a court of record having a seal.

§ 53.030. Certification of signature of officer to affidavit taken in another state or territory. When an affidavit is taken before a judge of a court in another state or in a territory of the United States, the genuineness of the signature of the judge, the existence of the court, and the fact that such judge is a member thereof shall be certified by the clerk of the court, under the seal thereof.

§ 53.040. Taking of affidavits in foreign countries. An affidavit taken in a foreign country to be used in this state shall be taken before an ambassador, minister, consul, vice consul or other consular agent of the United States, or any notary public or other person authorized by the laws of such country to administer oaths, or before any judge of a court of record of such foreign country, with the seal of the court attached, if there be one, and if there be none, then with a statement attached by the judge or clerk of the court to the effect that the court has no seal.

Foreign Depositions

§ 53.050. Short title. NRS 53.050 to 53.070, inclusive, may be cited as the Uniform Foreign Depositions Act.

§ 53.060. Authority to act. Whenever any mandate, writ or commission is issued out of any court of record in any other state, territory, district or foreign jurisdiction, or whenever upon notice or agreement it is required to take the testimony of a witness or witnesses in this state, witnesses may be compelled to appear and testify in the same manner and by the same process and proceeding as may be employed for the purpose of taking testimony in proceedings pending in this state.

§ 53.070. **Uniformity of interpretation.** NRS 53.050 to 53.070, inclusive, shall be so interpreted and construed as to effectuate their general purposes to make uniform the law of those states which enact them.

Justices' Courts

[NEV. JUSTICES' CT. R. CIV. P. 1]

Scope of Rules

These rules govern the procedure in the justices' courts in all suits of a civil nature, with the exceptions stated in Rule 81. They shall be construed to secure the just, speedy, and inexpensive determination of every action.

28. Persons Before Whom Depositions May Be Taken

(a) **Within the United States.** Within the United States or within a territory or insular possession subject to the dominion of the United States, depositions shall be taken before an officer authorized to administer oaths by the laws of the United States or of the place where the examination is held, or before a person appointed by the court in which the action is pending. A person so appointed has power to administer oaths and take testimony. Upon proof that the notice to take a deposition outside the State of Nevada has been given as provided in these rules, the clerk or justice shall issue a commission or letters rogatory in the form prescribed by the jurisdiction in which the deposition is to be taken, such form to be presented by the party seeking the deposition. Any error in the form or in the commission or letters is waived unless objection thereto be filed and served on or before the time fixed in the notice.

(b) **In foreign countries.** In a foreign country, depositions may be taken (1) on notice before a person authorized to administer oaths in the place in which the examination is held, either by the law thereof or by the law of the United States, or (2) before a person commissioned by the court, and a person so commissioned shall have the power by virtue of his commission to administer any necessary oath and take testimony, or (3) pursuant to a letter rogatory. A commission or a letter rogatory shall be issued on application and notice and on terms that are just and appropriate. It is not requisite to the issuance of a commission or a letter rogatory that the taking of the deposition in any other manner is impracticable or inconvenient; and both a commission and a letter rogatory may be issued in proper cases. A notice or commission may designate the person before whom the deposition is to be taken either by name or descriptive title. A letter rogatory may be addressed "To the Appropriate Authority in [here name the country]." Evidence obtained in response to a letter rogatory need not be excluded merely for the reason that it is not a verbatim transcript or that the testimony was not taken under oath or for any similar departure from the requirements for depositions taken within the United States under these rules.

(c) **Disqualification for interest.** No deposition shall be taken before a person who is a relative or employee or attorney or counsel of any of the parties, or is a relative or employee of such attorney or counsel, or is financially interested in the action.

District Courts

[NEV. R. CIV. P. (DIST. CT.) 1]

Scope of Rules

These rules govern the procedure in the district courts in all suits of a civil nature whether cognizable as cases at law or in equity, with the exceptions stated in Rule 81. They shall be construed to secure the just, speedy, and inexpensive determination of every action.

28. Persons Before Whom Depositions May Be Taken

(a) **Within the United States.** Within the United States or within a territory or insular possession subject to the dominion of the United States, depositions shall be taken before an officer authorized to administer oaths by the laws of the United States or of the place where the examination is held, or before a person appointed by the court in which the action is pending. A person so appointed has power to administer oaths and take testimony. Upon proof that the notice to take a deposition outside the State of Nevada has been given as provided in these rules, the clerk shall issue a commission or letters rogatory in the form prescribed by the jurisdiction in which the deposition is to be taken, such form to be presented by the party seeking the deposition. Any error in the form or in the commission or letters is waived unless objection thereto be filed and served on or before the time fixed in the notice.

(b) **In foreign countries.** In a foreign country, depositions may be taken (1) on notice before a person authorized to administer oaths in the place in which the examination is held, either by the law, thereof or by the law of the United States, or (2) before a person commissioned by the court, and a person so commissioned shall have the power by virtue of his commission to administer any necessary oath and take testimony, or (3) pursuant to a letter rogatory. A commission or a letter rogatory shall be issued on application and notice and on terms that are just and appropriate. It is not requisite to the issuance of a commission or a letter rogatory that the taking of the deposition in any other manner is impracticable or inconvenient; and both a commission and a letter rogatory may be issued in proper cases. A notice or commission may designate the person before whom the deposition is to be taken either by name or descriptive title. A letter rogatory may be addressed "To the Appropriate Authority in [here name the country]." Evidence obtained in response to a letter rogatory need not be excluded merely for the reason that it is not a verbatim transcript or that the testimony was not taken under oath or for any similar departure from the requirements for depositions taken within the United States under these rules.

(c) **Disqualification for interest.** No deposition shall be taken before a person who is a relative or employee or attorney or counsel of any of the parties, or is a relative or employee of such attorney or counsel, or is financially interested in the action.

NEW HAMPSHIRE

Witnesses

[N.H. REV. STAT. ANN.]

§ **516:4. Issue [of summonses] for depositions.** Any justice or notary may issue [summonses] for witnesses to appear before himself or any other justice or notary, to give depositions in any matter or cause in which the same may be lawfully taken.

Note: Every notary public has the same powers as a justice of the peace in relation to depositions and the administering of oaths. See *Authority and Duties,* N.H. REV. STAT. ANN. § 455:3.

§ **516:7. Penalty [for Neglect to Attend].** Every court, justice and notary, before whom a person has been summoned to appear and testify or to give a deposition, may bring the person neglecting or refusing to appear or to testify or to give his deposition, by attachment, before them, and if, on examination, he has no reasonable excuse, may find him guilty of a violation, and may order him to pay costs.

Note: Concerning the punishment for a "violation", see *Offenses,* N.H. REV. STAT. ANN. § 651:2.

§ **516:23. Party deponent.** No party shall be compelled, in testifying or giving a deposition, to disclose the names of the witnesses by whom nor the manner in which he proposes to prove his case, nor, in giving a deposition, to produce any writing which is material to his case or defense, unless the deposition is taken in his own behalf.

Depositions in Civil Cases

§ 517:2.   Before whom. Any justice or notary public in the state, any commissioner appointed under the laws of the state to take depositions in other states, any judge or justice of the peace or notary public in any other state or country, may take such deposition.

§ 517:3.   Disqualifications. No person shall write the testimony of a witness, or act as magistrate in taking the same, who would be disqualified to act as juror on the trial of the cause, for any reason except exemption from service as a juror.

§ 517:7.   Signing; oath. Every witness shall subscribe his deposition, and shall make oath that it contains the truth, the whole truth and nothing but the truth, relative to the cause for which it was taken.

§ 517:8.   Caption. The magistrate taking the deposition shall certify such oath, with the time and place of taking the deposition, the case and court in which it is to be used, that the adverse party was or was not present, was or was not notified, and that he did or did not object.

§ 517:9.   Annexing copy of notice. A copy of the notice left with the adverse party, his agent or attorney, with the return of the officer or affidavit of the person leaving such notice thereon, stating the time of leaving it, shall be annexed to the caption of the deposition, when the adverse party does not attend.

§ 517:10.   Sealing. Depositions so taken shall be sealed up by the magistrate taking the same, directed to the court or justice before whom they are to be used, with a brief description of the case, and shall be so delivered into court.

§ 517:11.   Deposition of party. Whenever the deposition of a party to an action has been taken it shall, within ten days thereafter, be filed in the office of the clerk of the court in which the action is pending. Either party may use the deposition upon the trial of the cause, unless the deponent is in attendance.

Depositions in Criminal Cases

§ 517:14-e.   Record. The justice presiding at a deposition taken [by the prosecution in a criminal case] shall cause a record to be made of the proceedings and shall cause a copy thereof to be furnished to the defendant. Such record or a copy thereof may be used in the trial of the case whenever in the discretion of the court the use thereof shall be deemed necessary for the promotion of justice.

Commissioners to Take Depositions

§ 517:5.   Appointment. Upon petition the superior court may appoint some suitable person as commissioner to take depositions outside this state, for use in causes pending in or returnable to said court.

§ 517:16. Procedure. After the appointment of such commissioner, the notice of the time and place of taking depositions before him, the proceedings in taking such depositions, the certificates to be made by him, and all other formalities with reference to taking, filing and using such depositions shall be the same, so far as applicable, as for taking other depositions in civil causes.

§ 517:17. Powers. Said commissioner shall have and exercise all the powers conferred by the laws of other states, territories and foreign countries upon commissioners or other persons authorized to take depositions in said other states, territories and foreign countries for use in causes pending in this state.

§ 517:18. Foreign. A commissioner or other person appointed by any court of record of any other state, territory or foreign country, for the purpose of taking depositions in this state for use in causes pending in such court of record, shall have the same powers of procuring the attendance of witnesses to give depositions before him, and of requiring the production of papers and the giving of such depositions, as justices of the peace within this state with reference to depositions for use in civil causes pending within the courts of this state.

Fees for Depositions

§ 517:19. Officials. Justices of the peace or other officers shall be allowed:

For a blank writ of summons, ten cents.

For swearing each witness and caption of deposition, thirty-four cents.

For writing a deposition, each page, seventeen cents.

For travel to swear witnesses each mile, six cents.

§ 517:20. Stenographers. When by agreement of the parties depositions are taken in shorthand and thereafter transcribed, or are taken down by the use of a typewriter, the court may allow as costs the whole or any part of the expense thereof, as justice may require.

NEW JERSEY

All oaths, affirmations and affidavits required to be made or taken by New Jersey law, or necessary or proper to be made, taken or used in any court of New Jersey, or for any lawful purpose, may be made and taken before, among others, notaries public and commissioners of deeds. See *Authority and Duties*, N.J. STAT. ANN. § 41:2-1.

[N.J. STAT. ANN.]

§ 41:2-17. Officers authorized to administer or take [oaths, affirmations or affidavits out of state]; jurat; certificate. Any oath, affirmation or affidavit required or authorized to be taken in any suit or legal proceeding in this state, or for any lawful purpose whatever, except official oaths and depositions required to be taken upon notice, when taken out of this state, may be taken before any notary public of the state, territory, nation, kingdom or country in which the same shall be taken, or before any officer who may be authorized by the laws of this state to take the acknowledgment of deeds in such state, territory, nation, kingdom or country; and a recital that he is such notary or officer in the jurat or certificate of such oath, affirmation or affidavit, and his official designation annexed to his signature, and attested under his official seal, shall be sufficient proof that the person before whom the same is taken is such notary or officer. When, however, any other certificate is required by law to be annexed to the certificate of such officer, other than a notary public, for the recording of a deed acknowledged before him, a like certificate shall be annexed to his certificate of the taking of such oath.

Civil Practice

Superior Court, County Courts and Surrogate's Courts

[N.J. R. CIV. PRAC. 4:12]

Persons Before Whom Depositions May Be Taken; Authority

4:12-1. Within the state. Within this State, depositions shall be taken before a person authorized by the laws of this State to administer oaths.

4:12-2. Without the state but within the United States. Outside this State but within the United States or within a territory or insular possession subject to the dominion of the United States, depositions shall be taken before a person authorized to administer oaths by the laws of this State, of the United States or of the place where the examination is held.

4:12-3. In foreign countries. In a foreign country depositions shall be taken (a) on notice before a secretary of embassy or legation, consul general, consul, vice consul, or consular agent of the United States, or (b) before such person or officer as may be appointed by commission or under letters rogatory. A commission or letters rogatory shall be issued only when necessary or convenient, on application and notice, and on such terms and with such directions as are appropriate. Officers may be designated in notices or commissions either by name or descriptive title and letters rogatory may be addressed "To the Appropriate Judicial Authority in (here name the country)".

4:12-4. Disqualification for interest. No deposition shall be taken before or by a person who is a relative, employee or attorney of a party or a relative or employee of such attorney or is financially interested in the action.

Criminal Practice

Superior Court and County Courts

Other Courts

[N.J. R. CRIM. PRAC. 3:13-2]

Depositions

(a) **When and how taken.** If it appears to the judge of the court in which the indictment or accusation is pending, that a material witness may be unable to attend or may be prevented from attending the trial of the indictment or accusation, or any hearing in connection therewith, the court, to prevent injustice, may upon motion and notice to the parties order that the testimony of such witness be taken orally by deposition as provided in civil actions and that any designated books, papers, documents or tangible objects, not privileged, be produced at the same time and place. If a witness is committted for failure to give bail to appear to testify at a trial or hearing, the court on written motion of the witness and upon notice to the parties may direct that his deposition be taken, and after the deposition has been subscribed the court may discharge the witness. The transcript of all depositions shall be filed with the county clerk as provided in civil actions.

(b) **Use.** [Omitted.]

(c) **Objections to admissibility.** Objections to receiving a deposition or part thereof in evidence may be made as provided in civil actions.

NEW MEXICO

Oaths and Affirmations

[N.M. STAT. ANN.]

§ 43-1-1. Administration of oath. Whenever any person shall be required to take an oath befoie he enters upon the discharge of any office, place of business, or on any lawful occasion, any person administering the oath shall do so in the following form, viz.: The person swearing shall, with his right hand uplifted, follow the words required in the oath as administered, beginning: I do solemnly swear, and closing: So help me God.

§ 43-1-2. Administration of affirmation in lieu of oath. Whenever any person is required to take or subscribe an oath and shall have conscientious scruples against taking the same, he shall be permitted, instead of such oath, to make a solemn affirmation, with uplifted right hand, in the following form, viz.: You do solemnly, sincerely and truly declare and affirm, and close with: And this I do under the pains and penalties of perjury, which affirmation shall be equally valid as if such person had taken an oath in the usual form; and every person guilty of falsely, willfully or corruptly declaring as aforesaid, shall be liable to punishment for the same as for perjury.

§ 43-1-3. Officers authorized to administer oaths and affirmations. The secretary of the state of New Mexico, county clerk, clerks of probate courts, clerks of district courts and all duly commissioned and acting notaries public, within the counties for which they are elected or commissioned, are hereby authorized and empowered to administer oaths and affirmations in all cases where magistrates and other officers within the state authorized to administer oaths may do so, under existing laws, and with like effect.

Civil Procedure

[N.M. R. CIV. P. 28]

Persons Before Whom Depositions May Be Taken

(a) **Within the United States.** Within the United States or within a territory or insular possession subject to the dominion of the United States, depositions shall be taken before an officer authorized to administer oaths by the laws of the United States or of the place where the examination is held, or before a person appointed by the court in which the action is pending. A person so appointed has power to administer oaths and take testimony.

(b) **In foreign countries.** In a foreign country, depositions may be taken (1) on notice before a person authorized to administer oaths in the place in which the examination is held, either by the law thereof or by the law of the United States, or (2) before a person commissioned by the court, and a person so commissioned shall have the power by virtue of his commission to administer any necessary oath and take testimony, or (3) pursuant to a letter rogatory. A commission or a letter rogatory shall be issued on application and notice and on terms that are just and appropriate. It is not requisite to the issuance of a commission or a letter rogatory that the taking of the deposition in any other manner is impracticable or inconvenient; and both a commission and a letter rogatory may be issued in proper cases. A notice or commission may designate the person before whom the deposition is to be taken either by name or descriptive title. A letter rogatory may be addressed "To the Appropriate Authority in (here name the country)." Evidence obtained in response to a letter rogatory need not be excluded merely for the reason that it is not a verbatim transcript or that the testimony was not taken under oath or for any similar departure from the requirements for depositions taken within the United States under these rules.

(c) Disqualification for interest. No deposition shall be taken before a person who is a relative or employee or attorney or counsel of any of the parties, or is a relative or employee of such attorney or counsel, or is financially interested in the action.

Criminal Procedure

[N.M. R. CRIM. P. 29]

o   o   o

(d) Persons before whom depositions may be taken.

(1) Within the United States. Within the United States or within a territory or insular possession subject to the dominion of the United States, depositions shall be taken before an officer authorized to administer oaths by the laws of the United States or of the place where the examination is held, or before a person appointed by the court in which the action is pending. A person so appointed has power to administer oaths and take testimony.

(2) In Foreign Countries. In a foreign country, depositions may be taken (i) on notice before a person authorized to administer oaths in the place in which the examination is held, either by the law thereof or by the law of the United States, or (ii) before a person commissioned by the court, and a person so commissioned shall have the power by virtue of his commission to administer any necessary oath and take testimony, or (iii) pursuant to a letter rogatory. A commission or a letter rogatory shall be issued on application and notice and on terms that are just and appropriate. It is not requisite to the issuance of a commission or a letter rogatory that the taking of the deposition in any other manner is impracticable or inconvenient; and both a commission and a letter rogatory may be issued in proper cases. A notice or commission may designate the person before whom the deposition is to be taken either by name or descriptive title. A letter rogatory may be addressed "To the Appropriate Authority in [here name the country]." Evidence obtained in response to a letter rogatory need not be excluded merely for the reason that it is not a verbatim transcript or that the testimony was not taken under oath or for any similar departure from the requirements for depositions taken within the United States under these rules.

(3) Disqualification for Interest. No deposition shall be taken before a person who is a relative, employee, attorney or counsel of any of the parties, or is a relative or employee of such attorney or counsel, or is interested in the action.

(e) Notice of examination: general requirements; nonstenographic recording.

o   o   o

(3) The court may upon motion order that the testimony at a deposition be recorded by other than stenographic means, in which event the order shall designate the manner of recording, preserving, and filing the deposition, and may include other provisions to assure that the recorded testimony will be accurate and trustworthy. If the order is made, a party may nevertheless arrange to have a stenographic transcription made at his own expense.

(f) **Record of examination.** The officer before whom the deposition is to be taken shall put the witness on oath and shall personally, or by someone acting under his direction and in his presence, record the testimony of the witness.

o   o   o

NEW YORK
Oaths and Affirmations

[N.Y. CIV. PRAC. LAW]

§ 2309. **Oaths and affirmations. (a) Persons authorized to administer.** Unless otherwise provided, an oath or affirmation may be administered by any person authorized to take acknowledgments of deeds by the real property law.° Any person authorized by the laws of this state to receive evidence may administer an oath or affirmation for that purpose. An oath to a juror or jurors may be administered by a clerk of court and his deputies. This section shall not apply to an oath of office.

(b) **Form.** An oath or affirmation shall be administered in a form calculated to awaken the conscience and impress the mind of the person taking it in accordance with his religious or ethical beliefs.

(c) **Oaths and affirmations taken without the state.** An oath or affirmation taken without the state shall be treated as if taken within the state if it is accompanied by such certificate or certificates as would be required to entitle a deed acknowledged without the state to be recorded within the state if such deed had been acknowledged before the officer who administered the oath or affirmation.

(d) **Form of certificate of oath or affirmation administered by officer of the armed forces of the United States.** The certificate of an oath or affirmation administered within or without the state or the United States, by an officer of the armed forces of the United States authorized by the real property law to take acknowledgment of deeds, shall state:

1. the rank and serial number of the officer before whom the oath or affirmation is taken and the command to which he is attached;

2. that the person taking the oath or affirmation was, at the time of taking it, a person enlisted or commissioned in or

serving in or with the armed forces of the United States or the dependent of such a person, or a person attached to or accompanying the armed forces of the United States; and

3. the serial number of the person who takes, or whose dependent takes the oath or affirmation, if such person is enlisted or commissioned in the armed forces of the United States. The place where such oath or affidavit is taken need not be disclosed.

° See *Acknowledgments*, N.Y. REAL PROP. LAW §§ 298 *et seq.*

Depositions

Rule 3113. Conduct of the examination. (a) Persons before whom depositions may be taken. Depositions may be taken before any of the following persons except an attorney, or employee of an attorney, for a party or prospective party and except a person who would be disqualified to act as a juror because of interest in the event or consanguinity or affinity to a party:

1. within the state, a person authorized by the laws of the state to administer oaths;

2. without the state but within the United States or within a territory or possession subject to the dominion of the United States, a person authorized to take acknowledgments of deeds outside of the state by the real property law of the state or to administer oaths by the laws of the United States or of the place where the deposition is taken; and

3. in a foreign country, any diplomatic or consular agent or representative of the United States, appointed or accredited to, and residing within, the country, or a person appointed by commission or under letters rogatory, or an officer of the armed forces authorized to take the acknowledgment of deeds.

Officers may be designated in notices or commissions either by name or descriptive title and letters rogatory may be addressed "To the Appropriate Authority in (here name the state or country)."

(b) Oath of witness; transcription of testimony; objections; continuous examination; written questions read by examining officer. The officer before whom the deposition is to be taken shall put the witness on oath and shall personally, or by someone acting under his direction, record the testimony. The testimony shall be transcribed. All objections made at the time of the examination to the qualifications of the officer taking the deposition or the person recording it, or to the manner of taking it, or to the testimony presented, or to the conduct of any person, and any other objection to the proceedings, shall be noted by the officer upon the deposition and the deposition shall proceed subject to the right of a person to apply for a protective order. The deposition shall be taken continuously and without unreasonable adjournment, unless the court otherwise orders or the witness and parties present otherwise agree. In lieu of participating in an oral examination, any party served with notice of taking a deposition may transmit written questions to the officer, who shall propound them to the witness and record the answers.

(c) **Examination and cross-examination.** Examination and cross-examination of deponents shall proceed as permitted in the trial of actions in open court. When the deposition of a party is taken at the instance of an adverse party, the deponent may be cross-examined by his own attorney. Cross-examination need not be limited to the subject matter of the examination in chief.

Rule 3114. Examination of witness who does not understand the English language. If the witness to be examined does not understand the English language, the examining party must, at his own expense, provide a translation of all questions and answers. Where the court settles questions, it may settle them in the foreign language and in English. It may use the services of one or more experts whose compensation shall be paid by the party seeking the examination and may be taxed as a disbursement.

Rule 3116. Signing deposition; physical preparation; copies.
(a) **Signing.** The deposition shall be submitted to the witness for examination and shall be read to or by him, and any changes in form or substance which the witness desires to make shall be entered at the end of the deposition with a statement of the reasons given by the witness for making them. The deposition shall then be signed by the witness before any officer authorized to administer an oath. If the witness fails to sign the deposition, the officer before whom the deposition was taken shall sign it and state on the record the fact of the witness' failure or refusal to sign, together with any reason given. The deposition may then be used as fully as though signed.

(b) **Certification and filing by officer.** The officer before whom the deposition was taken shall certify on the deposition that the witness was duly sworn by him and that the deposition is a true record of the testimony given by the witness. He shall list all appearances by the parties and attorneys. If the deposition was taken on written questions, he shall attach to it the copy of the notice and written questions received by him. He shall then securely seal the deposition in an envelope endorsed with the title of the action and the index number of the action, if one has been assigned, and marked "Deposition of (here insert name of witness)" and shall promptly file it with, or send it by registered or certified mail to the clerk of the court where the case is to be tried. The deposition shall always be open to the inspection of the parties, each of whom is entitled to make copies thereof. If a copy of the deposition is furnished to each party or if the parties stipulate to waive filing, the officer need not file the original but may deliver it to the party taking the deposition.

(c) Exhibits. Documentary evidence exhibited before the officer or exhibits marked for identification during the examination of the witness shall be annexed to and returned with the deposition. However, if requested by the party producing documentary evidence or on exhibit, the officer shall mark it for identification as an exhibit in the case, give each party an opportunity to copy or inspect it, and return it to the party offering it, and it may then be used in the same manner as if annexed to and returned with the deposition.

(d) Expenses of taking. Unless the court orders otherwise, the party taking the deposition shall bear the expense thereof.

(e) Errors of officer or person transcribing. Errors and irregularities of the officer or the person transcribing the deposition are waived unless a motion to suppress the deposition or some part thereof is made with reasonable promptness after such defect is, or with due diligence might have been, ascertained.

NORTH CAROLINA

[N.C. GEN. STAT.]

§ 8-75. Depositions in justices' courts. Any party in a civil action before a justice of the peace may take the depositions of all persons whose evidence he may desire to use in the action, and in order to do so may apply to the clerk of the superior court for a commission to take the same; or such deposition may be taken by a notary public of this or any other state, or of a foreign country, without a commission issuing from the court.

The proceedings in depositions in a civil action before a justice of the peace shall be in all respects as if such action were in the superior court.

When any such depositions are returned to the clerk, they shall be opened and passed upon by the clerk, and delivered to the justice of the peace before whom the trial is to be had; and the reading and using of said depositions shall conform to the rules of the superior court.

§ 8-76. Depositions before municipal authorities. Any board of alderman, board of town or county commissioners or any person interested in any proceeding, investigation, hearing or trial before such board, may take the depositions of all persons whose evidence may be desired for use in said proceeding, investigation, hearing or trial; and to do so, the chairman of such board or such person may apply in person or by attorney to the superior court clerk of that county in which such proceeding, investigation, hearing or trial is pending, for a commission to take the same, and said clerk, upon such application, shall issue such commission, or such deposition may be taken 1·, a notary public of this State or of any other state or foreign country without a commission issuing from the court; and the notice and proceedings upon the taking of said depositions shall be the same as provided for in civil actions; and if the person upon the notice of the taking of such deposition is to be served is absent from or cannot after due diligence be found within this State, but can be found within the county in which the deposition is to be taken, then, and in that case, said notice shall be personally served on such person by the commissioner appointed to take such deposition or by the notary taking such deposition, as the case may be; and when any such deposition is returned to the clerk it shall be opened and passed upon by him and delivered to such board, and the reading and using of such deposition shall conform to the rules of the superior court.

§ 8-77. **Depositions in quo warranto proceedings.** In all actions for the purpose of trying the title to the office of clerk of the superior court, register of deeds, county treasurer or sheriff of any county, it shall be competent and lawful to take the deposition of witnesses before a commissioner or commissioners to be appointed by the judge of the district wherein the case is to be tried, or the judge holding the court of said district, or the clerk of the court wherein the case is pending, or a notary public, under the same rules as to time of notice and as to the manner of taking and filing the same as is now provided by law for the taking of depositions in other cases; and such depositions, when so taken, shall be competent to be read on the trial of such action, without regard to the place of residence of such witness or distance of residence from said place of trial: Provided, that the provisions of this section shall not be construed to prevent the oral examination, by either party on the trial, of such witnesses as they may summon in their behalf.

§ 8-78. **Commissioner may subpoena witness and punish for contempt.** Commissioners to take depositions appointed by the courts of this State, or by the courts of the states or territories of the United States, arbitrators, referees, and all persons acting under a commission issuing from any court of record in this State, are hereby empowered, they or the clerks of the courts respectively in this State, to which such commission shall be returnable, to issue subpoenas, specifying the time and place for the attendance of witnesses before them, and to administer oaths to said witnesses, to the end that they may give their testimony. And any witness appearing before any of the said persons and refusing to give his testimony on oath touching such matters as he may be lawfully examined unto shall be committed, by warrant of the person before whom he shall so refuse, to the common jail of the county, there to remain until he may be willing to give his evidence; which warrant of commitment shall recite what authority the person has to take the testimony of such witness, and the refusal of the witness to give it.

§ 8-79. **Attendance before commissioner enforced.** The sheriff of the county where the witness may be shall execute all such subpoenas, and make due return thereof before the commissioner, or other person, before whom the witness is to appear, in the same manner, and under the same penalties, as in case of process of a like kind returnable to court; and when the witness shall be subpoenaed five days before the time of his required attendance, and shall fail to appear according to the subpoena and give evidence, the default shall be noted by the commissioner, arbitrator, or other person aforesaid; and in case the default be made before a commissioner acting under authority from courts without the State, the defaulting witness shall forfeit and pay to the party at whose instance he may be subpoenaed fifty dollars, and on the trial for such penalty the subpoena issued by the commissioner, or other person, as aforesaid, with the indorsement thereon of due service by the officer serving the same, together with the default noted as aforesaid and indorsed on the subpoena, shall be prima facie evidence of the forfeiture, and sufficient to entitle the plaintiff to judgment for the same, unless the witness may show his incapacity to have attended.

§ 8-80. **Remedies against defaulting witness before commissioner.** But in case the default be made before a commissioner, arbitrator, referee or other person, acting under a commission or authority from any of the courts of this State, then the same shall be certified under his hand, and returned with the subpoena to the court by which he was commissioned or empowered to take the evidence of such witness; and thereupon the court shall adjudge the defaulting witness to pay to the party at whose instance he was summoned the sum of forty dollars; but execution shall not issue therefor until the same be ordered by the court, after such proceedings had as shall give said witness an opportunity to show cause, if he can, against the issuing thereof.

§ 8-84. **Depositions taken in the State to be used in another state.**
(a) By Whom Obtained. In addition to the other remedies prescribed by law, a party to an action, suit or special proceeding, civil or criminal, pending in a court without the State, either in the United States or any of the possessions thereof, or any foreign country, may obtain, by the proceedings prescribed by this section, the testimony of a witness and in connection therewith the production of books and papers within the State to be used in the action, suit or special proceeding.

(b) Application Filed. Where a commission to take testimony within the State has been issued from the court in which the action, suit or special proceeding is pending, or where a notice has been given, or any other proceeding has been taken for the purpose of taking the testimony within the State pursuant to the laws of the state or country wherein the court is located, or pursuant to the laws of the United States or any of the possessions thereof, if it is a court of the United States, the person desiring such testimony, or the production of papers and documents, may present a verified petition to any justice of the Supreme Court, judge of the Court of Appeals, or judge of the superior court, stating generally the nature of the action or proceeding in which the testimony is sought to be taken, and that the testimony of the witness is material to the issue presented in such action or proceeding, and he shall set forth the substance of or have annexed to his petition a copy of the commission, order, notice, consent or other authority under which the deposition is taken. In case of an application for a subpoena to compel the production of books or papers, the petition shall specify the particular books or papers, the production of which is sought, and show that such books or papers are in the possession of or under the control of the witness and are material upon the issues presented in the action or special proceeding in which the deposition of the witness is sought to be taken.

(c) Subpoena Issued. Upon the filing of such petition, if the justice of the Supreme Court, judge of the Court of Appeals, or judge of the superior court is satisfied that the application is made in good faith to obtain testimony within the provisions of this section, he shall issue a subpoena to the witness, commanding him to appear before the commissioner named in the commission, or before a commissioner within the State, for the state, territory or foreign country in which the notice was given or the proceeding taken, or before the officer designated in the commission, notice or other paper, by his title or office, at a time and place specified in the subpoena, to testify in the action, suit or special proceeding. Where the subpoena directs the production of books or papers, it shall specify the particular books or papers to be produced, and shall specify whether the witness is required to deliver sworn copies of such books or papers to the commissioner or to produce the original thereof for inspection, but such books and original papers shall not be taken from the witness. This subpoena must be served upon the witness at least two days, or, in case of a subpoena requiring the production of books or papers, at least five days before the day on which the witness is commanded to appear. A party to an action or proceeding in which a deposition is sought to be taken, or a witness subpoenaed to attend and give his testimony, may apply to the court issuing such subpoena to vacate or modify the same.

(d) Witness Compelled to Attend and Testify. If the witness shall fail to obey the subpoena, or refuse to have an oath administered, or to testify or to produce a book or paper pursuant to a subpoena, or to subscribe his deposition, the justice or judge issuing the subpoena shall, if it is determined that a contempt has been committed, prescribe punishment as in case of a recalcitrant witness. Upon proof by affidavit that a person to whom a subpoena was issued has failed or refused to obey such subpoena, to be duly sworn or affirmed, to testify or answer a question propounded to him, to produce a book or paper which he has been subpoenaed to produce, or to subscribe to his deposition when correctly taken down, the justice or judge shall grant an order requiring such person to show cause before him, at a time and place specified, why he should not appear, be sworn or affirmed, testify, answer a question propounded, produce a book or paper, or subscribe to the deposition, as the case may be. Such affidavit shall set forth the nature of the action or special proceeding in which the testimony is sought to be taken, and a copy of the pleadings or other papers defining the issues in such action or special proceeding, or the facts to be proved therein. Upon the return of such order to show cause, the justice or judge shall, upon such affidavit and upon the original petition and upon such other facts as shall appear, determine whether such person should be required to appear, be sworn or affirmed, testify, answer the question propounded, produce the books or papers, or subscribe to his deposition, as the case may be, and may prescribe such terms and conditions as shall seem proper. Upon proof of a failure or refusal on the part of any person to comply with any order of the court made upon such determination, the justice or judge shall make an order requiring such person to show cause before him, at a time and place therein specified, why such person should not be punished for the offense as for a contempt. Upon the return of the order to show cause, the questions which arise must be determined as upon a motion. If such failure or refusal is established to the satisfaction of the justice or judge before whom the order to show cause is made returnable, he shall enforce the order and prescribe the punishment as hereinbefore provided.

(e) Deposit for Costs Required. The commissioner herein provided for shall not proceed to act under and by virtue of his appointment until the party seeking to obtain such deposition has deposited with him a sufficient sum of money to cover all costs and charges incident to the taking of the deposition, including such witness fees as are allowed to witnesses in this State for attendance upon the superior courts. From such deposit the commissioner shall retain whatever amount may be due him for services, pay the witness fees and other costs that may have been incurred by reason of taking such deposition, and if any balance remains in his hands, he shall pay the same to the party by whom it was advanced.

NORTH DAKOTA

[N.D. CENT. CODE]

§ 27-10-23. **Contempt of witness before notary public, officer, board, or tribunal.** If a witness fails to attend for examination when duly required to do so, or refuses to be sworn, or to answer as a witness, before a notary public or any other officer, board, or tribunal authorized by law to require his attendance for examination and to take testimony, such notary public, officer, board, or tribunal shall certify such fact to the judge of the district court of the county in which such witness resides or in which such witness may be present. Such judge, by order, then shall require such witness to attend before him for examination at a time and place specified in the order. Upon the return day of the order, the examination of the witness shall be conducted before the judge, and for the failure of such witness to attend, or to be sworn, or to answer as a witness, or for a refusal of such witness to do any act required of him by law, he may be punished as for a contempt in the manner provided in this chapter.

§ 31-04-02. "Affidavit" defined. An affidavit is a written declaration under oath made without notice to the adverse party.

§ 31-04-03. "Deposition" defined. A deposition is a written declaration under oath made upon notice to the adverse party for the purpose of enabling him to attend and cross-examine, or upon written interrogatories.

§ 31-06-16. Commission, how issued — Contents. Every commission issued in a criminal action for the examination of a witness outside of this state shall be issued under the seal of the court and under the signature of the clerk thereof. Such commission:

1. Shall be directed to some person designated as commissioner;
2. Shall authorize the person to whom it is directed to examine the witness named therein on oath and on the interrogatories thereto attached as provided in this chapter;
3. Shall authorize such person to take and certify the deposition of such witness and return it according to the instructions given with the commission; and
4. Shall have annexed to it a copy of section 31-06-18.

§ 31-06-18. Method of execution of commission by commissioner. The commissioner named in a commission for the taking of a deposition outside of this state on behalf of a defendant in a criminal action, unless otherwise specially directed, in executing the commission shall:

1. Administer an oath to the witness that his answers given to the interrogatories and cross interrogatories shall be the truth, the whole truth, and nothing but the truth;
2. Cause the examination of the witness to be reduced to writing and subscribed by him;
3. Write the answers of the witness as nearly as possible in the language in which he gives them, and he shall read to such witness each answer so taken down, and shall correct or add to it until it conforms to what the witness declares is the truth;
4. State that the witness declines to answer a question, if such is the case, and the reason assigned by the witness for declining to answer;

5. Certify and annex to the deposition any papers or documents, or copies thereof, which are produced before him and proved by the witness, and shall see that such papers or documents, or the copies thereof, are subscribed by the witness;

6. Subscribe his name to each sheet of the deposition and to each sheet of the papers or documents annexed to the deposition or to each sheet of the copies thereof;

7. Seal and address his commission and the deposition as directed by the endorsement on his commission; and

8. Deposit his commission and the deposition so sealed as soon as possible in the nearest post office if there is a direction on his commission to return them by mail. If any other direction is made to him as to their return, either by the written consent of the parties or by the court or judge, he shall comply with such direction.

[N.D. R. CIV. P. 28]

Rule 28—Persons Before Whom Depositions May Be Taken

(a) **Within the United States.** Within the United States or within a territory or insular possession subject to the dominion of the United States, depositions shall be taken before an officer authorized to administer oaths by the laws of this state or of the United States or of the place where the examination is held, or before a person appointed by the court in which the action is pending. A person so appointed has power to administer oaths and take testimony.

(b) **In foreign countries.** In a foreign state or country depositions shall be taken (1) on notice before a secretary of embassy or legation, consul general, consul, vice consul, or consular agent of the United States, or (2) before such person or officer as may be appointed by commission or under letters rogatory. A commission or letters rogatory shall be issued only when necessary or convenient, on application and notice, and on such terms and with such directions as are just and appropriate. Officers may be designated in notices or commissions either by name or descriptive title and letters rogatory may be addressed "To the Appropriate Judicial Authority in (here name the Country)".

(c) **Disqualification for interest.** No depositions shall be taken before a person who is a relative or employee or attorney or counsel of any of the parties, or is a relative or employee of such attorney or counsel, or is financially interested in the action.

OHIO

[OHIO REV. CODE ANN.]

§ 147.38. **Armed forces officers may administer oaths.** Any commissioned officer of the armed forces of the United States may administer oaths, take depositions, affidavits, and acknowledgments of deeds, mortgages, leases, and other conveyances of lands, and all powers of attorney of any person, or the dependent of any person, who for the time being is in the armed forces of the United States, wherever they may be, and of persons, and dependents thereof, serving with, employed by, or accompanying the armed forces outside the United States, in the same manner as a judge of a county court, commissioner of this state, or notary public might do.

Any oath administered and deposition or affidavit taken, or acknowledgment certified by such officer if otherwise in accordance with law, shall be as effectual for all purposes, as if administered, taken, or certified by any judge of a county court, commissioner of this state, or notary public.

§ 147.40. **Manner of taking depositions.** Depositions taken in pursuance of section 147.38 of the Revised Code, shall be taken on written interrogatories, on a written notice being given by the party desiring to take such depositions, which notice shall contain the names of the parties plaintiff and defendant, the court or tribunal in which the action is pending, the number of the regiment or battalion to which the witness belongs, and the names of the witnesses. Said notice shall be served upon the adverse party, or his agent or attorney of record, or left at his usual place of abode, with a copy of the interrogatories, at least twenty days prior to the taking of such depositions. If the party on whom such notice is served desires to file cross-interrogatories, a copy of the same shall be served on the adverse party, or his agent or attorney of record, or left at his usual place of abode, within six days after said notice of taking depositions has been served, and the party giving the notice to take depositions, shall forward with his said notice and interrogatories, the cross-interrogatories so served on him; and neither party, by himself, or his agent or attorney, shall be present at the time of taking such depositions.

§ 2319.03. **Use of affidavit.** An affidavit may be used to verify a pleading, to prove the service of the summons, notice, or other process in an action; or to obtain a provisional remedy, an examination of a witness, a stay of proceedings, or upon a motion, and in any other case permitted by law.

§ 2319.04. **Before whom affidavit may be made.** An affidavit may be made in or out of this state before any person authorized to take depositions, and unless it is a verification of a pleading it must be authenticated in the same way as a deposition.

Such affidavit may be made before any person authorized to administer oaths whether an attorney in the case or not.

§ 2319.09. **Uniform foreign depositions.** Whenever any mandate, writ, or commission is issued out of any court of record in any other state, territory, district, or foreign jurisdiction, or whenever upon notice or agreement it is required to take the testimony of a witness in this state, witnesses may be compelled to appear and testify in the same manner and by the same process and proceedings as are employed for the purpose of taking testimony in proceedings pending in this state.

This section shall be so interpreted and construed as to effectuate its general purpose to make the law of this state uniform with those states which enact similar legislation.

§ 2319.10. Officers authorized to take depositions. Depositions may be taken in this state before a judge or the clerk of the supreme court, a judge or clerk of the court of appeals, a judge or clerk of the court of common pleas, a probate judge, justice of the peace, notary public, mayor, master commissioner, official stenographer of any court in this state, or any person empowered by a special commission.

§ 2319.27. Fees for taking depositions; lien. The following fees shall be allowed for taking depositions in this state: Swearing each witness, four cents; for each subpoena, attachment, or order of commitment, fifty cents; for each hundred words contained in the deposition and certificate, ten cents.

The officer may retain the deposition until such fees are paid. He shall also tax the costs of the sheriff or other officer who serves the process, and fees of the witnesses, and, if directed by a person entitled thereto, may retain such depositions until his fees are paid.

§ 2319.28. Exceptions. Exceptions to depositions shall be in writing, shall specify the grounds of objection, and be filed with the papers in the cause.

Criminal Procedure

§ 2945.50. Deposition in criminal cases. At any time after an issue of fact is joined upon an indictment, information, or an affidavit, the prosecution or the defendant may apply in writing to the court in which such indictment, information, or affidavit is pending for a commission to take the depositions of any witness. The court or a judge thereof may grant such commission and make an order stating in what manner and for what length of time notice shall be given to the prosecution or to the defendant, before such witness shall be examined.

§ 2945.54. Conduct of examination. The examination of witnesses by deposition in criminal cases shall be taken and certified, and the return thereof to the court made as for taking depositions under sections 2319.05 to 2319.31, inclusive, of the Revised Code. The commissioners appointed under section 2945.50 of the Revised Code to take depositions shall receive such compensation as the court directs, to be paid out of the county treasury and taxed as part of the costs in the case.

Note: §§ 2319.05 to 2319.31 were repealed, effective in 1971, but the repealing act said that for the purpose of depositions in criminal cases under § 2945.54, §§ 2319.05 to 2319.31 should continue effective without change. Pertinent provisions include the following:

§ **2319.05.** (Repealed) The deposition of a witness may be used only:

(A) When it is made to appear to the satisfaction of the court that he does not reside in, or is absent from, the county where the action or proceeding is pending, or, by change of venue, is sent for trial;

(B) When he is dead, or, from age, infirmity, or imprisonment, is unable to attend court;

(C) When the testimony is required upon a motion, or where the oral examination of the witness is not required;

(D) When he is an attending physician or medical expert, although residing within the county in which the action is heard. This section shall not preclude either party from calling such a witness to appear personally at the trial.

Nothing contained in division (D) of section 2319.05 of the Revised Code shall prevent the taking and use of any deposition otherwise provided by law.

§ **2319.10.** (Repealed) Depositions may be taken in this state before a judge or the clerk of the supreme court, a judge or clerk of the court of appeals, a judge or clerk of the court of common pleas, a probate judge, judge of the county court, notary public, mayor, master commissioner, official stenographer of any court in this state, or any person empowered by a special commission.

§ **2319.20.** (Repealed) ° ° ° Such depositions must be sealed up, indorsed with the title of the action or proceeding, the name of the officer before whom taken, and addressed and transmitted by him to such county court judge, mayor or other judicial officer, arbitrators, referees, or masters.

Civil Procedure

[OHIO R. CIV. P. 28]

Persons Before Whom Depositions May Be Taken

(A) **Depositions within state.** Depositions may be taken in this state before: a person authorized to administer any oath by the laws of this state, a person appointed by the court in which the action is pending, or a person agreed upon by written stipulation of all the parties.

(B) **Depositions outside state.** Depositions may be taken outside this state before: a person authorized to administer oaths in the place where the deposition is taken, a person appointed by the court in which the action is pending, a person agreed upon by written stipulation of all the parties, or, in any foreign country, by any consular officer of the United States within his consular district.

(C) **Disqualification for interest.** Unless the parties agree otherwise as provided in Rule 29 depositions shall not be taken before a person who is a relative, employee or attorney of any of the parties, or is a relative or employee of such attorney, or is financially interested in the action.

OKLAHOMA

[OKLA. STAT. ANN.]

Tit. 12, § 435. Before whom [depositions] taken. Depositions may be taken in this State before a judge or clerk of a court of record, before a county clerk, justice of the peace, notary public, or before a master commissioner, or any person empowered by a special commission; but depositions taken in this State, to be used therein, must be taken by an officer or person whose authority is derived within the State.

Tit. 12, § 436. Depositions out of State. Depositions may be taken out of this State by a judge, justice or chancellor of any court of record, a justice of the peace, notary public, mayor or chief magistrate of any city or town corporate, or any person authorized by a special commission from this State.

Tit. 12, § 437. Officer to be disinterested. The officer before whom depositions are taken must not be a relative or attorney of either party, or otherwise interested in the event of the action or proceeding.

Tit. 12, § 438. Commission to take depositions. Any court of record of this State, or any judge thereof, is authorized to grant a commission to take depositions within or without the State. The commission must be issued to a person or persons therein named, by the clerk, under the seal of the court granting the same; and depositions under it must be taken upon written interrogatories, unless the parties otherwise agree.

Tit. 12, § 441. Manner of writing deposition. The deposition shall be written in the presence of the officer taking the same, either by the officer, the witness or some disinterested person, and subscribed by the witness, or the deposition may be taken in shorthand by the officer or some disinterested person, and if so taken and after being transcribed shall be subscribed by the witness as though taken in long hand in the first instance.

Tit. 12, § 442. Filing. The deposition, so taken, shall be sealed up and indorsed with the title of the cause and the name of the officer taking the same, and by him addressed and transmitted to the clerk of the court where the action or proceeding is pending. It shall remain under seal until opened by the clerk by order of the court, or at the request of a party to the action or proceeding, or his attorney.

Tit. 12, § 445.   Authentication of depositions. Depositions taken pursuant to this article, by any judicial or other officer herein authorized to take depositions, having a seal of office, whether resident in this State or elsewhere, shall be admitted in evidence, upon the certificate and signature of such officer, under the seal of the court of which he is an officer, or his official seal; and no other or further act of authentication shall be required. If the officer taking the same have no official seal, the deposition, if not taken in this State, shall be certified and signed by such officer, and shall be further authenticated, either by parol proof, adduced in court, or by the official certificate and seal of the Secretary of State or other officer of the State keeping the great seal thereof, or of the clerk or prothonotary of any court having a seal, attesting that such judicial or other officer was, at the time of taking the same, duly qualified, and acting as such officer. But if the deposition be taken within this State by an officer having no seal, or within or without this State under a special commission, it shall be sufficiently authenticated by the official signature of the officer or commissioner taking the same.

Tit. 12, § 446.   Certificate of officer. The officer taking the deposition shall annex thereto a certificate, showing the following facts: That the witness was first sworn to testify the truth, the whole truth, and nothing but the truth; that the deposition was reduced to writing or taken in shorthand and transcribed by some proper person, naming him; that the deposition was subscribed in the presence of the officer certifying thereto; that the deposition was taken at the time and place specified in the notice.

Tit. 12, § 1703.01.   Taking of depositions outside state for use in state. (a) A deposition to obtain testimony or documents or other things in an action or proceeding pending in this state may be taken outside this state:

(1) On reasonable notice in writing to all parties, setting forth the time and place for taking the deposition, the name and address of each person to be examined, if known, and if not known, a general description sufficient to identify him or the particular class or group to which he belongs, and the name or descriptive title of the person before whom the deposition will be taken.

(x) The deposition may be taken before a person authorized to administer oaths in the place in which the deposition is taken by the law thereof or by the law of this state, or the United States; or

(y) Before a person commissioned by the court, and a person so commissioned shall have the power by virtue of his commission to administer any necessary oath; or

(z)   Pursuant to a letter rogatory issued by the court.   A letter rogatory may be addressed "To the Appropriate Authority in (here name the state or county)."

(2)   In any manner, before any person, at any time or place, upon any notice, as stipulated by the parties.   A person designated by the stipulation has the power by virtue of his designation to administer any necessary oath.

(b)   A commission or a letter rogatory shall be issued after notice and application to the court, and on terms that are just and appropriate.   It is not requisite to the issuance of a commission or a letter rogatory that the taking of the deposition in any other manner is impracticable or inconvenient, and both a commission and a letter rogatory may be issued in proper cases.   Evidence obtained in a foreign country in response to a letter rogatory need not be excluded merely for the reason that it is not a verbatim transcript or that the testimony was not taken under oath or for any similar departure from the requirements for depositions taken within this state.

(c)   When no action or proceeding is pending, a court of this state may authorize a deposition of any person to be taken outside this state regarding any matter that may be cognizable in any court of this state.   The court may prescribe the manner in which and the terms upon which the deposition shall be taken.

Tit. 12, § 1703.02.   Taking of depositions within state for use outside state.   (a)   A court of this state may order a person who is domiciled or is found within this state to give his testimony or statement or to produce documents or other things for use in a proceeding in a tribunal outside this state.   The order may be made upon the application of any interested person or in response to a letter rogatory and may prescribe the practice and procedure, which may be in whole or in part the practice and procedure of the tribunal outside this state, for taking the testimony or statement or producing the documents or other things.   To the extent that the order does not prescribe otherwise, the practice and procedure shall be in accordance with that of the court of this state issuing the order.   The order may direct that the testimony or statement be given, or document or other thing produced, before a person appointed by the court.   The person appointed shall have power to administer any necessary oath.

(b)   A person within this state may give voluntarily his testimony or statement or produce documents or other things for use in a proceeding before a tribunal outside this state.

Foreign Depositions

Tit. 12, § 461.   Citation of Act.   This may be cited as the Uniform Foreign Depositions Act.

Tit. 12, § 462. Compelling witnesses to appear and testify— Manner, process and proceedings. Whenever any mandate, writ or commission is issued out of any court of record in any other state, territory, district or foreign jurisdiction, or whenever upon notice or agreement it is required to take the testimony of a witness or witnesses in this State, witnesses may be compelled to appear and testify in the same manner and by the same process and proceeding as may be employed for the purpose of taking testimony in proceedings pending in this State.

Tit. 12, § 463. Interpretation and construction. This Act shall be so interpreted and construed as to effectuate its general purposes to make uniform the law of those states which enact it.

Court Reporters

Tit. 20, § 1502. Duties of Board. The [State Board of Examiners of Official Shorthand Reporters] shall have the following duties:

a. conduct preliminary investigations to determine the qualifications of applicants seeking to attain the status of certified or licensed shorthand reporters;

b. conduct at least once a year, at a place and time to be published by ample notice given to all interested parties, an examination of those persons who seek to attain the status of certified or licensed shorthand reporters;

c. recommend to the Supreme Court for official enrollment as certified or licensed court reporters those persons who, on their examination, have established the requisite proficiency in taking testimony and proceedings and in preparing accurate transcription thereof;

d. conduct proceedings, on reasonable notice, the object of which is to recommend to the Supreme Court the suspension, cancellation, revocation or reinstatement of the enrollment of a certified or licensed court reporter or of the status of any acting court reporter, regular or temporary, on the following grounds:

1. conviction of a felony or misdemeanor involving moral delinquency;
2. misrepresentation in obtaining enrollment;
3. any violation of this act;
4. fraud, gross incompetence or neglect;
5. any other violation of duties;
6. nonpayment of renewal dues.

In all hearings or investigations on revocation, cancellation or suspension of enrollment each Board member shall be empowered to administer oaths and affirmations, subpoena witnesses and take evidence anywhere in the state, after giving reasonable notice to the party whose status is sought to be affected.

e.   adopt, with the approval of the Chief Justice, examination standards and rules governing enrollment, discipline, suspension, cancellation and revocation proceedings and any other matter within the Board's cognizance.

f.   keep a current roll of certified and licensed court reporters and a file on all disciplined court reporters, official or unofficial, regular or temporary.

Tit. 20, § 1503.   Examination for enrollment as certified or licensed shorthand reporter.

a.   Every applicant who seeks to be examined for enrollment as a certified or licensed shorthand reporter shall prove to the satisfaction of the Board that he is of legal age, meets the requisite standards of ethical fitness and has at least a high school education or its equivalent.

b.   Every applicant for enrollment as a certified shorthand reporter shall be required, on examination, to demonstrate proficiency in reporting testimony and proceedings at a speed of not less than two hundred (200) words per minute in taking a question-and-answer type dictation only, and no other type, and in preparing an accurate transcription thereof that is reasonably free from spelling errors. Any examination or test given shall be approved by the Supreme Court. The Board may not increase or decrease such minimum speed requirement, by rule or otherwise. Every applicant for enrollment as a licensed shorthand reporter shall be required, on examination, to demonstrate proficiency in reporting testimony and proceedings at a speed of not less than one hundred fifty (150) words per minute in taking a question-and-answer type dictation only, and no other type, and in preparing an accurate transcription thereof that is reasonably free from spelling errors. The Board may not increase or decrease such minimum speed requirement, by rule or otherwise.

c.   As used in paragraph b. hereof, the phrase, "proficiency in reporting testimony and proceedings" shall mean proficiency in verbatim reporting by use of any generally recognized system of symbols or abbreviations written with pen or pencil, stenotype or similar machines, or such other method as may be from time to time approved by the Supreme Court.

Tit. 20, § 1504.   Enrollment without examination. The following persons shall be entitled to enrollment as licensed court reporters without examination:

a.   any noncertified court reporter who was engaged and serving on March 1, 1969, as an official court reporter for the district or superior court;

b.   any person deemed by the Board to hold an equivalent license from another state who is a resident of Oklahoma, provided his credentials are found to be in proper order.

Tit. 20, § 1505. **Licensees from other states.** A person holding a license from another state which is deemed by the Board to be equivalent to that of an Oklahoma certified shorthand reporter may be enrolled without examination as an Oklahoma certified shorthand reporter upon satisfying the Board that his credentials are in proper order and that he is a resident of Oklahoma.

Tit. 20, § 1506. **Fees.** The Board shall charge the following fees:

a. Thirty-five Dollars ($35.00) for an examination fee;

b. Thirty-five Dollars ($35.00) for an application to enroll a licensed or certified shorthand reporter without an examination;

c. Ten Dollars ($10.00) as an annual renewal fee to be paid by all persons enrolled as certified or licensed shorthand reporters.

Tit. 20, § 1508. **Metal seals—use of abbreviations—powers of certified reporters.** Every person enrolled as a certified shorthand reporter shall be entitled to use the abbreviation C.S.R. after his name and shall receive from the Board, without additional charge, a metal seal with his name and the words "Oklahoma Certified Shorthand Reporter." Every person enrolled as a licensed shorthand reporter shall be entitled to use the abbreviation L.S.R. after his name and shall receive from the Board, without additional charge, a metal seal with his name and the words "Oklahoma Licensed Shorthand Reporter." Acting court reporters shall not be allowed the use of a seal. Certified shorthand reporters shall be authorized to issue affidavits in respect to their regular duties, to subpoena witnesses for depositions, administer oaths and affirmations, and to take depositions or other sworn statements, with authority equal to that of a notary public. Licensed shorthand reporters shall have the same authority while employed as official court reporters.

Tit. 20, § 1510. **Severability.** The provisions of this act are severable and if any part or provision hereof shall be held void the decision of the court so holding shall not affect or impair any of the remaining parts or provisions of this act.

OREGON

Oaths and Affirmations

[ORE. REV. STAT.]

§ 44.320. Authority to take testimony and administer oaths. Every court, judge, clerk of a court, justice of the peace or notary public is authorized to take testimony in any action, suit or proceeding, as are other persons in particular cases authorized by statute. Every such court or officer is authorized to administer oaths and affirmations generally, and every such other person in the particular case authorized.

§ **44.330. Form of oath generally.** An oath may be administered as follows: The person who swears holds up his hand, while the person administering the oath addresses him: "You do solemnly swear that the evidence you shall give in the issue (or matter) now pending between ——— and ——— shall be the truth, the whole truth and nothing but the truth, so help you God." If the oath is administered to any other than a witness, the same form and manner may be used.

§ **44.340. Variations in form of oath.** Whenever the court or officer before which a person is offered as a witness is satisfied that he has a peculiar mode of swearing, connected with or in addition to the usual form of administration, which, in his opinion is more solemn or obligatory, the court or officer may in its discretion adopt that mode. When a person is sworn who believes in any other than the Christian religion, he may be sworn according to the peculiar ceremonies of his religion.

§ **44.350. Who may affirm.** Any person who has conscientious scruples against taking an oath may make his solemn affirmation by assenting when addressed in the following form: "You do solemnly affirm that," etc., as in ORS 44.330.

§ **44.360. Affirmation equivalent to oath.** Whenever by statute an oath is required, an affirmation, as prescribed in ORS 44.350, is equivalent, and a false affirmation is perjury equally with a false oath.

Taking Testimony

§ **45.010. Testimony taken in three modes.** The testimony of a witness is taken by three modes:

(1) Affidavit.

(2) Deposition.

(3) Oral examination.

§ **45.020. Affidavit defined.** An affidavit is a written declaration under oath, made without notice to the adverse party.

§ **45.030. Deposition defined.** A deposition is a written declaration under oath, made upon notice to the adverse party for the purpose of enabling him to attend and cross-examine.

Affidavits and Depositions

§ **45.110. Affidavit or deposition, how taken.** In all affidavits and depositions the witness must be made to speak in the first person. Depositions shall be taken in the form of question and answer, unless the parties agree to a different mode.

§ **45.125. Authentication of affidavits taken in another state or country.** An affidavit taken in another state or territory of the

United States, the District of Columbia or in a foreign country must be authenticated as follows before it can be used in this state:

(1) Certified by a commissioner appointed by the Governor of this state to take affidavits in such place; or

(2) Certified by a judge of court, having a clerk and a seal, to have been taken and subscribed before him at a time and place specified, in which case the existence of the court, the fact that the judge is a member and the genuineness of his signature shall be certified by the clerk of the court, under the seal thereof; or

(3) Made and certified before a notary public having a seal, and acting as such by authority of any state or territory of the United States or the District of Columbia and his seal shall be affixed to the affidavit together with the date of the expiration of the notarial commission; or

(4) Made in a foreign country before any minister plenipotentiary, minister extraordinary, minister resident, charge d'affaires, commissioner, consul, vice consul, or consul general of the United States appointed to reside therein, and certified thereon by the signature of the officer taking it; or made before any officer authorized to administer oaths in such foreign country and certified by his signature and official seal.

§ 45.161. **Persons authorized to take depositions; notice to be given.** Such deposition shall be taken before a person authorized to administer oaths in the place where such deposition is taken on giving reasonable notice in writing to every other party to the action, suit or proceeding. ° ° °

§ 45.171. **Manner of taking deposition.** Any party may attend the examination and examine the witness upon oral interrogatories; or in lieu of participating in the oral examination any party served with notice of taking a deposition may transmit written interrogatories to the officer who shall propound them to the witness and record the answers verbatim. The deposition shall be written by the officer taking it, or by the witness, or by some disinterested person, in the presence and under the direction of the officer. When completed, it shall be read to or by the witness and subscribed by him. Before subscribing it, the witness shall be allowed, if he desires, to correct or explain any statement in the deposition, but the statement, although corrected and explained, shall remain a part of the deposition.

§ 45.230. **Certificate of officer taking deposition.** The officer taking the deposition shall append thereto his certificate, under his seal of office, if any, that the deposition was taken before him, at a place mentioned, between certain hours of a day and reduced to writing by a person named; that before proceeding to the examination, the witness was duly sworn to tell the truth, the whole truth, and nothing but the truth; that the deposition was read to or by the witness and was then subscribed by him.

§ 45.240. **Delivery or forwarding of deposition.** The officer taking the deposition shall inclose it in a sealed envelope, directed to the clerk of the court or the justice of the peace before whom the action, suit or proceeding is pending, or such other person as may by writing be agreed upon, and deliver or forward it accordingly, by mail or other usual channel of conveyance.

Depositions upon Commission or Before Commissioners

§ 45.320. **Deposition of witness out of state, how taken.** The deposition of a witness out of the state may be taken upon commission issued from the court, or without commission before a commissioner appointed by the Governor of this state pursuant to ORS 194.210.

§ 45.325. **Taking deposition in this state on written interrogatories.** Any party may also take the deposition of any person, witness or party in this state on written interrogatories attached to a commission, the same as provided for in ORS 45.330 and 45.340, but when such deposition is taken on written interrogatories no party shall be represented by counsel at the time of taking such deposition.

§ 45.330. **Issuance of commission.** The commission may be issued by the clerk of the court, or by a justice of the peace in a cause in his own court, on the application of either party, upon five days' previous notice to the other. It shall be issued to a person agreed upon by the parties, or if they do not agree, to a judge, justice of the peace, notary public or clerk of a court, selected by the officer issuing it.

§ 45.340. **Written and oral interrogatories.** Such interrogatories, direct and cross, as the parties may prepare, to be settled by the court in a summary manner as to form, if the parties disagree, may be annexed to the commission. The examination may be without written interrogatories when the parties agree to that mode.

§ 45.370. **Taking deposition before commissioner appointed by Governor.** The deposition of a witness in any other state or territory of the United States, or the District of Columbia, may also be taken before a commissioner appointed by the Governor of this state to take depositions in that place. ° ° ° Either party may attend the examination and examine the witness upon oral interrogatories, but if either party by written notice to the other, within three days from the service of the original notice, requires it, it shall be taken upon written interrogatories, to be settled, if not agreed upon, by the same officer and in the same manner as in case of a deposition upon commission; and in that case the deposition shall be taken, certified and directed by the commissioner in the same manner as a deposition upon commission.

Foreign Depositions

§ 45.910.   **Uniform Foreign Depositions Act.**   (1) This section may be cited as the Uniform Foreign Depositions Act.

(2) Whenever any mandate, writ or commission is issued out of any court of record in any other state, territory, district or foreign jurisdiction, or whenever upon notice or agreement it is required to take the testimony of a witness or witnesses in this state, witnesses may be compelled to appear and testify in the same manner and by the same process and proceeding as may be employed for the purpose of taking testimony in proceedings pending in this state.

(3) This section shall be so interpreted and construed as to effectuate its general purposes to make uniform the laws of those states which enact it.

PENNSYLVANIA

Foreign Depositions

[PA. STAT. ANN.]

Tit. 28, § 31.   Procedure in general.   Whenever any mandate, writ, or commission is issued out of any court of record of the United States, or any of its territories or possessions, or of any State of the United States, or of any foreign country, or of any jurisdiction outside of Pennsylvania, or whenever, upon notice or agreement, it is required to take the testimony of a witness or witnesses in this State, witnesses may be compelled to appear and testify in the same manner and by the same process and proceeding as may be employed for the purpose of taking testimony in proceedings pending in this State.

Tit. 28, § 32.   Construction of act.   This act shall be so interpreted and construed as to effectuate its general purposes to make uniform the law of those States which enact it.

Tit. 28, § 33.   Citation of act.   This act may be cited as the Uniform Foreign Depositions Act.

Civil Procedure

[PA. R. CIV. P.]

Rule 4015.   Persons Before Whom Depositions May Be Taken.
(a) In the United States or a territory or insular possession subject to the dominion of the United States, depositions shall be taken before an officer authorized to administer oaths by the laws of the United States or of this Commonwealth or of the place where the examination is held.

(b) In a foreign state or country, depositions shall be taken (1) before a secretary of embassy or legation, consul general, consul, vice-consul, or consular agent of the United States, or other person authorized to administer oaths by the laws of the United States, or (2) before such person or officer as may be appointed by commission or under letters rogatory. A commission or letters rogatory shall be issued only when necessary or convenient, on petition, and on such terms and with such directions as are appropriate. Officers may be designated in notices or commissions either by name or descriptive title and letters rogatory may be addressed "To the Appropriate Judicial Authority in [name of country]."

(c) No deposition shall be taken before a person who is a relative, employee or attorney of any of the parties, or who is a relative or employee of such attorney, or who is financially interested in the action.

Rule 4017.1. Videotape Depositions. (a) Any deposition to be taken upon oral deposition may be recorded by videotape without a stenographic transcript. Except as otherwise provided by this rule, the rules of this chapter governing the practice and procedure in depositions and discovery shall apply.

(b) Every notice or subpoena for the taking of a videotape deposition shall state that it is to be videotaped, the name and address of the person whose deposition is to be taken, the name and address of the person before whom it is to be taken, and the name and address of the videotape operator and of his employer. The operator may be an employee of the attorney taking the deposition.

(c) The deposition shall begin by the operator stating on camera (1) his name and address, (2) the name and address of his employer, (3) the date, time and place of the deposition, (4) the caption of the case, (5) the name of the witness, and (6) the party on whose behalf the deposition is being taken. The officer before whom the deposition is taken shall then identify himself and swear the witness on camera. At the conclusion of the deposition the operator shall state on camera that the deposition is concluded. When the length of the deposition requires the use of more than one tape, the end of each tape and the beginning of each succeeding tape shall be announced on camera by the operator.

(d) The deposition shall be timed by a digital clock on camera which shall show continually each hour, minute and second of each tape of the deposition.

(e) No signature of the witness shall be required.

(f) The attorney for the party taking the deposition shall take custody of and be responsible for the safeguarding of the videotape and shall permit the viewing of and shall provide a copy of the videotape or the audio portion thereof upon the request and at the cost of a party.

(g) In addition to the uses permitted by Rule 4020 a videotape deposition of a medical witness or any witness called as an expert, other than a party, may be used at trial for any purpose whether or not the witness is available to testify.

(h) At a trial or hearing that part of the audio portion of a videotape deposition which is offered in evidence and admitted, or which is excluded on objection, shall be transcribed in the same manner as the testimony of other witnesses. The videotape shall be marked as an exhibit and shall remain in the custody of the court.

PUERTO RICO
Affidavits

[P.R. LAWS ANN.]

Tit. 32, § 2065. In a State of United States. An affidavit taken in a State of the United States to be used in Puerto Rico may be taken before a commissioner appointed by the Governor of Puerto Rico to take affidavits and depositions in such State, or before any notary public in another State, or before any clerk of a court of record having a seal.

Tit. 32, § 2066. In foreign country. An affidavit, taken in a foreign country to be used in Puerto Rico may be taken before an ambassador, minister, consul, vice-consul, or consular agent of the United States, or before any clerk of a court of record having a seal, in such foreign country.

Civil Procedure

[P.R. R. CIV. P. (1958) 25 (tit. 32, App. II)]

Persons Before Whom Depositions May Be Taken

25.1. Within Puerto Rico and the United States. Within Puerto Rico, within the United States, or within any territory or possession subject to the dominion of the United States, depositions shall be taken before an officer authorized to administer oaths by the laws of Puerto Rico or of the place where the examination is held, or before a person appointed by the part of the court in which the action is pending. A person so appointed has power to administer oaths and take testimony.

25.2. In foreign countries. In a foreign state or country depositions shall be taken (1) on notice before a secretary of embassy or legation, consul general, consul, vice consul, or consular agent of the United States, or (2) before such person or officer as may be appointed by commission or under letters rogatory. A commission or letters rogatory shall be issued only when necessary or convenient, on application and notice, and on such terms and with such directions as are just and appropriate. Officers may be designated in notices or commissions either by name or descriptive title, and letters rogatory may be addressed "To the Appropriate Judicial Authority in (here name the country)."

25.3. Disqualification for interest. No deposition shall be taken before a person who is a relative within the fourth degree of consanguinity or the second degree of affinity, or employee or attorney of any of the parties, or is a relative within the degrees mentioned, or employee of such attorney, or is financially interested in the action.

Rule 27.6. Certification and filing by officer; copies; notice of filing. (a) The officer shall certify on the deposition that the witness was duly sworn by him and that the deposition is a true record of the testimony given by the witness. He shall then securely seal the deposition in an envelope indorsed with the title of the action and marked "Deposition of (here insert name of witness)," and shall promptly file it with the clerk of the part of the court in which the action is pending, or send it by registered mail to the clerk thereof for filing.

(b) Upon payment of reasonable charges therefor, the officer shall furnish a copy of the deposition to any party to the action or to the deponent.

(c) The party taking the deposition shall give prompt notice of its filing in the office of the clerk to all other parties.

RHODE ISLAND

[R.I. GEN. LAWS ANN.]

§ 9-17-3. Subpoenas issued by ° ° ° officials. Auditors, referees, masters in chancery, and commissioners may issue subpoenas to witnesses in all cases and matters pending before them, respectively; and justices of the peace and notaries public may issue subpoenas to witnesses in any case, civil or criminal, before any court, and in any matter before any body or person authorized by law to summon witnesses.

§ 9-18-1. Officials authorized to take depositions. Any justice of the supreme or superior court, justice of the peace or notary public, may take the deposition of any witness, to be used in the trial of any civil suit, action, petition or proceeding, in which he is not interested, nor counsel, nor the attorney of either party, and which shall then be commenced or pending in this state, or in any other state, or in the District of Columbia, or in any territory, government, or country.

§ 9-18-2. Notice to adverse party. Previous to the taking of any deposition as aforesaid within this state, the official authorized to take the same shall, in all cases, cause the adverse party or his attorney of record to be notified in writing of the time and place appointed for taking such depositions, so that he may attend and put interrogatories to the deponent if he think fit; provided, that if the person to be notified cannot be found and his residence be not known, and he has no attorney of record, the moving party or his attorney may make affidavit of such facts before any justice of the superior court at any time, and thereupon the justice shall prescribe the method in which notice shall be given to such person.

§ 9-18-3.　**Address and time of service of notice.**　The notification issued by the magistrate, officer, or commissioner who shall take such deposition shall be directed to any proper officer, or to any impartial or disinterested person, and shall be served a reasonable time, not less than twenty-four (24) hours, exclusive of Sundays and legal holidays, before the time of taking such deposition.

§ 9-18-4.　**Service and return of notice.**　The officer or other person charged as aforesaid with the service of such notification shall serve the same by reading it to the party to be cited, if to be found; and if not to be found, by leaving a copy thereof at his usual place of abode; and shall, in his return, state the manner and time of such service; and whenever such service shall be made by any person other than a sworn officer, he shall verify the same, under oath, before some officer authorized to administer oaths.

§ 9-18-5.　**Manner of taking depositions outside state for use in state.**　Depositions may be taken without this state to be used in the tribunals of this state, upon an order obtained on motion from the court in which the case is pending, and when ordered shall be taken either by the person and in the manner and with the formalities required by the law of the state, district, territory, or country in which the same shall be taken; or second, shall be taken, if taken in any other state, district, or territory of the United States, before a commissioner appointed by the governor of this state, or before a judge, chancellor, justice of the peace, notary public, or civil magistrate of such state, district, or territory, respectively, or, if taken out of the United States, before a resident official of the United States, or, if the deponent be in the military, air, or naval service of the United States, before a colonel, lieutenant-colonel, or major in the army or air force, or before any officer in the navy not below the grade and rank of lieutenant commander.　And in every such case under the second method, the party causing such depositions to be taken shall notify the adverse party, or his attorney of record, of the time and place appointed for taking the same; and such notification issued by the official before whom such deposition is to be taken shall be served, in the manner hereinbefore provided, such reasonable time before the taking of such deposition as will give the adverse party a full opportunity to be present in person or by attorney and put interrogatories to the deponent, if he think fit.

§ 9-18-6. Oath of deponent—reduction of deposition to writing. Every person, before deposing, shall be sworn to testify the truth, the whole truth, and nothing but the truth, and after giving such deposition shall subscribe his name thereto, if taken in longhand in the presence of the official before whom the same was taken. Such deposition may be reduced to writing by such official or by any person, including the deponent, under his direction and in his presence, or may be reduced to writing stenographically either by such official or by some person in his presence and under his direction, sworn by such official to correctly take down in shorthand, the evidence as given; and in the latter case a transcript thereof in longhand writing, typewriting, print, or other reproduction, sworn to by the person stenographically reporting the same and signed by the deponent, shall be received in evidence. The signature in the latter case shall be attested by the official taking the deposition or by some magistrate authorized to administer oaths whether in this state or elsewhere.

§ 9-18-7. Sealing and delivery to court. The deposition, so taken, shall be retained by such magistrate, officer, or commissioner until he deliver the same with his own hand to the court for which it is taken, or shall, together with a certificate of its having been duly taken, be by said magistrate, officer, or commissioner, sealed up and directed to such court and delivered to the clerk thereof, and remain so sealed until opened by order of the court or of some justice thereof, or by the clerk with the consent of the parties; and any person may be compelled to appear and depose as aforesaid within this state, in the same manner as to appear and testify in court.

§ 9-18-8. Deposition as evidence—use of certified copy. The deposition of any person taken pursuant to this chapter may be used as evidence in the trial of any judicial proceeding in any court, or town council, or before commissioners, masters in chancery, referees, or auditors, in which it shall have been taken to be used; ° ° °.

§ 9-18-9. Court grant of commission to take deposition. Any court may, on the motion of either party in any action, suit, or proceeding, civil or criminal, pending therein, in which a deposition may be used, or before any commissioners, referees, or auditors appointed by any such court or under a rule from it, grant a commission to take depositions according to law, whenever it may be necessary to prevent a failure or delay of justice, on such terms as such court, by general or special order, may direct; and the deposition, so taken, may be used in any state of the cause, on appeal or otherwise.

§ 9-18-11. Depositions for use in foreign tribunals. Depositions may be taken in this state, to be used on the trial of any cause pending in a tribunal of any other state, district, territory, or country, before any person residing in this state, to whom a commission shall be directed and sent by such tribunal, with the formalities prescribed in such commission, or, if there are none prescribed, then according to the laws of the jurisdiction whence said commission issues.

§ 9-29-3. **Deposition fees.** To all officers empowered to take depositions, there shall be allowed:

For every hour necessarily employed .... $.40

For every page of 200 words .... .30

For every mile's travel to the place of caption .... .10

§ 43-3-11. **Oaths and affirmations.** The word "oath" shall be construed to include affirmation; the word "sworn," affirmed; and the word "engaged," either sworn or affirmed.

[R.I. R. CIV. P. 28]

Persons before whom depositions may be taken. (a) Within the State. Within the state depositions shall be taken before an officer authorized to administer oaths by the law of the state or before a person appointed by the court. A person so appointed has the power to administer oaths and take testimony.

(b) Outside the State. Within another state, or within a territory or insular possession subject to the dominion of the United States, or in a foreign country, depositions may be taken (1) on notice before a person authorized to administer oaths in the place in which the examination is held, either by the law thereof or by the law of the United States, or (2) before a person commissioned by the court, and a person so commissioned shall have the power by virtue of his commission to administer any necessary oath and take testimony, or (3) pursuant to a letter rogatory. A commission or a letter rogatory shall be issued on application and notice and on terms that are just and appropriate. It is not requisite to the issuance of a commission or a letter rogatory that the taking of the deposition in any other manner is impracticable or inconvenient; and both a commission and a letter rogatory may be issued in proper cases. A notice or commission may designate the person before whom the deposition is to be taken either by name or descriptive title. A letter rogatory may be addressed "To the Appropriate Authority in (here name the state, territory, or country)." Evidence obtained in a foreign country in response to a letter rogatory need not be excluded merely for the reason that it is not a verbatim transcript or that the testimony was not taken under oath or for any similar departure from the requirements for depositions taken within the United States under these rules.

(c) Disqualification for Interest. No deposition shall be taken before a person who is a relative or employee or attorney or counsel of any of the parties, or is a relative or employee of such attorney or counsel, or is financially interested in the action.

SOUTH CAROLINA

Examination by Commission

[S.C. CODE ANN.]

§ 26-601. **Commissions to examine witnesses on application of party to suit.** Any judge or clerk of the circuit court may, on the application of any party to a suit pending in the court of common pleas for his county made to him by the party, either in person or by agent or attorney, grant commissions, under the seal of the court, directed to three or more commissioners, empowering them or any two of them to take the depositions in writing of the witness or witnesses therein mentioned who are:

(1) Resident without the limits of the State or of the county in which the trial is to be had or at a greater distance than one hundred miles from the court where such action has been instituted;

(2) About to remove without the limits of the State before the sitting of the next court or before the suit will stand ready for trial; or

(3) Whose presence cannot be procured by reason of indispensable attendance on some public official duty or professional duty as an attorney at such time or of such sickness or infirmity as incapacitates such witness or witnesses from traveling in order to appear and testify touching such matters as they may have in charge by such commission.

Such application shall be accompanied by an affidavit of the party applying declaring his belief of the materiality of any witness proposed to be so examined, together with the facts which may entitle the party to such commission.

Examination by Deposition

§ 26-705. **Before whom ° ° ° deposition taken.** [A] deposition may be taken before:

(1) Any circuit judge of this State;

(2) The clerk of any of the circuit courts of this State;

(3) Any magistrate or notary public of this State;

(4) Any chancellor, justice or judge of a Supreme or superior court, mayor or chief magistrate of a city, magistrate or judge of a county court or court of common pleas of any of the United States or of the Dominion of Canada or Kingdom of Great Britain; or

(5) Any notary public not being of counsel or attorney to either of the parties interested in the event of the cause.

§ 26-708. **Testimony to be reduced to writing.** Every person deposing as provided in this chapter shall be cautioned and sworn to testify the whole truth and carefully examined. His testimony shall be reduced to writing by the officer taking the deposition or by himself in the officer's presence and by no other person and shall, after it has been reduced to writing, be subscribed by the deponent. But this section shall not be construed to prevent the use of stenographers for the purpose of taking such testimony, but the testimony so taken by such stenographers shall be reduced to writing or typewritten and read over to the witness.

§ 26-709. **Disposition of deposition.** Every deposition taken under the provisions of [this chapter] shall be retained by the officer taking it until he delivers it with his own hand into the court for which it is taken or shall, together with a certificate of the reasons as aforesaid of taking it and of the notice, if any, given to the adverse party, be by such officer sealed up and directed to such court and forwarded to such court either by mail or express and shall remain under his seal until opened in court. ° ° °

SOUTH DAKOTA

Civil Procedure

[S.D. COMPILED LAWS ANN.]

Persons Before Whom Depositions May Be Taken

§ 15-6-28(a). **Taking depositions within the United States.** Within the United States or within a territory or insular possession subject to the dominion of the United States, depositions shall be taken before an officer authorized to administer oaths by the laws of this state, the United States or of the place where the examination is held, or before a person appointed by the court in which the action is pending. A person so appointed has power to administer oaths and take testimony.

§ 15-6-28(b). **Taking depositions in foreign countries.** In a foreign country, depositions may be taken

    (1)   on notice before a person authorized to administer oaths in the place in which the examination is held, either by the law thereof or by the law of the United States, or

    (2)   before a person commissioned by the court, and a person so commissioned shall have the power by virtue of his commission to administer any necessary oath and take testimony, or

    (3)   pursuant to a letter rogatory.

A commission or a letter rogatory shall be issued on application and notice and on terms that are just and appropriate. It is not requisite to the issuance of a commission or a letter rogatory that the taking of the deposition in any other manner is impracticable or inconvenient; and both a commission and a letter rogatory may be issued in proper cases. A notice or commission may designate the person before whom the deposition is to be taken either by name or descriptive title. A letter rogatory may be addressed "To the Appropriate Authority in (here name the country)." Evidence obtained in response to a letter rogatory need not be excluded merely for the reason that it is not a verbatim transcript or that the testimony was not taken under oath or for any similar departure from the requirements for depositions taken within the United States under this chapter.

§ 15-6-28(c). **Disqualification to take deposition for interest.** No deposition shall be taken before a person who is a relative or employee or attorney or counsel of any of the parties, or is a relative or employee of such attorney or counsel, or is financially interested in the action.

Taking Testimony

§ 19-3-1. **Means of testimony enumerated.** The testimony of witnesses is taken in three modes:

(1) By affidavit;

(2) By deposition;

(3) By oral examination.

§ 19-3-2. **Affidavit defined.** An affidavit is a written declaration under oath made without notice to the adverse party.

§ 19-3-3. **Deposition defined.** A deposition is a written declaration under oath made upon notice to the adverse party for the purpose of enabling him to attend and cross-examine; or upon written interrogatories.

§ 19-3-5. **Oath administered to witnesses.** Before testifying every witness must be sworn or affirmed as follows:

You do solemnly swear that the evidence you shall give relative to the matter in difference now in hearing between ———, plaintiff, and ———, defendant, shall be the truth, the whole truth and nothing but the truth, so help you God.

§ 19-3-6. **Affirmation in lieu of oath.** Any person having conscientious scruples against taking an oath shall be allowed to make affirmation, substituting for the word "swear" the word "affirm," and for the words "so help you God" the following: "This you do under the pains and penalties of perjury."

§ 19-3-7. **Interpreter provided if witness does not speak English.** When a witness does not understand and speak the English language the court shall procure and appoint a disinterested interpreter for him.

TENNESSEE

[TENN. CODE ANN.]

§ 8-1627. **Depositions taken by notaries of other states.** Notaries public, duly and lawfully commissioned by the proper authorities of other states and empowered by the law of such state to take depositions, are authorized to take depositions to be used in the courts of this state, upon the same terms that are provided for the taking of depositions by other officials in such states. But the certificate of said notary public shall show the date of the commencement and expiration of the commission under which he may be acting.

§ 24-906.   **Depositions for use in foreign courts.**   Whenever any mandate, writ, or commission is issued out of any court of record in any other state, territory, district, or foreign jurisdiction, or whenever upon notice or agreement it is required to take the testimony of a witness or witnesses in this state, witnesses may be compelled to appear and testify in the same manner and by the same process and proceeding as may be employed for the purpose of taking testimony in proceedings pending in this state. The person whose deposition is required under a foreign commission, or is taken upon agreement, is entitled to the same fees as a person summoned to give testimony in the circuit courts of this state.

§ 24-920.   **Persons authorized to take depositions.**   Depositions may be taken by any judge, justice of the peace, notary public, the clerk of any court, or any other person properly commissioned or appointed by the court or clerk, not being interested, of counsel, or related to either of the parties within the sixth degree, computing by the civil law.

§ 24-921.   **Place of taking by notary.**   When taken by any notary public of this state, it shall be in the county in which he resides; and the certificate of the notary shall show his locality.

§ 24-922.   **Subpoena of witnesses.**   The commissioner, notary public or person authorized to take depositions, has power to issue subpoena for witnesses, which may be served by the sheriff or any constable, and the certificate of the commissioner, or person authorized, that the witness failed to appear, together with the return of the officer, is proof of the facts.

§ 24-923.   **Penalty for failure of witness to appear.**   Any witness who fails to appear in such cases, according to the terms of the subpoena, or to answer the questions which may be lawfully put to him, is subject to the penalties provided for enforcing the attendance of witnesses to give testimony in court, and compelling them to testify. The penalty for nonattendance may be enforced by the tribunal having cognizance of the suit, upon scire facias, as in other cases.

§ 24-924.   **Power of officer over proceedings.**   Any person authorized to take depositions, is, while engaged in the discharge of his duties, vested with all the powers of a court to preserve order, prevent interruption, and control the conduct of the parties in the examination of the witness.

§ 24-925.   **Manner of taking deposition.**   The commissioner or notary, having first sworn the witness according to law, should require the questions to be reduced to writing before being put, and then read to the witness, and should take down his answers in writing, or cause the same to be done by the witness himself, as near as may be in the witness' own words.

§ 24-926. **Subsequent cross-examination.** After a deposition has been taken without cross-examination at the time, the witness may subsequently be cross-examined, upon notice to that effect.

§ 24-927. **Form of caption and certificate.** The caption and certificate shall be substantially as follows:

A B   In the ——— court, ——— county, Tennessee: Depositions of ——— and ———, witnesses for plaintiff (or C D   defendant) in the above case, taken upon notice (or interrogatories), on the ——— day of ———, 19—, at ———, in the presence of the plaintiff and defendant (show the fact). The said witness ———, aged ———, being duly sworn, deposed as follows:

The foregoing depositions were taken before me, as stated in the caption, and reduced to writing by me (or by the witnesses). And I certify that I am not interested in the cause, nor of kin or counsel to either of the parties, and that I sealed them up and delivered them to ——— [or delivered them to the express office, or put them in the postoffice], without being out of my possession, or altered after they were taken. Given under my hand the ——— day ———, 19—.

The last clause may be written across the back of the envelope on the sealed side, instead of inserting it in the certificate.

§ 24-928. **Use of shorthand or typewriter.** Persons authorized to take depositions may take them in shorthand, and subsequently reduce the same to manuscript or typewriting, or may take them directly on a typewriting machine; provided, that in case the deposition be taken in shorthand, the person taking it can truthfully certify, and does certify substantially, as follows: "I certify that, being a stenographer, I took the foregoing deposition in the exact language of the witness, and reduced it to typewriting [or manuscript]. That it was then read over by the witness in my presence [or was read over by me to the witness], and was approved and signed by him; and I also certify that I am not, in any capacity, in the regular employ of the party in whose behalf this deposition is taken, nor in the regular employ of his attorney; and I certify that I am not interested in the case, nor of kin or counsel to either of the parties, and that I sealed up said deposition and delivered it to ——— [or delivered it to the express office, or put it in the postoffice] without its being out of my possession, or altered after it was taken."

No deposition taken under this section shall be signed by the witness until it shall have been reduced to manuscript or typewriting. Nothing herein shall prevent the taking of depositions by stenogra-

phers in the regular employ of the litigant taking the deposition, or
his attorney, where the opposite party consents thereto.

§ 24-929. Employment of stenographer. In addition to the modes
of taking depositions now authorized by law, it shall be lawful
for any clerk of a court, justice of the peace, notary public, or
officer now empowered by law, to take depositions to employ, upon
request of either party, a reputable and competent stenographer or
typewriter, who may take down the testimony of the witness in
shorthand and thereafter transcribe it in longhand, or upon the
typewriter, or who may take the testimony upon the typewriter direct;
and when certified as provided in § 24-930, may be read as evidence.

§ 24-930. Affidavit and certificate to stenographer's transcript.
When the deposition of a witness is so taken, the stenographer, or
person taking down the testimony, shall append his affidavit, setting
forth that he took down the testimony correctly and correctly transcribed it and delivered it to the officer before whom the deposition
was taken; and that said testimony as delivered to the officer correctly sets forth the testimony of the witness or witnesses, and that
he is in no way interested in said suit or of kin or counsel to either
party; and thereupon the officer before whom the depositions were
taken shall certify in all respects as now required by law in case
of depositions taken by the officer himself in longhand, except that
instead of certifying that the testimony was reduced to writing by
himself or the witness, he shall certify to the employment of the
stenographer or typewriter taking the testimony, and that the same
was not altered after being received by him from the stenographer
or typewriter.

**§ 24-931. Compensation of officer and stenographer—waiver of
affidavit and certificate.** The party calling for the employment of the
stenographer or typewriter shall be liable for his compensation. The
officer's fees for taking the deposition shall be taxed as now fixed by
law; provided, that nothing in §§ 24-929—24-931 shall prevent the
waiver of the affidavit and certificate by agreement, or the taking of
depositions by consent, or in any of the other methods provided by
law.

§ 24-932. Forwarding to clerk. The depositions, when complete,
shall be enveloped, together with the commission, if any, and all
documents which may have been deposed to, sealed, with the commissioner's or notary's name written across the seal, and directed
to the clerk of the court where the cause is pending, with the title of
the cause indorsed thereon, and may be sent by mail, express, or
private conveyance. If sent by private conveyance, the person delivering it shall make affidavit before the clerk that he received the
deposition from the commissioner; that it has not been out of his
possession, or opened by him, or while in his possession.

Civil Procedure

[TENN. R. CIV. P. 28]

Persons Before Whom Depositions May Be Taken

§ 28.01. Within the United States or in territory subject to dominion of United States. Within the United States or within a territory or insular possession subject to the dominion of the United States, depositions shall be taken before an officer authorized to administer oaths by the laws of the United States or of the place where the examination is held, or before a person appointed by the court in which the action is pending. A person so appointed has power to administer oaths and take testimony.

§ 28.02. In foreign countries. In a foreign state or country depositions shall be taken (1) on notice before a secretary of embassy or legation, consul general, consul, vice consul, or consular agent of the United States, or (2) before such person or officer as may be appointed by commission or under letters rogatory. A commission or letters rogatory shall be issued only when necessary or convenient, on application and notice, and on such terms and with such directions as are just and appropriate. Officers may be designated in notices or commissions either by name or descriptive title and letters rogatory may be addressed "To the Appropriate Judicial Authority in (here name the country)."

§ 28.03. Disqualification for interest. Except as provided in Rule 29, no deposition shall be taken before a person who is a relative (within the sixth degree, computed by the civil law) or employee or attorney or counsel of any of the parties, or who is a relative (within the sixth degree, computed by the civil law) or employee of such attorney or counsel, or who is financially interested in the action.

TEXAS

[TEX. REV. CIV. STAT. ANN.]

Art. 2324a. Powers as to depositions, commissions, oaths and affidavits. Section 1. All official District Court reporters are authorized to take depositions of witnesses, and to receive, execute and return commissions, administer oaths and affidavits, in connection with such depositions, and make a certificate of such fact, and do all other things necessary in the taking of such depositions in accordance with existing laws.

Section 2. Said reporters shall have authority to perform the above mentioned acts only within any county within the judicial district that such reporter was appointed and serving in connection with his official business, in the State of Texas.

Section 3. This Act shall be cumulative of all existing laws providing for the method and manner of taking depositions.

Art. 5996e.   Official stenographer.   No district judge shall appoint as official stenographer of his district any person related within the third degree to the judge or district attorney of such district.

Art. 5996f.   Punishment.   Whoever violates any provision of the ° ° ° preceding [article] shall be guilty of a misdemeanor involving official misconduct, and shall be fined not less than one hundred nor more than one thousand dollars.

Civil Procedure

[TEX. R. CIV. P.]

District and County Courts

Rule 196.   Taking of written deposition.   Upon the appearance of the witness any officer authorized to take depositions shall proceed to take his answers to the questions and cross questions, if any, reduce to writing, and shall cause the same to be signed and sworn to by the witness.   The officer shall certify that the answers were signed and sworn to by the witness before him, and shall seal them up in an envelope, together with the questions and cross-questions, if any, write his name across the seal, and indorse on the envelope the names of the parties to the suit and of the witnesses, and shall direct the package to the clerk of the court or justice of the peace where the action is pending.   If the deposition be sent by mail, the officer taking the same shall certify on the envelope enclosing the depositions that he in person deposited same in the mail for transmission, stating the date when and the post office in which the same are so deposited.

Rule 197.   Interpreter.   The officer taking such written deposition shall have authority, when he deems it expedient, to summon and swear an interpreter to facilitate the taking of the deposition.

Rule 198.   Return of Depositions.   Depositions may be returned to the court either by mail, or by a party interested in taking the same, or by any other person.   If returned by mail, the clerk or justice taking them from the post office shall indorse on them that he received them from the post office, and sign his name thereto.   If not sent by mail, the person delivering them into court shall make affidavit before the clerk or justice that he received them from the hands of the officer before whom they were taken, that they have not been out of his possession since, and that they have undergone no alteration.   The party taking the deposition shall give prompt notice of its filing to all other parties.

Rule 199.   Oral Deposition.   The testimony of any witness and of any party to a suit may be taken in any civil case in any district or county court of this State by oral deposition and answer in any instance where depositions are now authorized to be taken.

Rule 205. Witness sworn. Every person so deposing shall be first cautioned and sworn to testify the truth, the whole truth and nothing but the truth.

Rule 206. Examination. The witness shall be carefully examined, his testimony shall be reduced to writing or typewriting by the officer taking the deposition, or by some person under his personal supervision, or by the deponent himself in the officer's presence, and by no other person, and shall, after it has been reduced to writing or typewriting, be subscribed by the deponent.

Rule 207. Objections to testimony. The officer taking such oral deposition shall not sustain objections to any of the testimony taken, nor exclude same; but any of the parties or attorneys engaged in taking the testimony may have any objections they may make recorded with the testimony and reserved for the action of the court in which the cause is pending, but the court shall not be confined to objections made at the taking of the testimony.

Rule 208. Depositions certified and returned. Such depositions shall be certified and returned by the officer taking the same, and opened and used as is provided in case of depositions on written questions. The party taking a deposition shall give prompt notice of its filing to all other parties.

Rule 209. Submission to witness; changes; signing. When the testimony is fully transcribed the deposition shall be submitted to the witness for examination and shall be read to or by him, unless such examination and reading are waived by the witness and by the parties; provided that when the witness is a party to the suit with an attorney of record the deposition officer shall notify such attorney of record in writing by registered mail that the deposition is ready for such examination and reading at the office of such deposition officer, and if the witness does not appear and examine, read and sign his deposition within twenty (20) days after the mailing of such notice the deposition shall be returned as provided herein for unsigned depositions.

Any changes in form or substance which the witness desires to make shall be entered upon the deposition by the officer with the statement of the reasons given by the witness for making them. The deposition shall then be signed by the witness, unless the parties by stipulation waive the signing or the witness is ill or cannot be found or refuses to sign. If the deposition is not signed by the witness, the officer shall sign it and state on the record the fact of the waiver or of the illness or absence of the witness or the fact of the refusal to sign together with the reason, if any, given therefor; and the deposition may then be used as fully as though signed; unless on motion to suppress, made as provided in Rule 212, the Court holds that the reasons given for the refusal to sign require rejection of the deposition in whole or in part.

Rule 210. Depositions opened. Depositions, after being filed, may be opened by the clerk or justice at the request of either party or his counsel; and the clerk or justice shall indorse on such depositions upon what day and at whose request they were opened, signing his name thereto, and they shall remain on file for the inspection of either party.

Criminal Procedure

[TEX. CODE CRIM. PRO. ANN.]

Art. 39.04. Applicability of civil rules. The rules prescribed in civil cases for issuance of commissions, subpoenaing witnesses, taking the depositions of witnesses and all other formalities governing depositions° shall, as to the manner and form of taking and returning the same and other formalities to the taking of the same, govern in criminal actions, when not in conflict with this Code.

° See TEX. R. CIV. P. 196 to 210, above.

Art. 39.05. Objections. The rules of procedure as to objections in depositions in civil actions shall govern in criminal actions when not in conflict with this Code.

Art. 39.07. Certificate. Where depositions are taken under commission in criminal actions, the officer or officers taking the same shall certify that the person deposing is the identical person named in the commission; or, if they cannot certify to the identity of the witness, there shall be an affidavit of some person attached to the deposition proving the identity of such witness, and the officer or officers shall certify that the person making the affidavit is known to them.

Art. 39.08. Authenticating the deposition. The official seal and signature of the officer taking the deposition shall be attached to the certificate authenticating the deposition.

Art. 39.09. Non-resident witnesses. Depositions of a witness residing out of the State may be taken before a judge or before a commissioner of deeds and depositions for this State, who resides within the State where the deposition is to be taken, or before a notary public of the place where such deposition is to be taken, or before any commissioned officer of the armed services or before any diplomatic or consular officer. The deposition of a non-resident witness who may be temporarily within the State, may be taken under the same rules which apply to the taking of depositions of other witnesses in the State.

Art. 39.10. Return. In all cases the return of depositions may be made as provided in civil actions.

UTAH

Examination on Commission

[UTAH CODE ANN.]

§ 77-47-1. In criminal action when witness is nonresident. When an issue of fact is joined upon an information or indictment, or before, if the court so orders, the defendant may have any material witness residing out of the state examined in his behalf as prescribed in this chapter, and not otherwise.

§ 77-47-9. Execution of commission. The commissioner, unless otherwise specifically directed, may execute the commission as follows:

(1) He must publicly administer an oath to the witness that his answers given to the interrogatories shall be the truth, the whole truth and nothing but the truth.

(2) He must cause the examination of the witness to be reduced to writing and subscribed by the witness.

(3) He must write the answers of the witness as nearly as possible in the language in which he shall give them, and read to him each answer as it is taken down, and correct or add to it until it conforms to what the witness declares is the truth.

(4) If the witness declines to answer a question, that fact, with the reason assigned by him for declining, must be stated.

(5) If any papers or documents are produced before him and proved by the witness, the same, or copies thereof, must be annexed to the deposition, subscribed by the witness and certified by the commissioner.

(6) The commissioner must subscribe his name to each sheet of the deposition, and annex the deposition, with the papers and documents proved by the witness, or copies thereof, to the commission, and must close it up under seal and address it as directed by the indorsement thereon.

(7) If there is a direction on the commission to return it by mail, the commissioner must immediately deposit it in the nearest post office.

(8) If any other direction is made by the written consent of the parties, or by the court or judge, on the commission as to its return, he must comply with the direction.

A copy of this section must be annexed to the commission.

§ 77-47-10. Return by agent. If the commission and return is delivered by the commissioner to an agent, the agent must deliver the same to the clerk to whom it is directed, or to the judge of the court in which the action is pending, by whom it may be received and opened, upon the agent's making affidavit that he received it from the hands of the commissioner, and that it has not been opened or altered since he received it.

Oaths, Affirmations and Declarations

§ 78-24-16. **Oaths—who may administer.** Every court, every judge, clerk and deputy clerk of any court, every justice, every notary public, and every officer or person authorized to take testimony in any action or proceeding, or to decide upon evidence, has power to administer oaths or affirmations.

§ 78-24-17. **Form.** An oath or affirmation in an action or proceeding may be administered, the person who swears or affirms expressing his assent when addressed, in the following form:

You do solemnly swear (or affirm) that the evidence you shall give in this issue (or matter) pending between ———— and ———— shall be the truth, the whole truth and nothing but the truth, so help you God (or, under the pains and penalties of perjury).

§ 78-24-18. **Affirmation or declaration instead of oath allowed.** Any person may at his option, instead of taking an oath, make his solemn affirmation or declaration, by assenting, when addressed in the following form:

"You do solemnly affirm (or declare) that," etc., as in the preceding section.

§ 78-24-19. **May be varied to suit witness' belief.** Whenever the court before which a person is offered as a witness is satisfied that he has a peculiar mode of swearing, connected with or in addition to the usual form, which in his opinion is more solemn or obligatory, the court may in its discretion adopt that mode.

If a person who is sworn believes in any other than the Christian religion, he may be sworn according to the peculiar ceremonies of his religion, if there are any.

Affidavits

§ 78-26-5. **Affidavits—before whom taken in this state.** An affidavit to be used before any court, judge or officer of this state may be taken before any judge or clerk of any court or any justice of the peace or any notary public in this state.

§ 78-26-6. **If in another state.** An affidavit taken in another state or territory of the United States, to be used in this state, may be taken before a commissioner appointed by the governor of this state to take affidavits and depositions in such other state or territory, or before any notary public in another state or territory, or before any judge or clerk of a court of record having a seal.

§ 78-26-7. **If in a foreign country.** An affidavit taken in a foreign country, to be used in this state, may be taken before an ambassador, minister, consul, vice consul or consular agent of the United States, or before any judge of a court of record having a seal, in such foreign country.

§ 78-26-8. If before foreign court or judge, clerk of court to certify. When an affidavit is taken before a judge or court in another state or territory, or in a foreign country, the genuineness of the signature of the judge, the existence of the court, and the fact that such judge is a member thereof, must be certified by the clerk of the court under the seal thereof.

Civil Procedure

[UTAH R. CIV. P. 28]

Persons Before Whom Depositions May Be Taken

(a) **Within the United States.** Within the United States or within a territory or insular possession subject to the dominion of the United States, depositions shall be taken before an officer authorized to administer oaths by the laws of the United States or of the place where the examination is held, or before a person appointed by the court in which the action is pending. A person so appointed has power to administer oaths and take testimony.

(b) **In foreign countries.** In a foreign country, depositions may be taken (1) on notice before a person authorized to administer oaths in the place in which the examination is held, either by the law thereof or by the law of the United States, or (2) before a person commissioned by the court, and a person so commissioned shall have the power by virtue of his commission to administer any necessary oath and take testimony, or (3) pursuant to a letter rogatory. A commission or a letter rogatory shall be issued on application and notice and on terms that are just and appropriate. It is not requisite to the issuance of a commission or a letter rogatory that the taking of the deposition in any other manner is impracticable or inconvenient; and both a commission and a letter rogatory may be issued in proper cases. A notice or commission may designate the person before whom the deposition is to be taken either by name or descriptive title. A letter rogatory may be addressed "To the Appropriate Authority in [here name the country]." Evidence obtained in response to a letter rogatory need not be excluded merely for the reason that it is not a verbatim transcript or that the testimony was not taken under oath or for any similar departure from the requirements for depositions taken within the United States under these rules.

(c) **Disqualification for interest.** No deposition shall be taken before a person who is a relative or employee or attorney or counsel of any of the parties, or is a relative or employee of such attorney or counsel, or is financially interested in the action.

VERMONT

Oaths and Affirmations

[VT. STAT. ANN.]

Tit. 12, § 5810. Oath to be administered to witnesses. You solemnly swear that the evidence you shall give, relative to the cause now under consideration, shall be the whole truth and nothing but the truth. So help you God.

Tit. 12, § 5811. Oath to be administered to interpreter of testimony. You solemnly swear that you will justly, truly and impartially interpret to A. B. the oath about to be administered to him, and the testimony he shall give relative to the cause now under consideration. So help you God.

Tit. 12, § 5851. Affirmation. In the administration of an oath, the word "swear" may be omitted, and the word "affirm" substituted, when the person to whom the obligation is administered is religiously scrupulous of swearing, or taking an oath in the prescribed form; and, in such case, the words "so help you God" may be omitted, and the words "under the pains and penalties of perjury" substituted; and a person so affirming shall be considered, for every legal purpose of privilege, qualification or liability, as having been duly sworn.

Civil Procedure

[VT. R. CIV. P. 28]

Persons Before Whom Depositions May Be Taken

(a) Within the State. Within the state depositions shall be taken before a justice of the peace or notary public or a person appointed by the court. A person so appointed has power to administer oaths and take testimony.

(b) Outside the State. Within another state, or within a territory or insular possession subject to the dominion of the United States, or in a foreign country, depositions may be taken (1) on notice before a person authorized to administer oaths in the place in which the examination is held, either by the law thereof or by the law of the United States, or (2) before a person appointed or commissioned by the court, and such a person shall have the power by virtue of his appointment or commission to administer any necessary oath and take testimony, or (3) pursuant to a letter rogatory. A commission or a letter rogatory shall be issued on application and notice and on terms that are just and appropriate. It is not requisite to the issuance of a commission or a letter rogatory that the taking of the deposition in any other manner is impracticable or inconvenient; and both a commission and a letter rogatory may be issued in proper cases. A notice or commission may designate the person before whom the deposition is to be taken either by name or descriptive title. A letter rogatory may be addressed "To the Appropriate Authority in (here name the state, territory or country)." Evidence obtained in a foreign country in response to a letter rogatory need not be excluded merely for the reason that it is not a verbatim transcript or that the testimony was not taken under oath or for any similar departure from the requirements for depositions taken within the United States under these rules.

(c) **Disqualification for interest.** No deposition shall be taken before a person who is a relative or employee or attorney or counsel of any of the parties, or is a relative or employee of such attorney or counsel, or is financially interested in the action.

(d) **Depositions for use in foreign jurisdictions.** Whenever the deposition of any person is to be taken in this state pursuant to the laws of another state or of the United States or of another country for use in proceedings there, any Superior Judge may, upon petition to the county court in the county where the deponent resides or is employed or transacts his business in person, make an order directing issuance of a subpoena as provided in Rule 45, in aid of the taking of the deposition, and may make any order in accordance with Rule 30(d), 37(a) or 37(b)(1).

Criminal Procedure

[VT. R. CRIM. P. 15]

✿   ✿   ✿

(d) **How taken.** Subject to such additional conditions as the court shall provide, a deposition [in a criminal case] shall be taken and filed in the maner provided in civil actions except as otherwise provided in these rules, provided that (1) in no event shall a deposition be taken of a party defendant without his consent and (2) the scope and manner of examination and cross-examination shall be such as would be allowed in the trial itself. The State shall make available to the defendant or his counsel for examination and use at the taking of the deposition any relevant written or recorded statement of the witness being deposed which is in the possession or control of the State and to which the defendant would be entitled at trial.

✿   ✿   ✿

(f) **Objections to admissibility.** Objections to receiving in evidence any deposition or part thereof may be made as provided in civil actions.

✿   ✿   ✿

(h) **Commission to examine witness out of state.** When an issue of fact is joined upon an information or indictment, on application of the defendant or prosecuting attorney the court may grant a commission to depose material witnesses residing out of the state as provided in this rule, and the prosecuting attorney may join in such commission and name material witnesses to be examined on the part of the state.

(i) **Deposition by agreement not precluded.** Nothing in this rule shall preclude the taking of a deposition, orally or upon written questions, or the use of a deposition, by agreement of the parties.

VIRGIN ISLANDS

Notaries public may administer oaths and affirmations, and perform such other acts as may be authorized by law. See *Authority and Duties,* V.I. CODE ANN. tit. 3, § 777. The authority to administer oaths qualifies notaries public to take depositions under CIV. R. 28 below.

[V.I. CODE ANN. tit. 5, App. I, CIV. R. 28]

Persons Before Whom Depositions May Be Taken

(a) WITHIN THE UNITED STATES. Within the United States or within a territory or insular possession subject to the dominion of the United States, depositions shall be taken before an officer authorized to administer oaths by the laws of the United States or of the place where the examination is held, or before a person appointed by the court in which the action is pending. A person so appointed has power to administer oaths and take testimony.

(b) IN FOREIGN COUNTRIES. In a foreign country, depositions may be taken (1) on notice before a person authorized to administer oaths in the place in which the examination is held, either by the law thereof or by the law of the United States, or (2) before a person commissioned by the court, and a person so commissioned shall have the power by virtue of his commission to administer any necessary oath and take testimony, or (3) pursuant to a letter rogatory. A commission or a letter rogatory shall be issued on application and notice and on terms that are just and appropriate. It is not requisite to the issuance of a commission or a letter rogatory that the taking of the deposition in any other manner is impracticable or inconvenient; and both a commission and a letter rogatory may be issued in proper cases. A notice or commission may designate the person before whom the deposition is to be taken either by name or descriptive title. A letter rogatory may be addressed "To the Appropriate Authority in [here name the country]." Evidence obtained in response to a letter rogatory need not be excluded merely for the reason that it is not a verbatim transcript or that the testimony was not taken under oath or for any similar departure from the requirements for depositions taken within the United States under these rules.

(c) DISQUALIFICATION FOR INTEREST. No deposition shall be taken before a person who is a relative or employee or attorney or counsel of any of the parties, or is a relative or employee of such attorney or counsel, or is financially interested in the action.

VIRGINIA

[VA. CODE ANN.]

§ 8-296. **How summons for witness issued, [° ° °].** A summons may be issued, directed as prescribed [by statute], commanding the officer to summon any person to attend on the day and at the place that such attendance is desired, to give evidence before a court, grand jury, arbitrators, umpire, justice, coroner, surveyor, notary, or any commissioner appointed by a court. The summons may be issued, ° ° °; if before a notary or other officer taking a deposition, by such notary or other officer at the instance of the attorney desiring the attendance of the person sought; ° ° °; and, in a proceeding pending before a court by the clerk of the court in which the proceeding is pending; .° ° °. It shall express on whose behalf, and in what case or about what matter, the witness is to attend.

§ 8-297. **Attendance before commissioners of other states.** The preceding section shall be deemed to authorize a summons to compel attendance before commissioners or other persons appointed by authority of another state, but only in case they be citizens of this State, and the summons requires the attendance of a witness at a place not out of his county or city.

§ 8-304. **Deposition of witness, by whom taken in this State; how certified.** In any pending case the deposition of a witness, whether a party to the suit or not, may be taken in this State, after the motion for judgment or bill has been filed, by a notary or commissioner in chancery; and, if certified under his hand, may be received without proof of the signature to such certificate.

§ 8-305. **Of nonresident witness.** The deposition of a witness, whether a party to the suit or not, who resides out of this State, or is out of it in the service thereof, or of the United States, may be taken before any commissioner appointed by the Governor of this State, or notary, or other officer authorized to take depositions in the state wherein the witness may be, or, if the deposition is to be taken in a foreign country, before any person that the parties may agree upon in writing, or any American minister plenipotentiary, charge d' affaires, consul-general, vice-consul, commercial agent appointed by the government of the United States, or any other representative of the United States in a foreign country, or the mayor, or other magistrate of any city, town, or corporation in such country, or any notary therein. Any person, before whom a deposition may be so taken, may administer an oath to the witness, and take and certify the deposition with his official seal annexed; and if he have none, then the genuineness of his signature shall be authenticated by some officer of the same state or country, under his official seal, unless the deposition is taken by a justice out of this State, but in the United States, or before some person agreed upon in writing by the parties, in which case his certificate shall be received without any seal annexed, or other authentication of his signature. When a deposition is taken before some person agreed upon in writing by the parties other than an officer authorized to take the deposition, such writing shall be returned with the deposition, and the deposition shall not be read unless such writing is so returned.

§ 8-306. **No commission to take deposition necessary.** No commission shall be necessary to take a deposition, whether within or without the State.

§ 8-314. **How deposition certified, returned, and filed.** A deposition, when completed, shall be certified and returned by the officer taking it, or sealed and sent to the clerk of the court wherein the suit or other proceeding, in which the deposition is taken, is pending, or to the commissioner or person before whom it is to be read; and when received, the clerk, commissioner, or other person to whom sent, after indorsing thereon the time it was so received, shall file it among the papers of the suit or other proceeding.

Foreign Depositions

§ 8-316.1. **Compelling attendance of witnesses for taking depositions to be used in foreign jurisdiction.** Whenever any mandate, writ or commission is issued out of any court of record in any other state, territory, district or foreign jurisdiction, or whenever upon notice or agreement it is required to take the testimony of a witness or witnesses in this State, witnesses may be compelled to appear and testify in the same manner and by the same process and proceeding as may be employed for the purpose of taking testimony in proceedings pending in this State.

§ 8-316.2. **Uniformity of interpretation; reciprocal privileges.** This article shall be so interpreted and construed as to effectuate its general purposes to make uniform the law of those states which enact it. The privilege extended to persons in other states by § 8-316.1 shall only apply to those states which extended the same privilege to persons in this State.

§ 8-316.3. **Short title.** This article may be cited as the Uniform Foreign Depositions Act.

Affidavits

Any oath or affidavit required by law, which is not of such nature that it must be made in court, may be administered by, or made before, among others, a notary. See *Authority and Duties*, VA. CODE ANN. § 49-4.

[VA. CODE ANN.]

§ 49-5. Officer of another state or country may take affidavit; authentication. An affidavit may also be made before any officer of any state or country authorized by its laws to administer an oath, and shall be deemed duly authenticated if it be subscribed by such officer and there be annexed to it a certificate of the clerk or any other officer of a court of record of such state or country, under an official seal, verifying the genuineness of the signature of the first mentioned officer and his authority to administer an oath, except that when such affidavit is made before a notary public of such other state or country the same shall be deemed and taken to be duly authenticated if it be subscribed by such notary with his official seal attached without being certified to by any clerk or other officer of a court of record.

§ 49-7. Affidavits by corporations and agents. An affidavit by or for a corporation may be made by its president, vice-president, general manager, cashier, treasurer or a director, without any special authorization therefor, or by any person authorized by a majority of its stockholders or directors to make the same; and when an affidavit is made by any person other than the principal authorized by law to make it, such person shall be deemed to have been the agent of the person so authorized until the contrary is made to appear.

Fees

An officer returning affidavits or depositions of witnesses must state at the foot thereof the fees therefor, to whom charged and, if paid, by whom. See *Fees Chargeable*, VA. CODE ANN. § 14.1-98.

WASHINGTON
County or Judicial District Court Commissioners
[WASH. REV. CODE ANN.]

§ 2.24.010. Appointment of court commissioner—qualifications—term of office. There may be appointed in each county or judicial district, by the judges of the superior court having jurisdiction therein, a court commissioner for said county or judicial district. Such commissioner shall be a citizen of the United States and an elector of the county or judicial district in which he may be appointed, and shall hold his office during the pleasure of the judges appointing him.

§ 2.24.020. Oath. Court commissioners appointed hereunder shall, before entering upon the duties of such office, take and subscribe an oath to support the Constitution of the United States, the Constitution of the state of Washington, and to perform the duties of such office fairly and impartially and to the best of his ability.

§ 2.24.040. Powers of commissioner—fees. Such court commissioner shall have power, authority and jurisdiction, concurrent with the superior court and the judge thereof, in the following particulars:

o   o   o

(10)   To take acknowledgments and proofs of deeds, mortgages and all other instruments requiring acknowledgment under the laws of this state, and to take affidavits and depositions in all cases.

(11)   To provide an official seal, upon which shall be engraved the words "Court Commissioner," and the name of the county for which he may be appointed, and to authenticate his official acts therewith in all cases where same is necessary.

(12)   To charge and collect, for his own use, the same fees for the official performance of official acts mentioned in subdivisions (4) and (10) herein as are provided by law for referees and notaries public.

Oaths and Affirmations

§ 5.28.010.   Who may administer.   That every court, judge, clerk of a court, justice of the peace or notary public, is authorized to take testimony in any action, suit or proceeding, and such other persons in particular cases as authorized by law.   Every such court or officer is authorized to administer oaths and affirmations generally, and every such other person in such particular case as authorized.

Comment

Superintendents, associate and assistant superintendents, business managers, records officers and camp superintendents of correctional institutions or facilities operated by the state may administer oaths. See *Acknowledgments*, WASH. REV. CODE ANN. § 64.08.090.

Probate

§ 11.20.030.   Commission to take testimony of witness.   If any witness be prevented by sickness from attending at the time any will is produced for probate, or reside out of the state or more than thirty miles from the place where the will is to be proven, such court may issue a commission annexed to such will, and directed to any judge, justice of the peace, notary public, or other person authorized to administer an oath, empowering him to take and certify the attestation of such witness.

Civil Rules for Superior Courts

[WASH. SUPER. CT. CIV. R. 28]

Persons Before Whom Depositions May Be Taken

Within the State.   Depositions within the state may be taken before the following officers:

(1)   Court Commissioners.

(2)   Superior Courts.

(3)   Judicial Officers.

(4) Judges of Supreme and Superior Courts.

(5) Inferior Judicial Officers.

(6) Notaries Public.

(7) Special Commissions.

(a) **Within the United States.** Within the United States or within a territory or insular possession subject to the dominion of the United States, depositions shall be taken before an officer authorized to administer oaths by the laws of the United States or of the place where the examination is held, or before a person appointed by the court in which the action is pending. A person so appointed has power to administer oaths and take testimony.

(b) **In foreign countries.** In a foreign country, depositions may be taken (1) on notice before a person authorized to administer oaths in the place in which the examination is held, either by the law thereof or by the law of the United States, or (2) before a person commissioned by the court, and a person so commissioned shall have the power by virtue of his commission to administer any necessary oath and take testimony, or (3) pursuant to a letter rogatory. A commission or a letter rogatory shall be issued on application and notice, and on terms that are just and appropriate. It is not requisite to the issuance of a commission or a letter rogatory that the taking of the deposition in any other manner is impracticable or inconvenient; and both a commission and a letter rogatory may be issued in proper cases. A notice or commission may designate the person before whom the deposition is to be taken either by name or descriptive title. A letter rogatory may be addressed "To the Appropriate Authority in [here name the country]." Evidence obtained in response to a letter rogatory need not be excluded merely for the reason that it is not a verbatim transcript or that the testimony was not taken under oath or for any similar departure from the requirements for depositions taken within the United States under these rules.

(c) **Disqualification for interest.** No deposition shall be taken before a person who is a relative or employee or attorney or counsel of any of the parties, or is a relative or employee of such attorney or counsel, or is financially interested in the action.

WEST VIRGINIA

[W. VA. CODE ANN.]

§ 56-3-5. To whom process directed; return of process; return of summons for witness. Process from any court, whether original, mesne or final, may be directed to the sheriff of any county. Any process shall be returnable, within ninety days after its date, except as provided in section six, article two [§ 56-2-6] of this chapter, to the court on any day of a term, or in the clerk's office to the first day of any rules, designated as the first or last Monday, as the case may be, in any month and year, except that a summons for a witness shall be returnable on whatever day his attendance is desired, and an order of attachment may be returnable to the next term of the court, although more than ninety days from the date of the order, and process awarded in court may be returnable as the court may direct.

§ 57-4-1. **Taking and certification of depositions—generally.** In any pending case the deposition of a witness, whether a party to the suit or not, may, without commission, be taken in or out of this State by a justice, or notary public, or by a commissioner in chancery, or before any officer authorized to take depositions in the county or state where they may be taken. And such depositions may be taken in shorthand, or stenographic characters or notes, and shall be written out in full and transcribed into the English language by the stenographer taking the same, and certified by the officer before whom the depositions are taken; and if certified by such officer under his hand and if further certified by him that such stenographic characters and notes were correctly taken and accurately transcribed by him, or under his direction and supervision, and that the witnesses were duly sworn, such depositions may be received and read in evidence without proof of the signature to such certificate and without the signature of the witness to such depositions. And in case the stenographer taking such depositions is not the officer before whom the same are being taken, then such stenographer, before proceeding to take any of said depositions, shall be sworn to take correctly and accurately transcribe the same, and the certificate of the officer before whom the depositions are taken shall state that the stenographer was so sworn.

§ 57-5-1. **Summons for witnesses.** A summons may be issued, directed as described in section five [§ 56-3-5],° article three, chapter fifty-six of this Code, commanding the officer to summon any person to attend on the day and at the place that such attendance is desired, to give evidence before a court, grand jury, arbitrators, umpire, justice, surveyor, notary public, or any commissioner appointed by a court. The summons may be issued, if the attendance be desired at a court, by the clerk thereof; if before a grand jury, by the prosecuting attorney or the clerk of the court, at the instance of the prosecuting attorney; and in other cases, by any person before whom, or the clerk of the circuit court of a county in which, the attendance is desired; or, if attendance be desired before a justice, by such or any other justice. The summons shall express on whose behalf, and in what case, or about what matter, the witness is to attend. This section shall be deemed to authorize a summons to compel attendance before commissioners or other persons appointed by authority of another state, but only in case they be citizens of this State, and the summons requires the attendance of a witness at a place not out of his county.

° For § 56-3-5, see above.

§ 57-5-6. Commitment to jail of person attending but refusing to testify or produce writing. If a person, after being served with ° ° ° summons, shall attend and yet refuse to be sworn, or to give evidence, or to produce any writing or document required, he may by order of the court whose clerk issued said summons, or of the person before whom he was summoned to attend, be committed to jail, there to remain until he shall, in custody of the jailer, give such evidence or produce such writing or document.

§ 57-5-7. Interpreters. Interpreters may be sworn truly to interpret, when necessary.

Oaths

§ 57-5-8. Who may administer oath to witness. Any person before whom a witness is to be examined may administer an oath to such witness.

§ 57-5-9. Administration of oaths or taking of affidavits; authentication of affidavit made in another state or country; oaths and affidavits of persons in military service. Any judge of this State may administer any oath that is or may be lawful for any person to take, including oaths of office, and also may swear any person to an affidavit, and administer an oath to any person in any proceeding.

Any oath or affidavit required by law, which is not of such a nature that it must be made otherwise or elsewhere may, unless otherwise provided, be administered by, or made before, a county commissioner, notary public, or a commissioner appointed by the governor, or by the clerk of any court, or, in case of a survey directed by a court in a case therein pending, by or before the surveyor directed to execute said order of survey.

An affidavit may also be made before any officer of another state or country authorized by its laws to administer an oath, and shall be deemed duly authenticated if it be subscribed by such officer, with his official seal annexed, and if he have none, the genuineness of his signature, and his authority to administer an oath, shall be authenticated by some officer of the same state or country under his official seal.

Any oath or affidavit required of a person in the military service of the United States (including the Women's Army Corps, Women's Appointed Volunteers for Emergency Service, Army Nurse Corps, Spars, Women's Reserve, or similar women's auxiliary unit officially connected with such military service of the United States), may be administered by or made before any commissioned officer of any branch of the military service of the United States, or any auxiliary unit officially connected with such military service. Such oath may be taken or affidavit made at any place either within or outside the United States of America, or any territory, possession or dependency thereof. The jurat to such oath and certificate to such affidavit need not state the place where the same is taken and shall require no seal to be affixed thereto. The certificate of the officer before whom such oath is taken or affidavit is made must state his rank, branch of military service, and identification number, and such certificate may be substantially in form and effect as follows:

IN THE MILITARY SERVICE OF THE UNITED STATES:

I, ———, being duly sworn on oath (affirmation), do swear (affirm) that I am a member of the military service of the United States (or of ———, an auxiliary to the military forces of the United States); that ° ° °, etc.

———

Taken, subscribed and sworn to before me, ———, a commissioned officer in the ——— service of the United States, by ———, a member of the military service of the United States (or of ———, an auxiliary to the military forces of the United States), this the ——— day of ———, 19—.

——— (Signature of officer)

———   ———

(Rank)   (Indentification Number)

Any oath or affidavit heretofore taken or made by any person in the military service in substantial compliance with this section shall be valid.

Divorce

§ 48-2-24. **Maturing of actions for divorce, annulment and separate maintenance; hearing; testimony and depositions; reference of action to commissioner.** Actions for divorce, annulment and separate maintenance shall mature in the same manner as other actions provided for in the Rules of Civil Procedure of the State of West Virginia, and when ready for hearing under said rules shall be tried before the court, in chambers, and all witnesses shall appear and testify at the hearing the same as witnesses in other civil actions. Such actions may be heard, when matured, and a judgment order entered, at any time irrespective of whether or not there is a term of court in session. The law governing the taking and reading of depositions, as provided for in the Rules of Civil Procedure, shall apply to depositions in the hearing of a divorce case. The court may, instead of proceeding with the action under this section, refer the same to a commissioner, or a special commissioner, of said court as provided for in section twenty-five [§ 48-2-25] of this article.

§ 48-2-25. **Reference to commissioner; taking of depositions; oral testimony before court.** Instead of proceeding with the action under the provisions of section twenty-four [§ 48-2-24] of this article, the court may, in its discretion, refer it to one of the commissioners of such court, or to a special commissioner, who shall take and return the testimony in such action, with a report of all such facts as the commissioner may be able to obtain as to property rights of the parties, their income, their character, conduct, health, habits, their children, their respective places of residence from the time of their marriage up to the time of such report, and any other matter deemed necessary by the court, together with his recommendation concerning whether a divorce, annulment or affirmation, as the case may be, should be granted, and concerning any other matter on which the court may request his recommendation. All such facts so reported and the recommendation of the commissioner shall be considered by the court in passing on the merits of the case, whether the same be referred to in the pleadings or evidence, or not. Except as otherwise expressly provided herein, the procedure in respect to the reference of such a case to a commissioner shall be governed in all respects by the rules applicable to references to commissioners generally.

If testimony is to be taken in a county other than that in which the action is pending, or of witnesses residing out of the State of West Virginia, the same shall be taken before some person duly authorized to take depositions in the county or state where taken. If such depositions are taken out of the county in which the action is pending, or without the State, the same shall be, by the person taking the same, filed with or forwarded to the clerk of the court wherein such action is pending, and on receipt of such depositions such clerk shall lay the same before the commissioner to whom such action has been referred, who shall consider the same in connection with his report hereinbefore mentioned. The person before whom depositions are taken hereunder shall be personally present at the time and place of taking depositions, and no deposition shall be taken or read in the action unless it appears therefrom that such person was personally present during the taking of the same. It is hereby made the duty of the person before whom such depositions are taken, to see that all witnesses are so examined as to elicit all facts within their knowledge pertaining to the action. If any person before whom any such depositions are taken certified falsely as to his presence at the taking of such depositions, he shall be guilty of a misdemeanor, and, on conviction thereof, shall be fined not less than fifty nor more than five hundred dollars.

The court in which such action is pending may so refer the same as often as, in its judgment, justice requires, and may, if it so elect, summon anyone to appear before such court, and give evidence with reference thereto, and base its findings on such oral evidence solely. The commissioner shall be allowed for his services the same compensation as is allowed in other court actions, and all costs, including stenographer's fees, shall be taxed as in other court actions.

Civil Procedure

[W. VA. R. CIV. P. 28]

Persons Before Whom Depositions May Be Taken

(a) *Within the United States.* Within the United States or within a territory or insular possession subject to the dominion of the United States, depositions shall be taken before an officer authorized to administer oaths by the laws of the United States or of this State or of the place where the examination is held, or before a person appointed by the court in which the action is pending. A person so appointed has power to administer oaths and take testimony.

(b) *In foreign countries.* In a foreign state or country depositions shall be taken (1) on notice before a secretary of embassy or legation, consul general, consul, vice consul, or consular agent of the United States, or (2) before such person or officer as may be appointed by commission or under letters rogatory. A commission or letters rogatory shall be issued only when necessary or convenient, on application and notice, and on such terms and with such directions as are just and appropriate. Officers may be designated in notices or commissions either by name or descriptive title and letters rogatory may be addressed "To the Appropriate Judicial Authority in [here name the country]."

(c) *Disqualification for interest.* No deposition shall be taken before a person who is a relative or employee or attorney or counsel of any of the parties, or is a relative or employee of such attorney or counsel, or is financially interested in the action.

(d) *Depositions for use in foreign jurisdictions.* Whenever the deposition of any person is to be taken in this State pursuant to the laws of another state or of the United States or of another country for use in proceedings there, any court having general civil jurisdiction in the county wherein the deponent resides or is employed or transacts his business in person may, upon petition, make an order directing issuance of a subpoena as provided in Rule 45, in aid of the taking of the deposition.

WISCONSIN

[WIS. STAT. ANN.]

§ 256.46. **Reporter not to take statements of injured persons.** No phonographic reporter for any court of record in the state of Wisconsin or any of his assistants shall be employed by any person or corporation to take the statement of any injured or other person in any way relating to the manner in which the person was injured or killed or the extent of personal injuries, and any reporter or assistant violating the provisions hereof shall be removed and shall not be permitted to testify in any court concerning any such statements taken in violation hereof. The taking, transcribing or reporting testimony given by deposition or otherwise according to law, is not prohibited by this section.

§ 887.025. **Testimonial oath.** (1) In all judicial proceedings the witnesses shall be sworn before testifying, and the oath may be administered substantially in the following form: Do you solemnly swear that the testimony which you shall give in [here indicate the action, proceeding or matter on trial or being inquired into], shall be the truth, the whole truth and nothing but the truth, so help you God.

(2) The assent to the oath by the person being sworn may be manifested by the uplifted hand.

§ 887.03. **Oath, how taken.** Any oath or affidavit required or authorized by law may be taken in any of the usual forms, and every person swearing, affirming or declaring in any such form shall be deemed to have been lawfully sworn.

§ 887.04. **Affirmations.** (1) Every person who shall declare that he has conscientious scruples against taking the oath, or swearing in the usual form, shall make his solemn declaration or affirmation, which may be in the following form: Do you solemnly, sincerely and truly declare and affirm that the testimony you shall give in [here indicate the action, proceeding or matter on trial or being inquired into] shall be the truth, the whole truth and nothing but the truth; and this you do under the pains and penalties of perjury.

(2) The assent to the affirmation by the person making it may be manifested by the uplifted hand.

§ 887.05. **Depositions, may be taken.** (1) Depositions (including that of a party taken on his own behalf) may be taken to be used before any court, magistrate or any other person authorized to hear testimony, in any civil action, matter or proceeding whatever, or on any motion therein.

(2) No deposition shall be taken before any officer or commissioner who is the attorney or of counsel for any party or person interested, or is himself otherwise interested in the action, matter or proceeding in or for which the deposition is taken, except by written consent of the parties.

§ 887.08. **Deposition; attendance of witness.** Any witness may be subpoenaed and compelled to give his deposition at any place within 20 miles of his abode, under the same penalties as he may be subpoenaed and compelled to attend as a witness in any court.

§ 887.09. **Oral depositions; when taken, before whom, notice, absence of officer.** (1) **Oral depositions in this state.** (a) Such deposition, in this state, may be taken by a municipal justice, notary public, court commissioner or other person authorized to take depositions, except as provided in § 887.12(4),* at any time after the action or proceeding is commenced or after a submission to arbitration.

(b)   One day's notice shall be sufficient to authorize the taking of depositions of additional witnesses desired to be examined, given during the course of the taking of any deposition where the parties on each side appear.

(c)   In case the officer designated shall not attend at the time and place noticed for taking the deposition, it may be taken before any other officer, authorized to take depositions, designated by the party who served the notice of taking deposition, and notice of such designation to the opposite party, in sufficient time to attend before the officer so designated if the opposite party shall have appeared at the time and place mentioned in the first notice; but if he shall not so appear, the moving party may, after waiting one hour, proceed to take such deposition before such other officer without further notice.

(2)   **Oral depositions without this state.**   (a)   Such deposition may be taken orally without this state by any notary public or justice of the peace or by any judge or justice, court commissioner or master in chancery of any court of record of the United States or any state or territory thereof, or by any commissioner appointed pursuant to s. 137.02, within the territory in which such officer is authorized to act.

(b)   In a foreign country such deposition may be taken before any judge or clerk of a court of such country, any notary public, or any consul, vice consul, deputy consul or consular agent of the United States, resident in such country, or by any officer authorized by the laws of the United States to take depositions.

(c)   Such deposition without the state may be taken, certified, returned, filed and used in the manner and under the provisions of law applicable to depositions taken within the state.

   * For § 887.12(4) see below.

§ 887.095.   Ex parte deposition in county court.   In proceedings in the county court where there is no contest, depositions may be taken for use therein in such manner as the court directs, either within or without the state.

§ 887.10.   Depositions; how taken and returned.   The deponent shall be sworn to testify the truth, the whole truth and nothing but the truth relating to the action, proceeding or matter for which his testimony is taken, and his testimony shall be taken in writing, or in shorthand by a stenographer approved by the officer taking the same, or by all parties in interest, and by or under the supervision of such stenographer typewritten or reduced to longhand.   There must be inserted therein every answer or declaration of the witness and every oral interrogatory which any party requires to be inserted.

The deposition must be read to or by the witness and subscribed by him, unless the parties represented shall stipulate, upon the record (which they may do), that the reading of the deposition to or by the deponent and his signature thereto are waived, and that the deposition may be used with like force and effect as if read and subscribed by him. The attendance of the deponent for the purpose of reading and subscribing his deposition may be compelled in the same manner that his attendance to be examined may be compelled. The deposition shall in all cases be delivered or transmitted by the officer by whom the same is taken to the clerk of the court, the magistrate, board or officer before whom the action, proceeding or matter is pending, securely sealed, and shall remain sealed until opened by such court, clerk, magistrate, board or officer.

§ 887.12. **Depositions; purpose, procedure, scope, use, effect and related matters.**

o   o   o

(4) Time, place, notice; officers empowered to take

(4) Such examinations shall be taken in counties within this state having a population of 500,000 or more before a court commissioner or judge at chambers and elsewhere before any officer authorized to take depositions by the laws of the state where the deposition is taken on previous notice to all adverse parties or their respective attorneys of at least 5 days. If the person to be examined is a nonresident party to the action or proceeding, or is an officer, director, or managing agent of a corporation that is a party, the court may upon just terms fix the time and place of such examination, and he shall attend at such time and place and submit to the examination, and, if required, attend for the reading and signing of such deposition, without service of subpoenas. Such examination shall not be compelled in any county other than that in which the person examined resides, except that any nonresident subject to examination may be examined in any county of this state in which he is personally served with notice and subpoena. The court may fix another place for such an examination in the case of a person who is physically unable to attend the examination in the county of his residence. When a party has instituted suit in any county of this state, he shall be subject to adverse examination in such county whether he resides in such county or not provided a subpoena is served upon him within such county. If such party is an out-of-state resident such service of subpoena upon his resident attorney shall confer jurisdiction upon him for purposes of the adverse examination.

o   o   o

Note: § 887.09(1)(a), above, refers to this section.

§ 887.20. **Deposition in municipal justice court.** The municipal justice before whom any civil cause is pending may, on any day on which a trial may be had, after an application has been made for adjournment and before making an order for an adjournment, on the application of either party, showing any cause provided by law therefor, proceed to take the deposition of any witness then in attendance before the municipal justice; and no prior notice shall be required.

§ 887.22. **Form of certificate.** The officer shall annex to the deposition a certificate substantially as follows:

STATE OF WISCONSIN,

ss.

———— County.

I, A. B. (add official designation), in and for said county, do hereby certify that the above deposition was taken before me at my office, in the ———— of ————, in said county, on the ———— day of ————, 19—, at ———— o'clock, ———— noon; that it was taken at the request of the plaintiff (or defendant, or other person procuring it), upon verbal (or written) interrogatories; that it was reduced to writing by myself (or by ————, a disinterested person, in my presence, and under my direction, or was taken in shorthand by ————, approved by me, or by all parties in interest and by him reduced to longhand); that it was taken to be used in the action of A. B. vs. C. D., now pending in ———— court (or to be used in some proceeding or matter, mentioning it), and that the reason for taking it was (here state the true reason); that ———— attended at the taking of such deposition (or that a notice, of which the annexed is a copy, was served upon ———— on the ———— day of ————, 19—; or that the deposition was taken in pursuance of the annexed stipulation); that said deponent, before examination, was sworn to testify the truth, the whole truth and nothing but the truth relative to said cause, and that said deposition was carefully read to (or by) said deponent and then subscribed by him (or the parties attending the taking of the deposition stipulated on the record, that the reading of the deposition by or to the deponent and his signature thereto is waived and that it may be used as if read and signed).

A. B. (adding official designation).

§ 887.26. **Depositions without this state by commission. (1) How taken.** In any civil action, proceeding or matter in which depositions may be taken within this state, the deposition of any witness without the state may be taken upon written interrogatories as provided in this section.

(4) Commission to take. A commission may issue from any court of record to take the deposition of any witness without the state, where an issue of fact has been joined or the time therefor has expired, for any cause which shall be deemed sufficient by the court, or when required for use on any trial or hearing or upon any motion or proceeding. The commission shall be signed by the clerk and sealed and shall be accompanied by a copy of subs. (4), (5) and (6).

(5) Procuring commission. (a) The party desiring a commission shall prepare interrogatories and state in the caption thereof the name of the commissioner proposed by him, the name of the witness and the residence of each with particularity, and shall serve a copy thereof on the opposite party, with a notice that, at the expiration of 10 days from the date of such service, a commission will be issued to take the deposition of the witness, specifying the reason for taking the same. Within such time the opposite party may file with the clerk and serve upon the other his objections, to the interrogatories proposed and to the competency of the witness and to the issuance of the commission and serve his cross-interrogatories; and state the name and residence of any person whom he desires to act as an additional commissioner, who must reside in the county in which the commissioner first named resides.

(b) At the expiration of the time limited, the moving party may file the notice and interrogatories, with proof of service thereof and his objections to the cross-interrogatories. He may also serve redirect interrogatories on the opposite party, who may, within 3 days after such service, file objections to such redirect interrogatories. Thereupon the commission shall be issued, with the interrogatories, direct, cross and redirect, and all objections, and transmitted to the commissioner first named by mail or express at the expense of the moving party. But when any defendant shall not have appeared and the time for him to plead has expired, no notice is required to be given such defendant, and the commission may issue on filing the direct interrogatories. No commission shall issue if the residences are not given as required.

(6) Duty of commissioner. (a) The commissioner first named shall fix the time and place for executing the commission and give the other commissioner one day's notice thereof, when he resides in the same place, and when not, one day's notice in addition for every 30 miles of distance between his place of residence and the place fixed for executing the commission. If the notice be by mail double time shall be allowed; but notice may be waived in writing or by appearance at the execution of the commission. If there be 2 commissioners the commission shall be executed in the county where they reside, unless they agree upon another. The commissioner first named shall have charge of and return the deposition, which return shall be in the form and manner directed by the commission or as provided by s. 887.22. If either commissioner shall not attend at the time and place so fixed, the other may execute the commission with like effect as if both were present, but he must certify in his return that the other had due notice but failed to attend.

(b)   One of the commissioners shall publicly administer an oath or affirmation to each witness that the answers which he shall make to each of the interrogatories propounded to him shall be the truth, the whole truth, and nothing but the truth. His answers to each interrogatory shall be reduced to writing. Each witness shall subscribe his name at the end of his answer and the commissioners shall subscribe their names at the foot of each page of the testimony. If any exhibit is produced and proved or referred to in the answer of any witness, it shall be marked as an exhibit, either by letter or number, by a commissioner, and referred to in the testimony of the witness, and annexed to and returned with the deposition. If the paper be a record or other document not in the control of either party, it shall be sufficient to annex a copy, stated by the witness in his answers to be a true copy thereof. The commissioners shall certify in their return that each witness, before giving his evidence, was duly sworn or affirmed, and shall state the time when the testimony was taken.

(c)   The proper commissioner shall inclose the commission, the interrogatories, and the deposition with the return annexed in a sealed envelope, with the title of the action indorsed thereon and immediately transmit the same by mail or express to the clerk of the court from which the commission issued.

(d)   Upon the receipt of such package, the clerk shall indorse the time and manner in which he received the same, and open it and file the contents thereof and give notice of the receipt of the same to the attorneys for the respective parties.

(7)   **Fees.**   The persons who take depositions and the witness shall be entitled to the fees allowed court commissioners under s. 252.17‡ and witnesses for similar service by the law of this state, or such as may be prescribed by the law of the state or country where taken.

‡ Concerning fees of court commissioners, see § 252.17, below.

(8)   **Translations.**   When the witness is unable to speak the English language, the judge of the court from which the commission issues may appoint some competent and disinterested person to translate the commission, rules, interrogatories and cross-interrogatories, or such part thereof as may be necessary, from the English into the language spoken by the witness; and such translation shall be sent to the commissioner in place of the original papers that have been translated. Upon the return of the commission and deposition, such judge shall in like manner cause the answers of the witness and the exhibits to be translated into English, as well as all other proceedings in a foreign language, and such translation to be filed. The translator shall append to all translations his affidavit that he knows the English and such foreign language, and that in making such translation he carefully and truly translated such proceedings

from the English into such foreign language or from the latter into English, and that such translation is correct.   Such translation shall have the same effect as if all the proceedings were in English, but the trial court, upon the deposition being offered in evidence, may admit the testimony of witnesses learned in such foreign language for the purpose of correcting errors therein; and, if it shall appear that the first translation was in any respect so incorrect as to mislead the witness, the court may, in discretion, continue the cause for the further taking of testimony.

Fees of Court Commissioners

§ 252.17.   **Fees of court commissioners.**   Court commissioners shall be entitled to the following fees:

° ° °

(8)   Attendance upon the taking of testimony or examination of witnesses in any matter or proceeding whatever, whether acting as a referee or otherwise, $15 for the first 2 hours thereof and $5 per hour thereafter, and also 75 cents per page for the original transcript of the testimony so taken and 30 cents per page for each copy thereof.   For purposes of this section a page other than the final page of a transcript shall consist of any 25 or more consecutive typewritten lines, double-spaced, on paper not less than 8½ inches in width, with a margin of not more than 1½ inches on the left and 5/8 of an inch on the right, exclusive of lines disclosing page numbering; type shall be standard pica with 10 letters to the inch.   Questions and answers shall each begin a new line.   Indentations for speakers or paragraphs shall be not more than 15 spaces from left margin.   The commissioner shall be paid $15 and the reporter shall be paid $10 per day for the attendance at each examination or adjourned hearing whether or not evidence is taken, but no attendance fee shall be paid to the reporter where the testimony taken at any examination or adjourned hearing results in a total page charge of $10 or more for the original transcript.   Where the reporter is present, no motion for adjournment shall be granted unless the movant first pays the reporter's and commissioner's attendance fee.   No attendance fee shall be allowed to a court reporter whose salary is paid in whole or in part by the state while taking testimony in the normal course of his official duties. Out of fees charged by the court commissioner under this subsection he shall be obligated to pay the reporter 45 cents per page for the original transcript and 25 cents per page for each copy.   The attorney requesting the examination shall be directly responsible to the court commissioner for the payments of all fees except for the fees to be paid by a party requesting an adjournment.   The attorney requesting the examination shall be directly responsible to the court commissioner for the payment of the original transcript of testimony costs and any attorney ordering a copy of the transcript shall be directly responsible for the payment of same to the court commissioner.   Original

of the testimony shall be filed by the commissioner only after payment of the commissioner's and reporter's fees. All moneys collected by the court commissioner pursuant to this section which are payable to the court reporter shall be held in trust by the commissioner, and the commissioner shall make payment forthwith of the moneys to the court reporter. The reporter shall enter into the transcript the time of commencement and conclusion of the hearing.

o   o   o

(14)   For every precept for a jury, subpoena for a witness or attachment for a witness, 25 cents.

o   o   o

(23)   For administering an oath, in cases where no fee is specifically provided for by law, and certifying the same when required, 12 cents.

o   o   o

(32)   For administering an oath to a witness, 10 cents.

o   o   o

(34)   For forwarding of all copies of testimony to any attorney ordering same, the cost of the first class mailing thereof and registering with return receipt requested.

WYOMING

Notaries public, among other officers, are authorized to administer oaths. See *Authority and Duties,* WYO. STAT. ANN. § 1-9. They are also specifically authorized to take depositions. See *Authority and Duties,* WYO. STAT. ANN. § 32-5.

[WYO. R. CIV. P. 28]

Persons Before Whom Depositions May Be Taken

(a)   *Within the United States.*   Within the United States or within a territory or insular possession subject to the dominion of the United States, depositions shall be taken before an officer authorized to administer oaths by the laws of this state or of the United States or of the place where the examination is held, or before a person appointed by the court in which the action is pending. A person so appointed has power to administer oaths and take testimony.

(b)   *In Foreign Countries.*   In a foreign country, depositions may be taken (1) on notice before a person authorized to administer oaths in the place in which the examination is held, either by the law thereof or by the law of the United States, or (2) before a person commissioned by the court, and a person so commissioned shall have the power by virtue of his commission to administer any necessary oath and take testimony, or (3) pursuant to a letter rogatory. A commission or a letter rogatory shall be issued on application and notice and on terms that are just and appropriate. It is not requisite to the issuance of a commission or a letter rogatory that the taking of the deposition in any other manner is impracticable or inconvenient; and both a commission and a letter rogatory may be issued in proper cases. A notice or commission may designate the person before whom the deposition is to be taken either by name or descriptive title. A letter rogatory may be addressed "To the Appropriate Authority in (here name the country)." Evidence obtained in response to a letter rogatory need not be excluded merely for the reason that it is not a verbatim transcript or that the testimony was not taken under oath or for any similar departure from the requirements for depositions taken within the United States under these rules.

(c) *Disqualification for Interest.* No deposition shall be taken before a person who is a relative, employee, attorney or counsel of any of the parties, or is financially interested in the action.

[WYO. R. CRIM. P. 17]

Depositions

(a) *When Taken.* If it appears that a prospective witness may be unable to attend or prevented from attending a trial or hearing, that his testimony is material and that it is necessary to take his deposition in order to prevent a failure of justice, the court at any time after the filing of an indictment or information may upon motion of any party and notice to the other parties order that his testimony be taken by deposition and that any designated books, papers or documents or tangible objects, not privileged, be produced at the same time and place. If a witness is committed for failure to give bail to appear to testify at a trial or hearing, the court on written motion of the witness and upon notice to the parties may direct his deposition be taken. After the deposition has been subscribed, the court may discharge the witness.

(b) *Notice of Taking.* The party at whose instance the deposition is to be taken shall give to every other party reasonable written notice of the time and place for taking the deposition. The notice shall state the name and address of each person to be examined. On motion of a party upon whom the notice is served, and for cause shown on notice and hearing, the court may extend or shorten the time for taking the deposition.

(c) *Defendant's Counsel and Payment of Expenses.* [Omitted.]

(d) *How Taken.* A deposition shall be taken in the manner provided in civil actions. The court at the request of a defendant may direct that a deposition be taken on written interrogatories in the manner provided in civil actions.

(e) *Use.* [Omitted.]

(f) *Objections to Admissibility.* Objections to receiving in evidence the deposition or part thereof may be made as provided in civil actions.

UNITED STATES

Civil Procedure

[FED. R. CIV. P. 28]

Persons Before Whom Depositions May Be Taken

(a) **Within the United States.** Within the United States or within a territory or insular possession subject to the dominion of the United States, depositions shall be taken before an officer authorized to administer oaths by the laws of the United States or of the place where the examination is held, or before a person appointed by the court in which the action is pending. A person so appointed has power to administer oaths and take testimony.

(b) **In foreign countries.** In a foreign country, depositions may be taken (1) on notice before a person authorized to administer oaths in the place in which the examination is held, either by the law thereof or by the law of the United States, or (2) before a person commissioned by the court, and a person so commissioned shall have the power by virtue of his commission to administer any necessary oath and take testimony, or (3) pursuant to a letter rogatory. A commission or a letter rogatory shall be issued on application and notice, and on terms that are just and appropriate. It is not requisite to the issuance of a commission or a letter rogatory that the taking of the deposition in any other manner is impracticable or inconvenient; and both a commission and a letter rogatory may be issued in proper cases. A notice or commission may designate the person before whom the deposition is to be taken either by name or descriptive title. A letter rogatory may be addressed "To the Appropriate Authority in [here name the country]." Evidence obtained in response to a letter rogatory need not be excluded merely for the reason that it is not a verbatim transcript or that the testimony was not taken under oath or for any similar departure from the requirements for depositions taken within the United States under these rules.

(c) **Disqualification for interest.** No deposition shall be taken before a person who is a relative or employee or attorney or counsel of any of the parties, or is a relative or employee of such attorney or counsel, or is financially interested in the action.

Rule 29. Stipulations regarding discovery procedure. Unless the court orders otherwise, the parties may by written stipulation (1) provide that depositions may be taken before any person, at any time or place, upon any notice, and in any manner and when so taken may be used like other depositions, and (2) modify the procedures provided by these rules for other methods of discovery, except that stipulations extending the time provided in Rules 33, 34, and 36 for responses to discovery may be made only with the approval of the court.

Rule 30. Depositions upon oral examination. (a) When Depositions may be taken. After commencement of the action, any party may take the testimony of any person, including a party, by deposition upon oral examination. Leave of court, granted with or without notice, must be obtained only if the plaintiff seeks to take a deposition prior to the expiration of 30 days after service of the summons and complaint upon any defendant or service made under Rule 4(e), except that leave is not required (1) if a defendant has served a notice of taking deposition or otherwise sought discovery, or (2) if special notice is given as provided in subdivision (b)(2) of this rule. The attendance of witnesses may be compelled by subpoena as provided in Rule 45. The deposition of a person confined in prison may be taken only by leave of court on such terms as the court prescribes.

(b) Notice of examination: general requirements; special notice; non-stenographic recording; production of documents and things; deposition of organization.

(1) A party desiring to take the deposition of any person upon oral examination shall give reasonable notice in writing to every other party to the action. The notice shall state the time and place for taking the deposition and the name and address of each person to be examined, if known, and, if the name is not known, a general description sufficient to identify him or the particular class or group to which he belongs. If a subpoena duces tecum is to be served on the person to be examined, the designation of the materials to be produced as set forth in the subpoena shall be attached to or included in the notice.

(2) Leave of court is not required for the taking of a deposition by plaintiff if the notice (A) states that the person to be examined is about to go out of the district where the action is pending and more than 100 miles from the place of trial, or is about to go out of the United States, or is bound on a voyage to sea, and will be unavailable for examination unless his deposition is taken before expiration of the 30-day period, and (B) sets forth facts to support the statement. The plaintiff's attorney shall sign the notice, and his signature constitutes a certification by him that to the best of his knowledge, information, and belief the statement and supporting facts are true. The sanctions provided by Rule 11 are applicable to the certification.

If a party shows that when he was served with notice under this subdivision (b)(2) he was unable through the exercise of diligence to obtain counsel to represent him at the taking of the deposition, the deposition may not be used against him.

(3) The court may for cause shown enlarge or shorten the time for taking the deposition.

(4)   The court may upon motion order that the testimony at a deposition be recorded by other than stenographic means, in which event the order shall designate the manner of recording, preserving, and filing the deposition, and may include other provisions to assure that the recorded testimony will be accurate and trustworthy.   If the order is made, a party may nevertheless arrange to have a stenographic transcription made at his own expense.

(5)   The notice to a party deponent may be accompanied by a request made in compliance with Rule 34 for the production of documents and tangible things at the taking of the deposition.   The procedure of Rule 34 shall apply to the request.

(6)   A party may in his notice and in a subpoena name as the deponent a public or private corporation or a partnership or association or governmental agency and describe with reasonable particularity the matters on which examination is requested.   In that event, the organization so named shall designate one or more officers, directors, or managing agents, or other persons who consent to testify on its behalf, and may set forth, for each person designated, the matters on which he will testify.   A subpoena shall advise a non-party organization of its duty to make such a designation.   The persons so designated shall testify as to matters known or reasonably available to the organization.   This subdivision (b) (6) does not preclude taking a deposition by any other procedure authorized in these rules.

(c)   **Examination and cross-examination; record of examination; oath; objections.**   Examination and cross-examination of witnesses may proceed as permitted at the trial under the provisions of Rule 43(b).   The officer before whom the deposition is to be taken shall put the witness on oath and shall personally, or by someone acting under his direction and in his presence, record the testimony of the witness.   The testimony shall be taken stenographically or recorded by any other means ordered in accordance with subdivision (b) (4) of this rule.   If requested by one of the parties, the testimony shall be transcribed.

All objections made at time of the examination to the qualifications of the officer taking the deposition, or to the manner of taking it, or to the evidence presented, or to the conduct of any party, and any other objection to the proceedings, shall be noted by the officer upon the deposition.   Evidence objected to shall be taken subject to the objections.   In lieu of participating in the oral examination, parties may serve written questions in a sealed envelope on the party taking the deposition and he shall transmit them to the officer, who shall propound them to the witness and record the answers verbatim.

(d)   **Motion to terminate or limit examination.**   At any time during the taking of the deposition, on motion of a party or of the deponent and upon a showing that the examination is being conducted in bad faith or in such manner as unreasonably to annoy, embarrass, or oppress the deponent or party, the court in which the action is pending or the court in the district where the deposition is being taken may order the officer conducting the examination to cease forthwith from taking the deposition, or may limit the scope and manner of the taking of the deposition as provided in Rule 26(c). If the order made terminates the examination, it shall be resumed thereafter only upon the order of the court in which the action is pending. Upon demand of the objecting party or deponent, the taking of the deposition shall be suspended for the time necessary to make a motion for an order. The provisions of Rule 37(a)(4) apply to the award of expenses incurred in relation to the motion.

(e) **Submission to witness; changes; signing.** When the testimony is fully transcribed the deposition shall be submitted to the witness for examination and shall be read to or by him, unless such examination and reading are waived by the witness and by the parties. Any changes in form or substance which the witness desires to make shall be entered upon the deposition by the officer with a statement of the reasons given by the witness for making them. The deposition shall then be signed by the witness, unless the parties by stipulation waive the signing or the witness is ill or cannot be found or refuses to sign. If the deposition is not signed by the witness within 30 days of its submission to him, the officer shall sign it and state on the record the fact of the waiver or of the illness or absence of the witness or the fact of the refusal to sign together with the reason, if any, given therefore; and the deposition may then be used as fully as though signed unless on a motion to suppress under Rule 32(d)(4) the court holds that the reasons given for the refusal to sign require rejection of the deposition in whole or in part.

(f) **Certification and filing by officer; exhibits; copies; notice of filing.**

(1) The officer shall certify on the deposition that the witness was duly sworn by him and that the deposition is a true record of the testimony given by the witness. He shall then securely seal the deposition in an envelope indorsed with the title of the action and marked "Deposition of [here insert name of witness]" and shall promptly file it with the court in which the action is pending or send it by registered or certified mail to the clerk thereof for filing.

Documents and things produced for inspection during the examination of the witness, shall, upon the request of a party, be marked for identification and annexed to and returned with the deposition, and may be inspected and copied by any party, except that (A) the person producing the materials may substitute copies to be marked for identification, if he affords to all parties fair opportunity to verify the copies by comparison with the originals, and (B) if the person producing the materials requests their return, the officer shall mark them, give each party an opportunity to inspect and copy them, and return them to the person producing them, and the materials may then be used in the same manner as if annexed to and returned with the deposition. Any party may move for an order that the original be annexed to and returned with the deposition to the court, pending final disposition of the case.

(2) Upon payment of reasonable charges therefor, the officer shall furnish a copy of the deposition to any party or to the deponent.

(3) The party taking the deposition shall give prompt notice of its filing to all other parties.

(g) **Failure to attend or to serve subpoena; expenses.**

(1) If the party giving the notice of the taking of a deposition fails to attend and proceed therewith and another party attends in person or by attorney pursuant to the notice, the court may order the party giving the notice to pay to such other party the reasonable expenses incurred by him and his attorney in attending, including reasonable attorney's fees.

(2) If the party giving the notice of the taking of a deposition of a witness fails to serve a subpoena upon him and the witness because of such failure does not attend, and if another party attends in person or by attorney because he expects the deposition of that witness to be taken, the court may order the party giving the notice to pay to such other party the reasonable expenses incurred by him and his attorney in attending, including reasonable attorney's fees.

Criminal Procedure

[FED. R. CRIM. P. 15]

Depositions. (a) **When taken.** If it appears that a prospective witness may be unable to attend or prevented from attending a trial or hearing, that his testimony is material and that it is necessary to take his deposition in order to prevent a failure of justice, the court at any time after the filing of an indictment or information may upon motion of a defendant and notice to the parties order that his testimony be taken by deposition and that any designated books, papers, documents or tangible objects, not privileged, be produced at the same time and place. If a witness is committed for failure to give bail to appear to testify at a trial or hearing, the court on written motion of the witness and upon notice to the parties may direct that his deposition be taken. After the deposition has been subscribed the court may discharge the witness.

(b) **Notice of taking.** The party at whose instance a deposition is to be taken shall give to every other party reasonable written notice of the time and place for taking the deposition. The notice shall state the name and address of each person to be examined. On motion of a party upon whom the notice is served, the court for cause shown may extend or shorten the time.

(c) **Defendant's counsel and payment of expenses.** [Omitted.]

(d) **How taken.** A deposition shall be taken in the manner provided in civil actions. The court at the request of a defendant may direct that a deposition be taken on written interrogatories in the manner provided in civil actions.

(e) **Use.** [Omitted.]

(f) **Objections to admissibility.** Objections to receiving in evidence a deposition or part thereof may be made as provided in civil actions.

CHAPTER 14:

COMMERCIAL PAPER UNDER THE UNIFORM COMMERCIAL CODE

CROSS-REFERENCE

For definitions of the various terms used in this chapter, consult the *Glossary*, page 853.

JURISDICTION:	LOCAL CITATION:		ORIGINAL EFFECTIVE DATE OF UCC:
	Article 3:	Article 4:	
Alabama	ALA. CODE tit. 7A, § 3-101 to 7A, § 3-805	ALA. CODE tit. 7A, § 4-101 to 7A, § 4-504	Jan. 1, 1967
Alaska	ALASKA STAT. § 45.05.246 to § 45.05.402	ALASKA STAT. § 45.05.404 to § 45.05.474	Jan. 1, 1963
Arizona	ARIZ. REV. STAT. ANN. § 44-2501 to § 44-2599	ARIZ. REV. STAT. ANN. § 44-2601 to § 44-2639	Jan. 1, 1968
Arkansas	ARK. STAT. ANN. § 85-3-101 to § 85-3-805	ARK. STAT. ANN. § 85-4-101 to § 85-4-504	Jan. 1, 1962
California	CAL. COMM. CODE § 3101 to § 3805	CAL. COMM. CODE § 4101 to § 4504	Jan. 1, 1965
Colorado	COLO. REV. STAT. ANN. § 4-3-101 to § 4-3-805	COLO. REV. STAT. ANN. § 4-4-101 to § 4-4-504	July 1, 1966
Connecticut	CONN. GEN. STAT. ANN. § 42a-3-101 to § 42a-3-805	CONN. GEN. STAT. ANN. § 42a-4-101 to § 42a-4-504	Oct. 1, 1961
Delaware	DEL. CODE. ANN. tit. 5A, § 3-101 to 5A, § 3-805	DEL. CODE. ANN. tit. 5A, § 4-101 to 5A, § 4-504	July 1, 1967
District of Columbia	D.C. CODE ENCYCL. ANN. § 28:3-101 to § 28:3-805	D.C. CODE ENCYCL. ANN. § 28:4-101 to § 28:4-504	Jan. 1, 1965

JURISDICTION:	LOCAL CITATION:		ORIGINAL EFFECTIVE DATE OF UCC:
	Article 3:	Article 4:	
Florida	FLA. STAT. ANN. § 673:3-101 to § 673:3-805	FLA. STAT. ANN. § 674:4-101 to § 674:4-504	Jan. 1, 1967
Georgia	GA. CODE ANN. § 109A-3-101 to § 109A-3-805	GA. CODE ANN. § 109A-4-101 to § 109A-4-504	Jan. 1, 1964
Hawaii	HAWAII REV. STAT. § 490:3-101 to § 490:3-805	HAWAII REV. STAT. § 490:4-101 to § 490:4-504	Jan. 1, 1967
Idaho	IDAHO CODE § 28-3-101 to § 28-3-805	IDAHO CODE § 28-4-101 to § 28-4-504	Jan. 1, 1968
Illinois	ILL. ANN. STAT. Ch. 26, § 3-101 to 26, § 3-805 (Smith-Hurd)	ILL. ANN. STAT. Ch. 26, § 4-101 to 26, § 4-504 (Smith-Hurd)	July 2, 1962
Indiana	IND. CODE § 26-1-3-101 to § 26-1-3-805	IND. CODE § 26-1-4-101 to § 26-1-4-504	July 1, 1964
Iowa	IOWA CODE ANN. § 554.3-101 to § 554.3-805	IOWA CODE ANN. § 554.4-101 to § 554.4-504	July 1, 1964
Kansas	KAN. STAT. ANN. § 84-3-101 to § 84-3-805	KAN. STAT. ANN. § 84-4-101 to § 84-4-504	Jan. 1, 1966
Kentucky	KY. REV. STAT. ANN. § 355.3-101 to § 355.3-805	KY. REV. STAT. ANN. § 355.4-101 to § 355.4-504	July 1, 1960

JURISDICTION:	LOCAL CITATION:		ORIGINAL EFFECTIVE DATE OF UCC:
	Article 3:	Article 4:	
Louisiana	LA. REV. STAT. § 10:3-101 to § 10:3-805	LA. REV. STAT. § 10:4-101 to § 10:4-504	Jan. 1, 1975
Maine	ME. REV. STAT. ANN. tit. 11, § 3-101 to 11, § 3-805	ME. REV. STAT. ANN. tit. 11, § 4-101 to 11, § 4-504	Dec. 31, 1964
Maryland	MD. ANN. CODE art. 95B, § 3-101 to 95B, § 3-805	MD. ANN. CODE art. 95B, § 4-101 to 95B, § 4-504	Feb. 1, 1964
Massachusetts	MASS. GEN. LAWS. ch. 106, § 3-101 to 106, § 3-805	MASS. GEN. LAWS. ch. 106, § 4-101 to 106, § 4-504	Oct. 1, 1958
Michigan	MICH. COMP. LAWS ANN. § 440.31-101 to § 440.38-805	MICH. COMP. LAWS ANN. § 440.4-101 to § 440.4-504	Jan. 1, 1964
Minnesota	MINN. STAT. ANN. § 336.3-101 to § 336.3-805	MINN. STAT. ANN. § 336.4-101 to § 336.4-504	July 1, 1966
Mississippi	MISS. CODE ANN. § 75-3-101 to § 75-3-805	MISS. CODE ANN. § 75-4-101 to § 75-4-504	Mar. 31, 1968
Missouri	MO. ANN. STAT. § 400.3-101 to § 400.3-805	MO. ANN. STAT. § 400.4-101 to § 400.4-504	July 1, 1965
Montana	MONT. REV. CODES ANN. § 87A-3-101 to § 87A-3-805	MONT. REV. CODES ANN. § 87A-4-101 to § 87A-4-504	Jan. 2, 1965

JURISDICTION:	LOCAL CITATION:		ORIGINAL EFFECTIVE DATE OF UCC:
	Article 3:	Article 4:	
Nebraska	NEB. REV. STAT. U.C.C. § 3-101 to § 3-805	NEB. REV. STAT. U.C.C. § 4-101 to § 4-504	Sept. 2, 1965
Nevada	NEV. REV. STAT. § 104.3-101 to § 104.3-805	NEV. REV. STAT. § 104.4-101 to § 104.4-504	Mar. 1, 1967
New Hampshire	N.H. REV. STAT. ANN. § 382-A:3-101 to § 382-A:3-805	N.H. REV. STAT. ANN. § 382-A:4-101 to § 382-A:4-504	July 1, 1961
New Jersey	N.J. STAT. ANN. § 12A:3-101 to § 12A:3-805	N.J. STAT. ANN. § 12A:4-101 to § 12A:4-504	Jan. 1, 1963
New Mexico	N.M. STAT. ANN. § 50A-3-101 to § 50A-3-805	N.M. STAT. ANN. § 50A-4-101 to § 50A-4-504	Jan. 1, 1962
New York	N.Y. U.C.C. § 3-101 to § 3-805	N.Y. U.C.C. § 4-101 to § 4-504	Sept. 27, 1964
North Carolina	N.C. GEN. STAT. § 25-3-101 to § 25-3-805	N.C. GEN. STAT. § 25-4-101 to § 25-4-504	July 1, 1967
North Dakota	N.D. CENT. CODE § 41-03-01 to § 41-03-81	N.D. CENT. CODE § 41-04-01 to § 41-04-38	July 1, 1966
Ohio	OHIO REV. CODE ANN. § 1303.01 to § 1303.78 (Page)	OHIO REV. CODE ANN. § 1304.01 to § 1304.34 (Page)	July 1, 1962

JURISDICTION:	LOCAL CITATION:		ORIGINAL EFFECTIVE DATE OF UCC:
	Article 3:	Article 4:	
Oklahoma	OKLA. STAT. ANN. tit. 12A, § 3-101 to 12A, § 3-805	OKLA. STAT. ANN. tit. 12A, § 4-101 to 12A, § 4-504	Jan. 1, 1963
Oregon	ORE. REV. STAT. § 73.1010 to § 73.8050	ORE. REV. STAT. § 74.1010 to § 74.5040	Sept. 1, 1963
Pennsylvania	PA. STAT. ANN. tit. 12A, § 3-101 to 12A, § 3-805	PA. STAT. ANN. tit. 12A, § 4-101 to 12A, § 4-504	July 1, 1954
Puerto Rico	None; not enacted.	None; not enacted.	None
Rhode Island	R.I. GEN. LAWS ANN. § 6A-3-101 to § 6A-3-805	R.I. GEN. LAWS ANN. § 6A-4-101 to § 6A-4-504	Jan. 2, 1962
South Carolina	S.C. CODE ANN. § 10.3-101 to § 10.3-805	S.C. CODE ANN. § 10.4-101 to § 10.4-504	Jan. 1, 1968
South Dakota	S.D. COMPILED LAWS ANN. § 57-9-1 to § 57-17-9	S.D. COMPILED LAWS ANN. § 57-18-1 to § 57-22-5	July 1, 1967
Tennessee	TENN. CODE ANN. § 47-3-101 to § 47-3-805	TENN. CODE ANN. § 47-4-101 to § 47-4-504	July 1, 1964
Texas	TEX. BUS. & COM. CODE § 3-101 to § 3-805	TEX. BUS. & COM. CODE § 4-101 to § 4-504	July 1, 1966

JURISDICTION:	LOCAL CITATION:		ORIGINAL EFFECTIVE DATE OF UCC:
	Article 3:	Article 4:	
Utah	UTAH CODE ANN. § 70A-3-101 to § 70A-3-805	UTAH CODE ANN. § 70A-4-101 to § 70A-4-504	Jan. 1, 1966
Vermont	VT. STAT. ANN. tit. 9A, § 3-101 to 9A, § 3-805	VT. STAT. ANN. tit. 9A, § 4-101 to 9A, § 4-504	Jan. 1, 1967
Virginia	VA. CODE ANN. § 8.3-101 to § 8.3-805	VA. CODE ANN. § 8.4-101 to § 8.4-504	Jan. 1, 1966
Virgin Islands	V.I. CODE ANN. tit. 11A, § 3-101 to 11A, § 3-805	V.I. CODE ANN. tit. 11A, § 4-101 to 11A, § 4-504	July 1, 1965
Washington	WASH. REV. CODE ANN. § 62A.3-101 to § 62A.3-805	WASH. REV. CODE ANN. § 62A.4-101 to § 62A.4-504	July 1, 1967
West Virginia	W. VA. CODE ANN. § 46-3-101 to § 46-3-805	W. VA. CODE ANN. § 46-4-101 to § 46-4-504	Jan. 1, 1964
Wisconsin	WIS. STAT. ANN. § 403.101 to § 403.805	WIS. STAT. ANN. § 404.101 to § 404.504	July 1, 1965
Wyoming	WYO. STAT. ANN. § 34:3-101 to § 34:3-805	WYO. STAT. ANN. § 34:4-101 to § 34:4-504	Jan. 2, 1962

§ 14.1   General.

A large number of state and other jurisdiction statutes place large importance on the functions of notaries public in relation to commercial paper, sometimes called negotiable instruments.   These functions are to some extent affected by the provisions of Articles 3 and 4 of the Uniform Commerical Code, which was recommended to the various state and other legislatures for adoption by the American Law Institute and the National Conference of Commissioners on Uniform State Laws.   First adopted and made effective in Pennsylvania in 1954, Massachusetts in 1958, and Kentucky in 1960, the other states and jurisdictions followed by adopting it, as modified to a relatively small degree by the legislatures of the adopting states and other jurisdictions.   The Uniform Commercial Code is now at least in part, the law in 50 states, the District of Columbia and the Virgin Islands.   The most recent adoption of the Uniform Commercial Code by one of the states was the adoption of a part of the Code, including Articles 3 and 4 which are pertinent here, by Louisiana, effective January 1, 1975. Article 3 concerns commercial paper and Article 4 concerns bank deposits and collections.   For specific references to Articles 3 and 4, as they have been enacted in the various states and other jurisdictions, see the Table of Jurisdictions and Citations, above.

§ 14.2   Presentment of bills for acceptance.

Presentment is a demand for acceptance or payment made upon the maker, acceptor, drawee or other payor by or on behalf of the holder.[1]   The holder of a bill or his agent, generally a notary public, must call upon the drawee, exhibit the bill to him and ask whether the drawee will pay it at its maturity.

Presentment for acceptance is necessary to charge the drawer and indorsers of a draft where the draft so provides,

---

[1] Uniform Commercial Code (hereinafter UCC) § 3-504(1).

or is payable elsewehere than at the residence or place of business of the drawee, or its date of payment depends upon such presentment. The holder may at his option present for acceptance any other draft payable at a stated date.[2]

Presentment may be made: (1) by mail, in which event the time of presentment is determined by the time of receipt of the mail; (2) through a clearing house; or (3) at the place of acceptance specified in the instrument or if there be none at the place of business or residence of the party to accept. If neither the party to accept nor anyone authorized to act for him is present or accessible at such place, presentment is excused.[3]

Presentment may be made to: (1) any one of two or more makers, acceptors, drawees or other payors; or (2) any person who has authority to make or refuse the acceptance. A draft accepted or a note made payable at a bank in the United States must be presented at such bank.[4]

§ 14.3 —Time.

Unless a different time is expressed in the instrument the time for presentment is determined as follows: (1) where an instrument is payable at or a fixed period after a stated date any presentment for acceptance must be made on or before the date it is payable; (2) where an instrument is payable after sight it must either be presented for acceptance or negotiated within a reasonable time after date or issue whichever is later; (3) with respect to the liability of any secondary party presentment for acceptance of any other instrument is due within a reasonable time after such party becomes liable thereon.[5]

A reasonable time for presentment is determined by the nature of the instrument, any usage of banking or trade and the facts of the particular case. Where any present-

---

[2] UCC § 3-501(1)(a).

[3] UCC § 3-504(2).

[4] UCC § 3-504 (3, 4).

[5] UCC § 3-503 (1).

ment is due on a day which is not a full business day for either the person making presentment or the party to accept, presentment is due on the next following day which is a full business day for both parties. Presentment to be sufficient must be made at a reasonable hour, and if at a bank during its banking day.[6]

§ 14.4   —Excused.

Delay in presentment is excused when the party is without notice that it is due or when the delay is caused by circumstances beyond his control and he exercises reasonable diligence after the cause of delay ceases to operate.[7]

Presentment is entirely excused when either: (1) the party to be charged has waived it expressly or by implication either before or after it is due; (2) such party has himself dishonored the instrument or has countermanded payment or otherwise has no reason to expect or right to require that the instrument be accepted; (3) by reasonable diligence the presentment cannot be made; (4) the maker, acceptor or drawee of any instrument except a documentary draft is dead or in insolvency proceedings instituted after the issue of the instrument; or (5) acceptance is refused but not for want of proper presentment.[8]

A waiver of protest is also a waiver of presentment. Where a waiver of presentment is embodied in the instrument itself it is binding upon all parties; but where it is written above the signature of an indorser it binds him only.[9]

§ 14.5   Dishonor by nonacceptance.

An instrument is dishonored when: (1) a necessary or optional presentment is made and due acceptance is refused or cannot be obtained within the prescribed time

---

6 UCC § 3-503 (2-4).   See *Legal Holidays* page 781.

7 UCC § 3-511 (1).

8 UCC § 3-511 (2, 3).

9 UCC § 3-511 (5, 6).

or in case of bank collections the instrument is seasonably returned by the midnight deadline; or (2) presentment is excused and the instrument is not duly accepted.[10]

Return of an instrument for lack of proper indorsement is not dishonor. A term in a draft or an indorsement thereof allowing a stated time for re-presentment in the event of any dishonor of the draft by nonacceptance if a time draft or by nonpayment if a sight draft gives the holder as against any secondary party bound by the term an option to waive the dishonor without affecting the liability of the secondary party. He may present again up to the end of the stated time.[11]

Where a draft has been dishonored by nonacceptance a later presentment for payment and any notice of dishonor and protest for nonpayment are excused unless in the meantime the instrument has been accepted.[12]

§ 14.6   Presentment for payment.

Unless excused (Section 3-511; see § 14.4) presentment for payment is necessary to charge any indorser. In the case of any drawer, the acceptor of a draft payable at a bank or the maker of a note payable at a bank, presentment for payment is necessary, but failure to make presentment discharges the drawer, acceptor or maker only as stated in Section 3-502(1)(b).[13]

Where the maker or acceptor of an instrument payable otherwise than on demand is able and ready to pay at every

---

[10] UCC § 3-507 (1).

[11] UCC § 3-507 (3, 4).

[12] UCC § 3-511 (4).

[13] UCC § 3-501 (1)(b, c). UCC § 3-502(1)(b) provides that where without excuse any necessary presentment or notice of dishonor is delayed beyond the time when it is due, any drawer or the acceptor of a draft payable at a bank or the maker of a note payable at a bank who because the drawee or payor bank becomes insolvent during the delay is deprived of funds maintained with the drawee or payor bank to cover the instrument may discharge his liability by written assignment to the holder of his rights against the drawee or payor bank in respect of such funds, but such drawer, acceptor or maker is not otherwise discharged.

place of payment specified in the instrument when it is due, it is equivalent to tender. Any party making tender of full payment to a holder when or after it is due is discharged to the extent of all subsequent liability for interest, costs and attorney's fees.[14]

§ 14.7 —Time.

Unless a different time is expressed in the instrument the time for presentment is determined as follows: (1) where an instrument shows the date on which it is payable presentment for payment is due on that date; (2) where an instrument is accelerated presentment for payment is due within a reasonable time after the acceleration; (3) with respect to the liability of any secondary party presentment for payment of any other instrument is due within a reasonable time after such party becomes liable thereon.[15]

A reasonable time for presentment is determined by the nature of the instrument, any usage of banking or trade and the facts of the particular case. In the case of an uncertified check which is drawn and payable within the United States and which is not a draft drawn by a bank the following are presumed to be reasonable periods within which to present for payment or to initiate bank collection: (1) with respect to the liability of the drawer, thirty days after date or issue whichever is later; and (2) with respect to the liability of an indorser, seven days after his indorsement.[16]

Where any presentment is due on a day which is not a full business day for either the person making presentment or the party to pay or accept, presentment is due on the next following day which is a full business day for both parties. Presentment to be sufficient must be made at a reasonable hour, and if at a bank during its banking day.[17]

---

[14] UCC § 3-604.

[15] UCC § 3-503(1).

[16] UCC § 3-503(2).

[17] UCC § 3-503(3, 4). See *Legal Holidays,* page 781.

§ 14.8   —Sufficiency.

Presentment is a demand for payment made upon the maker, acceptor, drawee or other payor by or on behalf of the holder. Presentment may be made by mail, in which event the time of presentment is determined by the time of receipt of the mail, or through a clearing house.[18] Presentment to be sufficient must be made at a reasonable hour, and if at a bank during its banking day.[19]

§ 14.9   —Place.

Presentment for payment may be made at the place of payment specified in the instrument or if there be none at the place of business or residence of the party to pay. If neither the party to pay nor anyone authorized to act for him is present or accessible at such place presentment is excused.[20]

§ 14.10   To whom made.

Presentment for payment may be made to any one of two or more makers, acceptors, drawees or other payors, or to any person who has authority to make or refuse the payment.[21]

The party to whom presentment is made may without dishonor require any or all of the following: (1) exhibition of the instrument; (2) reasonable identification of the person making presentment and evidence of his authority to make it if made for another; (3) that the instrument be produced for acceptance or payment at a place specified in it, or if there be none at any place reasonable in the circumstances; and (4) a signed receipt on the instrument for any partial or full payment and its surrender upon full payment. Failure to comply with any such requirement invalidates the

---

[18] UCC § 3-504(1, 2).

[19] UCC § 3-503(4).

[20] UCC § 3-504(2).

[21] UCC § 3-504(3).

presentment but the person presenting has a reasonable time in which to comply and the time for payment runs from the time of compliance.[22]

§ 14.11 —Delay excused.

Delay in presentment is excused when the party is without notice that it is due or when the delay is caused by circumstances beyond his control and he exercises reasonable diligence after the cause of the delay ceases to operate.[23]

§ 14.12 —Dispensed with.

Presentment is entirely excused when: (1) the party to be charged has waived it expressly or by implication either before or after it is due; (2) such party has himself dishonored the instrument or has countermanded payment or otherwise has no reason to expect or right to require that the instrument be accepted or paid; (3) by reasonable diligence the presentment cannot be made; (4) the maker, acceptor or drawee of any instrument except a documentary draft is dead or in insolvency proceedings instituted after the issue of the instrument; or (5) payment is refused but not for want of proper presentment.[24]

Where a draft has been dishonored by nonacceptance a later presentment for payment is excused unless in the meantime the instrument has been accepted. A waiver of protest is also a waiver of presentment. Where a waiver of presentment is embodied in the instrument itself it is binding upon all parties; but where it is written above the signature of an indorser it binds him only.[25]

§ 14.13 Dishonor by nonpayment.

An instrument is dishonored when: (1) a necessary or optional presentment is duly made and due payment is

---

22 UCC § 3-505.

23 UCC § 3-511(1).

24 UCC § 3-511(2, 3).

25 UCC § 3-511(4-6).

refused or cannot be obtained within the prescribed time or in case of bank collections the instrument is seasonably returned by the midnight deadline; or (2) presentment is excused and the instrument is not duly paid.[26]

§ 14.14 Protest.

A protest is a declaration in writing made by, among others, a notary public, on behalf of the holder of a bill or note, that acceptance or payment has been refused. This written declaration itself is also called a certificate of dishonor or the certificate of protest, which is only the evidence of the fact of protest. Although in a technical sense the term "protest" means only the formal declaration drawn up and signed by the notary, yet in commercial usage it includes all the steps necessary to charge the indorser.[27]

Unless excused (Section 3-511; see § 14.19) protest of any dishonor is necessary to charge the drawer and indorsers of any draft which on its face appears to be drawn or payable outside of the states, territories, dependencies and possessions of the United States, the District of Columbia, and the Commonwealth of Puerto Rico. The holder may at his option make protest of any dishonor of any other instrument and in the case of a foreign draft may on insolvency of the acceptor before maturity make protest for better security. Protest is not necessary to charge an indorser who has indorsed an instrument after maturity.[28]

§ 14.15 —Time for making.

With one exception any necessary protest is due by the time that notice of dishonor is due.[29] Any necessary notice of dishonor must be given by a bank before its midnight deadline and by any other person before midnight of the

---

[26] UCC § 3-507(1).

[27] See also the definition in the *Glossary*, page 862.

[28] UCC § 3-501(3, 4).

[29] UCC § 3-509(4, 5).

third business day after dishonor or receipt of notice of dishonor.[30] The exception is that if, before protest is due, an instrument has been noted for protest by the officer to make protest, the protest may be made at any time thereafter as of the date of the noting.[31]

§ 14.16 —Place.

Under the Code protest need not be made at the place where dishonor occurs.[32]

§ 14.17 —Contents of certificate.

The protest must identify the instrument and certify either that due presentment has been made or the reason why it is excused and that the instrument has been dishonored by nonacceptance or nonpayment. The protest may also certify that notice of dishonor has been given to all parties or to specified parties.[33]

A complete certificate of protest should ordinarily include the following items: (1) the notary's venire or locality within which he is authorized to act; (2) his name and title; (3) for whom he acted, or the holder's name; (4) a copy of the instrument presented; (5) the fact and manner of presentment and demand; (6) the time; (7) the place; (8) to whom presented, and of whom demand was made; (9) the fact of dishonor; (10) the fact of protest; (11) the reason assigned for refusal to honor; (12) who was notified; (13) the manner of notification; and (14) the notary's official seal and signature.[34]

---

[30] UCC § 3-508(2).

[31] UCC § 3-509(4, 5).

[32] UCC § 3-509, Official Comment 3.

[33] UCC § 3-509(2, 3).

[34] UCC § 3-509(2) says that the protest must identify the instrument and certify either that due presentment has been made or the reason why it is excused and that the instrument has been dishonored by nonacceptance or nonpayment. UCC § 3-509(3) says that the protest may also certify that notice of dishonor has been given to all parties or to specified parties.

§ 14.18 —Form of protest.

[This certificate follows a copy of the bill or note protested]

United States of America,

State of ———,

——— County, ss.

Be it known by this Instrument of Protest, that at the close of banking hours on ——— the ——— day of ———, 19—, I, G H, a notary public within and for said county of ———, did, at the request of ———, holder of the original ———, dated ———, a copy of which appears above, present the same to ——— at ——— in the city of ———, ———, and demanded payment (*or*, acceptance) thereof, which was refused. Said dishonor of said ——— occurred for the following assigned reason: ———.

Whereupon I protested the same for nonpayment (*or*, nonacceptance) and notified the following named drawer and indorsers thereof of said presentment and protest, by a separate notice to each, enclosed in (the same, or separate) envelope— and addressed as follows: ———; and deposited the same in the post office of ——— in said county, the same day, postage paid; and the following named drawer and indorsers thereof, by delivering to each of them such notices personally on the same or the next day ———.

Whereupon, I, the said notary, upon the authority aforesaid, have protested and do hereby solemnly protest as well against the drawer and indorsers of the said ——— as against all others whom it doth or may concern, for exchange, re-exchange, and all costs, charges, damages and interest, suffered or to be suffered, for the want of payment (*or*, acceptance) thereof, and I certify that I have no interest in the above-protested instrument.

Witness my hand and notarial seal this ——— day of ———, 19—.

Protest fees, $———.

(SEAL)   G H, Notary Public.

My commission expires ———.

§ 14.19   —Dispensed with.

Protest is entirely excused when either: (1) the party to be charged has waived it expressly or by implication either before or after it is due; (2) such party has himself dishonored the instrument or has countermanded payment or otherwise has no reason to expect or right to require that the instrument be accepted or paid; (3) By reasonable diligence the protest cannot be made; or (4) a draft has been dishonored by nonacceptance, unless the instrument has been accepted in the meantime.   Where a waiver of protest is embodied where it is written above the signature of an indorser it binds him only.[35]

§ 14.20   —Record.

Statutes in many states and other jurisdictions require, and well established custom in other states and jurisdictions permits, a notary to make a minute on the dishonored instrument, or in this register, of the presentment, refusal to accept or pay, the month, day and year, and his charges of protest.[36]   This is called noting, and must be done, if not at the very time, at least not later than the day of the dishonor.   The protest may be written out in full at any convenient time afterward.[37]

Because the notary may be called upon to testify in relation to his acts as notary by deposition or orally, it is important that he should keep a register or record containing detailed information with regard to the protesting of commercial paper.

§ 14.21   —National bank notes.

Whenever any national banking association fails to redeem in the lawful money of the United States any of its

---

35 UCC § 3-511(2, 6). See also § 14.14, above, wherein it is pointed out that there is no requirement of protest except dishonor of a draft which on its face appears to be either drawn or payable outside of the states, territories, dependencies, and possessions of the United States, the District of Columbia and the Commonwealth of Puerto Rico.

36 See *Records: State and Other Statutes*, page 227.

37 See *Authority and Duties: State and Other Statutes*, page 127.

circulating notes, upon demand of payment duly made during the usual hours of business, at the office of such association, or at its designated place of redemption, the holder may cause the same to be protested, in one package, by a notary public, unless the president or cashier of the association whose notes are presented for payment, or the president or cashier of the association at the place at which they are redeemable, offers to waive demand and notice of the protest, and, in pursuance of such offer, makes, signs, and delivers to the party making such demand an admission in writing, stating the time of the demand, the amount demanded, and the fact of the nonpayment thereof. The notary public, on making such protest, or upon receiving such admission, shall forthwith forward such admission or notice of protest to the Comptroller of the Currency, retaining a copy thereof. If, however, satisfactory proof is produced to the notary public that the payment of the notes demanded is restrained by order of any court of competent jurisdiction, he shall not protest the same. When the holder of any notes causes more than one note or package to be protested on the same day, he shall not receive pay for more than one protest.[38]

§ 14.22   Acceptance supra protest.

Acceptance is the drawee's signed engagement to honor the draft as presented. It must be written on the draft, and may consist of his signature alone. It becomes operative when completed by delivery or notification. A draft may be accepted although it has not been signed by the drawer or is otherwise incomplete or is overdue or has been dishonored.[39]

§ 14.23   Payment for honor.

Payment or satisfaction may be made with the consent of the holder by any person including a stranger to the

---

[38] 12 USC § 131.

[39] UCC § 3-410(1, 2)

instrument. Surrender of the instrument to such a person gives him the rights of a transferee.[40]

§ 14.24 Notice of dishonor.

Unless excused[41] notice of any dishonor is necessary to charge any indorser. In the case of any drawer, the acceptor of a draft payable at a bank or the maker of a note payable at a bank, notice of any dishonor is necessary, but failure to give such notice discharges such drawer, acceptor or maker only as stated in Section 3-502(1)(b);[42] however, notice of dishonor is not necessary to charge an indorser who has indorsed an instrument after maturity.[43] Notice operates for the benefit of all parties who have rights on the instrument against the party notified.[44]

§ 14.25 —Given by agent.

An agent or bank in whose hands the instrument is dishonored may give notice to his principal or customer or to another agent or bank from which the instrument was received.[45]

§ 14.26 —Essentials.

Notice may be given in any reasonable manner. It may be oral or written and in any terms which identify the instrument and state that it has been dishonored. A mis-

---

[40] UCC § 3-603(2).

[41] UCC § 3-511 provides that delay in notice of dishonor is excused when the party is without notice that it is due or when the delay is caused by circumstances beyond his control and he exercises reasonable diligence after the cause of the delay ceased to operate. When a draft has been dishonored by nonacceptance a later presentment for payment and any notice of dishonor is excused unless in the meantime the instrument has been accepted. A waiver of protest is also a waiver of notice of dishonor even though protest is not required.

[42] Concerning UCC § 3-502(1)(b), see § 7.7, n. 13.

[43] UCC § 3-501(2, 4).

[44] UCC § 3-508(8).

[45] UCC § 3-508(1).

description which does not mislead the party notified does not vitiate the notice. Sending the instrument bearing a stamp, ticket or writing stating that acceptance or payment has been refused or sending a notice of debit with respect to the instrument is sufficient.[46]

§ 14.27 —Form of notice of dishonor.

—— (Place)

—— (Date)

Take notice, that a bill of exchange (or, promissory note) for —— Dollars dated ——, drawn by ——, in favor of ——, on —— Bank (accepted by ——), indorsed by ——, payable ——, was this day presented for acceptance (or, payment), which was refused, and therefore was this day protested by the undersigned notary public for non-acceptance (or, nonpayment).

The holder therefore looks to you for payment thereof, together with interest, damages, costs, you being indorser (or, drawer) thereof.

To: ——

G H, Notary Public

My commission expires ——.

§ 14.28 —To whom given.

Notice of dishonor may be given to any person who may be liable on the instrument by or on behalf of the holder or any party who has himself received notice, or any other party who can be compelled to pay the instrument. In addition an agent or bank in whose hands the instrument is dishonored may given notice to his principal or customer or to another agent or bank from which the instrument was received.[47]

Notice to one partner is notice to each although the firm

---

46 UCC § 3-508(3).

47 UCC § 3-508(1).

has been dissolved. When any party is in insolvency proceedings instituted after the issue of the instrument, notice may be given either to the party or to the representative of his estate.[48]

§ 14.29   —Time of giving.

Any necessary notice must be given by a bank before its midnight deadline and by any other person before midnight of the third business day after dishonor or receipt of notice of dishonor. Written notice is given when sent although it is not received.[49]

§ 14.30   —Place.

When any party is dead or incompetent notice may be sent to his last known address or given to his personal representative.[50]

§ 14.31   —Waiver.

Where a waiver of notice of dishonor is embodied in the instrument itself it is binding upon all parties; but where it is written above the signature of an indorser it binds him only. A waiver of protest is also a waiver of presentment and of notice of dishonor even though protest is not required.[51]

§ 14.32   —Dispensed with.

Notice of dishonor is entirely excused when: (1) the party to be charged has waived it expressly or by implication either before or after it is due; (2) by reasonable diligence the notice cannot be given. Where a draft has been dishonored by nonacceptance a later presentment for pay-

---

48 UCC § 3-508(5, 6).

49 UCC § 3-508(2, 4).

50 UCC § 3-508(7).

51 UCC § 3-511(5, 6).

ment and any notice of dishonor are excused unless in the meantime the instrument has been accepted.[52]

§ 14.33 —Delay excused.

Delay in notice of dishonor is excused when the party is without notice that it is due or when the delay is caused by circumstances beyond his control and he exercises reasonable diligence after the cause of the delay ceases to operate.[53]

§ 14.34 Promissory note.

A promissory note is an unconditional promise in writing made by one person to another, signed by the maker engaging to pay on demand, or at a definite time, a sum certain in money to the order of such other or to bearer. The person who signs such unconditional written promise is called the maker and the person to whom the order is payable, the payee. If the payee transfers it to a third person by indorsement, the payee is the indorser and the third person, the indorsee. The following is an ordinary form of a promissory note:

FORM

——— (City) ——— (State)
——— (Date)

$———

On ——— (date) (or, ——— days, or, months, or, years, after date; or, on demand), for value received, I promise to pay to the order of CD (or, bearer) the sum of ——— Dollars, with interest thereon after date, at the rate of ———% per year, payable quarterly (or, semi-annually, or, annually) at the ——— Bank, of ———.

AB

---

[52] UCC § 3-511(2, 4).
[53] UCC § 3-511(1).

§ 14.35 Bill of exchange.

⅄ bill of exchange, or draft, is an unconditional, written and signed, order to pay a sum certain in money to someone, drawn by a person on a third party. The person who signs such order is called the drawer; the person who is directed to pay, the drawee; and after accepting the order, the drawee is also the acceptor. The following is an ordinary form of a bill of exchange:

FORM

—— (City) —— (State)

—— (Date)

—— days after date (or on demand; or, at sight) pay to the order of EF, —— Dollars, for value received, and charge to account of

AB

To: CD, —— (City) —— (State)

STATUTORY SUPPLEMENT

Selected Portions of
Uniform Commercial Code,

Article 3,

Commercial Paper°

§ 1-201. Definitions. (20) "Holder" means a person who is in possession of a document of title or an instrument or an investment security drawn, issued or indorsed to him or to his order or to bearer or in blank.

§ 3-104. Form of negotiable instruments; "draft;" "check;" "certificate of deposit;" "note." (1) Any writing to be a negotiable instrument within this Article must

(a) be signed by the maker or drawer; and

(b) contain an unconditional promise or order to pay a sum certain in money and no other promise, order, obligation

---

° Only the pertinent sections of the Article are included.

or power given by the maker or drawer except as authorized by this Article; and

(c)   be payable on demand or at a definite time; and

(d)   be payable to order or to bearer.

(2)   A writing which complies with the requirements of this section is

(a)   a "draft" ("bill of exchange") if it is an order;

(b)   a "check" if it is a draft drawn on a bank and payable on demand;

(c)   a "certificate of deposit" if it is an acknowledgment by a bank of receipt of money with an engagement to repay it;

(d)   a "note" if it is a promise other than a certificate of deposit.

(3)   As used in other Articles of this Act, and as the context may require, the terms "draft," "check," "certificate of deposit" and "note" may refer to instruments which are not negotiable within this Article as well as to instruments which are so negotiable.

§ 3-115.   **Incomplete Instruments.**   (1)   When a paper whose contents at the time of signing show that it is intended to become an instrument is signed while still incomplete in any necessary respect it cannot be enforced until completed, but when it is completed in accordance with authority given it is effective as completed.

(2)   If the completion is unauthorized the rules as to material alteration apply (Section 3-407), even though the paper was not delivered by the maker or drawer; but the burden of establishing that any completion is unauthorized is on the party so asserting.

Transfer and Negotiation

§ 3-201.   **Transfer: Right to Indorsement.**   (1)   Transfer of an instrument vests in the transferee such rights as the transferor has therein, except that a transferee who has himself been a party to any fraud or illegality affecting the instrument or who as a prior holder had notice of a defense or claim against it cannot improve his position by taking from a later holder in due course.

(2)   A transfer of a security interest in an instrument vests the foregoing rights in the transferee to the extent of the interest transferred.

(3)   Unless otherwise agreed any transfer for value of an instrument not then payable to bearer gives the transferee the specifically enforceable right to have the unqualified indorsement of the transferor. Negotiation takes effect only when the indorsement is made and until that time there is no presumption that the transferee is the owner.

§ 3-202. **Negotiation.** (1) Negotiation is the transfer of an instrument in such form that the transferee becomes a holder. If the instrument is payable to order it is negotiated by delivery with any necessary indorsement; if payable to bearer it is negotiated by delivery.

(2) An indorsement must be written by or on behalf of the holder and on the instrument or on a paper so firmly affixed thereto as to become a part thereof.

(3) An indorsement is effective for negotiation only when it conveys the entire instrument or any unpaid residue. If it purports to be of less it operates only as a partial assignment.

(4) Words of assignment, condition, waiver, guaranty, limitation or disclaimer of liability and the like accompanying an indorsement do not affect its character as an indorsement.

§ 3-204. **Special indorsement; blank indorsement.** (1) A special indorsement specifies the person to whom or to whose order it makes the instrument payable. Any instrument specially indorsed becomes payable to the order of the special indorsee and may be further negotiated only by his indorsement.

(2) An indorsement in blank specifies no particular indorsee and may consist of a mere signature. An instrument payable to order and indorsed in blank becomes payable to bearer and may be negotiated by delivery alone until specially indorsed.

(3) The holder may convert a blank indorsement into a special indorsement by writing over the signature of the indorser in blank any contract consistent with the character of the indorsement.

§ 3-205. **Restrictive indorsements.** An indorsement is restrictive which either

(a) is conditional; or

(b) purports to prohibit further transfer of the instrument; or

(c) includes the words "for collection," "for deposit," "pay any bank," or like terms signifying a purpose of deposit or collection; or

(d) otherwise states that it is for the benefit or use of the indorser or of another person.

§ 3-206. **Effect of restrictive indorsement.** (1) No restrictive indorsement prevents further transfer or negotiation of the instrument.

(2) An intermediary bank, or a payor bank which is not the depositary bank, is neither given notice nor otherwise affected by a restrictive indorsement of any person except the bank's immediate transferor or the person presenting for payment.

(3) Except for an intermediary bank, any transferee under an indorsement which is conditional or includes the words "for collection," "for deposit," "pay any bank," or like terms (sub-paragraphs

(a) and (c) of Section 3-205) must pay or apply any value given by him for or on the security of the instrument consistently with the indorsement and to the extent that he does so he becomes a holder for value. In addition such transferee is a holder in due course if he otherwise complies with the requirements of Section 3-302 on what constitutes a holder in due course.

(4) The first taker under an indorsement for the benefit of the indorser or another person (subparagraph (d) of Section 3-205) must pay or apply any value given by him for or on the security of the instrument consistently with the indorsement and to the extent that he does so he becomes a holder for value. In addition such taker is a holder in due course if he otherwise complies with the requirements of Section 3-302 on what constitutes a holder in due course. A later holder for value is neither given notice nor otherwise affected by such restrictive indorsement unless he has knowledge that a fiduciary or other person has negotiated the instrument in any transaction for his own benefit or otherwise in breach of duty (subsection (2) of Section 3-304).

Rights of a Holder

§ 3-302. **Holder in due course.** (1) A holder in due course is a holder who takes the instrument

    (a)   for value; and

    (b)   in good faith; and

    (c)   without notice that it is overdue or has been dishonored or of any defense against or claim to it on the part of any person.

(2) A payee may be a holder in due course.

(3) A holder does not become a holder in due course of an instrument:

    (a)   by purchase of it at judicial sale or by taking it under legal process; or

    (b)   by acquiring it in taking over an estate; or

    (c)   by purchasing it as part of a bulk transaction not in regular course of business of the transferor.

(4) A purchaser of a limited interest can be a holder in due course only to the extent of the interest purchased.

Liability of Parties

§ 3-402. **Signature in ambiguous capacity.** Unless the instrument clearly indicates that a signature is made in some other capacity it is an indorsement.

§ 3-409. **Draft not an assignment.** (1) A check or other draft does not of itself operate as an assignment of any funds in the hands of the drawee available for its payment, and the drawee is not liable on the instrument until he accepts it.

(2) Nothing in this section shall affect any liability in contract, tort or otherwise arising from any letter of credit or other obligation or representation which is not an acceptance.

§ 3-410. Definition and operation of acceptance. (1) Acceptance is the drawee's signed engagement to honor the draft as presented. It must be written on the draft, and may consist of his signature alone. It becomes operative when completed by delivery or notification.

(2) A draft may be accepted although it has not been signed by the drawer or is otherwise incomplete or is overdue or has been dishonored.

(3) Where the draft is payable at a fixed period after sight and the acceptor fails to date his acceptance the holder may complete it by supplying a date in good faith.

§ 3-411. Certification of a check. (1) Certification of a check is acceptance. Where a holder procures certification the drawer and all prior indorsers are discharged.

(2) Unless otherwise agreed a bank has no obligation to certify a check.

(3) A bank may certify a check before returning it for lack of proper indorsement. If it does so the drawer is discharged.

§ 3-412. Acceptance varying draft. (1) Where the drawee's proffered acceptance in any manner varies the draft as presented the holder may refuse the acceptance and treat the draft as dishonored in which case the drawee is entitled to have his acceptance cancelled.

(2) The terms of the draft are not varied by an acceptance to pay at any particular bank or place in the United States, unless the acceptance states that the draft is to be paid only at such bank or place.

(3) Where the holder assents to an acceptance varying the terms of the draft each drawer and indorser who does not affirmatively assent is discharged.

§ 3-413. Contract of maker, drawer and acceptor. (1) The maker or acceptor engages that he will pay the instrument according to its tenor at the time of his engagement or as completed pursuant to Section 3-115 on incomplete instruments.

(2) The drawer engages that upon dishonor of the draft and any necessary notice of dishonor or protest he will pay the amount of the draft to the holder or to any indorser who takes it up. The drawer may disclaim this liability by drawing without recourse.

(3) By making, drawing or accepting the party admits as against all subsequent parties including the drawee the existence of the payee and his then capacity to indorse.

§ 3-415. **Contract of accommodation party.** (1) An accommodation party is one who signs the instrument in any capacity for the purpose of lending his name to another party to it.

(2) When the instrument has been taken for value before it is due the accommodation party is liable in the capacity in which he has signed even though the taker knows of the accommodation.

(3) As against a holder in due course and without notice of the accommodation oral proof of the accommodation is not admissible to give the accommodation party the benefit of discharges dependent on his character as such. In other cases the accommodation character may be shown by oral proof.

(4) An indorsement which shows that it is not in the chain of title is notice of its accommodation character.

(5) An accommodation party is not liable to the party accommodated, and if he pays the instrument has a right of recourse on the instrument against such party.

Presentment, Notice of Dishonor and Protest

§ 3-501. **When presentment, notice of dishonor, and protest necessary or permissible.** (1) Unless excused (Section 3-511) presentment is necessary to charge secondary parties as follows:

   (a) presentment for acceptance is necessary to charge the drawer and indorsers of a draft where the draft so provides, or is payable elsewhere than at the residence or place of business of the drawee, or its date of payment depends upon such presentment. The holder may at his option present for acceptance any other draft payable at a stated date;

   (b) presentment for payment is necessary to charge any indorser;

   (c) in the case of any drawer, the acceptor of a draft payable at a bank or the maker of a note payable at a bank, presentment for payment is necessary, but failure to make presentment discharges such drawer, acceptor or maker only as stated in Section 3-502(1)(b).

(2) Unless excused (Section 3-511)

   (a) notice of any dishonor is necessary to charge any indorser;

   (b) in the case of any drawer, the acceptor of a draft payable at a bank or the maker of a note payable at a bank, notice of any dishonor is necessary, but failure to give such notice discharges such drawer, acceptor or maker only as stated in Section 3-502 (1) (b).

(3) Unless excused (Section 3-511) protest of any dishonor is necessary to charge the drawer and indorsers of any draft which on its face appears to be drawn or payable outside of the states and territories of the United States and the District of Columbia. The holder may at his option make protest of any dishonor of any other instrument and in the case of a foreign draft may on insolvency of the acceptor before maturity make protest for better security.

(4) Notwithstanding any provision of this section, neither presentment nor notice of dishonor nor protest is necessary to charge an indorser who has indorsed an instrument after maturity.

§ 3-502. **Unexcused delay; discharge.** (1) Where without excuse any necessary presentment or notice of dishonor is delayed beyond the time when it is due

(a) any indorser is discharged; and

(b) any drawer or the acceptor of a draft payable at a bank or the maker of a note payable at a bank who because the drawee or payor bank becomes insolvent during the delay is deprived of funds maintained with the drawee or payor bank to cover the instrument may discharge his liability by written assignment to the holder of his rights against the drawee or payor bank in respect of such funds, but such drawer, acceptor or maker is not otherwise discharged.

(2) Where without excuse a necessary protest is delayed beyond the time when it is due any drawer or indorser is discharged.

§ 3-503. **Time of presentment.** (1) Unless a different time is expressed in the instrument the time for any presentment is determined as follows:

(a) where an instrument is payable at or a fixed period after a stated date any presentment for acceptance must be made on or before the date it is payable;

(b) where an instrument is payable after sight it must either be presented for acceptance or negotiated within a reasonable time after date or issue whichever is later;

(c) where an instrument shows the date on which it is payable presentment for payment is due on that date;

(d) where an instrument is accelerated presentment for payment is due within a reasonable time after the acceleration;

(e) with respect to the liability of any secondary party presentment for acceptance or payment of any other instrument is due within a reasonable time after such party becomes liable thereon.

(2) A reasonable time for presentment is determined by the nature of the instrument, any usage of banking or trade and the facts of the particular case. In the case of an uncertified check which is drawn and payable within the United States and which is

not a draft drawn by a bank the following are presumed to be reasonable periods within which to present for payment or to initiate bank collection:

<blockquote>
(a)   with respect to the liability of the drawer, thirty days after date or issue whichever is later; and

(b)   with respect to the liability of an indorser, seven days after his indorsement.
</blockquote>

(3)   Where any presentment is due on a day which is not a full business day for either the person making presentment or the party to pay or accept, presentment is due on the next following day which is a full business day for both parties.

(4)   Presentment to be sufficient must be made at a reasonable hour, and if at a bank during its banking day.

§ 3-504.   **How presentment made.**   (1)   Presentment is a demand for acceptance or payment made upon the maker, acceptor, drawee or other payor by or on behalf of the holder.

(2)   Presentment may be made

<blockquote>
(a)   by mail, in which even the time of presentment is determined by the time of receipt of the mail; or

(b)   through a clearing house; or

(c)   at the place of acceptance or payment specified in the instrument or if there be none at the place of business or residence of the party to accept or pay. If neither the party to accept or pay nor anyone authorized to act for him is present or accessible at such place presentment is excused.
</blockquote>

(3)   It may be made

<blockquote>
(a)   to any one of two or more makers, acceptors, drawees or other payors; or

(b)   to any person who has authority to make or refuse the acceptance or payment.
</blockquote>

(4)   A draft accepted or a note made payable at a bank in the United States must be presented at such bank.

(5)   In the cases described in Section 4-210 presentment may be made in the manner and with the result stated in that section.

§ 3-505.   **Rights of party to whom presentment is made.**   (1)   The party to whom presentment is made may without dishonor require

<blockquote>
(a)   exhibition of the instrument; and

(b)   reasonable identification of the person making presentment and evidence of his authority to make it if made for another; and

(c)   that the instrument be produced for acceptance or pay-
</blockquote>

ment at a place specified in it, or if there be none at any place reasonable in the circumstances; and

(d) a signed receipt on the instrument for any partial or full payment and its surrender upon full payment.

(2) Failure to comply with any such requirement invalidates the presentment but the person presenting has a reasonable time in which to comply and the time for acceptance or payment runs from the time of compliance.

§ 3-507. **Dishonor; holder's right of recourse; term allowing re-presentment.** (1) An instrument is dishonored when

(a) a necessary or optional presentment is duly made and due acceptance or payment is refused or cannot be obtained within the prescribed time or in a case of bank collections the instrument is seasonably returned by the midnight deadline (Sec. 4-301); or

(b) presentment is excused and the instrument is not duly accepted or paid.

(2) Subject to any necessary notice of dishonor and protest, the holder has upon dishonor an immediate right of recourse against the drawers and indorsers.

(3) Return of an instrument for lack of proper indorsement is not dishonor.

(4) A term in a draft or an indorsement thereof allowing a stated time for re-presentment in the event of any dishonor of the draft by nonacceptance if a time draft or by nonpayment if a sight draft gives the holder as against any secondary party bound by the term an option to waive the dishonor without affecting the liability of the secondary party and he may present against up to the end of the stated time.

§ 3-508. **Notice of dishonor.** (1) Notice of dishonor may be given to any person who may be liable on the instrument by or on behalf of the holder or any party who has himself received notice, or any other party who can be compelled to pay the instrument. In addition an agent or bank in whose hands the instrument is dishonored may give notice to his principal or customer or to another agent or bank from which the instrument was received.

(2) Any necessary notice must be given by a bank before its midnight deadline and by any other person before midnight of the third business day after dishonor or receipt of notice of dishonor.

(3) Notice may be given in any reasonable manner. It may be oral or written and in any terms which identify the instrument and state that it has been dishonored. A misdescription which does not mislead the party notified does not vitiate the notice. Sending the instrument bearing a stamp, ticket or writing stating that acceptance

or payment has been refused or sending a notice of debit with respect to the instrument is sufficient.

(4) Written notice is given when sent although it is not received.

(5) Notice to one partner is notice to each although the firm has been dissolved.

(6) When any party is in insolvency proceedings instituted after the issue of the instrument notice may be given either to the party or to the representative of his estate.

(7) When any party is dead or incompetent notice may be sent to his last known address or given to his personal representative.

(8) Notice operates for the benefit of all parties who have rights on the instrument against the party notified.

Protest

§ 3-509. **Protest; noting for protest.** (1) A protest is a certificate of dishonor made under the hand and seal of a United States consul or vice consul or a notary public or other person authorized to certify dishonor by the law of the place where dishonor occurs. It may be made upon information satisfactory to such person.

(2) The protest must identify the instrument and certify either that due presentment has been made or the reason why it is excused and that the instrument has been dishonored by nonacceptance or nonpayment.

(3) The protest may also certify that notice of dishonor has been given to all parties or to specified parties.

(4) Subject to subsection (5) any necessary protest is due by the time that notice of dishonor is due.

(5) If, before protest is due, an instrument has been noted for protest by the officer to make protest, the protest may be made at any time thereafter as of the date of the noting.

§ 3-511. **Waived or excused presentment, protest or notice of dishonor or delay therein.** (1) Delay in presentment, protest or notice of dishonor is excused when the party is without notice that it is due or when the delay is caused by circumstances beyond his control and he exercises reasonable diligence after the cause of the delay ceases to operate.

(2) Presentment or notice or protest as the case may be is entirely excused when

    (a)   the party to be charged has waived it expressly or by implication either before or after it is due; or

    (b)   such party has himself dishonored the instrument or has countermanded payment or otherwise has no reason to expect or right to require that the instrument be accepted or paid; or

(c)   by reasonable diligence the presentment or protest cannot be made or the notice given.

(3)   Presentment is also entirely excused when

(a)   the maker, acceptor or drawee of any instrument except a documentary draft is dead or in insolvency proceedings instituted after the issue of the instrument; or

(b)   acceptance or payment is refused but not for want of proper presentment.

(4)   Where a draft has been dishonored by nonacceptance a later presentment for payment and any notice of dishonor and protest for nonpayment are excused unless in the meantime the instrument has been accepted.

(5)   A waiver of protest is also a waiver of presentment and of notice of dishonor even though protest is not required.

(6)   Where a waiver of presentment or notice or protest is embodied in the instrument itself it is binding upon all parties; but where it is written above the signature of an indorser it binds him only.

Discharge

§ 3-603.   **Payment or satisfaction.**   (1)   The liability of any party is discharged to the extent of his payment or satisfaction to the holder even though it is made with knowledge of a claim of another person to the instrument unless prior to such payment or satisfaction the person making the claim either supplies indemnity deemed adequate by the party seeking the discharge or enjoins payment or satisfaction by order of a court of competent jurisdiction in an action in which the adverse claimant and the holder are parties.   This subsection does not, however, result in the discharge of the liability

(a)   of a party who in bad faith pays or satisfies a holder who acquired the instrument by theft or who (unless having the rights of a holder in due course) holds through one who so acquired it; or

(b)   of a party (other than an intermediary bank or a payor bank which is not a depositary bank) who pays or satisfies the holder of an instrument, which has been restrictively indorsed in a manner not consistent with the terms of such restrictive indorsement.

(2)   Payment or satisfaction may be made with the consent of the holder by any person including a stranger to the instrument. Surrender of the instrument to such a person gives him the rights of a transferee (Sec. 3-201).

§ 3-604.   **Tender of payment.**   (1)   Any party making tender of full payment to a holder when or after it is due is discharged to the extent of all subsequent liability for interest, costs and attorney's fees.

(2) The holder's refusal of such tender wholly discharges any party who has a right of recourse against the party making the tender.

(3) Where the maker or acceptor of an instrument payable otherwise than on demand is able and ready to pay at every place of payment specified in the instrument when it is due, it is equivalent to tender.

CHAPTER 15: COMMISSIONERS OF DEEDS

APPOINTMENT AND POWERS

SECTION
    15.1 Appointment.
    15.2 Oath and seal.
    15.3 Powers.

APPOINTMENT AND POWERS

§ 15.1 Appointment.

A commissioner of deeds is an officer authorized by the laws of one state to perform certain duties in another state or country where he resides. As an example, a resident of Ohio may be appointed by the governor of Illinois to take acknowledgments, administer oaths, or perform other duties in Ohio, for use in Illinois. The statutes of most of the states expressly provide for such officers. They are appointed by the governor of the state for which they are to act, though in a few of the states the appointment of such commissioners must be by and with the advice and consent of the senate or the governor's council. The number to be appointed is ordinarily left to the discretion of the governor.

Commissioners are ordinarily appointed for a term of years, varying from two to seven; and in a few states, during the pleasure of the governor. Sometimes a bond is required.

§ 15.2 Oath and seal.

Many of the states require commissioners of deeds to take an oath of office for the faithful performance of their duties. Some states also require them to procure an official seal. The form of such seal, as prescribed by statutes, frequently consists of the following: the words "Commissioner of Deeds for the State of ———" (the state appointing him), the name of the commissioner, and the name of the state in which he has authority to act. Before entering upon the duties of his office, the commissioner must usually send to the secretary of state for which he is appointed his executed oath of office, an impression of his seal, and his signature.

§ 15.3   Powers.

Commissioners are commonly authorized to administer oaths, take depositions and affidavits, and take acknowledgments or proof of the execution of deeds, leases, mortgages, or other written instruments, to be used in evidence or recorded in the state from which the commission has been issued. If appointed for a foreign country, a commissioner may often certify to the existence of a patent, record, or other document recorded in a public office or under official custody in such country, and to the correctness of a copy thereof.

Frequently there are statutory provisions regulating the fees which commissioners may charge for their services in connection with administering oaths or taking depositions or acknowledgments.

All acts of a commissioner in the state for which he is appointed must be authenticated by his official seal and signature. Although not required by all states, it is advisable for the commissioner to add the date of the expiration of his commission.

COMMISSIONERS OF DEEDS:
STATE AND OTHER STATUTES

ALABAMA

[ALA. CODE]

Tit. 41, § 1. Appointment of commissioners in other states. The governor may appoint commissioners in other states and territories of the United States, to take and certify depositions, to receive the acknowledgment and take the proof of conveyances of property within this state, and the proof of wills executed by persons without the state, devising or bequeathing property within this state. Commissioners appointed under this section shall hold office for four years.

ALASKA

[ALASKA STAT.]

§ 44.53.010. Appointment [of commissioners], term of office, and powers. The governor may appoint as many commissioners in each state, territory, and district of the United States as he considers expedient. Each commissioner holds office for four years. Within the state, territory, or district for which appointed, each commissioner may take and certify

(1) the proof or acknowledgment of a conveyance of real property within the district or of any other written instrument to be used or operated in it;

(2) the acknowledgment of satisfaction of a judgment of a court of this district;

(3) an affidavit or deposition to be used in a court or before a judicial officer of the district.

§ 44.53.020. Qualifying for office. Before exercising his powers, a commissioner appointed under § 10 of this chapter shall have a seal of office, and take an oath before a judicial officer in the county, city, or town where he resides, that he will faithfully perform the duties of the office. The commissioner shall file the oath and an impression of the seal in the office of the Department of Administration. The Department of Administration shall collect $5 for each certificate of appointment and shall account for and deposit the amounts received in the state treasury.

ARIZONA

The former provisions concerning commissioners of deeds, ARIZ. REV. STAT. ANN. §§ 41-301 and 41-302, were repealed effective July 1, 1974.

ARKANSAS

[ARK. STAT. ANN.]

§ 12-1501. Appointment of commissioners in other states—Powers. The Governor of this State may nominate, appoint and commission, under the great seal of this State, in any other State or Territory of the United States, one or more commissioners, as he may think proper to continue in office, during the pleasure of the Governor for the time being, who shall have power to administer oaths, and affirmations, and to take depositions, affidavits, and the proof and acknowledgment of deeds or other instruments of writing, under seal to be used or recorded in this State.

§ 12-1502. Validity of acts. All oaths administered by the said commissioner, all affidavits and depositions taken by them, and all acknowledgments, etc., aforesaid, certified by them, shall be as effectual in law; to all intents and purposes, as if done and certified by any justice of the peace, or other authorized officer within this State.

§ 12-1503. Oath. Before any such commissioner shall proceed to discharge any of the duties of his said appointment he shall take and subscribe an oath before some justice of the peace, or other officer authorized to administer oaths in the State for which such commissioner shall be appointed, that he will well and faithfully discharge all the duties of his said appointment, which said oath, together with the signature and an impression of the seal of the said commissioner, shall be filed in the office of the Secretary of State within six [6] months after the taking of the same.

§ 28-204. Before whom affidavits made out of state—Formalities. An affidavit may be made out of this State before a commissioner appointed by the Governor of this State to take depositions, or before a judge of a court, mayor of a city, notary public, or justice of the peace, whose certificate shall be proof of the time and manner of its being made.

CALIFORNIA

[CAL. GOV'T CODE—(West)]

§ 8308. Commissioners of deeds; term. On and after the effective date of this section, no more commissioners of deeds shall be appointed pursuant to this chapter whether as to a new commission or as a renewal of an existing commission. Commissioners of deeds previously appointed pursuant to this chapter shall hold office for the term of four years from and after the date of their commissions.

Note: The operative date of the foregoing section is the same as the effective date of statutes generally enacted at the 1975 Regular Session of the California Legislature. The following section was repealed with the same operative date:

[CAL. GOV'T CODE—(West)]

§ 8300. Appointment; term of office [Repealed]. The Secretary of State may appoint in each state of the United States, or in any foreign country, one or more commissioner of deeds. They shall hold office for the term of four years from and after the date of their commission.

COLORADO

[COLO. REV. STAT. ANN.]

§ 38-30-130. **Governor may appoint commissioners of deeds.** The governor may appoint and commission, in any other state, in the District of Columbia, in each of the territories of the United States, and in any foreign country, one or more commissioners, who shall keep a seal of office, and continue in office during the pleasure of the governor, and shall have authority to take the acknowledgment, or proof of the execution of any deed or other conveyance, or lease of any lands lying in this state, or of any contract, letters of attorney, or any other writing under seal, or note to be used and recorded in this state, and such commissioners, appointed for any foreign country, shall also have authority to certify to the official character, signature or seal of any officer within their district who is authorized to take acknowledgments or declarations under oath.

§ 38-30-131. **Oath of commissioner of deeds.** Every such commissioner, before performing any duty or exercising any power by virtue of his appointment, shall take and subscribe an oath or affirmation before a judge or clerk of one of the courts of record of the district, territory, state or country in which such commissioner shall reside, or before any ambassador, minister, consul or vice-consul, consular agent, vice-consular agent, charge d'affaires or any diplomatic, consular or commercial agent or representative of the United States appointed for the foreign state or country in which such commissioner shall reside, well and faithfully to execute and perform all the duties of such commissioner under and by virtue of the laws of the state of Colorado, which oath, and an impression of the seal of office, together with his signature thereto, shall be filed in the office of the secretary of state of this state within six months after the date of appointment.

§ 38-30-132. **Effect of commissioner's acknowledgment.** Such acknowledgment or proof so taken according to the laws of this state, and certified by any such commissioner under his seal of office, annexed to or endorsed on such instrument, shall have the same force and effect as if the same had been made before a judge or any other officer authorized to perform such act in this state.

§ 38-30-133. **Commissioner shall have power to administer oath.** Every commissioner shall have power to administer any oath, which may be lawfully required in this state, to any person willing to take it, and to take and certify all depositions to be used in any of the courts of this state, in conformity with the laws thereof, either on interrogations proposed under commission from a court of this state, or by consent of parties, and all such acts shall be as valid as if done and certified according to law by a magistrate of this state.

§ 38-30-134. **Fees of commissioners.** Commissioners for like services, shall be allowed the same fees as are allowed by law to notaries public of this state.

Note: See *Fees Chargeable,* COLO. REV. STAT. ANN. § 12-55-110.

CONNECTICUT

[CONN. GEN. STAT. ANN.]

§ 4-21. **Commissioners for Connecticut.** The governor may appoint and commission a convenient number of commissioners in each of the other states of the United States, in any territory thereof and in the District of Columbia, for the term of five years, commencing with the date of their respective commissions, unless the appointments and commissions are sooner revoked. Each commissioner so appointed and commissioned shall have power to take the acknowledgment of deeds and of any instruments required by the laws of this state to be acknowledged, to administer oaths or affirmations, examine witnesses and take depositions relating to any cause pending, or to be brought, in any of the courts of this state; but no commissioner shall act as such until he has filed with the secretary an affidavit, signed and sworn to by him before proper authority, that he will faithfully perform his duties as such commissioner.

DELAWARE

The statutes are vague concerning commissioners of deeds. Acknowledgment and proof of a deed may be taken out of the state by any commissioner of deeds appointed by the Governor in any of the states or territories of the United States, in the District of Columbia, in the possessions of the United States, or in foreign countries, the deed to be certified in like manner under the hand and seal of the commissioner. See *Acknowledgments,* DEL. CODE ANN. tit. 25, § 129. There is no express provision for the appointment of commissioners of deeds, however.

DISTRICT OF COLUMBIA

There are no provisions for commissioners of deeds under the laws of the District of Columbia.

FLORIDA

[FLA. STAT. ANN.]

§ 118.01. **Appointment [of commissioners] and power to take acknowledgments.** The governor may name, appoint and commission one or more commissioners in each of such of the states and territories of the United States, the District of Columbia, and in any foreign country, as he may deem expedient; and such commissioner shall continue in office for four years, and shall have authority to take the acknowledgment and proof of the execution of any deed, mortgage or other conveyance of any lands, tenements or hereditaments lying or being in this state, and any contract, letter of attorney, or any other writing under seal to be used or recorded in this state, and such acknowledgment or proof taken or made in the manner directed by the laws of this state and certified by any one of the said commissioners before whom the same shall be taken or made under his seal, which certificate shall be endorsed on or annexed to said deed or instrument aforesaid, shall have the same force and effect, and be as good and available in law for all purposes, as if the same had been made or taken before the proper officer of this state.

§ 118.02. May administer oaths. Every commissioner appointed by virtue of this chapter may administer an oath to any person who shall be willing and desirous to make such oath before him, and such affidavit made before such commissioner shall be as good and effectual to all intents and purposes as if taken by any magistrate resident in this state and competent to take the same.

§ 118.03. Oath of office. Every commissioner appointed as aforesaid before he shall proceed to perform any duty under and by virtue of this law shall take and subscribe an oath before a notary public or justice of the peace in the city or county in which such commissioner shall reside, well and faithfully to execute and perform all the duties of such commissioner under and by virtue of the laws of this state, which oath shall be filed in the office of the department of state.

GEORGIA

[GA. CODE ANN.]

§ 71-301. Appointment [of commissioners] in other States and Territories. The Governor shall have power to appoint, in other States and Territories of the United States, commissioners to take and certify the acknowledgment or proof of deeds or other conveyances of property in this State, of depositions under commissions or otherwise, of powers of attorney, of wills executed by persons devising or bequeathing property within the State, and of other instruments in writing required to be attested under the laws of this State.

HAWAII

[HAWAII REV. STAT.]

§ 503-1. Appointment [of commissioners]. The governor may appoint commissioners in the states and territories of the United

States, and one or more commissioners in every foreign country, who shall hold office for three years from the date of their respective appointments, unless removed by the governor.

§ 503-2. **Oath and seal.** A commissioner who is appointed for a state or territory of the United States shall, within three months after his appointment, take and subscribe an oath before a justice of the peace or other magistrate of the city or county where he resides, or before a clerk of a court of record within the state or territory where he resides, faithfully to perform the duties of his office, and shall cause an official seal to be prepared upon which shall appear his name, the words: "Commissioner for Hawaii," and the name of the state or territory and city or county in which he resides. A commissioner who is appointed for a foreign country shall, before performing any duty of his office, take and subscribe an oath before a judge or clerk of a court of record of the country in which he resides or before an ambassador, minister, or consul of the United States appointed to reside in such country, faithfully to perform the duties of his office. In each case, a certificate of the commissioner's oath of office and his signature and an impression of his official seal shall be forthwith transmitted to and filed in the office of the lieutenant governor.

§ 503-3. **Powers; charges.** A commissioner may, in the state, territory, or country for which he is appointed, administer oaths and take depositions, affidavits, and acknowledgments of deeds and other instruments to be used or recorded in the State, and the proof of such deeds, if the grantor refuses to acknowledge the same; which shall be certified by him under his official seal. Charges made by commissioners for services rendered shall be at the rates authorized by statute for similar services rendered by notaries within the jurisdiction in which the services are performed. Duly certified records of the acts performed by a commissioner have the same force and effect as if performed by a notary within the State.

§ 503-4. **Records; what same shall contain.** Each commissioner so appointed besides the certificate of acknowledgment endorsed upon the instrument, shall keep a record of every acknowledgment, oath, deposition, and affidavit in a book of records. Each record shall set forth at least the date of acknowledgment, the parties to the instrument, the persons acknowledging, the date, and some memorandum as to the nature of the instrument acknowledged; and, as to oaths, depositions, and affidavits, the name or names of the party or parties making the same, the date and nature of the instrument and date of administering the oath.

§ 503-5. **Instructions to.** The lieutenant governor shall prepare and forward to each commissioner instructions and forms in conformity with law, and a copy of sections 503-1 to 503-4.

§ 503-6. **Construction of statutes.** This chapter shall not be construed as repealing or amending chapter 502.

Note: Chapter 502 pertains in part to acknowledgments.

IDAHO

The former provisions concerning commissioners of deeds, IDAHO CODE §§ 51-201 through 51-207, were repealed effective 1949.

ILLINOIS

There are no provisions for commissioners of deeds under the laws of Illinois.

INDIANA

[IND. CODE]

§ 4-2-5-1. **Appointment and commission—Number—Term.** The governor may appoint and commission in any other state or territory, or in any foreign country, such number of commissioners as he may think proper, who shall hold their office for the term of four [4] years unless such appointment be sooner revoked by the governor, who shall have power to revoke the same.

§ 4-2-5-2. **Powers.** Commissioners so appointed shall have power to take depositions and affidavits to be used in the courts of this state, and acknowledgment of deeds and other instruments, proper to be recorded in this state. But such depositions or acknowledgments shall not be valid unless attested by the official seal of such commissioner. But when so attested they shall have the same force and effect as if taken before a notary public in this state.

§ 4-2-5-3. **Oath and seal.** Before any commissioner shall enter upon the discharge of his duties as such, he shall take and subscribe an oath, before some officer authorized to administer oaths, that he will faithfully discharge his duties as such commissioner; which oath he shall forward to the governor, to be by him filed in the office of secretary of state. And he shall also procure such an official seal as will make a plain and distinct impression on paper.

§ 4-2-5-4. **Copy of act to commissioners.** It shall be the duty of the secretary of state to forward a copy of this act [4-2-5-1—4-2-5-4] to all commissioners now acting, or hereafter appointed.

§ 5-7-1-1. **Fees charged by secretary of state.** The secretary of state, Provided That no fees shall be charged against the United States, or this, or any other state, or any county of this state, nor against any officer of either of them, for any attestation, certificate or paper required by them for official use, shall be authorized to charge and collect on behalf of the state of Indiana, the following fees, to be paid by the parties requiring the service: ° ° ° for each commission to commissioner of deeds, and filing qualifications, five dollars [$5.00]; ° ° °.

Editorial comment

Concerning the fees which commissioners of deeds may charge, see *Fees Chargeable*, IND. CODE § 5-7-9-6.

IOWA

There are no provisions for commissioners of deeds under the laws of Iowa.

KANSAS

[KAN. STAT. ANN.]

§§ 28-140, 28-142, 28-143.　See *Fees* below.

§ 53-201.　**Commissioners in other states; appointment; powers.** The governor may appoint in each of the United States and territories and in the District of Columbia, and in foreign countries, one or more commissioners, to continue in office during the pleasure of the governor for the time being; and every such commissioner shall have power to administer oaths, and to take depositions and affidavits to be used in this state, and also to take the acknowledgments of deeds, powers of attorney or other instruments to be recorded in this state.

§ 53-202.　**Same; commissioners' acts effectual as if done within state.** All oaths administered by the said commissioners, all affidavits and depositions taken by them, and all acknowledgments aforesaid, certified by them, shall be as effectual in law, to all intents and purposes, as if done and certified by any authorized officer within this state.

§ 53-203.　**Oath, autograph and impression of seal of commissioner.** Before any commissioners, appointed as aforesaid, shall proceed to perform any of the duties of their office, they shall take and subscribe an oath, before any justice of the peace or other officer authorized to administer oaths, in the state or territory for which such commissioner may be appointed, that they will faithfully discharge all the duties of their office; which oath shall be filed in the office of the secretary of this state, within six months after the taking of the same, and also his autograph and impression of his seal of office.

Note: Concerning oath of office, see also *Appointment*, KAN. STAT. ANN. § 54-106.

Fees

§ 28-140.　**Posting list of fees; penalty for failure.** Each officer herein named shall cause a list of his fees to be posted in his office, in some conspicuous place, under penalty of three dollars for each day he shall neglect to do so.

§ 28-142. **Bill for fees or costs.** Any person liable for any costs or fees shall be entitled to receive, on demand, a certified bill of the same, in which the items of service and the charge thereof shall be specially stated.

§ 28-143. **Receipt for fees paid.** Every officer charging fees shall, if required by the person paying them, give him a receipt therefor, setting forth the items and the date of each.

KENTUCKY

[KY. REV. STAT. ANN.]

§ 14.090. **Fees.** (1) The Secretary of State shall charge and collect for the state the following fees:

For issuing commission with Seal of Commonwealth attached and all necessary forms to a commissioner of foreign deeds $5.00

° ° °

(2) No fee shall be collected for affixing the State Seal to a commission issued to any public officer other than commissioner of foreign deeds or notary public, or to a grant, or to a pardon of a felony.

§ 423.070. **Commissioners of foreign deeds; appointment, term.** The Governor may appoint and commission one or more commissioners of deeds in each state of the United States for a term of two years. Before entering on the duties of his office, each commissioner shall make and subscribe an affidavit, before an officer authorized to administer an oath, to well and truly execute and perform all the duties of his office. The affidavit must be filed in the office of the Secretary of State of this state.

§ 423.080. **Powers of commissioners.** Any commissioner of deeds appointed and qualified pursuant to KRS 423.070 may take the acknowledgment of proof of any instrument of writing, except wills, which instrument is required by the laws of this state to be recorded, and may examine and take the acknowledgment of married women to any such instrument. The examination, acknowledgment or proof of any such instrument taken by a commissioner, and certified under his official seal, in the manner required by the laws of this state, shall authorize the instrument to be recorded in the proper office. A commissioner of deeds may administer any oath or take any affirmation necessary to discharge his official duties, and may take and certify depositions to be read on the trial of any action or proceeding in any of the courts of this state.

LOUISIANA

[LA. REV. STAT.]

§ 35:451. **Appointment.** The governor may appoint one or more persons of known integrity and learning as commissioners for each one of the states and territories of the union, who shall reside therein.

§ 35:452. **Notarial powers of commissioner.** Any commissioner for the State of Louisiana, for any one of the states or territories of the United States shall, within the state or territory for which he is appointed, have all the powers of a notary public, whether the party or person making any acknowledgment, proof, oath, affirmation, or passing any act before him reside within that state or territory or not.

§ 35:453. **Acts to have force of notarial acts.** Acts passed before any commissioner and two witnesses, have the full force and effect of a notarial act passed within this state, and shall be deemed and taken to be such notarial act.

§ 35:454. **Certified copies of acts as proof of contents of original.** Copies of an act passed before a commissioner and by him certified to be a true copy of the original, shall not make proof of what is contained in the original except to the same extent to which a copy may be admissible in evidence as the copy of an act under private signature; but copies of originals certified as true copies from the originals by any notary public within the State of Louisiana with whom the original may be deposited, shall make like proof of what is contained in the original as is made by the copy of a notarial act certified as a true copy by the notary who is the depositary of the original.

§ 35:455. **Commissioners in foreign countries; powers.** Wherever "Commissioner" is used in this Chapter, it shall be construed to apply to and to include all persons authorized to act as commissioners for this state in any foreign country.

§ 35:456. **General powers of commissioners.** Commissioners shall take depositions in virtue of any commission that may be directed to them by the courts of this State. They may take the acknowledgment and proof of any deed, mortgage or conveyance of any lands, tenements or real property, lying and being in the State of Louisiana, and take the acknowledgment and proof of the execution of any instrument of writing for the sale, transfer or assignment of any property, movable or immovable, and of rights and debts, and also of any power of attorney, or other writing to be used or proved in this state, before any court or public officer, and administer an oath or affirmation for like purposes to any person desirous of making the same.

§ 35:457. **Authentication of signature, capacity and acts of public officers.** Commissioners may authenticate and attest the signature, official capacity and official acts of any judge, justice of the peace, or other public officer holding a commission or acting under the authority of the state or territory in which he resides, and for which he has been appointed.

§ 35:458. Duties in executing commissions. In executing commissions, commissioners shall conform in all respects to the legislation of this state in reference thereto, and shall sign every process verbal of deposition taken by them, and affix thereto their seal of office, bearing the impress of their names, official capacity, and the name of the state or territory within the jurisdiction of which they are authorized to act.

§ 35:459. Deposit of duplicates of signature and seal of office. The duplicate original of the signature and seal of office of each commissioner appointed in the different states and territories of the United States shall be deposited in the office of the secretary of state of Louisiana.

§ 35:460. Ambassadors, etc., in foreign countries authorized to act as commissioners; seal. All United States ambassadors, ministers, charges d'affaires, secretaries of legation, consuls general, consuls, vice consuls and commercial agents, in any foreign country, are authorized to act as commissioners, and are empowered to use their respective seals of office instead of the commissioner's seal hereinbefore described.

MAINE

[ME. REV. STAT. ANN.]

Tit. 33, § 251. Appointment; powers. The Governor may appoint one or more commissioners in any other of the United States and in any foreign country, who shall continue in office during his pleasure; and have authority to take the acknowledgment and proof of the execution of any deed, other conveyance or lease of lands lying in this State; and of any contract, letter of attorney or any other writing, under seal or not, to be used or recorded in this State.

Tit. 33, § 252. Legal effect of official acts. The acknowledgment or proof, taken according to the laws of this State and certified by any such commissioner under his seal of office, annexed to or indorsed on such instrument, shall have the same force and effect as if done by an officer authorized to perform such acts within this State.

Tit. 33, § 253. Administration of oaths and depositions. Every commissioner appointed under section 251 may administer any oath lawfully required in this State to any person willing to take it; and take and duly certify all depositions to be used in any of the courts in this State, in conformity to the laws thereof, on interrogatories proposed under commission from a court of this State, by consent of parties or on legal notice given to the opposite party. All such acts shall be as valid as if done and certified according to law by a magistrate in this State.

Tit. 33, § 254.   Qualifications and seal.   Every commissioner appointed under section 251, before performing any duty or exercising any power by virtue of his appointment, shall take and subscribe an oath or affirmation, before a judge or clerk of one of the superior courts of the state or country in which he resides, well and faithfully to execute and perform all his official duties under the laws of this State; which oath and a description of his seal of office shall be filed in the office of the Secretary of State.

MARYLAND

There are no provisions for commissioners of deeds under the laws of Maryland.

MASSACHUSETTS

[MASS. ANN. LAWS]

Ch. 222, § 4.   Commissioners in Other States and Countries.   The governor, with the advice and consent of the council, may appoint commissioners in the states, territories, districts and dependencies of the United States, and one or more commissioners in every foreign country, to hold office for three years from the date of their respective appointments.

Note: Before the delivery of a commission to a person appointed commissioner under this section, he must pay to the state secretary a fee of $25.00. See *Appointment,* MASS. ANN. LAWS ch. 30, § 13.

§ 5.   Oath, Signature, Seal, etc.   A person appointed commissioner in a state, territory, district or dependency of the United States shall, within three months after his appointment, take and subscribe an oath before a justice of the peace or other magistrate of the town or county where he resides, or before a clerk of a court of record within the state, territory, district or dependency where he resides, faithfully to perform the duties of his office, and shall cause an official seal to be prepared, upon which shall appear his name, the words "Commissioner for Massachusetts" and the name of the state, territory, district or dependency, and town or county where he resides.   A person appointed commissioner in a foreign country shall, before performing any duty of his office, take and subscribe an oath before a judge or clerk of a court of record of the county where he resides or before an ambassador, minister or consul of the United States, accredited to such country, faithfully to perform the duties of his office.   In each case, a certificate of the commissioner's oath of office and his signature and an impression of his official seal shall be forthwith transmitted to and filed in the office of the state secretary.

§ 6. **Powers and Duties.** A commissioner may, in his state, territory, district, dependency or country, administer oaths and take depositions, affidavits and acknowledgments of deeds and other instruments, to be used or recorded in this commonwealth, and the proof of such deeds, if the grantor refuses to acknowledge the same, all of which shall be certified by him under his official seal.

§ 7. **Instructions, etc.** The state secretary shall prepare and forward to each commissioner appointed under section four, instructions and forms in conformity to law, and a copy of the three preceding sections.

Ch. 262, § 42. **Commissioners in Other States, etc.** The fees of commissioners appointed under section four of chapter two hundred and twenty-two shall be as follows:

For administering oaths and certifying the same under their official seals, one dollar for each; for taking acknowledgments of deeds and other instruments and certifying the same under their official seals, one dollar for each; for each written page contained in any deposition or affidavit taken by them, fifty cents; for administering the oath or affirmation to each deponent, one dollar; for authenticating, sealing up and directing each deposition, one dollar; for services not hereinbefore specified, the same fees as are allowed to justices of the peace in this commonwealth for like services; but the court to which a deposition is returnable shall order further allowance therefor if it appears proper to do so.

MICHIGAN

There are no express provisions for the appointment of commissioners of deeds under the laws of Michigan. Commissioners appointed by the governor of the state for the purpose of taking acknowledgments are mentioned in the statutes, however. See *Acknowledgments*, MICH. COMP. LAWS ANN. § 565.10.

MINNESOTA

[MINN. CONST.]

Art. 5, § 4. **Powers and duties of governor.** The governor ° ° ° shall have power to appoint commissioners to take the acknowledgment of deeds or other instruments in writing, to be used in the State. ° ° °

MISSISSIPPI

All qualified electors and no others are eligible to office, except as otherwise provided in the state constitution. See *Qualifications*, MISS. CONST. art. 12, § 250.

[MISS. CONST.]

Art. 14, § 266.   No person holding or exercising the rights or powers of any office of honor or profit, either in his own right or as a deputy, or while otherwise acting for or in the name or by the authority of another, under any foreign government, or under the government of the United States, shall hold or exercise in any way the rights and powers of any office of honor or profit under the laws or authority of this state, except notaries, commissioners of deeds, and United States commissioners.

[MISS. CODE ANN.]

§ 7-1-17. Commissioners for other states.   The governor may appoint one or more commissioners, residing in each of the states and territories of the United States and in the District of Columbia or in any foreign country, who shall hold their office for the term of four years from the date of their commissions.   They shall have full power to administer oaths and affirmations, to take and certify depositions and affidavits to be used in this state, and to take and certify the acknowledgment and proof of all instruments of writing to be recorded in this state; and their acts shall be as effectual in law as if done and certified by any officer thereunto duly authorized in this state.   Before any commissioner so appointed shall proceed to perform any of the duties of his office, he shall take and subscribe an oath, before an officer authorized to administer oaths in the state or county for which such commissioner may be appointed, that he will faithfully discharge all the duties of the office, which oath shall be filed in the office of the secretary of state within six months after the taking and subscribing of the same.

MISSOURI

The state is entitled to a fee of $7.50 for the services of the secretary of state in issuing a commission to a commissioner of deeds. See *Appointment*, MO. ANN. STAT. § 28.160.

[MO. ANN. STAT.—(Vernon)]

§ 486.100. Appointment—powers generally.   The governor may appoint and commission in any other state, in the District of Columbia, in each of the territories of the United States, and in any foreign country, one or more commissioners, who shall continue in office during the pleasure of the governor, and shall have authority to take relinquishments of dower of married women, the acknowledgment or proof of the execution of any deed or other conveyance, or lease of any lands lying in this state, or of any contract, letters of attorney, or of any other writing, under seal or note, to be used and recorded in this state; and such commissioners appointed for any foreign country shall also have authority to certify to the official character, signature or seal of any officer within their district, who is authorized to take acknowledgments or declarations under oath.

§ 486.110. Official oath, etc. Every such commissioner, before performing any duty or exercising any power in virtue of his appointment, shall take and subscribe an oath or affirmation before some judge or clerk of any United States court of record or before some judge or clerk of any court of record in and of the state of Missouri, or before a judge or clerk of one of the courts of record of the district, territory, state or county in which said commissioner shall reside, well and faithfully to execute and perform all the duties of such commissioner, under and by virtue of the laws of the state of Missouri; which oath, and a description of his seal of office, if there be one, together with his signature thereto, shall be filed in the office of the secretary of state of this state within six months after the date of his appointmeant.

§ 486.120. Effect of authentication by commissioner. An acknowledgment or proof so taken according to the laws of this state, and certified to by any such commissioner, under his seal of office, if there is one annexed to or indorsed on the instrument, has the same force and effect as if the same had been made before a judge or magistrate, or any other officer authorized to perform the act in this state.

§ 486.130. Additional powers—oaths—depositions. Every commissioner shall have power to administer any oath which may be lawfully required in this state, to any person willing to take it; and to take and certify all depositions to be used in any of the courts of this state, in conformity to the laws thereof, either on interrogatories proposed under commission from a court of this state, or by consent of parties, or on legal notice given to the opposite party; and all such acts may be as valid as if done and certified according to law by a magistrate in this state.

§ 486.140. Fees. Commissioners shall for like services be allowed the same fees as clerks of courts of record.

MONTANA

[MONT. REV. CODES ANN.]

§ 56-201. Governor to appoint. The governor may appoint in each state of the United States, or in any foreign state, one or more commissioners of deeds, to hold office for the term of five years from and after the date of their commission, but the governor may remove from office any commissioner during the term for which he was appointed.

§ 56-202. General duties of. Every commissioner of deeds has power, within the state for which he was appointed:

1. To administer and certify oaths.
2. To take and certify depositions and affidavits.

3. To take and certify the acknowledgment of proof of powers of attorney, mortgages, transfers, grants, deeds, or other instruments for record.

4. To provide and keep an official seal, upon which must be engraved his name, the words "commissioner of Deeds for the State of Montana," and the name of the state for which he is commissioned.

5. To authenticate with his official seal all his official acts.

§ 56-203. Effect of acts done by commissioners. All oaths administered, depositions and affidavits taken, and all acknowledgments and proofs certified by commissioners of deeds, have the same force and effect, to all intents and purposes, as if done and certified in this state by any officer authorized by law to perform such acts.

§ 56-204. Oaths, when to be filed. The official oaths of commissioners of deeds, together with the impressions of their official seals, must be filed in the office of the secretary of state within six months after they are taken.

§ 56-205. Fees. The fees of commissioners of deeds are the same as those prescribed for notaries public.

Accord, § 25-113, which is worded substantially the same, and for that reason is omitted.

§ 56-206. Copy of this chapter to be transmitted to appointee. The secretary of state must transmit, with the commission to the appointee, a certified copy of this chapter, and of the section prescribing the fees of notaries public.

§ 56-207. Fee to be paid into state treasury. No commission must issue until the applicant pays into the state treasury the sum of five dollars.

NEBRASKA

The former provision concerning commissioners of deeds, NEB. REV. STAT. §§ 76-220 to 76-225, were repealed in 1969.

NEVADA

[NEV. REV. STAT.]

§ 240.170. Appointment and term. The governor may, when in his judgment it may be necessary, appoint in each of the United States, and in each of the territories and districts thereof, and in each foreign state, kingdom, province, territory and colony, one or more commissioners of deeds, to continue in office 4 years, unless sooner removed by him.

§ 240.180. Fee for commission. Before any commission shall be delivered to any appointee under the provisions of NRS 240.170 to

240.220, inclusive, a fee of $25 on the commission, exclusive of other legal charges thereon, shall be paid therefor to the secretary of state, and shall be accounted for by him and paid into the general fund of the State of Nevada.

§ 240.190. Oath of office. Before any appointed commissioner shall proceed to perform any of the duties of his office, he shall take and subscribe an oath that he will faithfully perform and discharge all of the duties of his office. The oath shall be filed in the office of the secretary of State of Nevada within 6 months after being taken and subscribed.

§ 240.200. Commission and copy of law transmitted to appointee. The secretary of state shall transmit a copy of NRS 240.170 to 240.-220, inclusive, with the commission to each person appointed under the provisions of NRS 240.170 to 240.220, inclusive.

§ 240.210. Powers of commissioners. Every commissioner of deeds appointed by the governor shall have power:

1.   To administer oaths.

2.   To take and certify depositions and affidavits to be used in this state.

3.   To take the acknowledgment or proof of any deed or other instrument to be recorded in this state, and duly certify the same under his hand and official seal.

§ 240.220. Legality of acts of commissioners. All oaths administered by commissioners of deeds, all depositions and affidavits taken by them, and all acknowledgments and proofs of deeds and other instruments, taken and certified by them under their seals as commissioners of deeds, shall have the same force and effect in law, for all purposes whatever, as if done and certified by any notary public or other officer, in and for this state, who is now or hereafter may be authorized by law to perform such act.

§ 240.230. Compensation of commissioners of deeds acting in Nevada; penalties. 1. Commissioners of deeds appointed by the governors of any of the states of the United States of America, or of any of the territories thereof, to reside in the State of Nevada, may receive for services rendered in this state the following compensation, and none other:

> For drawing an affidavit, deposition or other paper, for
> each folio $0.30
>
> For administering an oath or affirmation .... .25
>
> For putting his seal to such instruments .... .50
>
> For taking an acknowledgment or proof of deed or
> other instrument, to include the seal and the
> writing of the certificate, for the first signature 1.00
>
> For each additional signature .... .50

2. Each commissioner of deeds residing in this state shall be subject to all the penalties for official delinquency or extortions as are provided by law for official misconduct.

NEW HAMPSHIRE

[N.H. REV. STAT. ANN.]

§ 455:12. **Appointment.** The governor, with advice of the council, may appoint, in each state, district and territory of the United States, and in each foreign country to which the United States sends a representative, a commissioner or commissioners, to continue in office five years.

Note: A fee of $5.00 is payable to the secretary of state for the use of the state for every commission for an office of profit, except justice of the peace and notary public. See *Appointment,* N.H. REV. STAT. ANN. § 5:10.

§ 455:13. **Oath.** Before any commissioner shall perform any duty of his office he shall take and subscribe an oath, before a judge of some court of record, that he will well and faithfully perform all the duties of the office, which oath shall be filed by him in the office of the secretary of state within six months after taking the same.

§ 455:14. **Powers.** Such commissioner may administer oaths, take depositions and affidavits to be used in this state and notify parties of the time and place thereof, and take the acknowledgment of deeds or instruments to be used or recorded in this state, in the same manner and with the same effect as a justice of the peace of this state may do within the state.

§ 455:15. **For Other States; By Court Appointment.** Any commissioner for any other state who is authorized to take depositions, administer oaths and affirmations and take the acknowledgment of deeds within this state, to be used in such other state, and any commissioner appointed by the supreme or superior court or any justice thereof, shall have the power to administer oaths and affirmations, to issue writs of summons to a witness, to proceed against such witness upon his neglect to appear and give his deposition, and in all proceedings under his commission, that is vested in justices of the peace in like cases.

NEW JERSEY

Foreign Commissioners of Deeds

[N.J. STAT. ANN.]

§ 52:6-12. **Appointment by Secretary of State; number; designation and description; fees.** The Secretary of State may appoint such number of commissioners resident in each of the States and territories of the United States and the District of Columbia as he may deem expedient, except where such appointments are incompatible with the laws of the jurisdiction wherein such commissioners shall reside. Persons thus appointed shall be commissioned by the Governor.

Each commissioner so appointed shall be designated a "foreign commissioner of deeds for New Jersey," and may be so described in his appointment and commission or as a "commissioner for taking the acknowledgment or proof of deeds for New Jersey in (such State, territory or district)." He may use either of such designations in his certificates. The fees required to be paid for the issuance of any commission to a person appointed as foreign commissioner of deeds for New Jersey shall be paid to the Secretary of State, who shall account to the State Treasurer for the same.

Note: The office of foreign commissioner of deeds should not be confused with the office of commissioner of deeds. New Jersey law provides for both offices. Concerning commissioners of deeds, see *Acknowledgments*, N.J. STAT. ANN. §§ 52:6-1 to 52:6-11.

§ 52:6-13. Terms of office; removal by governor. Commissioners appointed by virtue of section 52:6-12 of this title shall hold office for a term of three years. They may be removed from office at the pleasure of the governor, and shall be removed if it is made to appear to the governor that they have been or are charging more or greater fees than are allowed by law.

§ 52:6-14. Removal from residence as vacating appointment. Except as provided in section 52:6-15 of this title, if a foreign commissioner removes out of the state, territory or district in which he resides at the time of his appointment, his commission shall thereupon be void.

§ 52:6-15. Foreign commissioners for Pennsylvania or New York resident in New Jersey. A foreign commissioner of deeds for New Jersey in and for either Pennsylvania or New York may reside in this state, but he shall not exercise or perform any of the duties of his office outside Pennsylvania or New York, as the case may be. The official acts of such a commissioner resident in this state and performed in either Pennsylvania or New York shall be as valid and effectual as if he had resided in Pennsylvania or New York, as the case may be.

§ 52:6-16. Fee to accompany application for commission. Each applicant for a commission as a foreign commissioner of deeds for New Jersey shall inclose with his application the fee required by section [22A:4-1]° of the title Fees and Costs, which shall be returned if a commission is not issued to him.

(°) The statute says "section 22:4-1." That former section has been transferred and renumbered as § 22A:4-1, however. The fee required for the commission is $15.00. The fee for filing the seal of a foreign commissioner of deeds is $1.00. See *Appointment*, N.J. STAT. ANN. § 22A:4-1.

§ 52:6-17. **Official oath; by whom administered; filing.** Each foreign commissioner of deeds shall, before he enters upon the duties of his office, take and subscribe an oath to perform well and faithfully the duties of his office in accordance with the laws of this state. The oath may be administered by the mayor or other chief magistrate of the city or by a judge of the supreme or superior court of the state where such commissioner shall be resident, and shall be filed in the office of the secretary of state.

§ 52:6-18. **Seal; impression of filed with secretary of state.** Each foreign commissioner of deeds shall attest his official acts by an official seal, an impression of which, in wax or other appropriate substance shall, with his official oath, be filed in the office of the secretary of state of this state.

Note: The fee for filing the seal of a foreign commissioner of deeds is $1.00. See *Appointment,* N.J. STAT. ANN. § 22A:4-1.

§ 52:6-19. **Official certificates; forms.** The forms of official certificates of foreign commissioners of deeds shall conform to the laws of this state.

§ 52:6-20. **Use and effect of official certificates.** The official certificates of a foreign commissioner of deeds attested by his official seal may be indorsed upon or annexed to any instrument of writing for use or record in this state, and shall be entitled to full faith and credit.

§ 52:6-21. **Laws and forms to be printed and sent to commissioners.** The secretary of state shall cause such parts of this article as relate to the duties of foreign commissioners of deeds, and also the forms of acknowledgment and proof of deeds, mortgages and conveyances used in this state, to be printed and sent to each such commissioner with his commission.

§ 52:6-22. **Lists of foreign commissioners; copies for county clerks or registers of deeds and mortgages.** The secretary of state shall annually within ten days after the adjournment of the legislature make out and cause to be printed a list of all foreign commissioners of deeds duly appointed and commissioned during the preceding year, with the dates of their appointments and the expiration of the terms of office, a copy of which he shall cause to be sent to the county clerk or register of deeds and mortgages of each county in the state.

Editorial comment
Concerning the fees which foreign commissioners of deeds may charge, see *Fees Chargeable*, N.J. STAT. ANN. § 22A:4-14.

NEW MEXICO

The former provisions concerning commissioners of deeds, N.M. STAT. ANN. §§ 35-2-1 to 35-2-6, were repealed in 1968.

NEW YORK

Commissioners of Deeds in other States, Territories and Foreign Countries

[N.Y. EXEC. LAW]

§ 96. Fees and refunds. Except as otherwise provided by section ninety-six-a of this chapter, the department of state shall collect the following fees:

⚬   ⚬   ⚬

6. For a certificate as to the official character of a commissioner of deeds residing in another state or foreign country, fifty cents.

⚬   ⚬   ⚬

§ 141. Commissioners of deeds in other states, territories and foreign countries. The secretary of state may, in his discretion, appoint and commission in any other state, territory or dependency, or in any foreign country, such number of commissioners of deeds as he may think proper, each of whom shall be a resident of or have his place of business in the city, county, municipality or other political subdivision from which chosen, and shall hold office for the term of four years, unless such appointment shall be sooner revoked by the secretary of state, who shall have power to revoke the same. A person applying for appointment as a commissioner of deeds shall state in his application the city, county, municipality or other political subdivision for which he desires to be appointed, and shall inclose with his application the sum of five dollars, which sum, if a commission shall be granted, shall be paid by the secretary of state into the state treasury, and if such commission shall not be granted, then the same shall be returned to the person making the application. Each commissioner, before performing any of the duties or exercising any of the powers of his office, shall take the constitutional oath of office, if appointed for a city or county within the United States, before a justice of the peace or some other magistrate in such city or county; and if for a territory or dependency, before a judge of a court of record in such territory or dependency; and if for a city, municipality or other political subdivision in a foreign country, before a person authorized by the laws of this state to administer an oath in such country, or before a clerk or judge of a court of record in such foreign country; and shall cause to be prepared an official seal on which shall be designated his name, the words, "commissioner of deeds for the state of New York," and the name of the city or county, and the state, country, municipality or other political subdivision from which appointed, and shall file a clear impression of such seal, his written signature and his oath certified by the officer before whom it was taken, in the office of the department of state. The secretary of state upon receipt of such impression, signature and oath, shall forward to such commissioner instructions and forms, and a copy of the appropriate sections of this chapter.

Note: The office of commissioner of deeds in other states, territories and foreign countries should not be confused with the office of commissioner of deeds within the state. New York law provides for both offices. Concerning commissioners of deeds within the state, see *Acknowledgments,* N.Y. EXEC. LAW §§ 139 to 140.

§ 142. **Powers of such commissioners.** Every such commissioner shall have authority, within the city, county, municipality or other political subdivision for which he is appointed, and in the manner in which such acts are performed by authorized officers within the state:

1. To take the acknowledgment or proof of the execution of a written instrument, except a bill of exchange, promissory note or will, to be read in evidence or recorded in this state.

2. To administer oaths.

3. If such commissioner is also an attorney at law regularly admitted to practice in this state, in his discretion, to the extent authorized by this section, to administer an oath to or take the acknowledgment of or proof of the execution of an instrument by his client with respect to any matter, claim, action or proceeding.

4. If appointed for a foreign country, to certify to the existence of a patent, record or other document recorded in a public office or under official custody in such foreign country, and to the correctness of a copy of such patent, record or document, or to the correctness of a copy of a certified copy of such patent, record or other document, which has been certified according to the form in use in such foreign country.

5. A written instrument acknowledged or proved, an oath administered, or a copy or a copy of a certified copy of a patent, record or other document certified, as heretofore provided in this section, may be read in evidence or recorded within this state, the same as if taken, administered or certified within the state before an officer authorized to take the acknowledgment or proof of a written instrument, to administer oaths, or to certify to the correctness of a public record, if there shall be annexed or subjoined thereto, or indorsed thereon a certificate of the commissioner before whom such acknowledgment or proof was taken, by whom the oath was administered, or by whom the correctness of such copy is certified, under his hand and official seal. Such certificate shall specify the day on which, and the city or other political subdivision, and the state or country or other place in which, the acknowledgment or proof was taken, or the oath administered, without which specification the

certificate shall be void. Except as provided in subdivision five of this section, such certificate shall be authenticated by the certificate of the secretary of state annexed or subjoined to the certificate of such commissioner, that such commissioner was, at the time of taking such acknowledgment or proof, of administering such oath, or of certifying to such patent record or document, or copy thereof, duly authorized therefor, that he is acquainted with the handwriting of such commissioner, or has compared the signature upon the certificate with the signature of such commissioner deposited in his office, that he has compared the impression of the seal affixed to such certificate with the impression of the seal of such commissioner deposited in his office, and that he believes the signature and the impression of the seal upon such certificate to be genuine. The certificate of a commissioner as to the correctness of a copy of a certified copy of a patent, record or other document, as provided by this section, shall be presumptive evidence that it was certified according to the form in use in such foreign country.

6. A commissioner of deeds appointed pursuant to the preceding section may during his term of office procure from the secretary of state, on payment to him of a fee of one dollar, a certificate of his appointment, prescribed by the secretary of state, stating among other things, the date of his appointment, the date of expiration thereof and the city, county, municipality or other political subdivision for which he is appointed, and containing the signature of the commissioner in his own handwriting and his official seal, and certifying that he has compared the signature on such certificate with the signature of such commissioner deposited in his office, that he has compared the impression of the seal affixed to such certificate with the impression of the seal of such commissioner deposited in his office and that he believes the signature and the impression of the seal upon such certificate to be genuine. Such a certificate may be filed by such commissioner in the office of any county clerk or register in the state upon the payment to such county clerk or register of a fee of one dollar. Upon the filing of such certificate in the office of a county clerk or register in this state, a written instrument acknowledged or proved, an oath administered, or a copy or copy of a certified copy of a patent, record or other document certified, by a commissioner pursuant to this section, shall be entitled to be read in evidence and shall be accepted for filing or recording and filed or recorded, as the case may be, in the office of such county clerk or register, on tender or payment of the lawful fees therefor, without having annexed or subjoined to the certificate of such commissioner contained thereon the authenticating certificate of the secretary of state as required by subdivision four of this section or by subdivision one of section three hundred eleven of the real property law or by any other provision of law.

§ 143. **Fees of such commissioners.** The fees of such commissioners shall be as follows:

1. If appointed for another state, territory or dependency, not to exceed four times the amount allowed by the laws of such state, territory or dependency for like services, and not to exceed in any case one dollar for taking the proof or acknowledgment of a written instrument, or administering an oath;

2. If appointed for Great Britain or Ireland, for administering or certifying an oath, one shilling sterling, and for taking the proof or acknowledgment of a written instrument, or for certifying to the existence or correctness of a copy of a patent, record or document, four shillings sterling;

3. If appointed for France or any other foreign country, for administering and certifying an oath, one franc and twenty-five centimes, and for taking the proof or acknowledgment of a written instrument, or for certifying to the existence or correctness of a copy of a patent, record or document, five francs.

[N.Y. REAL PROP. LAW]

§ 307. **When certificate to state time and place.** When the acknowledgment or proof is taken by a commissioner of deeds appointed pursuant to the laws of this state to take acknowledgments or proofs without this state, whether within or without the United States, the certificate must also state the day on which, and the city or other political subdivision, and the state or country or other place in which, the same was taken.

Editorial comment

Concerning the commissions of commissioners of deeds in other states, territories and foreign countries, see *Appointment*, N.Y. PUB. OFFICERS LAW § 8.

NORTH CAROLINA

The former provisions concerning commissioners of deeds, N.C. GEN. STAT. §§ 3-1 to 3-8, were repealed in 1971.

NORTH DAKOTA

[N.D. CENT. CODE]

§ 44-07-01. **Appointment of commissioner of deeds.** The governor may appoint in each of the states of the United States and the territories thereof one or more commissioners under the seal of this state, to continue in office for the term of six years, who shall have the power to:

1. Administer oaths;

2. Take depositions and affidavits to be used in this state; and

3. Take acknowledgments of any deed or other instrument to be used or recorded in this state.

§ 44-07-02. Seal required—Bond—Terms. Before any commissioner, appointed as provided in section 44-07-01, shall proceed to perform any of the duties of his office, he shall take and subscribe an oath before any clerk of a court of record, or other officer having an official seal and authorized to administer oaths in the state or territory for which such commissioner is appointed, that he will discharge faithfully all the duties of his office. Such oath shall be filed in the office of the secretary of state of this state. A commissioner of deeds shall provide and keep an official seal upon which must be engraved his name and the words, "Commissioner of Deeds for the State of North Dakota," and the name of the state or territory for which he is commissioned, with the date on which his commission expires. He shall file an impression of such seal in the office of the secretary of state of this state and shall furnish a bond to this state by a surety company, in the sum of five hundred dollars, conditioned that he will perform the duties of his office faithfully. Such appointee shall file such bond in the office of the secretary of state of this state, and shall pay into the state treasury the sum of ten dollars.

§ 44-07-03. Commissioner of deeds—Compensation for services. The commissioner of deeds shall be entitled to collect and charge for his services the same fees as are allowed a notary public in the state for which he is appointed.

OHIO

The statutes are vague concerning commissioners of deeds. The acknowledgment of an instrument may be made outside the state before a commissioner appointed by the governor for that purpose. See *Acknowledgments*, OHIO REV. CODE ANN. § 5301.05 (Page). There is no express provision for the appointment of such a commissioner, however.

OKLAHOMA

The statutes are vague concerning commissioners of deeds. The acknowledgment of an instrument taken out of the state but in the United States, United States possessions, or Canada including Newfoundland, may be taken before a commissioner of deeds appointed by the governor of the state for the county, state or territory where the same is taken. See *Acknowledgments*, OKLA. STAT. ANN. tit. 16, § 35. There is no express provision for the appointment of such a commissioner, however.

OREGON

The former provisions concerning commissioners of deeds, ORE. REV. STAT. §§ 194.210 to 194.220, were repealed in 1969.

PENNSYLVANIA

[PA. STAT. ANN.]

Tit. 21, § 971. Appointment of commissioners of deeds in other states. The governor of this commonwealth be and he is hereby authorized to name, appoint and commission one or more commissioners in each, or such of the other states of the United States, or in the District of Columbia, as he may deem expedient; which commissioners shall continue in office during the pleasure of the governor; and shall have authority to take the acknowledgments and proof of the execution of any deed, mortgage or other conveyance of any lands, tenements or hereditaments lying or being in this state; any contract, letter of attorney or any other writing under seal, to be used or recorded in this state, and such acknowledgment or proof taken or made in the manner directed by the laws of this state, and certified by any one of the said commissioners before whom the same shall be taken or made under his seal, which certificate shall be endorsed on or annexed to said deed or instrument aforesaid, shall have the same force and effect, and be as good and available in law for all purposes as if the same had been made or taken before a judge of the supreme court of the United States.

Tit. 21, § 972. Power to administer oaths. Every commissioner appointed by virtue of this act shall have full power and authority to administer an oath or affirmation to any person who shall be willing and desirous to make such oath or affirmation before him, and such affidavit or affirmation made before such commissioner shall and is hereby declared to be as good and effectual to all intents and purposes as if taken by any magistrate resident in this commonwealth, and competent to take the same.

Tit. 21, § 973. Oath of office. Every commissioner appointed as aforesaid, before he shall proceed to perform any duty under and by virtue of this law, shall take and subscribe an oath or affirmation before a justice of the peace, in the city or county in which such commissioner shall reside, well and faithfully to execute and perform all the duties of such commissioner under and by virtue of the laws of Pennsylvania, which oath or affirmation shall be filed in the office of the secretary of this commonwealth.

Tit. 21, § 975. Commissions to continue in force for five years. All commissions hereafter issued for the appointment of commissioners to take acknowledgment and proof of deeds and instruments under seal, depositions and other papers, under and by virtue of the act and its supplements, shall continue in force for five years from their date, and no longer, and may be revoked at any time by the governor; and shall each be subject to a tax of five dollars, which shall be paid to the secretary of the commonwealth at the time of issuing the commission, and accounted for as provided by law in the case of other fees.

Tit. 21, § 976. Appointment in the territories. The provisions of the several sections of [this] act ° ° ° be and they are hereby extended so as to authorize the governor of this commonwealth to appoint and commission in like manner and with like powers one or more commissioners in each of the territories of the United States.

Tit. 21, § 977. Fees of commissioners of deeds in other states. The commissioners appointed or hereafter to be appointed by the governor of this commonwealth, under the authority of [this] act ° ° ° be hereby authorized to demand as their compensation for taking each acknowledgment the fee of one dollar, and no more.

Tit. 21, § 978. Commissioners in foreign countries. The governor shall have power to appoint one or more commissioners in any foreign country, who shall continue in office during the pleasure of the governor, and shall have the authority to take the acknowledgment and proof of the execution of any deed or other conveyance or lease of any lands lying in this state, or of any contract, letters of attorney, or of any other writing, under seal or not, to be used and recorded in this state.

Tit. 21, § 979. Oath of office. Every such commissioner, before performing any duty, or exercising any power in virtue of his appointment, shall take and subscribe an oath or affirmation before a judge or clerk of one of the courts of record of the state, kingdom, or country in which said commissioner shall reside, well and faithfully to execute and perform all the duties of such commissioner, under and by virtue of the laws of the state of Pennsylvania, which oath, and a description of his seal of office, together with his signature thereto, shall be filed in the office of the secretary of this state.

Tit. 21, § 980. Fees. The fees for all such services shall be the same as for similar services rendered by commissioners of this state in other states of the Union, the same being reckoned in the money of the United States.

Tit. 21, § 981. Women as commissioners. From and after the passage of this act, women, being twenty-one years of age, shall be eligible to the office of commissioner to take the acknowledgment of deeds and instruments of writing under seal; and the governor of this commonwealth is hereby authorized to appoint and commission them as commissioners, in each or any of the states of the United States, or in the District of Columbia, as he may deem it expedient.

Tit. 21, § 982. New commission in case of marriage. Whenever any female commissioner shall marry, she shall, before the performance of any official act, return her commission to the governor, stating the fact of her marriage, and giving her married name; and the governor shall thereupon issue to her a new commission, conforming to the change of name and covering the term for which she was originally commissioned, without requiring any payment to the commonwealth other than that originally made; and upon issuing said new commission, the woman thus commissioned shall give a new bond, according to the change of name, with security as required by existing laws.

PUERTO RICO

[P.R. LAWS ANN.]

Tit. 4, § 951. Appointment in states and territories of United States and foreign countries. The Governor may appoint in each of the states and territories of the United States, or in any foreign state, one or more Commissioners, who shall hold their offices for four years from the date of their respective appointments unless sooner removed by the Governor.

Tit. 4, § 952. Oath of office; seal; commission. Every such Commissioner shall, within three months from his appointment, take and subscribe an oath or affirmation before a justice of the peace or other magistrate of the city or county where he resides or before a clerk of a court of record within the state or territory where he resides, faithfully to discharge the duties of his office, and shall cause to be prepared an official seal upon which shall appear his name, the words "Commissioner for Puerto Rico" and the name of the state or territory and city or county in which he resides. An impression of such seal, together with the Commissioner's oath of office and signature, shall forthwith be transmitted to and filed in the office of the Secretary of State of Puerto Rico, whereupon his commission shall be forwarded to him.

Tit. 4, § 953. Administration of oaths, depositions, affidavits, etc. Said Commissioner may, in the state or territory for which he is appointed, administer and certify oaths and take depositions, affidavits, and acknowledgments of deeds and other instruments, to be used or recorded in Puerto Rico, and the proof of such deeds when the grantor refuses to acknowledge the same; and all oaths, depositions, affidavits, acknowledgments, and proofs so administered or taken and certified by such Commissioner under his official seal, shall be as effectual as if administered or taken and certified by the proper officers of Puerto Rico and shall be received as evidence in all the courts of justice of Puerto Rico.

Tit. 4, § 954. Fees. Commissioners appointed under section 951 of this title shall be allowed the following fees:

For administering oaths and certifying the same under their official seal, one dollar for each; for taking acknowledgments of deeds and other instruments, and certifying the same under their official seals, one dollar for each; for each written page contained in any deposition or affidavit taken by them, fifty cents; for administering the oath or affirmation to each deponent, one dollar; for authenticating, sealing up, and directing each deposition, one dollar; for services not hereinbefore specified, the same fees as are followed to notaries public in the Commonwealth of Puerto Rico; but the court to which a deposition is returnable shall order further allowance therefor if it appears proper to do so.

RHODE ISLAND

[R.I. GEN. LAWS ANN.]

§ 42-31-1. **Appointment of commissioners.** The governor may appoint, in any foreign country and in any state of the United States and in any territory of the United States and in the District of Columbia, one (1) or more commissioners, under the seal of the state, to continue in office for the period of five (5) years.

§ 42-31-2. **Oath of office.** Before any commissioner shall perform any duty of his office, he shall take and subscribe an oath before some officer authorized to administer oaths in the state, country or territory, or District of Columbia, for which such commissioner is appointed, that he will faithfully discharge all the duties of his office; a certificate of which shall be filed in the office of the secretary of state of this state within six (6) months after the taking of the same.

§ 42-31-3. **Powers of commissioners.** Such commissioners may administer oaths and take depositions and affidavits to be used in this state; and may also take the acknowledgment of any deed or other instrument to be used or recorded in this state.

§ 42-31-4. **Effectiveness of acts of commissioners.** All oaths administered by such commissioners, and all affidavits and depositions taken by them, and all acknowledgments aforesaid certified by them, shall be as effectual in law, to all intents and purposes, as if certified by any judge, justice of the peace or notary public, within this state.

Editorial comment

Concerning the removal of, among others, commissioners of deeds, see *Appointment*, R.I. GEN. LAWS ANN. § 42-30-10.

SOUTH CAROLINA

The former provisions concerning commissioners of deeds, S.C. CODE ANN. §§ 49-51 to 49-55, were repealed in 1972.

SOUTH DAKOTA

[S.D. COMPILED LAWS ANN.]

§ 18-2-1. **Appointment by Governor—Tenure—Authority to take acknowledgment and proof.** The Governor shall have power to appoint one or more commissioners in any state of the United States or any of the territories belonging to the United States, who shall continue in office during the pleasure of the Governor and shall have authority to take acknowledgment and proof of the execution of any deed or other conveyance, or lease of any lands lying in this state, and of any contract, letter of attorney, or any other writing under seal or not, to be used or recorded in this state.

§ 18-2-2.   Official seal of commissioner—Contents.   Each commissioner appointed pursuant to § 18-2-1 shall have an official seal on which shall be engraved the words "Commissioner of South Dakota," with his surname at length and at least the initials of his Christian name; also the name of the state or territory in which he has been commissioned to act, which seal must be so engraved as to make a clear impression.

§ 18-2-3.   Oath of office—Filing of oath and seal with secretary of state.   Every such commissioner, before performing any duty or exercising any power by virtue of his appointment, must take and subscribe an oath or affirmation before some judge or clerk of some court of record having a seal of the state or territory in which such commissioner shall reside, well and faithfully to execute and perform all the duties of such commissioner under and by virtue of the laws of the state of South Dakota, with a description and impression of his seal of office to be filed in the office of the secretary of this state.

§ 18-2-4.   Administration of oaths by commissioner—Depositions—Validity.   Every commissioner appointed as mentioned in § 18-2-1 shall have power to administer any oath which may be lawfully required in this state to any person willing to take the same, and to take and duly certify all depositions to be used in any of the courts of this state in conformity to the laws thereof, either on interrogatories proposed under a commission from any court in this state or by consent of the parties, or on legal notice given to the opposite party; and all such acts shall be as valid as if done and certified to according to law by a proper officer in this state.

§ 18-2-5.   Force and effect of acknowledgments and proofs taken.   All acknowledgments and proofs as provided in § 18-2-1, taken according to the laws of this state and certified to by such commissioner under his seal of office and annexed to or endorsed upon such instrument, shall have the same force and effect as if the same had been taken before any officer authorized to perform such acts in this state.

TENNESSEE

The former provision concerning commissioners of deeds, TENN. CODE ANN. § 8-1701, was repealed in 1963.

TEXAS

[TEX. REV. CIV. STAT. ANN.]

Art. 1270. Appointment. The Governor is authorized to biennially appoint and commission one or more persons in each or any of the other states of the United States, the District of Columbia, and in each or any of the territories of the United States, and in each or any foreign country, upon the recommendation of the executive authority of said state, District of Columbia or territory or foreign country to serve as commissioner of deeds. Such commissioner shall hold office for two years.

Art. 1271. Oath. Such commissioner, before he shall proceed to perform any duty under and by virtue of this title, shall take and subscribe an oath or affirmation, before the clerk of any court of record in the city, county or country in which such commissioner may reside, well and faithfully to execute and perform all the duties of such commissioner under the laws of this State; which oath or affirmation, certified to by the clerk under his hand and seal of office, shall be filed in the office of the Secretary of State in this State.

Art. 1272. Seal. Every such commissioner shall provide for himself a seal with a star of five points, in the center, and the words, "Commissioner of the State of Texas," engraved thereon, which seal shall be used to certify all the official acts of such commissioner; and without the impress of said seal upon any instrument, or to certify any act of such commissioner, said act shall have no validity in this State.

Art. 1273. Authority. The commissioner of deeds shall have the same authority as to taking acknowledgments and proofs of written instruments, administering oaths, and taking depositions to be used or recorded in this State, as is conferred by law upon a notary public of this State.

UTAH

[UTAH CODE ANN.]

§ 21-4-2. Fees of commissioners of deeds. Every commissioner of deeds may collect for his own use the same fees as those provided for a notary public.

Accord, § 46-2-7. Concerning the fees provided for a notary public, see *Fees Chargeable,* UTAH CODE ANN. § 21-4-1.

§ 46-2-1. Appointment—Term—Removal. The governor may appoint and commission in each state and territory of the United States, except this state, and in any foreign country, one or more commissioners of deeds, to hold office for the term of four years from and after the date of their commissions, but the governor may remove from office any commissioner during the term for which he was appointed. The commission shall be filed with, and be recorded in the office of, the secretary of state.

§ 46-2-2. **Powers.** Every commissioner of deeds has power within the state or country for which he was appointed:

(1) To administer and certify oaths.

(2) To take and certify depositions and affidavits.

(3) To take and certify the acknowledgment or proof of powers of attorney, mortgages, transfers, grants, deeds or other instruments for record.

(4) To provide and keep an official seal, upon which must be engraved his name, the words "Commissioner of Deeds for the State of Utah," and the name of the state or country for which he is commissioned.

(5) To authenticate with his official seal all of his official acts.

§ 46-2-3. **Affix to signature place of residence and date commission expires.** To all acknowledgments, oaths, affirmations and instruments of every kind taken and certified by a commissioner of deeds he shall affix to his signature his official title and his place of residence and the date on which his commission expires.

§ 46-2-4. **Force and effect of official acts.** All oaths administered, depositions and affidavits taken, and all acknowledgments and proofs certified, by commissioners of deeds have the same force and effect, to all intents and purposes, as if done and certified in this state by any officer authorized by law to perform such acts.

§ 46-2-5. **Official oath.** Before a commissioner of deeds can perform any of the duties of his office, he shall take and subscribe an oath that he will faithfully perform his duties, which oath shall be taken and subscribed before some judge or clerk of a court of record in the state, territory or foreign country in which the commissioner is to exercise his functions, and shall be certified under the hand of the person taking it and the seal of his court.

§ 46-2-6. **Official oaths and impressions of seals to be filed with secretary of state.** The official oaths of commissioners of deeds and impressions of their official seals must be filed in the office of the secretary of state within six months after they are taken and adopted.

§ 46-2-8. **Copy of laws to accompany commission.** The secretary of state must transmit with the commission to the appointee a certified copy of this chapter, and of the laws prescribing the fees of notaries public.

§ 46-2-9. **Commissioners of other states and countries residing here.** Commissioners of deeds for other states or countries residing in this state shall file with the secretary of state a certified copy of their commissions, together with a statement of their places of residence.

VERMONT

[VT. STAT. ANN.]

Tit. 4, § 851. Appointment and powers of commissioners. The governor may appoint commissioners in other states and in foreign countries, who shall hold office for five years unless sooner removed by him. They may take depositions, affidavits and testimony to be used in any proceedings in [a county court held by the presiding judge alone, sitting without a jury], administer oaths and take the acknowledgment of deeds and other instruments to be used or recorded in this state, and their acts therein shall have the same force as though performed by a justice or master in chancery in this state.

Tit. 4, § 852. Oath and bond. Before entering upon his duties, each commissioner shall take and subscribe an oath of office before a magistrate of his locality and execute a bond to this state with sureties to the satisfaction of the governor in the sum of $500.00, conditioned for the faithful performance of his duties. The bond shall be kept in the office of the secretary of state, and an action may be maintained against any or all signers thereof, in the name of the state, for the benefit of a person injured by the act or neglect of the commissioner.

VIRGIN ISLANDS

There are no provisions for commissioners of deeds under the laws of the Virgin Islands.

VIRGINIA

[VA. CODE ANN.]

§ 47-5. Appointment; lists of commissioners to be published. The Governor shall appoint out of this State, and within the United States, or within Puerto Rico, Hawaii, or any other territory subject to the jurisdiction of the United States, or over which the United States exercises authority, so many commissioners for such states, countries, and districts as to him shall seem proper, who shall hold their office, at the pleasure of the Governor, for the term of two years, and he shall, within thirty days after the beginning of each regular session of the General Assembly, communicate to it the names and residence of the persons holding office under such appointment. Lists of such commissioners shall be published with the acts and resolutions of the General Assembly.

§ 47-6. Fee of Secretary of Commonwealth. The Secretary of the Commonwealth shall be entitled in each case to receive from the person appointed commissioner as aforesaid a fee of five dollars for making out and transmitting his commission to him.

Accord, § 14.1-103. See *Appointment*, VA. CODE ANN. § 14.1-103.

§ 47-7. Certificate of acknowledgment. A certificate of acknowledgment before any commissioner appointed under this chapter shall be under the form prescribed by §§ 55-113 and 55-120,° and shall have like effect for all purposes as a certificate of acknowledgment before and by a notary public.

(°) See *Acknowledgments*, VA. CODE ANN. §§ 55-113 *et seq.*

§ 49-2. Form of oath for out-of-state commissioners. Where a person residing in another state is appointed a commissioner by the Governor, he shall only be required to take and subscribe the following oath or affirmation:

"I, ———, swear (or affirm) that I will faithfully perform the duties of commissioner to the best of my ability. So help me God."

§ 49-3. Who may administer oaths to officers. ° ° ° A justice of the peace of another state may administer the oaths to be taken by a commissioner or other person residing therein.

> *Editorial comment*
> The deposition of a witness, whether a party to the suit or not, who resides out of the state or is out of it in the service thereof or of the United States, may be taken before, among others, any commissioner appointed by the Governor. Any person before whom a deposition may be so taken may administer an oath to the witness and take and certify the deposition with his official seal. See *Depositions*, VA. CODE ANN. § 8-305. Similarly, any oath or affidavit required by law, which is not of such nature that it must be made in court, may be administered by, or made before, among others, a commissioner appointed by the Governor. See *Authority and Duties*, VA. CODE ANN. § 49-4.
> An officer returning affidavits or depositions of witnesses must state at the foot thereof the fees therefor, to whom charged and, if paid, by whom. See *Fees Chargeable*, VA. CODE ANN. § 14.1-98.

WASHINGTON

[WASH. REV. CODE ANN.]

§ 42.28.120. Commissioners of deeds. The governor may appoint in each of the United States and the territories thereof, one or more commissioners, under the seal of this state, to continue in office for the term of four years, who shall have power to administer oaths, and to take depositions and affidavits, to be used in this state, and also to take the acknowledgment of any deed or other instrument to be used or recorded in the state.

§ 42.28.130. **Oath, seal, fee.** Before any commissioner appointed as aforesaid shall proceed to perform any of the duties of his office he shall take and subscribe an oath before any clerk of a court of record, or other officer having an official seal authorized to administer oaths in the state or territory for which such commissioner is appointed, that he will faithfully discharge all duties of his office, a certificate of which shall be filed in the office of the secretary of state, and shall provide and keep an official seal, upon which must be engraved his name and the words "Commissioner of Deeds for the State of Washington", and the name of the state or territory for which he is commissioned, with the date at which his commission expires, and shall pay into the state treasury the sum of five dollars for the special state library fund [state general fund].

WEST VIRGINIA

[W. VA. CODE ANN.]

§ 29-4-12. **Commissioners out of State; qualifications; fee.** The governor, if he deems it proper, may appoint any persons residing within or without this State and within the United States, its territories or possessions as commissioners to acknowledge signatures performed in or out of State by persons residing in or out of the State of West Virginia, covering deeds, leases and other writings pertaining to West Virginia property for recordation in the State of West Virginia.

Such commissioners shall hold office for ten years, unless sooner removed by the governor. Any commissioner in office upon the effective date of this act [June 3, 1974] shall continue therein until his term expires or until sooner removed in the manner prescribed by law.

Before performing any duties as such, the commissioner shall enter into a bond in the penalty sum of one thousand dollars with corporate surety to be approved by the secretary of state and filed in his office.

A fee of one hundred dollars for such commission issued shall be paid to the secretary of state.

Note: An additional $5.00 is payable to the secretary of state for services rendered in issuing a commission to a commissioner in another state. See *Appointment,* W. VA. CODE ANN. § 59-1-2.

§ 29-4-14. **Power of such commissioner to take acknowledgments.** Such commissioners, under regulations prescribed by law, may take, within or any place out of the State of West Virginia, the acknowledgments of deeds and other writings to be admitted to record in the State of West Virginia, but each such acknowledgment shall reflect where the acknowledgment was taken, as, for example, the State and county, the territory, etc.

§ 29-4-15.   Seal of such commissioner.   Every such commissioner shall provide an official seal, on which shall be inscribed his name and residence, and the words "commissioner for West Virginia." An impression of such seal, together with his signature, shall be forthwith transmitted to and filed in the office of the secretary of state.

§ 29-4-16.   Authentication of such commissioner's certificate. Every certificate of such commissioner shall be authenticated by his signature and official seal.

WISCONSIN

[WIS. STAT. ANN.]

§ 137.02.   Commissioners of deeds.   (1)   The governor shall have power to appoint one or more commissioners in any of the United States, or of the territories belonging to the United States and in foreign countries, who shall hold his office for the term of four years unless sooner removed. Every such commissioner shall take the official oath before a judge or clerk of one of the courts of record of the state or territory or country in which he shall reside, and file the same, with an impression of his seal of office and a statement of his post-office address, in the office of the secretary of state, and shall at the same time pay into the treasury the sum of five dollars; and thereupon his commission shall issue.

(2)   Such commissioner shall have authority to take the acknowledgment and proof of the execution of deeds, conveyances and leases of any lands lying in this state, or written instruments relating thereto, or of any contract or any other writing, sealed or unsealed, to be used or recorded in this state; to administer oaths required to be used in this state; to take and certify depositions to be used in the courts of this state, either under a commission, by consent of parties or on notice to the opposite party; and all such acts done pursuant to the laws of this state and certified under his hand and seal of office shall be as valid as if done by a proper officer of this state.

WYOMING

[WYO. STAT. ANN.]

§ 32-16.   Appointment; term; number; powers generally.   The governor may appoint in each of the United States and territories and in the District of Columbia, one or more commissioners to continue in office during the pleasure of the governor for the time being, and every such commissioner shall have the power to administer oaths, and take depositions and affidavits to be used in this state, and also to take acknowledgments of deeds, powers of attorney, or other instruments to be recorded in this state.

§ 32-17. Acts to be legally effectual. All oaths administered by the said commissioners, all affidavits and depositions taken by them, and all acknowledgments aforesaid, certified by them, shall be effectual in law, to all intents and purposes, as if done and certified by any other authorized officer within this state.

§ 32-18. Official seal and oath. Before any commissioner appointed as aforesaid, shall proceed to perform any of the duties of his office, he shall provide an official seal and take and subscribe an oath before any officer authorized to administer oaths, and having an official seal in the state or territory for which said commissioner was appointed, that he will faithfully discharge all the duties of his office, which oath together with his autograph and an impression of his seal of office he shall immediately file in the office of the secretary of state.

§ 32-19. Notice to county clerk of appointment, etc.—Duty of secretary of state. When any person has been appointed, and shall have qualified as commissioner under the provisions of this act [§§ 32-16 to 32-20], it shall be the duty of the secretary of state, within thirty days after he has received notice that such commissioner has so qualified, to forward to the county clerk of each county in this state a written notice which shall contain the name of the commissioner, the name of the state, territory or district for which such commissioner was appointed and qualified, the date of his appointment, the date on which he qualified and the date of the expiration of his term of office; and when any commissioner shall resign, or his appointment be revoked by the governor, the secretary shall, within thirty days thereafter, notify the county clerk of each county of such resignation or revocation.

§ 32-20. Same—Duty of clerk upon receipt of notice. The different county clerks in the state shall, on receipt of the notice above provided for, file the same and keep a list thereof, which list shall show the name of each person, who has been appointed and qualified as a commissioner, the name of the state, territory or district for which such person was appointed and qualified, the date of his appointment, the date on which he qualified, the date of the expiration of his term of office, and in case of resignation or the revocation of his appointment, it shall also be entered on said list.

APPENDIX:

LEGAL HOLIDAYS;
GLOSSARY OF DEFINITIONS

LEGAL HOLIDAYS

Legal holidays are creatures of statute. As such, they have precisely the meaning given them by the statute, no more and no less. At common law, in the absence of a specific statute, holidays have no legal significance. Some statutes, as is seen in the statutes quoted below, make specific provision for the delegation of authority to the Governor to declare other holidays, in addition to those expressly created by the statute. It is therefore important that a person interested in whether a particular day is a holiday and if so, what its significance is, should examine not only the chart of legal holidays which is provided below,[1] but must read the precise words of the various applicable state, federal, and other statutes which create the holidays and which are quoted below.[2] In addition to legal holidays, a large number of states, the federal government, and other jurisdictions, have days of special observance or commemoration which are not legal holidays, but which have more or less special significance within the jurisdiction. In some instances, a particular day will be a legal holiday in one state and only a day of special observance or commemoration in another state. A substantial portion of such statutes are also quoted below, so that

---

[1] See *Chart of Legal Holidays,* pages 767-780..

[2] See *Legal Holidays: State and Other Statutes,* page 781.

the meaning of such days which may be observed locally may be clarified.

This information concerning various state and other holidays is important to the notary public in connection with his duties under the Uniform Commercial Code (U.C.C.). In the context of commercial paper, there is superimposed on the various state, federal, and other statutes quoted below, the provisions concerning legal holidays in U.C.C. § 3-503(3), which is uniformly in effect in each of the states, the District of Columbia, and the Virgin Islands.   Under § 3-503(3), where any presentment is due on a day which is not a full business day for either the person making the presentment or the party to pay or accept, e.g., a holiday, presentment is due on the next following day which is a full business day for both parties.   This provision in the U.C.C. replaces the former analogous Uniform Negotiable Instruments Law §§ 85 and 146.   U.C.C. § 3-503(3) is intended to make allowance for the increasing practice of closing banks or businesses on Saturday or other days of the week.   It is not intended to mean that any drawee or obligor can avoid dishonor of instruments by extended closing.

Holiday	Alabama	Alaska	Arizona	Arkansas
Monday, if Holiday falls on Sunday	x	x		
Christmas Day (Dec. 25)	x	x	x	x
Thanksgiving Day	x	x	x	x
Veterans' Day (Nov. 11)		x	x	x
Columbus Day (Oct. 12)			x	
Labor Day (1st Monday in Sept.)	x	x	x	x
Independence Day (July 4)	x	x	x	x
Jefferson Davis' Birthday (June 3)				
Last Monday in May		x	x	x
National Memorial Day (May 30)				
Confederate Memorial Day (May 10)				
Mardi Gras (Shrove Tuesday)	x			
Thomas Jefferson's Birthday (Apr. 13)	x			
Third Monday in Feb. (Presidents' Day)	x	x	x	x
Washington's Birthday (Feb. 22)				
Lincoln's Birthday (Feb. 12)		x	x	
Robert E. Lee's Birthday (Jan. 19)				x
New Year's Day (Jan. 1)	x	x	x	x
Sunday	x	x	x	

Other Legal Holidays and Remarks

Alabama: Robert E. Lee's birthday observed third Monday in January; Confederate Memorial day observed fourth Monday in April; Jefferson Davis' birthday observed first Monday in June; Columbus day and Fraternal day observed second Monday in October; Veteran's day observed fourth Monday in October.

Alaska: Seward's day observed last Monday in March; Alaska day observed October 18.

Arizona: Admission day, February 14; Mother's day, second Sunday in May; Father's day, third Sunday in June; General election day.

Arkansas: End of World War II, August 14 (§ 69-104). See also Memorial days which are not legal holidays.

Other Legal Holidays and Remarks	Admission day, September 9; Good Friday, 12 noon to 3 p.m.; State wide election day; Columbus day observed second Monday in October.	Columbus day observed second Monday in October; general election day; Colorado day, first Monday in August; Veteran's day observed fourth Monday in October.	Martin Luther King day, second Sunday in January; Columbus day observed second Monday in October.
Monday, if Holiday falls on Sunday	x	x	
Christmas Day (Dec. 25)	x	x	x
Thanksgiving Day	x	x	x
Veterans' Day (Nov. 11)	x		x
Columbus Day (Oct. 12)			x
Labor Day (1st Monday in Sept.)	x	x	x
Independence Day (July 4)	x	x	x
Jefferson Davis' Birthday (June 3)			
Last Monday in May	x	x	x
National Memorial Day (May 30)			
Confederate Memorial Day (May 10)			
Mardi Gras (Shrove Tuesday)			
Thomas Jefferson's Birthday (Apr. 13)			
Third Monday in Feb. (Presidents' Day)	x	x	x
Washington's Birthday (Feb. 22)			
Lincoln's Birthday (Feb. 12)	x	x	x
Robert E. Lee's Birthday (Jan. 19)			
New Year's Day (Jan. 1)	x	x	x
Sunday	x		
	California	Colorado	Connecticut

State	1	2	3	4	5	6	7	8	9	10	11	12	13	14	15	Notes
Delaware	x	x	x			x	x		x			x			x	Good Friday; Saturdays; Biennial general election day; Lincoln's birthday observed first Monday in February; Columbus day observed second Monday in October; Veteran's day observed fourth Monday in October. See also provision concerning Sussex county (tit. 1, § 501).
District of Columbia	x	x	x			x	x		x	x			x		x	Saturday after 12:00 noon; Presidential inauguration day every fourth year. See also Provisions concerning financial institutions.
Florida	x	x	x	x		x	x	x	x		x	x		x	x	Good Friday; General election day; Confederate Memorial day observed April 26; Columbus day and Farmer's day observed second Monday in October.
Georgia		x	x	x	x	x	x	x	x			x		x	x	Columbus day observed second Monday in October. See also special days for public schools.
Hawaii	x	x	x	x		x	x		x			x			x	Kuhio day; Good Friday; Kamehameha day; Admission day; Discoverers' Day observed second Monday in October; General election days. See also Baha'i New Year's Day.
Idaho		x	x	x		x	x		x			x			x	Columbus day observed second Monday in October.

Other Legal Holidays and Remarks	Illinois — Columbus day observed second Monday in October; General election day for House of Representatives; Saturday after 12:00 noon; day selected by a bank; Good Friday; Martin Luther King, Jr.'s, birthday observed January 15.	Indiana — Good Friday; Columbus day observed second Monday in October; Election day.	Iowa — See also Mother's day, Independence Sunday, Columbus day, Herbert Hoover day, Youth Honor day.	Kansas — Columbus day observed second Monday in October; Veterans' day observed fourth Monday in October. See also Family day.
Monday, if Holiday falls on Sunday		x		
Christmas Day (Dec. 25)	x	x	x	x
Thanksgiving Day	x	x	x	x
Veterans' Day (Nov. 11)	x	x	x	
Columbus Day (Oct. 12)				
Labor Day (1st Monday in Sept.)	x	x	x	x
Independence Day (July 4)	x	x	x	x
Jefferson Davis' Birthday (June 3)				
Last Monday in May		x	x	x
National Memorial Day (May 30)	x			
Confederate Memorial Day (May 10)				
Mardi Gras (Shrove Tuesday)				
Thomas Jefferson's Birthday (Apr. 13)				
Third Monday in Feb. (Presidents' Day)	x	x	x	x
Washington's Birthday (Feb. 22)				
Lincoln's Birthday (Feb. 12)	x	x	x	x
Robert E. Lee's Birthday (Jan. 19)				
New Year's Day (Jan. 1)	x	x	x	x
Sunday		x		

State														Notes
Kentucky	x	x	x	x	x	x	x		x		x	x	x	Franklin D. Roosevelt day, January 30; Confederate Memorial day and Jefferson Davis day combined on June 3; Columbus day observed second Monday in October; the Tuesday after the first Monday in November in presidential election years.
Louisiana	x	x	x	x	x	x	x		x			x	x	Battle of New Orleans, January 8; Good Friday; Huey P. Long day, August 30; Columbus day observed second Monday in October; All Saints day, November 1; Inauguration day in Baton Rouge; in certain parishes Saturdays and Wednesdays. See also Mardis Gras (§ 1:55 A(3)), second Friday of Holiday in Dixie (§ 1:55 A(5)).
Maine	x		x	x	x	x			x				x	Presidential election day; Patriot's day third Monday in April; state wide primary election day; state election day; special state wide election day; Columbus day observed second Monday in October.
Maryland	x		x	x	x	x	x		x		x	x	x	Maryland day March 25; Good Friday; Defenders' day September 12; Columbus day observed second Monday in October; Veterans' day observed fourth Monday in October; General and congressional election days throughout the state. See also Martin Luther King day; John Hanson's birthday (art. 13, § 9).

	Other Legal Holidays and Remarks			
	Massachusetts	Michigan	Minnesota	Mississippi
	Third Monday in April; second and fourth Mondays in October. In Suffolk county March 17 and June 17.	Columbus day observed second Monday in October; Saturday after 12 noon; national and state general election days. See also Casimir Pulaski day.	Columbus day observed second Monday in October; Friday if certain holidays fall on Saturday.	Robert E. Lee's birthday observed third Monday in January; Confederate Memorial day observed last Monday in April; Jefferson Davis' birthday observed first Monday in June.
Monday, if Holiday falls on Sunday	×	×	×	×
Christmas Day (Dec. 25)	×	×	×	×
Thanksgiving Day	×	×	×	×
Veterans' Day (Nov. 11)		×	×	×
Columbus Day (Oct. 12)				
Labor Day (1st Monday in Sept.)	×	×	×	×
Independence Day (July 4)	×	×	×	×
Jefferson Davis' Birthday (June 3)				
Last Monday in May	×	×	×	
National Memorial Day (May 30)			,	
Confederate Memorial Day (May 10)				
Mardi Gras (Shrove Tuesday)				
Thomas Jefferson's Birthday (Apr. 13)				
Third Monday in Feb. (Presidents' Day)	×	×	×	×
Washington's Birthday (Feb. 22)				
Lincoln's Birthday (Feb. 12)		×		
Robert E. Lee's Birthday (Jan. 19)				
New Year's Day (Jan. 1)	×	×	×	×
Sunday				

State														Notes
Missouri	x	x	x	x	x	x	x		x	x			x	x	May 8; Columbus day observed second Monday in October; general primary and general state election days. See also Jefferson day, Missouri day, Truman day and Law day.
Montana		x	x	x	x	x	x		x	x			x	x	Columbus day observed second Monday in October; state general election day. See also special provisions concerning banks (§ 19-107) and Good Roads day (§ 32-4401).
Nebraska		x	x	x	x	x	x		x	x			x	x	Arbor day, April 22; Columbus day observed second Monday in October; Veterans day observed fourth Monday in October. See also special provisions concerning banks (§§ 62-301, 62-301.01) and Veterans day.
Nevada		x		x	x	x	x		x	x			x	x	Veterans' day observed fourth Monday in October; Nevada day, October 31. If certain holidays occur on Saturday, the preceding Friday is observed. See also Mother's day, Law day, Nevada All-Indian Stampede days, and Nevada Mineral Industry week.
New Hampshire		x		x	x	x	x	x	x	x			x	x	Fast day, fourth Monday in April; biennial election day; Columbus day observed second Monday in October. See also provisions concerning banking organizations. (§ 288:3).

	New Jersey	New Mexico	New York
Other Legal Holidays and Remarks	Good Friday; Columbus day observed second Monday in October; Veteran's day observed fourth Monday in October; general election day; Saturday. See also Mother's day, Father's day, Crispus Attucks day, American Flag Week, and New Jersey day.	Columbus day observed second Monday in October; Armistice day & Veterans' day observed fourth Monday in October. See also Arbor day, Onate day, and Bataan day.	Columbus day observed second Monday in October; Veterans' day observed fourth Monday in October; general election day; Saturday's after noon.
Monday, if Holiday falls on Sunday	✕	✕	✕
Christmas Day (Dec. 25)	✕	✕	✕
Thanksgiving Day	✕	✕	✕
Veterans' Day (Nov. 11)			
Columbus Day (Oct. 12)			
Labor Day (1st Monday in Sept.)	✕	✕	✕
Independence Day (July 4)	✕	✕	✕
Jefferson Davis' Birthday (June 3)			
Last Monday in May	✕	✕	✕
National Memorial Day (May 30)			
Confederate Memorial Day (May 10)			
Mardi Gras (Shrove Tuesday)			
Thomas Jefferson's Birthday (Apr. 13)			
Third Monday in Feb. (Presidents' Day)	✕	✕	✕
Washington's Birthday (Feb. 22)			
Lincoln's Birthday (Feb. 12)	✕	✕	✕
Robert E. Lee's Birthday (Jan. 19)			
New Year's Day (Jan. 1)	✕	✕	✕
Sunday			

State														Notes
North Carolina	x	x	x	x	x	x	x	x	x		x		x	Anniversary of signing Halifax Resolves, April 12; anniversary of Mecklenburg Declaration of Independence, May 20; Easter Monday; Columbus day observed second Monday in October; general election day. See also Arbor week.
North Dakota	x	x	x	x	x	x			x		x		x	Good Friday; state wide election day; for bank purposes, Friday if holiday falls on Saturday.
Ohio	x	x	x	x	x	x			x		x		x	Columbus day observed second Monday in October; Saturdays after noon. See also provisions concerning schools (§ 5.23) and financial institutions (§ 5.40); Martin Luther King day observed third Monday in January.
Oklahoma	x	x	x	x	x	x			x		x		x	Columbus day observed second Monday in October. See also additional holidays (tit. 25, § 82.2).
Oregon	x	x	x	x	x	x			x		x		x	Lincoln's birthday observed first Monday in February. See also days of commemoration (§ 187.025).
Pennsylvania	x	x	x	x	x				x	x	x			Good Friday; Memorial day observed last Monday in May; Flag day, June 14; Columbus day observed second Monday in October; election day; Saturdays after noon. See also Arbor day and William Penn's birthday.

	Puerto Rico
Other Legal Holidays and Remarks	Discovery day observed second Monday in October; Armistice day observed fourth Monday in October; March 22; Good Friday; Island wide election day; January 6; January 11, birthday of Eugenio Maria de Hostos; second Sunday in April, Antonio R. Barcelo day; April 16, Jose de Diego day; July 17, Munoz Rivera day; July 25, Day of the Constitution; July 27, Dr. Jose Celso Barbosa's birthday; November 19, discovery of Puerto Rico; Labor day also consecrated to memory of Santiago Iglesias Pantin. See also Ernesto Ramos Antonini day, Ramon Emeterio Betances day, and Police day.
Monday, if Holiday falls on Sunday	×
Christmas Day (Dec. 25)	×
Thanksgiving Day	×
Veterans' Day (Nov. 11)	
Columbus Day (Oct. 12)	
Labor Day (1st Monday in Sept.)	×
Independence Day (July 4)	×
Jefferson Davis' Birthday (June 3)	
Last Monday in May	×
National Memorial Day (May 30)	
Confederate Memorial Day (May 10)	
Mardi Gras (Shrove Tuesday)	
Thomas Jefferson's Birthday (Apr. 13)	
Third Monday in Feb. (Presidents' Day)	×
Washington's Birthday (Feb. 22)	
Lincoln's Birthday (Feb. 12)	
Robert E. Lee's Birthday (Jan. 19)	
New Year's Day (Jan. 1)	×
Sunday	×

State	Notes
Rhode Island	May 4, Rhode Island Independence day; second Monday in August, Victory day; Columbus day observed second Monday in October; Armistice day observed fourth Monday in October; State election day, Tuesday next after first Monday in November. See also various other days of special observance.
South Carolina	General election days; December 26; Thursday of state fair week in Berkeley, Dorchester and Florence counties. See also provisions for additional holidays for banks and cash depositories (§ 64-154) and savings and loan and building and loan associations (§ 64-163).
South Dakota	Second Monday in October, Pioneers' day; preceding Friday if holiday occurs on Saturday.
Tennessee	Good Friday; preceding Friday if holiday occurs on Saturday; state wide election day, Saturday after noon; Columbus day observed second Monday in October. See also special observance days.
Texas	March 2; April 21; August 27, Lyndon B. Johnson's birthday; second Monday in October; fourth Monday in October; state wide election day. See also Texas Pioneers' day, Stephen F. Austin day, General Pulaski Memorial day.

	Utah	Vermont	Virgin Islands
Other Legal Holidays and Remarks	Arbor day, last Friday in April; Pioneer day, July 24; Columbus day observed second Monday in October; Veterans' day observed fourth Monday in October.	Town meeting day, first Tuesday in March; Bennington battle day, August 16; Columbus day observed second Monday in October; Friday if holiday occurs on succeeding Saturday. See also Arbor Day.	Three King's day, January 6; Martin Luther King's birthday, January 15; Franklin D. Roosevelt's birthday observed last Monday in January; Lincoln's birthday observed second Monday in February; Transfer day, last Monday in March; Holy Thursday; Good Friday; Easter Monday; Organic Act day, third Monday in
Monday, if Holiday falls on Sunday	×	×	×
Christmas Day (Dec. 25)	×	×	×
Thanksgiving Day	×	×	×
Veterans' Day (Nov. 11)		×	
Columbus Day (Oct. 12)			
Labor Day (1st Monday in Sept.)	×	×	×
Independence Day (July 4)	×	×	×
Jefferson Davis' Birthday (June 3)			
Last Monday in May	×	×	×
National Memorial Day (May 30)			
Confederate Memorial Day (May 10)			
Mardi Gras (Shrove Tuesday)			
Thomas Jefferson's Birthday (Apr. 13)			
Third Monday in Feb. (Presidents' Day)	×	×	×
Washington's Birthday (Feb. 22)			
Lincoln's Birthday (Feb. 12)	×	×	
Robert E. Lee's Birthday (Jan. 19)			
New Year's Day (Jan. 1)	×	×	×
Sunday	×		×

State																			Notes
Virgin Islands (Continued)																		x	June; Supplication day, fourth Monday in July; Columbus day and Puerto Rico Friendship day observed second Monday in October; Local Thanksgiving day, third Monday in October; Veteran's day observed fourth Monday in October; Liberty day, first Monday in November; Christmas Second day, December 26. See also West Indies Solidarity day and Teachers' day.
Virginia	x		x			x			x			x		x		x	x	x	x	Lee-Jackson day, third Monday in January; Confederate Memorial day observed last Monday in May; Columbus day observed second Monday in October; Election day; Friday if holiday occurs on succeeding Saturday. See also Saturday closing of banks, Mother's day, Citizenship day, Arbor day, Dogwood day, First Lady's day.
Washington		x	x			x		x	x			x		x		x	x	x	x	Columbus day observed second Monday in October; state wide general election day.
West Virginia		x	x			x			x			x		x		x	x	x	x	West Virginia day, June 20; Columbus day observed second Monday in October; election day throughout the district or municipality wherein held.

Other Legal Holidays and Remarks	Wisconsin	Wyoming	United States
	Columbus day observed second Monday in October; Veterans' day observed fourth Monday in October; September primary election day; November general election day. See also provisions concerning Good Friday (§ 256.-17), municipal elections (§ 256.17), Indian Rights day, and various holiday proclamations.	Columbus day observed second Monday in October; general election day. See also Arbor day, Wyoming day.	Columbus day observed second Monday in October; Friday if holiday occurs on succeeding Saturday. See also provisions concerning Inauguration day (5 U.S.C. § 6103 (c)), and various national observances.
Monday, if Holiday falls on Sunday		x	
Christmas Day (Dec. 25)	x	x	x
Thanksgiving Day	x	x	x
Veterans' Day (Nov. 11)		x	x
Columbus Day (Oct. 12)			
Labor Day (1st Monday in Sept.)	x	x	x
Independence Day (July 4)	x	x	x
Jefferson Davis' Birthday (June 3)			
Last Monday in May	x	x	x
National Memorial Day (May 30)			
Confederate Memorial Day (May 10)			
Mardi Gras (Shrove Tuesday)			
Thomas Jefferson's Birthday (Apr. 13)			
Third Monday in Feb. (Presidents' Day)	x	x	x
Washington's Birthday (Feb. 22)			
Lincoln's Birthday (Feb. 12)			
Robert E. Lee's Birthday (Jan. 19)			
New Year's Day (Jan. 1)	x	x	x
Sunday			

LEGAL HOLIDAYS:
STATE AND OTHER
STATUTES

ALABAMA

[ALA. CODE—(Approved April 20, 1971)]

Tit. 39, § 184. Holidays enumerated; observance of Veterans' day; bank closings. (1) Sunday, Christmas day, New Year's day, Robert E. Lee's birthday, George Washington's birthday, Thomas Jefferson's birthday, Mardi Gras, Confederate Memorial day, Jefferson Davis' birthday, the Fourth day of July, Labor day, Columbus day and Fraternal day, Veterans' day and the day designated by the governor for public thanksgiving, shall each be deemed a holiday. If any holiday falls on Sunday, the following day is the holiday. Veterans' day shall be observed by the closing of all state, county, and municipal offices, and the public schools on such day. The superintendent of banks, with the concurrence of not less than two members of the state banking board, may authorize any state bank to close on National Memorial day, May 30, and on such other days as may be declared by the governor to be state holidays in honor of a special event. In the event any authorized state holiday falls on Friday, the superintendent of banks may authorize the Saturday following that Friday to be a holiday. The superintendent may also authorize the closing of banks at 12:00 noon on the day prior to Christmas day, and the day prior to New Year's day, if such days fall on business days.

(2) Of the above enumerated legal public holidays, the following shall be observed on the dates herein prescribed:

Robert E. Lee's birthday—the third Monday in January.

George Washington's birthday—the third Monday in February.

Confederate Memorial day—the fourth Monday in April.

Jefferson Davis' birthday—the first Monday in June.

Columbus day and Fraternal day—the second Monday in October.

Veterans' day—the fourth Monday in October.

ALASKA

[ALASKA STAT.—(Twice amended in 1973)]

§ 44.12.010. Legal holidays. The following days are legal holidays: (1) the first of January, known as New Year's Day; (2) the 12th of February, known as Lincoln's Birthday; (3) the third Monday in February, known as Washington's Birthday; (4) the last Monday of March, known as Seward's Day; (5) the last Monday in May, known as Memorial Day; (6) the fourth of July, known as

Independence Day; (7) the first Monday in September, known as Labor Day; (8) the eighteenth of October, known as Alaska Day; (9) the 11th of November, known as Veterans' Day; (10) the fourth Thursday in November, known as Thanksgiving Day; (11) the 25th of December, known as Christmas Day; (12) every Sunday; (13) every day designated by public proclamation by the President of the United States or the governor of the state as a legal holiday.

§ **44.12.020.** **Holiday falling on Sunday.** If a holiday listed in § 10 of this chapter, except § 10(12), falls on a Sunday, Sunday and the following Monday are both legal holidays.

ARIZONA

[ARIZ. REV. STAT. ANN.—(Amended in 1973)]

§ **1-301.** **Holidays enumerated.** A. The following days shall be holidays:

1. Sunday of each week.
2. January 1, "New Year's Day".
3. February 12, "Lincoln Day".
4. February 14, "Admission Day".
5. Third Monday in February, "Washington's Birthday".
6. Second Sunday in May, "Mothers' Day".
7. Last Monday in May, "Memorial Day".
8. Third Sunday in June, "Fathers' Day".
9. July 4, "Independence Day".
10. First Monday in September, "Labor Day".
11. Second Monday in October, "Columbus Day".
12. "General Election Day".
13. November 11, "Veterans' Day".
14. Fourth Thursday in November, "Thanksgiving Day".
15. December 25, "Christmas Day".

B. When any of the holidays enumerated in subsection A falls on a Sunday, the following Monday shall be observed as a holiday, with the exception of the holidays enumerated in paragraphs 1, 6 and 8.

§ **1-302.** **Closing of offices and courts; transaction of certain judicial business.** A. Public offices shall not be open, and no court of justice shall be open or any judicial business transacted on a legal holiday, except for the following purposes:

1. To give upon its request, instructions to a jury deliberating on its verdict.
2. To receive a verdict or discharge a jury.
3. For the exercise of the powers of a magistrate in a criminal action or in a proceeding of a criminal nature.

B. Injunctions, attachments, process for claim and delivery and
writs of prohibition may be issued and served on any day.

ARKANSAS

[ARK. STAT. ANN.—(Amended in 1973)]

§ 69-101. **Legal holidays.** The following days are hereby declared to be legal holidays:

New Year's Day—January 1.
Robert E. Lee's Birthday—January 19.
George Washington's Birthday—the third Monday in February.
Memorial Day—the last Monday in May.
Independence Day—July 4.
Labor Day—the first Monday in September.
Veterans Day—November 11.
Thanksgiving Day—the fourth Thursday in November.
Christmas Day—December 25.

§ 69-102. **Memorial days—commemoration on proclamation.** The
following days shall not be legal holidays, but shall be memorial
days to be commemorated by the issuance of appropriate proclama-
tions by the governor:

January 26th—General Douglas MacArthur Day
February 12th—Lincoln's Birthday
Friday Preceding Easter—Good Friday
June 3rd—Jefferson Davis Birthday
October 12th—Columbus Day
First Saturday in February—Arbor Day.

§ 69-103. **Commercial paper payable day after holiday—holiday
falling on Sunday.** All bills of exchange, drafts or promissory notes,
which shall become payable on a legal holiday shall be payable
on the day next succeeding such holiday. In case any legal holiday
which falls upon Sunday, the next succeeding Monday shall be a
legal holiday in its stead.

§ 69-104. **End of World War Two—August 14th designated as
holiday.** The 14th day of August of this year and each succeeding
year during the existence of this state is hereby set aside and
dedicated as a holiday to every intent and purpose as if said date
was a Sunday or the first day of a week for the purpose of commemorating the ending of World War Two and as a perpetual
memorial day to the memory of the men and women who gave
their lives for this nation during said war.

§ 69-110. **Confederate flag day.** The Saturday immediately preceding Easter Sunday of each year is hereby designated as "Con-

federate Flag Day" in this state, and no person, firm or corporation shall hereafter display any confederate flag or replica thereof in connection with any advertisement of any commercial enterprise, or display such flag or replica thereof, or in any manner for any purpose except to honor the Confederate States of America.

§ 69-111. Violations of provisions of Act—penalty. Any person, firm or corporation, violating the provisions of this Act [§§ 69-110, 69-111] shall be guilty of a misdemeanor and upon conviction shall be fined not less than one hundred dollars ($100.00) nor more than one thousand dollars ($1,000.00).

§ 69-112. State offices to be closed on holidays—exceptions. Hereafter [Hereafter] [after July 18, 1971], all State offices shall be closed on all days declared to be legal holidays under the laws of this State and all persons employed thereby shall not be required to work on such legal holidays. Provided, this Act [§§ 69-101, 69-112, 69-113] shall not apply to those State and county offices and employees that are essential to the preservation and protection of the public peace, health and safety, nor to the offices of the various Constitutional officers who may use their own discretion in the matter of closing their offices on legal holidays.

CALIFORNIA

[CAL. GOV'T CODE—(West) (Amended in 1973)]

§ 6700. State holidays. The holidays in this state are:

(a) Every Sunday.

(b) January 1st.

(c) February 12th, known as "Lincoln Day."

(d) The third Monday in February.

(e) The last Monday in May.

(f) July 4th.

(g) First Monday in September.

(h) September 9th, known as "Admission Day."

(i) The second Monday in October, known as "Columbus Day."

(j) November 11th, known as "Veterans Day."

(k) December 25th.

(l) Good Friday from 12 noon until 3 p.m.

(m) Every day on which an election is held throughout the state.

(n) Every day appointed by the President or Governor for a public fast, thanksgiving, or holiday.

Except for the Thursday in November appointed as Thanksgiving Day, this subdivision shall not apply to a city, county or district unless made applicable by charter, or by ordinance or resolution of the governing body thereof.

§ 6701. **Holidays falling on Saturdays and Sundays.** If January 1st, February 12th, July 4th, September 9th, November 11th, or December 25th falls upon a Sunday, the Monday following is a holiday. If November 11th falls upon a Saturday, the preceding Friday is a holiday.

§ 6702. **Saturday half-holiday; closing city offices on holidays.** Every Saturday from noon to midnight is a holiday as regards the transaction of business in the public offices of the state and political divisions where laws, ordinances, or charters provide that public offices shall be closed on holidays. This section shall not be construed to prevent or invalidate the issuance, filing, service, execution, or recording of any legal process or written instrument during such period. Public offices of a city shall be closed on those holidays enumerated in Section 6700 unless otherwise provided by charter, ordinance or resolution.

COLORADO

[COLO. REV. STAT. ANN.—(Effective in 1971)]

§ 24-11-101. **Legal holidays—effect.** (1) The following days, viz: The first day of January, commonly called New Year's day; the third Monday in February, commonly called Washington's birthday; the last Monday in May, commonly called Memorial day; the fourth day of July, commonly called Independence day; the first Monday in September, commonly called Labor day; the second Monday in October, commonly called Columbus day; the fourth Monday in October, commonly called Veteran's day; the day of the general election in November or such other day as a general election may be held; the fourth Thursday in November, commonly called Thanksgiving day; the twenty-fifth of December, commonly called Christmas day; and any day appointed or recommended by the governor of this state or the president of the United States as a day of fasting or prayer, or thanksgiving, are hereby declared to be legal holidays; and shall, for all purposes whatsoever, as regards the presenting for payment or acceptance and of the protesting and giving notice of the dishonor of bills of exchange, drafts, bank checks, promissory notes, or other negotiable instruments, also for the holding of courts, be treated and considered as is the first day of the week commonly called Sunday.

§ 67-1-2. **Additional holidays—effect.** (1) The following days, viz: The twelfth day of February, commonly called Lincoln's birthday; and the first Monday of August, which shall be observed as Colorado day, are hereby declared to be legal holidays and shall, for all purposes as regards the holding of courts, be treated and considered as the first day of the week commonly called Sunday. In case any of said holidays shall fall upon a Sunday, then the Monday following shall be considered as the holiday, and in case the return or adjourned day in any suit, matter, or hearing before any court shall come on any of such days, such suit, matter, or proceeding, commenced or adjourned as aforesaid, shall not by reason of coming on any such day, abate, but the same shall stand continued to the next succeeding day, at the same place and time, unless the next day shall be the first day of the week, when in such case the same shall stand continued to the next succeeding, secular or business day, at the same time and place. Nothing in this section shall prevent the issuing or serving of process on any of the days above mentioned or on Sunday.

CONNECTICUT

[CONN. GEN. STAT. ANN.—(Amended in 1973)]

§ 1-4. Days designated as legal holidays. In each year the first day of January (known as New Year's Day), the second Sunday of January (known as Martin Luther King Day), the twelfth day of February (known as Lincoln Day), the third Monday in February (known as Washington's Birthday), the last Monday in May (known as Memorial Day or Decoration Day), the fourth day of July (known as Independence Day), the first Monday in September (known as Labor Day), the second Monday in October (known as Columbus Day), the eleventh day of November (known as Veterans' Day) and the twenty-fifth day of December (known as Chirstmas), or, whenever any of such days, which are not designated above to occur on Sunday or Monday, occurs upon Sunday, the Monday next following such day, and any day appointed or recommended by the governor of this state or the president of the United States as a day of thanksgiving, fasting or religious observance, shall each be a legal holiday, provided the provisions of section 5-254 shall not apply to Martin Luther King Day. When any such holiday occurs on a school day, there shall be no session of the public schools on such day.

DELAWARE

[DEL. CODE ANN.—(Effective 1971)]

Tit. 1, § 501. The following days shall be legal holidays in this State: the first of January, known as New Year's Day; the first Monday in February, known as Lincoln's Birthday; the third Monday in February, known as Washington's Birthday; Good Friday; the last Monday in May, known as Memorial Day; the fourth of July, known as Independence Day; the first Monday in September, known as Labor Day; the second Monday in October, known as Columbus Day; the fourth Monday in October, known as Veterans Day; the fourth Thursday in November, known as Thanksgiving Day; the twenty-fifth of December, known as Christmas; Saturdays; the day of the General Election as it biennially occurs; and in Sussex County,

Return Day, the second day after the General Election, after 12 noon.

If any of the legal holidays fall on Sunday, the Monday following shall be a legal holiday. If any of the legal holidays other than Saturday fall on Saturday, the Friday preceding shall be a legal holiday.

§ 502. Validity of acts, transactions, legal procedures, etc. (a) No contract made, instrument executed, or act done on any of the legal holidays designated in section 501 of this title shall be thereby rendered invalid, and nothing in that section shall be construed to prevent or invalidate the entry, issuance, service or execution of any writ, summons, confession, judgment, order or decree, or other legal process whatever, or the proceedings of any court or judge or Board of Canvass on any of such holidays.

(b) Any bank or trust company may, at its option, either close or remain open for business on the legal holidays designated in section 501 of this title. As to any bank or trust company electing to remain open on any such holidays, such day or days shall not constitute a holiday within the meaning of the provisions of the negotiable instrument law or any other law of this state and such bank or trust company shall incur no liability by reason of remaining open on such holiday. If any bank or trust company elects to close on any of such holidays, any act authorized, required or permitted to be performed at or by such bank or trust company may be performed on the next succeeding banking day (as the same is defined in section 291 of Title 6) and no liability or loss of rights of any kind shall result from remaining closed notwithstanding the provisions of any law of this state to the contrary. The provisions of this section shall not operate to invalidate or prohibit the doing on any of such holidays of any act by any person or bank or trust company, and nothing in any laws of this state shall, in any manner whatsoever, affect the validity or render void or voidable the payment, certification or acceptance of a check or any other negotiable instrument or any other transaction by any person or bank or trust company, because done or performed during any of such holidays, notwithstanding the provisions of any other law of this state to the contrary.

(c) For the purpose of this section, each branch or office of a bank shall be deemed a separate bank.

DISTRICT OF COLUMBIA

[D.C. CODE ENCYCL. ANN.—(Effective 1965)]

§ 28-2701. Holidays designated—time for performing acts extended. The following days in each year, namely, the first day of January, commonly called New Year's Day; the twenty-second day of February, known as Washington's Birthday; the Fourth of July; the thirtieth day of May, commonly called Decoration Day; the first Monday in September, known as Labor Day; the twenty-fifth day of December, commonly called Christmas Day; every Saturday, after twelve o'clock noon; any day appointed or recommended by the President of the United States as a day of public feasting or thanksgiving, and the day of the inauguration of the President, in every fourth year are holidays in the District for all purposes. When a day set apart as a legal holiday falls on Sunday the next succeeding day is a holiday. In such cases, and when a Sunday and a holiday fall on successive days, all commercial paper falling due on any of those days shall, for all purposes of presenting for payment or acceptance, be deemed to mature and be presentable for payment or acceptance on the next secular business day succeeding. Every Saturday is a holiday in the District for (1) every bank or banking institution having an office or banking house located within the District, (2) every Federal savings and loan association whose main office is in the District, and (3) every building association, building and loan association, or savings and loan association, incorporated or unincorporated, organized and operating under the laws of and having an office located within the District. An act which would otherwise be required, authorized, or permitted to be performed on Saturday in the District at the office or banking house of, or by, any such bank or bank institution, Federal savings and loan association, building association, building and loan association, or savings and loan association, if Saturday were not a holiday, shall or may be so performed on the next succeeding business day, and liability or loss of rights of any kind may not result from such delay.

FLORIDA

[FLA. STAT. ANN.—(Amended in 1973)]

§ 683.01. Legal holidays. (1) The legal holidays, which are also public holidays, are the following:

(a) Sunday, the first day of each week.

(b) New Year's Day, January 1.

(c) Birthday of Robert E. Lee, January 19.

(d) Washington's birthday, the third Monday in February.

(e) Good Friday.

(f) Confederate Memorial Day, April 26.

(g) Memorial Day, the last Monday in May.

(h) Birthday of Jefferson Davis, June 3.

(i) Independence Day, July 4.

(j) Labor Day, the first Monday in September.

(k) Columbus Day and Farmer's Day, the second Monday in October.

(l) Veterans' day, November 11.

(m)　General Election Day.

(n)　Thanksgiving Day, the fourth Thursday in November.

(o)　Christmas Day, December 25.

(p)　Shrove Tuesday (sometimes also known as Mardi Gras), in counties where carnival associations are organized for the purpose of celebrating the same.

(2)　Whenever any legal holiday shall fall upon a Sunday, the Monday next following shall be deemed a public holiday for all and any of the purposes aforesaid.

§ 683.02.　Meaning of term "legal holidays" as used in contracts. Whenever, in contracts to be performed in the state, reference is made to "legal holidays," the term shall be, understood to include those holidays designated in section 683.01, Florida Statutes, and such others as may be designated by law.

GEORGIA

[GA. CODE ANN.—(Amended in 1972)]

§ 14-1809.　Public and legal holidays designated. (a)　The following days are declared to be public and legal holidays in Georgia: The 1st day of January known as New Year's Day; the 19th day of January known as Lee's Birthday; the 22nd day of February known as Washington's Birthday; the 26th day of April known as Confederate Memorial Day; the 30th day of May known as National Memorial Day; the 3rd day of June known as Jefferson Davis' Birthday; the 4th day of July known as Independence Day; the 1st Monday in September known as Labor Day; the 12th day of October known as Columbus Day; the 11th day of November known as Veterans' Day; the 4th Thursday in November known as Thanksgiving Day; and the 25th day of December known as Christmas Day; and any day proclaimed or designated by the Governor of the State of Georgia or the President of the United State as a day of fasting and prayer or other religious observance are hereby declared public and legal holidays in the State of Georgia.　Whenever a public or legal holiday occurs on a Sunday, the following Monday shall be observed as a public and legal holiday.

(b)　Beginning with the calendar year 1971, George Washington's Birthday shall be observed on the 3rd Monday in February; National Memorial Day shall be observed on the last Monday in May; and Columbus Day shall be observed on the 2nd Monday in October.

§ 32-1503.　Observance of special days. The county and local boards of education shall see that the following days are observed either by holidays or appropriate exercises and it shall be the duty of the State Superintendent of Schools to arrange programs for the proper observance of these occasions, and of the superintendent and teachers to direct the attention of the pupils to these dates and topics by practical exercises:

1. Thanksgiving Day, last Thursday in November.
2. Uncle Remus Day, December 9.
3. Lee's Birthday, January 19.
4. Georgia Day, February 12.
5. Washington's Birthday, February 22.
6. Arbor and Bird Day, third Friday in February.
7. Memorial Day, April 26.
8. Alexander H. Stephens' Birthday.
9. Crawford W. Long's Birthday.

§ 32-1504. Temperance Day designated; program in schools. The 4th Friday in March of each year shall be designated and known as Temperance Day in the public schools. On Temperance Day at least two hours shall be devoted in the public schools to a program, which shall be educational in nature, teaching the good of temperance and prohibition, and the evils of intemperance and disobedience to law.

HAWAII

[HAWAII REV. STAT.—(Amended in 1971)]

§ 8-1. Holidays designated. The following days of each year are set apart and established as state holidays:

The first day of January, New Year's Day;

The third Monday in February, President's Day;

The twenty-sixth day of March, Kuhio Day;

The Friday preceding Easter Sunday, Good Friday;

The last Monday in May, Memorial Day;

The eleventh day of June, Kamehameha Day;

The fourth day of July, Independence Day;

The third Friday in August, Admission Day;

The first Monday in September, Labor Day;

The second Monday in October, Discoverers' Day;

The fourth Monday in October, Veterans' Day;

The twenty-fifth day of December, Christmas Day;

All election days, except primary election day, in the county wherein the election is held;

Any day designated by proclamation by the President of the United States as a day of thanksgiving, fasting or religious observance;

Any day designated by proclamation by the governor as a holiday.

§ 8-2. Observance of holidays falling on Sundays and Saturdays. If any of the State's legal holidays fall on Sunday, the following

Monday shall be observed as a holiday. If the day falls on Saturday and is also observed as a national holiday, the preceding Friday shall be observed as a holiday.

§ 8-4.5. **Baha'i New Year's Day.** The 21st day of March shall be known as Baha'i New Year's Day, provided that this day is not and shall not be construed to be a state holiday.

§ 1-32. **Acts to be done on holidays.** Whenever any act of a secular nature other than a work of necessity or mercy is appointed by law or contract to be performed upon a particular day, which day falls upon a Sunday or holiday, the act may be performed upon the next business day with the same effect as if it had been performed upon the appointed day. When so provided by the rules of court, the act also may be performed upon the next business day with the same effect as if it had been performed upon the appointed day if the appointed day falls on a Saturday.

§ 502-32. **Instrument recorded as of time of delivery; office hours.** Every instrument entitled by law to be recorded, shall be recorded in the order and as of the time when the same is delivered to the registrar for that purpose, and shall be considered as recorded from the time of such delivery; provided, that it shall not be lawful for the registrar to accept or enter for record and record any instrument or other paper on any Sunday or legal holiday, or on any Saturday that the registrar's office remains closed pursuant to law, or on any other day except between the hours of 8:00 a.m. and 4:00 P.M.

IDAHO

[IDAHO CODE—(Amended in 1973)]

§ 73-108. **Holidays enumerated.** Holidays, within the meaning of these compiled laws, are:

Every Sunday;
January 1 (New Year's Day);
Third Monday in February (Washington's Birthday);
Last Monday in May (Decoration Day);
July 4 (Independence Day);
First Monday in September (Labor Day);
Second Monday in October (Columbus Day);
November 11 (Veterans Day);
Fourth Thursday in November (Thanksgiving Day);
December 25 (Chirstmas);

Every day appointed by the President of the United States, or by the governor of this state, for a public fast, thanksgiving, or holiday.

Any reference in a law of the state of Idaho to the observance

of a legal public holiday on a day other than the day prescribed
for the observance of such a holiday by this section shall, on and
after the effective date of this act, be considered a reference to the
day for the observance of such holiday prescribed in this section.

ILLINOIS

[ILL. ANN. STAT.—(Smith-Hurd) (Effective in 1973)]

**Ch. 98, § 18.   Holidays and half holidays—days selected by banks
to remain closed—acts done during other than regular banking hours.**
The first day of January, commonly called New Year's Day, the third
Monday in February, the 30th day of May, the fourth day of July,
the second Monday in October, the twenty-fifth day of December,
commonly called Christmas Day, the first Monday in September, to
be known as Labor Day, the twelfth of February, November 11 to
be known as Veterans Day, any day appointed or recommended by
the Governor of this State or the President of the United States as
a day of fast or Thanksgiving, any day proclaimed by the Governor,
the days upon which the general elections for members of the House
of Representatives are held, and in cities of 200,000 inhabitants or
more from 12 o'clock noon to 12 o'clock midnight of the last day of
the week commonly called Saturday, are legal holidays and half
holidays, the term half holidays including the period from noon to
midnight of each Saturday which is not a holiday. All such holidays,
the half holidays and any day selected by a bank doing business
within the State to remain closed, as hereinafter provided, shall, for
all purposes whatsoever, as regards the presenting for payment or
acceptance, the maturity and protesting and giving of notice of the
dishonor of bills of exchange, bank checks and promissory notes and
other negotiable or commercial paper or instrument, be treated and
considered as is the first day of the week, commonly called Sunday.
When any such holidays fall on Sunday, the Monday next following
shall be held and considered such holiday. All notes, bills, drafts,
checks or other evidence of indebtedness, falling due or maturing on
either of such days, shall be deemed as due or maturing upon the
day following, and when 2 or more of these days come together,
or immediately succeeding each other, then such instruments, paper
or indebtedness shall be deemed as due or having matured on the
day following the last of such days. Any bank doing business
within the State may select any one day of the week to remain
closed upon adoption of a resolution by the Board of Directors of
such bank designating the day selected and upon filing and publishing a copy of such resolution as hereinafter required. Any such
resolution shall be deemed effective for the purposes of this Section
only when a copy thereof certified by an officer having charge of
the records of such bank is filed with the Recorder of Deeds of the
county in which such bank is located and published once each
week for 3 successive weeks in a newspaper of general circulation in

such county. Any such selection shall remain in full force and effect until a copy of a later resolution of the Board of Directors of such bank, certified in like manner, terminating or altering any such prior selection shall be filed and published in the same manner as such prior resolution. Any day which any bank doing business within the State shall select to remain closed pursuant to this Section shall, with respect to such bank be treated and considered as is the first day of the week, commonly called Sunday, as hereinbefore provided.

Any act authorized, required or permitted to be performed at or by or with respect to any bank doing business within the State on a day which it has selected to remain closed under this Section may be so performed on the next succeeding business day and no liability or loss of rights of any kind shall result from such delay.

Nothing in this Act shall in any manner affect the validity of, or render void or voidable, the payment, certification, or acceptance of a check or other negotiable instrument, or any other transaction by a bank in this State, because done or performed on any Saturday, Sunday, holiday, or any day selected by a bank to remain closed, or during any time other than regular banking hours; but no bank in this State, which by law or custom is entitled to remain open or to close for the whole or any part of any day selected by it to remain open or to close, is compelled to close, or to remain open for the transaction of business or to perform any of the acts or transactions aforesaid except at its own option.

§ 19. **Veterans Day holiday.** The eleventh day of November of each year shall be a holiday, to be known as Veterans Day, which shall be observed throughout the State as a day on which to hold appropriate exercises in commemoration of the victory of the United States Army, United States Navy, and the United States Air Force in all wars.

§ 20. **Commercial paper on Veterans Day.** Veterans Day shall, for all purposes whatever, as regards the presenting for payment or acceptance and of protesting and giving notice of the dishonor of bills of exchange, bank checks and promissory notes, and as regards days of grace upon commercial paper, be treated and considered as is the first day of the week, commonly called Sunday.

§ 20a. **Lincoln's Birthday.** The twelfth day of February of each year shall be a legal holiday to be known as Lincoln's Birthday, which shall be observed as a day on which to hold appropriate exercises in commemoration of our illustrious President. When February twelfth shall fall on a Sunday, the Monday next following shall be held and considered such holiday.

§ 20b. **Good Friday.** The Friday immediately before Easter Sunday of each year, known as Good Friday, shall be a legal holiday in this State. Said day shall, for all purposes whatever, as regards the presenting for payment or acceptance and of protesting and giving notice of the dishonor of bills of exchange, bank checks and promissory notes, be treated and considered as is the first day of the week, commonly called Sunday.

§ 20c.   Christopher Columbus Day. The second Monday in October of each year shall be a holiday, to be known as "Christopher Columbus Day" and which shall be observed throughout the State as a day on which to hold appropriate ceremonies and exercises in commemoration of the discoveror of the New World and his discovery of October 12, 1492.

§ 20d.   Dr. Martin Luther King's birthday—proclamation. The fifteenth of January of each year is a holiday to be observed throughout the State and to be known as the birthday of Dr. Martin Luther King, Jr.

When January fifteenth falls on a Sunday, the holiday shall be celebrated on the following Monday.

Within 10 days prior to the birthday of Dr. Martin Luther King, Jr. in each year, the Governor shall issue a proclamation announcing the holiday and designating the official events which shall be held in honor of the memory of Dr. Martin Luther King, Jr. and his contributions to this nation.

INDIANA

[IND. CODE—(Amended in 1972)]

§ 1-1-9-1.   Legal holidays. The following are legal holidays within the state of Indiana for all purposes: New Year's Day, January 1; the twelfth day of February, commonly called Lincoln's Birthday; Washington's Birthday, the third Monday in February; the movable feast day of Good Friday; Memorial Day, the last Monday in May; Independence Day, July 4; Labor Day, the first Monday in September; Columbus Day, the second Monday in October; Veterans' Day, November 11; Thanksgiving Day, the fourth Thursday in November; Christmas Day, December 25; the day of any general, national, state or city election or primary; and the first day of the week, commonly called Sunday.

When any of these holidays, other than Sunday, comes on Sunday, the Monday next succeeding shall be the legal holiday.

The provisions of this section shall not affect any action taken by the general assembly while in regular or special session and any action taken by the general assembly on any such holiday shall be valid for all purposes.

Any reference in a law of the state of Indiana, in effect on the effective date of this amendatory act, to the observance of a legal public holiday on a day other than the day prescribed for the observance of such holiday by this amendatory act, shall on and after the effective date of this amendatory chapter be considered as a reference to the day for the observance of such holiday prescribed in this section as last amended.

IOWA

[IOWA CODE ANN.—(Effective 1973)]

§ 33.1. **Legal public holidays.** The following are legal public holidays:

1. New Year Day, January first.
2. Lincoln's Birthday, February twelfth.
3. Washington's Birthday, the third Monday in February.
4. Memorial Day, the last Monday in May.
5. Independence Day, July fourth.
6. Labor Day, the first Monday in September.
7. Veterans' Day, November 11.
8. Thanksgiving Day, the fourth Thursday in November.
9. Christmas Day, December twenty-fifth.

§ 31.4. **Mother's Day.** The governor of this state is hereby authorized and requested to issue annually a proclamation calling upon our state officials to display the American flag on all state and school buildings, and the people of the state to display the flag at their homes, lodges, churches, and places of business, on the second Sunday in May, known as Mothers' Day, as a public expression of reverence for the homes of our state, and to urge the celebration of Mothers' Day in said proclamation in such a way as will deepen home ties, and inspire better homes and closer union between the commonwealth, its homes, and their sons and daughters.

§ 31.5. **Independence Sunday.** The governor is hereby authorized and requested to issue annually a proclamation, calling upon the citizens of Iowa to assemble themselves in their respective communities for the purpose of holding suitable religious-patriotic services and the display of the American colors, in commemoration of the signing of the Declaration of Independence, on Independence Sunday, which is hereby established as the Sunday preceding the Fourth of July of each year, or on the Fourth when that date falls on Sunday.

§ 31.6. **Columbus Day.** The governor of this state is hereby authorized and requested to issue annually a proclamation, calling upon our state officials to display the American flag on all state and school buildings and the people of the state to display the flag at their homes, lodges, churches, and places of business on the twelfth day of October, known as Columbus Day; to commemorate the life and history of Christopher Columbus and to urge that services and exercises be had in churches, halls and other suitable places expressive of the public sentiment befitting the anniversary of the discovery of America.

§ 31.7. Veterans' Day. The governor is hereby authorized and requested to issue annually a proclamation designating the eleventh day of November as Veterans' Day and calling upon the people of Iowa to observe it as a legal holiday in honor of those who have been members of the armed forces of the United States, and urging state officials to display the American flag on all state and school buildings and the people of the state to display the flag at their homes, lodges, churches and places of business; that business activities be held to the necessary minimum; and that appropriate services and exercises be had expressive of the public sentiments befitting the occasion.

§ 31.8. Youth Honor Day. The governor of this state is hereby requested and authorized to issue annually a proclamation designating the thirty-first day of October of each year as "Youth Honor Day".

§ 31.9. Herbert Hoover Day. The Sunday which falls on or nearest the tenth day of August of each year is hereby designated as Herbert Hoover Day, which shall be a recognition day in honor of the late President Herbert Hoover. The governor is hereby authorized and requested to issue annually a proclamation designating such Sunday as Herbert Hoover Day and calling on the people and officials of the state of Iowa to commemorate the life and principles of Herbert Hoover, to display the American flag, and to hold appropriate services and ceremonies.

§ 541.202. Negotiating instrument on holiday. Nothing in any law of this state shall in any manner whatsoever affect the validity of, or render void or voidable, the payment, certification, or acceptance of a check or other negotiable instrument or any other transaction by a bank or trust company in this state because done or performed on any legal holiday or during any time other than regular banking hours, if such payment, certification, acceptance or other transaction could have been validly done or performed on any other day; provided that nothing herein shall be construed to compel any bank or trust company in this state, which by law or custom is entitled to close for the whole or any part of any legal holiday, to keep open for the transaction of business or to perform any of the acts or transactions aforesaid on any legal holiday except at its own option.

§ 617.8. Holidays. No person shall be held to answer or appear in any court on any day now or hereafter made a legal holiday.

KANSAS

[KAN. STAT. ANN.—(Effective 1971)]

§ 35-107. Legal public holidays designated. (a) On and after January 1, 1971, the following days are declared to be legal public holidays and are to be observed as such:

New Year's Day, January 1;
Lincoln's Birthday, the twelfth day in February;
Washington's Birthday, the third Monday in February;
Memorial Day, the last Monday in May;
Independence Day, July 4;
Labor Day, the first Monday in September;
Columbus Day, the second Monday in October;
Veterans' Day, the fourth Monday in October;
Thanksgiving Day, the fourth Thursday in November;
Christmas Day, December 25.

(b)   Any reference in the laws of this state concerning observance of legal holidays shall on and after January 1, 1971, be considered as a reference to the day or days prescribed in subsection (a) hereof for the observance of such legal holiday or holidays.

§ 35-108.   **Commercial paper, agreements, written instruments and judicial proceedings not affected.**   The provisions of this act shall not be construed to affect commercial paper, the making or execution of agreements or instruments in writing or interfere with judicial proceedings.

§ 35-201.   **Family day.**   That the Sunday following Thanksgiving Day in November of each year shall be set aside and designated as "Family Day"; and public and private organizations and individuals in this state are urged to take appropriate action on this day to properly recognize and dedicate this Family Day.

§ 52-717.   **Bank transactions on Saturday afternoon or holiday.** No provision of any law of this state shall be so construed as to prevent banks from paying checks, drafts, or other bills of exchange upon Saturday afternoon, or upon any legal holiday: *Provided,* Such payments would be legal if made at other times.

KENTUCKY

[KY. REV. STAT. ANN.—(Effective in 1971)]

§ 2.110.   **Holidays.**   (1) The 1st day of January (New Year's Day), the 19th day of January (Robert E. Lee Day), the 30th day of January (Franklin D. Roosevelt Day), the 12th day of February (Lincoln's Birthday), the third Monday in February (Washington's Birthday), the last Monday in May (Memorial Day), the 3rd day of June (Confederate Memorial Day, and Jefferson Davis Day), the 4th day of July (Independence Day), the first Monday in September (Labor Day), the second Monday in October (Columbus Day), the fourth Monday in October (Veterans Day), the 25th day of December (Christmas Day) of each year, and all days appointed by the President of the United States or by the Governor as days of thanksgiving, are holidays, on which all the public offices of this Commonwealth may be closed; and, subject to the provisions of subsection (2) of this section, shall be considered as Sunday for all purposes regarding the presenting for payment or acceptance, and of protesting for and giving notice of the dishonor of bills of exchange, bank checks and promissory notes, placed by law upon the footing of bills of exchange. If any of the days named as holidays occur on Sunday, the next days thereafter shall be observed as a holiday but bills of exchange or other papers may be presented for payment or acceptance on the Saturday preceding the holiday and proceeded on accordingly.

(2) Any bank, trust company, or combined bank and trust company may, at its option, either close or remain open for business on the 19th day of January (Robert E. Lee Day), the 30th day of January (Franklin D. Roosevelt Day), the 12th day of February (Lincoln's Birthday), the third Monday in February (Washington's Birthday), the 3rd day of June (Confederate Memorial Day, and Jefferson Davis Day), the second Monday in October (Columbus Day), and the fourth Monday in October (Veterans Day). Any bank, trust company, or combined bank and trust company electing to remain open on such of the above mentioned holidays may do so and as to such bank, trust company, or combined bank and trust company such day or days shall not constitute a holiday within the meaning of the provisions of the negotiable instrument law or any other law of the Commonwealth and such bank, trust company, or combined bank and trust company shall incur no liability by reason of remaining open on such holiday, provided that any bank, trust company, or any combined bank and trust company, electing to remain open on any of the above mentioned holidays which occurs on a Monday, Tuesday, Wednesday, Thursday or Friday shall remain closed the following Saturday, or shall comply with KRS 287.197. If any such bank, trust company, or combined bank and trust company elects to close on such holidays, any act authorized, required or permitted to be performed at or by such bank, trust company, or combined bank and trust company, may be performed on the next succeeding business day and no liability or loss of rights of any kind shall result from remaining closed notwithstanding the provisions of any law of this Commonwealth to the contrary. The provisions of this section shall not operate to invalidate or prohibit the doing on any of the aforementioned legal holidays of any act by any person or bank or trust company, or combined bank and trust company, and nothing in this section shall, in any manner whatsoever affect the validity of or render void or voidable the payment, certification or acceptance of a check or any other negotiable instrument or any other transaction by any person or bank or trust company or combined bank and trust company because done or performed during any of the aforesaid holidays, notwithstanding the provisions of any other law of this Commonwealth to the contrary.

(3)   No person shall be compelled to labor on the first Monday in September (Labor Day) by any person.

§ 2.190.   Presidential election day (effective in 1972). The Tuesday after the first Monday in November in presidential election years shall be a state holiday on which all state offices, all schools and all state universities and colleges shall be closed, and which shall be treated as Sunday for all purposes of banking and negotiable instruments law. Any employee who is required to work on said state holiday shall receive compensatory pay or time off.

LOUISIANA

[LA. REV. STAT.—(Amended in 1973)]

§ 1:55.   Days of public rest, legal holidays and half-holidays. A.   The following shall be days of public rest and legal holidays and half-holidays:

(1)   The following shall be days of public rest and legal holidays: Sundays; January 1, New Year's Day; January 8, Battle of New Orleans; January 19, Robert E. Lee Day; third Monday in February, Washington's Birthday; Good Friday; the last Monday in May, National Memorial Day; June 3, Confederate Memorial Day; July 4, Independence Day; August 30, Huey P. Long Day; the first Monday in September, Labor Day; the second Monday in October, Christopher Columbus Day; November 1, All Saints' Day; November 11, Veterans' Day; the fourth Thursday in November, Thanksgiving Day; December 25, Christmas Day; Inauguration Day in the city of Baton Rouge; provided, however, that in the parish of Orleans, the city of Baton Rouge, in each of the parishes comprising the second and sixth congressional districts, except the parish of Ascension, and in each of the parishes comprising the fourteenth and thirty-first judicial districts of the state, the whole of every Saturday shall be a legal holiday, and in the parishes of Catahoula, Caldwell, West Carroll, Concordia, East Carroll, Franklin, Madison, Morehouse, Ouachita, Richland, Tensas, Union, Jackson, Avoyelles, West Feliciana, Rapides, Natchitoches, Grant, LaSalle, Winn, Lincoln and East Baton Rouge, the whole of every Saturday shall be a holiday for all banking institutions, and in the parishes of Sabine and Vernon each Wednesday and Saturday, from 12:00 o'clock noon until 12:00 o'clock midnight, shall be a half-holiday for all banking institutions. All banks and trust companies, however, may, each at its option, remain open and exercise all of its regular banking functions and duties upon January 8; January 19; Washington's Birthday; Good Friday; National Memorial Day; June 3; August 30; Christopher Columbus Day; November 1; and Veterans' Day; however, when on any of said last named days any bank or trust company does actually remain open it shall, as to transactions on such day, to exactly the same extent as if such day were not otherwise a legal holiday, be not

subject to any of the provisions of R.S. 7:85 and R.S. 7:251 or any other laws of Louisiana covering the matters of maturity of negotiable instruments and demand, notice, presentment, acceptance or protest thereof on legal holidays and half-holidays, and all instruments payable to or at such bank upon such day shall become due on such day; and provided, further, that the option of remaining open shall not apply to Saturdays or Wednesdays which are holidays or half-holidays, or to Mardi Gras when the same has been declared a legal holiday; and provided still further that nothing in any law of this state shall in any manner whatsoever affect the validity of or render void or voidable the payment, certification or acceptance of a check or other negotiable instrument or any other transaction by a bank in Louisiana because done on any holiday or half-holiday or because done on any day upon which such bank, if remaining open because of the option given it herein, if the payment, certification, acceptance or other transaction could have been validly done on any other day.

(2)   In all parishes of the state the governing authorities thereof shall have the option to declare the whole of every Saturday a holiday, and until the whole of Saturday is so declared a holiday in any parish, Saturday from 12 o'clock noon until 12 o'clock midnight shall be a half-holiday; provided that in the city of Baton Rouge and in the Parish of Orleans the whole of every Saturday is a holiday; provided further, that the governing authority of the Parish of Washington may declare the whole of Wednesday or the whole of Saturday a holiday, and if the Parish of Washington declares the whole of Wednesday a holiday, no part of Saturday shall be a holiday in that parish.   In no parish shall the whole of Wednesday be a holiday when the immediately preceding day is a holiday.

(3)   In the parishes of Orleans, St. Bernard, Jefferson, Plaquemines, St. Charles, St. James, St. John the Baptist, East Baton Rouge, Lafayette, St. Tammany, Iberia, St. Martin, Ascension and Washington and in all municipalities, Mardi Gras shall be a holiday when the governing authorities so declare by ordinance. The school boards of the parishes of Acadia and Lafayette may declare Mardi Gras and the day of International Rice Festival in Crowley a holiday for public school children of those parishes.

(4)   Whenever December 25, January 1, or July 4 falls on a Sunday, the next day is a holiday.

When December 25, or July 4 falls on a Saturday, the preceding Friday is a holiday when the governing authorities so declare by ordinance.

(5)   The governing authorities of all parishes in the state shall have the option to declare the second Friday of Holiday in Dixie a legal holiday.   The school boards in all parishes shall have the option to declare such day a holiday for public school children.

B. Legal holidays shall be observed by the departments of the state as follows:

(1) In so far as may be practicable in the administration of the government, no employee shall work on New Year's Day, Mardi Gras Day, Good Friday, Independence Day, Labor Day, Veterans' Day, Thanksgiving Day, Christmas Day, Inauguration Day once in every four years in the city of Baton Rouge, or General Election Day every two years.

(2) Robert E. Lee Day, Washington's Birthday, National Memorial Day, Confederate Memorial Day, and Huey P. Long Day shall be observed only in such manner as the Governor may proclaim, considering the pressure of the state's business.

(3) The Governor, by executive proclamation, may authorize the observance of such other holidays and half-holidays as he may deem in keeping with efficient administration.

C. It shall be lawful to file and record suits, deeds, mortgages and liens, to issue and serve citations, to make sheriff's sales by virtue of any execution, and to take and to execute all other legal proceedings on Wednesday and Saturday holidays and half-holidays.

D. Notwithstanding the provisions of R.S. 6:65 or any other law to the contrary, all banking institutions and savings and loan associations located within the parishes of Terrebonne, Lafourche, Iberia, Pointe Coupee, West Baton Rouge, St. Mary, and Iberville, and all banking institutions located within the parish of Lafayette, shall be closed during any year on Saturdays, Sundays, New Year's Day, Mardi Gras, Independence Day, Labor Day, Thanksgiving and Christmas; provided, however, that when New Year's Day, Independence Day or Christmas fall on a Sunday, said banking institutions and savings and loan associations shall be closed on the next day, and said financial institutions may, each at its option, remain open and exercise all of its regular functions and duties upon January 8; January 19; the third Monday in February, Washington's Birthday; Good Friday; the last Monday in May, National Memorial Day; June 3; August 30; the second Monday in October, Christopher Columbus Day; November 1; and November 11, Veterans' Day; and further provided that when on any of said last named days any said financial institution does actually remain open it shall, as to transactions on such day, to exactly the same extent as if such day were not otherwise a legal holiday, be not subject to any of the provisions of R.S. 7:85 and R.S. 7:251, or any other laws of Louisiana, covering the matters of maturity of negotiable instruments and demands, notice, presentment, acceptance or protest thereof on legal holidays and half-holidays, and all instruments payable to or at such bank upon such day shall become due on such day; and provided further that the option of remaining open shall not apply to Saturdays or Wednesdays which are holidays or half-holidays, or to Mardi Gras when the same has been declared a legal holiday; and provided further that nothing in any law of this state shall in any manner whatsoever affect the validity of, or render void or voidable, the payment, certification of acceptance of a check or other negotiable instrument, or any other transaction by a bank in Louisiana because done on any holiday or half-holiday or because done on any day upon which such financial institution if remaining open because of the option given it herein, if the payment, certification, acceptance, or other transaction could have been validly done on any other day, provided, however, that in the parishes of Beauregard, Sabine, Vernon, Evangeline and DeSoto the banking institutions may elect to make the whole of Saturdays holidays and close, in lieu of half-holidays on Wednesdays and half-holidays on Saturdays.

MAINE

[ME. REV. STAT. ANN.—(Effective in 1974)]

Tit. 4, § 1051. Legal holidays. No court shall be held on Sunday or any day designated for the annual Thanksgiving; or for the choice of Presidential Electors; New Year's Day, January 1st; Washington's Birthday, the 3rd Monday in February; Patriot's Day, the 3rd Monday in April; Memorial Day, the last Monday in May; the 4th of July; Labor Day, the first Monday of September; the day of the state-wide primary election; the day of the state election; the day of any special state-wide election; Columbus Day, the 2nd Monday in October; Veterans Day, November 11th; or on Christmas Day; and when the time fixed for a term of court falls on any of said days, it shall stand adjourned until the next day, which shall be deemed the first day of the term for all purposes. The public offices in county buildings may be closed to business on the above-named holidays. When any one of the above-named holidays falls on Sunday, the Monday following shall be observed as a holiday, with all the privileges applying to any of the days above named.

MARYLAND

[MD. ANN. CODE—(Twice amended in 1973)]

Art. 13, § 9. Enumeration; emergency closing of banking institutions. The following days in each and every year, namely the first day of January, commonly called "New Years' Day"; the 12th day of February, known as "Lincoln's Birthday"; the third Monday in February, known as "Washington's Birthday"; the 25th day of March known as "Maryland Day"; "Good Friday"; the first Monday in September, commonly called "Labor Day"; the last Monday in May, commonly called "Memorial Day"; the 4th day of July, called "Independence Day"; the 12th day of September, known as "Defenders' Day"; the second Monday in October, known as "Columbus Day"; the fourth Monday in October, known as "Veterans' Day"; the fourth Thursday in November, known as "Thanksgiving Day"; the 25th day of December, called "Christmas Day"; and all days of general and congressional elections throughout the State and all special days that may be appointed or recommended by the State and on all special days that may be appointed or recommended by the Governor of this State or the President of the United States, as days of thanksgiving or fasting and prayer, or other religious observance or for the general cessation of business, shall be regarded as legal holidays, and shall be duly observed as such, and shall for all purposes whatsoever as regards the presenting for payment or acceptance and of the protesting and giving notice of dishonor of bills of exchange, bank checks, drafts and promissory notes, to be treated and considered as the first day of the week, commonly called Sunday, and all such bills, drafts, checks, and notes presented for payment or acceptance on these said days, shall be deemed to be presented for acceptance or payment on the secular or business day next succeeding such holiday. The 15th day of January of each and every year shall be proclaimed by the Governor as "Martin Luther King Day" and shall be a day of prayer in honor of Martin Luther King. The 13th day of April of each and every year shall be proclaimed by the Governor as "John Hanson's Birthday" and be dedicated to the memory of the statesman, John Hanson. The Governor of this State shall have the power by proclamation to appoint a day or days for the general cessation of business in any one or more of the political subdivisions of the State, in case of emergency from fire, flood or otherwise, with the same legal consequences as hereinabove provided. In case of emergency from fire, flood, storm, snow, robbery, riot, or other cause of any kind whatsoever in any part of the State, the Governor shall have the further power by proclamation to appoint a day or days during which banking institutions (as defined in Article 11 of the Annotated Code of Maryland) within the area or areas designated in the proclamation may remain closed, in which case the appointed day or days shall be treated and considered as the first day of the week, commonly called Sunday, with the same legal consequences as hereinabove provided. If the emergency condition is confined to one or more particular banking institutions or branch offices, the proclamation shall be limited to the institutions or offices so designated. In the event an emergency condition arises and it is not practicable to obtain a proclamation prior to actual closing, the institutions so affected may, by the action of the chairman of the board of directors or the president of the institution, effect a closing; and such closing shall have the same force and effect as a proclamation. In such instances where the chairman of the board or the president elects to effect an emergency closing he shall, as soon as possible, but in no event later than twenty-four (24) hours after closing, notify the Governor or his representative of the reasons for closing. In any case, the emergency closing shall have the force and effect of a proclamation only (a) until the first of the following events occurs: (1) the issuance of a proclamation by the Governor pertaining to the emergency closing, (2) notice to the institution that the Governor declines to issue a proclamation, or (3) reopening of the institution by the chairman of the board or the president; or (b) until five o'clock on the third day (excluding Saturdays, Sundays and legal holidays) following the day on which the chairman or the president closed the institution.

§ 10.   **Banks may close on Saturdays; Saturdays as legal holidays.** It shall be lawful for any banking institution as defined in Article 11 of the Annotated Code of Maryland to remain closed on any one or more or all Saturdays, as it may by resolution of its board of directors determine, from time to time.   Any Saturday on which any banking institution shall remain closed in accordance with the provisions of this section shall, as to such banking institution, constitute a legal holiday within the meaning of such term as used in and for all purposes of § 9 of this article.   Interest on any bill of exchange, draft or promissory note presentable for such payment on any Saturday on which such banking institution shall remain closed in accordance with the provisions of this section shall be computed down to and including any such Saturday only, provided such bill of exchange, draft or promissory note is presented on the next succeeding secular day.

§ 11.   **Monday to be treated as holiday when enumerated holidays fall on Sunday.**   Whenever the 1st day of January, the 12th day of February, the 25th day of March, the 4th day of July, the 12th day of September, or the 25th day of December shall occur on Sunday, the Monday next following shall be deemed and treated as a public holiday for all or any of the purposes aforesaid; provided, however, that in such case all bills of exchange, bank checks, drafts and promissory notes which would otherwise be presentable for acceptance or for payment on either of the Mondays so observed as holiday, shall be deemed to be presentable for acceptance or for payment on the secular or business day next succeeding such Monday, and such Mondays, so observed for all purposes whatever as regards the presenting for payment and acceptance and of the protesting and giving notice of the dishonor of bills of exchange, bank checks, drafts and promissory notes be also treated and considered as is the first day of the week, commonly called Sunday.

§ 12.   **Election to remain open on certain days otherwise holidays.** Notwithstanding any of the provisions of §§ 9 and 11 of this subtitle, any banking institution as determined by a resolution of its board of directors may elect to remain open for business on any day of the year except Sundays, New Year's Day, Washington's Birthday, Good Friday, the last Monday in May, commonly called Memorial Day, the fourth day of July, Labor Day, the second Monday in October, known as Columbus Day, the fourth Monday in October known as

Veterans' Day, Thanksgiving Day and Christmas. Any day which but for the action of the board of directors of any bank would be a legal holiday shall not be a legal holiday for that banking institution. All laws concerning legal holidays shall apply or not apply to any banking institution acting under the provisions of this section according to the action of its board of directors in declaring such day to be or not to be a legal holiday.

MASSACHUSETTS

[MASS. ANN. LAWS—(Effective in 1971)]

Ch. 4, § 7.

        o   o   o

"*Legal Holiday.*" Eighteen, "Legal holiday" shall include January the first, July the fourth and Christmas day, or the day following when any of said days occur on Sunday, and the third Monday in February, the third Monday in April, the last Monday in May, the first Monday in September, the second Monday in October, the fourth Monday in October, and Thanksgiving Day. "Legal holiday" shall also include, with respect to Suffolk county only, March the seventeenth and June the seventeenth, or the day following when said days occur on Sunday; provided, however, that the words "legal holiday" as used in section forty-five of chapter one hundred and forty-nine shall not include March the seventeenth, or the day following when said day occurs on Sunday.

        o   o   o

MICHIGAN

[MICH. COMP. LAWS ANN.—(Amended in 1973)]

§ 435.101. **Public holidays for bills and notes; transaction of business, holding of courts, adjournment of cases; Saturdays.** Sec. 1. The following days namely: January 1, New Year's Day; February 12, Lincoln's birthday; the third Monday of February, Washington's birthday; the last Monday of May, Memorial or Decoration day; July 4; the first Monday in September, Labor day; the second Monday in October, Columbus day; November 11, Veteran's day; December 25, Christmas day; every Saturday from 12 noon until 12 midnight, which is designated a half holiday; all national and state general election days, as defined in the state election law; and the fourth Thursday of November, Thanksgiving day, for all purposes whatever as regards the presenting for payment or acceptance and the protesting and giving notice of the dishonor of bills of exchange, bank checks, and promissory notes, also for the holding of courts, except as hereinafter provided, shall be treated and considered as the first day of the week, commonly called Sunday, and as public holidays or half holidays. All such bills, checks, and notes otherwise presentable for acceptance of payment on any of the days shall be deemed to be payable and presentable for acceptance or payment on the secular or business day next succeeding such holiday or half holiday. Nothing in any law in this state shall in any manner whatsoever affect the validity of, or render void or voidable, the payment, certification, or acceptance of a check or other negotiable instrument or any other transaction by a bank in this state, because done or performed on any Saturday between 12 noon and midnight, if such payment, certification, acceptance, or other transaction would be valid if done or performed before 12 noon on such Saturday. Nothing herein shall be construed to compel any bank, savings and loan association, or building and loan association in this state, which by law or custom is entitled to close at 12 noon on any Saturday, to keep open for the transaction of business or to perform any of the acts or transactions aforesaid, on any Saturday after such hour except at its own option. In construing this section, every Saturday, unless a whole holiday, shall for the holding of court and the transaction of any business authorized by the laws of this state be deemed a secular or business day. In case the return or adjourn day in any suit, matter, or hearing before any court, officer, referee, or arbitrators, shall come on any of the days first above named except Sunday, such suit, matter, or proceeding, commenced or adjourned, shall not, by reason of coming on any such days except Sunday, abate, but the same shall stand continued on the next succeeding day, at the same time and place unless the next day be the first day of the week, or a holiday, in which case the same shall stand continued to the next day succeeding the first day of the week or holiday, at the same time and place. Whenever the first day of the general term of any circuit court, as fixed by the order of a circuit judge shall fall upon either of the days first above named or whenever any circuit court shall be adjourned to any of the days first above named, such court may be adjourned to the next succeeding secular day. Nothing herein contained shall be construed to prevent or invalidate the entry, issuance, service, or execution of any writ, summons, or confession of judgment, or other legal process whatever, holding courts or the transaction of any lawful business except banking on any of the Saturday afternoons herein designated as half holidays, nor to prevent any bank, savings and loan association, or building and loan association from keeping its doors open or transacting its business on any Saturday afternoons, if by vote of its directors it elects to do so. The legislative body of any county or city may, by ordinance or resolution, provide for the closing of county or municipal offices for any or for all purposes on every Saturday.

§ 435.102. Holiday on Sunday, observance on Monday. Sec. 2. Whenever January 1; February 12; July 4; November 11; or December 25 shall fall upon Sunday, the next Monday following shall be deemed a public holiday for any or all of the purposes aforesaid. In such cases all bills of exchange, checks, and promissory notes made after the passage of this act which would otherwise be presentable for acceptance or payment on such Monday shall be deemed to be presentable for acceptance or payment on the secular business day next succeeding the holiday.

§ 435.141. **Designation of Casimir Pulaski Day.** Sec. 1. October 11 of each year shall be known as the "Casimir Pulaski Day".

MINNESOTA

[MINN. STAT. ANN.]

§ 645.44.

°   °   °

Subd. 5. Holidays. "Holiday" includes New Year's Day, January 1; Washington's and Lincoln's Birthday, the third Monday in February; Memorial Day, the last Monday in May; Independence Day, July 4; Labor Day, the first Monday in September; Christopher Columbus Day, the second Monday in October; Veterans Day, the fourth Monday in October; Thanksgiving Day, the fourth Thursday in November; and Christmas Day, December 25; provided, when New Year's Day, January 1; or Independence Day, July 4; or Christmas Day, December 25; falls on Sunday, the following day shall be a holiday and, provided, when New Year's Day, January 1; or Independence Day, July 4; or Christmas Day, December 25; falls on Saturday, the preceding day shall be a holiday. No public business shall be transacted on any holiday, except in cases of necessity and except in cases of public business transacted by the legislature, nor shall any civil process be served thereon.

°   °   °

MISSISSIPPI

[MISS. CODE ANN.—(Effective in 1971)]

§ 3-3-7. **Legal holidays.** The following are declared to be legal holidays, viz: the first day of January (New Year's Day); the third Monday of January (Robert E. Lee's birthday); the third Monday of February (Washington's birthday); the last Monday of April (Confederate Memorial Day); the first Monday of June (Jefferson Davis' birthday), the fourth day of July (Independence Day); the first Monday of September (Labor Day); the eleventh day of November (Armistice or Veterans' Day); the day fixed by proclamation by the governor of Mississippi as a day of thanksgiving which shall be fixed to correspond to the date proclaimed by the President of the United States (Thanksgiving Day); and the twenty-fifth day of December (Christmas Day). Provided, however, that in the event any holiday hereinbefore declared legal shall fall on Sunday, then the next following day shall be a legal holiday.

Insofar as possible, Armistice Day shall be observed by appropriate exercises in all the public schools in the State of Mississippi at the eleventh hour in the morning of the eleventh day of the eleventh month of the year.

MISSOURI

[MO. ANN. STAT.—(Vernon) (Amended in 1973)]

§ 9.010. Public holidays. The first day of January, the twelfth day of February, the third Monday in February, the eighth day of May, the last Monday in May, the fourth day of July, the first Monday in September, the second Monday in October, the eleventh day of November, any general primary election day, any general state election day, the fourth Thursday in November, and the twenty-fifth of December, are declared and established public holidays; and when any of such holidays falls upon Sunday, the Monday next following shall be considered the holiday. There shall be no holiday for state employees on the fourth Monday of October.

§ 9.020. Designation of certain holidays. In each year the twelfth day of February is known as "Lincoln Day" and the thirteenth day of April is known as "Jefferson Day" and the second Monday in October is known as "Columbus Day".

§ 9.030. Governor to proclaim "Jefferson Day". The governor shall annually issue a proclamation setting apart April thirteenth as "Jefferson Day", and recommending that it be observed by the people with appropriate exercises in the public schools and otherwise to the end that the memory of the public service and the humanitarian principles of Thomas Jefferson may be perpetuated.

§ 9.035. May 8, Truman Day. The governor shall issue annually a proclamation setting apart the eighth day of May as "Truman Day" and recommending to the people of the state that the day be appropriately observed in honor of and out of respect for Harry S. Truman, the thirty-third president of the United States, a distinguished public servant and the only Missourian ever to be elected to this high office.

§ 9.040. "Missouri Day", date of — how observed. The third Wednesday of October of each year is known and designated as "Missouri Day" and is set apart as a day commemorative of Missouri history to be observed by the teachers and pupils of schools with the appropriate exercises. The people of the state of Missouri, and the educational, commercial, political, civic, religious and fraternal organizations of the state of Missouri are requested to devote some part of the day to the methodical consideration of the products of the mines, fields, and forests of the state and to the consideration of the achievements of the sons and daughters of Missouri in commerce, literature, statesmanship, science and art, and in other departments of activity in which the state has rendered service to mankind.

§ 9.050. May 1, Law Day. In order to rededicate Missourians to the principles of the democratic form of government; to emphasize that ours is a government of law and not of men; and to further our philosophy that, "The Welfare of the People shall be the Supreme Law", May first of each year shall be designated as Law Day U.S.A. It is not the purpose of this section to declare another legal holiday, but a day to solemnly declare allegiance to the principles of democracy, and respect for law.

MONTANA

[MONT. REV. CODES ANN.—(Amended in 1974)]

§ 19-107. (10) Legal holidays and business days defined. The following are legal holidays in the state of Montana:

(1) Each Sunday.
(2) New Year's Day, January 1.
(3) Lincoln's Birthday, February 12.
(4) Washington's Birthday, the third Monday in February.
(5) Memorial Day, the last Monday in May.
(6) Independence Day, July 4.
(7) Labor Day, the first Monday in September.
(8) Columbus Day, the second Monday in October.
(9) Veterans' Day, November 11.
(10) Thanksgiving Day, the fourth Thursday in November.
(11) Christmas Day, December 25.
(12) State general election day.

If any of the above-enumerated holidays (except Sunday) fall upon a Sunday, the Monday following is a holiday. All other days are business days.

Whenever any bank in the state of Montana elects to remain closed and refrains from the transaction of business on Saturday, pursuant to authority for permissive closing on Saturdays by virtue of the laws of the state, legal holidays for such bank during the year of such election are hereby limited to the following holidays:

(1) Each Sunday.
(2) New Year's Day, January 1.
(3) Memorial Day, the last Monday in May.
(4) Independence Day, July 4.
(5) Labor Day, the first Monday in September.
(6) Thanksgiving Day, the fourth Thursday in November.
(7) Christmas Day, December 25.

(8) On such days as banks are closed in accordance with sections 5-1058 to 5-1062.

Any bank practicing Saturday closing in compliance with law may remain closed and refrain from the transaction of business on Saturdays, notwithstanding that a Saturday may coincide with a legal holiday other than one of the holidays designated above for banks practicing Saturday closing in compliance with law, and provided further that it shall be optional for any bank, whether practicing Saturday closing or not, to observe as a holiday and to be closed on any day upon which a general election is held throughout the state of Montana and on Veterans' Day, November 11, and on any local holiday which historically or traditionally or by proclamation of a local executive official or governing body is established as a day upon which businesses are generally closed in the community in which the bank is located.

§ 5-1042. (6014.126) **Transaction on holidays.** Nothing in any law of this state shall in any manner whatsoever affect the validity of, or render void or voidable, the payment, certification or acceptance of a check or other negotiable instrument, or any other transaction by a bank in this state, because done or performed during any time other than regular banking hours or on a legal holiday; provided, that nothing shall be construed herein to compel any bank in this state, which by law or custom is entitled to close at twelve noon on any Saturday, or for the whole or part of any legal holiday, to keep open for transaction of business, or to perform any of the acts or transactions aforesaid on any Saturday after such hour or on any legal holiday except at its option.

§ 32-4401. **Good Roads day.** The third Tuesday in June is hereby designated "Good Roads day." The governor may annually, by public proclamation, request the people of the state to contribute toward the improvement and safety of public highways.

NEBRASKA

[NEB. REV. STAT.—(Amended in 1969)]

§ 62-301. **Holidays, enumerated.** (1) For the purposes of the Uniform Commercial Code and section 62-302, the following days shall be holidays: New Year's Day, January 1; Lincoln's birthday, February 12; Washington's birthday, the third Monday in February; Arbor Day, April 22; Memorial Day, the last Monday in May; Independence Day, July 4; Labor Day, the first Monday in September; Columbus Day, the second Monday in October; Veterans Day, the fourth Monday in October; Thanksgiving Day, the fourth Thursday in November; and Christmas Day, December 25. If any of such dates fall on Sunday, the following Monday shall be a holiday.

(2) Any bank doing business in this state may, by a brief written

notice at, on, or near its front door, fully dispense with or restrict, to such extent as it may determine, the hours within which it will be open for business.

(3) Any bank may close on Saturday if it states such fact by a brief written notice at, on, or near its front door. Where such bank shall, in observance of such a notice, not be open for general business, such day shall, with respect to the particular bank, be the equivalent of a holiday, as fully as if such day were listed in subsection (1) of this section, and any act authorized, required, or permitted to be performed at, by, or with respect to such bank which shall, in observance of such notice not be open for general business, acting in its own behalf or in any capacity whatever, may be performed on the next succeeding business day and no liability or loss of rights on the part of any person shall result from such delay.

(4) Any bank which, by the notice provided for by subsection (3) of this section, has created the holiday for such bank may, without destroying the legal effect of the holiday for it and solely for the convenience of its customers, remain open all or part of said day in a limited fashion by treating every transaction with its customers on said day as though said transaction had taken place immediately upon the opening of such bank on the first following business day.

§ 62-301.01. Holidays; transactions with bank; validity. Nothing in any law of this state shall in any manner affect the validity of, or render void or voidable any transaction by a bank in this state because done or performed during any time other than regular banking hours; *Provided*, that nothing herein shall be construed to compel any bank in this state which by law or custom is entitled to close at a fixed hour on any day or for the whole or any part of any holiday, to keep open for the transaction of business on any day after such hour, or on any holiday, except at its own option.

§ 84-104.01. (Effective in 1973) Veterans Day; proclamation by Governor; prohibition of transaction of business by state departments; manner of observance. The Governor shall issue his proclamation each year designating Veterans Day and calling upon the public schools and citizens of Nebraska to observe such day as a patriotic day. Veterans Day shall be November 11, annually, unless such date falls on Saturday, or Sunday, in which event the Governor may declare the preceding Friday or the following Monday as Veterans Day. No business shall be transacted on that day at any department of the State of Nebraska, except for necessary maintenance, highway construction inspection or in case of emergency. In pursuance to such proclamation, suitable exercises having reference to the wars and military campaigns of the United States, of Nebraska's role therein, and honoring the veterans of such wars and campaigns may be held in all schools of the state, both public and private.

NEVADA

[NEV. REV. STAT.—(Amended in 1971)]

§ 236.015. **Legal holidays; closing of state and county offices, courts, banks, savings and loan associations, public schools and University of Nevada System.** 1. On and after January 1, 1971, the following days are declared to be legal holidays for state and county government offices:

> January 1 (New Year's Day)
>
> Third Monday in February (Washington's Birthday)
>
> Last Monday in May (Memorial Day)
>
> July 4 (Independence Day)
>
> First Monday in September (Labor Day)
>
> Fourth Monday in October (Veterans' Day)
>
> October 31 (Nevada Day)
>
> Fourth Thursday in November (Thanksgiving Day)
>
> December 25 (Christmas Day)
>
> Any day that may be appointed by the President of the United States or by the governor for public fast, thanksgiving or as a legal holiday.

2. All state and county offices, courts, banks, savings and loan associations, public schools and the University of Nevada System shall close on the legal holidays enumerated in subsection 1 unless in the case of appointed holidays all or a part thereof are specifically exempted.

3. If January 1, July 4, October 31 or December 25 falls upon a:

(a) Sunday, the Monday following shall be observed as a legal holiday.

(b) Saturday, the Friday preceding shall be observed as a legal holiday.

Days of Observance

§ 236.020. **Mother's Day.** The governor of this state is authorized and requested to issue annually a proclamation calling upon the state officials to display the United States flag on all state and school buildings, and the people of the state to display the flag at their homes, lodges, churches and places of business, and other suitable places, on the 2nd Sunday in May, known as "Mother's Day," founded by Anna Jarvis of Philadelphia, as a public expression of love and reverence for the mothers of our state and other women serving it, and as an inspiration for better homes and closer ties between the home and the state.

§ 236.030. **Law Day U.S.A.** 1. May 1 of each year shall be designated as Law Day U.S.A.

2. It is not the purpose of this section to declare a legal holiday, but a day to declare solemn allegiance to the principles of democracy and respect for law.

§ 236.040. **Nevada All-Indian Stampede Days.** The governor of this state is authorized and requested to issue annually a proclamation designating the third week of July as "Nevada All-Indian Stampede Days" to be celebrated in Fallon, Nevada, in commemoration of the Indian people and their efforts to maintain their culture, customs and traditions.

§ 236.050. **Nevada Mineral Industry Week.** 1. The governor shall annually proclaim the first week in February to be Nevada Mineral Industry Week to commemorate the important role mining has had in the history and economy of the state.

2. The proclamation shall call upon news media, educators and state officials to call the attention of the citizens of Nevada to the history of mining in the state and the role it plays in the development of the culture and economy of its people.

§ 1.130. **Nonjudicial days; transaction of judicial business.** 1. No court except a justice's court or a municipal court shall be opened nor shall any judicial business be transacted except by a justice's court or municipal court on Sunday, or on any day declared to be a legal holiday according to the provisions of NRS 236.015, except for the following purposes:

(a) To give, upon their request, instructions to a jury then deliberating on their verdict.

(b) To receive a verdict or discharge a jury.

(c) For the exercise of the power of a magistrate in a criminal action or in a proceeding of a criminal nature.

(d) For the issue of a writ of attachment, which may be issued on each and all of the days above enumerated upon the plaintiff, or some person in his behalf, setting forth in the affidavit required by law for obtaining the writ the additional averment as follows: That the affiant has good reason to believe, and does believe, that it will be too late for the purpose of acquiring a lien by the writ to wait until subsequent day for the issuance of the same. All proceedings instituted, and all writs issued, and all official acts done on any of the days above specified, under and by virtue of this section, shall have all the validity, force and effect of proceedings commenced on other days, whether a lien be obtained or a levy made under and by virtue of the writ.

2. Nothing herein contained shall affect private transactions of any nature whatsoever.

§ 10.030. **Performance of secular acts.** Whenever any act of a secular nature, other than a work of necessity or mercy, is appointed by law or contract to be performed upon a particular day, which day falls upon a holiday or a nonjudicial day, it may be performed upon the next business day with the same effect as if it had been performed upon the day appointed; and if such act is to be performed at a particular hour it may be performed at the same hour of the next business day.

NEW HAMPSHIRE

[N.H. REV. STAT. ANN.—(Amended in 1973)]

§ 288:1. **Holidays.** Thanksgiving Day whenever appointed, the fourth Monday in April known as Fast Day, the first Monday in September known as Labor Day, the day on which the biennial election is held, January first, the third Monday in February known as Washington's Birthday, the thirtieth day in May known as Memorial Day, July fourth, the second Monday in October known as Columbus Day, the eleventh day in November known as Veterans Day and Christmas Day are legal holidays.

§ 288:2. **Falling on Sunday.** When either of the days mentioned in section one hereof falls on Sunday, the following day shall be observed as a holiday.

§ 288:3. **Banking organizations, closing on Saturdays.** Any banking organization which for the purposes of this section shall include not only state banks, savings banks, trust companies, and other companies, associations and businesses described in section 1 of chapter 384, RSA, but also any national banking association, federal savings and loan association or federal credit union doing business in this state, may remain closed on any or all Saturdays as it may determine from time to time. Any Saturday on which a banking organization remains closed shall be with respect to such banking organization a holiday and not a business day. Any act authorized, required or permitted to be performed at or by or with respect to any banking organization as herein defined, on a Saturday, may be so performed on the next succeeding business day, and no liability or loss of rights of any kind shall result from such delay.

§ 275:28. **Holidays.** No employee shall be required to work in any mill or factory on any legal holiday, except to perform such work as is both absolutely necessary and can lawfully be performed on the Lord's Day.

§ 275:29. **Penalty.** Whoever violates RSA 275:28 shall be guilty of a misdemeanor if a natural person, or guilty of a felony if any other person.

NEW JERSEY

[N.J. STAT. ANN.—(Effective in 1971)]

§ 36:1-1. **Presentation or payment of bills; checks and notes; transaction of public business; state and county offices closed.** The following days in each year shall, for all purposes whatsoever as regards the presenting for payment or acceptance, and of the protesting and giving notice of dishonor, of bills of exchange, bank checks and promissory notes be treated and considered as the first day of the week, commonly called Sunday, and as public holidays: January 1, known as New Year's Day; February 12, known as Lincoln's Birthday; the third Monday in February, known as Washington's Birthday; the day designated and known as Good Friday; the last Monday in May, known as Memorial Day; July 4, known as Independence Day; the first Monday in September, known as Labor Day; the second Monday in October, known as Columbus Day; the fourth Monday in October, known as Veteran's Day; the fourth Thursday in November, known as Thanksgiving Day; December 25, known as Christmas Day; any general election day in this State; every Saturday; and any day heretofore or hereafter appointed, ordered or recommended by the Governor of this State, or the President of the United States, as a day of fasting and prayer, or other religious observance, or as a bank holiday or holidays. All such bills, checks and notes, otherwise presentable for acceptance or payment on any of the days herein enumerated, shall be deemed to be payable and be presentable for acceptance or payment on the secular or business day next succeeding any such holiday.

Whenever any of the days herein enumerated can and shall fall on a Sunday, the Monday next following shall, for any of the purposes herein enumerated be deemed a public holiday; and bills of exchange, checks and promissory notes which otherwise would be presentable for acceptance or payment on such Monday, shall be deemed to be presentable for acceptance or payment on the secular or business day next succeeding such holiday.

In construing this section, every Saturday shall, until 12 o'clock noon, be deemed a secular or business day, except as is hereinbefore provided in regard to bills of exchange, bank checks and promissory notes, and the days herein enumerated except bank holidays and Saturdays shall be considered as the first day of the week, commonly called Sunday, and public holidays, for all purposes whatsoever as regards the transaction of business in the public offices of this State, or counties of this State; but on all other days or half days, except Sunday or as otherwise provided by law, such offices shall be kept open for the transaction of business.

§ 36:1-2. **Transaction of business on holidays.** Any person or corporation may transact either private or public business in this state on any designated holiday or half holiday, in the same manner as on any other day of the week on which it is lawful to transact such business.

§ 36:1-3. **Sales of real and personal property on Saturday.** Any sale of real or personal property made by any public officer, or by any citizen of this state, on any Saturday, shall be as valid as though such sale was made on any other day of the week on which it is lawful to sell and transfer real or personal property.

§ 36:1-4. Transactions by bank or trust company after twelve o'clock noon on Saturdays. The payment, certification or acceptance of any check or other negotiable instrument or any other transaction by any bank or trust company, or banking institution shall not be void or voidable or invalid because done or performed on Saturday between twelve o'clock noon and midnight, if such payment, certification, acceptance or other transaction would be valid if done or performed before twelve o'clock noon on such Saturday. Nothing herein contained shall be construed to compel any bank to keep open, or to perform any of the acts or transactions aforesaid, on any Saturday after twelve o'clock noon except at its own option.

§ 36:1-5. Mother's day. For the purpose of paying a special tribute to mothers, the second Sunday of May in each year is designated as a day for the general observance of that purpose and shall be known as Mother's Day.

§ 36:1-6. Father's day. For the purpose of paying a special tribute to fathers, the third Sunday of June in each year is designated as a day for the general observance of that purpose and shall be known as Father's Day.

§ 36:2-1. Crispus Attucks Day. In order to pay respect to Crispus Attucks, the first American patriot to give his life in our country's war of freedom, the fifth day of March, in each year, is designated as a day for the general observance of that purpose and shall be known as Crispus Attucks Day; *provided, however,* that when said day shall fall on any secular or business day of the week, no business transaction, allowable or permissible on such secular or business day, shall be prohibited.

§ 36:2-2. American Flag Week. The Governor of the State of New Jersey is requested, annually, to issue an appropriate proclamation designating the period of June 7 through June 14 of each year as American Flag Week, and calling upon all citizens of the State to display the flag of the United States of America on those days.

§ 36:2-3. New Jersey Day. The Governor of the State of New Jersey is requested to issue annually an appropriate proclamation designating April 17 as New Jersey Day and calling upon all citizens and residents of this State to commemorate and observe said day as the anniversary of the beginning of unified government in New Jersey by directing, and participating in, programs recalling our heritage and its meaning to New Jersey today and in the future.

NEW MEXICO

[N.M. STAT. ANN.—(Amended in 1971)]

Note: N.M. Laws 1973, ch. 165, amended this section to change Memorial day to May 30 and Armistice day and Veterans' day to

November 11, effective only if Congress passes legislation making such changes.

§ 56-1-2. Legal holidays—designation. Legal public holidays in New Mexico are:

New Year's Day, January 1;

Lincoln's Birthday, February 12;

Washington's Birthday, third Monday in February;

Memorial Day, last Monday in May;

Independence Day, July 4;

Labor Day, first Monday in September;

Columbus Day, second Monday in October;

Armistice Day and Veterans' Day, fourth Monday in October;

Thanksgiving Day, fourth Thursday in November; and

Christmas Day, December 25.

§ 56-1-1. Arbor Day—Establishment—Observance. The second Friday in March of each year shall be set apart and known as Arbor Day, to be observed by the people of this state in the planting of forest trees for the benefit and adornment of public and private grounds, places and ways, and in such other efforts and undertakings as shall be in harmony with the general character of the day so established: Provided, that the actual planting of trees may be done on the day designated or at such other most convenient times as may best conform to local climatic conditions, such other time to be designated and due notice thereof given by the several county superintendents of schools for their respective counties.

The day as above designated shall be a holiday in all public schools of the state, and school officers and teachers are required to have the schools, under their respective charge, observe the day by planting of trees or other appropriate exercises.

Annually, at the proper season, the governor shall issue a proclamation, calling the attention of the people to the provisions of this section and recommending and enjoining its due observance. The respective county superintendents of schools shall also promote by all proper means the observance of the day, and the said county superintendents of schools shall make annual reports to the governor of the state of the action taken in this behalf in their respective counties.

§ 56-1-3. Legal holidays—Sundays—effect on commercial paper.
A. Whenever a legal public holiday falls on Sunday, the following Monday is a legal public holiday.

B. Any bill, check or note presentable for acceptance or payment on a legal public holiday or on a Sunday is payable and presentable for acceptance or payment on the next business day after the legal public holiday or Sunday.

§ 56-1-4. August 3rd designated Ernie Pyle Day. In appreciation of the splendid work as a writer and war correspondent, and the great credit reflected upon the state of New Mexico by Ernie Pyle, one of her outstanding citizens, his birthday, August 3rd, of each year, is hereby designated as Ernie Pyle Day, upon which appropriate ceremonies shall be held in his honor and in honor of all members of the armed forces of the United States serving so valiantly in the present [sic] World War.

§ 56-1-5. Onate Day. The governor shall designate for the benefit of the state of New Mexico in connection with an annual celebration held in the Espanola Valley each year during the month of July, a day during said month to be known as Onate Day.

§ 56-1-6.1. Bataan Day. In honor of the brave and patriotic New Mexicans composing the 200th and 515th Coast Artillery Regiments (anti-aircraft) who served in the Phillippine Islands during World War Two, fighting insuperable odds and enduring every deprivation, and who, following surrender, entered upon a tragic "death march," the day of April 9 is designated "Bataan Day."

NEW YORK

[N.Y. GEN. CONSTR. LAW—(McKinney) (Effective in 1971)]

§ 24. Public holidays; half-holidays. The term public holiday includes the following days in each year: the first day of January, known as New Year's day; the twelfth day of February, known as Lincoln's birthday; the third Monday in February, known as Washington's birthday; the last Monday in May, known as Memorial day; the fourth day of July, known as Independence day; the first Monday in September, known as Labor day; the second Monday in October, known as Columbus day; the fourth Monday in October, known as Veterans' day; the fourth Thursday in November, known as Thanksgiving day; and the twenty-fifth day of December, known as Christmas day, and if any of such days is Sunday, the next day thereafter; each general election day, and each day appointed by the president of the United States or by the governor of this state as a day of general thanksgiving, general fasting and prayer, or other general religious observances. The term half-holiday includes the period from noon to midnight of each Saturday which is not a public holiday.

§ 25. Public holiday, Saturday or Sunday in contractual obligations; extension of time where performance of act authorized or required by contract is due on Saturday, Sunday or public holiday. 1. Where a contract by its terms authorizes or requires the payment of money or the performance of a condition on a Saturday, Sunday or a public holiday, or authorizes or requires the payment of money or the performance of a condition within or before or after a period of time computed from a certain day, and such period of time ends on a Saturday, Sunday or a public holiday, unless the contract expressly or impliedly indicates a different intent, such payment may be made or condition performed on the next succeeding business day, and if the period ends at a specified hour, such payment may be made or condition performed, at or before the same hour of such next succeeding business day, with the same force and effect as if made or performed in accordance with the terms of the contract.

2.   Where time is extended by virtue of the provisions of this section, such extended time shall not be included in the computation of interest unless the contract so provides, except that when the period is specified as a number of months, such extended time shall be included in the computation of interest unless the contract otherwise provides.

NORTH CAROLINA

[N.C. GEN. STAT.—(Amended in 1973)]

§ 103-4. **Dates of public holidays.** (a) The following are declared to be legal public holidays:

(1) New Year's Day, January 1.

(2) Robert E. Lee's Birthday, January 19.

(3) Washington's Birthday, the third Monday in February.

(4) Anniversary of signing of Halifax Resolves, April 12.

(5) Confederate Memorial Day, May 10.

(6) Anniversary of Mecklenburg Declaration of Independence, May 20.

(7) Memorial Day, the last Monday in May.

(8) Easter Monday.

(9) Independence Day, July 4.

(10) Labor Day, the first Monday in September.

(11) Columbus Day, the second Monday in October.

(12) Veterans Day, November 11.

(13) Tuesday after the first Monday in November in years in which a general election is to be held.

(14) Thanksgiving Day, the fourth Thursday in November.

(15) Christmas Day, December 25.

Provided that Easter Monday and Memorial Day, the last Monday in May, shall be a holiday for all State and national banks only.

(b) Whenever any public holiday shall fall upon Sunday, the Monday following shall be a public holiday.

§ 103-5. **Acts to be done on Sunday or holidays.** Where the day or the last day for doing an act required or permitted by law to be done falls on Sunday or a holiday the act may be done on the next succeeding secular or business day and where the courthouse in any county is closed on Saturday or any other day by order of the board of county commissioners of said county and the day or the last day required for filing an advance bid or the filing of any pleading or written instrument of any kind with any officer having an office in the courthouse, or the performance of any act required or permitted to be done in said courthouse falls on Saturday or other day during which said courthouse is closed as aforesaid, then said Saturday or other day during which said courthouse is closed as aforesaid shall be deemed a holiday; and said advance bid, pleading or other written instrument may be filed, and any act required or permitted to be done in the courthouse may be done on the next day during which the courthouse is open for business.

§ 103-6. **Arbor Week.** The week in March of each year containing March 15 is hereby designated as Arbor Week in North Carolina.

NORTH DAKOTA

[N.D. CENT. CODE—(Twice amended in 1973)]

§ 1-03-01. **Holidays.** Holidays are as follows:

1. Every Sunday.
2. The first day of January, which is New Year's Day.
3. The third Monday in February, in recognition of the birthday of George Washington.
4. The fourth day of July, which is the anniversary of the Declaration of Independence.
5. The twenty-fifth day of December, which is Christmas Day.
6. The last Monday in May, which is Memorial Day.
7. The first Monday in September, which is Labor Day.
8. The eleventh day of November, which is Veterans' Day.
9. The fourth Thursday in November, which is Thanksgiving Day.
10. The Friday next preceding Easter Sunday and commonly known as Good Friday.
11. Every day on which an election is held throughout the state.
12. Every day appointed by the President of the United States or by the governor of this state for a public holiday.

Nothing in this section shall be construed to prevent the holding of legislative sessions or the taking of final action on any legislative matter upon any of such holidays other than Sunday. Any action heretofore taken upon any legislation matter upon any such holiday shall be valid and legal for all purposes. All state offices and offices of political subdivisions in the state shall remain open for business as usual on election days.

§ 1-03-02. **When day following holiday shall be a holiday.** If the first day of January, the twelfth day of February, the fourth day of July, or the twenty-fifth day of December falls upon a Sunday, the Monday following shall be the holiday.

§ 1-03-02.1. **When holiday falls on a Saturday—bank holiday.** If any of the holidays enumerated in section 1-03-02 fall on a Saturday, the Friday immediately before shall be the holiday for purposes of the banks of this state.

§ 1-03-04. **Business days.** All days other than those mentioned in sections 1-03-01, 1-03-02, and 1-03-02.1 are to be deemed business days for all purposes; provided, however, that any bank may remain closed on any one business day of each week, as it may from time to time elect. Any day upon which a bank is so closed shall be, with respect to such bank, a holiday and not a business day. Any act authorized, required, or permitted to be performed at or by or with respect to such bank on such day, may be performed on the next succeeding business day, and no liability or loss of rights shall result from such delay.

Provided, further, that notice of intention on the part of any bank to remain closed on a business day of the week shall be posted in a conspicuous place in the lobby of the bank at least thirty days prior to the establishment of such practice and similar notice shall be given when a bank elects to change the day of the week on which it remains closed.

Any state bank establishing the practice, as hereinbefore provided, of closing one day a week shall give thirty days' notice in writing to the state examiner, in addition to posting the notice in the lobby.

OHIO

[OHIO REV. CODE ANN.—(Page) (Effective in 1975)]

§ 1.14. **First day excluded and last day included in computing time; exceptions; legal holiday defined.** The time within which an act is required by law to be done shall be computed by excluding the first and including the last day; except that when the last day falls on Sunday or a legal holiday, then the act may be done on the next succeeding day which is not Sunday or a legal holiday.

When a public office in which an act, required by law, is to be performed is closed to the public for the entire day which constitutes the last day for doing such act or before its usual closing time on such day, then such act may be performed on the next succeeding day which is not a Sunday or a legal holiday as defined in this section.

"Legal holiday" as used in this section means the following days:

(A) The first day of January, known as New Year's day;

(B) The third Monday in January, known as Martin Luther King day;

(C) The third Monday in February, known as Washington-Lincoln day;

(D) The last Monday in May, known as Decoration or Memorial day;

(E) The fourth day of July, known as Independence day;

(F) The first Monday in September, known as Labor day;

(G) The second Monday in October, known as Columbus day;

(H) The eleventh day of November, known as Veterans' day;

(I) The fourth Thursday in November, known as Thanksgiving day;

(J) The twenty-fifth day of December, known as Christmas day;

(K) Any day appointed and recommended by the governor of this state or the president of the United States as a holiday.

If any day designated in this section as a legal holiday falls on Sunday, the next succeeding day is a legal holiday.

§ 5.21. **Labor day; Columbus day; Veterans' day.** The first Monday in September of each year shall be known as "Labor day" and for all purposes shall be considered as the first day of the week.

The second Monday in October of each year shall be known as "Columbus day" and is a legal holiday.

The eleventh day of November of each year shall be known as "Veterans' day" and is a legal holiday. If said day falls on Sunday, the following Monday is the legal holiday.

§ 5.22. **Arbor day.** The governor shall, by proclamation, designate the last Friday of each April as "Arbor Day."

§ 5.23. **Holidays to be commemorated in schools.** The twelfth day of February, known as Lincoln's birthday, the twenty-second day of February, known as Washington's birthday, the thirtieth day of May, known as Memorial day, and the eleventh day of November, known as Veterans' day, shall be commemorated in the schools.

§ 5.30. **Saturday afternoon is legal holiday.** Every Saturday afternoon is a legal holiday, beginning at twelve noon and ending at twelve midnight. No section of the Revised Code and no decision of any court shall affect the validity of any check, bill of exchange, order, promissory note, due bill, mortgage, or other writing obligatory made, signed, negotiated, transferred, assigned, or paid by any person, corporation, or bank upon said holiday, or any other transaction had thereon.

§ 5.40. **Financial institutions may transact business on holidays and outside of hours.** Any financial institution doing business in this state may outside of regular banking hours on any day, or at any time on a day which is in whole or in part a holiday, pay, certify, or accept negotiable or nonnegotiable instruments including a demand instrument dated on the holiday on which it is presented for payment, certification, or acceptance, and transact any other business which would be valid if done on a business day during regular banking hours. This section does not affect any law relative to the time of maturity or presentment of negotiable instruments or the validity of any law relative to transactions by persons or corporations.

This section does not require a financial institution which remains open for business on all or a part of any holiday to perform any act on that day in its capacity as collection agent which would not be required of it if it were closed on such holiday or part holiday.

OKLAHOMA

[OKLA. STAT. ANN.—(Amended in 1971)]

Tit. 25, § 82.1. Designation and dates of holidays. The designation and dates of holidays in Oklahoma shall be as follows: Each Sunday, New Year's Day on the 1st day of January, Washington's Birthday on the third Monday in February, Memorial Day on the last Monday in May, Independence Day on the 4th day of July, Labor Day on the first Monday in September, Columbus Day on the second Monday in October, Veterans' Day on the 11th day of November, Thanksgiving Day on the fourth Thursday in November, Christmas on the 25th day of December; and if any of such holidays other than Sunday at any time fall on Sunday, the succeeding Monday shall be a holiday in that year. Any act authorized, required or permitted to be performed on a holiday as designated in this section may be performed on the next succeeding business day and no liability or loss of rights of any kind shall result from such delay.

§ 82.2. (Amended in 1972) Additional holidays—acts performable —optional closing by banks and offices. The following additional days are designated as holidays:

Jefferson Day on the 13th day of April; Oklahoma Day on the 22d day of April; Mother's Day on the second Sunday in May; Indian Day on the first Saturday after the full moon in September; Cherokee Strip Day on the 16th day of September; Will Rogers' Day on the 4th day of November; Citizenship Recognition Day on such date as may be fixed by the Governor; Oklahoma Historical Day on the 10th day of October; Senior Citizens' Day the 9th day of June; each day in which a state election is held throughout the State of Oklahoma; and such other days as may be designated by the President of the United States or the Governor of the State of Oklahoma. Notwithstanding the day designated for Veterans' Day by Section 82.1 of this title, any bank, savings and loan association or credit union may observe the fourth Monday in October as Veterans' Day. Any act authorized, required or permitted to be performed on any holiday as designated in this section may and shall be performed on said day the same as on any business day; provided any state, national or federal reserve bank, building and loan association, credit union, state, federal, county or municipal office may close on any day designated in this section as a holiday, and, upon such bank, building and loan association, credit union, or public office being closed on such day, any act authorized, required or permitted to be performed at or by such bank, building and loan association, credit union, public office or public official may be performed on the next succeeding business day and no liability or loss of rights of any kind shall result from such delay.

§ 86. Will Rogers Day. The fourth day of November each year is hereby declared a public holiday, to be known as "Will Rogers Day". Provided, this Act shall not affect the legality of judicial proceedings, the service of process, making or execution of agreements or instruments in writing, or the transaction of other business on said day.

§ 88. Oklahoma week. That the week beginning with November 11th through November 16th (Statehood Day) of each year is hereby designated as "Oklahoma Week".

That every city in Oklahoma, every business, every organization, every man, woman and child are hereby urged during this week to conduct a personal campaign to let the world know that "we are proud of Oklahoma, and prouder to be Oklahomans."

§ 89. Official day for Indian tribes. The Governor of the State of Oklahoma shall declare an official day for each Indian tribe in the State of Oklahoma. The particular designated day for each Indian tribe shall be selected by the respective Indian tribes.

§ 90.1. Oklahoma Heritage Week. The week in each year in which November 16 falls is hereby declared to be "Oklahoma Heritage Week," beginning on a Sunday when November 16 falls on such day or a following day of the week through Saturday.

OREGON

[ORE. REV. STAT.—(Amended in 1973)]

§ 187.010. Legal holidays; acts deferred to next business day.
(1) The following days are legal holidays in this state:
(a) Each Sunday.
(b) New Year's Day on January 1.
(c) Memorial Day on the last Monday in May.
(d) Independence Day on July 4.
(e) Labor Day on the first Monday in September.
(f) Veterans Day on November 11.
(g) Thanksgiving Day on the fourth Thursday in November.
(h) Christmas Day on December 25.

If any of such holidays, other than Sunday, at any time fall on Sunday, the succeeding Monday shall be a holiday in that year.

(2) Any act authorized, required or permitted to be performed on a holiday as designated in this section may be performed on the next succeeding business day; and no liability or loss of rights of any kind shall result from such delay.

§ 187.020. **Additional legal holidays.** In addition to those specified in ORS 187.010, the following days are legal holidays in this state:

(1) Lincoln's Birthday on the first Monday in February.

(2) Washington's Birthday on the third Monday in February.

(3) Every day appointed by the President of the United States or by the Governor as a holiday.

If any of such holidays at any time fall on Sunday, the succeeding Monday shall be a holiday in that year.

§ 187.025. **Days of commemoration.** The following days shall be days of commemoration but not legal holidays and shall be suitably observed in schools:

(1) Admission of Oregon into the Union on February 14.

(2) Columbus Day on October 12.

§ 187.030. **Banks closing on Saturdays and holidays; negotiable instruments payable on holidays, effect on time of payment.** (1) Any bank which elects to close on Saturdays under any Act permitting such closure shall not remain closed on any holiday enumerated in ORS 187.020 when such holiday occurs on Friday or the observance of which occurs on Monday.

(2) Any bank, which term, for the purposes of this section, includes any state bank, national bank, federal reserve bank, trust company, safe deposit company, mutual savings bank and savings and loan association, doing business in this state, may, at its sole option, remain open for business on any holiday as designated in ORS 187.020; but any act authorized, required or permitted to be performed at or by or with respect to any bank, as herein defined, may be performed on the next succeeding business day, and no liability or loss of rights of any kind shall result from such performance of business on such holiday.

(3) Negotiable instruments falling due on any holiday designated in ORS 187.010 or 187.020 shall be due and payable on the next succeeding business day.

PENNSYLVANIA

[PA. STAT. ANN.—(Amended in 1973)]

Tit. 44, § 11. Holidays designated; bank holidays; presentation and paying of instruments. The following days and half days, namely: the first day of January, commonly called New Year's Day, the twelfth day of February, known as Lincoln's Birthday, the third Monday of February, known as Washington's Birthday, Good Friday, the last Monday in May, known as Memorial Day, the fourteenth day of June, known as Flag Day, the fourth of July, called Independence Day, the first Monday of September, known as Labor Day, the second Monday in October, known as Columbus Day, the first Tuesday after the first Monday of November, Election Day, the eleventh day of November, known as Veterans' Day, the fourth Thursday in November, known as Thanksgiving Day, the twenty-fifth day of December, known as Christmas Day; and every Saturday, after twelve o'clock noon until twelve o'clock midnight, each of which Saturdays is hereby designated a half holiday; and any day appointed or recommended by the Governor of this State or the President of the United States as a day of thanksgiving or fastings and prayer, or other religious observance; and in the event of a financial crisis in the State or Nation, any day or days appointed by the Governor of this State or the President of the United States as a bank holiday; and in the event of public calamity in any part of the State through fire, flood, famine, violence, riot, insurrection, or enemy action, any day or days appointed by the Governor of this State as a bank holiday for banking institutions affected by such public calamity shall, for all purposes whatever as regards the presenting for payment or acceptance, and as regards the protesting and giving notice of the dishonor of bills of exchange, checks, drafts, and promissory notes, made after the passage of this act, be treated and considered as the first day of the week, commonly called Sunday, and as public holidays and half holidays; and all such bills, checks, drafts, and notes otherwise presentable for acceptance or payment on any of the said days, shall be deemed to be payable and be presentable for acceptance or payment on the secular or business day next succeeding such holiday or half holiday; except checks, drafts, bills of exchange, and promissory notes, payable at sight or on demand, which would otherwise be payable on any half holiday Saturday, shall be deemed to be payable at or before twelve o'clock noon of such half holiday: Provided, however, That for the purpose of protesting or otherwise holding liable any party to any bill of exchange, check, draft, or promissory note, and which shall not have been paid before twelve o'clock noon of any Saturday designated a half holiday as aforesaid, a demand for acceptance or payment thereof shall not be made, and notice of protest or dishonor thereof shall not be given, until the next succeeding secular or business day: And provided further, That when any person, firm, corporation or company shall, on any Saturday designated a half holiday, receive for collection any check, bill of exchange, draft, or promissory note, such person, firm, corporation, or company shall not be deemed guilty of any neglect or omission of duty, nor incur any liability, in not presenting for payment or acceptance or collection such check, bill of exchange, draft or promissory note, on that day: And provided further, That, in construing this section, every Saturday designated a half holiday shall, until twelve o'clock noon, be deemed a secular or business day; and the days and half days aforesaid, so designated as holidays and half holidays, shall be considered as public holidays and half holidays for all purposes whatsoever as regards the transaction of business, except that any day or days appointed as a bank holiday shall be regarded as secular or business days for all other purposes than those mentioned in this act: And provided further, That nothing herein contained shall be construed to prevent or invalidate the entry, issuance, service, or execution of any writ, summons, confession of judgment, or other legal process whatever, on any of the holidays or half holidays herein designated as holidays; nor to prevent any banking institution from keeping its doors open or transacting its business, on any Saturday afternoon, if by a vote of its directors it shall elect to do so, unless such Saturday is appointed as a bank holiday under the provisions of this act: And provided further, That any banking institution may, by a vote of its directors, or in the case of a private bank by action of the private banker or bankers, notice of which shall have been posted in its banking house for not less than fifteen days before the taking effect thereof, observe any Saturday throughout the year as a full holiday with like effect hereunder as though such day had been designated as a full holiday by the provisions of this act, and may in the same manner, observe as a full holiday any Monday next following the first day of January, the fourth day of July or the twenty-fifth day of December whenever any of such holidays shall occur on a Saturday with like effect hereunder as though such day had been designated as a full holiday by the provisions of this act.

§ 15. **Execution of legal process; banks may transact business; bank holidays; optional observance of Saturdays and certain Mondays by banks.** Nothing herein contained shall be construed to prevent or invalidate the entry, issuance, service, or execution of any writ, summons, confession of judgment, or other legal process whatever, on any of the holidays or half holidays herein designated as holidays; nor to prevent any banking institution from keeping its doors open or transacting its business, on any Saturday afternoon, if by a vote of its directors it shall elect to do so, unless such Saturday is appointed as a bank holiday under the provisions of this act: And provided further, That any banking institution may, by a vote of its directors, or in the case of a private bank by action of the private banker or bankers, notice of which shall have been posted in its banking house for not less than fifteen days before the taking effect thereof, observe any Saturday throughout the year as a full holiday with like effect hereunder as though such day had been designated as a full holiday by the provisions of this act, and may in the same manner, observe as a full holiday any Monday next following the first day of January, [the thirtieth day of May, the fourth day of

July] or the twenty-fifth day of December whenever any of such holidays shall occur on a Saturday with like effect hereunder as though such day had been designated as a full holiday by the provisions of this act.

§ 16.   When Monday a holiday; validity of acts on Saturday afternoon and certain holidays; option of banks as to keeping open. (a)   Whenever the first day of January, the twelfth day of February, the fourteenth day of June, the fourth day of July, the eleventh day of November or the twenty-fifth day of December, shall any of them occur on Sunday, the following day (Monday) shall be deemed and declared a public holiday. All bills of exchange, checks, drafts, or promissory notes, falling due on any of the Mondays observed as holidays, shall be due and payable on the next succeeding secular or business day; and all Mondays observed as holidays shall, for all purposes whatever as regards the presenting for payment or acceptance, and as regards the protesting and giving notice of the dishonor of bills of exchange, checks, drafts, and promissory notes, made after the passage of this act, be treated and considered as if the first day of the week, commonly called Sunday.

(b)   Nothing in any law of this Commonwealth shall in any manner whatsoever affect the validity of, or render void or voidable, the payment, certification, or acceptance of a check or other negotiable instrument or any other transaction by a banking institution in this State because done or performed or transacted on any Saturday between twelve o'clock noon and midnight, provided such payment, certification, acceptance or other transaction would be valid if done or performed on or before twelve o'clock on Saturday.

(c)   Nothing in any law of this Commonwealth shall in any manner whatsoever affect the validity of, or render void or voidable the payment, certification, or acceptance of, any bill of exchange, check, draft, promissory note, or other negotiable instrument, or any other transaction by a banking institution in this State, because done or performed or transacted on any of the following legal holidays: the twelfth day of February, the third Monday in February, Good Friday, the fourteenth day of June, the second Monday in October, or the first Tuesday after the first Monday of November, the eleventh day of November or whenever any of said days shall occur on Sunday, done or performed or transacted on the following day (Monday): Provided, Such payment, certification, acceptance, or other transaction would be valid if done or performed on a secular or business day: Provided further, however, That for the purpose of protesting or otherwise holding liable any party to any bill of exchange, check, draft, promissory note, or other negotiable instrument which shall not have been paid on any of said holidays, a demand for acceptance or payment thereof shall not be made, and notice of protest or dishonor thereof shall not be given, until the next succeeding secular or business day. Nothing herein shall be construed to require any banking institution to keep open for the transaction of business on any of said holidays, or to require any banking institution which elects to be open for business on all or any part of any of said holidays, to do or perform any act or transaction on such holiday; but all acts and transactions done or performed on any such holiday shall be at the option of such banking institution.

§ 19. **Arbor Day.** The governor of this commonwealth be requested to appoint a day to be designated as "Arbor Day," in Pennsylvania, and to recommend, by proclamation to the people, on the day named, the planting of trees and shrubbery in public school grounds and along public highways throughout the state.

§ 19.1. **Governor to appoint day as Arbor Day; observance.** The Governor each year shall appoint an appropriate day to be designated as Arbor Day and shall recommend by proclamation to the people that such day be suitably observed by widespread planting of trees and shrubs and by group and community programs stressing the value and importance of trees and forests.

§ 19.2. **Last Friday in April.** The day designated as Arbor Day shall be the last Friday in April.

§ 21. **Election days made legal half-holidays.** The third Tuesday of February of each year, and the first Tuesday after the first Monday of November of each year, be and the same are hereby designated as legal half-holidays from twelve o'clock noon until midnight of such days, and shall for all purposes whatsoever as regards the presenting for payment or acceptance, and as regards the protesting and giving notice of the dishonor of bills of exchange, checks, drafts and promissory notes, made after the passage of this act, be treated and considered as the first day of the week, commonly called Sunday, and as public holidays, and half-holidays, and all such bills, checks, drafts and notes otherwise presentable for acceptance or payment on any of the said days, shall be deemed to be payable and be presentable for acceptance or payment at or before twelve o'clock noon on such half-holidays.

Note: Concerning election day as a holiday, see also § 11.

§ 22. **Birthday of William Penn; observance on October 24.** The Governor shall annually issue his proclamation designating and calling upon the public schools, other educational institutions of the State, and the citizens of Pennsylvania to observe the birthday of William Penn, the great Founder and Governor of Pennsylvania. Said birthday of William Penn shall be observed on the twenty-fourth day of October of each year, unless such day falls on Saturday or Sunday, in which event the Governor may designate the preceding Friday or the following Monday. In pursuance to said proclamation of the Governor, appropriate exercises with respect to the life of William Penn, the Founder and Proprietor and Governor of Pennsylvania, and the principles advocated by him in founding Pennsylvania, shall be held in the public schools and other educational institutions under the Commonwealth.

Note: This section is repealed in part, insofar as it pertains to public schools and other educational institutions.

PUERTO RICO

[P.R. LAWS ANN.]

Tit. 1, § 71. Holidays generally. Holidays, within the meaning of sections 71-73 of this title, are every Sunday, the first day of January, the twenty-second day of February, the twenty-second day of March, Good Friday, the thirtieth day of May, the fourth day of July, the twenty-fifth day of July, the first Monday of September, to be known as Labor Day, the twenty-fifth day of December, every day on which an election is held throughout the island and every day appointed by the President of the United States, by the Governor of Puerto Rico or by the Legislative Assembly, for a public fast, thanksgiving, or holiday. When any such day falls upon a Sunday, the Monday following is a holiday.

§ 84. (Effective in 1971) Transference of holidays. The weekends listed below shall be held every year during the day and month set, immediately, after the holiday.

1. Washington's Birthday; shall be held on the third Monday of February.

2. Memorial Day; shall be held on the last Monday of May.

3. Discovery Day; shall be held on the second Monday of October.

4. Armistice Day; shall be held on the second Monday of October.

§ 73. Day of performance falling upon holiday. Whenever any act is appointed by law or contract to be performed upon a particular day, which day falls upon a holiday, such act may be performed upon the next business day with the same effect as if it had been performed upon the day appointed.

§ 74. January 6. The sixth day of January of each year is hereby declared to be an official and legal holiday in the Commonwealth of Puerto Rico.

§ 75. January 11; birthday of Eugenio Maria de Hostos. January 11, the date of the anniversary of the birth of the illustrious Puerto Rican educator, philosopher, sociologist, writer, and patriot, is hereby declared a legal holiday every year.

§ 76. Second Sunday of April; Antonio R. Barcelo Day. The second Sunday of April of 1941, and of each succeeding year is hereby declared a legal holiday, and such day shall be known as Antonio R. Barcelo Day.

§ 77. **April 16; Jose de Diego Day.** The sixteenth day of the month of April of each year shall be known in Puerto Rico as "Jose de Diego Day", and is hereby declared to be a legal holiday.

§ 78. **July 17; Luis Munoz Rivera Day.** The 17th day of July of each year shall be commemorated in Puerto Rico as "Munoz Rivera Day," the same being hereby declared a legal holiday.

§ 79. **July 25; Day of the Constitution.** July 25 of each year is hereby declared a legal holiday designated as Day of the Constitution.

§ 80. **July 27; birthday of Dr. Jose Celso Barbosa.** The twenty-seventh day of July of each year is hereby declared an official and legal holiday in Puerto Rico, and during such day all public offices of Puerto Rico, Commonwealth and Municipal, shall remain closed.

§ 81. **First Monday of September; Santiago Iglesias Pantin Day.** In addition to the declaration of Congress setting apart the first Monday of September of each year as Labor Day, the first Monday of September of 1940, and of each subsequent year is hereby declared a holiday consecrated to the memory of the eminent citizen, Santiago Iglesias Pantin.

§ 82. **October 12; Columbus Day.** The twelfth day of October of each year is hereby declared to be and shall be kept as a legal holiday in Puerto Rico under the name of "Columbus Day."

§ 83. **November 19; discovery of Puerto Rico.** The nineteenth day of November is declared a holiday in Puerto Rico.

§ 130. **Ernesto Ramos Antonini Day.** The 24th day of April of each year shall be observed as "Ernesto Ramos Antonini Day" throughout the Commonwealth of Puerto Rico.

The Department of Education shall adopt the necessary measures for the effectuation of the purpose of this act through the organization of acts and ceremonies as a tribute in memory of this eminent public man, attorney, orator and artist.

§ 131. **Ramon Emeterio Betances Day.** April 8 of each year shall be commemorated as "Ramon Emeterio Betances Day" in all public schools of the Commonwealth of Puerto Rico.

The Department of Education shall take the necessary measures for the effectuation of the purpose of this section through the organization of acts and ceremonies as a tribute in memory of this eminent public man, orator and physician.

§ 132. **Police Day.** (a) The 21st day of February of each year is hereby declared as Puerto Rico's Police Day.

RHODE ISLAND

[R.I. GEN. LAWS ANN.—(Amended in 1969)]

§ 25-1-1. General holidays enumerated. The first day of January (as New Year's day), the third Monday of February (as Washington's birthday), the fourth day of May (as Rhode Island Independence day), the last Monday of May (as Memorial day), the fourth day of July (as Independence day), the second Monday of August (as Victory day), the first Monday of September (as Labor day), the second Monday of October (as Columbus day), the fourth Monday of October (as Armistice day), the twenty-fifth day of December (as Christmas day), and each of said days in every year, or when either of the said days falls on the first day of the week, then the day following it, the Tuesday next after the first Monday in November in each year in which a general election of state officers is held (as election day), the first day of every week (commonly called Sunday), and such other days as the governor or general assembly of this state or the president or the congress of the United States shall appoint as holidays for any purpose, days of thanksgiving, or days of solemn fast, shall be holiday.

§ 25-1-2. Thanksgiving day. The governor shall annually appoint a day of public thanksgiving, and shall announce the same by proclamation to the people of the state.

§ 25-1-3. Saturday bank closing—filing of resolution. Any bank, savings bank, trust company, safe deposit company, building-loan association, national banking association or federal savings and loan association doing business within the state of Rhode Island or any branch or office of any such institution may remain closed on any Saturday or Saturdays upon the adoption of a resolution to close by the board of directors or the board of trustees thereof and upon filing a copy of the same as hereinafter required. Any such resolution shall be deemed effective for the purposes of this section and § 25-1-4 only when a copy thereof certified by the proper officer of such institution is filed in the office of the director of business regulation of this state, and any such resolution shall remain in full force and effect until a copy of a later resolution, certified in like manner, terminating any such prior resolution, is filed in such office of the director of business regulation.

§ 25-1-4. Effect of Saturday closing on rights and obligations. Any Saturday upon which any such bank, savings bank, trust company, safe deposit company, building-loan association, national banking association or federal savings and loan association, or any branch or office thereof, shall remain closed pursuant to the provisions of §§ 25-1-3 and 25-1-4 shall, with respect to such closed institution, branch or office thereof, be a holiday for the purpose of chapter 3 of title 6A. If any such bank, savings bank, trust company, safe deposit company, building-loan association, national banking association or federal savings and loan association, or any branch or office thereof, shall close on any Saturday pursuant to the provisions of § 25-1-3, any act which would otherwise be required to be performed on any such Saturday at or by such institution, or any branch or office thereof, if such institution, branch or office thereof were not so closed, shall be performed on the next succeeding business day, and any act which would otherwise be authorized or permitted to be performed on any such Saturday at or by such institution, or any branch or office thereof, if such institution, branch or office thereof were not so closed, may be so performed on the next succeeding business day. No liability or loss of rights of any kind shall result from the failure to perform any of such acts on any such Saturday.

§ 25-1-5. **Saturday closing of public offices.** The several administrative offices of state, city and town governments may remain closed on any Saturday or Saturdays by executive order of the governor in the case of state administrative government and by the adoption of a resolution upon the part of the city and/or town council in the case of a city or town. Any Saturday upon which the several administrative offices of state, city and town governments, or any branch, division or independent agency thereof, shall remain closed pursuant to the provisions of this section shall, with respect to such closed administrative office, branch, division or independent agency thereof, be a holiday for the purpose of chapter 3 of title 6A. If any state, city and/or town administrative offices, or any branch, division or independent agency thereof, shall close on any Saturday pursuant to the provisions of this section, any act which would otherwise be required to be performed on any such Saturday at or by such administrative office, or any branch, division or independent agency thereof, if such administrative office, branch, division or independent agency thereof were not so closed, shall be so performed on the next succeeding business day, and any act which would otherwise be authorized or permitted to be performed on any such Saturday at or by such administrative office, or any branch, division or independent agency thereof, if such administrative office, branch, division or independent agency thereof were not so closed, may be so performed on the next succeeding business day. No liability or loss of rights of any kind shall result from the failure to perform any of such acts on any such Saturday.

§ 25-1-6. **(Amended in 1972) Work on holidays prohibited—exceptions—time and half.** No person, firm or corporation shall require or permit an employee to work and no person shall engage in gainful activities in any store, mill or factory, or in any commercial occupation, or in the work of transportation or communication, or in the work of industrial process on Sundays or on any of the following holidays, to wit, New Year's day, May 4, 1976, the 200th anniversary of the independence of the state of Rhode Island, Memorial day, Fourth of July, Victory day, Labor day, Columbus day, Armistice day, Thanksgiving day (but only in such years as the governor shall by public proclamation designate such day as a legal holiday) and Christmas day except to perform such work as is both absolutely necessary and can lawfully be performed on Sunday; provided, however, that nothing herein contained shall prohibit the director of labor from granting a permit to perform such work upon written application therefor at least ten (10) days previous to the Sunday or holiday therein referred to or for such less time as the necessity of the occasion may require in the discretion of the director of labor, which application shall contain a sworn statement by or on behalf of such person, firm or corporation of the particular necessity to perform such work and the economic hardship which would otherwise prevail as declared in said application; and provided, that all employees working during Sundays and holidays under a permit granted by the director of labor shall receive from their employer at least time and a half for work so performed; provided further that nothing herein shall be a ground for discharge or other penalty upon any employee for refusing to work for any person, firm or corporation upon any of the holidays enumerated herein, and provided further, nothing herein contained shall prohibit any licensing board of any city or town of the state or any state licensing board or commission from granting a permit to hold athletic meets, contests, race meets, or athletic exhibitions on any of the aforesaid holidays, and any person, association or corporation receiving a permit to operate any such event shall have the right to employ the necessary persons to conduct such event, and nothing herein contained shall prohibit any person from engaging in or being employed in connection with the holding or operation of any such event so licensed.

§ 25-1-7. **Penalty for violations.**   Any person, firm or corporation convicted of violating any of the provisions of § 25-1-6 shall be punished by a fine of twenty-five dollars ($25.00) for each employee involved and each separate offense committed, but in no event shall the fine be less than two hundred dollars ($200).

§ 25-1-8. **Enforcement of work prohibition.**   The department of labor shall enforce and administer the provisions of §§ 25-1-6 and 25-1-7.   All actions, suits, complaints and prosecutions for the violation of any of the provisions of said sections shall be brought by and in the name of the director of labor or his duly authorized representatives.

Other Days of Special Observance

§ 25-2-1. **Rhode Island Independence day.**   The fourth day of May in each and every year hereafter is hereby established, in this state, as a day for celebration of Rhode Island independence;—being a just tribute to the memory of the members of our general assembly, who, on the fourth day of May, 1776—in the statehouse at Providence, passed an act renouncing allegiance of the colony to the British crown, and by the provisions of that act declaring it sovereign and independent;—the first official act of its kind by any of the thirteen (13) American colonies.

§ 25-2-4. Narragansett Indian day. The last Saturday before the second Sunday in August shall annually be set apart as a day to be known as the "Rhode Island Indian Day of the Narragansett Tribe of Indians," said day to be observed by the people of this state with appropriate exercises in public places and otherwise commemorative of the Narragansett Tribe of Indians.

§ 25-2-7. Veteran Firemen's Muster day. The governor shall annually issue a proclamation calling for proper observance of Veteran Firemen's Muster day, so-called.

§ 25-2-8. Disabled American veterans day. The 7th day of December shall annually be set apart as a day to be known as "Disabled American veterans day" said day to be observed by the people of this state with appropriate exercises in public places and otherwise commemorating the disabled American veterans and to be named as "D. A. V. Day."

§ 25-2-9. V. F. W. loyalty day. The governor shall annually issue a proclamation calling for proper observance of the first day of May in each and every year as V. F. W. loyalty day, so-called.

§ 25-2-10. Itam—vets daisy day. The first Saturday of June in each and every year shall be set apart as the "Italian American war veterans of the United States Incorporated field daisy day." To be known as "Itam—Vets daisy day," said day to be observed by the people of this state with appropriate exercises.

§ 25-2-11. Founders day of Italian American War Veterans of the United States Incorporated. The 15th day of February in each and every year shall be set apart as a day to be known as "Founders day of the Italian American War Veterans of the United States Incorporated," said day to be observed by the people of this state with appropriate exercises in public places and otherwise commemorating the founding of said organization and its members.

§ 25-2-12. National police day and week. The fifteenth (15th) day of May in each and every year thereafter is hereby established in this state as a day for celebration of "National police day."

The calendar week containing May fifteenth (15) in each year is hereby designated as "National police week," and is set apart as a period during which the state and its cities and towns may conduct appropriate exercises in honor of those men who have given their lives in the war against crime while protecting the lives and property of our citizens.

§ 25-2-15. General Casimir Pulaski day. The eleventh day of October shall be set apart as a day to be known as "General Casimir Pulaski day." Said day to be observed by the people of this state with appropriate exercises in public places.

SOUTH CAROLINA

[S.C. CODE ANN.—(Amended in 1973)]

§ 64-151. List of legal holidays. National Thanksgiving days, all general election days and also the first day of January, the nineteenth day of January, the third Monday in February (George Washington's birthday), the tenth day of May, the third day of June, the fourth day of July, the first Monday in September, the eleventh day of November and the twenty-fifth and twenty-sixth days of December in each year shall be legal holidays.

§ 64-151.1. Christmas Eve may be declared holiday for State employees. The Governor of South Carolina is empowered to declare Christmas Eve of each year a holiday for State government employees.

§ 64-152.1. Thursday of State Fair week may be declared holiday in Berkeley, Dorchester and Florence Counties. The county supervisor and the town council of any municipality in Berkeley, Dorchester and Florence Counties may, upon one publication of notice fifteen days in advance in a newspaper of general circulation in the county, declare Thursday of State Fair week a legal holiday concerning the conduct of its business.

§ 64-153. Certain Mondays declared holidays; presentment of bills, notes and checks. Whenever any of the legal holidays mentioned in § 64-151 shall fall upon Sunday the Monday next following shall be deemed a public holiday for all of the purposes aforesaid. But in such case all bills of exchange, checks and promissory notes which would otherwise be presentable for acceptance or payment on any such Monday shall be deemed to be presentable for acceptance or payment on the secular or business day next succeeding the holiday.

§ 64-154. Additional holidays for banks and cash depositories. In addition to the holidays enumerated in §§ 64-151 to 64-153 and 64-158 the Governor, at the request of the chairman of the State Board of Bank Control and the president of the South Carolina Bankers' Association, may declare any other day or days of the year legal holidays for banks and cash depositories.

§ 64-155. All first Mondays in month business days for certain purposes. Notwithstanding the provisions of §§ 64-151 and 64-153, each first Monday in any month shall be a legal day for judicial or sheriff's sales or the transaction of any legal business.

§ 64-157. When paper maturing on Sunday or legal holiday collectible. Any commercial paper or other security which shall mature and become payable and collectible on Sunday or on any legal holiday shall be deemed and taken and treated as maturing and becoming payable and collectible on the next day thereafter if such next day shall not be Sunday or a legal holiday, in which latter event it shall be deemed, taken and treated as due, maturing and collectible on the first day thereafter which is not a Sunday or a legal holiday.

§ 64-163. Additional holidays for savings and loan and building and loan associations in case of special events. In addition to the holidays enumerated in §§ 64-151 to 64-153 and 64-158, the Governor at the request of the President of the South Carolina Savings and Loan League and the Chairman of the State Board of Bank Control may, in case of special events, declare any other day or days of the year legal holidays for savings and loan and building and loan associations.

SOUTH DAKOTA

[S.D. COMPILED LAWS ANN.—(Amended in 1974)]

§ 1-5-1. Holidays enumerated. The first day of every week, known as Sunday; the first day of January, commonly known as New Year's Day; the third Monday in February, the anniversary of the birthdays of Lincoln and Washington; the last Monday in May, commonly known as Memorial Day; the fourth day of July, commonly known as Independence Day; the first Monday in September, commonly known as Labor Day; the second Monday in October, commonly known as Pioneers' Day; the eleventh day of November, known as Veterans' Day; the fourth Thursday in November, commonly known as Thanksgiving Day; and the twenty-fifth day of December, commonly known as Christmas Day; and every day appointed by the President of the United States, or by the Governor of this state for a public fast, thanksgiving, or holiday shall be observed in this state as a legal holiday.

If the fourth day of July, the first day of January, the eleventh day of November or the twenty-fifth day of December falls upon a Sunday, the Monday following is a legal holiday and shall be so observed; and if any such day fall upon a Saturday, the preceding Friday is a legal holiday and shall be so observed.

§ 1-5-2. Business and official acts permitted on holidays. Any public or private business may be transacted or legal process or notices of any kind may be served or published on any of said days or next succeeding days designated herein as holidays, excepting Sundays, provided, that for good cause, a judge in whose court an action has been or is about to be brought, may endorse upon any process or notice permission to serve the same on Sunday, and if so endorsed, service thereof on Sunday shall be valid.

TENNESSEE

[TENN. CODE ANN.—(Effective in 1973)]

§ 55-101. Legal holidays. The first day of January; the twenty-second day of February, known as "Washington Day"; the thirtieth day of May,, known as "Memorial" or "Decoration Day"; the fourth of July; the first Monday in September, known as "Labor Day"; the eleventh day of November, known as "Veterans' Day"; the fourth Thursday in November, known as "Thanksgiving Day"; the twenty-fifth day of December; and Good Friday; and when any one of these days shall fall on Sunday then the following Monday shall be substituted; and when any of these days shall fall on Saturday, then the preceding Friday shall be substituted; also, all days appointed by the governor or by the President of the United States, as days of fasting or thanksgiving, and all days set apart by law for holding county, state, or national elections, throughout this state, are made legal holidays, and the period from noon to midnight of each Saturday which is not a holiday is made a half-holiday, on which holidays and half-holidays all public offices of this state may be closed and business of every character, at the option of the parties in interest of the same, may be suspended. On and after January 1, 1971, the second Monday in October, known as "Columbus Day," shall be and is hereby declared to be a legal holiday and all public offices of this state may be closed and business of every character, at the option of the parties in interest of the same, may be suspended. On and after January 1, 1971, "Washington Day" will be observed on the third Monday in February; "Memorial" or "Decoration Day" will be observed on the last Monday in May.

§ 55-204. Proclamation of special observance days. Each year it shall be the duty of the governor of this state to proclaim the following as days of special observance; the nineteenth day of January, "Robert E. Lee Day"; the twelfth day of February, "Abraham Lincoln Day"; the fifteenth day of March, "Andrew Jackson Day"; the third day of June, "Memorial or Confederate Decoration Day"; the thirteenth day of July, "Nathan Bedford Forrest Day"; and the eleventh day of November, "Veterans' Day"; the governor shall invite the people of this state to observe the said days in schools, churches, and other suitable places with appropriate ceremonies expressive of the public sentiment befitting the anniversary of such dates.

TEXAS

[TEX. REV. CIV. STAT. ANN.—(Effective in 1973)]

Art. 4591. Enumeration. The first day of January, the 19th day of January, the third Monday in February, the second day of March, the 21st day of April, the last Monday in May, the fourth day of July, the 27th day of August, the first Monday in September, the second Monday in October, the fourth Monday in October, the fourth Thursday in November, and the 25th day of December, of each year, and every day on which an election is held throughout the state, are declared legal holidays, on which all the public offices of the state may be closed and shall be considered and treated as Sunday for all purposes regarding the presenting for the payment or acceptance and of protesting for and giving notice of the dishonor of bills of exchange, bank checks and promissory notes placed by the law upon the footing of bills of exchange. The nineteenth day of January shall be known as "Confederate Heroes Day" in honor of Jefferson Davis, Robert E. Lee and other Confederate heroes.

Art. 4591a. Texas Pioneers' Day. The 12th of August of each year hereafter shall be designated and observed as Texas Pioneers' Day, and the Governor of Texas shall issue a proclamation at least thirty days in advance of such date each year, in which he shall call upon the people of the State of Texas to assemble in mass-meetings preferably to be held in the open air and in the form of Pioneers' Picnics and Old Settlers' Reunions and similar celebrations, to do honor to the memory of the heroic pioneers who by their sacrifices and hardships converted the primeval wilderness into the great empire of peace and plenty which we today enjoy;

The purpose of these celebrations shall be patriotic and educational, to preserve the traditions and memories of pioneer days, and in nowise of a political, sectarian or partisan nature;

The State association of Texas Pioneers is hereby requested to assume the initiative in the organization of Pioneer Day celebrations each year and to prepare and circulate suitable programs for the observance of the same.

Nothing in this resolution shall be construed to make Texas Pioneers' Day a legal holiday.

Art. 4591b. Stephen F. Austin day; designation and commemoration. That the Third day of November of each year is hereby designated and fixed, and is to be hereafter known as, "Father of Texas Day" in memory of Stephen F. Austin, the real and true Father of Texas, and that said day and date be regularly observed by appropriate and patriotic programs, being given in the Public Schools and other places that will properly commemorate the birthday of that great pioneer patriot, Stephen F. Austin, and thereby inspire a greater love for our beloved Lone Star State; provided, however, that said day shall not be a legal holiday.

Art. 4591c. General Pulaski Memorial Day. Therefore be it Resolved, by the Legislature of the State of Texas, that the Governor of the State of Texas is authorized and directed to issue a proclamation calling upon officials of the Government to display the flag of the United States on all governmental buildings on October 11th of each year and inviting the people of the State of Texas to observe the day in schools and churches, or other suitable places, with appropriate ceremonies in commemoration of the death of General Casimir Pulaski.

Art. 4591e. Veterans Day; designation changed from Armistice Day. The holiday of November 11th, heretofore known as Armistice Day, is hereby designated and is to be hereafter known as Veterans Day, dedicated to the cause of world peace and to honoring the veterans of all wars in which Texans and other Americans have fought.

UTAH

[UTAH CODE ANN.—(Approved in 1970)]

§ 63-13-2. Legal holidays. Governor authorized to declare additional days.

o   o   o

(2) For the period beginning with January 1, 1971, the following-named days are legal holidays in this state: Every Sunday; the 1st day of January, called New Year's Day; the 12th day of February, the anniversary of the birth of Abraham Lincoln; the 3rd Monday of February, observed as the anniversary of the birth of George Washington; the last Friday in April, called Arbor Day; the last Monday of May, called Memorial Day; the 4th day of July, called Independence Day; the 24th day of July, called Pioneer Day; the 1st Monday of September, called Labor Day; the 2nd Monday of October, called Columbus Day; the 4th Monday of October, called Veterans' Day; the 4th Thursday of November, called Thanksgiving Day; the 25th day of December, called Christmas; and all days which may be set apart by the president of the United States, or the governor of this state by proclamation as days of fast or thanksgiving. If any of the holidays provided for in this subsection (2), except the first mentioned, namely Sunday, shall fall on Sunday, then the following Monday shall be the holiday.

(3) The governor is further hereby authorized and empowered, whenever in his opinion extraordinary conditions exist justifying such action, by proclamation to declare legal holidays in addition to those holidays provided for in subsections (1) and (2) of this section and to limit such holidays to certain classes of business and activities to be designated by him, but no such holidays shall extend for a longer period than sixty consecutive days. Any such holidays may be renewed for one or more periods not exceeding thirty days each as the governor may deem necessary, and any such holidays may by like proclamation be terminated before the expiration of the period for which they were declared.

VERMONT

[VT. STAT. ANN.—(Twice amended in 1973; effective in 1974)]

Tit. 1, § 371. Legal holidays. (a) The following shall be legal holidays:

New Year's Day, January 1;

Lincoln's Birthday, February 12;

Washington's Birthday, the third Monday in February;

Town meeting day, the first Tuesday in March;

Memorial Day, the last Monday in May;

Independence Day, July 4;

Bennington Battle Day, August 16;

Labor Day, the first Monday in September;

Columbus Day, the second Monday in October;

Veterans' Day, November 11;

Thanksgiving Day, the fourth Thursday in November;

Christmas Day, December 25.

(b)   All state departments, agencies and offices shall observe any legal holiday which falls on a Saturday on the preceding Friday and any legal holiday which falls on a Sunday on the following Monday.

§ 372. Arbor Day. The first Friday in the month of May of each year is hereby designated as "Arbor Day".

VIRGIN ISLANDS

[V.I. CODE ANN.—(Twice amended in 1971)]

Tit. 1, § 171. Legal holidays; serving liquor on Good Friday; performance of acts under law or contract. (a)   The following days are legal holidays in the Virgin Islands:

Every Sunday

January 1 (New Year's Day)

January 6 (Three King's Day)

January 15 (Martin Luther King's Birthday)

Last Monday in January (Franklin D. Roosevelt's Birthday)

Second Monday in February (Lincoln's Birthday)

Third Monday in February (Washington's Birthday)

Last Monday in March (Transfer Day)

Holy Thursday

Good Friday

Easter Monday

Last Monday in May (Memorial Day)

Third Monday in June (Organic Act Day)

July 4 (Independence Day)

The Fourth Monday in July (Supplication Day)

First Monday in September (Labor Day)

Second Monday in October (Columbus Day and Puerto Rico Friendship Day)

Third Monday in October (Local Thanksgiving Day)
Fourth Monday in October (Veteran's Day)
First Monday in November (Liberty Day)
Fourth Thursday in November (Thanksgiving Day)
December 25 (Christmas Day)
December 26 (Christmas Second Day)

and such other days as the President or the Governor may by proclamation declare to be holidays. Whenever any holiday (other than Sunday) falls upon a Sunday, the Monday following shall be a legal holiday.

(b) Distilled liquor and drinks prepared therewith shall not be served in public places of refreshments between the hours of 9:00 o'clock in the morning and 4:00 o'clock in the afternoon on Good Friday. Whoever violates this subsection shall be fined not more than $200 or imprisoned not more than one year, or both.

(c) Whenever any act is appointed by law or contract to be performed upon a particular day, which day falls upon a holiday, that act may be performed upon the next business day with the same effect as if it had been performed upon the day appointed.

§ 171a. **Exemption of banks and trust companies from Thursday half-holidays; option; validity of non-regular banking-hour transactions.** The Thursday half-holidays provided by law shall not be applicable to banks and banking business, provided, however, that any bank, trust company or national banking association may, at its option, observe Thursday afternoons as half-holidays, effective July 3, 1958. Nothing in any law of the Virgin Islands shall in any manner whatsoever affect the validity of, or render void or voidable, the payment, certification, or acceptance of a check or other negotiable instrument or any other transaction by a bank or trust company in the Virgin Islands, because done or performed during any time other than regular banknig hours.

Note: Thursday half-holidays were formerly provided for in § 171, but reference to them was omitted in 1971 amendment, Act No. 2924.

§ 171b. **Banks and trust companies may close one business day each week.** Any bank or trust company and any national banking association or any branch or branches of any of them transacting business in the Virgin Islands may close on any one business day or any part thereof of each week and shall have this right even though there shall fall in such week a legal holiday.

§ 171c. **West Indies Solidarity Day.** The first Monday in September shall be observed as West Indies Solidarity Day throughout the Virgin Islands.

§ 172. **Teachers' Day.** The first Friday of the month of May of each year shall be observed as Teachers' Day throughout the

Virgin Islands. On that day, preferential attention shall be given in the schools to the holding of the public acts and demonstrations which, as homage to school teachers, may be announced as provided in sections 173-175 of this title.

VIRGINIA

[VA. CODE ANN.—(Amended in 1973)]

§ 2.1-21. Legal holidays. In each year the first day of January (New Year's Day), the third Monday in January (Lee-Jackson Day), the third Monday in February (George Washington Day), the last Monday in May (Confederate Memorial Day), the fourth day of July (Independence Day), the first Monday in September (Labor Day), the second Monday in October (Columbus Day), the eleventh day of November (Veterans Day), the Tuesday next following the first Monday in November (Election Day), the fourth Thursday in November (Thanksgiving Day), the twenty-fifth day of December (Christmas Day), or, whenever any of such days shall fall on Saturday, the Friday next preceding such day, or whenever any of such days shall fall on Sunday, the Monday next following such day, and any day so appointed by the Governor of this State or the President of the United States, shall be a legal holiday as to the transaction of all business.

§ 2.1-22. Acts, business transactions, legal proceedings, etc., on holidays valid. No contract made, instrument executed, or act done on any of the legal holidays named in the preceding section (§ 2.1-21), or on any Saturday, whether before or after twelve o'clock, noon, shall be thereby rendered invalid, and nothing in such section shall be construed to prevent or invalidate the entry, issuance, service or execution of any writ, summons, confession, judgment, order or decree, or other legal process whatever, or the session of the proceedings of any court or judge on any of such legal holidays or Saturdays, either before or after twelve o'clock, noon, nor to prevent any bank, banker, banking corporation, firm or association from keeping their doors open and transacting any lawful business on any of such legal holidays or Saturdays.

§ 2.1-23. Saturday closing of banks. It shall be lawful for any bank as defined in § 6.1-4, including national banking associations and federal reserve banks, to permit any one or more or all of its offices to remain closed on any one or more or all Saturdays, as the bank, by resolution of its board of directors, may from time to time determine. Any Saturday on which an office of a bank shall remain closed, as herein permitted, shall as to such office, constitute a legal holiday, and any act authorized, required or permitted to be performed at, by or with respect to any such office on a Saturday on which the office is so closed, may be performed on the next succeeding business day and no liability or loss of rights of any kind shall result from such delay.

§ 2.1-24. Display of flags on Mother's Day. The Governor is authorized to issue annually a proclamation calling upon State officials to display the flag of the United States and of the Commonwealth on all public buildings, and the people of the State to display such flags at their homes and other suitable places on the second Sunday in May, known as "Mother's Day," as a public expression of love and reverence for the mothers of this State.

§ 2.1-24.1. Citizenship Day and Constitution Week. The Governor shall annually issue a proclamation setting apart the seventeenth day of September as Citizenship Day and September seventeen through twenty-three as Constitution Week and recommending that they be observed by the State with appropriate exercises in the schools and otherwise so that the eventful day on which the Constitution of the United States was formally adopted may forever remain enshrined in the hearts and minds of all citizens and so that they may be reminded on that date annually of the blessings of liberty which they enjoy by the adoption of the United States Constitution, the Bill of Rights and all other amendments thereto.

§ 2.1-25. Arbor Day. The second Friday in March of each year shall be designated and known as "Arbor Day."

§ 2.1-26. Dogwood Day. The third Saturday in April of each year shall be known and designated as "Dogwood Day."

§ 2.1-27. First Lady's Day in Virginia. Martha Washington's birthday, the second day of June, nineteen hundred sixty, and the same day of each succeeding year is designated as First Lady's Day in Virginia in special tribute to Martha Washington as America's first Lady and to each of her successors as First Ladies of this Nation; and upon this date, in perpetuity, all citizens, groups and appropriate agencies in and of the Commonwealth of Virginia and of the Nation are urged to reflect upon and give appropriate recognition to the magnificent contribution of this Nation's First Ladies to the heritage of the United States of America.

WASHINGTON

[WASH. REV. CODE ANN.—(Amended in 1973)]

§ 1.16.050. "Legal holidays". The following are legal holidays: Sunday; the first day of January, commonly called New Year's Day; the twelfth day of February, being the anniversary of the birth of Abraham Lincoln; the third Monday of February, being celebrated as the anniversary of the birth of George Washington; the thirtieth day of May, commonly known as Memorial Day; the fourth day of July, being the anniversary of the Declaration of Independence; the first Monday in September, to be known as Labor Day; the second Monday of October, to be known as Columbus Day; the eleventh day of November, to be known as Veterans' Day; the fourth Thursday in November, to be known as Thanksgiving Day; the twenty-fifth day of December, commonly called Christmas Day; the day on which any general election is held throughout the state; and any day designated by public proclamation of the chief executive of the state as a legal holiday.

If any of the above specified state legal holidays are also federal legal holidays but observed on different dates, only the state legal holidays shall be recognized as a paid legal holiday for employees of the state and its political subdivisions.

Whenever any legal holiday, other than Sunday, falls upon a Sunday, the following Monday shall be a legal holiday.

WEST VIRGINIA

[W. VA. CODE ANN.—(Amended in 1973)]

§ 2-2-1. **Legal holidays; official acts or court proceedings.** The following days shall be regarded, treated and observed as legal holidays, viz: The first day of January, commonly called "New Year's Day"; the twelfth day of February, commonly called "Lincoln's Birthday"; the third Monday of February, commonly called "Washington's Birthday"; the last Monday of May, commonly called "Memorial Day"; the twentieth day of June, commonly called "West Virginia Day"; the fourth day of July, commonly called "Independence Day"; the first Monday of September, commonly called "Labor Day"; the second Monday of October, commonly called "Columbus Day"; the eleventh day of November, hereafter referred to as "Veterans Day"; the fourth Thursday of November, commonly called "Thanksgiving Day"; the twenty-fifth day of December, commonly called "Christmas Day"; any national, state or other election day throughout the district or municipality wherein held; and all days which may be appointed or recommended by the governor of this State, or the president of the United States, as days of thanksgiving, or for the general cessation of business; and when any of said days or dates falls on Sunday, then the succeeding Monday shall be regarded, treated and observed as such legal holiday. When the return day of any summons or other court proceeding or any notice or time fixed for holding any court or doing any official act shall fall on any of said holidays, the ensuing day which is not a Saturday, Sunday or legal holiday shall be taken as meant and intended: Provided, that [nothing] herein contained shall increase nor diminish the legal school holidays provided for in section two [§ 18A-5-2], article five, chapter eighteen-A of this Code.

§ 2-2-2. **When acts to be done fall on Saturday, Sunday or legal holiday; adjournments from day to day.** When a proceeding is directed to take place or any act to be done on any particular day of the month or within any period of time prescribed or allowed, including those provided by article two [§ 55-2-1 et seq.], chapter fifty-five of this Code, if that day or the last day falls on a Saturday, Sunday or legal holiday, the next day which is not a Saturday, Sunday or legal holiday shall be deemed to be the one intended, and when the day upon which a term of court is directed by law to commence, falls on a Saturday, Sunday or legal holiday, the following day which is not a Saturday, Sunday or legal holiday shall be deemed to be the day intended. When an adjournment is authorized from day to day, an adjournment from Friday to Monday will be legal.

§ 2-2-3. **Computation of time.** The time or period prescribed or allowed within which an act is to be done shall be computed by excluding the first day and including the last; or if the last be a Saturday, Sunday or legal holiday, it shall also be excluded, and any such Saturday shall be a legal holiday solely for the purpose of Rule 6(a) of the Rules of Civil Procedure for Trial Courts of Record; but the provisions of this section shall not be deemed to change any rule of law applicable to bills of exchange or negotiable notes.

WISCONSIN

[WIS. STAT. ANN.—(Effective in 1972)]

§ **256.17. Legal holidays.** January 1, the 3rd Monday in February (which shall be the day of celebration for February 12 and 22), the last Monday in May (which shall be the day of celebration for May 30), July 4, the 1st Monday in September which shall be known as Labor Day, the 2nd Monday in October, the 4th Monday in October (which shall be the day of celebration for November 11), the 4th Thursday in November, December 25, the day of holding the September primary election, and the day of holding the general election in November are legal holidays. On Good Friday the period from 11 a.m. to 3 p.m. shall uniformly be observed for the purpose of worship. In every city of the 1st class the day of holding any municipal election is a legal holiday, and in every such city the afternoon of each day upon which a primary election is held for the nomination of candidates for city offices is a half holiday and in counties having a population of 500,000 or more the county board may by ordinance provide that all county employes shall have a half holiday on the day of such primary election and a holiday on the day of such municipal election, and that employes whose duties require that they work on such days be given equivalent time off on other days. Whenever any of said days falls on Sunday, the succeeding Monday shall be the legal holiday.

§ **256.175. Indian Rights Day.** July 4 is designated as "Indian Rights Day," and in conjunction with the celebration of Independence Day, appropriate exercises or celebrations may be held in commemoration of the granting by congress of home rule and a bill of rights to the American Indians. When July 4 falls on Sunday, exercises or celebrations of Indian Rights Day may be held on either the third or the fifth.

§ 14.16. Holiday proclamations.

(1) **Arbor and Bird Day.** The governor, by proclamation, may set apart one day each year to be designated as Arbor and Bird Day, and may request its observance by all schools, colleges and other institutions by the planting of trees, the adornment of school and public grounds and by suitable exercises having for their object the advancement of the study of arboriculture, the promotion of a spirit of protection to birds and trees and the cultivation of an appreciative sentiment concerning them.

(2) **Citizenship Day.** The governor may also set aside, by proclamation, the 3rd Sunday in May in each year to be designated as Citizenship Day, and shall request its observance by all circuit court judges, county boards, municipalities, colleges and other institutions, by suitable exercises for all those persons who have recently become enfranchised either by naturalization or by reaching their majority on the necessity of exercising responsible, vigilant and intelligent citizenship to safeguard and maintain our inalienable American liberties, freedom of person, stability, strength, endurance of our democratic institutions, ideals and leadership.

(3) **Labor Day.** The governor may also set apart, by proclamation, one day in each year to be observed as Labor Day.

(4) **Veterans Day.** The governor shall annually issue a proclamation calling attention to the fact that the 4th Monday in October (which shall be the day of celebration for November 11) is the anniversary of Veterans Day, and requesting the people throughout the state to observe by appropriate exercises the hour at which the armistice following World War I was concluded.

(5) **Mother's Day.** The governor may annually proclaim the 2nd Sunday in May as Mother's Day and urge the people and organizations to display the American flag as a public expression of love and reverence for the mothers of our state and as a symbol of a united effort to inspire betters homes and closer union between the state, its homes and its sons and daughters.

(6) **Gold Star Mother's Day.** The governor may annually proclaim the last Sunday in September as Gold Star Mother's Day and call upon the people and organizations to display the American flag and hold appropriate meetings in their homes, churches and other suitable places as a public expression of love, sorrow and reverence for the gold star mothers of our state.

(7) **American History Month.** To emphasize the spirit of America and Americanism and to remind the citizens of this state of the

history of our nation and its free institutions, the month of February in each year is designated "American History Month" and the governor is directed to annually issue a suitable proclamation for the observance thereof.

WYOMING

[WYO. STAT. ANN.—(Amended in 1973)]

§ 8-51. **Legal holidays; dismissal of schools.** New Year's Day, January 1; the observance of Washington's and Lincoln's birthdays, to be held on the third Monday in February; Memorial Day, to be held on the last Monday in May; Independence Day, the fourth day of July; Labor Day to be observed on the first Monday in September; Columbus Day, the second Monday in October; Veterans Day to be observed on November 11; Thanksgiving Day to be observed on the fourth Thursday in November; Christmas Day, December 25; all days upon which general elections are held and upon declaration by the governor of this state, any date appointed or declared by the president of the United States as an occasion of national mourning, rejoicing or observance of national emergency are hereby declared legal holidays in and for the State of Wyoming. If New Year's Day, Independence Day, or Christmas Day, or any of them fall upon a Sunday, the Monday following shall be a legal holiday. Provided, that on Washington's and Lincoln's birthdays, Columbus Day, Veterans Day and all days upon which general elections are held, the public schools of any district shall not be dismissed except by order of the board of trustees of said district but proper exercises shall be held in the schools on these respective days to emphasize their significance and importance.

§ 8-52. **Arbor day.** The governor shall annually, in the spring, designate by official proclamation, an Arbor day, to be observed by the schools and for economic tree planting.

§ 8-53. **Wyoming day.** In recognition of the action of the Wyoming territorial governor on December 10, 1869 in approving the first law found anywhere in legislative history which extends the right of suffrage to women, the tenth day of December of each year is designated as "Wyoming day". Such day shall be observed in the schools, clubs and similar groups by appropriate exercises commemorating the history of the territory and state and the lives of its pioneers, and fostering in all ways the loyalty and good citizenship of its people.

UNITED STATES

[5 U.S.C.—(Effective in 1971)]

§ 6103. **Holidays.** (a) The following are legal public holidays: New Year's Day, January 1.

Washington's Birthday, the third Monday in February.

Memorial Day, the last Monday in May.

Independence Day, July 4.

Labor Day, the first Monday in September.

Columbus Day, the second Monday in October.

Veterans Day, November 11.

Thanksgiving Day, the fourth Thursday in November.

Christmas Day, December 25.

(b) For the purpose of statutes relating to pay and leave of employees, with respect to a legal public holiday and any other day declared to be a holiday by Federal statute or Executive order, the following rules apply:

(1) Instead of a holiday that occurs on a Saturday, the Friday immediately before is a legal public holiday for—

(A) employees whose basic workweek is Monday through Friday; and

(B) the purpose of section 6309 of this title.

(2) Instead of a holiday that occurs on a regular weekly nonworkday of an employee whose basic workweek is other than Monday through Friday, except the regular weekly nonworkday administratively scheduled for the employee instead of Sunday, the workday immediately before that regular weekly nonworkday is a legal public holiday for the employee.

This subsection except subparagraph (B) of paragraph (1), does not apply to an employee whose basic workweek is Monday through Saturday.

(c) January 20 of each fourth year after 1965, Inauguration Day, is a legal public holiday for the purpose of statutes relating to pay and leave of employees as defined by Section 2105 of this title and individuals employed by the government of the District of Columbia employed in the District of Columbia, Montgomery and Prince Georges Counties in Maryland, Arlington and Fairfax Counties in Virginia, and the cities of Alexandria and Falls Church in Virginia. When January 20 of any fourth year after 1965 falls on Sunday, the next succeeding day selected for the public observance of the inauguration of the President is a legal public holiday for the purpose of this subsection.

[26 U.S.C.]

§ 7503. Time for Performance of Acts Where Last Day Falls on Saturday, Sunday, or Legal Holiday. When the last day prescribed under authority of the internal revenue laws for performing any act falls on Saturday, Sunday, or a legal holiday, the performance of such act shall be considered timely if it is performed on the next succeeding day which is not a Saturday, Sunday, or a legal holiday.

For purposes of this section, the last day for the performance of any act shall be determined by including any authorized extension of time; the term "legal holiday" means a legal holiday in the District of Columbia; and in the case of any return, statement, or other document required to be filed, or any other act required under authority of the internal revenue laws to be performed, at any office of the Secretary or his delegate, or at any other office of the United States or any agency thereof, located outside the District of Columbia but within an internal revenue district, the term "legal holiday" also means a Statewide legal holiday in the State where such office is located.

National Observances

[36 U.S.C.]

§ 141. **Display of flag on Mother's Day.** The President of the United States is authorized and requested to issue a proclamation calling upon the Government officials to display the United States flag on all Government buildings, and the people of the United States to display the flag at their homes or other suitable places, on the second Sunday in May, as a public expression of our love and reverence for the mothers of our country.

§ 142. **Mother's Day.** The second Sunday in May shall hereafter be designated and known as Mother's Day, and it shall be the duty of the President to request its observance as provided for in this resolution [§§ 141, 142 of this title].

§ 142a. **Father's Day.** The third Sunday in June of each year is hereby designated as "Father's Day". The President is authorized and requested to issue a proclamation calling on the appropriate Government officials to display the flag of the United States on all Government buildings on such day, inviting the governments of the States and communities and the people of the United States to observe such day with appropriate ceremonies, and urging our people to offer public and private expressions of such day to the abiding love and gratitude which they bear for their fathers.

§ 143. **Child Health Day.** The President of the United States is hereby authorized and requested to issue annually a proclamation setting apart the first Monday in October, of each year as Child Health Day and inviting all agencies and organizations interested in child welfare to unite upon that day in the observance of such exercises as will awaken the people of the Nation to the fundamental necessity of a year-round program for the protection and development of the health of the Nation's children.

§ 145. **National Maritime Day.** May 22 of each year shall hereafter be designated and known as National Maritime Day, and the President is authorized and requested annually to issue a proclamation calling upon the people of the United States to observe such

National Maritime Day by displaying the flag at their homes or other suitable places and Government officials to display the flag on all Government buildings on May 22 of each year.

§ 146. **Columbus Day.** The President of the United States is authorized and requested to issue a proclamation designating October 12 of each year as Columbus Day and calling upon officials of the Government to display the flag of the United States on all Government buildings on said date and inviting the people of the United States to observe the day in schools and churches, or other suitable places, with appropriate ceremonies expressive of the public sentiment befitting the anniversary of the discovery of America.

§ 147. **Display of flag on Gold Star Mother's Day.** The President of the United States is hereby authorized and requested to issue a proclamation calling upon the Government officials to display the United States flag on all Government buildings, and the people of the United States to display the flag and to hold appropriate meetings at their homes, churches, or other suitable places, on the last Sunday in September, as a public expression of the love, sorrow, and reverence of the people of the United States for the American Gold Star Mothers.

§ 148. **Gold Star Mother's Day.** The last Sunday in September shall hereafter be designated and known as "Gold Star Mother's Day," and it shall be the duty of the President to request its observance as provided for in this resolution [§§ 147, 148 of this title].

§ 149. **Commemoration of Thomas Jefferson's birthday.** The President of the United States of America is authorized and directed to issue a proclamation calling upon officials of the Government to display the flag of the United States on all Government buildings on April 13 of each year, and inviting the people of the United States to observe the day in schools and churches, or other suitable places, with appropriate ceremonies in commemoration of the birth of Thomas Jefferson.

§ 151. **National Aviation Day.** The President of the United States is authorized to designate August 19 of each year as National Aviation Day, and to issue a proclamation calling upon officials of the Government to display the flag of the United States on all Government buildings on that day, and inviting the people of the United States to observe the day with appropriate exercises to further and stimulate interest in aviation in the United States.

§ 151a. **Pan American Aviation Day.** The President of the United States is authorized to designate December 17 of each year as Pan American Aviation Day and to issue a proclamation calling upon all officials of the Government, Governors of the forty-eight [fifty] States, or possessions, and all citizens to participate in the observance of this day to further and stimulate interest in aviation in the American countries as an important stimulus to the further development of more rapid communications and cultural development between the nations of the Western Hemisphere.

§ 153. **Citizenship Day.** The 17th day of September of each year is hereby designated as "Citizenship Day" in commemoration of the formation and signing, on September 17, 1787, of the Constitution of the United States and in recognition of all who, by coming of age or by naturalization have attained the status of citizenship, and the President of the United States is hereby authorized to issue annually a proclamation calling upon officials of the Government to display the flag of the United States on all Government buildings on such day, and inviting the people of the United States to observe the day in schools and churches, or other suitable places, with appropriate ceremonies.

That the civil and educational authorities of States, counties, cities, and towns be, and they are hereby, urged to make plans for the proper observance of this day and for the full instruction of citizens in their responsibilities and opportunities as citizens of the United States and of the States and localities in which they reside.

Nothing herein [§§ 153, 154 of this title] shall be construed as changing, or attempting to change, the time or mode of any of the many altogether commendable observances of similar nature now being held from time to time, or periodically, but, to the contrary, such practices are hereby praised and encouraged.

§ 169. **Wright Brothers Day.** The 17th day of December of each year is hereby designated as "Wright Brothers Day," in commemoration of the first successful flights in a heavier than air, mechanically propelled airplane, which were made by Orville and Wilbur Wright on December 17, 1903, near Kitty Hawk, North Carolina. The President is authorized and requested to issue annually a proclamation inviting the people of the United States to observe such day with appropriate ceremonies and activities.

GLOSSARY OF DEFINITIONS

Selected from COCHRAN'S LAW LEXICON, 5th edition revised by Wesley Gilmer, Jr., Copyright 1973 by The W. H. Anderson Company, Cincinnati.

Acceptance, the receipt of a thing, offered by another, with the intention of retaining it. (2) The agreeing to terms or proposals by which a bargain is concluded and the parties are bound. (3) An agreement by the person, on whom a draft, or bill of exchange is drawn, to pay the same according to its terms, generally expressed by writing the word "accepted" across the face and signing his name under it. Before acceptance he is called the drawee, after it, the acceptor. An acceptance may be general (absolute); or qualified, *i.e.,* conditional, or partial. An acceptance may be implied from the acts of the drawee warranting the inference that he intends to pay, and it may be expressed in writing on another paper, or by giving previous written authority to draw the draft and agreeing to accept the same. If the drawee refuses to accept a bill drawn on him, it is dishonored, and the holder must look to the drawer.

Accommodation paper, a promissory note, or bill of exchange which a party makes, indorses, or accepts without consideration, for the benefit of another, who receives money on it and is to provide for its payment when due. The want of consideration is a valid defense to an action brought on such paper by the person accommodated, but is no defense to an action by a third person who is a bona fide holder for value.

Acknowledgment, the act of going before a competent officer or court and declaring the execution of a deed or other instrument. The acknowledgment is certified by the officer, and his certificate is sometimes called the acknowledgment. Acknowledgment of deeds, mortgages, and instruments conveying an interest in real property is required by the laws of most of the states, to entitle them to be recorded, and to dispense with other proof of their execution.

Affidavit, a written statement of fact, signed and sworn to before a person having authority to administer an oath.

Affirmation, a solemn declaration without oath. The privilege of affirming in judicial proceedings is now generally extended to all persons who object to taking an oath.

Attorney at law, a person licensed by a court to practice the profession of law. Such a license authorizes him to appear in court, give legal advice, draft written instruments, and do many other things which constitute the practice of law (*q.v.*).

Average, a contribution, or adjustment of loss, made by merchants when goods have been thrown overboard for the safety of a ship. It is either general, *i.e.*, where the loss having been incurred for the general benefit, the owners of the ship and all that have cargo on board contribute proportionately toward making good the loss; or particular, where the loss has been accidental, or not for the general benefit, and therefore there is no general contribution. An average bond is an instrument executed by the several persons liable to contribute, empowering an arbitrator to assess the amount of their contributions. (2) Petty average, a small duty paid to masters of ships over and above the freight; known also as primage and average. (3) Formerly a service which an English tenant owed to his lord by doing work with his work beasts.

Bill, a written statement of one's claim or account against another. (2) An unconditional, written and signed, order to pay a sum certain in money to someone, drawn by a person on a third party, *e.g., a bill of exchange,* also called a draft. If it is drawn on a bank and payable on demand, it is a check. U.C.C. § 3-104. (3) The original draft of a law presented to a legislative body for enactment. It is a bill until passed, and then becomes an act, or statute. The term is applied to some special acts after their passage; *e.g., bill of attainder, bill of indemnity,* etc. (4) A document evidencing the receipt of goods for shipment, *i.e., a bill of lading,* issued by a person engaged in the business of transporting or forwarding goods. U.C.C. § 1-201. (5) The written statement of an offense charged against a person, which is presented to a grand jury. If satisfied by the evidence that the charge is probably true, it is endorsed, "a true bill," and called an indictment.

Bill of discovery, an application to a court which asks for the discovery of facts resting within the knowledge of the person against whom the bill is filed, or of deeds, writings, or other things, in his custody or control, and material to enable the party filing the bill to prosecute or defend some action at law. Under modern rules of practice, this procedure is less formal and is usually called Discovery (*q.v.*).

Bill of exchange, see *Bill (2).*

Bottomry, or **Bummaree,** a species of mortgage or hypothecation of a ship, by which the ship is pledged as security for the repayment of a sum of money. If the ship be totally lost, the lender loses his money; but if the ship arrives safely, he recovers his principal, together with the interest agreed upon, which is at a high rate corresponding to the risk. The contract may be called a bottomry bill or a bottomry bond. See also, *Respondentia.*

Certified copy, a paper which is verified to be a faithful replica of a document which is in the custody of the officer making the certification. It is signed by the officer and usually has an official seal affixed to it.

Charter-party, the written contract by which the owner of a ship or other vessel hires her out to another person for a particular period or voyage.

Check or **Cheque,** an unconditional order to pay a sum certain in money to order or to bearer, drawn on a bank and payable on demand, which is signed by the drawer. U.C.C. § 3-104.

Citation, a reference to a constitution, statute, precedent case or other persuasive material used in legal writing. (2) A summons to appear in court. (3) A compliment or award.

Citizen, a flexible term descriptive of a person who has the freedom and privileges of a city, county, state or nation. (2) A person who is a member of a body politic, owes allegiance to its government and may claim the protection of its government.

Citizen of the United States, any person born in the United States, or born out of the United States, if his parents were citizens, or one of foreign birth and parentage who has become naturalized. All persons born or naturalized in the United States, and subject to the jurisdiction thereof, are citizens of the United States and of the State wherein they reside. U.S. Const. Amend. XIV, Sec. 1.

City or **Municipal corporation,** a public corporation established as a subdivision of a state for local governmental purposes, with various powers of government vested in its own officials.

Commercial law, that branch of the law which concerns the relationships of persons engaged in business.

Commercial paper, negotiable instruments *(q.v.), e.g.,* checks and promissory notes.

Commission, an authorization or order to do some act, *e.g.,* to take depositions or to hold an inquest of lunacy. (2) The evidence of an officer's appointment and authority to discharge the duties of his office. (3) A body of persons appointed with necessary powers to do certain things. (4) The act of perpetrating an offense. (5) The compensation of a person employed to sell goods, usually a percentage on the amount realized from the sale.

Commissioner, a court officer who is authorized to perform certain judicial or administrative functions and report his actions to the court for ratification. (2) The title given by law to the heads of bureaus in certain departments of the United States government and to state officials charged with special duties.

Common law, an ambiguous term. (1) A system of jurisprudence founded on principles of justice which are determined by reasoning and administration consistent with the usage, customs and institutions of the people and which are suitable to the genius of the people and their social, political and economic condition. The rules deduced from this system continually change and expand with the progress of society. (2) That system of law which does not rest for its authority upon any express statutes, but derives its force and authority from universal consent and immemorial usage, and which is evidenced by the decisions of the courts of law, technically so called, in contra-distinction to those of equity and the ecclesiastical courts.

Conflict of laws, the variance between the laws of two states or countries relating to the subject matter of a suit brought in one of them, when the parties to the suit, or some of them, or the subject matter, belong to the other. See also, *Lex loci.*

Conveyance, the transfer of the title to property from one person to another. (2) The instrument for affecting such transfer.

Corporation, an articificial person composed of individuals. It usually has a corporate name and perpetual duration. Sometimes its duration is a fixed term of years. It substitutes for the individuals who compose it. See also *Municipal Corporation* and *Professional Service Corporation.*

County, a civil division of a state for judicial, administrative and political purposes.

Cross-examination, the questioning of a witness by the party opposed to the party which called the witness for direct examination. This usually occurs after the direct examination but on occasion may be otherwise allowed. The form of the questions on cross-examination is designed for the purpose of eliciting evidence from a hostile witness.

Curtesy, the estate which a husband has in his wife's fee simple or fee tail estates, general or special, after her death. In many jurisdictions, the extent and nature of this right are modified and defined by various statutes. Under the common law, the husband had an estate for his life. Three things were necessary to this estate: A legal marriage, seizin of the wife, and birth of issue, capable of inheriting, alive and during the mother's life.

Custom of merchants, see *Law merchant.*

De be'ne es'se, a technical phrase applied to a thing done provisionally, and out of due course, *e.g.,* evidence taken in advance of a trial, where there is danger that it may be lost, owing to the age, infirmity, or intended absence of the witness.

Dedi′mus potesta′tem, *l.* (we have given the power), formerly a writ or commission empowering the persons to whom it is directed to do a certain act.

Deed, a written instrument designed for the purpose of conveying real property from a present owner to a new owner. (2) Sometimes any written instrument.

Dep′osition, a written record of oral testimony, in the form of questions and answers, made before a public officer, for use in a lawsuit. They are used for the purpose of discovery of information, or for the purpose of being read as evidence at a trial, or for both purposes.

Discovery, a pliant method by which the opposing parties to a lawsuit may obtain full and exact factual information concerning the entire area of their controversy, via pre-trial depositions, interrogatories, requests for admissions, inspection of books and documents, physical and mental examinations and inspection of land or other property. The purpose of these pre-trial procedures is to disclose the genuine points of factual dispute and facilitate adequate preparation for trial. Either party may compel the other party to disclose the relevant facts that are in his possession, prior to the trial. Fed. R. Civ. P. 26-37.

Dishonor, to refuse to accept or pay a draft or to pay a promissory note when duly presented. An instrument (*q.v.*) is dishonored when a necessary or optional presentment is duly made and due acceptance or payment is refused, or cannot be obtained within the prescribed time, or in case of bank collections, the instrument is seasonably returned by the midnight deadline; or presentment is excused and the instrument is not duly accepted or paid. U.C.C. § 3-507(1).

Dower, the common law life estate which a widow has in one-third of all the lands of which her husband was seized in fee simple, or fee tail, at any time during coverture. Dower is modified and defined by various state statutes.

Draft, a preliminary or rough copy of a legal document. (2) See *Bill* (2).

Drawee, a person to whom a bill or draft is directed *e.g.*, the drawee of a check is the bank on which it is drawn. See also, *Bill* (2).

Drawer, the person who draws a bill or draft, *e.g.*, the drawer of a check is the person who signs it. See also, *Bill* (2).

Encumbrance, see *Incumbrance*.

Endorsement, see *Indorsement.*

Fair, a flexible term for just, impartial, evenhanded, candid or reasonable. (2) An event attended by persons having goods and chattels to exhibit and sell, held at stated intervals, or on special occasions.

Felony, a type of crime which is of a relatively serious nature, usually various offenses in various jurisdictions, for which the maximum penalty can be death or imprisonment in the state penitentiary, regardless of such lesser penalty as may in fact be imposed. Occasionally defined by various state statutes. (2) Formerly, every offense at common law which caused a forfeiture of lands or goods, besides being punishable by death, imprisonment or other severe penalty.

Folio, a flexible term for a measurement of written material according to the number of words contained therein. Frequently, although not invariably, considered to be 100 words. KAN. STAT. ANN. § 28-128 defines folio as consisting of 100 words and provides that two figures should be counted as one word.

General warranty, a covenant or undertaking that a grantor and his heirs and personal representatives will forever warrant and defend real property for the grantee, his heirs, pesonal representatives and assigns, against the claims and demands of all persons whatever. Cf. *Special warranty.*

Guarantor, a person who makes a guaranty. See also, *Surety.*

Guaranty, or **Guarantee,** a promise to a person to be answerable for the payment of a debt, or the performance of a duty by another, in case he should fail to perform his engagement. It may be for a single act, or be a continuing guaranty, covering all transactions of like kind and to a like amount, until revoked by the guarantor.

Holiday, a flexible term for a day specially designated by some governmental authority as a day of exemption from labor, or from the performance of legal business. Legal holidays, often recognized in the United States, are Sundays, New Year's Day, Presidents' Holiday, Memorial Day, Independence Day (Fourth of July), Labor Day, Veterans' Day, a day of National Thanksgiving, and Christmas Day.

Hypothecation, the deposit of stocks, bonds or negotiable securities with another, to secure the repayment of a loan, with power to sell the same in case the debt is not paid, and to pay the loan out of the proceeds. (2) In an older and unusual sense, a species of pledge in which the pledgor retained possession of the thing pledged. Analogous to mortgage *(q.v.)* and security agreement *(q.v.).*

Incumbrance, a claim, lien or liability attached to property, *e.g.,* a mortgage or a judgment.

Indorsement, something written on the back of an instrument in writing, and having relation to it. (2) Especially, the writing put on the back of a bill, or promissory note, and signed, by which the party signing, called the indorser, transfers the property in the bill or note to another, called the indorsee. Indorsement may, however, be in blank, *i.e.,* not specifying the name of the indorsee, in which case it may be transferred from hand to hand without further indorsement, and is payable to bearer. Indorsement may also be made without recourse, and thereby, the indorser relieves himself from liability in case the bill or note is not paid.

International law, is either public or private. (1) The former regulates the conduct of independent nations toward each other. (2) The latter decides the tribunal before which, and the law by which, private rights shall be determined. See also, *Conflict of laws.*

Ju'rat, a certificate or memorandum of the time, place, and person before whom an affidavit is sworn.

Jurisdiction, the authority of a court to hear and decide an action or lawsuit. (2) The geographical district over which the power of a court extends. Jurisdiction is limited when the court has power to act only in certain specified cases; general, or residual, when it may act in all cases in which the parties are before it, except for those cases which are within the exclusive jurisdiction of another court; concurrent, when the same cause may be entertained by one court or another; original, when the court has power to try the case in the first instance; appellate, when the court hears cases only on appeal, certiorari, or writ of error from another court; exclusive, when no other court has power to hear and decide the same matter.

Law merchant, or **Custom of merchants,** the general body of commercial usages which have become an established part of the law of the United States and England, and which relate chiefly to the transactions of merchants, mariners, and those engaged in trade. Unless displaced by the particular provisions of the Act, the principles of law and equity, including, among other things, the law merchant, shall supplement its provisions. U.C.C. § 1-103.

Lex lo'ci, the law of the place where a contract is made, *i.e.,* Lex loci contractus; or thing is done, *i.e.,* Lex loci actus; tort is committed, *i.e.,* Lex loci delicti; or where the thing, *i.e.,* real estate, is situated, *i.e.,* Lex loci rei sitae. It is usually applied in suits relating to such contracts, transactions, torts, and real estate.

Lien, a security device, by which there is created a right (1) to retain that which is in a person's possession, belonging to another, until certain demands of the person in possession are satisfied; or (2) to charge property in another's possession with payment of a debt, e.g., a vendor's lien (q.v.). It may be either (a) particular, arising out of some charge or claim connected with the identical thing; (b) general, in respect of all dealings of a similar nature between the parties; or (c) conventional, by agreement, express or implied, between the parties, e.g., a mortgage; or (d) by operation of law, e.g., a lien for taxes or an attorney's lien.

Maker, a person who signs a promissory note, and by so doing, engages to pay it according to its tenor.

Misdemeanor, any crime or offense not amounting to a felony (q.v.).

Mortgage (mor gag), (a dead pledge), a conveyance of real or personal property to a person called the mortgagee, to secure the payment of money by the mortgagor and to become void upon the performance of such act. At common law, such conveyances became absolute upon failure to perform the condition, but in equity, the mortgagor is permitted to redeem. The manner in which the equity of redemption may be barred is regulated by various state statutes. A legal mortgage is one created by the conveyance or assignment of the property to the mortgagee. An equitable mortgage is one in which the mortgagor does not actually convey the property, but does some act by which he manifests his intention to bind it as security. Cf. *Lien* and *Security agreement.*

Municipal corporation, see *City.*

Negotiability, that quality of certain written instruments by which a transferor may convey to an innocent transferee a better title than he has himself. See also, *Negotiable instrument* and *Negotiation (1).*

Negotiable instrument, a writing which is signed by the maker or drawer, and contains an unconditional promise or order to pay a sum certain in money and no other promise, order, obligation or power given by the maker or drawer, except as authorized by law, which is payable on demand or at a definite time, and which is payable to order or bearer. U.C.C. § 3-104(1). See also, *Negotiability* and *Negotiation (1).*

Negotiate, to perform a negotiation (q.v.).

Negotiation, the transfer of an instrument (q.v.) in such form that the transferee becomes a holder (q.v.). If the instrument is payable to order, it is negotiated by delivery with any necessary indorsement; if payable to bearer, it is negotiated by delivery. U.C.C. § 3-202(1). See also, *Negotiability* and *Negotiable instrument.* (2) Preliminary communications between parties, which seek to determine whether the parties can make a mutually agreeable sale, purchase, bargain or contract.

Notary, or **Notary public,** a minor public official, whose duties and powers vary in the different states. Commonly authorized to administer oaths, to take affidavits, acknowledgments and depositions, and to protest notes and bills of exchange for nonpayment.

Note, a promissory note *(q.v.).* (2) A memorandum. To note a dishonored bill is for a notary public to initial it, giving the date and the reason assigned for its not being paid.

Nuncu'pative will, an oral disposition of property, intended to take effect upon death, made during a final illness, in the presence of witnesses. It usually disposes of personal property only. Regulated by various state statutes, which may require that it be reduced to writing.

Oath, various solemn affirmations, declarations or promises, made under a sense of responsibility to God, for the truth of what is stated, or the faithful performance of what is undertaken. Under various statutes, different forms of affirmation or solemn declaration are allowed in lieu of oaths, where an oath is not binding on the conscience of the individual, or the witness has conscientious scruples against making oaths. Oaths are judicial, *i.e.,* made in the course of judicial proceedings, or extrajudicial, *i.e.,* voluntary or outside of judicial proceedings, evidentiary, *i.e.,* relating to past facts, or promissory, *i.e.,* relating to the future performance of acts or duties, *e.g.,* those of a judge, director or other official.

Oath of office, various declarations of promises, made by persons who are about to enter upon the duties of a public office, concerning their performance of that office. An oath of office is required, by federal and state constitutions, and by various statutes, to be made by major and minor officials, *e.g.,* President of the United States, governor, judge, notary public, juror, executor, administrator, guardian and court commissioner. The oath of office required of the President of the United States is prescribed by U.S. Const., Art. II, Sec. I.

Obligee, a person to whom is due an obligation *(q.v.).*

Obligor, a person who is bound to perform an obligation *(q.v.).*

O're te'nus, *l.,* by word of mouth.

Parish, in Louisiana, a civil division, corresponding to the county in other states.

Payee, a person to whom a promissory note, check or bill of exchange is made payable.

Payment, the satisfaction of a debt, or obligation to pay money. It may be made in money, or anything of value which is unconditionally accepted by the payee as a substitute therefor.

Practice of law, any service rendered, which involves legal knowledge or legal advice, *e.g.*, representation, counsel, advocacy, or drafting of instruments, which is rendered in respect to the rights, duties, obligations, liabilities or business affairs of someone requiring the services. Often defined by various rules of court, and occasionally by various state statutes. See also, *Attorney at Law.*

Professional service corporation, a corporation *(q.v.)* which is organized by individuals who are licensed to render a professional service, *e.g.*, attorneys, dentists or physicians, for the purpose of rendering those professional services to the public via the corporate organization, and not as individual practitioners. Usually authorized and regulated, and often defined, by various state statutes.

Promissory note, an unconditional promise in writing, made by one person to another, signed by the maker, engaging to pay on demand or at a definite time, a sum certain in money, to the order of such other, or to bearer. U.C.C. § 3-104(1), (2). Occasionally called note of hand.

Protest, a solemn declaration of opinion, usually of dissent. (2) An express reservation, whereby a person protects himself against the effects of any admission that might be implied from his act, *e.g.*, payment under protest. (3) In commercial paper transactions, a certificate of dishonor *(q.v.)*, made under the hand and seal of a United States consul, or vice consul or a notary public, or other person authorized to certify dishonor by the law of the place where dishonor occurs. It may be made upon information satisfactory to such person. U.C.C. § 3-509(1). (4) A document drawn by the master of a ship, and formally attested, stating the circumstances under which damage has happened to the ship, or her cargo.

Qua'si, *l.*, as if; almost. Often used to indicate significant similarity or likeness to the word that follows, while denoting that the word that follows must be considered in a flexible sense.

Quitclaim deed, a written instrument that transfers a party's rights or claims, concerning particular property, whatever those rights or claims might be. It is usually used to voluntarily divest a party of his or her undetermined rights and claims, and to merge them into the title of an owner, who desires to perfect his title to the property.

Real property, Real estate, or **Realty,** all land and buildings, including estates and interests in land and buildings which are held for life, but not for years, or some greater estate therein.

Scroll, formerly, a mark made with a pen, intended to take the place of a seal.

Seal, an impression on wax, paper, or other substance capable of being impressed, made for the purpose of authenticating the document to which it is attached. (2) The metal die, or other instrument, with which the impression is made. Cf. *Scroll.*

Security agreement, an agreement *(q.v.)* which creates or provides for a security interest *(q.v.)*. U.C.C. § 9-105(1)(h).

Security interest, an interest *(q.v.)* in personal property of fixtures which secures payment or performance of an obligation. The term also includes any interest of a buyer of accounts, chattel paper, or contract rights. U.C.C. § 1-201(37).

Special warranty, a covenant or undertaking that a grantor and his heirs and personal representatives will forever warrant and defend real property for the grantee, his heirs, personal representatives and assigns, against the claims and demands of the grantor and all persons claiming by, through or under him. Cf. *General warranty.*

Statute, a law enacted, for prospective application, by the legislative body of a nation or a state. It may be (a) declaratory, *i.e.,* one which does not alter the existing law, as opposed to remedial or amending; (b) enabling, *i.e.,* removing restrictions, as opposed to disabling. Statutes may also be either public, or private, the latter including those which have a special application to particular persons or places.

Subpoena *(sub pena),* a court order or writ, commanding attendance in a court, under a penalty for the failure to do so. A subpoena ad testificandum is personally served upon a witness to compel him to attend a trial, or deposition, and give evidence. (2) A subpoena duces tecum is personally served upon a person who has in his possession a book, instrument, or tangible item, the production of which in evidence is desired, commanding him to bring it with him, and produce it at the trial or deposition. Cf. *Citation* and *Summons.*

Summons, a court order, or writ, commanding the sheriff to notify a party therein named to appear in court on, or before, a specified date, and defend the complaint in an action commenced against him. It should also notify the party that, in case of his failure to do so, judgment by default will be rendered against him, for the relief demanded in the complaint.

Surety, a person who makes himself responsible for the fulfillment of another's obligation, in case the latter, who is called the principal, fails himself to fulfill it. It includes a guarantor, U.C.C. § 1-201 (40). See also, *Guarantor* and *Guaranty.*

INDEX

(References are to Sections)